CRITICAL SURVEY
OF
SHORT FICTION

CRITICAL SURVEY
OF
SHORT FICTION

Supplement

Edited by
FRANK N. MAGILL

SALEM PRESS
Pasadena, California   Englewood Cliffs, New Jersey

Library of Congress Cataloging-in-Publication Data
Critical survey of short fiction. Supplement.
   Bibliography: p.
   Includes index.
   1. Short story—Dictionaries. 2. Short story—
Bio-bibliography. I. Magill, Frank Northen,
1907-   .
PN3321.C7 Suppl.   809.3'1'03   87-16261
ISBN 0-89356-218-1

PUBLISHER'S NOTE

The present volume is a supplement to the *Critical Survey of Short Fiction* (1981). It is being published in conjunction with comparable supplements to the other sets in Magill's Salem Press genre series, which together constitute a forty-five-volume, worldwide survey of the major figures in the fields of short fiction, poetry, long fiction, and drama.

The primary purpose of this supplement is to extend coverage to significant writers of short fiction who were not included in the earlier volumes. Of the forty-nine writers included in the supplement (thirteen of whom are women), most are from the twentieth century; also included, however, are several writers from earlier periods, from the fourteenth century (Giovanni Boccaccio) to the nineteenth (Johann Wolfgang von Goethe, Sir Walter Scott, and Nikolai Leskov). Slightly less than a third of the writers included are from the United States; in all, seventeen countries are represented on the list, which includes writers from England, Scotland, and Ireland, Canada and Australia, Eastern and Western Europe, South Africa and India, China and Japan, Brazil, and the Soviet Union.

The title of the original survey established a distinction between short fiction and the short story proper, the former term being the more inclusive. That distinction has been maintained in the supplement. Many of the writers included in the supplement are indeed practitioners of the classic short story: the Englishman H. E. Bates, the Canadian Morley Callaghan, the Australian Henry Lawson, and the Americans Alice Adams, Ann Beattie, and Raymond Carver, to name only a few. At the same time, however, the list includes many writers whose work falls outside the boundaries of the traditional short story: the philosophical tales of Voltaire, the antistories of Donald Barthelme and the whimsical meditations of Richard Brautigan, the idiosyncratic sketches and miniatures of Robert Walser and the much different miniatures of Varlam Shalamov, chronicler of the Kolyma labor camps.

The fantastic tale has played a particularly important role in the history of short fiction, and it is striking to note how many of the writers included here, from widely different literary traditions, make use of the fantastic. Dino Buzzati, Charles Waddell Chesnutt, Stephen King, Tommaso Landolfi, Ursula K. Le Guin, Stanisław Lem, Clarice Lispector, Christoph Meckel, P'u Sung-ling, Bruno Schulz, Leslie Marmon Silko, Sylvia Townsend Warner—all are tellers of strange tales, and the list could easily be extended to include others, such as Alexander Pushkin, who occasionally dip into the fantastic.

The format of the individual articles in this volume is consistent with that of the earlier volumes. (The *Critical Survey of Short Fiction* was the initial set in Magill's Salem Press genre series; following its publication, slight modifications were made in the format, which became standard for all subsequent volumes.) Pertinent top matter is followed by a listing of the writer's principal collections of short fiction, with dates of first publication, a brief survey of work in literary forms other than short fiction, a summary of the subject's professional achievements, a biographical sketch, and a critical analysis of the subject's canon, which is the body of the article. Following these critical overviews is a list of major publications other than short fiction and a bibliography of significant criticism.

In addition, the supplement updates information provided in the *Critical Survey of Short Fiction*. For writers who were living when those earlier volumes were published, the supplement provides a record of subsequent publications and awards and, when applicable, a death date. These listings appear in a separate section following the articles on individual writers.

A comprehensive Index to the volume supplements the original *Critical Survey of Short Fiction* index, listing all major authors, titles, and terms discussed. Entries for authors who appear in the volume are in boldface type, followed by an alphabetical listing of those of their works which are analyzed in the text.

CONTRIBUTORS

Michael Adams

A. Owen Aldridge

Bryan Aubrey

Ben Befu

Richard P. Benton

Gerhard Brand

Keith H. Brower

Carl Brucker

Rebecca R. Butler

Rosemary M. Canfield-Reisman

John Carpenter

Julian W. Connolly

Natalia Costa-Zalessow

Timothy C. Frazer

Todd C. Hanlin

Mark Harman

David V. Harrington

Terry Heller

Jane Hill

Ronald L. Johnson

Ralph R. Joly

Paul Kane

Karen A. Kildahl

Paula Kopacz

John Lang

Harry Lawton

Michael Loudon

Hugh McLean

Paul Marx

Charles E. May

Walter E. Meyers

Vasa D. Mihailovich

S. S. Moorty

Brian Murray

William Peden

Richard Rice

Joseph Rosenblum

Madison U. Sowell

Mary J. Sturm

Mark A. Weinstein

Barbara Wiedemann

Patricia A. R. Williams

LIST OF AUTHORS

CRITICAL SURVEY OF SHORT FICTION

ALICE ADAMS

Born: Fredericksburg, Virginia; August 14, 1926

Principal short fiction
Beautiful Girl, 1979; *To See You Again*, 1982; *Return Trips*, 1985.

Other literary forms
Though Alice Adams was first successful in short fiction, she also has produced several novels, including *Families and Survivors* (1974), *Listening to Billie* (1978), *Rich Rewards* (1980), and *Superior Women* (1984). Adams' novels work out the same kinds of themes and treat the same basic character types as are found in her stories, but the longer novel form often provides Adams more leisure to follow her characters' lives at greater lengths and to work out solutions to her central problems in greater detail. At the end of *Superior Women*, for example, her characters end their lives of divorce and unhappy love affairs together in a communal relationship on a Georgia farm, where they run a shelter for battered and abandoned wives. Years of pain, of trial and error, have led them to reject both the male-female couple relationship and the nuclear family. They find instead peace, friendship, and commitment as they provide one another the love and support they have sought all of their lives.

Achievements
Adams did not publish her first collection of stories until she was in her fifties, but she has quickly assumed a place among the leading practitioners of the genre. Her stories frequently appear in *The New Yorker* and have been selected for annual collections of outstanding short fiction. Like writers as diverse as Ann Beattie and Raymond Carver, Adams is a chronicler of contemporary life. Her tone is characteristically understated, often ironic, yet currents of emotion flow beneath the surface of her stories. In 1982, Adams received the O. Henry Special Award for Continuing Achievement, given for only the third time; her predecessors were Joyce Carol Oates (in 1970) and John Updike (in 1976).

Biography
Alice Boyd Adams was born in Fredericksburg, Virginia, on August 14, 1926, the daughter of Nicholson Adams, a professor, and Agatha (née Boyd) Adams, a writer. She received a B.A. degree from Radcliffe College. She has held various office jobs, including that of secretary, clerk, and bookkeeper.

In 1946, she was married. The union, which ended in divorce in 1958, produced a son, Peter. Her stories have appeared in *The New Yorker*, *The Atlantic*, *Redbook*, *McCall's Magazine*, and *The Paris Review*.

Analysis

Most of Alice Adams' stories revolve around common themes, and her characters, mostly educated, upper-middle-class women, are defined by a set of common traits and situations which reappear in somewhat different combinations. They find their lives flawed, often by unhappy relationships with lovers, husbands, parents, friends, sometimes with combinations of these, usually with a living antagonist, occasionally with one already dead. Often, they resolve these problems, but sometimes they do not.

Frequently, the tensions of Adams' plots are resolved when her central, female characters learn something new or find a new source of strength which enables them to part from unsatisfactory husbands, lovers, or friends. Claire, in "Home Is Where" (in *Beautiful Girl*), leaves both an unsatisfactory marriage and a miserable love affair in San Francisco, where she feels "ugly—drained, discolored, old," to spend the summer with her parents in her North Carolina hometown, where she had been young and "if not beautiful, sought after." Refreshed and stimulated by the sensual landscape and a summertime affair, Claire returns to San Francisco to divorce her husband, take leave of her unpleasant lover, and, eventually, to remarry, this time happily. Cynthia, in "The Break-in" (*To See You Again*), finds herself so different from her fiancé, Roger, when he automatically blames the burglary of his home on "Mexicans," that she leaves him without a word, "going home." The narrator of "True Colors" (*To See You Again*) discovers, in Las Vegas, David's ugly side as an obsessive gambler and leaves him: "From then on I was going to be all right, I thought." Clover Baskerville in "The Party-Givers" (*To See You Again*) leaves behind her malicious friends when she realizes that she need not call them if she does not want to see them. All these characters have learned that "home is where" the heart not simply "is," but also chooses to be.

Adams' heroines must also sometimes free their hearts from painful entanglements with the dead. In "Lost Luggage" (*To See You Again*), a widow unable to get on with her life loses in her luggage a notebook she has kept as therapy to deal with her husband's death, even though they did not love each other much, and he had little time for her. Her life begins again when she starts a new notebook which "will fit easily" into a "carry-on traveling bag." Charlotte O'Mara's visit after many years to "Berkeley House" (*To See You Again*) helps to rid her of her obsession with both the house and the memory of her dead parents' unhappy marriage. In "Legends" (*To See You Again*), Jane Phelps's exhaustive but therapeutic discussion of her long affair with the late legendary Randolph Clavell helps her to decide that enough has been said about Clavell, and she and her interlocutor agree to direct the interview toward her own work as a sculptor. In "Sintra" (*Return Trips*), Arden Kinnel finally frees herself from the memory of her dead lover Luiz when she learns to live with being alone. For the women in these stories, a dead past is luggage that must be lost before they can live in the present or face the future with confidence.

Sometimes the renewal of Adams' characters gives them the strength not to escape from unhappy relationships and situations but to live with them. In "Time in Santa Fe" (*Return Trips*), Emma, worried by everyone around her, her mother, her husband, her daughter, even her ailing cat, visits her old friend David, who comforts her despite his own pain over the possible terminal illness of his lover Jeffrey; from their friendship, she returns to face her troubles feeling "rich." The narrator in "Return Trips," from the title story of that collection, traveling to her husband's homeland in Greece (he is uninterested in her past), feels less alone and isolated as they drive near the place in Yugoslavia where in her youth she was loved by Paul, a young poet.

Adams' heroines sometimes reach out from their lonely and isolated lives to find sympathetic bonds with poor or troubled people from other cultures. In "Greyhound People" (*To See You Again*), a divorced, middle-aged woman's discovery of kinship with her (mostly black and poor) fellow commuters, along with her discovery that her commuter ticket will take her anywhere in California, is so liberating that she can finally break free of her repressive, domineering roommate and friend, Hortense. In "Verlie I Say unto You" (*Beautiful Girl*), Jessica Todd's sensitivity to her black maid Verlie's humanity underscores a fundamental difference between herself and her insensitive husband (see also "The Break-in" in this regard). In "Mexican Dust" (*To See You Again*), Marian comes to prefer the company of the Mexican peasants to that of her husband, friends, and other Americans as they bus through Mexico on vacation; she abandons her party and returns to Seattle, where she plans to study Spanish, presumably to prepare for a return to Mexico alone. In fact, one sign of a strong character in Adams' stories is a marked sensitivity to other cultures. Elizabeth, in the story of that name, purchases her Mexican beach house in the name of her Mexican servant Aurelia and leaves Aurelia in full possession of the house at her death. The central focus in "La Señora" (*Return Trips*) is the friendship between a wealthy, elderly American woman who vacations annually at a Mexican resort, and Teodola, the Mexican maid in charge of her hotel room. (Adams' own concern for the human plight of those of other cultures can be seen in "Teresa," in *Return Trips*, a story about the privation, terror, and grief of a Mexican peasant woman.)

At the same time, Adams' stories also show the restraints between people that can result from regional and class differences. In "New Best Friends" (*Return Trips*), Sarah and Jonathan, a Northern couple transplanted to the South, after failed attempts to find new friends and an especially painful rejection by the very Southern McElroys, find that "we're low, very low, on their priority list." In "A Southern Spelling Bee" (*To See You Again*), Avery Todd, a young girl taken in by her father's relations while her own family is much in trouble, is still, years later, though grown up, married, brilliant, and successful, trying to win the approval of her relations, to overcome their unfair prejudice against her in the Southern spelling bee she endured as a child. "Truth or Consequences" (*To See You Again*) recounts the class bias among Southern whites. As a penalty for losing the game referred to in the title of the story, young Emily is required to kiss Carstairs Jones, one of the "truck children" from uneducated families who are bused to school from the countryside. Though the incident prompts Jones himself to academic achievement, social mobility, and, ultimately, celebrity status across the nation, the trauma of the incident and the ribbing that she took from her upper-middle-class schoolmates haunt Emily for years.

In two of Adams' most effective stories, female protagonists learn to live confidently in themselves: "Molly's Dog" (*Return Trips*) and "A Public Pool" (*Return Trips*). In the former, Molly returns with her homosexual friend Sandy to a small oceanside cabin, where she experienced a love affair so intense she cannot think of it without weeping. A friendly dog attaches itself to them on the beach and follows them as they leave; Molly pleads with Sandy to go back, but he drives faster, and the dog, though running, falls back and shrinks in the distance. Molly and Sandy quarrel over the dog, and Molly, realizing that she is much too dependent on men, comes to see less of Sandy back in San Francisco. She finally learns to think of the dog without pain but cannot forget it, and the place by the ocean becomes in her memory "a place where she had lost, or left something of infinite value. A place to which she would not go back."

In "A Public Pool," the protagonist, though working-class, neither part of the literary or artistic world nor so well educated as many of Adams' women characters, shares with many of them a dissatisfaction with her body and a sense of being cut off and alone. She cannot bear to meet people or look even for a job ("we wouldn't even have room for you," she imagines an employer saying), so that life at age thirty is a grim existence in a cold apartment with a penurious mother. Though swimming offers an escape from home and a chance for meeting new people, it also has its fears: exposing her body in the locker room and enduring the rebukes of strangers—of the faster swimmers whose lane she blocks, of the blond-bearded man who goes by so swiftly that he splashes her, and of a large black woman who tells her that she should stay by the side of the pool. After a few months of lap swimming, her body changes and her fear of others lessens. An early remark of the blond-bearded man made her babble nervously, but now she responds to his conventional questions with brief assent. On the day the black lady compliments her on her stroke and they leave the pool together, at least for a moment, she is finally able to find a job and thinks of moving out of her mother's apartment. She walks happily about the neighborhood, thinking that she and the black woman might become friends. At that moment, she meets in the street the blond-bearded man, who smells of Juicy Fruit and is wearing "sharp" clothes from Sears. He invites her for coffee, but, "overwhelmed" by the smell of Juicy Fruit and realizing that "I hate sharp clothes," she makes her excuses. Like other Adams women, she has felt loneliness, but also like many other women in these stories, she finds new strength that will mitigate her isolation by giving her independence. Yet here it is primarily achieved by herself, and, appropriately, Adams' always masterful use of language here is especially striking. As Adams' character goes off independently from the blond-bearded man, she says confidently, "I leave him standing there. I swim away."

Not all of these stories, however, end so conclusively; in others, it is unclear whether the heroines' chosen resolutions to the problems confronting them will be satisfactory. The young housewife of "You Are What You Own: A Notebook" (*Return Trips*) lives in a house crammed with her domineering mother's furniture, which the girl seems doomed to polish for all eternity. Her boring graduate student husband complains that she does not polish the furniture enough and even starts to do it himself. She escapes in fantasy, fictionalizing the artists who live in a house down the street from her, assigning them her own names (not knowing their real ones) and indulging with them in imagined conversations. At the end of the story—recorded in her notebook—she tells her husband in a letter that she is leaving him the furniture and leaving to look for a job in San Francisco. Did she go? Is she capable? Similarly, the lonely young wife in "To See You Again" uses the image of a beautiful adolescent boy in her class to re-create the image of her husband as he was when they fell in love—slim and energetic, not as he is now, overweight and frequently paralyzed by chronic, severe depression. The story ends with her fantasizing that somehow she has escaped her grim life with him, that things are as they once were, her husband somehow reclaimed in the body of the young student.

The story plots summarized here raise a possible objection to Adams' fiction—that many of her female characters are too obsessed with the attention of men, even to the point where the women's own highly successful careers seem to matter little. This issue, however, must be placed in historical perspective. Most of the women in her stories, like Adams herself, grew up and entered adulthood during the period after World War II, when women's roles in American society were constricted, when women were sent home from their wartime jobs to take on what seemed then an almost patriotic duty, submitting themselves to the roles of wife and mother. From this point of view, Adams' female characters are victims of that culture, dependent on men and falling desperately in love with them because they were expected to do just that. Given these crushing expectations, it is no wonder that Adams' heroines feel lost when bereft, by divorce or widowhood, of the men in their lives. The young people in these stories often reach out to surrogate parents, usually mothers, when the incredible strain on the postwar nuclear family cracks and splinters it (someone in "Roses, Rhodendrons," in *Beautiful Girl*, says "we all need more than one set of parents—our relations with the original set are too intense, and need dissipating").

Emblematic of the plight of this generation is Ardis Bascombe in "Beautiful Girl," an ironic title because Ardis, though in her youth beautiful and popular, is now fleshy, drinking herself to death in her San Francisco apartment, failed as a wife and, as her filthy kitchen attests, failed as a homemaker. She had been independent enough to leave her unhappy marriage, but like other women of her generation, despite her intelligence, idealism, courage, and sophistication, she was unable to make a new life. The life of this beautiful girl demonstrates graphically the destructive pressures on postwar women.

Adams' stories, then, representing a time span of more than twenty-five years, present a composite portrait of women struggling with the pressures and pain of a particular moment in history. In their intensely personal ways, they accommodate themselves to their circumstances, but with varying degrees of success. The time frames of Adams' stories and Adams' own writing career, moreover, suggest that with the passage of time comes hope. "Beautiful Girl," after all, in which one finds the helplessness of Ardis Bascombe's middle age, is from the earliest volume of stories, while "A Public Pool" is from a later volume and depicts a woman of a later generation. Looking at Alice Adams' stories together teaches one that women, and American society in general, have emerged from the grim reality of Ardis' grimy kitchen to that extraordinary moment when the woman from "A Public Pool," once almost pathologically shy, considers a man's offer of a cup of coffee and exercises a splendid freedom in refusing.

Other major works

NOVELS: *Families and Survivors*, 1974; *Listening to Billie*, 1978; *Rich Rewards*, 1980; *Superior Women*, 1984.

Bibliography

Chell, Cara. "Succeeding in Their Times: Alice Adams on Women and Work," in *Soundings*. LXVIII (Spring, 1985), pp. 62-71.
Gold, Lois. "Life After Radcliffe," in *The New York Times Book Review*. LXXXIX (September 23, 1984), p. 9.

Timothy C. Frazer

RYŪNOSUKE AKUTAGAWA
Ryūnosuke Niihara

Born: Tokyo, Japan; March 1, 1892
Died: Tokyo, Japan; July 27, 1927

Principal short fiction

Kappa, 1927 (English translation, 1970); *Aru ahō no isshō*, 1927 (*A Fool's Life*, 1971); *Rashomon and Other Stories*, 1930, 1952, 1964; *Tales Grotesque and Curious*, 1930; *Hell Screen and Other Stories*, 1952; *Japanese Short Stories*, 1961; *Exotic Japanese Stories: The Beautiful and the Grotesque*, 1964.

Other literary forms

Ryūnosuke Akutagawa is known mainly for his short stories, most of which were based on Japanese tales from the twelfth and thirteenth centuries, but he also wrote poetry and essays on literature.

Achievements

Akutagawa gained attention even as a student in English literature at Tokyo University, publishing a short story about a priest with an enormous nose in 1916. Natsumi Sōseki, the foremost novelist of the day, wrote Akutagawa praising his concise style and predicting that if he could write twenty or thirty more such stories he would become famous. He was well recognized as a literary figure by 1918, an unusual accomplishment for such a young writer. Such was his fame that in 1935 the Akutagawa Prize was established in his name. It recognizes promising new writers and is one of the most prestigious litcrary awards in Japan. Akutagawa is generally considered to be one of the outstanding literary figures in the prewar era, along with Sōseki and Mori Ogai, and he achieved this in spite of a brief career. His stories are considered classics in modern Japanese literature.

Biography

Ryūnosuke Akutagawa was the son of a dairyman named Niihara Toshizo. Akutagawa's mother went insane seven months after his birth, and she remained so until her death in 1902. At a time when insanity was assumed to be hereditary, Akutagawa feared it most of his life. In fact, he referred to his mother in his suicide note in 1927. Akutagawa was adopted by his mother's brother and reared by his foster mother and a maiden aunt. He was a good student, well-read in both Japanese and European literature, including Guy de Maupassant, Anatole France, August Strindberg, and Fyodor Dostoevski.

In 1913, Akutagawa entered the English Literature Department at Tokyo Imperial University, where he published his writing in a university literary magazine. His first important short story, "Rashōmon," appeared in November of 1915, and other modern versions of ancient Japanese tales followed.

Akutagawa was graduated in 1916 and briefly held a teaching job, but he soon quit to devote his full time to writing the short stories which already had given him fame.

Akutagawa married Tsukamoto Fumiko in 1918, and in the next few years, well established as a writer, he wrote some of his best stories. These stories were based on old tales from Chinese, Japanese, and Western literature. In 1922, however, he left this genre behind him. It may be that his literary transition and the psychological problems he had were related to his seeming loss of imagination in the early 1920's.

By 1923, Akutagawa's health was deteriorating, and he complained of nervous exhaustion, cramps, and other ailments. Despite his earlier criticisms of the self-confessional I-novel, after 1924 his writing underwent a profound change as he stopped writing imaginative period pieces and turned to contemporary subjects and his own life, especially his childhood. Possibly, he was too ill to muster the creative energy to continue his storytelling. Critics and even some friends had long urged him to reveal himself in his writing, but perhaps he feared facing the insanity that had separated him from his mother when he was a young boy.

From 1923 until his suicide in 1927, Akutagawa turned to contemporary themes that reflected his deteriorating health and increasing depression. In February, 1927, he began a famous literary dispute with Jun'ichirō Tanizaki that lasted until his death in July that year. This "plot controversy" started in a literary magazine where Akutagawa questioned the artistic value of a plot in novels. Tanizaki had denounced unstructured confessional writing in which the author describes his state of mind, ironically a position with which Akutagawa would have agreed in his early career. Month by month in the spring of 1927, they debated structure versus a quality Akutagawa called "purity," but in truth there was little lucidity in the debate, although it aroused great interest in literary circles. The debate ended with Akutagawa's death, which helped make it a turning point in Japanese fiction as writers sought new forms of expression.

With his own artistic shift in 1924, Akutagawa sensed more keenly than most writers the end of his era. He left the brilliant storytelling and plot structure behind in the last three years as he turned to gloomy autobiography that traced his descent into despair and self-destruction. He had become the tormented artist in "Jigokuhen" ("Hell Screen"), one of his most poignant works. Physically and mentally broken, he committed suicide by poisoning in 1927, leaving behind a long, depressing suicide note that has become a classic in itself.

Analysis

Ryūnosuke Akutagawa has come to typify the Taishō era (1912-1926) in Japanese literature, because of his challenge to the confessional and revealing I-novels that prevailed before World War I, and the fact that his suicide seemed to end the era, paving the way for prewar proletarian literature. Akutagawa, perhaps influenced by his wide reading of Western authors such as Edgar Allan Poe, used the short story genre from the start. I-novelists also wrote short stories, and in fact the Japanese term *shōsetsu* is used for both the novel and the short story, but Akutagawa rejected self-disclosure and stressed the narrative element. He saw the writer as a storyteller, and his own stories are twice removed from reality, for they are eclectic, based on other stories in classical Japanese and Chinese literature and stories by Western authors. Frequently, many elements from other works are carefully brought together in new combinations to create a self-contained structure, as Akutagawa let the story define reality in his work. Using old tales allowed him to define reality in symbolic terms and to apply the insights of modern psychology without dealing with the issue of the self.

Mining older literature was a tradition in Japanese literature, a tradition that had disappeared in the confessional novels that dominated early twentieth century Japanese literature. Akutagawa's concise polished style emerged precociously in the stories he published while a student of English literature at Tokyo Imperial University.

One of them, "Rashōmon," appeared in November, 1915, in a university literary magazine, *Teikoku Bungaku* (imperial literature). Akutagawa borrowed from a twelfth century tale and other sources, setting the story in Kyoto during a period of social and economic chaos. The story begins at a dilapidated gate (the Rashōmon of the title) during a rainstorm. A man seeking shelter from the storm encounters an old woman who is plucking the hair from corpses to use as wigs which she will sell. He, too, descends into depravity as he steals her clothes to sell. Akutagawa mined literature for details which evoke the decadent spirit of the age, adding psychological elements to give the story a modern relevance. In this syncretism, he did not seek to re-create the past but to use it to symbolize a modern theme of social breakdown and the disappearance of universal values.

Although many of his early stories contain sickening details, not all are morbid. His first popular success, "Hana" ("The Nose"), is a story about a Buddhist priest who has an enormous drooping nose which people pity. Embarrassed, he discovers a difficult treatment that shortens it, only to find that those who had previously taken pity on his plight now openly ridicule him for his vanity.

When the nose swells again to its former size one night, the priest is pleased that no one will laugh at him again. This grotesque but humorous story caught the attention of Sōseki, who praised it for its unusual subject and clear style. "The Nose" was reprinted in *Shinshōsetsu* (new fiction), a major literary review, and Akutagawa became a recognized new writer.

Akutagawa enhanced his reputation with nearly one hundred stories between 1916 and 1924. One of his most famous, "Kumo no ito" ("The Spider's Thread"), explores the theme of self-interest. A robber, Kandata, has been sent to hell for his crimes. Yet the all-compassionate Buddha can save even criminals. Because Kandata had once spared a spider, it spins a thread that drops into hell. Kandata begins to climb up on it, but looking below, he sees other sinners following him. Selfishly, he yells at them to let go lest the thread break. This self-centered thought indeed does break the thread, and he falls back into hell with the others, a victim of selfishness. In this story, as in many others, Akutagawa used a variety of sources, causing some critics to doubt his creativity.

Such criticism is unfair, because Akutagawa, while eclectic in his sources of inspiration, recasts tales into a new, more evocative form. An excellent example of his inspired adaptations is "Hell Screen." This powerful story is about an artist, Yoshihide, who puts his art before his family, striving for an inhuman perfection. In the story, Yoshihide is commissioned by his lord to paint a series of screens depicting hell. A slave to accuracy, Yoshihide has his models tortured in varied ways to depict their agony. The last scene requires the burning of a court lady inside a carriage. The lord agrees to stage the hideous scene, but he places Yoshihide's only daughter inside because she has spurned his advances. Horrified, Yoshihide nevertheless finishes the screen. He hangs himself, however, in remorse. The screen is recognized as a masterpiece, as was Akutagawa's moral tale.

Another well-known story from this period is "Yabu no naka" ("In a Grove"), which was made into a famous film by Akira Kurosawa in 1950, using the title "Rashōmon" from the earlier story and blending the two tales. Again using an old story, he gives conflicting versions of a rape-murder, leaving the reader to guess which is true. The story illustrates the difficulty of finding absolute truth, as each individual describes the incident from a different self-serving perspective. A samurai and his wife encounter a bandit in the forest who, according to the dead samurai speaking through a medium, ties him up and forces him to witness the rape of his wife, who appears to be a willing victim, urging the bandit to kill her weak husband. According to the samurai, the bandit is shocked at the woman's intensity, and he runs off. Humiliated, the samurai uses his wife's dagger to kill himself. Both the bandit and the wife then give their testimony, which glorifies their own actions and contradicts the original version. All the versions of the incident are left unresolved.

In 1924, Akutagawa made a major shift in his writing that signaled a new literary viewpoint. It also coincided with a personal crisis as he fell in love with a poet and began to experience long episodes of depression, trying to reconcile his family commitment with artistic creativity. In 1926, he published a volume of poetry that, for the first time, dealt directly with his own feelings. It marked his turn from stories to the realistic and biographical fiction that characterizes the last years of his life. His literary conversion and death were interpreted as the end of an era and a reflection of the modern debate about plot and expression and the relationship of the narrator to the novel.

Akutagawa's most important fictional work in his last year was *Kappa*, a satire about elves who appear in Japanese folklore, although the long story is similar to Anatole France's novel *L'Île des pingouins* (1908; *Penguin Island*, 1914). The grotesque kappa—part human, bird, and reptile—seem to reverse the human order of things, but they also have human problems, such as war and unemployment. Some of these problems have bizarre solutions; for example, the unemployed are eaten. Akutagawa's other stories describe mental breakdown and physical decline, reflecting his deepening gloom.

One of the best of Akutagawa's autobiographical works, "Haguruma" ("Cogwheels"), was published posthumously. He wrote of his mental tension and schizophrenic fears of imaginary cogwheels that blocked his vision. In his story, it is difficult to tell reality from hallucination, a reflection of his mental state. It ends with the demented plea, "Will no one have the goodness to strangle me in my sleep?" Another posthumous story written in his final days, describes corpses, ennui, and death.

Akutagawa's suicide note itself is well-known in Japan. Entitled "Aru kyuyu e okuru shuki" ("Memories Sent to an Old Friend"), it was addressed to Kume Masao. Akutagawa described his reasons for suicide, revealing that for two years he had constantly thought of killing himself, debating the way to carry it out with least trouble to his family. He ruled out a gun since it would leave an untidy mess, and he did not have the courage for the sword. In the end, he took an overdose of sleeping medicine and ended his tormented life on July 27, 1927. His death shocked the literary world but was no surprise to those who knew him well, for he had often talked of suicide.

Ryūnosuke Akutagawa was the first modern Japanese writer to attract wide attention abroad, and his personal literary conversion and dispute with Tanizaki reflect the modern debate over the direction of the novel. Akutagawa, the consummate storyteller, sensed the weakness in his own writing in his last years, and his dramatic death drew attention to the literary controversy he had begun with Tanizaki. His death signified the end of a period of Japanese literature when writers thought they could balance and reconcile life and art through aesthetic control. Because he was so famous and talented, most of his fellow writers were stunned by his death, and many were forced to reexamine their assumptions about literature. His last works are tragic, and the brutal honesty of his charting of his own demise has gained for him fame in modern Japanese literature. This fame is institutionalized in the Akutagawa Prize, the most sought-after source of recognition for young writers in Japan.

Other major work

MISCELLANEOUS: *Akutagawa Ryūnosuke zenshū*, 1967-1969 (eleven volumes).

Bibliography

Hibbett, Howard. "Akutagawa Ryunosuke and the Negative Ideal," in *Personality in Japanese History*, 1970. Edited by Albert Craig and Donald Shively.

Keene, Donald. "Akutagawa Ryunosuke," in *Dawn to the West: Japanese Literature of the Modern Era*, 1984.

Tsuruta, Kinya. "Akutagawa Ryūnosuke and I-Novelists," in *Monumenta Nipponica*. XXV, nos. 1-2 (1970), pp. 13-27.

Yu, Beongcheon. *Akutagawa Ryunosuke*, 1972.

Richard Rice

MARGARET ATWOOD

Born: Ottawa, Canada; November 18, 1939

Principal short fiction
Dancing Girls and Other Stories, 1977; *Bluebeard's Egg and Other Stories*, 1983.

Other literary forms
Margaret Atwood is the author of more than twenty books, including poetry, novels, children's literature, and nonfiction. In Canada, she is most admired for her poetry; elsewhere, she is better known as a novelist, particularly for *Surfacing* (1972) and *The Handmaid's Tale* (1986). Her other novels include *The Edible Woman* (1969), *Lady Oracle* (1976), *Life Before Man* (1979), and *Bodily Harm* (1982). Among her ten volumes of poetry are *The Circle Game* (1966), *The Animals in That Country* (1968), *The Journals of Susanna Moodie* (1970), *You Are Happy* (1975), and *Two-Headed Poems* (1978). In 1972, she published *Survival: A Thematic Guide to Canadian Literature*, a controversial critical work on Canadian literature, and in 1982, *Second Words: Selected Critical Prose*.

Achievements
Atwood is a prolific and controversial writer of international prominence whose works have been translated into many languages. She is the recipient of numerous honors, prizes, and awards, including the Governor General's Award for Poetry in 1967 for *The Circle Game*. Her works have become the focus of much critical attention, and several book-length studies have appeared. Assessments of her poetry are consistently positive, but assessments of her fiction run the gamut from inflation to denigration. She seems a writer difficult for critics to ignore, but also a writer difficult to get into focus, perhaps in part because of her preference for volatile subject matter: sexism, colonialism, capitalism, racism. She has been criticized for a sameness of tone (coldly detached, bitter, cynical) and for repetitiveness of situations, themes, and characters (all bored and destructive). Her short stories in particular have been criticized for being too spare and undeveloped, for relying too heavily on devices which succeed in poetry (metaphor, image, symbol) but which cannot substitute for the palpable reality readers expect to find in fiction. The consensus view, however, is that Atwood is an unsparing, brilliant observer of the social, political, and cultural scene, and one of North America's leading writers.

Biography
Margaret Atwood was born in Ottawa, Ontario, Canada on November 18,

1939. She grew up in northern Ontario, Quebec, and Toronto. Following graduation from Victoria College, University of Toronto, she attended Radcliffe College on a Woodrow Wilson Fellowship, receiving a master's degree in English in 1962. She has taught at a number of Canadian universities and has traveled extensively. She lives in Toronto with writer Graeme Gibson and their daughter, Jess.

Analysis

Inevitably, not all stories in a short story collection will be uniformly successful or significant. The six stories discussed here (three from each collection) have all received a measure of critical acclaim, develop themes which are pervasive in Margaret Atwood's work, and provide some indication of her range as writer.

In *Dancing Girls and Other Stories*, a gift for comic and satiric invention is evident from the first story, "The Man from Mars." Christine, an unattractive undergraduate at a Canadian university, is literally pursued by an odd looking, desperately poor exchange student. The daily chases of a bizarre little Oriental man in hot pursuit of a rather large Christine (a mouse chasing an elephant as Atwood describes it) attract the attention of other students and make Christine interesting to her male acquaintances for the first time. They begin to ask her out, curious as to the mysterious sources of her charm. She begins to feel and actually to be more attractive. As months pass, however, Christine begins to fantasize about this strange man about whom she knows nothing. Is he perhaps a sex maniac, a murderer? Eventually, through the overreactions and interventions of others, complaints are made to the police and the inscrutable foreigner is deported, leaving Christine with mingled feelings of relief and regret. She is graduated and settles into a drab government job and a sterile existence. Years pass. A war breaks out somewhere in the Far East and vividly revives thoughts of the foreigner. His country is the scene of fighting, but Christine cannot remember the name of his city. She becomes obsessed with worry, studying maps, pouring over photographs of soldiers, photographs of the wounded and the dead which appear in newspapers and magazines, compulsively searching the television screen for even a brief glimpse of his face. Finally, it is too much. Christine stops looking at pictures, gives away her television set, and does nothing except read nineteenth century novels.

The story is rich in comedy and in social satire, much of it directed against attitudes which make "a person from another culture" as alien as a "Man from Mars." Christine's affluent parents think of themselves as liberal and progressive. They have traveled, bringing back a sundial from England, a domestic servant from the West Indies. Christine's mother believes herself to be both tolerant and generous for employing foreigners as domestic servants in her home; as she observes, it is difficult to tell whether people from other

cultures are insane. Christine also typifies supposedly enlightened, liberal attitudes, having been president of the United Nations Club in high school,
and in college a member of the forensics team, debating such topics as the
obsolescence of war. While the story is on the whole a comic and satiric look
at the limits of shallow liberalism, there is, however, also some pathos in the
end. It seems that the encounter with the alien is the most interesting or
significant thing that has ever happened to Christine, and that her only feeling of human relationship is for a person with whom she had no real relationship. At the story's conclusion, she seems lost, now past either hope or love,
retreating into the unreal but safe world of John Galsworthy and Anthony
Trollope.

Another encounter with the alien occurs in the collection's title story,
"Dancing Girls," which is set in the United States during the 1960's. Ann, a
graduate student from Toronto, has a room in a seedy boardinghouse. Mrs.
Nolan, its American proprietor, befriends Ann because a Canadian does not
look "foreign." Mrs. Nolan's other tenants are mathematicians from Hong
Kong and an Arab who is becoming crazed with loneliness and isolation.
Ann's only other acquaintances are Lelah, a Turkish woman studying Russian
literature, and Jetske, a Dutch woman studying urban design. Ann also is
studying urban design because she has fantasies of rearranging Toronto. She
frequently envisions the open, green spaces she will create, but she seems to
have the same limitation as "The City Planners" in Atwood's poem of that
name. People are a problem: They ruin her aesthetically perfect designs,
clutter and litter the landscape. Finally, she decides that people such as Mrs.
Nolan, Mrs. Nolan's unruly children, and the entire collection of exotics who
live in the boardinghouse will have to be excluded from urban Utopia by a
high wire fence. Yet an event in the story causes Ann to change her mind.
The Arab whose room is next to hers throws a rowdy party one night for two
other Arab students and three "dancing girls." Ann sits in her room in the
dark, fascinated, listening to the music, drinking sherry, but with her door se-
curely bolted. As the noise level of the party escalates, Mrs. Nolan calls the
police but cannot wait for them to arrive. Overcome by xenophobic and pu-
ritanical zeal, she drives the room's occupants out of her house and down the
street with a broom.

Ann finally sees Mrs. Nolan for what she evidently is, a "fat crazy woman,"
intent on destroying some "harmless hospitality." Ann regrets that she lacked
courage to open the door and so missed seeing what Mrs. Nolan referred to
as the "dancing girls" (either Mrs. Nolan's euphemism for prostitutes or a reflection of her confused ideas about Middle Eastern culture). The story concludes with Ann again envisioning her ideal city, but this time there are many
people and no fence. At the center of Ann's fantasy now are the foreigners
she has met, with Lelah and Jetske as the "dancing girls." The implication is
clear: Ann has resolved her ambivalent feelings about foreigners, has broken

out of the need for exclusion and enclosure, and has rejected the racism, tribalism, and paranoia of a Mrs. Nolan, who sees the world in terms of "us" versus "them."

The question of human warmth and life and where it is to be found is more acutely raised in "Polarities," a strange, somewhat abstract story which also comments on the theme of alienation. Louise, a graduate student of literature, and Morrison, a faculty member, are both at the same western provincial university (probably in Alberta). Both are "aliens": Morrison is American and therefore regarded as an outsider and a usurper of a job which should have been given to a Canadian; Louise is a fragile person searching for a place of refuge against human coldness. Louise, a student of William Blake, has developed her own private mythology of circles, magnetic grids, and north-south polarities. Her friends, who believe that private mythologies belong in poetry, judge her to be insane and admit her to a mental institution. At first Morrison is not sure what to believe. Finally, he discovers that he loves her, but only because she is by now truly crazy, defenseless, "drugged into manageability." Examining his feelings for Louise and reflecting on Louise's uncanny notebook entries about him, Morrison is forced to confront some unpleasant realities. He realizes that his own true nature is to be a user and a taker rather than a lover and a giver, and that all of his "efforts to remain human" have led only to "futile work and sterile love." He gets in his car and drives. At the story's end, he is staring into the chill, uninhabitable interior of Canada's far north, a perfect metaphor for the coldness of the human heart that the story has revealed, and an ironic reversal of the story's epigraph, with its hopeful reference to humans who somehow "have won from space/ This unchill, habitable interior." The polarities between Louise's initial vision of a warmly enclosing circle of friends, and Morrison's final bleak vision of what William Butler Yeats called "the desolation of reality," seem irreconcilable in this story.

The final story in *Dancing Girls and Other Stories* is the most ambitious and complex in this collection. "Giving Birth" is about a physical process, but it is also about language and the relationship between fiction and reality. The narrator (possibly Atwood herself, who gave birth to a daughter in 1976) tells a story of a happily pregnant woman named Jeanie. Jeanie diligently attends natural-childbirth classes and cheerfully anticipates the experience of birth and motherhood. A thoroughly modern woman, she does "not intend to go through hell. Hell comes from the wrong attitude." Yet Jeanie is shadowed by a phantom pregnant woman, clearly a projection of the vague apprehensions and deep fears which Jeanie has repressed. When the day arrives, Jeanie calmly rides to the hospital with her husband and her carefully packed suitcase; the other woman is picked up on a street corner carrying a brown paper bag. As Jeanie waits cheerfully for a room, the other woman is screaming with pain. While Jeanie is taken to the labor room in a wheelchair, the other woman is rolled by on a table with her eyes closed and a tube in her arm: "Something is wrong."

In this story, Atwood suggests that such mysterious human ordeals as birth or death cannot ever be adequately prepared for or ever fully communicated through language: "When there is no pain she feels nothing, when there is pain, she feels nothing because there is no *she*. This, finally, is the disappearance of language." For what happens to the shadowy woman, the narrator says, "there is no word in the language." The story is concerned with the archaic ineptness of language. Why the expression, "giving birth?" "Who gives it? And to whom is it given?" Why speak this way at all when birth is an event, not a thing? Why is there no corollary expression, "giving death?" The narrator believes some things need to be renamed, but she is not the one for the task: "These are the only words I have, I'm stuck with them, stuck in them." Her task is to descend into the ancient tar pits of language (to use Atwood's metaphor) and to retrieve an experience before it becomes layered over by time and ultimately changed or lost. Jeanie is thus revealed to be an earlier version of the narrator herself; the telling of the story thus gives birth to Jeanie, just as Jeanie gave birth to the narrator: ("It was to me, after all, that birth was given, Jeanie gave it, I am the result.") The story is finally concerned with birth in several senses: the biological birth of an infant, the birth of successive selves wrought by experience and time, and the birth of a work of literature which attempts to rescue and fix experience from the chaos and flux of being.

A frequent theme in Atwood's fiction and poetry is the power struggle between men and women. At times, the conflict seems to verge on insanity, as in "Under Glass," "Lives of the Poets," "Loulou: Or, The Domestic Life of the Language," and "Ugly Puss." The title story in *Bluebeard's Egg and Other Stories*, however, seems less bleak. In a reversal of sexual stereotypes, Sally loves her husband, Ed, because he is beautiful and dumb. She is a dominating, manipulating woman (of the type seen also in "The Resplendent Quetzal"), and her relationship to her husband seems to be that of doting mother to overprotected child, despite the fact that he is a successful and respected cardiologist, and she has no meaningful identity outside her marriage. Bored, Sally takes a writing class where she is admonished to explore her inner world. Yet she is "fed up with her inner world; she doesn't need to explore it. In her inner world is Ed, like a doll within a Russian wooden doll and in Ed is Ed's inner world, which she can't get at." The more she speculates about Ed's inner world, the more perplexed she becomes. Required to write a version of the Bluebeard fable, Sally decides to retell the story from the point of view of the egg, because it reminds her of Ed's head, both "so closed and unaware." Sally is shocked into a new assessment of Ed, however, when she witnesses a scene of sexual intimacy between her husband and her best friend. Ed is after all not an inert object, a given; instead, he is a mysterious, frightening potential. Sally is no longer complacent, no longer certain she wants to know what lies beneath the surface.

The first and last stories in *Bluebeard's Egg and Other Stories* reveal Atwood in an atypically mellow mood. "Significant Moments in the Life of My Mother" is a loving celebration of the narrator's (presumably Atwood's) mother and father and of an earlier, simpler time. Yet it is never sentimental because Atwood never loses her steely grip on reality. Looking at an old photograph of her mother and friends, the narrator is interested in

> the background . . . a world already hurtling towards ruin, unknown to them: the theory of relativity has been discovered, acid is accumulating at the roots of trees, the bull-frogs are doomed. But they smile with something that from this distance you could almost call gallantry, their right legs thrust forward in parody of a chorus line.

The "significant moments" of the title inevitably include some significant moments in the life of the narrator as well. Amusing discrepancies between mother's and daughter's versions of reality emerge, but not all are amusing. For example, the narrator sees that her compulsive need to be solicitous toward men may be the result of early, "lethal" conditioning; her mother sees "merely cute" childhood behavior. The narrator recalls the shock she felt when her mother expressed a wish to be in some future incarnation an archeologist—inconceivable that she could wish to be anything else than the narrator's mother. Yet when the narrator became a mother herself, she gained a new perspective and "this moment altered for me." What finally emerges between mother and narrator/daughter is not communication but growing estrangement. Recalling herself as a university student, she feels as though she has become as unfathomable to her mother as "a visitor from outer space, a time-traveller come back from the future, bearing news of a great disaster." There are distances too great for maternal love to cross. Atwood is too much of a realist to omit this fact.

The final story, "Unearthing Suite," another seemingly autobiographical reminiscence, begins with the parents' pleased announcement that they have purchased their funeral urns. Their daughter is stunned—they are far more alive than she. Mother at seventy-three figure skates, swims daily in glacial lakes, and sweeps leaves off steeply pitched roofs. Father pursues dozens of interests at once: botany, zoology, history, politics, carpentry, gardening. From her torpor, the narrator wonders at their vitality, and, above all, at their enviable poise in the face of life's grim realities, those past as well as those yet to come. Perhaps the answer is that they have always remained close to the earth, making earthworks in the wild, moving granite, digging in gardens, and always responding joyously to earth's little unexpected gifts such as the visit of a rare fisher bird at the story's end, for them the equivalent of a visit "by an unknown but by no means minor god." The narrator appreciates her parents' wise tranquillity. She cannot, however, share it.

Atwood's stories are frequently explorations of human limitation, presentations of people as victims of history, biology, or cultural conditioning. The theme of isolation and alienation recurs: There are borders and fences; generational gaps, which make parents and children strangers to each other; failed communication between women and men; gaps between language and felt experience. It is easy to overstate the pessimism which is present in her writings, to see only the wreckage of lives and relationships with which her work is strewn. It is therefore important not to lose sight of the human strength and tenacity (a favorite Atwood word) which also informs her work. She does not imply that human experience is beyond understanding, that evil is necessarily beyond redemption, or that human beings are beyond transformation. Her wit, humor, irony, imagination, and sharp intelligence save her and her readers from despair, if anything can. To write at all in this negative age seems in itself an act of courage and affirmation, an act Margaret Atwood gives no sign of renouncing.

Other major works

NOVELS: *The Edible Woman*, 1969; *Surfacing*, 1972; *Lady Oracle*, 1976; *Life Before Man*, 1979; *Bodily Harm*, 1982; *The Handmaid's Tale*, 1986.

POETRY: *The Circle Game*, 1966; *The Animals in That Country*, 1968; *The Journals of Susanna Moodie*, 1970; *You Are Happy*, 1975; *Two-Headed Poems*, 1978.

NONFICTION: *Survival: A Thematic Guide to Canadian Literature*, 1972; *Second Words: Selected Critical Prose*, 1982.

Bibliography
Davidson, Arnold E., and Cathy N. Davidson, eds. *The Art of Margaret Atwood: Essays in Criticism*, 1981.
Grace, Sherrill. *Violent Duality: A Study of Margaret Atwood*, 1980.
Rosenberg, Jerome H. *Margaret Atwood*, 1984.

Karen A. Kildahl

DONALD BARTHELME

Born: Philadelphia, Pennsylvania; April 7, 1931

Principal short fiction

Come Back, Dr. Caligari, 1964; *Unspeakable Practices, Unnatural Acts*, 1968; *City Life*, 1970; *Sadness*, 1972; *Amateurs*, 1976; *Great Days*, 1979; *Sixty Stories*, 1981; *Overnight to Many Distant Cities*, 1984.

Other literary forms

Although Donald Barthelme is best known as one of the most influential and innovative short-story writers in contemporary literature, he has also established himself as a major experimental novelist. His first novel, *Snow White* (1967), is a satiric collage based loosely on the famous fairy tale; his next two novels, *The Dead Father* (1975) and *Paradise* (1986), push his experiments with breaking up linear narrative and playing with language to further metafictional extremes. Barthelme has also published one collection of nonfiction pieces titled *Guilty Pleasures* (1974) and a children's book, *The Slightly Irregular Fire Engine: Or, The Hithering Dithering Djinn* (1971).

Achievements

While some of Barthelme's colleagues, most notably John Gardner, have suggested that he goes for the clever rather than the profound, others, most influentially William H. Gass, have placed him at the very center of modern consciousness. Many critics have argued that he has had more impact on innovative American fiction than any other writer in the 1960's and 1970's. He is most often placed in the tradition of such modernist writers as Franz Kafka, Jorge Luis Borges, and Eugène Ionesco, and in the category of such contemporary minimalist or postmodernist writers as John Barth, Robert Coover, William H. Gass, and Raymond Federman.

Most of Barthelme's stories since his first one appeared in 1963 have been published in *The New Yorker*, a fact which has led some critics to accuse him of a kind of urbane chic which is concerned only with the surface of modern life. In spite of this accusation and the fact that his work over the years has exhibited a sameness, Barthelme is without doubt a significant force in modern fiction who cannot be ignored. He received a Guggenheim Fellowship in 1966 and a National Institute of Arts and Letters Award in 1972. Although he has twice been nominated for a National Book Award, he has only won it once, for his children's book *The Slightly Irregular Fire Engine*.

Biography

Donald Barthelme was born in Philadelphia, Pennsylvania, on April 7,

1931, the oldest of five children. When he was two, his parents moved to Houston, Texas, where his father, an architect, opened a firm. During his early schooling, Barthelme wrote for school newspapers and literary magazines. He entered the University of Houston in 1949 to study journalism; while there, he edited the campus newspaper and the yearbook and won several awards for his writing. He worked for a short time for the *Houston Post*, but was drafted in 1953 at the very end of the Korean War. On returning to Houston, he began work again for the *Houston Post* before going back to the University of Houston to work for the public relations department there, writing speeches for the university president.

In 1956, Barthelme founded the literary magazine *Forum* at the University of Houston, where he published the writing of a number of major writers and thinkers such as Gregory Bateson, Leslie Fiedler, and Jean-Paul Sartre. In 1962, he moved to New York and became managing editor of *Location*, a new literary and art review, which, although it lasted only two issues, gained immediate recognition for publishing such writers as William H. Gass, Marshall McLuhan, and Kenneth Koch. His first story was published in *The New Yorker* in 1963, and he has been writing professionally ever since. Barthelme has been a visiting professor of creative writing at the State University of New York at Buffalo, at Boston University, at the City College of New York, and at the University of Houston.

Analysis

The fiction of Donald Barthelme requires a major readjustment for readers who come to it accustomed to the leisurely linear story line of the traditional novel or the conventional short story. To plunge into a Barthelme story is to immerse oneself in the flotsam and jetsam of contemporary society, for his stories are not so much plotted tales as they are parodies and satires based on the public junk and commercial media hype that clutters up and covers over our private lives. Because they are satires, many of the stories are based not on the lives of individuals but on the means by which that abstraction called society or the public is manipulated. Consequently, some of Barthelme's pieces insist that the reader have a background knowledge of contemporary philosophic thought (albeit philosophic thought that has become cheapened by public chat), while others are based on popular culture.

Barthelme is not really interested in the personal lives of his characters; in fact, few seem to have personal lives. Rather, he wishes to present modern men and women as the products of the media and the language that surround them. Furthermore, he is not so much interested in art that serves merely to reflect or imitate the world outside itself as he is concerned to create artworks which are interesting in and for themselves. In an article titled "After Joyce" in the second and last issue of the journal *Location*, Barthelme argued that artists should not perceive their books as simply mirrors reflecting something else but as objects in themselves. As a result of this focus on the work as an object in the world, many of his stories feature graphics, engravings, and typographic manipulation. They seek to use language not as a clear medium through which the so-called real world can be perceived but as a medium that itself is ultimate reality. Many readers have consequently complained that Barthelme's stories are without subject matter, without character, without plot, and without concern for the reader's understanding.

To understand what Barthelme is attempting in his fiction, it is necessary to understand the pervasive postmodernist view that underlies it. For Barthelme, as well as for such innovative colleagues as Coover, Gass, and Barth, what is considered everyday reality is the result of a fiction-making process; reality is not so much "out there" as it is created out of language and languagelike structures of various communication media. Thus, literary fictions constitute an analogue of the means by which people create what they call reality. To write fiction is to engage self-consciously in the process by which reality is constructed, for the fiction writer makes the tacit explicit.

The primary effect of this mode of thought on contemporary fiction is that the story tends to loosen its illusion of reality to explore instead the reality of its own illusion. Rather than presenting itself as if it were real—a mimetic mirroring of external reality—postmodernist fiction often makes its own artistic conventions and devices the subject of the story as well as its theme. The basic problem with such fiction is that it is often called unreadable, for readers are unaccustomed to having those fictional conventions which are usually invisible suddenly laid bare, foregrounded, and manipulated by the author.

For Barthelme, the problem of language is the problem of reality, for reality is the result of language processes. The problem of words, Barthelme realizes, is that so much contemporary language is used up, has become trash, dreck. In Barthelme's first novel, *Snow White*, a character notes that when the per-capita production of trash reaches one hundred percent, the pressing question turns from disposing of it to appreciating its qualities. "We want to be on the leading edge of the trash phenomenon . . . and that's why we pay particular attention, too, to those aspects of language that may be seen as a model of the trash phenomenon." Barthelme takes as his primary task the recycling of language, making meaningful metaphors out of the castoffs of our technological culture. As a result of his literalizing of clichéd analogies for satiric effect, much of Barthelme's fiction seems cartoonlike, not only in terms of the flatness of his characters but also because of the exaggeration of situation and the concretization of metaphor. Barthelme has noted that if photography forced painters to reinvent painting, then films have forced fiction writers to reinvent fiction. Since films tell a realistic narrative so well, the fiction writer must develop a new principle for storytelling. Collage, says

Barthelme, is the central principle of all art in the twentieth century. The point of collage, says Barthelme, is that unlike things are stuck together to make a new reality; mixing bits of this and that together, Barthelme says, to make something that did not exist before is an "oddly hopeful endeavor."

One of the implications of this collage process in Barthelme's work is a radical shift from the usual temporal, cause-and-effect processes of fiction to the more spatial and metaphoric processes of poetry. The most basic example of Barthelme's use of this mode is "The Balloon," from his second collection, the premise of which is that a large balloon has encompassed the city. The persona of the story says that it is wrong to speak of situations which might imply a set of circumstances that would lead to a resolution. In this story there is no situation and no resolution—only the balloon, a concrete, particular thing to which people react and which they try to explain. The balloon is an extended metaphor for the Barthelme story itself, to which people try to find some means of access and which creates varied critical responses and opinions.

In another story from *Unspeakable Practices, Unnatural Acts*, "The Dolt," the spatial nature of Barthelme's art is further developed. The central character is preparing for the National Writers Examination and reads to his wife a story that he is writing which has a beginning and an end but no middle. "I sympathize," says Barthelme. "I myself have those problems. Endings are elusive, middles are ·nowhere to be found, but worst of all is to begin, to begin, to begin."

In what is perhaps Barthelme's most autobiographical story, "See the Moon," the persona cites what is often taken to be a central tenet of Barthelme's aesthetic: "Fragments are the only forms I trust." The narrator talks about the future of his child caught between procreative playthings at one end and the Educational Testing Service at the other, directed in the middle by the Minnesota Multiphastic Muzzle Map. Thinking about how he will respond to questions his son will ask, he points to a wall filled with fragments, fragments he has hope will one day merge, blur, and cohere into something meaningful, a work of art. Like Barthelme himself, however, the narrator knows that there was no particular point at which he stopped being "promising."

In another well-known story, "The Indian Uprising," the narrator aims for "strings of language" that extend in every direction to "bind the world into a rushing, ribald whole." He asserts, moreover, that the only forms of discourse of which he approves are the litany and the list. Indeed, the list is one of Barthelme's favorite devices, in which disparate items are yoked together in strings that end only arbitrarily. Barthelme strains at the outer limits of language but seems forever caught in the inevitable trap of temporality, for meaning is restricted to time regardless of one's efforts to escape it. A story from *City Life* that seems a self-conscious capitulation to this fact, even as it parodies the problem of the temporality of story, "The Glass Mountain" is a series of one hundred numbered statements in which the character tries to climb the glass mountain.

The themes and motifs of Barthelme's fifth and sixth collections of stories, *Amateurs* and *Great Days*, are quite similar to those in his earlier collections. In *Amateurs*, "At the End of the Mechanical Age" deals with an "actuality straining to become a metaphor," while "The Great Hug" equates the making of a balloon with the making of an artwork. The only new technique manifested in *Great Days* is the use of the extended dialogue form which Barthelme began in his novel *The Dead Father* and developed further in *Paradise*. In such stories as "The Crisis," "The New Music," and the title story, the narrative develops by means of counterpointing two voices who do not so much speak with each other as they speak past each other in a series of typical Barthelme *non sequiturs*.

If Barthelme is on the leading edge of the "trash phenomenon"—if fragments are the only form he trusts—then he is truly trapped in an artistic situation in which he is sentenced to repeat his language experiments over and over again. In a story from *Come Back, Dr. Caligari* titled "Shower of Gold," the existential point of view that underlies much of Barthelme's fiction is ridiculed by the litanylike use of such "trashed" and overused words as "*de trop*," "nausea," "bad faith," "anguish," and "despair." At the end of the story, the central character says, "In this kind of world, absurd if you will, possibilities nevertheless proliferate and escalate all around us and there are opportunities for beginning again."

One wonders, however, if Barthelme has not exhausted the already exhausted possibilities of his fiction. Given his technique and his point of view, there is no way to begin again, except to begin the same way over and over. There is no teleology, no promise for the future in Barthelme's worldview, only the satiric opportunity made possible by the inevitable absurdities of the past and the present.

The central problem of Barthelme's use of irony and parody in which one parodies oneself and therefore asserts nothing is best summed up in his story "Kierkegaard Unfair to Schlegel," from *City Life*. The persona, in referring to Søren Kierkegaard's *The Concept of Irony*, notes that the effect of irony is to deprive the object of its reality. Kierkegaard's worry that the ironist has nothing to put in the place of what he has destroyed seems often to be Barthelme's worry, too. The limitation of the ironist, says Kierkegaard, is that the actuality created by the ironist is a comment on a former actuality rather than a new actuality. Even as Barthelme says that collage is not simply a comment on an old object but rather the creation of a new one, there is the inevitable fear that few cases ever reach such a level.

The problem is summed up in another well-known story, "Me and Mrs. Mandible" from Barthelme's first collection, in which a thirty-five-year-old man is mistakenly taken to be eleven years old and is placed in a schoolroom charged with the atmosphere of aborted sexuality. The cause of his immediate problem, and indeed the original source or cause of all of Barthelme's stories, is the narrator's realization that although people "read signs as promises," the truth is that "signs are signs and some of them are lies." In a world in which one cannot take signs as promises, all the props are kicked out from under one and all the old, comfortable assumptions are destroyed.

The short story seems a more appropriate form for Barthelme's vision than the novel, for historically the short form has been less bound to the conventions of realism than the long form. The short story has also always been more aligned with the spatial techniques of poetry than the novel, lying in what Barthelme calls that ineffable realm between math and religion where truth resides. Perhaps the best definition of Barthelme's view of the short story can be found in one of his best-known stories, "Robert Kennedy Saved from Drowning." In this parody of pop journalism style which satirizes nonfiction's pretensions to truth, Robert Kennedy quotes the French writer Georges Poulet, who talks about "recognizing in the instant which lives and dies, which surges out of nothingness and which ends in dreams, an intensity and depth of significance which ordinarily attaches only to the whole of existence."

Barthelme's fiction continually blurs the line between fiction and analytical discourse about fiction, for his stories, by disavowing that the function of fiction is a mimetic mirroring of external reality, by self-consciously focusing on linguistic and quasi-linguistic constructs, throws into question accepted definitions of reality itself. The best that can be said about Barthelme's work is that it is a genuine effort to come to terms with the modern world as the world of communication; the worst that can be said is that it is too cute, too clever, too cocktail-party chic. Even Barthelme himself has said that the greatest fault in his fiction is its lack of emotion, which he admits is one of the very legitimate reasons people come to fiction.

The basic fictional issue overshadowing the work of Donald Barthelme is this: If reality is itself a process of fictional creation by metaphor-making man, then the modern writer who wishes to write about reality can truthfully only write about that very process. To write only about this process, however, is to run the risk of dealing with language on a level that leaves the reader gasping for something tangible and real, even if that reality is only an illusion.

Other major works

NOVELS: *Snow White*, 1967; *The Dead Father*, 1975; *Paradise*, 1986.

NONFICTION: *Guilty Pleasures*, 1974.

CHILDREN'S LITERATURE: *The Slightly Irregular Fire Engine: Or, The Hithering Dithering Djinn*, 1971.

Bibliography

Gordon, Lois G. *Donald Barthelme*, 1981.

Klinkowitz, Jerome. *Literary Disruptions: The Making of a Post-Contemporary Fiction*, 1975, 1980.

McCaffery, Larry. *The Metafictional Muse*, 1982.

Molesworth, Charles F. *Donald Barthelme's Fiction: The Ironist Saved from Drowning*, 1982.

Stengel, Wayne B. *The Shape of Art in the Short Stories of Donald Barthelme*, 1985.

Stott, William. "Donald Barthelme and the Death of Fiction," in *Prospects*. I (1975), pp. 369-386.

Charles E. May

H. E. BATES

Born: Rushden, England; May 16, 1905
Died: Canterbury, England; January 29, 1974

Principal short fiction

The Seekers, 1926; *Day's End and Other Stories*, 1928; *Seven Tales and Alexander*, 1929; *The Black Boxer: Tales*, 1932; *Thirty Tales*, 1934; *The Woman Who Had Imagination and Other Stories*, 1934; *Cut and Come Again: Fourteen Stories*, 1935; *Something Short and Sweet: Stories*, 1937; *Country Tales: Collected Short Stories*, 1938; *The Flying Goat: Stories*, 1939; *My Uncle Silas: Stories*, 1939; *The Beauty of the Dead and Other Stories*, 1940; *The Greatest People in the World and Other Stories*, 1942; *How Sleep the Brave and Other Stories*, 1943; *The Bride Comes to Evensford and Other Tales*, 1949; *Dear Life*, 1949; *Colonel Julian and Other Stories*, 1951; *The Daffodil Sky*, 1955; *The Sleepless Moon*, 1956; *Death of a Huntsman: Four Short Novels*, 1957 (U.S. edition, *Summer in Salandar*, 1957); *Sugar for the Horse*, 1957; *The Watercress Girl and Other Stories*, 1959; *An Aspidistra in Babylon: Four Novellas*, 1960 (U.S. edition, *The Grapes of Paradise*, 1960); *The Golden Oriole: Five Novellas*, 1961; *Now Sleeps the Crimson Petal and Other Stories*, 1961 (U.S. edition, *The Enchantress and Other Stories*, 1961); *Seven by Five: Stories, 1926-1961*, 1963 (U.S. edition, *The Best of H. E. Bates*, 1963); *The Fabulous Mrs. V.*, 1964; *The Wedding Party*, 1965; *The Four Beauties*, 1968; *The Wild Cherry Tree*, 1968; *The Good Corn and Other Stories*, 1974; *The Yellow Meads of Asphodel*, 1976.

Other literary forms

H. E. Bates's major literary achievements are, without much question, his short stories. He was also a successful and prolific novelist; among his best and most representative work in this form are *The Two Sisters* (1926), *The Poacher* (1935), *Fair Stood the Wind for France* (1944), *The Purple Plain* (1947), *Love for Lydia* (1952), and *The Darling Buds of May* (1958). Other works include several juveniles; books of verse; *The Modern Short Story: A Critical Survey* (1941); and a three-volume autobiography: *The Vanished World* (1969), *The Blossoming World* (1971), and *The World in Ripeness* (1972).

Achievements

Bates's creative output was prodigious—approximately a book a year for almost a half century. In spite of this formidable productivity, Bates from the beginning was a demanding taskmaster who held himself accountable to a high standard. Inevitably, there is a temptation to think that any writer as prolific as Bates cannot match the quality with the quantity of his work. The temptation is misleading, however, and its conclusion is erroneous. There are, indeed, misses and near-misses among his 250 collected stories. Yet, in spite of his amazing productivity, Bates was from first to last a dedicated craftsman and a keen observer of the human situation.

Biography

Herbert Ernest Bates was born and reared in what he later described as the "serene pastures" of the Nene Valley in the Northamptonshire village of Rushden, which later furnished subject, setting, and themes for much of his fiction. From a working-class family, he grew up in a period of transition often mirrored in his stories, in which one finds the contrast between rural and urban values; the individual up against the dehumanizing influence of the factory, and industrial blight clashing with the natural beauty of the Midlands. He entered school in Rushden when he was four; in a few years, he was "voraciously reading" the works of Arthur Conan Doyle and Edgar Wallace, unconsciously assimilating methods and techniques that, later, emerged as "guiding principle[s] when . . . [he] began to handle the short story." After failing an examination for a fellowship to a private school, Bates entered the grammar school at nearby Kettering, where his "solitary ambition . . . was to become a painter." Subsequently praised by one of his teachers, he "suddenly knew," he wrote years later, that he "was or was going to be, a writer."

After leaving school before his seventeenth birthday, Bates worked briefly for a newspaper (which he hated); became a competent amateur athlete between jobs; labored in a warehouse; and subsequently "discovered" Stephen Crane, the first of a group of "chosen idols" which included Ivan Turgenev, Anton Chekhov, Guy de Maupassant, and Joseph Conrad. It was to Crane, Bates said years later, that "I really owe my first conscious hunger to begin writing."

The Two Sisters, his first novel, for the most part written at the warehouse, was published when Bates was twenty; his second collection of short stories, *Day's End and Other Stories*, was published two years later; he married Marjorie Helen Cox in 1931 and subsequently moved to Little Chart, in the green and golden meadowlands of Kent (where he and his wife would live until Bates's final illness and death in Canterbury). The next few years were among the most productive—and significant—of Bates's career. In addition to several novels, he published eight collections of short fiction, rounding out the decade with two radically different collections: *My Uncle Silas*, which includes fourteen brisk tales centering on a robust ninety-three-year-old rascal based on the author's recollections of his great-uncle, and *The Flying Goat*, the least impressive of Bates's early collections.

In the summer of 1941, Bates received a commission as a writer in the Royal Air Force; out of this grew two small collections, as much reportage as fiction, published under the pseudonym of Flying Officer "X." These pieces mark a turning point in Bates's career and were immediately popular in England, a popularity that became international with *Fair Stood the Wind for France*, an American Book-of-the-Month Club selection, and *The Purple Plain*, the first of his novels to be made into a motion picture. For various reasons, Bates then virtually abandoned the short story for several years but returned with *Colonel Julian and Other Stories* in 1951. He vowed that he would "never, never write another novel" (a vow, incidentally, soon forgotten) and returned in 1955 to his "first love, the short story" with *The Daffodil Sky*, an impressive collection and apparently the one which Bates valued the most. *The Watercress Girl and Other Stories*, thirteen stories concerned primarily with children, or with an adult's recollections of childhood experiences, contains half a dozen or more stories that are among his best work. His remaining collections—including *Now Sleeps the Crimson Petal and Other Stories*, *The Wedding Party*, *The Wild Cherry Tree*, and the posthumous *The Yellow Meads of Asphodel*—added relatively little to his by then established reputation as one of the major twentieth century writers of short fiction.

Following the success of the first of the Larkin family series, Bates devoted more and more of his energy to the novel. Though he occasionally returned to stories of rural and village life and would resurrect Uncle Silas from time to time, these later collections are for the most part less important than those of his earlier years. He was made Commander of the British Empire shortly before his death in Canterbury on January 29, 1974.

Analysis

H. E. Bates's relatively few unsuccessful stories (in which Angus Wilson finds "some sense of sentimentality... that spoils what would otherwise be perfection") are animated by Bates's unwavering sense of wonderment in life, his feeling for the beauty in nature, and his insatiable appetite for pondering and re-creating the variety and richness of the human experience. Before Bates's second collection, *Day's End and Other Stories*, what E. M. Forster called the battle against the "tyranny of plot" had already been won by pioneers from Chekhov, Maupassant, and Crane to James Joyce, A. E. Coppard, Katherine Mansfield, and Sherwood Anderson. Bates admired Chekhov for freeing the short story from the nineteenth century sin of wordiness, for his simplicity, and for implying rather than commenting; he had learned, too, from what he called Crane's "sharp and dominant" lyricism, his "painterly quality," and his depicting of life not in "wooly, grand, or 'literary' prose, but in pictures." Perhaps the most important influences on Bates's early short fiction, however, were his conversations with Coppard on the relationship between film and the short story: " 'I want to see it,' Coppard had insisted. 'I must see it.' "

This is not to suggest that the works in *Day's End and Other Stories* are essentially derivative or imitative. Bates was already finding his own narrative voice, his own subject matter, and his own methods; his major concerns were with character, mood, and the evocation of a sense of time and place. He was to insist later, "I never had the slightest interest in plots; . . . the idea of plot is completely foreign to my. . . conception of the short story."

Most of the twenty-five stories in *Day's End and Other Stories* are set in the English Midlands that Bates knew so intimately; all but five or six are concerned with simple country folk, offering highly concentrated glimpses into the lives of his characters—single-episode sketches illuminated by muted revelations not unlike those of Joyce's *Dubliners* (1914). The world of *Day's End and Other Stories* is one in which a Creator—benign or malevolent—has no place; no divinity shapes his people's lives: Spiritual poverty, frustration, and isolation are as much a part of one's destiny as are their opposites, just as cold and rain, drought and decay, are as much a part of Nature as their opposites. The collection's stories are short and simple annals of the poor, the lonely, and the unfulfilled. Yet almost without exception, the pictorial and lyric quality of the collection is remarkable, as a distinguished fiction writer was to comment a quarter of a century later: "In lucid, effortless prose, Bates can write for the fiftieth time of a field in summer as though he had never seen a field before."

Throughout his long and productive career, Bates would explore other fields, utilize more traditional storytelling techniques and methods, and find more melodramatic or exotic settings. At the same time, he would continue to examine, recall, and write about the particular part of England that is the world of most of the collection's stories.

The title story of *The Black Boxer*, the first of Bates's collections published after his marriage, is interesting, particularly because of its atypical subject matter. The main character is an American black twenty years older than the local favorite he knocks out at a match at a county fairground. "The Hessian Prisoner," perhaps the best as well as the best known of the collection's stories, is similarly unusual, centering as it does on the death of a young German prisoner of war and the English couple in whose farm the prisoner is interned. More characteristic are "The Mower" and "A Flower Piece," the first depicting a conflict between a farmer and his hired man, a competition reverberating with the farmer's wife's repressed sexual attraction for her husband's worker, the second being a delicious little parody of genteel, middle-class mores. Such contrasts, so characteristic of Bates's early fiction, become more sharply defined in *The Woman Who Had Imagination and Other Stories*. "Sally Go Round the Moon" and "The Story Without an End," for example, are dark depictions of loneliness, lovelessness, and decadence; after such excursions into the depths, the quiet good humor of a brief sketch such as "Time" comes as a welcome relief, as does "The Lily," another sketch introducing Uncle Silas, who would become Bates's most popular character.

Something Short and Sweet is the darkest and perhaps the finest of Bates's prewar collections. In "Cloudburst," Bates examines a farm couple's futile efforts to save their barley crop from a devastating storm; the story is powerful and unerring in its specificity. At the other extreme are several stories involving grotesques who would be at home in the worlds of Flannery O'Connor or James Purdy: The most memorable of these include "Purchase's Living Wonders," a fablelike account of a midget; "The Palace," a study of loneliness, frustration, and isolation set in The Palace, a London landmark converted into an internment camp for Austrian and German prisoners during World War I; and "Breeze Anstey," possibly the best story in the collection, a memorable depiction of lesbianism.

Though published in the same year, *My Uncle Silas* and *The Flying Goat* are completely unrelated. The first contains fourteen brisk tales, narrative sketches, and reminiscences centering on a robust ninety-three-year-old based on Bates's recollections of a relative. The result is a pleasing, unpretentious, happy book, far removed in subject matter and tone from many of Bates's brooding stories of the 1930's. The sketches have about them the flavor and gusto of the oral tradition of folktales ranging from the fabliaux of the Middle Ages to A. B. Longstreet's *Georgia Scenes, Characters, Incidents, Etc. in the First Half Century of the Republic* (1835) and Mark Twain's frontier tales. Uncle Silas, called "reprobate, rapscallion, crafty as a monkey, liar, gardener of much cunning, drinker of infinite capacity," is one of Bates's most memorable characters. *The Flying Goat*, on the other hand, is the least important of Bates's prewar collections; apparently fully aware of its limitations, he included only one of its stories, "The Ox," in *Seven by Five*, the first important anthology of his short fiction. "I have rarely enjoyed writing as I did in . . . [that] decade," he would recall in *The World in Ripeness*, "when I produced half a dozen volumes of short stories."

More varied in setting than its predecessors—four of the fifteen stories take place outside England—and in one way or other concerned with the war and its aftermath, *Colonel Julian and Other Stories* is a memorable and disturbing collection. Soldier or civilian, young or old, male or female, most of the characters in *Colonel Julian and Other Stories* have reached the end of their rope in one way or another, because of the war, fatigue or disappointment, or some congenital inability to confront life on its terms rather than on their own. With the exception of two genuinely humorous Uncle Silas stories, *Colonel Julian and Other Stories* constitutes a kind of postwar anatomy of loneliness and despair. Some characters, such as the masculine protagonist of "A Girl Named Peter," are denied love because of physical or emotional traits over which they can exercise little or no control. Some, such as the lovers of "The Lighthouse," are frustrated by custom, tradition, or contemporary mores, others by fear or the sheer perversity of things as they are. Still others, such as the protagonist of "The Frontier," merely give up:

He had been travelling up and down there, in the same way, for twenty years. . . . He had learned, very early, that in the East time . . . does not matter; that it is better not to get excited; that what does not happen today will happen tomorrow and that death, it is very probable, will come between. His chief concern was not to shout, not to worry, not to get excited, but to grow and manufacture a tolerably excellent grade of tea.

All of Bates's people are similarly far from heroic: There is a sixtyish major with three different pairs of false teeth and a shrewish wife, a naïve farmer who finds only temporary relief by way of the agony columns, and a sensitive young woman badgered beyond endurance in a world of philistines. They are not ignoble, however, and long after their fate has been settled, they tend to linger disturbingly in the reader's mind.

Less dramatic and a return to more familiar Bates territory and subject matter is "The Little Farm," a Midlands story depicting the dismal aftermath of a naïve countryman's obtaining, through a want ad, a "young lady house-keeper." Quite different in form and content is "A Christmas Story," revolving around a small-town teacher, a bashful young man, and the local Babbitts. Effectively low-key and unassuming, this depiction of one person's life of quiet desperation is unforgettable.

The Daffodil Sky and *The Watercress Girl and Other Stories* are others of Bates's finest collections. The first is impressive in its variety: The protagonist of the title piece is a young Midlands countryman who begins to live only after a chance encounter with a lusty Lawrentian woman "full of the uncanny instinct of the blood"; not an ungentle man, he reacts with his blood, not his reason, and as the violent climax of the story-within-the-story indicates, the blood can save or destroy with equal indifference. In a very different mood, "The Good Corn," depicting the tensions between a Midlands farmer and his wife, has an unmistakable ring of authenticity and does not suffer by comparison with the best of D. H. Lawrence; there is an especially marvelous final scene reminiscent of the ritualistic baptism-by-sunlight episode of *Sons and Lovers* (1913). Best of all, perhaps, is the quiet, poignant creation of mood and characters of "The Maker of Coffins," which depicts a single episode in the life of a no-longer-young man who in his childhood had aspired to be a violinist. Without a single false note, the story ends as quietly and effectively as the young man's music, "like the sounds of pigeons' voices echoing each other far away in summer trees, and in the sound . . . was . . . love."

Unique among Bates's collections, the thirteen stories of *The Watercress Girl and Other Stories* are concerned primarily with children or with an adult's recollection of childhood; it contains several classic Bates stories. "The Cowslip Field," for example, is characteristic, representing a few moments in the lives of a young boy and Pacey, a small, eccentric woman. As in many of Bates's single-scene stories, nothing dramatic occurs externally: Child and adult wander through the flowering countryside and pick flowers; the boy makes a small chain of blossoms; Pacey lets down her long hair. The boy places the blossoms on Pacey's forehead, and he suddenly, unthinking, removes her glasses. Before him stands a "strange transformed woman he does not know." There, the story ends, after a moment of grace and happiness in what the reader knows will be a harsh future. The story is a small masterwork, alive and joyous but poignant in the reader's awareness that the magic and beauty of the moment are ephemeral.

As already noted, Bates's remaining collections—*Now Sleeps the Crimson Petal and Other Stories*, *The Wedding Party*, *The Wild Cherry Tree*, and *The Yellow Meads of Asphodel*—do relatively little to add to his reputation as one of the major twentieth century writers of short fiction. Following the success of the first of the Larkin family series—*The Darling Buds of May* and *A Breath of French Air* (1959)—Bates tended to devote more and more of his energies to the novel. Though he occasionally returned to the nostalgic re-creation of rural and village life and would resurrect Uncle Silas from time to time, his later collections tend to vary more widely, both in subject matter and importance, than their predecessors. Yet Bates never lost his enthusiasm for the short story. Relatively early in his career, in the preface to the first important anthology of his short fiction, he had written: "The best I can hope is that [the reader] will read these stories with something of the spirit in which they were written: for pleasure and out of a passionate interest in human lives." That "pleasure" and "passionate interest" animated Bates's short fiction from his first collection to his last.

Other major works

NOVELS: *The Two Sisters*, 1926; *Catherine Foster*, 1929; *Charlotte's Row*, 1931; *The Fallow Land*, 1932; *The Poacher*, 1935; *A House of Women*, 1936; *Spella Ho*, 1938; *Fair Stood the Wind for France*, 1944; *The Cruise of the Breadwinner*, 1946; *The Purple Plain*, 1947; *The Jacaranda Tree*, 1949; *The Scarlet Sword*, 1950; *Love for Lydia*, 1952; *The Nature of Love: Three Short Novels*, 1953; *The Feast of July*, 1954; *The Sleepless Moon*, 1956; *Death of a Huntsman: Four Short Novels*, 1957; *The Darling Buds of May*, 1958; *A Breath of French Air*, 1959; *An Aspidistra in Babylon: Four Novellas*, 1960; *When the Green Woods Laugh*, 1960; *The Day of the Tortoise*, 1961; *A Crown of Wild Myrtle*, 1962; *The Golden Oriole: Five Novellas*, 1962; *Oh! To Be in England*, 1963; *A Moment in Time*, 1964; *The Distant Horns of Summer*, 1967; *A Little of What You Fancy*, 1970; *The Triple Echo*, 1970.

PLAY: *The Last Bread*, 1926.

NONFICTION: *Through the Woods*, 1936; *Down the River*, 1937; *The Modern Short Story: A Critical Survey*, 1941; *In the Heart of the Country*, 1942; *Country Life*, 1943; *O More Than Happy Countryman*, 1943; *Edward Garnett*, 1950; *The Country of White Clover*, 1952; *The Face of England*, 1952; *The Vanished World: An Autobiography*, 1969; *The Blossoming World: An Autobiography*, 1971; *The World in Ripeness: An Autobiography*, 1972.

Bibliography

Gindin, James. "A. E. Coppard and H. E. Bates," in *The English Short Story, 1880-1945*, 1985. Edited by Joseph Flora.
Vannatta, Dennis. *H. E. Bates*, 1983.

William Peden

ANN BEATTIE

Born: Washington, D.C.; September 8, 1947

Principal short fiction
Distortions, 1976; *Secrets and Surprises*, 1978; *Jacklighting*, 1981; *The Burning House*, 1982; *Where You'll Find Me*, 1986.

Other literary forms
While Ann Beattie's reputation rests primarily on her short stories, particularly those that first appeared in *The New Yorker*, she has also written three novels. The first, *Chilly Scenes of Winter* (1976), appeared simultaneously with *Distortions*, a rare occurrence in the publishing world, especially for a first-time author. Her second novel, *Falling in Place* (1980), is her most ambitious and her best. In *Love Always* (1985), she uses an approach that is closer to that of her short stories than in either of the previous novels. The subject matter is narrower, and the characters are more distanced from the narrative voice. In 1986 and 1987, she worked on her first nonfiction project, the text to accompany a monograph containing twenty-six color plates of the paintings of Alex Katz.

Achievements
Beattie has been called the most imitated short-story writer in the United States, an amazing claim for a woman whose publishing career began only in the early 1970's. Along with such writers as Raymond Carver, she is a premier practitioner of minimalism, the school of fiction writing that John Barth has characterized as the "less is more" school. In 1977, she was named Briggs-Copeland Lecturer in English at Harvard, where she was apparently uncomfortable. She used a Guggenheim grant to leave Harvard and move back to Connecticut, where she had attended graduate school. She has also received an award of excellence from the American Academy and Institute of Arts and Letters (1980).

Biography
Born on September 8, 1947, Ann Beattie grew up with television, rock music, and all the other accoutrements of the baby-boomers. The child of a retired Health, Education, and Welfare Department administrator, Beattie took a B.A. in English at American University in 1969 and completed her M.A. at the University of Connecticut in 1970. She began, but did not complete, work on her Ph.D. She was married to, and is now divorced from, singer David Gates, who also writes for *Newsweek*. Before her appointment at Harvard, Beattie taught at the University of Virginia in Charlottesville.

After living in the Connecticut suburbs and in New York City, she returned to Charlottesville and the university in 1985. She appeared as a waitress in the film version of *Chilly Scenes of Winter* and, after her divorce, was named one of the most eligible single women in America.

Analysis

Ann Beattie has been called the spokesperson for a new lost generation, a sort of Ernest Hemingway for those who came of age during the 1960's and 1970's. Many of her themes and much about her style support the assertion that she, like Hemingway, voices a pervasive and universal feeling of despair and alienation, a lament for lost values and lost chances for constructive action. Yet to limit one's understanding of Beattie's work to this narrow interpretation is a mistake.

Beattie shares much with writers such as Jane Austen, who ironically portrayed the manners and social customs of her era, and with psychological realists such as Henry James, who delved into the meanings behind the subtle nuances of character and conflict. Her primary themes are loneliness and friendship, family life, love and death, materialism, art, and, for want of a better term, the contemporary scene. Her short fiction tends to be spare and straightforward. Her vocabulary and her sentence structure are quite accessible, or minimalist, to use a more literary label. Even when the stories contain symbols, their use is most often direct and self-reflexive.

Her combination of subject matter and style leads to a rather flat rendering of the world, and Beattie is sometimes criticized for that flatness. Because her narrators usually maintain a significant distance from the stories and their characters, critics and readers sometimes assume that Beattie is advocating such remove and reserve as the most feasible posture in contemporary life. Even her most ironic characters and narrative voices, however, experience a profound longing for a different world. Despite the ennui that dominates the texture of their lives, Beattie's characters hold on to the hope of renewal and redemption, often with great fierceness, even though the fierceness frequently suggests that these people are clutching at hope so hard that they are white-knuckling their way through life. If members of the generation about which she writes are indeed lost, they have not accepted their condition, even though they recognize it. They are still searching for the way out, for a place in which to find themselves or to be found.

"Dwarf House," the first story in *Distortions*, establishes an interest in the grotesque, the bizarre, and the slightly askew that surfaces several times in this first of Beattie's collections. The main characters of the story are James and MacDonald, brothers who struggle to find understanding and respect for each other and to deal with their possessive and intrusive mother. Because James, the older of the two, is a dwarf, Beattie immediately plays upon the collection's title and places the story beyond the plane of realism.

The irony of the story develops as the reader realizes that MacDonald's supposedly normal life is as distorted as the life of his sibling. When Mac-Donald goes to visit James in the dwarf house where he lives, along with several other dwarves and one giant, he finds himself repulsed by the foreign environment. Yet, when he gets home, he cannot face his own "normal" world without his martinis. He is as alienated and isolated at home and at work as he would be if he were a dwarf. Beattie uses the ludicrous, the exaggerated scenario of James's life, complete with his wedding to a fellow dwarf, conducted by a hippie minister and culminating in the releasing of a caged parrot as a symbol of hope and the new freedom of married life, to bring into focus the less obvious distortions of regular American life.

MacDonald is typical of many Beattie characters. He is relatively young—in his late twenties—and well-educated. He works, but his work provides little challenge or stimulation. He has enough money to live as he wants, but he struggles to define what it is he does want. His wife is his equal—young, well-educated, hip—but they have less than nothing to talk about.

MacDonald wants to make his brother's life more normal—that is, get him out of the dwarf house, the one place where James has ever been happy, and back into their mother's home, where James and MacDonald will both be miserable. MacDonald is motivated not by malice toward James but by an overdeveloped sense of guilt and responsibility toward his mother, a trait he shares with many of Beattie's young male characters. By the story's end, the reader cannot say who is better off: James, whose life is distorted but productive and satisfying to him, or MacDonald, who has everything a man could want but still lacks an understanding of what it is he should do with what he has.

In stories such as "Wally Whistles Dixie" and "It's Just Another Day in Big Bear City, California," Beattie plays with the almost unbelievable and the downright bizarre, illustrating that the line between the real and the fantastic is often fuzzy. For all of its science-fiction overtones, the second of these stories is finally a story of family life in a world where the complexities of life have so escalated as to drive the most ordinary parents over the brink.

The absolute fragility and terror of family life is a pervasive Beattie theme, and in "The Lifeguard," the final story in *Distortions*, she portrays the offbeat and grotesque elements that permeate the collection in a sharply realistic setting, where their humor and irony disappear. The impact of these elements is, then, all the more forceful for the reader's sense of sudden dislocation. Without warning, the book becomes too real for comfort at the same time it continues to use shades of the unreal to make its point.

"The Lifeguard" tells the story of the Warner family and their summer vacation. The mother, Toby, finds herself fantasizing about the young college student who is the lifeguard on the beach. Yet when her children Penelope and Andrew die in a boat deliberately set afire by their playmate Duncan

Collins, the inappropriateness and incapacity of the lifeguard and of her infatuation are too vividly brought home to Toby. The monstrousness of Duncan Collins' action is but another kind of distortion; there are no simple lives in a distorted world.

If *Distortions* emphasizes the outward manifestations of the disordered contemporary world, *Secrets and Surprises*, the second collection, turns inward, as its title suggests. "A Vintage Thunderbird" features a woman who comes to New York to have an abortion against the wishes of her husband. The friends to whom she turns, Karen and Nick, have their own problems in love. By mirroring the sense of loss that follows the abortion with the sense of loss felt by Karen and Nick when she sells the vintage car of the title, Beattie addresses the connection between spiritual and emotional needs and material needs.

Very few of the people in Beattie's fiction suffer for want of material goods; almost all suffer from lack of spiritual and emotional fulfillment. The interesting aspect of this dichotomy is that the characters do not, as a rule, actively pursue material well-being. Their money is often inherited, as are their houses and many of their other possessions. The main character in "Shifting," for example, inherits an old Volvo from an uncle to whom she was never very close. The money earned by these characters is almost always earned halfheartedly, without conspicuous ambition or enthusiasm. These are not yuppies, who have substituted acquisition for all human emotion; they are people who, by accident of birth or circumstance, have not had to acquire material wealth; for whatever reason, wealth comes to them.

What does not come is peace, satisfaction, and contentment. When a material object does provide emotional pleasure, as the Thunderbird does for Karen and Nick, Beattie's characters tend to confuse the emotion with the symbol and to conclude, erroneously, that ridding themselves of the object will also rid them of the gnawing doubts that seem to accompany contentment and satisfaction. It is sometimes as frightening, Beattie seems to suggest, to be attached to things as to people.

An important theme that runs throughout Beattie's work, quite evident in *Secrets and Surprises*, is the crucial importance of children in this world. When a mother's life is about to fall apart, drift away into apathy and nothingness, as is the case in stories such as "Octascope" and "Weekend," her children redeem her, give her stability and impetus to go forward. In "Starley" and "The Lawn Party," failed fathers seek redemptive power in their children, and even though they are too weak to benefit fully, their effort reinforces the role of children.

Perhaps overly inhibited by their own sense of irony, the adults in these stories are amazed by children's ability to overlook or to ignore life's ironies. If, Beattie suggests, the world presents one with irony, it is best to face that world with the straightforward faith of a child. That straightforwardness and faith appear to be the only truly successful tools for shaping life to one's desires in the world according to Beattie.

In *The Burning House*, Beattie's third collection, she turns to the darker, more richly textured veins of her standard subject matter to produce stories that are less humorous but more humane, less ironic but wiser than those in the earlier collections. Infidelity, divorce, love gone bad—all standard Beattie themes—are connected to parenthood and its attendant responsibilities, to homosexuality, to death, and to birth defects. The affairs and the abortions that were entered into, if not concluded, with a "me-generation" bravado suddenly collide with more traditional values and goals.

Many of Beattie's characters, both married and single, have lovers. In fact, having a lover or having had one at some time during a marriage is almost standard. In "The Cinderella Waltz," Beattie adds a further complication to the *de rigueur* extramarital affair by making the husband's lover a male. Yet, in much the same way that she makes the unusual work in a story such as "Dwarf House," Beattie manages to make this story more about the pain and suffering of the people involved than about the nontraditional quality of the love relationship.

The wife in "The Cinderella Waltz," left to understand what has happened to her marriage and to help her young daughter to reach her own understanding, finds herself drawn into a quiet, resigned acceptance of her husband's relationship with his lover. She laments the loss of innocence in the world, for her child and for them all, but she chooses to go forward with the two men as part of her life and the child's. She rejects—really never even considers—the negative, destructive responses that many women would have.

"The Cinderella Waltz" ends with images of enormous fragility—glass elevators and glass slippers. Yet they are images that her characters embrace and cling to, recognizing that fragile hope is better than none. The cautious nature of such optimism is often mistaken for pessimism in Beattie's work, but her intention is clearly as affirmative as it is tentative.

Another story from *The Burning House*, "Winter: 1978," offers a glimpse of most of Beattie's concerns and techniques. An unusually long story for Beattie, "Winter: 1978" features a selfish mother who is hosting a wake for her younger son, who has drowned in a midwinter boating accident. His death is mystifying, for there were life preservers floating easily within his reach, a fact that suggests the ultimate despair and surrender often present in Beattie's characters. An older son blames the mother for placing too much guilt and responsibility on the dead son, but he himself has done nothing to assume some of that burden. His former wife, their child, his current girlfriend, and his best friend are all present at the wake. The best friend's girlfriend is alone back in California, having her uterus cauterized. His former wife seems inordinately grief-stricken until it is revealed that the dead man was her lover. During the course of the wake, which lasts several days, she becomes the lover of her former husband's best friend.

This extremely baroque and convoluted situation contains much that is ironically humorous, but it also reflects deep pain on the part of all the characters, not only the pain of having lost a loved one but also the pain of reexamining their own lives and measuring them against the idea of death. That sort of existential questioning, rarely overt but frequently suggested, contributes to the idea of a lost generation brought to life on the pages of Beattie's fiction.

Yet Beattie rarely leaves her characters in perpetual existential angst, as is the case in a Hemingway story such as "A Clean, Well-Lighted Place," an embodiment of the existential despair and the longing for some minute, self-created order and refuge typical of the original literary lost generation. Instead, Beattie often opts for a neoromantic, minimalist version of hope and redemption, of continued searching as opposed to acquiescence.

"Winter: 1978" concludes with the absentee father, the surviving son, taking his own child upstairs for a bedtime story. The little boy, like the daughter in "The Cinderella Waltz," is far too wise to take comfort from the imaginary world of the story; he has been exposed to far too much of the confused adult world of his parents. On this occasion, however, he pretends to believe, and he encourages his father's tale about the evolution of deer. According to the story, deer have such sad eyes because they were once dinosaurs and cannot escape the sadness that comes with having once been something else.

This story serves as a metaphor for the melancholy cast of characters in this and Beattie's other collections of short fiction. Almost all of her characters have a Keatsian longing to connect with a better, more sublime existence that seems to be part of their generational collective consciousness. Far too aware and too ironic to follow the feeling and thereby to transcend reality, they linger in their unsatisfactory lesser world and struggle to accommodate their longing to their reality.

Quite often, a benefit emerges from this pervasive mind-set. Friendship is sacred in Beattie's world. One of the few true joys and comforts is the bond between platonic friends. (The equally numerous sexual relationships offer less comfort.) Yet even this strong, positive bond of friendship can turn sour if the friends do not have almost identical and almost stable values.

In "Playback," Holly is a woman struggling back from the total collapse of her life. Divorced and separated from her child, Holly relies on her friends to help her decide whether to start a new life with Ash, her lover. Her best friend, the narrator of the story, destroys a message from Ash, saying to herself that she is protecting Holly's best interests, but equally aware that she acts out of jealousy. The narrator cannot have the man she loves; therefore, she does not want Holly to have Ash.

At the end of this story, Ash appears to persuade Holly, despite her not having responded to his message. When the narrator sees him running up the driveway toward Holly, carrying a huge bunch of red gladiolas like a torch, she knows that her own insecurities cannot prevent Holly's taking the chance on love. Thus, Beattie suggests, friendship may be safer than love, but the rewards of love are greater.

More than her other collections, *Where You'll Find Me* displays Beattie's awareness of her own reputation as a writer. In particular, in a story called "Snow," she appears to write a definition of the kind of story her work has come to define. Less than three pages long, the story takes a single image, that of snow, and uses it not only as a symbol of the lost love the narrator is contemplating but also as a metaphor for storytelling as practiced by the author.

The remembered lover has explained to the narrator at one point that "any life will seem dramatic if you omit mention of most of it." The narrator then tells a story, actually one paragraph within this story, about her return to the place where the lovers had lived in order to be with a dying friend. She offers her story-within-the-story as an example of the way in which her lover said stories should be told.

The narrator goes on to say that such efforts are futile, bare bones without a pattern to establish meaning. For her, the single image, snow in this case, does more to evoke the experience of her life with the man than does the dramatized story with the details omitted. In the story's final paragraph, the narrator concludes that even the single image is too complex for complete comprehension. The mind itself, let alone the narratives it creates, is incapable of fully rendering human experience and emotion. The best a writer, a storyteller, can do is to present the essence of the experience in the concrete terms in which his or her consciousness has recorded it.

What the reader inevitably receives, then, is minimal, to return to John Barth's theory. It is equally important, however, that Barth argues that the minimal can be more than enough. The characters in this fourth collection are generally older and wiser than their predecessors. They have, as a rule, survived an enormous loss and are still hoping for a richer, more rewarding life, or at least one in which they feel less out of place and alone.

Andrea, the real-estate agent who is the main character of "Janus," is typical. Safely married to a husband who is interesting and financially secure, she is also successful in her career. The two of them take great pleasure in the things that they have accumulated. Yet Andrea takes most pleasure in a relatively inexpensive and quite ordinary-looking ceramic bowl, a gift from a former lover who asked her to change her life, to live with him.

Although she has long since turned him down, Andrea finds herself growing increasingly obsessed with the bowl. She begins to believe that all of her career success comes from the bowl's being precisely placed in the homes that she shows to her clients. A mystery to her, the bowl seems to be connected to the most real, the most private parts of herself. She loves the bowl as she loves nothing else.

She fears for its safety. She is terrified at the thought that it might disappear. She has lost the chance that the lover represents, choosing instead stasis and comfort, remaining intransigent about honoring her previous commitments. Sometimes she goes into her living room late at night and sits alone contemplating the bowl. She thinks, "In its way, it was perfect; the world cut in half, deep and smoothly empty."

Such is the world that Beattie observes, but Beattie is, after all, an artist, not a real-estate agent. All that Andrea can do is contemplate. Beattie can fill the bowl, to use a metaphor, with whatever she chooses. She can capture, again and again, the story behind the "one small flash of blue, a vanishing point on the horizon," that Andrea can only watch disappear.

Barth's description of the impulse behind minimalism, the desire "to strip away the superfluous in order to reveal the necessary, the essential," is a fair assessment of Beattie's work. Yet it is equally important to recall what necessary and essential elements remain after the superfluous has been stripped away. They are love, friendship, family, children, music, and creativity. Beattie fills the bowl of her fiction with much the same fruits that other writers have used.

Her characters are rarely as confident and as successful as their creator, but they want the same things that her fiction portrays as necessary and essential. The narrator in "Snow" also addresses a question sometimes raised about Beattie's characters and her stories when she says that people remember moments instead of years, and use seconds and symbols to summarize experiences.

There is, inarguably, a sameness in these stories. Some readers are annoyed that they cannot remember individual stories clearly, keep one separate from the other. The titles do little to help with this problem, but that is perhaps intentional on the author's part. Beattie may be working on the principle formulated by the narrator in "Snow." She may expect that her readers will not remember exactly what "Playback" is about or even if the character who carries the torch of gladiolas is in that story or that book. She is probably quite confident, however, that they will remember that image and the enormous hope it embodies.

Beattie's short stories are filled with such seconds and symbols. Her fiction is a lesson in the psychological reality of a certain segment of American life: well-educated, upper-middle-class men and women of the baby-boom generation. Although she sometimes writes about other people, it is these with whom she is most often identified. While the scope of her short fiction may be somewhat narrow, her finely detailed canvases yield a rich reward.

Other major works

NOVELS: *Chilly Scenes of Winter*, 1976; *Falling in Place*, 1980; *Love Always*, 1985.

NONFICTION: *Alex Katz*, 1987.

CHILDREN'S LITERATURE: *Spectacle*, 1985.

Bibliography

Barth, John. "A Few Words About Minimalism," in *The New York Times Book Review*. XXVIII (December, 1986), pp. 1-2.

Bell, Pearl K. "Literary Waifs," in *Commentary*. LXVII (February, 1979), pp. 69-71.

Epstein, Joseph. "Ann Beattie and the Hippoisie," in *Commentary*. LXXV (March, 1983), pp. 54-58.

Gelfant, Blanche H. "Ann Beattie's Magic Slate: Or, The End of the Sixties," in *New England Review*. I (1979), pp. 374-384.

Gerlach, John. "Through *The Octascope*: A View of Ann Beattie," in *Studies in Short Fiction*. XVII (Fall, 1980), pp. 489-494.

Jane Hill

GIOVANNI BOCCACCIO

Born: Florence or Certaldo, Italy; June or July, 1313
Died: Certaldo, Italy; December 21, 1375

Principal short fiction
Decameron: O, Prencipe Galeotto, 1349-1351 (*The Decameron*, 1620).

Other literary forms
Although Giovanni Boccaccio's greatest work is the masterfully framed collection of one hundred Italian short stories known as *The Decameron*, he also left a large and significant corpus of poetry. His earliest poetry, written in Naples, is in Italian and includes the *Rime* (c. 1330-1340; poems), which comprises more than one hundred lyrics, mostly sonnets and not all of sure attribution. These short poems are largely dedicated to the poet's beloved Fiammetta, who is identified in some of Boccaccio's pseudoautobiographical writings as Maria d'Aquino; supposedly, she was the illegitimate daughter of King Robert of Naples, but more probably she was the invention of the poet. Similarly, the longer poem *La caccia di Diana* (c. 1334; Diana's hunt), *Il filostrato* (c. 1335; *The Filostrato*, 1873), *Il filocolo* (c. 1336; *Labor of Love*, 1566), and *Teseida* (1340-1341; *The Book of Theseus*, 1974) are all poems ostensibly inspired by Boccaccio's ardor for Fiammetta, whose name means "little flame." Other poems that were composed in the 1340's also treat the formidable power of love and include the *Comedia delle ninfe*, entitled *Il ninfale d'Ameto* by fifteenth century copyists (1341-1342; the comedy of the nymphs of Florence), *L'amorosa visione* (1342-1343; English translation, 1986), *Elegia di Madonna Fiammetta* (1343-1344; *Amourous Fiammetta*, 1587), and *Il ninfale fiesolano* (1344-1346; *The Nymph of Fiesole*, 1597).

Achievements
Boccaccio created many literary firsts in Italian letters. He is often credited, for example, with the first Italian hunting poem (*La caccia di Diana*), the first Italian verse romance by a nonminstrel (*The Filostrato*), the first Italian prose romance (*Labor of Love*), and the first Italian idyll (*The Nymph of Fiesole*). Many scholars also regard Boccaccio as the greatest narrator Europe has produced. Such high esteem for the Tuscan author assuredly arises from his masterpiece, *The Decameron*, which has provided a model or source material for many notable European and English authors, from Marguerite de Navarre and Lope de Vega Carpio to Gotthold Ephraim Lessing and Alfred, Lord Tennyson. Even if Boccaccio had never composed his magnum opus, however, he would still enjoy significant acclaim in European literary history for his presumedly minor writings. For example, many consider his *Amourous Fiammetta* to be the first modern (that is, post-

classical) psychological novel. Certainly his *Il ninfale d'Ameto* anticipates Renaissance bucolic literature. Contemporary medieval authors also looked to Boccaccio for inspiration. In *The Filostrato*, Geoffrey Chaucer found ample material for his *Troilus and Criseyde* (1382), and in *The Book of Theseus* Chaucer discovered the source for "The Knight's Tale." Boccaccio's encyclopedic works in Latin resulted in his being regarded as one of the most prominent Trecento humanists. Indeed, it was as a Latin humanist, rather than as a raconteur of vernacular tales, that Boccaccio was primarily remembered during the first century following his demise.

Biography

The exact place and date of the birth of Giovanni Boccaccio are not known. Until the first half of the twentieth century, it was believed that he was born in Paris of a noble Frenchwoman; scholars now regard that story as another one of the author's fictional tales. Most likely, he was born in Florence or Certaldo, Italy, in June or July, 1313, the natural son of Boccaccio di Chellino and an unidentified Tuscan woman. His father, an agent for a powerful Florentine banking family (the Bardi), recognized Giovanni early as his son; the boy, as a result, passed both his infancy and his childhood in his father's house. Boccaccio's teacher in his youth was Giovanni Mazzuoli da Strada, undoubtedly an admirer of Dante, whose *La divina commedia* (c. 1320; *The Divine Comedy*) greatly influenced Boccaccio's own writings.

In his early teens, sometime between 1325 and 1328, Boccaccio was sent to Naples to learn the merchant trade and banking business as an apprentice to the Neapolitan branch of the Bardi Company. The Bardi family, as the financiers of King Robert of Anjou, exerted a powerful influence at the Angevin court in Naples. The experiences Boccaccio enjoyed with the Neapolitan aristrocracy and with the breathtaking countryside and beautiful sea are reflected in many of his early poems. During his sojourn in Naples, Boccaccio also studied canon law, between 1330 or 1331 and 1334. While studying business and law, however, he anxiously sought cultural experiences to broaden his awareness of belles lettres. Largely self-taught in matters literary, he soon began to study the writings of his somewhat older contemporary, Francesco Petrarca, known as Petrarch. Later, the two men became friends and met on a number of occasions (1350 in Florence, 1351 in Padua, 1359 in Milano, 1363 in Venice, and 1368 in Padua again).

Boccaccio left Naples and returned to Florence between 1340 and 1341 because of a financial crisis in the Bardi empire. Although Boccaccio rued having to leave Naples, so often associated in his imagination and writings with love and adventure and poetry, his highly bourgeois Florentine experience added an important and desirable dimension of realism to his work. Unfortunately, very little is documented about Boccaccio's life between 1340 and 1348, although it is known (from one of Petrarch's letters) that he was in Ravenna between 1345 and 1346 and that he sent a letter from Forlì in 1347. He was back in Florence in 1348, where he witnessed at first hand the horrible ravages of the Black Death, or bubonic plague. Between 1349 and 1351, he gave final form to *The Decameron*, which takes as its *mise en scène* Florence and the Tuscan countryside during the plague of 1348.

After his father's death in 1349, Boccaccio assumed many more familial responsibilities and financial burdens. As his fame as an author and scholar burgeoned, his fellow Florentines began to honor him with various ambassadorial duties, starting with his 1350 assignment as ambassador to the lords of Romagna. Such posts, however, did little to alleviate the financial difficulties caused by the collapse of the Bardi Company. Boccaccio longed to return to the pleasant life he had known in Naples, but visits there in 1355 and again in 1362 and 1370 to 1371 were extremely disappointing. Between 1360 and 1362, he studied Greek, the first among the literati of his time to do so seriously; from that time until his death, his home became the center for Italian humanism. Sometime around 1361 or 1362, he left Florence to take up residence in the family home in Certaldo, where he died, on December 21, 1375, the year after the death of his friend and fellow humanist, Petrarch.

Analysis

Giovanni Boccaccio's short fiction, one hundred *novelle*, or tales, is collectively and contemporaneously his longest work of fiction, known in both Italian and English as *The Decameron*. That fact must be kept foremost in mind in any serious analysis of the tales. In other words, Boccaccio's individual short stories are best understood when examined as part of a much larger work of fiction which has an elaborate *cornice*, or frame, striking symmetry, and selective and oft-repeated themes.

The word *decameron*, Greek for "ten days," refers to the number of days Boccaccio's fictional characters (three young men and seven young women) dedicate to swapping tales with one another in the tranquil Tuscan countryside away from the plague-infested city of Florence. The work's subtitle, "Prencipe Galeotto" (Prince Galahalt), refers to the panderer Galahalt, who brought Guinevere and Lancelot together, and emphasizes that Boccaccio's book—dedicated to women—is written, not unlike many of his early poems, in the service of love. As the narration of the First Day begins, three men— Panfilo ("all love"), Filostrato ("overcome by love"), and Dioneo ("the lascivious"), alluding to the love goddess Venus, daughter of Dione—come by chance one Tuesday upon seven women, who are between the ages of eighteen and twenty-eight, in the Church of Santa Maria Novella. The year is 1348, and the Black Death is the macabre background for what happens in the course of the telling of the tales. The seven women—Pampinea ("the vigorous"), Fiammetta (whose name echoes that of Boccaccio's beloved), Filomena ("lover of song"), Emilia ("the flatterer"), Lauretta (in homage to

Petrarch's beloved Laura), Neifile ("new in love"), and Elissa (another name for Vergil's tragic heroine Dido)—anxiously wish to remove themselves from the diseased and strife-torn city and repair to the healthful and peaceful countryside. The young men agree to accompany the ladies, and the following day (a Wednesday) the group leaves for a villa in nearby and idyllic Fiesole. To better enjoy what is essentially a fortnight's holiday, Pampinea suggests that they tell stories in the late afternoon when it is too hot to play or go on walks. It is decided that one of them will be chosen as king or queen for each day, and he or she will select a theme for the stories to be told on that day. Only Dioneo, who tells the last tale each day, has the liberty of ignoring the general theme if he so desires. They then proceed to tell ten stories per day over a two-week period, refraining from tale-telling on Fridays and Saturdays out of reverence for Christ's crucifixion and in order to prepare properly for the Sabbath. On a Wednesday, the day following the last day of telling tales and exactly two weeks from the day the group left Florence, they return to their respective homes.

The emphasis on order and propriety, the presentation of the countryside as a *locus amoenus*, the repetition of the number ten (considered a symbol of perfection in the Middle Ages), and even the total number of tales (one hundred, equal to the number of cantos in Dante's *The Divine Comedy*) are all aspects of the work which contrast sharply with the disorder, impropriety, and lack of harmony which characterized Florence during the 1348 plague. The author graphically depicts, in the opening pages of the book, examples of the social chaos caused by the plethora of plague-induced deaths. The pleasant pastime of telling tales in the shade of trees and the skillful ordering of the stories serve, in other words, as an obvious antidote or salutary response to the breakdown of society which resulted from the deadly pestilence which swept Italy and much of Europe in the mid-fourteenth century. Further supporting the notion that *The Decameron* presents an ordered universe as an alternative to the chaos and anarchy created by the plague is Boccaccio's insistence that his storytellers, though they may occasionally tell ribald tales, are uniformly chaste and proper in their behavior toward one another.

The stories told on each of the ten days which make up *The Decameron* explore a predetermined subject or theme. On the First Day, everyone is free to choose a topic—one is the character "Abraam giudeo" ("Abraham the Jew"). On the Second Day, the stories treat those, such as the subject of "Andreuccio da Perugia" ("Andreuccio of Perugia"), who realize unexpected happiness after serious misfortune. Then, on the Third Day, the stories discuss people who have accomplished difficult goals or who have repossessed something once lost, among which is the tale "Alibech" ("Alibech and Rustico"). The next day, the narrators tell love stories which end unhappily (see "Tancredi, Prenze di Salerno" and its English translation). On the Fifth

Day, they tell love stories which, depict misfortune but end felicitously (see
"Nastagio degli Onesti" and the English translation). The stories told on the
Sixth Day deal with the role of intelligence in helping one avoid problems—
one of the most famous among these is "Cisti fornaio" ("Cisti the Baker").
On the Seventh Day, the stories relate tricks which wives play on husbands
(see "Petronella mette un so amante in un doglio," or "Petronella and the
Barrel"), and on the Eighth Day, the stories recount tricks men and women
play on each other, as in "Calandrino" ("Calandrino and the Heliotrope").
On the Ninth Day, once again everyone is free to choose a topic (one is
described in "Le vasi una badessa in fretta ed al buio per trovare una sua
monaca a lei accusata" and its translation, "The Abbess and the Nun").
Finally, on the Tenth Day, the narrators tell of men and women who have
performed magnanimous deeds and acquired renown in so doing (see "Il
Marchese di Saluzzo," or "The Marchese di Saluzzo and Griselda").

In addition to the pronounced framing technique created by the introductions to the various days and by the themes themselves, there seems to be a
degree of subtle thematic framing within the stories themselves from first to
last. The first story of the First Day, "Ser Cepparello," tells how a most
wicked man—clearly a *figura diaboli*, or type of the devil—deceived a friar
with a false confession and came to be reputed a saint. On one hand, the tale
ridicules gullible priests and credulous common folk, but on the other hand,
it presents the undeniable power of human cunning. The tenth story of the
Tenth Day recounts the story of how the Marquis of Saluzzo marries the
peasant Griselda and subjects her to inhuman trials to ascertain her devotion; for example, he pretends to have their two children killed. His cruelty is
ostensibly designed to test her love or respect for him; her extraordinary patience in responding to his bestiality assuredly makes of her a *figura Christi*,
or type of Christ. From the comedic devil figure of Cepparello to the tragic
Christ figure of Griselda there appears to be in *The Decameron* a revelation
of the breadth of the human condition and the wide-ranging possibilities of
human experience. Nevertheless, Boccaccio explores a variation on at least
one of two themes in almost all of his stories: the power of human intelligence (for good or bad) and the effect of love or human passion (for the
well-being or detriment of those involved). At times, these themes are inter-
mingled, as in so many of the stories of the Seventh Day having to do with
the ingenious tricks wives play on their (usually cuckolded) spouses.

Often when treating the advantages of human wit, the author provides a
Florentine or Tuscan setting to his story. For example, in the Sixth Day,
"Cisti the Baker" is set in Florence and illustrates the rise and power of the
hardworking and hard-thinking merchant class Boccaccio knew so well in his
hometown. Similarly, "Guido Cavalcanti," told on the same day, has Florence
as its setting and reveals the barbed wit of one of the city's native sons. There
are also tales told of Florentines who are dull-witted; examples would include

the various Eighth Day and Ninth Day stories about the simple-minded painter Calandrino, who is constantly being tricked by his supposed friends Bruno and Buffalmacco. Those who outsmart him, however, are fellow Florentines. By contrast, many of the highly adventurous tales are set in cities far away from Florence, often in exotic locations. Not surprisingly, Naples figures prominently in perhaps the most notable of the adventure tales—that is, "Andreuccio of Perugia," the story of a provincial young man who goes to a big city (Naples) to buy horses and ends up suffering a series of misfortunes only to return home with a ruby of great value. In the tale, Naples symbolizes adventure and daring and is undoubtedly meant to recall the city of the author's youth.

Boccaccio's love tales repeatedly, though not exclusively, present realistic women in place of the idealized and angelic women Dante was wont to exalt. In stories scattered throughout *The Decameron*, but especially in those of the Third Day and Fifth Day, the physical and pleasurable union of man and woman is portrayed as the healthy and correct goal of human love. While some interpret such unabashed celebration of mankind's sexuality as a sure indication that *The Decameron* is a Renaissance work, it should be remembered that approximately ninety percent of Boccaccio's tales derive from medieval sources. G. H. McWilliam, in the introduction to his excellent English translation of *The Decameron*, reviews with insight the problem of how to classify the book with regard to historical period. He points out that the harsh judgment leveled against friars and monks, whether they are philanderers or simoniacs, has numerous precedents in the literature of the Middle Ages, including Dante's thoroughly medieval *Divine Comedy*. This is not to say, however, that *The Decameron* does not look to the future, for it most certainly does. For one thing, when Boccaccio attacks the superstitious religious beliefs and corrupt ecclesiastical practices of his times, he does so with more severity than did his predecessors; for another, he presents the centrality of sexuality to the human condition without recourse to sermons or condemnations of the same. In both ways, he draws closer to the spirit of a new age and distances himself from the Middle Ages. His overriding purpose in the tales, however, is to illuminate the spectrum of mankind's experiences and to point, in a world accustomed to pain and disease, a way to happiness and health. Boccaccio's medium is always the well-worded and exquisitely framed story; his best medicine, more often than not, is laughter or the praise of life.

Other major works

POETRY: *Rime*, c. 1330-1340; *La caccia di Diana*, c. 1334; *Il filostrato*, c. 1335 (*The Filostrato*, 1873); *Il filocolo*, c. 1336 (*Labor of Love*, 1566); *Teseida*, 1340-1341 (*The Book of Theseus*, 1974); *Il ninfale d'Ameto*, 1341-1342 (also known as *Commedia delle ninfe*); *L'amorosa visione*, 1342-1343

(English translation, 1986); *Elegia di Madonna Fiammetta*, 1343-1344 (*Amourous Fiammetta*, 1587); *Il ninfale fiesolano*, 1344-1346 (*The Nymph of Fiesole*, 1597); *Buccolicum carmen*, c. 1351-1366 (*Boccaccio's Olympia*, 1913).

NONFICTION: *Genealogia deorum gentilium*, c. 1350-1375; *Trattatello in laude di Dante*, 1351, 1360, 1373 (*Life of Dante*, 1898); *Corbaccio*, c. 1355 (*The Corbaccio*, 1975); *De casibus virorum illustrium*, 1355-1374 (*The Fall of Princes*, 1431-1438); *De montibus, silvis, fontibus lacubus, fluminubus, stagnis seu paludibus, et de nominbus maris*, c. 1355-1374; *De mulieribus claris*, c. 1361-1375 (*Concerning Famous Women*, 1943); *Esposizioni sopra la Comedia di Dante*, 1373-1374.

Bibliography

Branca, Vittore. *Boccaccio: The Man and His Works*, 1976. Translated by Richard Monges.

Cottino-Jones, Marga. *An Anatomy of Boccaccio's Style*, 1968.

Lee, A. C. *The Decameron: Its Sources and Analogues*, 1909, 1972.

Wright, Herbert G. *Boccaccio in England from Chaucer to Tennyson*, 1957.

Madison U. Sowell

RICHARD BRAUTIGAN

Born: Tacoma, Washington; January 30, 1935
Died: Bolinas, California; September, 1984

Principal short fiction
Trout Fishing in America, 1967; *Revenge of the Lawn: Stories, 1962-1970*, 1971; *The Tokyo-Montana Express*, 1980.

Other literary forms
Richard Brautigan's fragmented prose style makes any effort to classify his work into long and short fiction difficult and somewhat arbitrary. Brautigan himself called all of his prose works novels, with the single exception of *Revenge of the Lawn*, but critics have understandably referred to his books as "un-novels" or "Brautigans," works that seem approachable only on their own terms because they deliberately confront the realistic tradition of the novel by disregarding causality and character development.

Nevertheless, *Trout Fishing in America* and *The Tokyo-Montana Express* can be grouped with *Revenge of the Lawn* as examples of Brautigan's short fiction. Although arguably unified by point of view, setting, theme, and recurrent characters, *Trout Fishing in America* and *The Tokyo-Montana Express* lack any semblance of coherent plot and many of the individual selections which compose each book possess an integrity independent of context. Brautigan's other novels are distinguished by at least a thin strand of continuous narrative. The most important of these longer fictions are *A Confederate General from Big Sur* (1964), *In Watermelon Sugar* (1968), and *The Abortion: An Historical Romance* (1971). The best known of his eleven poetry collections are *The Pill Versus the Springhill Mine Disaster* (1968), *Rommel Drives on Deep into Egypt* (1970), and *June 30th, June 30th* (1978).

Achievements
After *Trout Fishing in America* was published by Don Allen's Four Season Foundation in 1967, it became a favorite of the counterculture movement that was peaking during that "summer of love." Brautigan was awarded a National Endowment for the Arts grant the following year. At the suggestion of Kurt Vonnegut, Jr., Seymour Lawrence bought the rights to *Trout Fishing in America* and promoted it nationally. The novel became a best-seller, eventually selling more than two million copies in twelve languages. The popularity spread to *A Confederate General from Big Sur*, *In Watermelon Sugar*, and *Revenge of the Lawn*, all of which sold hundreds of thousands of copies.

Brautigan's fortunes declined dramatically in the 1970's as the counterculture movement faded. One critic called *The Hawkline Monster: A Gothic Western* (1974) "a terrible book, deeply unfunny, in no need of having been written," and subsequent books met with similar critical hostility. By the end of the decade, Brautigan was being frequently dismissed as an anachronism. American sales also began to fall, and before his death, Brautigan was having difficulty getting his books published. As his popularity declined in the United States, however, he was discovered in Japan, increasing the foreign sales of his work.

Biography

Born in Tacoma, Washington, in the midst of the Great Depression, Richard Brautigan moved to San Francisco in 1956, arriving in time to be a peripheral part of the Beat movement. He managed to publish several volumes of poetry although none sold well and many were simply given away. Some were printed on packages of seeds. In 1961, during an extended camping trip in the Snake River country of Idaho, Brautigan wrote *Trout Fishing in America*, but he was unable to get his unusual book published until 1967. A more traditional novel, *A Confederate General from Big Sur*, sold only 743 copies in 1964. In 1967, while serving for a year as poet-in-residence at the California Institute of Technology, Brautigan began to develop an underground following. In the next few years, *Trout Fishing in America* made Brautigan rich and famous, and the media identified him as the literary spokesman of the counterculture. From 1972 to 1980, Brautigan produced a series of unsuccessful parodic novels and refused all lecture invitations and interview requests, dividing his time between his Montana ranch and Japan, where interest in his writing was increasing. He returned to the lecture circuit in 1980, but the years of popularity were irrecoverably behind him. His friends reported that this diminishing readership depressed Brautigan, and in September, 1984, he shot himself. The body was discovered in Brautigan's home in Bolinas, California, on October 25, 1984.

Analysis

Richard Brautigan's short fiction explores the imagination's power to transform reality. In some stories, this means contrasting a gritty, naturalistic portrait of cheap materialism, personal defeat, and latent violence with a vision of the lost American Eden or a nostalgic remembrance of childhood's innocence. Collectively, the stories describe a search for good in contemporary America, but because they sympathize with the defeated, they suggest that such a search is futile. Brautigan's stories stoically accept the conditions of existence, withholding judgment while suggesting that the imagination holds the only possible hope for transcendence.

The stories are self-consciously artificial, continually calling attention to the process of their creation. The typographical experimentation, outrageous figures of speech, extreme compression, and deceptively simplistic syntax work through a disengaged narrative voice to create prose that has been compared to skywriting. The conscious artificiality of Brautigan's stylistic mannerisms has led some critics to dismiss his work as whimsical, coy, naïve, and self-indulgent.

Although *Trout Fishing in America* became popular as a counterculture book during the late 1960's, it was written in 1961 as a late expression of the San Francisco Beat movement. Brautigan, like other Beats, had been conditioned by the experience of the Great Depression and World War II, historical examples of deprivation and violence, and he saw in these experiences deep truths that belied America's complacent prosperity. In contrast to the radicals of the 1930's and the New Left of the 1960's, Brautigan and other Beats sought social change not through collective action but through personal transformation.

Thus, *Trout Fishing in America* is an antididactic book, an effort to document America from a disengaged, thoroughly nonpolitical point of view. Although the America it documents is spiritually decayed, the forty-seven stories that compose *Trout Fishing in America* do not promote a program of social reform. Instead, the book's underlying philosophy, derived from Zen Buddhist belief, assumes that life is essentially determined and that social progress is an illusion. Brautigan expounds a politics of the imagination in which social activism is supplanted by the individual imagination's ability to create a vision of freedom, a vision of an America that is "often only a place in the mind." To this extent, the explicit theme of Kurt Vonnegut's *Mother Night*, which was published in 1961, as *Trout Fishing in America* was being written, suits Brautigan's book: "We are what we pretend to be, so we must be careful what we pretend to be." Brautigan's unnamed narrator uses his imagination to "fish" for something of value in the stream of contemporary America, but like his comically failed fisherman Alonso Hagen in "Fishing on the Streets of Eternity," his effort becomes "an interesting experiment in total loss."

Stylistically, *Trout Fishing in America* seems without literary precedent, a documentary collage of prose poems and cultural allusions that exhibits no interest in character, plot development, or psychological motivation. Literary parodies (of Ernest Hemingway, John Steinbeck, Henry David Thoreau) are juxtaposed to references to historical figures (Richard Nixon, "Pretty Boy" Floyd, Andrew Carnegie, Caryl Chessman, Deanna Durbin) and the signatures of popular culture (bumper stickers, diaries, tombstone engravings, recipes, warning signs). Woven through this cultural stew is the protean phrase "Trout Fishing in America," which is applied to people, places, a hotel, a pen nib, a state of mind, and the book itself.

"The Cover for Trout Fishing in America," the opening piece, exemplifies the book's self-consciousness and introduces Brautigan's ironic view of America. By describing the book's cover photograph, Brautigan reminds his reader that *Trout Fishing in America* is itself an artifact, a component of the society he is documenting. He then juxtaposes a statue of Benjamin Franklin, the prototypical American optimist, to the derelicts who sadly wait in the park hoping for a handout. Although the concluding quotation from Franz Kafka, "I like the Americans because they are healthy and optimistic," is ironic, Brautigan's matter-of-fact presentation prevents the piece from being read as social protest. Instead, the book implies that optimism, no matter how ill-founded, is a part of the American condition.

In a complementary way, "The Kool-Aid Wino" demonstrates the imagination's power to overcome the limitations of existence. The Kool-Aid Wino is a child who is restricted from picking beans or engaging in active play by a hernia. His family is too poor to afford an operation or even a truss, so the Kool-Aid Wino spends his days lovingly preparing a watered-down, sugarless version of Kool-Aid "like a famous brain surgeon removing a disordered portion of the imagination." Through his ceremonious preparation and consumption he creates "his own Kool-Aid reality" and is "able to illuminate himself by it." The story celebrates the human capacity to transcend reality while simultaneously portraying the sad deprivations that make such imaginative escape necessary.

In "Trout Fishing on the Bevel," Brautigan's narrator describes fishing a stream that runs past two graveyards, one for the rich and one for the poor. Like many of Brautigan's short fictions, "Trout Fishing on the Bevel" meditates on loneliness, poverty, death, and the desire to transcend them. The narrator describes the weathered boards, "like heels of stale bread," that mark the graves of the poor and imagines darkly humorous inscriptions ("Beloved Worked-to-Death Mother Of") that disclose the painful reality usually disguised by euphemisms. In contrast, the graves of the rich are marked with "marble hors d'oeuvres like horses trotting up the fancy paths to the sky." Admittedly "bothered" by "the poverty of the dead," the narrator has "a vision of going over to the poor graveyard and gathering up grass and fruit jars and tin cans and markers and wilted flowers and bugs and weeds and clods and going home and putting a hook in the vise and tying a fly with all that stuff and then going outside and casting it up into the sky, watching it float over clouds and then into the evening star." It is one of Brautigan's clearest statements of his artistic purpose, expressing his desire to construct from the forgotten or overlooked bits of life an art that can imaginatively free his reader from the particular loneliness of existence.

"The Cleveland Wrecking Yard" is placed near the end of *Trout Fishing in America*, and it provides a caricature of America's obsessive materialism. At the Cleveland Wrecking Yard, a microcosm of America, the narrator finds a trout stream for sale, stacked up in lengths beside toilets and other used plumbing supplies, but he does not condemn this outrageous "commodification" of nature; instead, he sees the Cleveland Wrecking Yard as a repository for tarnished dreams that can only be revitalized with imagination. Indeed, the process by which discarded items can be recycled parallels the way in which Brautigan salvages the scraps of American culture to construct *Trout Fishing in America*.

Many of the stories collected in *Revenge of the Lawn* deal with childhood, portraying it as a fragile refuge, a time when people are more open to the transforming power of imagination. The stories contrast this freedom with the crippling disillusionments that accompany maturation and the sadder ways adults use imagination to escape reality.

The title story, however, shows Brautigan at his most playful, demonstrating an ability to use comic misdirection and a deadpan narrative voice in the manner of Mark Twain. This rambling, autobiographical remembrance focuses on his grandmother, his grandfather, and a man named Jack. The grandfather, "a minor Washington mystic," went mad after he correctly "prophesied the exact date when World War I would start." In his madness he returns to an eternal childhood in which he is six years old. He is replaced by Jack, an itinerant salesman of lots in Florida, who hawks "a vision of eternal oranges and sunshine." These contrasting visionaries are set against the grandmother, a bootlegger, who sells a utilitarian sort of bottled vision. The action of the story revolves around Jack's relationship to nature, specifically the lawn which he has destroyed by driving on it, a pear tree which grows in the yard, the bees that are attracted to the pears, and the grandmother's geese. The geese eat some fermenting mash and pass out in the yard. The grandmother, comically assuming that the geese are dead, plucks them. They recover and are standing about "like some helpless, primitive American advertisement for aspirin," when Jack, distracted by the sight, drives into the house. In a concluding note, the narrator writes that his earliest memory is an image of Jack setting fire to the tree "while the fruit was still green on the branches." "Revenge of the Lawn" demonstrates Brautigan's ability to write comic narrative while satirizing man's foolish attempts to manage nature.

"Corporal" is a bittersweet inverted Horatio Alger story in which the narrator recounts his wartime involvement in a paper drive. The young patriots were to earn military ranks according to the amount of paper they collected. The narrator's initial eagerness was thwarted, however, when he realized that "the kids who wore the best clothes and had lots of spending money and got to eat hot lunch every day" had an unfair advantage, for these kids "were already generals," and "they strutted their military airs around the playground." Like so many of Brautigan's characters, the narrator admitted defeat and entered "the disenchanted paper shadows of America where failure is a bounced check or a bad report card or a letter ending a love affair and all the words that hurt people when they read them." "Corporal" evokes the opposing worlds of good and bad paper, the childlike creative dream and the stifling economic and social reality. The story painfully portrays the disappointments that constitute so much of life, and emphasizes, in a manner that is particularly relevant for an author who places imaginative creation at the center of life, the precariousness of a life lived in the mind.

The last piece in *Revenge of the Lawn* is one of the most openly autobiographical. "The World War I Los Angeles Airplane" is Brautigan's response to the death of his father-in-law, but this piece, despite its specificity, effectively communicates Brautigan's general sense of life as a process of attrition (the first word of *A Confederate General from Big Sur*). "The World War I Los Angeles Airplane" exemplifies Brautigan's disregard for traditional narrative method and his love of lists, for after a brief introduction, the story presents a numbered catalog of thirty-three separate thoughts. In an elliptical manner, these distinct statements chronicle the life of a defeated man. Most suggestive is the contrast between his father-in-law's experience as a pilot in World War I, when "he had been followed by a rainbow across the skies of France," and the quiet alcoholism of his final years of inactivity, when he watched daytime television and "used sweet wine in place of life because he didn't have any more life to use." The father-in-law's retreat from life parallels the Kool-Aid Wino's, except that in "The World War I Los Angeles Airplane" there is no intimation that the escape is illuminating.

During the 1970's, Brautigan announced his intention to write a novel parodying a popular genre each year. *The Hawkline Monster, Willard and His Bowling Trophies: A Perverse Mystery* (1975), *Sombrero Fallout: A Japanese Novel* (1976), and *Dreaming of Babylon: A Private Eye Novel, 1942* (1977) were critical disasters for Brautigan. By the time he published *The Tokyo-Montana Express* in 1980, his literary reputation had been ruined, and he had been deserted by most of his readers. His status as a counterculture hero, which was always based on a misunderstanding of his work, had become irrelevant, except as another barrier standing between him and the readers of the 1980's. Although Brautigan resumed lecturing to promote *The Tokyo-Montana Express*, he was unable to recapture the broad acceptance that had made him a best-selling author a decade before. Nevertheless, *The Tokyo-Montana Express*, for all of its unevenness, marked a healthy return to the effective short fiction evident in *Trout Fishing in America* and *Revenge of the Lawn*.

The Tokyo-Montana Express contains 131 individual prose pieces. A few of these approximate the traditional form of the short story, but most would more accurately be called anecdotes, vignettes, or prose poems. Overall, Brautigan's tendency toward compression is more evident in *The Tokyo-Montana Express* than in his earlier work. He is also more restrained in his use of bizarre figures of speech, and the disengaged flatness of his prose is more consistent.

As in all of his short fiction, Brautigan's primary concern in *The Tokyo-Montana Express* is the imagination. In *Trout Fishing in America*, he figuratively "fishes" for a vision of America; in *The Tokyo-Montana Express*, he travels an imaginary transpacific railroad, a vehicle for the metaphysical commutation of ideas between East and West. Written after a period during which he spent most of his time either in Japan or on his farm in Montana, Brautigan's collection examines the cultures of East and West, repeatedly showing the ironic similarities and in the end suggesting that Montana's big sky country may be a geographically appropriate setting for the philosophy of Japan.

In *The Tokyo-Montana Express*, Brautigan's involvement with Zen Buddhist thought is more explicit than in his earlier work, expressing itself in the stoic attitude of the narrative voice he employs. One paradox expressed in the collection is that while all experiences are equally worthy of examination, all experiences are also ultimately insignificant. The narrator's emotional disengagement cannot disguise a sadness that is much more prevalent here than in Brautigan's earlier work. Indeed, the narrator in *The Tokyo-Montana Express* expects very little of life, accepts the inevitable process of attrition, assumes that any meaning must originate in the individual imagination, and exhibits great faith in the integrity of that imagination.

"Another Texas Ghost Story" recounts the life of a man who, while growing up on a remote Texas ranch, is visited at night by a ghost. Forty years later at a family reunion, he accidentally admits his childhood experience to his brother and two sisters only to discover that they too had seen the apparition when they were children. They were all afraid to mention it at the time because they were afraid they would be thought crazy. In "Another Texas Ghost Story," Brautigan connects childhood and imagination and implies that societal pressure makes us less receptive to the wonder around us.

"Werewolf Raspberries" is an example of the extreme compression of many pieces in *The Tokyo-Montana Express*. Its seventy-nine words, interrupted by ellipses, seem like the fragmented remains of a more complete narrative, yet this abbreviated prose poem manages to communicate a complex story. Set in the spring of 1940 with a Glenn Miller recording playing in the background, the narrative voice in "Werewolf Raspberries" addresses a young man whose single-minded romantic desire to give his girl "a great big kiss" has been inexplicably thwarted by the raspberries' "little teeth shining in the moonlight." The piece concludes with the ironic remonstrance that "If you had played your cards right, you could have been killed at Pearl Harbor instead." On one level, this brief prose poem expresses a nostalgic feel for dreams lost to the inevitable imperfections and accidents of existence, but the final comment ironically compares the harmless adolescent dream of romance with the lethal, but equally adolescent, dream of glory.

"The Menu/1965" is the longest piece in *The Tokyo-Montana Express*, and it shows Brautigan extracting significance from a strange but mundane object, in this case the monthly menu prepared for residents of San Quentin's Death Row. The narrator resists judging the significance of this artifact; instead, he reports several other people's reactions to this strange juxtaposition of dining and death. At the end, the narrator and the intellectual father of a friend become entranced in "a long conversation where the menu became a kind of thought diving bell going deeper and deeper, deeper and deeper until we were at the cold flat bottom of the sea, staring fish-like at the colored Easter eggs that were going to be served next Sunday on Death Row." The allusion to Easter portrays the condemned prisoners as Christlike sacrifices, but the primary focus of the story is the fascination of the object and the manner in which it triggers the imagination.

All of Brautigan's short fictions are meant to become "thought diving bells" for the reader, and often, as in "The Menu/1965," the process of mental exploration begins with the contemplation of a simple object or event. In the end, Brautigan's creative process stands as an exemplum of a method for confronting life's attrition.

Other major works

NOVELS: *A Confederate General from Big Sur*, 1964; *In Watermelon Sugar*, 1968; *The Abortion: An Historical Romance*, 1971; *The Hawkline Monster: A Gothic Western*, 1974; *Willard and His Bowling Trophies: A Perverse Mystery*, 1975; *Sombrero Fallout: A Japanese Novel*, 1976; *Dreaming of Babylon: A Private Eye Novel, 1942*, 1977; *So the Wind Won't Blow It All Away*, 1982.

POETRY: *The Return of the Rivers*, 1957; *The Galilee Hitch-Hiker*, 1958; *Lay the Marble Tea, Twenty-four Poems*, 1959; *The Octopus Frontier*, 1960; *All Watched over by Machines of Loving Grace*, 1967; *The Pill Versus the Springhill Mine Disaster*, 1968; *Rommel Drives on Deep into Egypt*, 1970; *June 30th, June 30th*, 1978.

Bibliography

Adams, Robert. "Brautigan Was Here," in the *New York Review of Books*. April 22, 1971, pp. 24-26.

Foster, Edward Halsey. *Richard Brautigan*, 1983.

Hendin, Josephine. *Vulnerable People*, 1978.

Hicks, Jack. *In the Singer's Temple: Prose Fiction of Barthelme, Gaines, Brautigan, Piercy, Kesey, and Kosinski*, 1981.

Malley, Terence. *Richard Brautigan*, 1972.

Putz, Manfred. *The Story of Identity: American Fiction of the Sixties*, 1979.

Tanner, Tony. "Fragments and Fantasies," in *City of Words: American Fiction 1950-1970*, 1971.

Carl Brucker

DINO BUZZATI
Dino Buzzati Traverso

Born: San Pellegrino, near Belluno, Italy; October 16, 1906
Died: Milan, Italy; January 28, 1972

Principal short fiction

I sette messaggeri, 1942; *Paura alla Scala*, 1949; *Il crollo della Baliverna*, 1954; *Esperimento di magia*, 1958; *Sessanta racconti*, 1958; *Egregio signore, siamo spiacenti di . . .*, 1960; *Catastrophe: The Strange Stories of Dino Buzzati*, 1966; *Il colombre*, 1966; *La boutique del mistero*, 1968; *Le notti difficili*, 1971; *180 racconti*, 1982; *Restless Nights*, 1983; *The Siren: A Selection from Dino Buzzati*, 1984.

Other literary forms

Dino Buzzati is best known as a novelist. His third novel, *Il deserto dei Tartari* (1940; *The Tartar Steppe*, 1952), critically acclaimed as his masterwork, has been translated into the major European languages as well as Japanese. Structured along the themes of time, obsession, solitude, waiting, and renunciation, it is set against the majestic beauty and mystery of rugged and timeless mountains. In *The Tartar Steppe*, these themes, present in the novella *Bàrnabo delle montagne* (1933; *Bàrnabo of the Mountains*, 1984) and the novel *Il segreto del Bosco Vecchio* (1935), become more existentialist. The protagonist's life, symbolic of life in general, is viewed as a perennial waiting, in which hope for heroic deeds results only in failure and final renunciation—for the inevitable destiny of all humans is death, symbolized in the novel by the Tartars.

Buzzati's *Il grande ritratto* (1960; *Larger than Life*, 1962) and *Un amore* (1963; *A Love Affair*, 1964) have different outward environments: The first has a science-fiction frame, the second is founded on erotic realism but is actually an artistic transposition of the author's painful personal experiences dating back to the 1940's. Inwardly, however, Buzzati's usual themes remain visible: solitude, anguish, and alienation, in a foreboding and mysterious atmosphere and ending in death.

Buzzati wrote fifteen plays. Twelve premiered in Milan; one in Naples, *L'uomo che andrà in America* (1962; the man who will go to America); one in Spoleto, *Le finestre* (1959; the windows); and one, *Una ragazza arrivò* (1959; a girl arrived), aired on Italian Radio. Most of Buzzati's plays reflect the tormented, often nightmarish, atmosphere that characterizes his fiction. Perhaps the best known is *Un caso clinico* (1953; a clinical case), based on his story "Sette piani" ("Seven Floors"). After a successful run in Italy, it was staged in Berlin in 1954 and in Paris in 1955 by Albert Camus. His complete dramatic works were published together in the volume *Teatro* (1980; plays).

Buzzati's successful children's book *La famosa invasione degli orsi in Sicilia* (1945; *The Bears' Famous Invasion of Sicily*, 1947) contains the author's own drawings, originally created to entertain his sister's children.

Buzzati also wrote poetry that deals mainly with the absurdity of modern life. He produced a modern rendering of the Orpheus myth in *Poema a fumetti* (1969; comic-strip poem), in which the classic Greek poet Orpheus is transformed into Orfi, a rock-and-roll singer. It was awarded the Paese Sera Prize for best comic strip in 1969.

Buzzati's prose collection *In quel preciso momento* (1950; at that very moment) is difficult to define; it contains only a few stories, while the rest are notes or poignant reflections on his own actions and feelings as well as those of others, in which he captures all the themes found in his writings.

Buzzati's journalistic essays, written for the Milanese newspaper *Corriere della Sera*, subsequently appeared in book form. They are original in style, with a marked tendency for the fantastic and bizarre, especially in *I misteri dell'Italia* (1978; Italy's mysteries).

Achievements

Dino Buzzati's works often take a surrealistic and metaphysical turn and can be compared to the fantasies of Franz Kafka. His closest affinity is with the Romantic tradition of E. T. A. Hoffmann and Edgar Allan Poe. His short stories and novels—philosophical and symbolic tales of life's relentless passing, full of metaphysical allegories, strange events, and pessimism—are unique in Italian literature, both for their themes and for their style. Buzzati's characters, overwhelmed by cosmic fear, find themselves in a state of isolation and perpetual waiting. Buzzati's pessimism, however, is somewhat tempered by a vague Christian element, the hope of ultimate redemption from evil through the exercise of free will. Since death is viewed as the only possible conclusion to life, man's ability to die with dignity constitutes his greatest heroic deed.

Some critics saw Buzzati's existentialism as a snobbish and egotistic attitude. Indeed, Buzzati's works are not easily appreciated by the unprepared reader, who will remain perplexed before the strange, often hidden and allegoric meaning of his prose. At the same time, however, the stories are capitvating. He manages to maintain a sense of continuous suspense, capturing the reader's attention yet leaving him perplexed.

Translated into several languages, Buzzati's works became extremely popular in France, where a Buzzati society, Association Internationale des Amis de Dino Buzzati, was established in 1976. His masterpiece *The Tartar Steppe* influenced Julien Gracq's novel *Le Rivage des Syrtes* (1951; the shore of the Syrtes) and resulted in a French-Italian coproduction of a film directed by Valerio Zurlini in 1976.

Buzzati received the Gargano Prize in 1951 for *In quel preciso momento*, the Naples Prize in 1957 for *Il crollo della Baliverna*, the Strega Prize in 1958 for *Sessanta racconti*, and the All'Amalia Prize in 1970 for his narrative works in general. He is considered to be one of the most important writers of modern Italy.

Biography

Dino Buzzati was born at San Pellegrino, near Belluno, in the Dolomite Alps, where his family possessed a summerhouse. The mountains, to which he returned every summer, played an important part in his life (he became a passionate Alpine climber and skier) and influenced his narratives. He received all of his schooling, including a law degree, in Milan, where the Buzzati family resided even after the death, in 1920, of his father, Giulio Cesare Buzzati, a professor of international law. As a teenager, together with his friend Arturo Brambilla, Buzzati developed a passion for Egyptology and an intense interest in the designs of illustrator Arthur Rackham.

In 1928, Buzzati began a journalistic career for *Corriere della Sera*, the leading Italian newspaper, eventually becoming a chief editor. During World War II, he was war correspondent with the Italian navy. Although he was only thirty-five years old, he feared that he was losing his youth and his strength, that he would no longer be able to climb his beloved mountains. Indeed, Buzzati would constantly measure his physical strength against the mountain: Every year the Dolomites seemed to him to become taller and more difficult to climb, while he worried over the slightest difficulty, and, like his characters, expected only catastrophes.

Buzzati was married late in life, at the age of sixty. His wife, Almerina Antoniazzi, became curator of his many papers, including sixty-three volumes of his diary, after he died of cancer in 1972.

Analysis

Dino Buzzati's stories can be read on two levels: as strange tales, full of mysterious events, or as symbolic depictions of life's elusive reality. The period in which the action takes place is frequently vague; even when a precise date is given, there is a timeless quality about his stories. More important is the problem of existence itself, the inner torments that derive from the problem of facing reality.

In "Seven Messengers" (included in *Restless Nights*), which gave the title to the first collection of Buzzati's short fiction, *I sette messaggeri*, a prince sets out to explore his father's kingdom in the company of seven knights, who serve him as messengers and links to his father, his capital, and his house. As the prince advances toward the frontier, however, the messengers take longer and longer to return, and the letters they bring him seem to recall distant things. One day, the prince realizes that the messenger about to depart for the capital will return only in thirty-four years, by which time the prince will

be very old or even dead. Nevertheless, he continues his trip toward the border, with ever-increasing curiosity, to explore the unknown regions. Symbolically, the prince's trip is the journey of life. Day by day, one becomes more
and more distant from one's parents and childhood sentiments, full of eagerness to discover what lies ahead, even if the ultimate goal is death.

In "Seven Floors," from the same collection, a man with a minor illness is
sent to a hospital, where he learns that the patients are housed on each of
the seven floors according to the gravity of their state: The top floor, the seventh, is for mild cases; each lower floor is for increasingly severe cases; and
the dying are moved to the first floor, where the blinds go down at the moment of death. The man, assigned to the seventh floor, is assured that he will
be cured in two or three weeks. After ten days, however, he is asked, as a
favor, to yield his room to a woman, who is arriving with two children who
will be housed in the two adjacent rooms. He consents, only to discover that
he is to be moved to the sixth floor—since no other rooms are available on
the seventh floor—but is assured that this is only a temporary arrangement.
Gradually, however, he descends from floor to floor under different pretexts
and with ever-increasing alarm, until he arrives on the first floor, where he
watches the blinds go down in his room. Again, this man's strange adventure
is symbolic of life: Each period brings one, often without awareness, closer
to death.

In, "Paura alla Scala" ("The Scala Scare"), from the collection of that
title, an old pianist who has trouble understanding his composer son and his
new music goes to the Scala Theater for the premiere of a new opera. On his
way, he finds the city strangely empty of people. He meets a former student,
who makes an incomprehensible remark about the pianist's son and his
friends. The opera, with its disturbing and violent music, added to the po-
lemics as to its political allusions, increases the general tension among the
audience. During intermission, a gentleman tries to warn the pianist about
his son's impudence but does not finish his sentence. At the reception after
the performance, there is much talk about a revolt in progress, and it is
decided that it is unsafe to go home during the night. The fearful audience
settles down to wait. Soon the audience splits into two groups: those favoring
the rebellion and those condemning it, while some individuals oscillate between the two. Tension rises as the night progresses, and the old pianist, worried about his son, who is at home, decides to leave. Everyone watches him
as he leaves on unsteady legs, the result of the generously flowing champagne
at the reception. He reaches the center of the square in front of the Scala
Theater and is seen falling flat on his face with outstretched hands, as if
felled by a machine gun. Everyone stares at him, but no one moves. When
dawn finally arrives, a lone cyclist drives past; then, an old street sweeper
starts sweeping the square, and other people follow: The city is awakening to
another day. The old pianist wakes up, full of amazement, gets on his feet,

and trots home. An old flower-woman, dressed in black, enters the foyer, passing among the liverish-looking assembly and offering a gardenia. After establishing this mounting suspense, Buzzati ends the story abruptly, leaving the reader to wonder what, if anything, has happened.

Similarly, in "Qualcosa era successo" ("Catastrophe"), from *Il crollo della Baliverna*, Buzzati describes, from a passenger's point of view, a ten-hour, nonstop journey by express train. Contact with the rest of the world is only indirect, through the view out the train windows. It soon becomes evident, however, that something unusual is happening out there, for all the people seem to communicate alarm to one another. Subsequently, large crowds, as if in flight from danger, begin to move in the opposite direction from that in which the train is traveling, and the stations which the train passes are crowded. Yet none of the silent passengers manages to read the headline of the newspapers waved at them. A passenger grabs one, but it tears away, leaving in her hand only the letters -TION of the headline. When the train finally rolls into the station of the big city and comes to a stop, the passengers find a deserted place with no humans in sight.

This story was interpreted as symbolic of the fear of war or nuclear disaster. Buzzati, however, gives the reader a clue when he makes his protagonist exclaim that trains are just like life itself.

In "Il colombre" ("The Colomber"), from the collection of the same title, Stefano becomes a ship's captain, in spite of his father's warning never to go to sea and to beware of the mysterious fish, the colomber, which never abandons his victim. Stefano spends all of his life in restless navigating, attracted to the sea, where the colomber, or ruin, he knows, awaits him. He becomes old, never having enjoyed his riches, and decides to go out and face his enemy. When he does, he finds that the colomber was chasing after him only to give him a pearl which would have given him luck, power, love, and peace of mind. It is too late for Stefano: He has wasted his life.

In "La giacca stregata" ("The Bewitched Jacket"), from the same collection, a man discovers that every time he puts his hand into the pocket of his new suit, for which he has not yet paid, he finds a ten-thousand lire bill. He starts extracting money but soon realizes that there is a direct relationship between this action and the tragic criminal events he reads about in the newspapers. Still, he is unable to resist, until an old woman who lives in the same apartment house as he kills herself because she lost her only means of support, her monthly pension money, the sum of which corresponds exactly to the amount the man took from his magic pocket that day. Horrified, he drives to the mountains and burns the jacket, but hears a voice saying, "Too late, too late," though no one is in sight. His car (bought with the mysterious money) is gone, as are his houses and savings in town. He is a ruined man; he also knows that one day the tailor who made that suit for him will demand payment. In this fantastic story, one sees that man is responsible for his actions and will have to pay for them when the last rendering of accounts comes.

Particularly interesting are two surrealistic stories in which a metamorphosis occurs. Unlike Franz Kafka's novella *Die Verwandlung* (1915; *Metamorphosis*, 1936), in which one confronts a character who has undergone an unexplained transformation, Buzzati's stories show the transformations as they occur and offer reasons for them. In "Suicidio al parco" (suicide in the park), also from *Il colombre*, a young man's obsession with fancy cars reaches the point at which he speaks only of cars and ignores his loving, beautiful wife, Faustina. One day, a friend sees him in an unusual, fancy car, which he drives with passion. When asked about Faustina, he is vague, claiming that she has gone back to her parents. Some years later, the friend reads in the newspaper about a car that, driverless, drove through several street blocks, avoiding automobiles and pedestrians, and smashed itself against an old ruin in the park. Immediately, he thinks of Faustina and confronts her husband, who confesses that she, to make him happy, sacrificed herself by becoming a car. On the day of the accident, the thankless husband was on his way to sell the car, which had become old. Faustina, the car, therefore committed suicide. This story criticizes modern obsessions, here with fancy cars: Men become so attached to them that they treat them better than their own wives.

A wife's metamorphosis is painfully observed by her husband in "La moglie con le ali" ("The Count's Wife"), from Buzzati's last collection, *Le notti difficili*. The count is much older than his pretty wife, Lucina, and is very jealous of her. One day, he notices a strange growth on his wife's back, which becomes larger until it turns into full-fledged wings that reach the ground. Extremely worried and fearing scandal in his provincial town, he keeps her locked up and hidden at home. Upon the advice of his mother, a priest is consulted, who suggests that he test the wings: If Lucina can fly, the wings must be a gift of God rather than of the Devil. That night Lucina flies, joyful to be free, but she is locked up again so that she will not be seen. She resolves to continue her flights secretly. One autumn day, she is almost killed by a hunter. To save herself, she cries to the young hunter, whom she recognizes as a friend, not to shoot, and makes herself known. That evening, when the Count comes home, he finds the wings gone. Only the priest suspects that Lucina met the Devil and lost her wings.

Buzzati's stories are always original, even when based on old literary or pseudoreligious schemes, for he gives them his personal stamp. They are entertaining and at the same time extremely moral. Touching upon problems that are timeless, they are not restricted by national boundaries. Buzzati is, indeed, a master in the art of storytelling.

Other major works

NOVELS: *Bàrnabo delle montagne*, 1933 (*Bàrnabo of the Mountains*, 1984); *Il segreto del Bosco Vecchio*, 1935; *Il deserto dei Tartari*, 1940 (*The Tartar Steppe*, 1952); *Il grande ritratto*, 1960 (*Larger than Life*, 1962); *Un amore*, 1963 (*A Love Affair*, 1964).

PLAYS: *Piccola passeggiata*, 1942; *La rivolta contro i poveri*, 1946; *Un caso clinico*, 1953; *Le finestre*, 1959; *Una ragazza arrivò*, 1959; *L'uomo che andrà in America*, 1962; *La fine del borghese*, 1966; *Teatro*, 1980.

LIBRETTOS: *Ferrovia soprelevata*, 1955 (music by Luciano Chailly); *Procedura penale*, 1959 (music by Chailly); *Il mantello*, 1960 (music by Chailly); *Battono alla porta*, 1961 (based on Riccardo Malpiero's short story); *Era proibito*, 1963 (music by Chailly).

POETRY: *Il capitano Pic ed altre poesie*, 1965; *Due poemetti*, 1967; *Poema a fumetti*, 1969; *Le Poesie*, 1982.

NONFICTION: *Cronache terrestri*, 1972; *Dino Buzzati al Giro d'Italia*, 1981; *Cronache nere*, 1984; *Lettere a Brambilla*, 1985.

CHILDREN'S LITERATURE: *La famosa invasione degli orsi in Sicilia*, 1945 (*The Bears' Famous Invasion of Sicily*, 1947); *I dispiaceri del re*, 1980.

MISCELLANEOUS: *Il libro delle pipe*, 1945 (with Eppe Ramazzotti); *In quel preciso momento*, 1950 (includes stories and autobiographical sketches); *I miracoli di Val Morel*, 1971 (includes thirty-nine of Buzzati's paintings with his text); *Romanzi e racconti*, 1975; *I misteri dell'Italia*, 1978 (includes essays and stories).

Bibliography

Baumann, Barbara. *Dino Buzzati: Untersuchungen zur Thematik in seinem Erzählwerk*, 1980.

Biasin, Gian-Paolo. "The Secret Fears of Man: Dino Buzzati," in *Italian Quarterly*. VI, no. 22 (1962), pp. 78-93.

Crotti, Ilaria. *Buzzati*, 1977.

Gianfranceschi, Fausto. *Dino Buzzati*, 1967.

Laganà Gion, Antonella. *Dino Buzzati: Un autore da rileggere*, 1983.

Mignone, Mario B. *Anormalità e angoscia nella narrativa di Dino Buzzati*, 1981.

Panafieu, Yves. *Dino Buzzati: Un autoritratto*, 1973.

Veronese-Arslan, Antonia. *Invito alla lettura di Buzzati*, 1974.

Natalia Costa-Zalessow

MORLEY CALLAGHAN

Born: Toronto, Canada; September 22, 1903

Principal short fiction

A Native Argosy, 1929; *Now That April's Here and Other Stories*, 1936; *Morley Callaghan's Stories*, 1959; *The Lost and Found Stories of Morley Callaghan*, 1985.

Other literary forms

Although Morley Callaghan is a masterful short-story writer, he has also won recognition for his many novels, the most highly regarded being *Such Is My Beloved* (1934), *The Loved and the Lost* (1951), and *Close to the Sun Again* (1977). He is also the author of a novella (*No Man's Meat*, 1931), a children's book (*Luke Baldwin's Vow*, 1948), and three plays (*To Tell the Truth*, 1949; *Going Home*, 1949; and *Season of the Witch*, 1976). He has recorded some of his stories for children and others have been filmed. Starting his career as a journalist, Callaghan contributed articles and essays to newspapers and journals throughout his life. His nonfiction works include *Winter* (1974) and *That Summer in Paris: Memories of Tangled Friendships with Hemingway, Fitzgerald, and Some Others* (1963), an entertaining account of the heady days in Paris in 1929, when he socialized with Ernest Hemingway, F. Scott Fitzgerald, James Joyce, and other writers.

Achievements

In the 1920's, Callaghan's stories impressed Hemingway, who introduced them to Ezra Pound. Pound subsequently printed them in his magazine, *The Exile*. The stories also impressed Fitzgerald, who presented them to Maxwell Perkins, his editor at Scribner's. Perkins later published Callaghan's stories as well as some of his novels. Although considered a highly promising writer in the 1920's and 1930's, Callaghan neither developed a large audience nor achieved the type of reputation that his works warrant. Edmund Wilson has commented that he is "perhaps the most unjustly neglected novelist in the English-speaking world." Even so, he is the recipient of several awards: Canada's Governor General's Literary Award (1951), the Gold Medal of the Royal Society of Canada (1958), the Lorne Pierce Medal (1960), the Canada Council Molson Prize (1970), the Royal Bank of Canada Award (1970), and the Companion of the Order of Canada (1982). He was also nominated for a Nobel Prize. His fiction is praised for its direct, unornamented prose, for its sympathetic portrayal of ordinary people, and for its honest treatment of the problems of contemporary life.

Biography

Born in Toronto, Canada, on September 22, 1903, Edward Morley Callaghan was reared by Roman Catholic parents of Irish descent. He grew up interested in sports, especially boxing and baseball, but at a young age he also displayed a talent for writing, selling at age seventeen his first article, a description of Yonge and Albert streets in Toronto, to the *Star Weekly* for twelve dollars. In 1921, he entered St. Michael's College of the University of Toronto, and during the summers and part-time during the school year, he was a reporter for the Toronto *Daily Star*, the same newspaper that employed Ernest Hemingway, who encouraged him in his attempts at fiction writing. Receiving his B.A. in 1925, he enrolled in Osgoode Hall Law School in Toronto. He continued to write short stories, mailing them to Hemingway, who was then in Paris. Some of these stories, through Hemingway's assistance, appeared in various little magazines, such as *This Quarter, transition*, and *The Exile*. In 1928, the year that Callaghan finished law school and was admitted to the Ontario bar, Maxwell Perkins, of Scribner's, published several of his stories in *Scribner's Magazine* and agreed to print his first novel, *Strange Fugitive* (1928), as well as a collection of short stories, *A Native Argosy*. Forsaking law, Callaghan decided to be a writer. After marrying Loretto Florence Dee in 1929, he traveled to Paris, where he met with Hemingway and became acquainted with Fitzgerald and Joyce. He later recorded this volatile period in *That Summer in Paris*. Leaving Paris in the autumn, he returned to Toronto, which became his home except for occasional stays in Pennsylvania and New York, where he socialized with Sherwood Anderson, Thomas Wolfe, James T. Farrell, Sinclair Lewis, and other writers. During this early period, from 1928 to 1937, Callaghan published a novel or a collection of short stories almost yearly. From 1937 to 1948, he neglected his fiction and devoted his time to radio programming and writing essays. It has been suggested that the events of that time—the rise of Nazism, the Spanish Civil War, the purges of Stalin, and World War II—contributed to his lack of interest in fiction. In 1948, he resumed writing novels and short stories, which appeared regularly in leading magazines. In his later years, he increasingly devoted his energy to novels and his nonfiction works.

Analysis

Over his long career, Morley Callaghan has published more than one hundred short stories, in such magazines as *The New Yorker, Scribner's Magazine, Esquire, Harper's Bazaar, The Saturday Evening Post, The Atlantic Monthly*, and numerous other magazines. Many of these have been collected in his four volumes of short stories.

While there are variations and exceptions, Callaghan's stories generally have recognizable characteristics. Foremost of these is the style: Most noticeably in the early works, Callaghan employs short declarative sentences, colloquial dialogue, and plain, unadorned language. As he remarked in *That Summer in Paris*, he attempts to "tell the truth cleanly." This sparse, economical, straightforward style has been compared to Hemingway's. Perhaps Callaghan was influenced by Hemingway (he admired and respected the older author) but it is likely that Callaghan's work on a newspaper shaped his writing, just as Hemingway's style was honed by his years of reporting.

Like a journalist, Callaghan presents the events in his stories objectively, neither condemning nor praising his character. By precisely recording his observations, Callaghan allows his readers to form their own judgments. He strives "to strip the language, and make the style, the method, all the psychological ramifications, the ambience of the relationships, all the one thing, so the reader couldn't make separations. Cézanne's apples. The appleness of the apples. Yet just apples." In other words, he endeavors to capture the essence of the moment.

Although Callaghan's stories are often set in Canada, he should not be classified as a regional writer. His appeal ranges beyond the borders of his country. The themes he treats are universal and are not limited to Canadian issues; in fact, he has been criticized for not addressing Canadian problems more forcefully. Many of his stories examine human relationships, and they therefore revolve around psychological issues rather than physical actions. They depict the ordinary person and his or her desire for happiness. This desire is often frustrated by environmental forces such as unemployment and injustice and by internal drives such as fear and sex. In the early stories, the characters, inarticulate and of less than normal intelligence, are on the edge of society: the poor, the retarded, the criminal, and the insane. The characters in Callaghan's later stories are more likely to be educated, but they still struggle in their quest for a better life.

In 1928, Scribner's published Callaghan's first novel, *Strange Fugitive*, and followed this a year later with *A Native Argosy*, a collection of short fiction containing fourteen stories and two novellas. These stories are some of the most naturalistic produced by Callaghan, and the characters, themes, and style resemble that found in work by other naturalistic writers, such as Stephen Crane, Theodore Dreiser, and Frank Norris. Influenced by Charles Darwin, Karl Marx, and Sigmund Freud, these authors applied the principles of scientific determinism to their fiction. Man is viewed as an animal trapped in a constant struggle to survive. He is limited by forces that are beyond his control and even beyond his understanding. Callaghan, like the other naturalistic writers, presents the material in an objective and documentary manner, eschewing moral judgments and optimistic endings.

The first story in the collection, "A Country Passion," originally printed in *transition*, portrays an inarticulate character who is ultimately destroyed by a combination of his instincts and society's strictures. Jim Cline loves Ettie Corley, a retarded girl twenty-nine years his junior, who will soon be sent to an asylum. He wants to marry the sixteen-year-old girl, but the minister forbids it because Jim has been in jail, as the reader learns later, for stealing chickens and for fighting. Although unable to marry, Jim nevertheless "had come to an agreement with her any way," and now he faces a charge of seduction which carries a life sentence. Jim's interest in Ettie is more than sexual. Out of concern for her, Jim has bought coal and food for Ettie's family in the winter and clothes for her. She needs him; as the minister comments, "she's had the worst home in town and something should have been done about it long ago." Nevertheless, the culture will not accept their union. After being arrested, Jim escapes from jail, harboring the vague notion that "if he could get out he could explain his idea to everybody and get people behind him" and his problem would be solved. Unable to concentrate, he cannot formulate his idea. He is caught and will presumably spend the rest of his life in jail, while Ettie will spend hers in an institution. Though Jim and Ettie struggle to attain happiness, they cannot overcome the forces that oppose them. The depressing outcome is relieved partly by their achieving, even for a brief moment, a sharing of their affection.

The naturalistic tone is found throughout the collection. In "Amuck in the Bush," Gus Rapp is portrayed as an animal, controlled by his instincts. Fired from his lumberyard job, he seeks revenge by attacking the boss's wife and five-year-old daughter. The attack is savage, and only because of his own awkwardness does he not kill them. After the attack, he appears as a mute and uncomprehending animal as he crashes through the forest. Eventually, he is drawn back to the town, where he is captured and roped to a lamppost.

Many of the characters in *A Native Argosy* are dissatisfied and troubled by vague, unarticulated desires. In "A Wedding Dress," Lena Schwartz has waited fifteen years to marry. Finally, when her fiancé has a good job, the wedding is scheduled. She longs for a dress that will show her to her advantage and make her desirable to her future husband. Unaware of her own actions, she steals an expensive dress from a store. Regretting the deed, she nevertheless tries on the fancy but ill-fitting dress. Still wearing it, she is arrested. Her fiancé bails her out and takes her into his custody. In "An Escapade," a middle-aged woman is lonely and repressed. Because of the titillating gossip of her bridge-club friends, Rose Carew misses the service at her Catholic church in order to attend another service being held in a theater. During the service, she is sexually attracted to the man next to her. She does not, however, recognize the emotion; she only knows that she is uncomfortable. She hurriedly leaves, goes to her Catholic church, and prays until she recovers her equanimity. Both of these characters yearn for a change in their lives, but they cannot articulate their desires and are unable to initiate actions that might bring about the desired results.

Throughout Callaghan's work appear stories that contain characters, settings, and conflicts that are familiar to Catholics. In "A Predicament," a young priest hearing confessions must deal with a drunk who has wandered into the confessional booth. The man, thinking that he is on a streetcar, waits for his stop. The priest, ignoring him, hears confessions from the other booth, but it soon becomes apparent that the man will not go away and will probably cause a disturbance. The priest, young and somewhat insecure, is afraid of any embarrassment. To resolve the issue, the priest slips into the role of a streetcar conductor and announces to the man, "Step lively there; this is King and Yonge. Do you want to go past your stop?" The drunk quietly leaves. The priest is at first satisfied with his solution, but then his dishonesty bothers him. Earlier, he had chided a woman for telling lies, instructing her that lies lead to worse sins. Unsure of his position, he thinks that he should seek the bishop's advice but then decides to wait until he can consider his actions more closely. Thus, he postpones what might be a soul-searching encounter. Callaghan, gently and with humor, has shown that priests are no strangers to human weaknesses.

In *A Native Argosy*, Callaghan included two novellas. One of these, *In His Own Country*, presents a man who attempts to find a synthesis between religion and science. Although Bill Lawson dreams of becoming a latter-day Saint Thomas Aquinas, he is unsuited for the project because of his overwhelming ignorance. Indeed, the task throws him into a catatonic state. Flora, his wife, is concerned first with the income that the project might generate, then with his neglect of her, and finally with his well-being: He does not eat, shave, or take care of his clothes. She longs for the days when they would enjoy the evenings together. Eventually, he quits his job because the small hypocrisies associated with newspaper work taint him, or so he reasons, and render him unsuitable for his grand task. He grows increasingly bewildered as he tries to summarize what is known about geology, chemistry, and the other sciences. At one point, he argues that he can reduce all life to a simple chemical formula. He even converts to Catholicism in order to understand religion better. Finally, returning from a long walk, he discovers his wife with an old beau and dashes out of the house. Flora searches for him, but failing to find him, she retreats to her father's farm, a three-hour walk from town. Later, Bill is found incoherent on a bench. At first not expected to live, he is force-fed by his mother and eventually Flora returns to care for him. The town treats Bill as a marvel and admires him for the philosophical thoughts they assume that he is thinking. The ending is ambiguous. Is Bill a prophet, a saint, or a madman?

Flora as the point-of-view character is well chosen. Limited in intelligence, she makes no attempt to comprehend Bill's thoughts, which ultimately drive him to insanity. The sparse, economical prose style matches the limited perceptions of Flora. Bill and Flora belong to the roster of marginal characters in *A Native Argosy* who lack control over their own lives.

Callaghan's second collection of short stories, *Now That April's Here and*

Other Stories, contains thirty-five stories that were published in magazines from 1929 to 1935. This later work shows the influence of Christian humanism, a belief in a Christian interpretation of the world coupled with a focus on man's happiness and an emphasis on the realization of man's potential. In 1933, Callaghan spent many hours with Jacques Maritain, the French theologian and philosopher, who was then a visiting scholar at the University of Toronto. Maritain is credited with developing Christian existential thought as a response to Jean-Paul Sartre's essentially atheistic existentialism. His influence led Callaghan to moderate the strongly pessimistic tone of his fiction.

Less naturalistic in tone than the earlier tales, these stories present characters who, while they still cannot greatly alter the course of their lives, can occasionally achieve a measure of peace, contentment, and dignity. Unlike the inarticulate characters of the previous volume, these later characters are more intelligent. Matching this change in the characterization, Callaghan's style is more complex; the sentences are longer and of greater variety as opposed to the pared-down style of the earlier volume. Yet while the style is more mature and the stories more optimistic, there is less variety than in the earlier volume. The stories presented in this collection for the most part follow a set pattern. The equilibrium of the opening is interrupted by a crisis; after the crisis is met, an equilibrium is again established, but some insight is achieved, all within the span of a few hours.

Many of the selections in *Now That April's Here and Other Stories* depict the struggles of young lovers to overcome the effects of the Depression. In "The Blue Kimono," George and his wife, Marthe, had come to the city for better opportunities, but since they have arrived in the city, their situation has worsened. Frustrated, George blames his wife for his unemployment. One night, he awakens and discovers Marthe tending their son. The woman is frightened, but George is too frustrated to notice his wife's concern; all he sees is her tattered blue kimono. He had bought it when they were first married and now it seems to mock his attempts to secure a job. Gradually, his wife communicates her fears to him; the boy's symptoms resemble those of infantile paralysis. Immediately, the husband forgets his problems and tries to entertain the little boy. When the boy finally responds to the aspirin, the couple, who have weathered the crisis, are drawn closer. The wife thinks that she can mend the kimono so that it would not appear so ragged. Through their love for each other and for their son, the two have, for a moment, eliminated the tension caused by their poverty. In "The Blue Kimono" as in "A Wedding Dress," Callaghan uses clothing symbolically. These items suggest a happier moment and reveal the discrepancy between the characters' dreams and the reality that makes those dreams unattainable.

In this volume, as in *A Native Argosy*, Callaghan includes stories that utilize a situation that is familiar to Catholics. In "A Sick Call," Father Macdowell, an elderly priest, who is often chosen to hear confessions because nothing shocks him, is called to the bedside of a sick woman. Even though she has left the church, she, afraid of dying, wants to be absolved of her sins. Her husband, John, however, who rejects all religion, opposes the priest's visit. John is afraid that she will draw close to the Church and thereby reject him, thus destroying the love they share. Yet the priest's advanced age, his gentleness, and his selective deafness secure for him a place at the side of the woman's bed. In order to hear her confession, Father Macdowell requests that John leave, but John refuses. Father Macdowell seemingly accepts defeat and in preparation for departing asks the husband for a glass of water. As John complies, the priest quickly hears the woman's confession and grants absolution. John, returning as the priest is making the sign of the Cross, knows that he has been tricked.

The priest leaves with a sense of satisfaction, yet gradually he grows concerned that he came between the wife and her husband. The priest recognizes John's love for her and remarks on the beauty of such strong love, but then he dismisses it, calling it pagan. He begins to doubt his convictions, however, and allows that perhaps the pagan love is valid. In "A Sick Call," Callaghan has again presented a priest with human failings; Father Macdowell relies on subterfuge in order to hear a confession. Yet the story is more than a character study of a priest; it is a discussion of what is sacred, and the answer is left ambiguous. Callaghan implies that sacredness is not the sole property of religion.

After a ten-year hiatus in writing fiction, Callaghan resumed writing novels and short stories in the late 1940's. In 1959, he published his third collection of short stories, *Morley Callaghan's Stories*. For this, he selected his favorite stories from 1926 to 1953. Twelve had appeared earlier in *A Native Argosy*, thirty-two in *Now That April's Here and Other Stories*; the remaining thirteen, previously uncollected, had been written between 1936 and 1953. Callaghan in the prologue writes of the stories, "these are the ones that touch times and moods and people I like to remember now. Looking back on them I can see that I have been concerned with the problems of many kinds of people but I have neglected the very, very rich." These stories, as well as those in the other collections, show a sympathy for the beleaguered ordinary man and an understanding of his problems.

In "The Cheat's Remorse" (reprinted in the 1938 edition of Edward O'Brien's *Best Short Stories*), Callaghan focuses on people who have been adversely affected by the Depression. Phil, out of work, is drinking coffee in a diner. Although he has a possibility of a job, he needs a clean shirt before he can go for the interview. Yet his shirts are at the laundry, and he lacks the money to get them. At the diner, he notices a wealthy drunk drop a dollar when he pays the bill for sandwich he did not even eat. Phil waits until the man leaves. As he stoops to pick up the money, however, a young woman places her foot on it. She, too, has been waiting for the drunk to leave, and she, too, needs the money. Phil offers to flip a coin to resolve the issue. The woman loses. Having used his trick coin, Phil cheated her. Yet immediately he regrets it, tries to give her the dollar, and even confesses his guilt, but she refuses. She argues perceptively that a single dollar could not begin to alleviate her problems but it might make some difference to him. Although she is correct, he feels so bad that at the conclusion he is eyeing a tavern, planning to assuage his guilt with alcohol.

The characters are affected by economic forces over which they have little or no control. Thus the story has some affinities with the earlier naturalistic tales from *A Native Argosy*. In "The Cheat's Remorse," both the best and the worst are depicted. Phil, selfishly, willingly cheats the woman, but the woman, ignoring her need, offers to help Phil. So even though she is affected by the same forces, she maintains her humanity and dignity.

Callaghan has effectively written stories from the point of view of characters who are limited in intelligence, and he just as effectively can employ a child's point of view. In "A Cap for Steve," Steve, a painfully shy young boy, is obsessed with baseball. His father belittles the sport, however, not realizing that baseball is Steve's only pleasure. Grudgingly, his father takes him to a baseball game during which Steve acquires the cap of one of the star players. The cap changes Steve into a leader. Yet he loses the cap and becomes despondent. Later he discovers another boy, a lawyer's son, wearing his cap, and he and his father call on the boy's father. The difference between the two families is apparent immediately. Steve's family is barely surviving, while the boy's is wealthy. Since the lawyer's son bought the cap from another, the lawyer offers to sell it to Steve for the price he paid, five dollars. Even though five dollars represents a sacrifice for Steve and his father, they agree. Then the lawyer offers to buy back the cap because his son values it. At twenty dollars, Steve's father agrees. Stunned, Steve will not walk with his father on the return home. Steve's father realizes that he does not know his son and resolves to be more of a father. The boy accepts his father's apology and is willing to forget the cap as "the price [he] was willing to pay to be able to count on his father's admiration and approval."

Although the story is set in the Depression and illustrates class differences, the focus is on the father-and-son relationship. The father does not accept his son until he comes close to losing his love, but the boy is willing to forgive his father's indifference for the chance at a closer relationship. The emphasis is on the love that can survive under adverse conditions.

In 1985, Callaghan published a fourth volume of collected stories, *The Lost and Found Stories of Morley Callaghan*. The twenty-six stories in this volume were originally published in leading magazines in the 1930's, 1940's and 1950's. During the preparation of *Morley Callaghan's Stories*, they had been overlooked, and in 1984, they were "found." The stories are similar in tone, style, and theme to the work that appears in the other collections.

In Callaghan, the inarticulate and the forgotten—the rural and urban poor, the insane, and the mentally weak—have found a voice. Throughout his career, in a straightforward narrative style, he has told their story. Although Callaghan might not have received the recognition he deserves, he nevertheless should be studied. As one reviewer has written, Callaghan "sits across the path of Canadian literature like an old Labrador, you're not sure how to approach him, but you can't ignore him."

Other major works

NOVELS: *Strange Fugitive*, 1928; *It's Never Over*, 1930; *No Man's Meat*, 1931 (novella); *A Broken Journey*, 1932; *Such Is My Beloved*, 1934; *They Shall Inherit the Earth*, 1935; *More Joy in Heaven*, 1937; *The Varsity Story*, 1948; *The Loved and the Lost*, 1951; *The Many Colored Coat*, 1960; *A Passion in Rome*, 1961; *A Fine and Private Place*, 1975; *Close to the Sun Again*, 1977; *The Enchanted Pimp*, 1978; *A Time for Judas*, 1983; *Our Lady of the Snows*, 1985.

PLAYS: *To Tell the Truth*, 1949 (originally titled "Just Ask George"); *Going Home*, 1949 (originally titled "Turn Home Again"); *Season of the Witch*, 1976.

NONFICTION: *That Summer in Paris: Memories of Tangled Friendships with Hemingway, Fitzgerald, and Some Others*, 1963; *Winter*, 1974.

CHILDREN'S LITERATURE: *Luke Baldwin's Vow*, 1948.

Bibliography

Conron, Brandon. *Morley Callaghan*, 1966.
_____, ed. *Morley Callaghan*, 1975.
Hoar, Victor. *Morley Callaghan*, 1969.
Wilson, Edmund. *O Canada: An American's Notes on Canadian Culture*, 1964.

Barbara Wiedemann

RAYMOND CARVER

Born: Clatskanie, Oregon; May 25, 1938

Principal short fiction
Put Yourself in My Shoes, 1974; *Will You Please Be Quiet, Please?*, 1976; *Furious Seasons and Other Stories*, 1977; *What We Talk About When We Talk About Love*, 1981; *The Pheasant*, 1982; *Cathedral*, 1983; *If It Please You*, 1984; *The Stories of Raymond Carver*, 1985.

Other literary forms
Raymond Carver's work in the short story is his major contribution to contemporary American literature. In addition, however, he published three volumes of poetry in small press editions before his first collection of stories appeared. *Near Klamath*, containing twenty-six of his poems, was published in 1968 by the California State College, Sacramento, English Club. *Winter Insomnia* (1970) and *At Night the Salmon Move* (1976) were published by small presses in Santa Cruz and Santa Barbara, California. Random House has more recently published two collections of Carver's poetry, *Where Water Comes Together with Other Water* (1985) and *Ultramarine* (1986). Carver's nonfiction pieces, two essays on writing and influences on his work, are included in an anthology of stories, poems, and essays entitled *Fires* (1983).

Achievements
Carver was proclaimed an overnight sensation when his second collection of stories, *Will You Please Be Quiet, Please?*, was nominated for a National Book Award in 1977, even though, at that time, he was in his late thirties and had been writing on and off for ten years. It was only with his fourth collection, however, *What We Talk About When We Talk About Love*, that critics and colleagues realized that Carver's vision of contemporary American society and his unique control of the short-story form made him, in the words of critic Frank Kermode, "a full-grown master." John Barth has termed Carver one of the leading examples of what he has playfully called hyperrealistic minimalism, or the "less-is-more" school of the contemporary short story, which includes other short-story writers, such as Ann Beattie, Bobbie Ann Mason, Mary Robison, and Frederick Barthelme. While some dissenting critics claim that "less is less" in Carver's fiction, there is general agreement that he belongs in a line of major short-story writers beginning with Anton Chekhov and extending through Ernest Hemingway.

Biography
Raymond Carver was born on May 25, 1938, in a small town in northwestern Oregon, although his father moved the family to Yakima, Washington, to

work as a logger before Carver was of school age. Carver has said that growing up in the rugged and rural Pacific Northwest made him want to be a "writer from the West." He married when he was nineteen and soon after became a father. In his essay in the *Fires* anthology on influences on his career, he says, somewhat mordantly, that nothing had as much influence on his career as the fact that he had two children.

In 1958, Carver and his family moved to California, where he enrolled at Chico State College. While there, he founded a literary magazine and enrolled in a creative writing class taught by the late John Gardner, the second most important influence on his career. In 1960, he transferred to Humboldt State College in the northwestern part of the state, where he received his bachelor's degree in 1963. Soon after, he left for the University of Iowa Writers Workshop with a small graduate study grant of five hundred dollars, but he returned to California before the end of the academic year.

Carver's first big break came in 1970, when he received a National Endowment for the Arts Discovery Award for Poetry. With that money, he had the time to write and revise many of the stories that appeared in *Will You Please Be Quiet, Please?* Soon, he began publishing in such magazines as *Esquire* and *Harper's Bazaar*. He also began taking some one-year lecturing positions at California universities. Although Carver was receiving further recognition by having his stories selected to appear in the O. Henry Award collections during this period, a continuing problem with alcohol was getting worse. In 1977, the year his second collection of stories was nominated for the National Book Award, he was dying of his alcoholism, he has said, and had to be hospitalized several times. He stopped drinking on June 2, 1977, and began his recovery.

Carver received a Guggenheim Fellowship in 1979 and put together the collection *What We Talk About When We Talk About Love*, which Alfred A. Knopf published in 1981. With this book, Carver arrived as a major force in contemporary fiction. His collection *Cathedral*, published in 1983, only confirms that judgment. Following his divorce from his first wife in the late 1970's, Carver met and began living with the writer Tess Gallagher. They divide their time between living in a home in Syracuse, New York, and a home in Port Angeles, Washington.

Analysis

The short stories of Raymond Carver are not stories to which one can be indifferent. Whether one raves about them or is repulsed by them, they are bound to elicit powerful responses. His first two collections can truly be called shocking, for both in their subject matter and in their style, they assault the reader with the violence of their characters and the reticence of their language.

Will You Please Be Quiet, Please? contains twenty-two stories which were

originally published in a variety of periodicals during the fourteen-year period between 1963 and 1976. They provide stark black-and-white images of
lives of quiet desperation in a language often compared to that of Hemingway, a language which seems simple and straightforward but which is actually
highly studied and stylized.

In "Neighbors," a cryptic story representative of the collection, a young
couple are asked to look after a neighbor couple's apartment while they are
away. After the husband visits the apartment the first few times to feed the
cat, he comes back wanting sex with his wife. Each time he visits the apartment he stays longer, going through drawers, using the bathroom, trying on
clothes. Near the end of the story, the reader discovers that the wife is similarly fascinated with the apartment, and they go over together, thinking
fantastically that the neighbors may not come back. When they lock the door
and realize that they have left the key inside, they are horrified; the story
ends with them leaning against the door, braced as if against a wind.

The voyeurism suggested by the story, in which people become fascinated
with the idea of exchanging lives with others, is repeated in other stories in
the collection, such as "The Idea," in which a woman watches a couple next
door play out a voyeuristic game in which the husband goes outside to watch
his wife undress. Although the neighbor scorns such behavior, calling the
woman who exhibits herself trash, the story suggests, as does "The Neighbors," that fantasy life is inevitably superior to reality. "Are You a Doctor?"
has a similar theme: A man is mistakenly called by a woman who then invites
him over. After his visit, in which a strange sort of companionship is established, his wife calls from out of town; he responds to her in such a distanced
way that she says that he does not sound like himself. Indeed, he is not himself, for he has played the role of another and thus feels alienated from his
everyday reality.

In many of these stories, the characters are somehow thrown out of their
everyday routine and are caught in a kind of "in-between" situation. This
theme can perhaps best be seen in the title story of the collection. In "Will
You Please Be Quiet, Please?" Ralph, the central character, pushes his wife
Marian to admit that she has had sex with a man after a party two or three
years previously. The discovery drives Ralph out into the night, in spite of his
wife's pleas for forgiveness, for a nightmarish odyssey of drinking, gambling,
and finally being mugged. When he returns home, he locks himself in the
bathroom while his wife pleads from outside for him to open the door. His
only response is the title of the story, "Will you please be quiet, please?" He
finally gives in when he goes to bed, however, and she presses her body
against him. The story ends with him marveling at the impossible changes he
felt moving over him. Like many of the pieces in the collection, the story captures a moment when things fall apart, never to be the same again.

Whereas the stories in *Will You Please Be Quiet, Please?* are relatively drained of imagery and thus are reminiscent of the style of the stories of Hemingway, they are not as drastically drained as his *What We Talk About When We Talk About Love*, in which language is used so sparingly and the plots are so minimal that the stories at first seem to be mere patterns with no flesh and life in them. The stories are often so short and lean that they seem to have plot only as they are reconstructed in the reader's memory. Whatever theme they may have is embodied in the bare outlines of the event and in the spare dialogue of characters who are so overcome by events and so lacking in language that the theme is unsayable. Characters frequently have no names or only first names and are so briefly described that they appear to have no physical presence at all; certainly they have no distinct identity, but rather are shadowy presences trapped in their own inarticulateness.

The first story in the collection, "Why Don't You Dance?" is a paradigm of Carver's method, for the plot is minimal, the event is mysterious, and character is negligible. A man puts all of his furniture out in his front yard and runs an extension cord to it so that things work just as they did when they were inside. A young couple stop by, look at the furniture, try out the bed, have a drink, and the girl dances with the owner. The conversation is functional, devoted primarily toward making purchases in a perfectly banal way. At the conclusion, the young wife is telling someone about the event: "She kept talking. She told everyone. There was more to it, and she was trying to get it talked out. After a time, she quit trying." The problem in the story, as with many Carver stories, is that the event cannot be "talked out." It is completely objectified in the spare description of the event itself. Although there is no exposition in the story, the reader knows that a marriage is over, that the secret life of the house has been externalized on the front lawn, that the owner has made a desperate metaphor of his marriage, and that the hopeful young couple play out a mock scenario of that marriage which presages their own.

Things not said because they are unsayable also underlie "Gazebo," a story of a shadowy couple named simply Holly and Duane, who have taken over as managers of a motel. As Duane says, everything is just fine with their lives— that is, until he begins a purely sexual relationship with the Mexican maid. When Holly finds out, the couple stop registering guests, stop answering the phone, stop cleaning the pool, and instead merely drink, until the owners say they are coming to close the place down. "We knew our days were numbered," says Duane. "We had fouled up our lives and we were getting ready for a shake-up." As in other Carver stories, the event is more than can be articulated or escaped, and the couple serve as a stark metaphor for marriage, infidelity, nostalgia for lost dreams, and, inevitably, divorce in the modern American landscape.

"Tell the Women We're Going" and "So Much Water Close to Home," perhaps the most shocking stories in the collection, combine sexuality and

violence in an extreme way, suggesting the often inextricable relationship between these two primal emotions. "Tell the Women We're Going" is only a
summary account of the marriages of two friends, Bill and Jerry, and filled
with banality and backyard barbecues—until Bill and Jerry go for a ride during one of these barbecues, follow two girls, and Jerry kills the two girls for
no apparent reason. There is no particular aberration in Jerry that makes
him bludgeon the two girls with a rock; it is simply that he has reached a
point of helplessness, or disappointment, or boredom, or frustrated need, or
resentment, or a combination of all these emotions, making the murder
inevitable; any attempt to explain the event away would reduce its complexity.

Whereas this story ends with violence, "So Much Water Close to Home"
begins with a scene of sexual violence for which the story then works out the
implications. The event is related by the wife of a man who goes on a fishing
trip in the backcountry with some friends. When they reach their campsite,
they see the nude body of a young girl wedged in some branches that stick
out over the water. The men make various excuses for not doing anything;
they set up camp, fish, play cards, and drink for two days before hiking out
and calling someone about the body. When the wife hears about this, she becomes both alienated from her husband and obsessed with the event, even
going to the girl's funeral. When she comes back home after the funeral,
however, he looks at her and says, "I think I know what you need," and
begins to unbutton her blouse. Her distracted yet urgent response, which
ends the story, is: "That's right . . . . Hurry." Again the stark event is sufficient, for the reader knows that the wife has seen herself in the dead girl, has
seen herself violated and dehumanized, reduced to body and made a thing to
be ignored by a group of men playing their men-only escape games. At the
same time, however, after having seen the dead girl, the wife sees sex as the
means of a desperate and futile effort to hang on to life.

All the stories in this important Carver collection have more the ambience
of dream than of reality. They are unconcerned with social issues, yet they
are not parables in the usual sense. Even as the characters are more representative than real, they are still feeling figments of Carver's imagination.
They give the reader the sense of emotional reality which reaches the profound level of myth, but they refuse to give the reader the sense of physical
or simple psychological reality. The characters inhabit a real, albeit sparsely
delineated, world that, even as it is concrete, seems primarily oneiric.

The central theme of Carver's stories in these first two collections is the
tenuous union between men and women and the mysterious separations that
always seem hovering on the horizon. In the title story of *What We Talk
About When We Talk About Love*, two couples, having a drink before going
out to dinner, talk about their previous marriages. One woman says that her
ex-husband loved her so much that he dragged her around the room, saying,

"I love you, you bitch." When she finally left him, he drank rat poison and later finished the job by shooting himself in the mouth. Her present husband, Mel, says, "If you call that love, you can have it." Mel does most of the talking, though, as he ponders aloud the transient and elusive nature of love. For example, he tells about an old couple who are in the hospital after an auto accident. The old man becomes depressed because his bandages and casts will not permit him to turn around and see his wife in the bed next to him. Mel is so impressed and insistent about this that even when the conversation dies down and the liquor is gone, no one moves in the room, not even when the room gets dark.

Raymond Carver's stories are all bleak snapshots of the American marital scene but told in such a way that the universal human mystery of union and separation is exposed, if not revealed. The stories may be related in a terse, laconic voice that refuses to become involved, but it is not a voice that suggests heartlessness or dehumanization. Rather, it is a voice that makes readers care because they recognize, although perhaps in a vague, inchoate way, the same mysterious sources of fear in themselves. The charge is often lodged against contemporary short fiction that it is dehumanized and therefore cold and unfeeling. The so-called dehumanized reality that one sees in the stories in *What We Talk About When We Talk About Love*, however, actually reveals a humanity that goes deeper than the ordinary, everyday understanding of that term. The kind of humanity that Carver's stories reveal can neither be understood nor be cured by the supermarket psychology that often tries to pass for human understanding; it can only be captured in the true and painful event of human beings who come together and come apart.

Most critics agree that the stories in Carver's collection *Cathedral* are more hopeful, more "generous," as one critic has observed, than those in *What We Talk About When We Talk About Love*. Carver himself has agreed, suggesting that the bare-bones stories in the latter collection do not represent his chosen style, whereas the more developed stories in *Cathedral* do. After the latter collection, he says he thought it was time to move on to a fuller exploration of human relationships. In spite of the objective tone of Carver's stories, they correspond to his own life and seem to represent closely his own changing emotional state. While the stories in *What We Talk About When We Talk About Love* were written during his alcoholic period, when his marriage and his life seemed to be breaking up, the *Cathedral* stories, for the most part, reflect the way back up again.

The twelve stories in *Cathedral* suggest a sense of hope lacking in the earlier stories. The title piece, which has frequently been anthologized, seems most representative of this new point of view. The story is told by a man whose wife is visited by a blind man for whom she once worked. The narrator has certain stereotyped views of the blind, is somewhat jealous of his wife's friendship with the man, and is generally hostile and sarcastic about the visit.

The evening reaches its lethargic, yet somewhat tense, climax when, after the wife goes to sleep, the husband and the blind man "watch" a television show about cathedrals. When the blind man asks the husband to describe a cathedral for him, he cannot do it, and when the blind man asks him if he is religious, he says he does not believe in anything. It is then that the blind man suggests that they draw a cathedral together, and as the husband draws, with the blind man's hand on his own, a mysterious religious communion is established. Although the narrator cannot articulate the feeling, he says that, although he was in his house, he did not feel as if he were inside anything. "It's really something," he says. The unarticulated "something" which the story embodies suggests a human at-oneness as something to believe in which is often denied in the earlier stories.

The most striking example of the shift in Carver's value system, however, can be seen in one of the longest stories in the collection, "A Small, Good Thing," for the story is a rewriting and an expansion of a story which earlier appeared as a brief and cryptic story titled "The Bath" in *What We Talk About When We Talk About Love*. Both stories deal with a couple whose son is hit by a car on his eighth birthday and is hospitalized in a coma. This horrifying event is made ironically more intolerable by the fact that the couple receive annoying anonymous phone calls from a baker, from whom the wife earlier ordered a custom-made cake.

"The Bath" is told in the neutralized style typical of the first two collections. Characterization is minimal, and the information given the reader is slight. The repeated calls of the baker suggest the bleak and callous indifference of the world outside, and the story ends with a final phone call from the hospital which suggests that the child has died. In "A Small, Good Thing," Carver develops the emotional life of the couple in more sympathetic detail, suggesting that their prayers for their son bind them together in a genuine human communion that they have never felt before.

The most radical difference in the two stories, however, is that, whereas the child's death abruptly and coldly ends the first one, in the second story the couple go to visit the baker after the death. Although they go filled with hatred for this man who unknowingly has made their sorrow even more unbearable, when they tell the baker what has happened, he invites them in to share his fresh bread. "Eating is a small, good thing in a time like this," he says, and the three talk, with the baker sharing their sorrow as well as his own loneliness with them. Both the baker and the couple seem somehow reconciled in a broader human community, and they talk into the early morning, not thinking of leaving.

On the basis of several collections of short stories, Raymond Carver has truly established himself as a significant force in the renaissance of the short story in American literature in the 1980's. Although he has said that he began writing in the short form simply because he did not have time for the extended effort required to produce a novel, it may be that, like other writers before him, such as Anton Chekhov, Katherine Mansfield, and Eudora Welty, his vision and his technique are more suited to the short story than to the novel. Regardless of whether this is true, there is little doubt that many of Carver's stories are perfect representations of a fictional form that has the ability to capture a subtle emotional complex in a brief but powerful way.

Other major works

PLAY: *Carnations*, 1962.

SCREENPLAY: *Dostoevsky: A Screenplay*, 1985 (with Tess Gallagher).

POETRY: *Near Klamath*, 1968; *Winter Insomnia*, 1970; *At Night the Salmon Move*, 1976; *Two Poems*, 1982; *This Water*, 1985; *Where Water Comes Together with Other Water*, 1985; *Ultramarine*, 1986.

MISCELLANEOUS: *Fires: Essays, Poems, Stories*, 1983.

Bibliography

Boxer, David, and Cassandra Phillips. "Will You Please Be Quiet, Please? Voyeurism, Dissociation, and the Art of Raymond Carver," in *The Iowa Review*. X (Summer, 1979), pp. 75-90.

Carver, Raymond. "The Art of Fiction [an interview with Mona Simpson]," in *The Paris Review*. No. 88 (Summer, 1983), pp. 192-221.

Stull, William L. "Beyond Hopelessville: Another Side of Raymond Carver," in *Philological Quarterly*. LXIV (Winter, 1985), pp. 1-15.

Charles E. May

CHARLES WADDELL CHESNUTT

Born: Cleveland, Ohio; June 20, 1858
Died: Cleveland, Ohio; November 15, 1932

Principal short fiction
The Conjure Woman, 1899; *The Wife of His Youth and Other Stories of the Color Line*, 1899.

Other literary forms
Charles Waddell Chesnutt achieved his literary reputation and stature as a short-story writer. His scholarly bent and indelible concern for human conditions in American society, however, occasionally moved him to experiment in other literary forms. Based on his study of race relations in the American South, he wrote the novel *The Marrow of Tradition* (1901). As a result of the critical acclaim for this novel and for his first, *The House Behind the Cedars* (1900), Chesnutt became known not only as a short-story writer but as a first-rate novelist as well. He wrote two other novels, *The Colonel's Dream* (1905) and "The Quarry," which remains unpublished.

In 1885, Chesnutt published several poems in *The Cleveland Voice*. The acceptance of his essay "What Is a White Man?" by the *Independent* in May of 1889 began his career as an essayist. Illustrating his diverse talent still further and becoming an impassioned voice for human justice, he wrote essays for a major portion of his life. Chesnutt demonstrated his skill as a biographer when he prepared *Life of Frederick Douglass* (1899) for the Beacon biography series.

Achievements
One of Chesnutt's most significant achievements was his own education. Self-taught in the higher principles of algebra, the intricate details of history, the linguistic dicta of Latin, and the tenets of natural philosophy, he crowned this series of intellectual achievements by passing the Ohio bar examination after teaching himself law for two years.

A man of outstanding social reputation, Chesnutt received an invitation to Mark Twain's seventieth birthday party, an invitation "extended to about one hundred and fifty of America's most distinguished writers of imaginative literature." The party was held on December 5, 1905, at Delmonico's, in New York City. Chesnutt's greatest public honor was being chosen as the recipient of the Joel E. Springarn Medal, an award annually bestowed on an American citizen of African descent for distinguished service.

Biography
Charles Waddell Chesnutt was born in Cleveland, Ohio, on June 20, 1858.

He attended Cleveland public schools and the Howard School in Fayetteville, North Carolina. Having distinguished himself academically early in his schooling, Chesnutt was taken into the tutelage of two established educators, Robert Harris of the Howard School and his brother, Cicero Harris, of Charlotte, North Carolina. He later succeeded Cicero Harris as principal of the school in Charlotte in 1877 and followed this venture with an appointment to the Normal School in Fayetteville to train teachers for colored schools.

On June 6, 1878, Chesnutt was married to Susan Perry. Shortly after his marriage, he began his training as a stenographer. Even at this time, however, his interest in writing competed for his energies. He spent his spare time writing essays, poems, short stories, and sketches. His public writing career began in December of 1885 with the printing of the story "Uncle Peter's House" in the *Cleveland News and Herald*. Several years passed and "The Goophered Grapevine" was accepted by *The Atlantic Monthly* and published in 1888. Continuing his dual career as a man of letters and a businessman/attorney for more than a decade after his reception as a literary artist, Chesnutt decided, on September 30, 1899, to devote himself full-time to his literary career. From that moment on he enjoyed a full and productive career as a man of letters.

At the turn of the century, Chesnutt became more politically active as a spokesman for racial justice. He toured the South and its educational institution such as Tuskegee Institute and Atlanta University. He joined forces with black leaders such as Booker T. Washington and W. E. B. Du Bois. In May of 1909, he became a member of the National Negro Committee, which later became the National Association for the Advancement of Colored People (NAACP). The last two decades of Chesnutt's life were less active because his health began to fail him in 1919. He was, however, elected to the Cleveland Chamber of Commerce in 1912. Chesnutt continued to write until his death on November 15, 1932.

Analysis

The short fiction of Charles Waddell Chesnutt embraces traditions characteristic of both formal and folk art. Indeed, the elements of Chesnutt's narrative technique evolved in a fashion that conspicuously parallels the historical shaping of the formal short story itself. The typical Chesnutt narrative, like the classic short story, assumes its heritage from a rich oral tradition immersed in folkways, mannerisms, and beliefs. Holding true to the historical development of the short story as an artistic form, his early imaginative narratives were episodic in nature. The next stage of development in Chesnutt's short fiction was a parody of the fable form with a folkloric variation. Having become proficient at telling a story with a unified effect, Chesnutt achieved the symbolic resonance characteristic of the Romantic tale, yet his awareness of the plight of his people urged him toward an increasingly realistic depiction of social conditions. As a mature writer, Chesnutt achieved depth of characterization, distinguishable thematic features, and a rare skillfulness in creation of mood, while a shrewdly moralizing tone allowed him to achieve his dual goal as artist and social activist.

Chesnutt's journal stories constituted the first phase of his writing career, but when *The Atlantic Monthly* published "The Goophered Grapevine" in 1888, the serious aspects of his artistic skill became apparent. "The Goophered Grapevine" belongs to a tradition in Chesnutt's writings which captures the fable form with a folkloric variation. These stories also unfold with a didactic strain which matures significantly in Chesnutt's later writings. To understand clearly the series of stories in *The Conjure Woman*, of which "The Goophered Grapevine" is one, the reader must comprehend the allegorical features in the principal narrative situation and the thematic intent of the mythic incidents from Afro-American lore.

The Conjure Woman contains narratives revealed through the accounts of a Northern white person's rendition of the tales of Uncle Julius, a former slave. This storytelling device lays the foundation for Chesnutt's sociological commentary. The real and perceived voices represent the perspectives he wishes to expose, those of the white capitalist and the impoverished, disadvantaged Afro-American. The primary persona is that of the capitalist, while the perceived voice is that of the struggling poor. Chesnutt skillfully melds the two perspectives.

Chesnutt's two volumes of short stories contain pieces which are unified in theme, tone, and mood. Each volume also contains a piece which might be considered the lead story. In *The Conjure Woman*, the preeminent story is "The Goophered Grapevine." This story embodies the overriding thematic intent of the narratives in this collection. Chesnutt points out the foibles of the capitalistic quest in the post–Civil War South, a venture pursued at the expense of the newly freed Afro-American slave. He illustrates this point in "The Goophered Grapevine" by skillfully intertwining Aunt Peggy's gains as a result of her conjurations and Henry's destruction as a result of man's inhumanity to man. Chesnutt discloses his ultimate point when the plantation owner, McAdoo, is deceived by a Yankee horticulturist and his grape vineyard becomes totally unproductive.

Running episodes such as Aunt Peggy's conjurations to keep the field hands from consuming the grape crop and the seasonal benefit McAdoo gains from selling Henry serve to illustrate the interplay between a monied white capitalist and his less privileged black human resources. McAdoo used Aunt Peggy to deny his field laborers any benefit from the land they worked, and he sold Henry every spring to increase his cash flow and prepare for the next gardening season.

The central metaphor in "The Goophered Grapevine" is the bewitched vineyard. To illustrate and condemn man's inhumanity to man, Chesnutt contrasts the black conjure woman's protection of the grape vineyard with the white Yankee's destruction of it. McAdoo's exploitation of Henry serves to justify McAdoo's ultimate ruin. Through allegory, Chesnutt is able to draw attention to the immorality of capitalistic gain through a sacrifice of basic humanity to one's fellowman.

Following the theme of inhumanity established in "The Goophered Grapevine," "Po' Sandy" highlights the abuse of a former slave laborer. Accordingly, a situation with a folkloric variation is used to convey this message. Sandy, Master Marabo's field hand, is shifted from relative to relative at various points during the year to perform various duties. During the course of these transactions, he is separated from his second common-law wife, Tenie. (His first wife has been sent to work at a distant plantation.) Tenie is a conjurer. She transforms Sandy into a tree, and she changes him back to his original state periodically so that they can be together. With Sandy's apparent disappearance, Master Marabo decides to send Tenie away to nurse his ailing daughter-in-law. There is therefore no one left to watch Sandy, the tree. The dehumanizing effects of industrialization creep into the story line at this point. The "tree" is to be used as lumber for a kitchen at the Marabo home. Tenie returns just in time to try to stop this transformation at the lumber mill, but she is deemed "mad."

Sandy's spirit thereafter haunts the Marabo kitchen, and no one wants to work there. The complaints are so extensive that the kitchen is dismantled and the lumber donated toward the building of a school. This structure is then haunted, too. The point is that industrialization and economic gain diminish essential human concerns and can lead to destruction. The destruction of Sandy's marital relationships in order to increase his usefulness as a field worker justifies this defiant spirit. In his depiction of Sandy as a tree, Chesnutt illustrates an enslaved spirit desperately seeking freedom.

"The Conjurer's Revenge," also contained in *The Conjure Woman*, illustrates Chesnutt's mastery of the exemplum. The allegory in this work conveys a strong message, and Chesnutt's evolving skill in characterization becomes apparent. The characters' actions, rather than the situation, contain the didactic message of the story. Some qualities of the fable unfold as the various dimensions of characters are portrayed. Consequently, "The Conjurer's Revenge" is a good example of Chesnutt's short imaginative sketch. These qualities are also most characteristic of Chesnutt's early short fiction.

"The Conjurer's Revenge" begins when Primus, a field hand, discovers the conjure man's hog alone in a bush one evening. Concerned for the hog and not knowing to whom the animal belongs, Primus carries it to the plantation where he works. Unfortunately, the conjurer identifies Primus as a thief and transforms Primus into a mule. Chesnutt uses this transformation to reveal Primus' personality. As a mule, Primus displays jealousy when other men show an attraction to his woman, Sally. The mule's reaction is one of shocking violence in instances when Sally is approached by other men. The mule has a tremendous appetite for food and drink, an apparent compensation for his unhappiness. Laying the foundation for his exemplum, Chesnutt brings these human foibles to the forefront and illustrates the consequences of even the mildest appearance of dishonesty.

The conjurer's character is also developed more fully as the story progresses. After attending a religious revival, he becomes ill, confesses his act of vengeance, and repents. During the conjurer's metamorphosis, Chesnutt captures the remorse, grief, and forgiveness in this character. He also reveals the benefits of human compassion and concern for one's fellowman. A hardened heart undergoes reform and develops an ability to demonstrate sensitivity. Nevertheless, the conjurer suffers the consequences of his evil deed: He is mistakenly given poison by a companion and dies before he completely restores Primus' human features, a deed he undertakes after repenting. The conjurer dies prematurely, and Primus lives with a clubfoot for the rest of his life.

Features of Chesnutt's more mature writing emerge in the series of narratives which make up *The Wife of His Youth and Other Stories of the Color Line*. The stories in this collection center on the identity crisis experienced by Afro-Americans, portraying their true human qualities in the face of the grotesque distortions wrought by racism. In order to achieve his goal, Chesnutt abandons his earlier imaginative posture and embraces realism as a means to unfold his message. The dimensions of his characters are therefore appropriately self-revealing. The characters respond to the stresses and pressures in their external environment with genuine emotion; Mr. Ryder in "The Wife of His Youth" is no exception.

"The Wife of His Youth" follows the structural pattern which appears to typify the narratives in the collection. This pattern evolves in three phases: crisis, character response, and resolution. The crisis in "The Wife of His Youth" is Mr. Ryder's attempt to reconcile his new and old ways of life. He has moved North from a Southern plantation and entered black middle-class society. Adapting to the customs, traditions, and mores of this stratum of society is a stressful challenge for Mr. Ryder. Tensions exist between his old life and his new life. He fears being unable to appear as if he belongs to this "blue vein" society and exposing his lowly background. This probable eventuality is his constant preoccupation.

The "blue veins" were primarily lighter-skinned blacks who were better educated and more advantaged than their darker counterparts. Relishing their perceived superiority, they segregated themselves from their brothers and sisters. It is within this web of social clamoring and essential self-denial that Mr. Ryder finds himself. The inherent contradictions of this life-style present a crisis for him, although a resolution is attained during the course of the narrative.

Mr. Ryder's efforts to fit into this society are thwarted when his slave wife appears at his doorstep on the day before a major social event that he has planned. He is about to introduce the Blue Vein Society to a widow, Mrs. Dixon, upon whom he has set his affections. The appearance of Liza Jane, his slave wife, forces Mr. Ryder to confront his new life. This situation also allows Chesnutt to assume his typically moralizing tone. Mr. Ryder moves from self-denial to self-pride as he decides to present Liza Jane to his society friends instead of Mrs. Dixon. The narrative ends on a note of personal triumph for Mr. Ryder as he proudly introduces the wife of his youth to society.

Chesnutt does not totally relinquish his allegiance to the use of myth in *The Wife of His Youth and Other Stories of the Color Line*. The myth of the ascent journey, or the quest for freedom, is evident in several stories in the collection, among them "The Passing of Grandison" and "Wellington's Wives." Following the structured pattern of crisis, character response, and resolution, "The Passing of Grandison" is a commentary on the newly emerging moral values of the postbellum South. Colonel Owens, a plantation owner, has a son, Dick, who is in love with a belle named Charity Lomax. Charity's human values reflect the principles of human equality and freedom, and the challenge that she presents to Dick Owens becomes the crisis of the narrative.

Dick is scheduled to take a trip North, and his father insists on his being escorted by one of the servants. Grandison is selected to accompany his young master. Charity Lomax challenges Dick to find a way to entice Grandison to remain in the North and receive his well-deserved liberation. Charity's request conflicts with the values held by Dick and Grandison. Dick believes that slave/master relationships are essential to the survival of the South. Grandison holds that servants should be unequivocally loyal to their masters.

In spite of Dick's attempts to connect Grandison unobtrusively with the abolitionist movement in the North, the former slave remains loyal to Dick. Grandison's steadfastness perplexes Dick because his proposed marriage to Charity is at risk if he does not succeed in freeing Grandison. After a series of faulty attempts, Dick succeeds in losing Grandison. Dick then returns home alone and triumphant. Grandison ultimately returns to the plantation. He had previously proven himself so trustworthy that goodwill toward him is restored. To make the characterization of Grandison realistic, however, Chesnutt must have him pursue his freedom.

In a surprise ending typical of Chesnutt, Grandison plans the escape of all of his relatives who remain on the plantation. They succeed, and in the last scene of the narrative, Colonel Owens spots them from a distance on a boat journeying to a new destination. "The Passing of Grandison" successfully achieves the social and artistic goals of *The Wife of His Youth and Other Stories of the Color Line*. Chesnutt creates characters with convincing human qualities and captures their responses to the stresses and pressures of their environment. While so doing, he advocates the quest for human freedom.

"Uncle Wellington's Wives" contains several of the thematic dimensions mentioned above. The story concerns the self-identity of the Afro-American and the freedom quest. Wellington Braboy, a light-skinned mulatto, is determined to move North and seek his freedom. His crisis is the result of a lack of resources, primarily financial, to achieve his goal.

Braboy is portrayed as having a distorted view of loyalty and commitment. He justifies stealing money from his slave wife's life savings by saying that, as her husband, he is entitled to the money. On the other hand, he denies his responsibility to his slave wife once he reaches the North. He denies the legality of a slave marriage in order to marry a white woman.

Chesnutt takes Braboy on a journey of purgation and catharsis as he moves toward resolution. After being subjected to much ridicule and humiliation as a result of his mixed marriage, Braboy must honestly confront himself and come to terms with his true identity. Abandoned by his wife for her former white husband, Braboy returns to the South. This journey is also a symbolic return to himself; his temporary escape from himself has failed.

Milly, Braboy's first wife, does not deny her love for him, in spite of his previous actions. Milly receives and accepts him with a forgiving spirit. Chesnutt capitalizes on the contrast between Braboy's African and Anglo wives. The African wife loves him unconditionally because she has the capacity to know and understand him, regardless of his foibles. Braboy's Anglo wife was frustrated by what she considered to be irreparable inadequacies in his character and abandoned him.

In his character development, Chesnutt repeatedly sought to dispel some of the stereotypical thinking about Afro-Americans. An example of his success in this effort is found in "Cicely's Dream," set in the period of Reconstruction. Cicely Green is depicted as a young woman of considerable ambition. Like most Afro-Americans, she has had very little education and is apparently limited in her capacity to achieve. She does have, however, many dreams.

Cicely's crisis begins when she discovers a wounded man on her way home one day. The man is delirious and has no recollection of who he is. Cicely and her grandmother care for the man until his physical health is restored, but he is still mentally distraught. The tenderness and sensitivity displayed by Cicely keep the stranger reasonably content. Over a period of time, they become close and eventually pledge their love to each other. Chesnutt portrays a caring, giving relationship between the two lovers, one which is not complicated by any caste system which would destroy love through separation of the lovers. This relationship, therefore, provides a poignant contrast to the relationships among blacks during the days of slavery, and Chesnutt thereby exposes an unexplored dimension of the Afro-American.

Typically, however, there is a surprise ending: Martha Chandler, an Afro-American teacher, enters the picture. She teaches Cicely and other black youths for one school term. During the final program of the term, the teacher reveals her story of lost love. Her lover had been killed in the Civil War. Cicely's lover's memory is jolted by the teacher's story, and he proves to be the teacher's long-lost love. The happy reunion is a celebration of purely committed love. Again, Chesnutt examines qualities in the Afro-American which had largely been ignored. He emphasizes the innate humanity of the Afro-American in a natural and realistic way, combining great artistic skill with a forceful moral vision.

Other major works

NOVELS: *The House Behind the Cedars*, 1900; *The Marrow of Tradition*, 1901; *The Colonel's Dream*, 1905.

NONFICTION: *Life of Frederick Douglass*, 1899.

Bibliography

Chesnutt, Helen M. *Charles Waddell Chesnutt: Pioneer of the Color Line*, 1952.

Heermance, J. Noel. *Charles W. Chesnutt: America's First Great Black Novelist*, 1974.

Render, Sylvia Lyons. *Charles W. Chesnutt*, 1980.

Patricia A. R. Williams

OSAMU DAZAI
Shūji Tsushima

Born: Kanagi, Japan; June 19, 1909
Died: Tokyo, Japan; June 19, 1948

Principal short fiction
Bannen, 1936; *Tokyo hakkei*, 1941; *Kajitsu*, 1944; *Otogizōshi*, 1945; *Shinshaku shokoku banashi*, 1945; *Fuyu no hanabi*, 1947; *Dazai Osamu: Selected Stories and Sketches*, 1983.

Other literary forms
Osamu Dazai's international fame is based almost exclusively on a short novel, *Shayō* (1947; *The Setting Sun*, 1956). Translations also exist of a defensive fictional autobiography, *Ningen shikkaku* (1948; *No Longer Human*, 1958), and an equally personal travelogue, *Tsugaru* (1944; English translation, 1985; also as *Return to Tsugaru: Travels of a Purple Tramp*, 1985). Dazai published two plays as well as a number of essays, and like all Japanese authors, he experimented with the haiku. His total literary output is with regard to genre almost as versatile as it is prolific, but comparatively little has been translated into English or any other Western language.

Achievements
During his life, Dazai was much more of a cult figure than an institutional model, and for this reason he did not receive the major awards available in his milieu. After his death, however, he was accorded widespread homage. A literary journal has instituted an annual Osamu Dazai prize, televised memorial services at Dazai's graveside take place annually, and at least three memorial sites have been established throughout Japan.

Biography
All forms of autobiographical fiction are popular in Japan, especially the "I" novel, and Osamu Dazai's fictional reenactment of his own life has become the hallmark of his style. Indeed, his personal entourage, including his wives, mistresses, intimate friends, and members of his immediate family, repeatedly turn up in his fiction under their own names or thinly disguised pseudonyms. A bare chronology of the principal events in Dazai's life would be a somewhat sordid account of sexual encounters, family disputes, drugs, drinking, and attempted suicides. Only when accompanied by introspective analysis, artistic reflections, and literary parallels, as they are in the author's fiction, do these events become material of universal human interest.

Dazai was a poor little rich boy born Shūji Tsushima in the northernmost district of the main island of Japan. At the age of nineteen, shortly after meeting a geisha, Hatsuyo, he unsuccessfully attempted suicide. Four months later, he began the study of French literature at Tokyo University. In the same year, he made a joint suicide attempt with a waitress; he recovered, but she died. In the following month, he married Hatsuyo. Along with magazine editing and short-story writing, he engaged in leftist political activities. In 1933, he used for the first time his pen name, Osamu Dazai, with a story that won a newspaper prize. Three years later, he published his first collection of stories, and entered a mental hospital. In 1937, he again unsuccessfully attempted suicide, this time with Hatsuyo; shortly thereafter, their union was dissolved, and he entered into an arranged marriage with a woman from his own social class. During the war, he was disqualified by ill health from active military service, but he engaged in various noncombatant activities while continuing to write. For some time, he carried on a correspondence with a young woman, Ota Shizuko, on literary subjects, and shortly after their initial meeting in 1941, she became his mistress. In 1947, while writing *The Setting Sun*, he established a liaison with a beautician, Yamazaki Tomie, while still involved with and living with his wife. Shortly after completing *No Longer Human*, the most explicit of his confessional fiction, Dazai committed suicide with Tomie by drowning, leaving behind several notes, including one to his wife.

Analysis

Osamu Dazai's longer narratives are easier than his stories for Western readers to approach. In the blending of autobiography and fiction, he resembles Marcel Proust and Thomas Wolfe. The protagonist of most of his fiction is perennially the same character, a loser in society who, nevertheless, wins the sympathy of the reader. As such, he has been compared to Tom Sawyer and Holden Caulfield. He has equal resemblance to a stock character in classical Russian fiction, the useless man. Since Dazai knew the work of Ivan Goncharov, who portrayed this type in the novel *Oblomov* (1859; English translation, 1915), it would not be farfetched to describe Dazai's perennial persona as a decadent Oblomov. He is, however, a greater misfit in society, and he never succeeds in solving his problems. In *No Longer Human*, Dazai describes himself as a man "who dreads human beings," and in reference to city crowds in "Tokyo Hakkei" ("Eight Views of Tokyo"), he is reminded of the question posed by a Western author, "What is love?" and the answer, "To dream of beautiful things and do dirty ones." He is placed by critic Phyllis I. Lyons "in the school of irresponsibility and decadence." All this makes him appeal to youth both in Japan and elsewhere. As a rebel against convention, he highlights the antagonism between rich and poor and the clash between parents and children. In his youth, he had frequently acted the part of a buffoon, and he sometimes portrays this aspect of his personality in his fiction. His tone varies between self-dramatization and self-satire. In two of his works based on plots from William Shakespeare and Friedrich Schiller, however, he radically departs from his ostensible autobiographical mold. Although various episodes in Dazai's fiction treat human debasement, there is nothing prurient in his descriptions, which are frequently laconic or subtle. Occasionally, he resembles Honoré de Balzac with endless references to crude and minor details of life, debts, expenditures, and financial waste. In one of his stories, "Kuno no nenkan" ("An Almanac of Pain"), he suggests that he does not have thoughts, only likes and dislikes, and that he wants "to record in fragmentary form just those realities I cannot forget." Because of writing these personal fragments instead of formal history or philosophy, he describes himself in the same work as "a writer of the marketplace." In *Return to Tsugaru*, he remarks that "the gods spare no love for a man who goes burdened under the bad karma of having to sell manuscripts filled with details of his family in order to make a living." One of his themes is the problems of family life, but he frequently maintains that only individuals count. Edward Seidensticker regards Dazai as "a superb comic writer," but little of this comic genius is apparent in translation. It consists in caricature of himself as well as others and the portrayal of absurd situations rather than satire. Dazai is perhaps the outstanding example in any literature of solipsistic intertextuality or the constant quotation of previous works from his own pen. In *Return to Tsugaru*, for example, he quotes frequently and extensively from his own stories as well as from histories and guidebooks by other authors. Indeed, key passages from his early stories reappear over and over in his later works.

Despite the wide variety of style and subject matter in Dazai's short stories, they may be divided into two main categories, fantasy and autobiography. The latter group belongs to a special Japanese genre, *shishōsetsu*, or personal fiction. In stories about his own physical and psychological development, Dazai adheres closely to historical fact but arranges details to suit his aesthetic purpose. Among his recurring themes are the individual and the family, friendship, the search for identity, class barriers and distinctions, and the ambivalence of personality. "Omoide" ("Recollections") embodies all these themes in a Proust-like, somewhat lugubrious reminiscence of childhood. Blending the tones of irony and confession, he describes such episodes as sexual initiation and the trading of books for bird eggs and such feelings as loneliness and longing for parental love. A later story, "Gangu" ("Toys"), concerns his return home after a long absence. Here, he uses a narrative artifice of taking the reader into his confidence while assuming that the action takes place at the moment he is speaking or thinking. He goes back to the early stages of infancy and introduces one of his common scatological motifs of making water. His fantasies seem more real than his actual surroundings. In "Anitachi" ("My Older Brothers"), he portrays his histrionic involvement with French satanism and the role of a dandy, which he defines as a handsome, accomplished man loved by more than one woman. This and other narratives of his behavior with women do not measure up to the level of rakishness associated with contemporary France or even with the known details of his own activities. He portrays himself as bashful, inept, and inadequate in his sexual relationships, nearly all of which are with women of a lower social class.

Dazai several times describes his abortive suicide attempts. The title of the translation of "Ubasute" ("Putting Granny Out to Die"), refers to an ancient custom of exposing old people to the elements when they are no longer able to cope with life, but the story itself concerns his attempted suicide with Hatsuyo. En route to a mountain inn, he rehashes various derogatory terms that have been applied to him, "liar, swellhead, lecher, idler, squanderer," and then makes a sincere prayer in the toilet, a typical combination of incongruous elements. Dazai suggests that, although he represents a composite of unsavory qualities, he is still superior to the common lot. The reader wonders, however, whether Dazai's life story would have been worthy of attention if he had not belonged to a wealthy and influential family and whether a proletarian would have written it in the same style. His "Eight Views of Tokyo" is another example of a title not descriptive of the contents. Although it promises an account of urban life in the manner of Charles Dickens or Balzac, the work itself consists of further true confessions. It mentions only casually a project to write about Tokyo that was never carried out. Dazai includes an epigraph, "For one who has suffered," and introduces the marketplace theme by referring to his ten volumes of "mediocre writings" already published. He bids farewell to his youth, denies the accusation that he has joined the ranks of the philistines, and vaguely alludes to his radical political activities. Most important, he announces a spiritual crisis in the form of a "serious aspiration to become a writer." He affirms that his autobiographical style is inseparable from his art, an unambiguous declaration that the first-person narrator in most of his works is indeed himself. Striking a pose like Balzac, he observes that he himself has become one of the sights of Tokyo.

In the realm of fantasy, Dazai draws on native classical sources. "Gyofukuki" ("Transformation") combines the thoughts of a young girl about the death of a young man in a mountain pool with a folktale about a man who turned into a serpent after eating several trout. After her drunken father attempts to rape her, the girl commits suicide in the pool, fantasizing in the process that she has been transformed into a carp. The story has no connection with Franz Kafka's *Die Verwandlung* (1915; *The Metamorphosis*, 1936) but has some resemblance to Ovid's retelling of classical legends. "Sarugashima" ("The Island of Monkeys") is more like Kafka and has an outlook less gloomy. The narrator engages in dialogue with a group of monkeys after a sea voyage. Looking back on his own childhood, he seems to interpret his present incarnation as a sign of immortality or transmigration. Suddenly he realizes that people are coming to gape at him. He agrees with the most compatible of the monkeys that it is better to choose unknown dangers over boring regularity. The story concludes with a news item that two monkeys have escaped from the London Zoo. Another simian tale, "Saruzuka" ("The Mound of the Monkey's Grave"), resembles a Voltairean *conte philosophique*. A young couple flee from their parents because religious differences in the two households have kept them from marrying. They are accompanied by a monkey who acts as their servant. When a child is born, the monkey demonstrates an affection equal to that of the father and mother. One day, in the absence of the parents, the monkey, in giving the child a bath, immerses it in boiling water, not realizing the fatal consequences of the deed. He later commits suicide at the child's grave, and the parents abandon the world for religion. Dazai, intervening in the narrative, asks which sect they have chosen. The tragic story loses its point, he observes, if the original faith of either parent must be adopted by the other.

"Kohei" ("Currency") conforms to an extensive Western genre, the thingaresque, a form of narrative in which the protagonist, either an animal or inanimate object, provides an intensely realistic portrayal of the social conditions in which it exists. The genre derives from Lucius Apuleius' *The Golden Ass* (second century A.D.) and was also used by Dazai's forerunner Natsume Sōseki in his *Wagahai wa Neko de aru* (1905-1906; *I Am a Cat*, 1961). Dazai's story concerns the experiences of a one-hundred-yen note as it is passed from hand to hand in Tokyo in the aftermath of World War II. The story is exceptional in having absolutely nothing to do with the personal life of the author, but it does illustrate an aspect of Dazai's style described by James O'Brien as ironic reversal: Much of the story illustrates a woman's greed, but it concludes with the noble sacrifice of a prostitute. "Kobutori"; ("Taking the Wen Away"), based on an ancient tale, describes a Rip Van Winkle situation in which old man with a large wen climbs a hill at night in a drunken condition and encounters ten red demons, contentedly drunk like himself. As the old man joins them in a delirious dance, they insist that he return another time and let them take his wen with them as a pledge. A rich old man also with a wen, hearing this story, goes to the same place, but his measured cadences displease the demons and they prepare to leave. He catches one of them, entreating that his wen be removed, but they think he is asking for its return. They give him that of the first man, and he then has two. Dazai concludes that the story has no moral except to point up the currents of comedy and tragedy in life.

Dazai's two streams of autobiography and fantasy are brought together in "Dasu Gemeine" ("Das Gemeine"), whose title includes the German word for "vulgarity," but the strands are interwoven in such a way that no coherent plot structure can be discerned. For this reason, the story, one of Dazai's most difficult, is sometimes considered as an example of Dadaism or deliberate mystification. It is both a pastiche of Western literature and an account of the efforts of Dazai and his collaborators to establish a literary journal. It begins humorously with the narrator, Sanojiro, contemplating a double suicide until jilted by his paramour. He then becomes involved with a waitress at a sake stand. As a means of expressing spring joy, he composes a poem opposite in tone to the *ubi sunt* theme of French Renaissance poetry. Later, Dazai himself, as a character in the story, intones, "The rain falls on the town," paraphrasing a famous line by Arthur Rimbaud. He asks his fellow editors whether they prefer strawberries prepared for the market or purely natural ones, an allegory for literary works as well as a reflection of his theme of the marketplace. At the end of the story, the narrator, while questioning his identity, is run over by a train and records his death in the manner of the protagonist of "Transformation." Here, as in the rest of Dazai's works, the emphasis is on the individual rather than society. His stories as well as his longer fiction use his own personality to portray various contradictions in the human condition.

Other major works

NOVELS: *Shin Hamuretto*, 1941; *Seigi to bishō*, 1942; *Udaijin Sanetomo*, 1943; *Pandora no hako*, 1945 (originally titled "Hibari no koe"); *Sekibetsu*, 1945; *Shayō*, 1947 (*The Setting Sun*, 1956); *Ningen shikkaku*, 1948 (*No Longer Human*, 1958).

PLAYS: *Fuyu no hanabi*, 1946; *Haru no kaeha*, 1946.

NONFICTION: *Tsugaru*, 1944 (English translation, 1985; also as *Return to Tsugaru: Travels of a Purple Tramp*, 1985).

MISCELLANEOUS: *Dazai Osamu zenshū*, 1967-1968 (thirteen volumes).

Bibliography

Keene, Donald. "The Artistry of Dazai Osamu," in *East-West Review*. I (Winter, 1965), pp. 233-253.

Lyons, Phyllis I. *The Saga of Dazai Osamu: A Critical Study with Translations*, 1985.

O'Brien, James. *Dazai Osamu*, 1975.

_____. *Dazai Osamu: Selected Stories and Sketches*, 1983.

Ueda, Makoto. *Modern Japanese Writers and the Nature of Literature*, 1976.

A. Owen Aldridge

JOHANN WOLFGANG VON GOETHE

Born: Frankfurt am Main, Germany; August 28, 1749
Died: Weimar, Germany; March 22, 1832

Principal short fiction

Die Leiden des jungen Werthers, 1774 (*The Sorrows of Young Werther*, 1779); *Unterhaltungen deutscher Ausgewanderten*, 1795 (*Conversations of German Emigrants*, 1854); *Novelle*, 1826 (English translation, 1837).

Other literary forms

Johann Wolfgang von Goethe's genius extended beyond the short story to embrace all the major genres: the novel, drama, and lyric poetry, as well as nonfiction. Much of his work is autobiographical yet goes well beyond the personal in its focus on the individual's place in society and the struggle of the artist to express his humanity in the face of opposing forces, both external and internal. His novels *Wilhelm Meisters Lehrjahre* (1795-1796; *Wilhelm Meister's Apprenticeship*, 1825), *Die Wahlverwandtschaften* (1809; *Elective Affinities*, 1872), and *Wilhelm Meisters Wanderjahre: Oder, Die Entsagenden* (1821, 1829; *Wilhelm Meister's Travels*, 1882) are the prototypical *Bildungsroman*; his diverse lyrics and ballads are among the best in Western literature; and his nonfiction works—even extending to scientific treatises—chronicle some of the most important socioliterary thought of his day, especially his correspondence with Friedrich Schiller. Perhaps his crowning achievement, the Faust plays summarize the artistic and philosophical preoccupations not only of Goethe's Romantic age but, in many senses, of the twentieth century as well.

Achievements

Before World War II, Goethe was read by virtually the entire German populace. Even in the English world, where he has been neglected, largely because of the difficulty in translating the nuances of so sensitive an artisan, it has been commonplace to assign him a position in the literary pantheon of Homer, Dante, and William Shakespeare. Moreover, Goethe has had paramount influence on German literature, influencing writers such as Friedrich Hölderlin, Hermann Hesse, Thomas Mann, and Franz Kafka. In the English world, his influence is seen on Thomas Carlyle, Charles Dickens, Samuel Butler, and James Joyce; in the French world, on Romain Rolland and André Gide. Nothing escaped his observation; everything he wrote bears the stamp of monumental genius, whether one speaks of his short stories, novels, poems, or plays. Among modern readers, Goethe has been undergoing reappraisal, if not decline, particularly among younger Germans. This opposition, perhaps more social and political than aesthetic, is especially true for Marxists, who have historically resisted writing of nonpolitical orientation. In a day when human survival is at stake, Goethe can seem distant to the contemporary generation. Often his idiom is not so much difficult as it is ethereal; his message, in its optimism, more Victorian than modern. He consorted with aristocrats, despised the French Revolution, admired Napoleon. At times, he is viewed as moralistic, if not arrogant. On the other hand, he has often suffered from excess admiration. Ultimately his value may rest with the profundity of his psychological insights, his sense of the human quest with its pain, his mastery of lyric form. His work needs to be judged for itself, independent of biases. Certainly he has much to offer, given the Renaissance scope of his interests and achievements. His collected works comprise 143 volumes; his writings on science, fourteen volumes alone. If *Faust* were his only work, it would be sufficient to assure him a high place in literary annals with its affirmation of the human spirit and its confidence that humanity can transcend its errors.

Biography

Johann Wolfgang von Goethe was born into an upper-middle-class family in Frankfurt am Main, Germany, on August 28, 1749. Given a largely private education that included a rigorous study of ancient and modern languages, he came into contact with the theater at a very early age, with the French occupation of the city for three years during the Napoleonic wars. At the age of sixteen, he studied law at Leipzig but was interrupted by a debilitating illness that nearly took his life. Two years later, he went on to the University of Strasbourg, where he completed his studies. While there, he met Johann Gottfried Herder, who introduced him to Homer, Shakespeare, Ossian, and folk literature. Herder also converted Goethe to the tenets of a new artistic credo which would become known as Romanticism. All these elements loom large in Goethe's work.

On his return to Frankfurt, Goethe engaged in law and writing. In 1773, he achieved immediate renown among his countrymen with the play *Götz von Berlichingen mit der eisernen Hand* (*Götz von Berlichingen with the Iron Hand*, 1799). A year later, his reputation took on international stature with *The Sorrows of Young Werther*, his most noted work with the exception of *Faust*. In 1775, Goethe attracted the attention of the young Duke of Saxe-Weimar, who invited him to the capital city, Weimar. Except for a two-year interval when Goethe visited Italy, he would remain at Weimar all of his life. It was at Weimar that Goethe fell in love with the married Charlotte von Stein, a woman of high refinement and intellectual capability. Realizing that the ten-year affair was a romance without a future, Goethe departed for Italy in 1786, where he remained for nearly two years. The Italian sojourn affected him greatly and marks his embrace of classicism and his retreat from Herder's influence. Classicist norms are evident in his plays *Egmont* (1788; English translation, 1837), *Iphigenie auf Tauris* (1779, revised 1787; *Iphigenia in Tauris*, 1793), and *Torquato Tasso* (1790; English translation, 1827).

Several years after his return to Weimar, Goethe entered into the principal friendship of his life, with fellow artist Friedrich Schiller; each served as critic and motivator to the other until Schiller's death in 1805. On one occasion, Goethe confessed to Schiller that he owed him a second youth. Keenly intelligent, perhaps overly punctilious, Goethe seems to have intimidated many of his contemporaries. Hence, his last years were largely lonely ones. Nevertheless, during these years he produced some of his greatest works, among them *Faust*, a labor of love for nearly sixty years and, by common assent, some of the world's most sublime lyric verse. Literature, however, was not his only forte, for he was accomplished in fields as wide-ranging as botany and optics, mineralogy and anatomy. He died in 1832, already a legend in his lifetime.

Analysis

Johann Wolfgang von Goethe did not invent the novella, or short fiction, genre in German literature, though he is rightfully given credit as its first master. Before Goethe, no German writer had given serious thought to composing a crafted fictional work. Initially, Goethe borrowed his materials. It is in his adaptations, however, that these sources became transformed. In short fiction, Goethe's method usually followed the example of Giovanni Boccaccio, with his frame method of telling a series of stories within a social context. This appealed to Goethe's sense of formal integrity, or effecting of unity. Even in his novels, Goethe often interpolates short stories into his narratives, where they function largely to amplify the central theme.

It can be said that in Goethe's short fiction no two stories are ever quite alike, some of them being parabolic; others, psychological or sociological; a few, fables; still others, allegories. At times, Goethe is highly symbolic; at others, not so at all. His stories are often dilemma-centered and, consequently, demanding of resolution. If any overarching similarity exists in these stories, it may rest in the theme of love. In one story or another, love in one of its guises is surely present, whether of man for man, of man and woman for each other, or of human love for nature's world.

The Sorrows of Young Werther represents Goethe's entry into the realm of short fiction, here in the form of the novella. The plot is essentially uneventful; the protagonist, Werther, is engaged in writing letters after-the-fact to his friend, Wilhelm, describing the waning fortunes of his enamoredness for the engaged, and later married, Lotte, daughter of a town official. Werther, realizing that his passion is an impossible one, seeks egress through diplomatic service elsewhere. Things do not go well even with a move, however, and he finds himself snubbed for his middle-class origins. He returns to his town, only to find that Lotte has married Albert. Distraught, Werther contemplates suicide. On a final visit to Lotte during Albert's absence, they read together from Macpherson's *Ossian*, and, overcome with the plight of the poem's anguished lovers, Werther kisses Lotte, who becomes alarmed and refuses to see him again. Werther leaves. Lotte's intimation of impending tragedy is confirmed later that evening when Werther takes his life.

Goethe was only twenty-four when he wrote this work, which would find its way into every European salon. Like nearly everything he wrote, the story has autobiographical roots; Goethe and Werther share even the same birthday. Goethe had been in love with Charlotte Buff, the fiancée of another man, named Kestner. Like Werther, Goethe left the community to escape his passion. He had also contemplated suicide, and he made that part of the story upon learning of the suicide of an acquaintance, an attaché named Karl Wilhelm Jerusalem. Jerusalem had fallen in love with a married woman and had undergone social snubbing.

Despite their parallel experiences, however, it is important to distinguish Goethe from his protagonist. Goethe intends a psychological portraiture of a mind in distress, moving inexorably toward self-destruction. Goethe, who in many ways possessed the "two souls" of rationality and intuition, is admonishing readers to avoid excesses of passion, which can render beautiful feelings into ugliness when no limits are imposed. Although there is much in this novella that is characteristic of the lyrical Goethe—the rhapsodizing of spring, for example—Goethe's emphasis is clear: Feelings have potential for producing good, but because the line between good and evil is not always a clear one, danger abounds. *The Sorrows of Young Werther* begins as a story of love; it ends as a story of death.

Historically, the importance of this early work lies in its departure from eighteenth century norms of rationality, with their proscriptions of objective criteria, particularly as to language. *The Sorrows of Young Werther* is powerfully told through imagery, not abstraction. While there were other epistolary novels in the century, this work gave readers an unparalleled look at an individual character, thus anticipating the modern novel, with its interior, or psychological, rendering.

Though he was very young at the time that he wrote *The Sorrows of Young Werther*, Goethe also shows himself in command of form: The novella divides into two parts having an ironic relationship. The first part deals with Werther's arrival up to his departure from the town and anticipates the tragedy of the second part. Both parts involve escape, one by going away, the other by self-inflicted gunshot. Neither escape proves to be a proper resolution. The telling irony of this novella is that Werther wants his suicide to represent the ultimate altruism of self-sacrifice. On the contrary, it represents the ultimate egotism. A sterile act, it changes nothing. Genuine love sacrifices by yielding, not by abrogating. Readers may be sorry for Werther, but neither can they absolve him.

Each part is also orchestrated in terms of the seasons. In the first part, it is spring and summer; in the second, autumn and winter. The seasons reflect the cycles of maturation and decline, birth and death. Hence they amplify the course of the novella's action.

"Das Märchen" ("The Fairy Tale") reflects Goethe's fondness for the German folklore tradition. This tale, or *Erzählung*, originally appeared in *Conversations of German Emigrants*, comprising stories that Goethe wrote as imaginative pieces requiring the suspension of disbelief for their enjoyment. In this type of story, anything can happen and usually does. If the reader will be patient with the story, theme always emerges, for the archetypal elements are never lacking.

In "The Fairy Tale," a river divides two realms. A ferryman transports passengers from the east bank to the west bank. A giant's shadow returns visitors to the east bank. Those traveling westward visit Lily, whose realm suggests death. A Serpent, in this tale a heroic creature, sacrifices itself to make a bridge for the wayfarers from the east bank, or the realm of life. The story is replete with polarities, not only between East and West but also between light and darkness, the living and the dead, vegetables and minerals. Paradoxes extend to characters. The same Lily whose touch can kill can also restore life. The Man-with-the-Lamp, who comes from the East, appears to represent truth, which is that superlative goals can be reached only through collective effort, or self-abnegation. The Lily, however beautiful, cannot function meaningfully until the Prince (another character) dies willingly in her embrace, or as an act of love. Without love, life is sterility; existence, death. With the Serpent's act of self-sacrifice, a bridge is built. Separation ceases between the realms. Pilgrims move freely. The journey is life. Life (the East) and Death (the West) are reconciled in the context of existence lived in love (the bridge). Meanings abound in a story as symbolic as this: Each is necessary to the other (the sociological); love is the one true regenerative power (the moral); Nature is paradoxically both destroyer and procreator (the mythic).

Along with "The Fairy Tale," *Novelle* is the most renowned of Goethe's short fictions. Here, a princess takes an excursion into the countryside to see the ruins of a family castle destined to be restored. She is accompanied by the squire, Honorio, while her husband is away on a hunt. Proceeding initially through the town marketplace, they notice a caged tiger and lion surrounded by attention-getting placards focused on their ferocity, though the animals appear docile enough to the casual observer. As the day unfolds, a fire breaks out in the town, and the Princess turns back, only to encounter the tiger, who has escaped (along with the lion) in the aftermath of the fire. The tiger, which follows her, is killed by Honorio. At this point, a woman and her flute-playing son appear, protesting the killing of the "tamed" tiger. (She and her husband own the tiger and lion.) Soon, the Prince and his party, attracted by the fire, meet the Princess and spy the dead tiger. Just then, the woman's husband appears and begs the Prince to spare the life of the lion, who is nearby. The Prince agrees to this if it can be done safely. Playing his flute and singing his song, the child meets the escaped lion and woos him to his lap, before removing a thorn from one of its paws. The story ends with the child continuing his song with its admonition to employ love and melody to tame the wild.

This story, simple in format, is complex when it comes to interpretation. Like much of what Goethe wrote in his last years, the story is highly symbolic. It is certain that the story, on one level, involves the mutual animosity of man and nature. Ironically, however, it is man who proves to be the aggressor, hence the appropriateness of the story's opening with the hunting expedition. In this connection, the motif of appearance and reality functions pervasively. That the tiger and lion prove docile and the humans aggressive suggests that man has not yet come to terms with his own repressed animality. In short, the story may be seen to have sociological implications: societies and nations preying upon each other. Through the child's song, Goethe hints at the source of man's healing of the internal "thorn": the transforming power of love, which can render antagonist into friend. Goethe is on the side of the peasantry in this tale, and herein lies an ecological theme as well. The owners of the tiger and lion succeed over nature, not through the power of a gun, but through the dynamic of empathy. Their simple, harmonious lives provide a model for man's proper relation to the natural world.

Other major works

NOVELS: *Wilhelm Meisters Lehrjahre*, 1795-1796 (four volumes; *Wilhelm Meister's Apprenticeship*, 1825); *Die Wahlverwandtschaften*, 1809 (*Elective Affinities*, 1872); *Wilhelm Meisters Wanderjahre: Oder, Die Entsagenden*, 1821, 1829 (two volumes; *Wilhelm Meister's Travels*, 1882).

PLAYS: *Die Laune des Verliebten*, wr. 1767, pr. 1779 (*The Wayward Lover*, 1879); *Die Mitschuldigen*, first version wr. 1768, pr. 1780, second version wr. 1769, pr. 1777 (*The Fellow-Culprits*, 1879); *Götz von Berlichingen mit der eisernen Hand*, 1773 (*Götz von Berlichingen with the Iron Hand*, 1799); *Götter, Helden, und Wieland*, 1774; *Clavigo*, 1774 (English translation, 1798, 1897); *Erwin und Elmire*, 1775 (libretto, music by Duchess Anna Amalia of Saxe-Weimar); *Stella*, first version 1776, second version 1806 (English translation, 1798); *Claudine von Villa Bella*, first version 1776, second version 1788 (libretto); *Die Geschwister*, 1776; *Iphigenie auf Tauris*, first version 1779, second version 1787 (*Iphigenia in Tauris*, 1793); *Jery und Bätely*, 1780 (libretto); *Die Fischerinn*, 1782 (libretto, music by Corona Schröter; *The Fisherwoman*, 1899); *Scherz, List und Rache*, 1784 (libretto); *Der Triumph der Empfindsamkeit*, 1787; *Egmont*, 1788 (English translation, 1837); *Torquato Tasso*, 1790 (English translation, 1827); *Faust: Ein Fragment*, 1790 (*Faust: A Fragment*, 1980); *Der Gross-Cophta*, 1792; *Der Bürgergeneral*,

1793; *Was wir bringen*, 1802; *Die natürliche Tochter*, 1803; *Faust: Eine Tragödie*, 1808 (*The Tragedy of Faust*, 1823); *Pandora*, 1808; *Die Wette*, wr. 1812, pb. 1837; *Des Epimenides Erwachen*, 1814; *Faust: Eine Tragödie, zweiter Teil*, 1833 (*The Tragedy of Faust, Part Two*, 1838).

POETRY: *Neue Lieder*, 1770 (*New Poems*, 1853); *Sesenheimer Liederbuch*, 1775-1789, 1854 (*Sesenheim Songs*, 1853); *Römische Elegien*, 1793 (*Roman Elegies*, 1876); *Reinecke Fuchs*, 1794 (*Reynard the Fox*, 1855); *Epigramme: Venedig 1790*, 1796 (*Venetian Epigrams*, 1853); *Xenien*, 1796 (with Friedrich Schiller; *Epigrams*, 1853); *Hermann und Dorothea*, 1797 (*Herman and Dorothea*, 1801); *Balladen*, 1798 (with Schiller; *Ballads*, 1853); *Neueste Gedichte*, 1800 (*Newest Poems*, 1853); *Gedichte*, 1812, 1815 (two volumes; *The Poems of Goethe*, 1853); *Sonette*, 1819 (*Sonnets*, 1853); *Westöstlicher Divan*, 1819 (*West-eastern Divan*, 1877).

NONFICTION: *Von deutscher Baukunst*, 1773 (*On German Architecture*, 1921); *Versuch die Metamorphose der Pflanzen zu erklären*, 1790 (*The Metamorphosis of Plants*, 1946); *Beyträge zur Optik*, 1791, 1792 (two volumes); *Winckelmann und sein Jahrhundert*, 1805; *Zur Farbenlehre*, 1810 (*Theory of Colors*, 1840); *Aus meinem Leben: Dichtung und Wahrheit*, 1811-1814 (six volumes; *The Autobiography of Goethe*, 1824); *Italienische Reise*, 1816, 1817 (two volumes; *Travels in Italy*, 1883); *Zur Naturwissenschaft überhaupt, besonders zur Morphologe*, 1817, 1824 (two volumes); *Campagne in Frankreich, 1792*, 1822 (*Campaign in France in the Year 1792*, 1849); *Die Belagerung von Mainz, 1793*, 1822 (*The Siege of Mainz in the year 1793*, 1849); *Essays on Art*, 1845; *Goethe on Art*, 1980.

MISCELLANEOUS: *Works*, 1848-1890 (fourteen volumes); *Goethes Werke*, 1887-1919 (133 volumes).

Bibliography

Bielschowsky, Albert. *The Life of Goethe*, 1905-1908.

Croce, Benedetto. *Goethe*, 1923.

Dieckmann, Liselotte. *Johann Wolfgang Goethe*, 1974.

Fairley, Barker. *A Study of Goethe*, 1947.

Goedeke, Karl. *Goethes Leben und Schriften*, 1874.

Gray, Ronald D. *Goethe: A Critical Interpretation*, 1967.

Hatfield, Henry C. *Goethe: A Critical Introduction*, 1964.

Peacock, Ronald. *Goethe's Major Plays*, 1959.

Staiger, Emil. *Goethe*, 1952-1959.

Vietor, Karl. *Goethe*, 1949.

Ralph R. Joly

NADINE GORDIMER

Born: Springs, South Africa; November 20, 1923

Principal short fiction

Face to Face: Short Stories, 1949; *The Soft Voice of the Serpent and Other Stories*, 1952; *Six Feet of the Country*, 1956; *Friday's Footprint and Other Stories*, 1960; *Not for Publication and Other Stories*, 1965; *Livingstone's Companions: Stories*, 1971; *Selected Stories*, 1975; *A Soldier's Embrace*, 1980; *Something Out There*, 1984.

Other literary forms

Nadine Gordimer has published nine novels, including the acclaimed *A World of Strangers* (1958), *Occasion for Loving* (1963), *The Conservationist* (1974), *Burger's Daughter* (1979), and *July's People* (1981). She has also contributed to South African scholarship with her books *On the Mines* (1973; with David Goldblatt) and *The Black Interpreters* (1973). In 1967, Gordimer wrote a study of the literature of her homeland, *South African Writing Today*, which she also edited, with Lionel Abrahams.

Achievements

As a courageous chronicler of life in South Africa, Gordimer is known throughout the world. She received the W. H. Smith and Son Prize in 1971 for *Friday's Footprint and Other Stories*. Two years later, she won the James Tait Black Memorial Prize for *A Guest of Honour* (1970). The next year, *The Conservationist* shared with Stanley Middleton's *Holiday* (1974) the prestigious Booker Prize. Gordimer has also been a recipient of France's Grand Aigle d'Or. She is best known in the United States for her short stories, which have consistently received critical acclaim. One American reviewer summed up her importance in literature, writing, "Gordimer is in the great mainstream of the short story—Maupassant, Chekhov, Turgenev, James, Hemingway, Porter." Most of Gordimer's fiction has been published in paperback form, enabling a greater number of readers and critics to recognize and enjoy her work.

Biography

Nadine Gordimer grew up a hybrid and a rebel. Both parents were immigrants to South Africa; her mother was English, her father an Eastern European Jew. In Springs, the gold-mining town near Johannesburg, where she spent her early years, Gordimer frequently played hooky from her convent school. When she did attend, she would sometimes walk out. She found it difficult to tolerate all the pressures for conformity.

In the middle-class environment in which Gordimer grew up, a girl could aspire only to marry and rear a family. After leaving school and then working at a clerical job for a few years, she would be singled out as a prospective wife by a young man who had come from a family very much like her own, and from there, within months would actualize the greatest dreams of young womanhood: She would have her engagement party, her linen shower, and her wedding ceremony, and she would bear her first child. None of these dreams would be served by a girl's education; books, in perhaps leading her mind astray, would interfere with the years of her preparation for the mold.

At an early age, however, Gordimer did not fit the mold—she was an avid reader. By nine, she was already writing, and at fourteen she won a writing prize. Her favorite authors were Anton Chekhov, W. Somerset Maugham, Guy de Maupassant, D. H. Lawrence, and the Americans Katherine Anne Porter, O. Henry, and Eudora Welty. As she became a young woman, she became increasingly interested in politics and the plight of black South Africans. She did not, however, launch her writing career as a way to bring change.

A male friend was an important influence on her. He told her that she was ignorant and too accepting of society's values. Gordimer has written, "It was through him, too, that I roused myself sufficiently to insist on going to the university." Since she was twenty-two at the time and still being supported by her father, her family did not appreciate her desire to attend the university.

She commuted to Johannesburg and the University of Witwatersrand. While at the university, she met Uys Krige, an Afrikaans poet who had broken free of his Afrikaner heritage, lived in France and Spain, and served with the International Brigade in the Spanish Civil War. He, too, was a profound influence on her. She had been "a bolter," as she has put it, at school; she was in the process of bolting from her family and class and the culture of white South Africa, and Krige gave her a final push. She would be committed to honesty alone. She began to send stories to England and the United States. They were well received, and she began to build her reputation as a short-story writer and novelist.

After eight novels and two hundred short stories, in the late 1970's Gordimer turned to a new medium. She wrote screenplays of four of her stories—"Praise," "Oral History," "Country Lovers," and "A Chip of Glass Ruby"; she also participated in the production of three others. Taken together, the films present a compelling vision of Gordimer's South Africa. A filmed interview of Gordimer by Joachim Braun often accompanies the showing of her films. In this interview, Gordimer has many interesting things to say about both her work and the tragic state of her country.

Analysis

Although Nadine Gordimer is a distinguished novelist, her finest achievements are her short stories. About *Selected Stories*, drawn from her earlier volumes of stories, a reviewer has said, "the stories are marked by the courage of moral vision and the beauty of artistic complexity. Gordimer examines, with passionate precision, the intricacies both of individual lives and of the wide-ranging political and historical forces that contain them." About the stories in *A Soldier's Embrace*, a reviewer wrote, "Their themes are universal: love and change, political transition, family, memory, madness and infidelity, to name a few. . . . What makes Nadine Gordimer such a valuable— and increasingly valued—novelist and short story writer is her ability to meet the demands of her political conscience without becoming a propagandist and the challenges of her literary commitment without becoming a disengaged esthete."

It would be easy for Gordimer to declare self-exile. Unlike James Joyce, however, she has chosen not to abandon the inhospitable country of her birth. She accepts the obligation of citizenship to help make one's country better. She does this by practicing her art, for it is an art that enables her diverse countrymen to understand better themselves and one another.

The settings and characters in Gordimer's stories cut across the whole spectrum of South African life. She writes about black village life and black urban experiences. She writes about the ruling Afrikaans-speaking whites, English-speaking whites, Indians, and others. Her protagonists are as likely to be males as females, and reviewers have commented on her uncanny ability to make her male characters fully realized. With amazing range and knowledge, she sheds light on the intricacies of individual lives and on the historical and political forces that shape them.

Among Gordimer's most gripping stories are those in which blacks and whites are at cross-purposes. "Is There Nowhere Else Where We Can Meet?" from *The Soft Voice of the Serpent and Other Stories*, is one of the simplest and best of this group. On a country road, a young white woman's handbag is torn from her by a passing native, whose bedraggled condition had evoked the woman's pity. The day is very cold, yet he is shoeless and dressed in rags. When she attains safety and has brought her fear under control, she decides not to seek aid and inform the police. "What did I fight for?" she thinks. "Why didn't I give him the money and let him go? His red eyes, and the smell and those cracks in his feet, fissures, erosion."

The title piece of Gordimer's 1956 collection, *Six Feet of the Country*, is another exceptional story. A young black laborer walks from Rhodesia to find work in South Africa, where he has family who are employed on a weekend farm of a white Johannesburg couple. When he arrives at the farm, the illegal immigrant becomes ill and dies. There ensues a prolonged entanglement with the authorities, who insist on having the body so that it can be examined and the bureaucratic requirement for a statement of the cause of death can be fulfilled. With great reluctance, the family surrenders the body.

When at last the casket is returned to the farm for burial, they discover that the body in it is that of a stranger. In the course of spinning out a plot about the fate of a corpse, Gordimer provides great insight into the lives of the farm laborers, the proprietors, and the police official, and she also reveals the relative inability of the native laborers to deal with illness and the bureaucracy.

"A Chip of Glass Ruby," in *Not for Publication and Other Stories*, is about an Indian family in the Transvaal. The wife and mother is loving and un-assuming and a very competent manager of a household that includes nine children. To the chagrin of her husband, Bamjee, she is also a political activ-ist. It makes no sense to him that she takes grave risks for blacks, who are re-garded as lower even than Indians. During the course of the story, she is arrested and imprisoned and participates in a prison hunger strike. Bamjee, a poor, small-time fruit and vegetable dealer, cannot understand any of this: He asks, " 'What for?' Again and again: 'What for?' " His birthday comes, and he himself does not even remember. The eldest daughter brings word from her mother, in the prison, however, that his birthday must not be for-gotten. Bamjee is moved and begins to have a glimmer of understanding of the wonderful woman who is his wife. As the daughter explains: "It's because she always remembers; remembers everything—people without somewhere to live, hungry kids, boys who can't get educated—remembers all the time. That's how Ma is."

Two of Gordimer's best stories about white South African life and culture appear in *Livingstone's Companions*. "The Intruder" focuses on the deca-dence of an upper-class man of English descent. After shedding his last wife, hard-drinking, stay-out-late James Seago takes up with the beautiful teenage daughter of Mrs. Clegg, a woman of his age who affects a bohemian moral-ity. Seago refers to the daughter, Marie, whom he uses sexually and enjoys having in his lap as he drinks, as his teenage doll, his marmoset, his rabbit. Because he has financial problems, Seago is plausibly able to postpone committing himself to her in marriage. Once they are married, Seago's ir-responsible life of nightly partying does not change. Having married his pet, however, he must live with her, and so they set up housekeeping in an un-pleasant flat. Marie becomes pregnant. The arrival of a child will force changes in Seago's way of life: For one thing, they will have to find living quarters more suitable for a child; for another, his wife-pet will have to give her primary attention to the child, not him. Arriving home early one morn-ing after a night of partying, they fall into bed exhausted. A few hours later, Marie awakens hungry. She wanders out of the bedroom and finds the rest of the flat a wreck. All the kitchen staples have been spilled or thrown about; toothpaste is smeared about the bathroom. In the living room, on one of the sofa cushions, is "a slime of contraceptive jelly with hair-combings—hers." Gordimer only hints at the perpetrator. It seems more than likely, though, that it is James Seago, who again is rebelling at the prospect of being forced into a responsible mode of life.

In "Abroad," the main character is an Afrikaner. Manie Swemmer is a likable, middle-aged widower who has worked hard his entire life at construction and with cars. His grown sons have moved to neighboring black-run Zambia, known as Northern Rhodesia while still a British colony. Manie decides to take the train up to Zambia and visit his sons. Arriving in Lusaka, the capital, Manie is met by his younger son, Willie. Having expected to stay with Willie, Manie is surprised to learn that Willie does not have quarters of his own but is staying at a friend's, where there is no room for his father. To his dismay, Manie learns that all the local hotels are booked. The irrepressible Manie, though, manages to talk the manager of the Regent into placing him in a room that already has been rented as a single. The problem is that it is rented to an Indian, albeit an educated Indian. Although Manie has been given a key to the room and has placed his belongings inside, when he returns later, the Indian, from the inside, has bolted the door and locked out the Afrikaner. Manie then is offered a bed in a room intended for black guests. The blacks have not yet arrived, and Manie uses the door bolt to lock them out. "Abroad" is a beautiful story about a well-meaning Afrikaner who is excited by the racial mixing of the new nation and who wants to stretch himself to his liberal limit. His feelings toward blacks, though, are still conditioned by his South African base, where all blacks are automatically regarded as inferior. "I've only just got here, give me a bit of time," Manie tells the desk clerk. "You can't expect to put me in with a native, right away, first thing."

Upon gaining its independence from Portugal in 1975, Mozambique became another black-ruled neighbor of South Africa. "A Soldier's Embrace," the title story of Gordimer's 1980 collection, is about the changeover, the exultation, and the disillusionment of a liberal white couple. The story begins with a brilliant scene of the celebration of the victory of the guerrillas who have been fighting the colonial power. Swept up by the street crowd, the woman finds herself embraced by two soldiers, one a white peasant youth, the other a black guerrilla. She puts an arm around each and kisses each on the cheek. Under the new regime, one is certain, a human being will be a human being; all groups will be treated equally. Although many whites take flight to Europe, the woman and her husband, a lawyer, are eager to participate in building the new nation. Weeks and months pass, however, and, despite the friends the lawyer has among highly placed blacks, the government does not ask the lawyer for his services. There is an atmosphere of hostility toward whites. There is looting and violence. When a friend in nearby Rhodesia, soon to be Zimbabwe, offers the lawyer a position in that country, with reluctance and relief he and his wife pack and go. The couple has wanted the country in which they have spent their adult years to be black-run; when that comes about, they find that there is no role for them.

In the novel *July's People*, Gordimer imagines a full-scale race war in South Africa, essentially the black majority against the better-equipped white ruling minority. In the novella that provides the title for Gordimer's volume of short fiction *Something Out There*, a race war looms but has not yet erupted. Acts of violence are taking place; any one of them might well precipitate such a war. In the novella, the "something out there" is a baboon. Gordimer's intention is to suggest that the response of white South Africans to the baboon corresponds to the irrational way they have been responding to the carefully thought through symbolic acts of violence by guerrillas. Those acts of violence are handwriting on the wall announcing the coming of race war, which still could be prevented if the writing were read intelligently.

All that the whites want, however, is to be left alone. They want the animal "to be confined in its appropriate place, that's all, zoo or even circus." They want South African blacks to be confined in their appropriate places—locations and townships, black homelands, villages in the bush. As the baboon is "canny about where it was possible somehow to exist off the pickings of plenty," so, too, is the South African black majority, before the cataclysm, somehow able to exist off pickings of white wealth. That wealth will not be shared, only protected; "while charity does not move those who have everything to spare, fear will"—the fear of the baboon, the fear of the guerrilla.

What is the fate of the baboon? It is finally shot and slowly bleeds to death from its wounds. The implication is clear: A similar fate awaits the guerrillas. Gordimer's prime minister speaks: "This government will not stand by and see the peace of mind of its peoples destroyed. . . . We shall not hesitate to strike with all our might at those who harbour terrorists. . . ." The four guerrillas who are the novella's human protagonists, in counterpoint to the movements of the baboon, succeed in blowing up a power station; three escape, and it is made clear that they will carry out further attacks. The meaning in this plot—though not in all Gordimer plots on this subject—is that a ruthless government will be a match for those attempting to destroy it.

That the white population is greatly outnumbered makes no difference. They have the honed intelligence, the technology, the will to defend to the death what they have. Racial justice is an idea with which only a few whites—the man and woman on the power-station mission—are concerned. Protecting privilege and property is what most whites care most about. They cannot understand the few who act from disinterested motives. A minor character in "Something Out There" is a decent white police sergeant. He is totally mystified by the white guerrillas whom he interrogates: "There's something wrong with all these people who become enemies of their own country. . . . They're enemies because they can't enjoy their lives the way a normal white person in South Africa does."

One of the black guerrillas is dispassionate, determined, fearless Vusi, whose life is dedicated to bringing about black majority rule. Vusi says, "They can't stop us because we can't stop. Never. Every time, when I'm waiting, I know I'm coming nearer." A Vusi, however, is rare. "At the Rendezvous of Victory," another story in this volume, looks ahead to the ultimate black victory. It is about the man who served as commander in chief of the liberation army, known as General Giant. As a warrior, he was invaluable; as a cabinet minister after victory, he is a great burden to his prime minister. He led his people to victory and freedom; in freedom, his chief interest is women.

Gordimer is no sentimentalist. Her clear vision and honesty are chief among the reasons for which she is a great writer. It is a rare black character who is altogether admirable; it is a rare Afrikaner who is not a full human being. In "A City of the Dead, a City of the Living," a young black man who has committed illegal acts for his people's liberation and who is on the run from the police is given shelter by a township family. With their small house already overcrowded, the family is inconvenienced, but the husband knows his duty. His wife, nursing her fifth child, does not like the idea of taking in a stranger, but the man is pleasant and helpful, and she softens. She softens and begins to feel attracted to him. She goes to the police to inform on him, thus betraying the cause of her people's liberation.

"Sins of the Third Age," surprisingly, is not a political story. It is about a couple who survived World War II as displaced persons. Nothing remained of their pasts. They met and in a strange country began to build their lives together. Gordimer is wonderfully evocative as she suggests the passing of years and the deepening of their love. The wife's job as an interpreter takes her on frequent trips, many times to Rome and Milan. On one of her trips, she gets the idea that they should buy a home in Italy for their retirement, near a Piedmontese village. He retires first and goes to Italy to prepare the house. After several months, he appears suddenly and announces, "I've met somebody." His affair eventually ends, but the betrayal destroys the vitality of the marriage. To have done otherwise than to take her husband for granted would have been betrayal on her part. She trusted, and she loses.

"Blinder" is still another fine story in the 1984 volume. It is about an aging servant woman's loss of her lover, a man who was the main consolation of her life. Ephraim's first loyalty, however, was to his wife and children in his home village; the wife got his earnings, and after his death, her children get his bicycle. When Ephraim suddenly dies, Rose's white family expected her to increase her drinking, to go on a "blinder." Instead, she plays hostess to Ephraim's wife, who has come to the city to see about a pension.

Reading a story of Gordimer's is always exciting, because one does not know what will have caught her interest—urban or rural blacks, urban or rural Boers, leisured or working or revolutionary whites, an African or a European setting. It is a great surprise, for example, to discover a story in the form of a letter from a dead Prague father to the son who predeceased him. It is a made-up letter in which Hermann Kafka tells off ungrateful, congenitally unhappy Franz. It follows the story about General Giant; it comes before a story about a young man who is recruited to spy on South African white liberals.

As she has demonstrated again and again during more than thirty years of writing, Gordimer does not restrict her focus to people and scenes that are the most familiar. One marvels in reading "A City of the Dead, a City of the Living" at what the author, a well-off white woman, knows of black-township life, at the total credibility of characters Samson Moreke and his wife, Nanike. In "Something Out There," she has created not only the heroic Vusi but also the younger Eddie, a revolutionary made by the Soweto suppression of 1976. One of the finest passages in the novella tells of Eddie's impulsive leaving of base for an exciting day as a young black in the streets of downtown Johannesburg. Gordimer's rendering of the places and scenes familiar to blacks is completely credible. Similar knowledge and credibility is characteristic of all of her short fiction. "A City of the Dead, a City of the Living," "Sins of the Third Age," and "Blinder," in the 1984 volume, could easily be included among the twenty best short stories of the twentieth century. Indeed, all the stories discussed here might well be included in such a list.

Other major works

NOVELS: *The Lying Days*, 1953; *A World of Strangers*, 1958; *Occasion for Loving*, 1963; *The Late Bourgeois World*, 1966; *A Guest of Honour*, 1970; *The Conservationist*, 1974; *Burger's Daughter*, 1979; *July's People*, 1981; *A Sport of Nature*, 1987.

NONFICTION: *South African Writing Today*, 1967 (edited with Lionel Abrahams); *On the Mines*, 1973 (with David Goldblatt); *The Black Interpreters*, 1973.

Bibliography

Cooke, John. *The Novels of Nadine Gordimer: Private Lives, Public Landscapes*, 1985.

Eckstein, B. "Pleasure and Joy: Political Activism in Nadine Gordimer's Short Stories," in *World Literature Today*. LIX (Summer, 1985), pp. 343-346.

Gordimer, Nadine. "The Bolter and the Invincible Summer," in *Antaeus*. XLV/XLVI (Spring/Summer, 1982), pp. 105-113.

Greenstein, S. M. "Miranda's Story: Nadine Gordimer and the Literature of Empire," in *Novel*. XXVIII (Spring, 1985), pp. 227-242.

Haugh, Robert F. *Nadine Gordimer: The Meticulous Vision*, 1974.

O'Brien, Conor Cruise. Review of *Burger's Daughter* in *The New York*

Review of Books. XXVI (October 25, 1979), p. 27.

Servan-Schreiber, C. "Learning to Live with Injustice," in *World Press Review.* XXVII (January, 1980), p. 30.

Tyler, Anne. Review of *July's People* in *The New York Times Book Review.* LXXXIV (June 7, 1981), p. 1.

Paul Marx

MARK HELPRIN

Born: New York, New York; June 28, 1947

Principal short fiction

A Dove of the East and Other Stories, 1975; *Ellis Island and Other Stories*, 1981.

Other literary forms

Though Mark Helprin is best known as a writer of short fiction, the genre in which he has excelled, he is also the author of two substantial novels: *Refiner's Fire: The Life and Adventures of Marshall Pearl, a Foundling* (1977) and *Winter's Tale* (1983).

Achievements

Hailed as a gifted voice when his first book of short stories appeared, Helprin confirmed such judgments with *Ellis Island and Other Stories*, a volume that won the National Jewish Book Award in 1982. That same year, the American Academy and Institute of Arts and Letters awarded Helprin its Prix de Rome. Among his other honors are a Guggenheim Fellowship and nominations for both the PEN/Faulkner Award and the American Book Award for Fiction. Helprin is one of the most accomplished of the younger generation of Jewish American writers, and his fiction self-consciously attempts to extend and deepen the significant contribution those writers have made to American literature since World War II.

Biography

Mark Helprin was born in New York City on June 28, 1947. He earned a B.A. from Harvard University in 1969 and an M.A. from Harvard's Center for Middle Eastern Studies in 1972. While still an undergraduate, he sold his first story to *The New Yorker*, where most of his short fiction continues to appear. After completing his studies at Harvard, he emigrated to Israel, where from 1972 to 1973 he served in the Israeli army and air force. He has also served in the British Merchant Navy and is a skilled mountain climber. Since returning to the United States in 1973, he has devoted himself primarily to the writing of fiction—except for a year of postgraduate work at Magdalen College, Oxford University, in 1976-1977. There, he studied history under Hugh Trevor-Roper, focusing on Renaissance voyages of exploration. Helprin married Lisa Kennedy on June 28, 1980, has a daughter, and resides in New York City.

Analysis

Mark Helprin is an author whose imaginative resources seem inexhaustible. His prose has economy, grace, and a rich yet accessible metaphorical texture, qualities that combine to make his stories eminently readable. Helprin writes of an astonishing range of times and places and characters in stories that often move from realistic narrative toward fable. Yet his fiction is unified by what William J. Scheick has called Helprin's "fascination with the human spirit's impulse for transcendence." Helprin himself once remarked, "I write only for one reason—and that's a religious one. Everything I write is keyed and can be understood as . . . devotional literature." At their best, his stories disclose a world of values that does not simply reflect a personal metaphysics but also links Helprin's work to both the Jewish religious tradition and to the Transcendentalist heritage of Ralph Waldo Emerson, Walt Whitman, and Henry David Thoreau.

Not surprisingly, those stories often turn on moments of revelation, on various epiphanies. The beauty of nature and the beauty of human action combine to awaken many of his characters to a world that transcends human making. Helprin has noted that "vision and redemption" are two of the principal elements in his writing. Throughout that fiction, he moves his readers toward an enlarged conception of both their own capacities and the wondrous transformations of the world they inhabit.

While Helprin's voice is essentially an affirmative one, his affirmations are usually earned—the product not simply of visionary moments but also of experiences of suffering, anguish, and loss. His characters are frequently presented as survivors, sustained by their memories of an earlier love or by their commitments to art. War is one of the most common events in these characters' lives. Like Stephen Crane and Ernest Hemingway, whose influence is often apparent in Helprin's style and subject matter, Helprin makes the experience of war one of his central metaphors.

The most important lessons his characters learn through their varied experiences are spiritual, moral, and emotional. One of the major attractions of Helprin's writing, in fact, is its moral energy and its author's willingness to make assertions of value. "Without sacrifice the world would be nothing," one story begins. In his visionary novel *Winter's Tale*, which projects a transfigured urban world, Helprin describes the four gates that lead to the just city: acceptance of responsibility, the desire to explore, devotion to beauty, and selfless love. These qualities might be said to define the central themes of Helprin's stories as well.

Helprin's first book, *A Dove of the East and Other Stories*, contains twenty stories, many of them so brief that they depend almost entirely on the creation of a mood rather than on the development of plot or character or theme. For the book's epigraph Helprin uses a line from canto 2 of Dante's *Inferno*: *Amor mi mosse, che mi fa parlare* ("Love that has moved me causes me to speak"), words that anticipate the book's concern with the redemptive power of love. Helprin has called Dante his single greatest influence, and many of Helprin's portraits of female characters suggest that they function—much as Beatrice did for Dante—to mediate the spiritual vision his male characters strive to attain.

In "Katrina, Katrin'," for example, two young clerks returning home from work are discussing women and marriage, when one of them suddenly launches into an account of his loss of Katrina, to whom he had been engaged some two or three years earlier. Biferman's tale of Katrina's illness and death links this story with the Romantic tradition and its fascination with doomed love and with the strength of human fidelity despite the power of death. Moreover, through allusions to the biblical Song of Solomon, Helprin recalls an even more ancient tradition that conceived of love in terms of both profound passion and passionate commitment, a conception of love all too rare in an age of casual sexual liaisons and disposable spouses. "Katrina, Katrin'" leaves the reader not only with a sense of Biferman's tragic loss but also with a sense of love's shimmering possibilities.

An even greater emphasis on life's possibilities infuses "Katherine Comes to Yellow Sky," which Helprin plays off against a similarly titled story by Stephen Crane. In contrast to Crane's "The Bride Comes to Yellow Sky," in which the bride remains nameless and the story is told from the perspective of its male characters, Helprin focuses on Katherine, who arrives in Yellow Sky alone. Here Helprin employs two of his most recurrent symbols—light and a mountain landscape—to emphasize Katherine's potential for personal growth and transcendence. Katherine is a dreamer, in fact something of a visionary, who has come west after her parents' death to begin a new life. In Yellow Sky, with its "lantern mountains glowing gold in all directions, catching the future sun" and its peaks still gleaming after the sun has set, Katherine finds herself in the presence of "the source." Her journey's end is essentially a beginning. What Helprin says about Katherine's dreams might be said about his own approach to fiction. Katherine, he writes, "believed incessantly in what she imagined. . . . And strangely enough these substanceless dreams . . . gave her a strength, practicality, and understanding which many a substantial man would never have." For Helprin, the imagination projects and confirms life's promise.

Among the best of the briefer stories in *A Dove of the East and Other Stories* are "Ruin," "The Home Front," and "First Russian Summer." In both "Ruin" and "The Home Front," violence is a central, though understated, element. The latter story, set during the Civil War, is again reminiscent of Crane, as Helprin depicts a group of soldiers assigned to burial detail, awaiting a June battle. During an idyllic interlude, the men fraternize with a unit of nurses and luxuriate in the beauty of nature. The air of unreality the war has assumed is soon shattered, however, when the men are commanded to dig five enormous pits. In these mass graves, they later bury more than a thousand dead. The story concludes with a reference to "the high indifferent stars" that oversee the bloodshed below, an image that parallels the "high cold star on a winter's night" in Crane's "The Open Boat."

"The Home Front" is informed by Helprin's awareness of the potential for violence in human nature and the indifference with which the physical world often greets human need. Both humanity and nature have other dimensions, however, as additional stories in *A Dove of the East and Other Stories* suggest. In "First Russian Summer," for example, an eighty-year-old man named Levi recalls the words of his grandfather some seventy years earlier. Gazing upon forest and mountain, his grandfather had urged the boy to note "the shape of things and how astonishing they are" and had commended the trees, "not any painting or books or music," as "the finest thing on earth." The aged Levi has retained his grandfather's conviction that nature is a miracle which attests God's creative power. Yet he knows that he lives in "a world blind to the fact of its own creation." Levi's desire, like Helprin's, is to awaken humanity to the mystery that attends its being.

The most accomplished stories in this first collection are "A Jew of Persia" and the title story, which open and close the book. "A Jew of Persia" combines the fable with elements of literary realism, for it makes use of the supernatural as Nathaniel Hawthorne does in his tales and romances, or as Isaac Singer does in his stories. Here, Helprin presents the reader with a protagonist who struggles with the Devil himself, a conflict that begins in the mountains of Persia and ends in a barbershop in Tel Aviv, where Najime slays his adversary.

Helprin endows Najime with qualities that are central to his own artistic vision. The Jew not only possesses courage and ingenuity but also demonstrates vital piety. Before his final confrontation with the Devil, Najime prays for the strength both to recognize evil and to resist it, and he finds himself endangered in Tel Aviv precisely because he had earlier thwarted an attempt to rob him of the wealth of his village—gold and silver which he had been conveying to the Persian capital to help other Jews emigrate to Israel. Najime resists the robbers not to preserve his own life or his own property but to fulfill his communal responsibilities. Similarly, in Tel Aviv he acts to free the residents of the Ha Tikva Quarter from the misfortunes that have overtaken them on his account. As Helprin presents him, Najime is a heroic figure: not only a survivor but also a savior. In addition to his courage and piety, his greatest weapons are "the strength of the past" and "the power of memory," qualities that Helprin stresses in story after story. "A Jew of Persia" establishes Helprin's relationship to traditional Jewish characters and concerns, including the dramatic conflict between good and evil. Najime's triumphant encounter with the Devil also sounds the note of optimism that predominates in this collection.

In "A Dove of the East," that optimism is again present, though somewhat muted. Like "A Jew of Persia," this story is set in Israel, where its protagonist, Leon Orlovsky, herds cattle on the Golan Heights. Originally from Paris, Leon has become a skilled horseman and an excellent scout. On the day the story opens, he discovers an injured dove that his horse accidentally trampled during a frenzied ride prompted by Leon's desire to exorcise his memories. In a long flashback, Helprin reveals Leon's history: his training as a chemist, his love for Ann in Paris, their courtship and marriage, and her disappearance during World War II. Though Leon is endangering the cattle by remaining with the dove, he refuses to abandon it, seeing in the dove an emblem of suffering humanity. Like the bird he nurses, Leon himself "is moved by quiet love," and his fidelity to the dove's need reflects his continuing commitment to Ann, with whom he still hopes to be reunited. Like the war-torn Nick Adams of "Big Two-Hearted River," Leon carefully ritualizes his daily activities, for such self-discipline helps to insulate him from the ravages of modern history. Though bereft of Ann and unable to save the injured dove, Leon nevertheless affirms love and compassion while awaiting "a day when his unraveled life would again be whole."

Ellis Island and Other Stories, published some six years after Helprin's first collection, shows a marked increase in artistic achievement. The book contains the title story (a novella), in addition to ten others. Four of those ten deal with war or the threat of war, while two others present characters who must cope with the accidental deaths of their loved ones. In almost all these stories ("White Gardens" is a notable exception) both plot and characterization are much more fully developed than in many of the briefer mood pieces in *A Dove of the East and Other Stories*.

This second volume opens with one of Helprin's most visionary tales, "The Schreuderspitze," whose central character, a photographer named Wallich, has recently lost his wife and son in an automobile accident. To escape his grief, Wallich moves to a tiny Alpine village, where he takes up mountain climbing. "He was pulled so far over on one side by the death of his family," Helprin writes, "he was so bent and crippled by the pain of it, that he was going to Garmisch-Partenkirchen to suffer a parallel ordeal through which he would balance what had befallen him."

To prepare for his ascent of the Schreuderspitze, Wallich begins a rigorous period of physical training and ascetic self-discipline that lasts nearly two years. The story culminates, however, not in Wallich's actual ascent of the mountain but in a climb undertaken in a series of dreams that extends over three nights. In this dream-vision, Wallich mounts into the *Eiswelt*, the ice world, with an ever-increasing sense of mastery and control. There he achieves a state of mystical insight in which he recognizes "that there was life after death, that the dead rose into a mischievous world of pure light, that something most mysterious lay beyond the enfolding darkness, something wonderful." These discoveries Wallich associates with the quality of light in the *Eiswelt*, but he also links them to the artistry of Beethoven's symphonies, which he compares to "a ladder of mountains" leading into "a heaven of light and the dead." In its use of this imagery of mountains and light, "The Schreuderspitze" resembles "Katherine Comes to Yellow Sky." Like Katherine, Wallich is nourished by his dreams, for they enable him to rise "above time, above the world" to a Blakean vision of eternity ("Starry wheels sat in fiery white coronas"). Restored by this experience, Wallich returns to Munich to reenter an everyday world now imbued with the extraordinary.

"The Schreuderspitze," perhaps more than any other story in *Ellis Island and Other Stories*, bears the imprint of Helprin's religious concerns. Moreover, by grounding Wallich's vision in his encounter with the sublime in nature, Helprin places the story squarely in the Romantic tradition. Like his Transcendentalist predecessors, Helprin seeks to promote the reign of wonder as one means of recovering a sense of the sacred, an awareness of mystery.

"Letters from the *Samantha*," one of the most intriguing stories in *Ellis Island and Other Stories*, records this eruption of the mysterious in a minor rather than a major key. Influenced by Edgar Allan Poe, this story is told through a series of letters that recount events on board the *Samantha* after it rescues a large monkey adrift at sea. From the first, the creature undermines the ship's morale, and its presence sets many of the sailors against the vessel's master, one Samson Low, the author of the letters. Deciding that the ape must again be set adrift, Low finds himself strangling the creature when it resists him. Although Low informs his crew that the monkey is not a symbol and that no significance invests its coming and going, the power of Helprin's tale lies in just such suggestiveness. As the master's name indicates, Samson Low is himself a fallen creature who destroys what he cannot understand. Locked in battle, Low and the monkey mirror each other: "I gripped so hard that my own teeth were bared and I made sounds similar to his. He put his hands around my neck as if to strangle me back." This tale, which immediately follows "The Schreuderspitze," counterpoints the initial story. Low's movement, in contrast to Wallich's, is downward.

Several of the stories in *Ellis Island and Other Stories*—"Martin Bayer," "A Vermont Tale," "Tamar"—create or build upon a sense of nostalgia. They are tales that record the loss of innocence, the vanishing of an ideal, while at the same time they affirm the value of that ideal. "A Vermont Tale," for example, recalls the month-long visit the narrator and his younger sister make to his grandparents' farm while his parents contemplate divorce. Though the month is January, with its "murderous ice," the narrator's prose celebrates nature's grandeur. The highlight of this visit is the grandfather's lengthy tale of a pair of Arctic loons. As the old man describes the birds, he humanizes them, so that the marital difficulties he identifies in their relationship seem to parallel those of the narrator's parents. In the grandfather's dramatic and moving story, the unfaithful male loon is ultimately reunited with its mate. Helprin's tale ends, however, not on this optimistic note but rather with the boy's recognition that his parents' marriage will not follow his grandfather's plot. Yet the ideal of fidelity remains, an ideal that this story discovers, significantly, in nature itself.

Several of the other stories in Helprin's second collection of short fiction return to the concern for war and its effects that is so evident in his first collection. Two of those stories, moreover, appear to draw upon Helprin's own experiences in the Israeli army. The first of these, "North Light," although nominally a first-person narrative, is dominated by the "we" of the soldiers' shared perspective. In only five pages, the story explores the psychology of warfare as an army unit is held back from the battlefield. Helprin's analysis of the anger that this delay generates—an anger that will be the men's salvation in combat—is thoroughly convincing.

The other war story set in Israel, "A Room of Frail Dancers," focuses on a soldier named Rieser, whose brigade has just been demobilized. The title of this story becomes a metaphor for human existence itself, especially when Rieser images the dancers as "figures of imperfection in constant striving." The frailty of the dancers suggests the fragility of the order they establish, though Helprin's title also hints at humanity's perennial desire to achieve the grace and harmony associated with dance. Rieser's own frailty is evinced when he pronounces the dancers' movements "purposeless" and commits suicide.

Another story whose title functions metaphorically is "Palais de Justice." Whereas Rieser's struggle is largely internal, the conflict in this story involves a sculling contest between an attorney in his early sixties and a scornful young man. Using the wisdom of experience, the aging attorney unexpectedly triumphs over his adversary, whom he identifies with the barbarism and violence of the twentieth century, a century contemptuous of tradition and of the older generation that transmits its values: a theme Helprin also addresses in "First Russian Summer." The Palais de Justice is also "the palace of the world," Helprin suggests, and he implies as well that every individual has a responsibility to affirm the humane values embodied in this story's protagonist.

The novella that gives Helprin's second collection its title is a comic mixture of realism and fantasy. Divided into four sections, "Ellis Island" recounts the first-person narrator's arrival in the United States and his initial experiences there. The plot is complicated and its events often implausible, but the novella's central thematic concern is the narrator's discovery of selfless love. As is often the case in Helprin's fiction, this discovery is made possible by the protagonist's encounter with a woman, in this case with two women: Elise, a striking Danish immigrant with whom he falls in love on Ellis Island, and Hava, who attempts to teach him the tailor's trade once he reaches New York City. When Elise, his "pillar of fire" (the title of the novella's first section), is refused entry into the United States because she has no one to support her, the narrator agrees to find a job as a tailor to secure her freedom.

After having undergone several amazing changes of identity on Ellis Island, the narrator continues his extraordinary adventures in New York City, adventures that display Helprin's imagination at its most whimsical. Once the narrator obtains a position as a tailor (a trade about which he knows nothing), he meets Hava. It is from Hava, whose name is the Hebrew word for Eve, that he learns the lesson of selflessness, for she works twice as hard as usual to complete his tailoring along with her own. The narrator moves in with Hava, is ironically given the certificate of employment he needs not for winning a job but for quitting it, and begins a career as a journalist. His very success, however, causes him to forget Elise. Only after he and Hava are married does he recall his pledge "to redeem Elise." Returning to Ellis Island he learns that she has died while aiding those aboard a typhus-ridden ship. Her death, he recognizes, demands of him "a life of careful amends."

In this novella, as elsewhere in his fiction, Helprin does not shy away from the didactic. Even in so whimsical a tale, he manifests his pervasive concern for health of heart and soul. "Hardened hearts and dead souls" are the price that people pay for ignoring the demands of justice and compassion and self-sacrifice. "To give to another without reward," writes Helprin's narrator, "is the only way to compensate for our mortality, and perhaps the binding principle of this world."

It is the pursuit of such binding principles that energizes Helprin's fiction. His stories record his character's encounters with or longing for those perennial absolutes: love, goodness, beauty, justice, God. They also celebrate what "Palais de Justice" calls "this intricate and marvelously fashioned world." Though at times too rarefied in plot and character, at their best these stories become windows on the infinite, while grounded in the particular. They thus confirm the claim Helprin makes on his readers in the epigraph to *Winter's Tale*: "I have been to another world, and come back. Listen to me."

Other major works
NOVELS: *Refiner's Fire: The Life and Adventures of Marshall Pearl, a Foundling*, 1977; *Winter's Tale*, 1983.

Bibliography
Bell, Pearl K. "New Jewish Voices," in *Commentary*. LXXI (June, 1981), pp. 62-66.
Broyard, Anatole. "Mysterious Short Story," in *The New York Times Book Review*. LXXXVI (March 1, 1981), p. 35.
Buckley, Christopher. "A Talk with Mark Helprin: 'I May Be an Anomaly,'" in *The New York Times Book Review*. LXXXVI (March 25, 1984), p. 16.

Green, David B. "An Intimate Look at a Superb Storyteller," in *Vogue*. March, 1982, pp. 430-431.

Kakutani, Michiko. "The Making of a Writer: Tell a Yarn or No Dinner," in *The New York Times*. March 5, 1981, p. C17.

Steinberg, Sybil S. "Mark Helprin," in *Publishers Weekly*. CCXIX (February 13, 1981), pp. 12-13.

John Lang

STEPHEN KING

Born: Portland, Maine; September 21, 1947

Principal short fiction
Night Shift, 1978; *Different Seasons*, 1982; *Skeleton Crew*, 1985.

Other literary forms
Stephen King is certainly best known as a writer of horror novels, the field in which most of his writing has been published. Since the printing of *Carrie* in 1974, he has steadily produced novels with enormous success both in print and in film adaptations, including *'Salem's Lot* (1975), *The Shining* (1977), *The Stand* (1978), *The Dead Zone* (1979), *Firestarter* (1980), *Cujo* (1981), *Christine* (1983), and *Pet Sematary* (1983). King has also published three fantasies, *The Dark Tower: The Gunslinger* (1982, illustrated by Michael Whelan), *Cycle of the Werewolf* (1983), and *The Eyes of the Dragon* (1984, 1987); a mixture of criticism and autobiography in *Danse Macabre* (1981); and some early works under the pen name Richard Bachman.

Achievements
Almost from the start of his very prolific career, King was praised by critics as America's greatest living writer of horror fiction. Reviewers across the country also drew attention to his skill as a storyteller, in addition to his ability to paint gruesome scenes. Hollywood shared the opinion, as the long string of successful films based on King's novels proves. As might have been expected with so prolific a writer, King had his detractors, who claimed that he plotted in formulas, especially that of the monster machine. Nevertheless, much of his fiction is rooted in the concrete reality of the Maine he knows and loves, a reality that serves as an anchor for his fantasy.

Biography
Only two years after Stephen William King was born in Portland, Maine, in 1947, his father deserted the family. Still, King's father had a profound if indirect influence. Among his father's abandoned belongings was a collection of supernatural fiction, including a book of stories by H. P. Lovecraft. Although King admits that the books introduced him to a different world, their influence was a long time coming in his own work.

King was reared in Maine and attended college at the University of Maine at Orono, from which he was graduated in 1970 with a teaching degree in English. Although he began submitting stories for publication almost immediately, he succeeded in selling them only occasionally. His first four novels (none of them horror stories) remain unpublished. It was only in 1973, in a time of financial difficulty, that he decided, at his wife's urging, to rewrite a short story as a horror novel: He had no great hopes for the book, but to his surprise, *Carrie* was accepted and made the best-seller lists, an accomplishment achieved by each of his successive works.

Analysis

On first reading, Stephen King's short fiction will probably remind the reader of the longer works that Hollywood has popularized, because his short stories combine the elements of theme and setting that have proved successful again and again. Consider, for example, a horror theme that has been particularly associated with King since the publication of *Christine*: the machine that becomes a monster. The 1958 Plymouth of that novel had several prefigurations in King's short fiction. The earliest appearance of the theme seems to have been "The Mangler," in which the terror machine is a steam-driven ironer and folder at a commercial laundry. This particular treatment worked in demonic possession as the reason for the machine's hostility; later versions, such as "Trucks" and "Uncle Otto's Truck," dropped any attempt to give a plausible reason for the malevolence. King frequently leaves the reasons for bizarre occurrences mysterious, thus easing the strain on the reader's suspension of disbelief. King does not confine the theme of human artifacts gaining power over their makers to automobiles but has dealt with it in forms as varied as mirrors and word processors ("The Reaper's Image" and "Word Processor of the God"). Even toys, whether model soldiers ("Battleground") or a clockwork monkey ("The Monkey"), can be agents for evil in these stories.

If King has been somewhat typecast as a writer of horror fiction, his short fiction shows that he has the range and skill to move beyond that genre and even to blend several kinds of popular fiction in enjoyable ways. He does not need the monstrous machine, being as much at home with the products of Olympus as with those of Detroit. "Mrs. Todd's Shortcut" has as its central character a Maine housewife who gradually metamorphoses into the goddess Diana. Another example (and a humorous one) is "The Lawnmower Man," in which the god Pan goes into the lawn-care business in present-day New England. Figures from and allusions to classical mythology are not frequent in King's stories, but they are handled effectively when they appear.

The stories mentioned so far have all relied on the supernatural, but as Edgar Allan Poe knew, the writer of horror does not need ghosts and goblins: The workings of the human mind can terrify the reader. Similarly, some of King's most effective pieces are those that show a mind gripped by madness. "The Man Who Loved Flowers" is a powerful story that depends on a strong contrast between a spring setting in which youth, love, and flowers bloom and a resolution in which the lovers' meeting has an unexpected (though thoroughly foreshadowed) conclusion. Even more impressive are the stories that follow a mind through its descent into insanity. These include brief tales such as "Survivor Type," a story with only a single character in which the madman is also the victim, and "Cain Rose Up," which in very few pages gives a plausible picture of the making of a mass murderer. When King has greater room to expand, the progress from sanity to mania comes in almost imperceptible steps. Two longer stories both illustrate a frightening contagiousness about madness: In "The Ballad of the Flexible Bullet," a talented but psychotic writer slowly draws his editor into the circle of his hallucinations—unintentionally and by mail. The best and perhaps most chilling example of this kind, however, is one that King himself thought overlong: "Apt Pupil." It is difficult to agree with King about the length of the story, because the step-by-step change of an ordinary American boy to a random murderer requires a treatment of this length. In his California town, the boy discovers a German war criminal in hiding; his curiosity about World War II and the atrocities of the prison camps moves inexorably toward mania as the boy blackmails the old man into telling stories that fan a bloody ferocity in the German while they kindle one in the boy. The two characters, young and old, course toward the same destination at the slow pace of a ceremonial march.

King's short fiction exhibits his versatility better than his novels. Many of his stories show that he can move at will outside the limits of horror fiction. For the fan of the gangster story, there is "The Wedding Gig," set during Prohibition in the milieu of the Chicago mobs. Nothing supernatural happens here: It is a straightforward revenge story in a well-realized time and place. The fan of an even more specialized form, the prison-breakout story, will enjoy the human persistence and ingenuity of "Rita Hayworth and Shawshank Redemption." Finally, as a sample of an adventure story depending on a plain conflict of human wills, consider "The Ledge," in which two men make an unusual wager for the love of a woman. It is a model short story in which every word and every action focuses on the advancement of the plot.

Similarly, few would connect the name of Stephen King with science fiction, yet as early as 1974 he was using the familiar themes of that genre with a deft touch. "Night Surf" is a variation of the end-of-the-world story, made more ironic by the fact that the disease that sweeps the earth is not the plague or a germ bred in some laboratory but a new strain of flu. Two stories in *Skeleton Crew* are set in the future: One, "Beachworld," takes place on an alien planet that proves to be menacingly alive; the other, "The Jaunt," concerns a technological advance that allows teleportation, and its scientific patter should please even the most experienced reader of *Analog* or *Galaxy*. Although the setting of "The Mist" is the familiar Maine vacation country, the theme is that of Mary Shelley's *Frankenstein* (1818): the horror of science out of control. The action of the story concerns a handful of people besieged in a village supermarket, but always in the background is the knowledge that the shapes that attack from the mist were unloosed by an army experiment. Perhaps King's most interesting science-fiction story is "I Am the Doorway." Although it came early in his career (1971), it achieves a chilling mixture of horror theme and science-fiction form in its tale of an astronaut infected by an alien being.

Connoisseurs of more restrained horror, the frightening tale recollected in tranquillity, as it were, will enjoy two stories set in a very strange and very exclusive New York City club: "The Man Who Would Not Shake Hands" and "The Breathing Method." These stories have an almost nineteenth century pace to them; one would not be at all surprised to find that the teller of the story was Joseph Conrad's Marlow.

When King's versatility is admitted, it must also be admitted that the popular taste has fixed the label "horror fiction" firmly on his works. King is not uncomfortable with the label, and he honestly delivers what the label promises: all varieties of horror fiction, replete with tigers, giant rats, vampires, werewolves, and things without names. Yet surely one aspect of his work that makes him popular is his careful planting of his stories in his native soil. If stories such as "The Reach" were his only works in print, King would be called a regional realist. It is a tender story of an old woman's death on an island off the Maine coast, and every detail lends an unmistakable feeling of place. Any writer can add concreteness to a work of fiction by specifying a brand of beer or a year and model of car, but it requires more than ordinary skill and dedication to describe a coast so that it is not any coast, but a Maine coast, or to describe a woods as not any woods but clearly and precisely a Maine woods. This is a skill that Stephen King has, and it is a skill that shines from many of his short stories, whether it be "Jerusalem's Lot," a horror piece reminiscent of Lovecraft, or "The Mist," mentioned above.

In the tales set in Maine, especially those in or near the fictional town of Castle Rock, even minor characters reappear from story to story, lending verisimilitude to a fantastic plot and almost a sense of familiarity to a realistic plot. Stories such as "Nona," the tale of a college dropout entranced by woman or witch or shapechanger, show how effective a writer King can be with a horror theme in a setting well known and well loved. Stories such as "The Body," an entirely realistic story of boys growing up in that setting, show that Stephen King need never depend on horror to write a story worth reading.

Other major works

NOVELS: *Carrie*, 1974; *'Salem's Lot*, 1975; *The Shining*, 1977; *Rage*, 1977 (as Richard Bachman); *The Stand*, 1978; *The Dead Zone*, 1979; *The Long Walk*, 1979 (as Bachman); *Firestarter*, 1980; *Cujo*, 1981; *Roadwork*, 1981 (as Bachman); *The Dark Tower: The Gunslinger*, 1982 (illustrated by Michael Whelan); *The Running Man*, 1982 (as Bachman); *Cycle of the Werewolf*, 1983 (novelette); *Christine*, 1983; *Pet Sematary*, 1983; *The Eyes of the Dragon*, 1984, 1987; *Thinner*, 1984 (as Bachman); *The Bachman Books: Four Early Novels by Stephen King*, 1985 (includes *Rage*, *The Long Walk*, *Roadwork*, and *The Running Man*); *It*, 1986; *Misery*, 1987; *The Tommyknockers*, 1987.

SCREENPLAYS: *Creepshow*, 1982 (adaptation of his book); *Cat's Eye*, 1984; *Silver Bullet*, 1985 (adaptation of *Cycle of the Werewolf*); *Maximum Overdrive*, 1986 (adaptation of his short story "Truck").

NONFICTION: *Danse Macabre*, 1981.

Bibliography

Underwood, Tim, and Chuck Miller, eds. *Fear Itself: The Horror Fiction of Stephen King*, 1982.

Winter, Douglas E. *Stephen King: Starmont Reader's Guide Sixteen*, 1982.

Walter E. Meyers

TOMMASO LANDOLFI

Born: Pico, near Frosinone, Italy; August 9, 1908
Died: Rome, Italy; July 7, 1979

Principal short fiction

Dialogo dei massimi sistemi, 1937; *Il Mar delle Blatte*, 1939; *La spada*, 1942; *Le due zitelle*, 1945 (*The Two Old Maids*, 1961); *Cancroregina*, 1950 (*Cancerqueen*, 1971); *Ombre*, 1954; *Se non la realtà*, 1960; *Racconti*, 1961; *In società*, 1962; *Tre racconti*, 1964; *Gogol's Wife and Other Stories*, 1963; *Racconti impossibili*, 1966; *Cancerqueen and Other Stories*, 1971; *Le labrene*, 1974; *A caso*, 1975.

Other literary forms

While Tommaso Landolfi has written mainly short stories and short works called *novelle*, he has also published some long fiction. Examples include *La pietra lunare* (1937; the moonstone) and *Un amore del nostro tempo* (1965; a love story of our time). He has written for the theater: *Landolfo VI di Benevento* (1958; Landolph VI) and *Faust '67* (1969). He has published two highly regarded volumes of poetry: *Viola di morte* (1972; the violet shade of death) and *Il tradimento* (1977; betrayal). In Italy, he also enjoys a reputation as an observant literary critic and a witty and ironic essayist. A selection of critical essays are gathered in *Gogol a Roma* (1971; Gogol in Rome), while *Del meno* (1978; this and that) is a collection of columns which Landolfi published over the years on the "terza pagina" (the literary page) of the *Corriere della Sera*. To this steady and voluminous activity must be added the writer's numerous translations from French, German, and Russian literature.

Achievements

Landolfi is a unique and eccentric writer who fits into no obvious category of Italian literature, past or present. Italian fiction in the twentieth century follows the tradition laid down by the nineteenth century masters, Alessandro Manzoni and Giovanni Verga, both of whom dealt directly with the historical forces at work on human society and who emphasized realistic description of the social backdrop. Landolfi appears to have had no interest in dealing overtly with those historical crises of his time which had such a formative influence on his own generation (Fascism and World War II). Instead, Landolfi's cosmopolitanism is reflected in his continuous output as a translator—mainly from Russian, but also from French and German literature, which always paralleled his literary production. In the 1930's, Landolfi was associated with the hermetic movement in Italian poetry and prose, as a part of that generation of writers who, in response to the pressures of the Fascist regime, turned in upon themselves to rediscover a poetic voice or simply to maintain private integrity, while they also looked to foreign traditions in search of stylistic and thematic mentors. In those years, Landolfi, who had taken a degree in Russian literature at the University of Florence, continued to reside in that city and published his early fiction in reviews such as *Letteratura* and *Campo di Marte*. The hermetics made their anti-Fascist comments obliquely, never attacking the regime directly, but rather withdrawing from its vulgarity, militancy, and stridency.

In the immediate postwar period, Landolfi found himself increasingly isolated in a climate of intensifying political commitment and mounting claims made on all writers for allegiance. Such withdrawal from fashion was a conscious choice on Landolfi's part, resulting in a slow recognition of the quality of his work. His columns in the *Corriere della Sera*, however, earned for him a wider audience, and his achievements over a broad area of the literary landscape were certainly acknowledged in Italy, where he received the country's major literary prizes, including the Pirandello Prize for Drama (1968) and the Viareggio Prize, for both fiction (1958) and poetry (1972).

Biography

The biographical facts pertaining to Tommaso Landolfi can be briefly stated. His was a life without major incident, which he chose to live in obscurity, away from the glare of publicity. Landolfi is known for consciously establishing barriers between himself and any would-be biographer. This jealously guarded privacy amounted to something of an obsession.

He was born in Pico (in the province of Frosinone) in 1908. His mother died in his second year, and as a young adolescent he was sent away to boarding school. He later attended the University of Florence, from which he was graduated, having specialized in Russian literature. He spent most of the 1930's in Florence, participating in the literary activities of the time, publishing his early fiction. It is known that, on the eve of World War II, he was arrested and spent some time in prison for activities deemed inappropriate by the regime. Landolfi's political demeanor, however, took the form of a rather generic anti-Fascism rather than that of an overt militancy. During the war, he lived with his father in his ancestral home in Pico, which at different times during the war was occupied both by German forces and by Moroccan troops of the Free French Army. Landolfi married later in life, fathered two children, and devoted himself to literature. He divided the years after the war between Pico and Rome, where he died in 1979.

Analysis

It is appropriate to begin with a psychological portrait of the man before proceeding to an analysis of the writer's principal themes and works. For one who made such a cult of privacy, Tommaso Landolfi proved remarkably confessional, revealing much of a complicated inner life, the details of which are far richer than the external events of his career. In this respect, the critic's task was made much easier with the publication in the 1950's and the 1960's of such autobiographical works as *La bière du pecheur* (1953; the sinner's bier/coffin), *Rien va* (1963; no more), and *Des mois* (1968; months). These works are not strictly diaries; they are more like private jottings in which the writer reminisces, but also attempts to define personal responses to crises in his own life and to clarify his position vis-à-vis all human experience. These volumes have their nineteenth century antecedents Giacomo Leopardi's *Zibaldone* (1898-1900; notebooks) and Charles Baudelaire's *Mon cœur mis à nu* (1887; *My Heart Laid Bare*, 1950).

The following psychological patterns are quite visible in Landolfi's personality and in the fiction that they have nourished. The loss of his mother before his second birthday left scars on the psyche of the child and adolescent that were to stay with him the rest of his life, bestowing on him a profound sense of privation and an equally strong sense of guilt. To the child's trauma one can trace the origins of an ambivalence toward women, who, on the one hand, stirred in the writer erotic and even violent impulses, and, on the other, as repositories of a sacred motherhood suggested an ineffable purity accessible only through dream and memory. In the absence of the mother stood the father—in reality an affectionate if gruff man with a taste for solitude, and a forthright anti-Fascist. The fictional father figure loomed menacingly over vulnerable offspring, often in a gloomy manor in an abandoned corner of the provinces. The son may never have fully pardoned the father for sending his hypersensitive child to a private boarding school at the age of twelve: For the second time in his young life, Landolfi felt rejected, cast off and set afloat in a hostile universe. Thereafter the fiction bristled with the theme of Oedipal conflict and incestuous temptation. In the novella *La morte del re di Francia* (the death of the King of France, published in *Gogol's Wife and Other Stories*), the father, So-and-So, broods over his daughter Rosalba's ripening adolescence and supervises her daily bath, while he is also the object of her erotic dream. In the fable *Racconto d'autunno* (1947; an autumn tale), an old man keeps his daughter imprisoned in an isolated villa, where she serves as a high priestess to an almost necrophiliac cult of his dead wife. The Landolfian antihero is solitary and impotent in a much larger than sexual sense: His essential form of communication is the monologue, which he commits to the page of his diary. He is convinced of his own uselessness in an existence that he finds insufficient.

The Two Old Maids, published just after the war, offers few concessions to the fashion of contemporary realism. Both the setting and the style of this novella place it within the tradition of nineteenth century fiction, which Landolfi acknowledges, and from which he detaches himself in the second sentence. The reader can be thankful, he writes, that he (the author) would not dream of describing this house and district in every detail. His satire of a literature to which he remains devoted and of a way of life that he knows rather too intimately remains unerring. The district is "disheartening"; dust lies on the buildings and trees. In the apartment which the reader is invited to enter, the old maids Lilla and Nena sacrifice their lives to their seemingly indestructible mother, who dominates them to her dying day.

The hero of this tale is the monkey, the family pet, more or less domesticated and living, as all objects of love do (says Landolfi), in a large cage. The sisters have inherited him from their brother, a sea captain, who brought him back from one of his voyages; and they lavish on him an affection that is their memorial to the departed mariner. The monkey is the only male in the house, summing up in his diminutive frame the roles of father, brother, even husband, and certainly that of the children the barren sisters never bore. Like a child or lover, he likes to sleep in Lilla's lap and sometimes clutch her breasts when she lies down for a nap. The animal introduces a contrapuntal principle of virility and spontaneity into a shared existence predicated on a pious suppression of instinct.

The crisis comes when the monkey, Tombo, is accused by the Mother Superior of the convent next door of stealing the consecrated host and drinking the communion wine from the chapel. Nena vehemently denies these charges, but on closer inspection she learns that the ingenious Tombo can indeed unlock his cage, make his way over the wall into the convent garden, and pay a visit to the chapel. Following him, Nena hides herself in that sacred place together with a young nun and observes with her own eyes the sacrilegious trespass of the monkey. What she sees horrifies her far more than the accusations of stealing heard from the Mother Superior. Every gesture that the little creature makes—the way he wraps himself in the holy corporal as if it were a stole, the pouring of the wine into the chalice, the salutation to a nonexistent congregation—can spell only one thing: "Tombo was saying Mass!" For such desecration he is immediately condemned. Nena declares, "He must die."

If the tale is read simply as social satire, then the monkey's comic imitations of the gestures of the priest do not go beyond a parody of the mass and the devalued rituals of the Church. Tombo, however, is not the damnable heretic for which he is mistaken. In effect, his visits to the chapel are his way of following in his mistresses' footsteps, of identifying with their faith, of adoring their God as best he might. Tombo's mass, with its gibbering replication of the priest's devotions, is not heretical simply because it is an untidy imitation and not in Latin. It is, rather, a reminder of masses conducted in primitive conditions in distant colonies under missionary supervision, scruffy but sincere: the sort of thing that her brother the sea captain might have witnessed, had Nena the piety to remember that.

The demise of the monkey is finally consummated. Landolfi communicates the terror of an animal that knows no guilt, but knows it is about to die, betrayed for having dared to love. Nena victoriously snuffs out a flickering life, and in her victory achieves a terrible irony. By his crucifixion she elevates the blasphemer Tombo to actual martyrdom. The last event in the sisters' life is over, and until their death all can return to normal, or, as Landolfi puts it, a gray dust can settle over everything once more.

Cancerqueen is linked thematically to Landolfi's previous fiction in that it explores the human search for freedom along with the foundering of that quest. It marks at the same time an anticipated development in his career and a point of crisis. It is in part an exercise in science fiction which suggests that the writer's imagination was finally working its way free of earthbound experience and needed to test itself against the dimensions of space. The tale is divided into two parts. The first recounts the author's meeting with a mad scientist who invites him on a voyage to the moon aboard his spaceship, christened *Cancerqueen*. This fantasy is told in chronological order in punctilious detail, as if it belonged to the tradition of narrative realism. Part 2 is composed of a diary in which the protagonist, marooned alone in the spaceship, jots down his thoughts on his isolation, on life in general, on his fears and obsessions. Artistically this part marks a rupture with the first forty pages of the tale; it also provides an interesting indication of the diaristic direction of Landolfi's prose less than three years before the publication of *La bière du pecheur*. This diary also indicates the growing inversion of Landolfi's point of view and his preference to write in the first person singular and to adopt the form of the monologue.

The protagonist is a failed writer forced to return to his native village and house as a result of gambling debts and disappointments in love. He receives a visit from an escapee from the local insane asylum, who tries to interest him in a bizarre story of his invention of a wonderful machine designed to fly them to the moon. Can there be any method in this madman? Is he the victim of the prejudice of rival professionals jealous of his superior genius? Is he an expression of human fears of science and fascination with the forces beyond human control—the fears that humanity's moral development has not kept pace with technological advance? Might this maniac not represent the gambler's instinct in Landolfi come to whisper in his ear that it is better to risk all for a flight through the cosmos than to accept stagnation and death in a moldering mansion without hope or a future?

The author is tempted, and the two men rush out of the house to embark on their "singular excursion" into the mountains in search of the treasured creation of Filano (the mysterious visitor and architect of *Cancerqueen*). The remarkable description of this journey by moonlight up steep slopes, across vertiginous peaks, and over dizzying chasms is another example of Landolfi's fascination with the wild nature of his native hills around Pico. They are built into the texture of many of his tales, and he invests them with a strange, gothic beauty, attractive and terrifying. The journey ends with a descent into a cave at the pit of which is the miraculous *Cancerqueen*, a creation of almost mythic dimension and faith more than of scientific calculation. She—and she must be granted her sex—is presented not as a triumph of physics, but rather is anthropomorphized as an extension of the human imagination now poised to conquer space.

The human imagination, however, is impeded by human paranoia. Filano goes mad and, concluding that the voyage will be jeopardized by the extra weight of his companion, determines to jettison him. In the ensuing struggle it is Filano who is plunged into the void, with the protagonist facing space alone. Not quite alone, however, for the laws of physics decree that the ejected Filano cling eternally to the sides of his beloved craft, and he is transformed into an irremovable mute companion on a voyage without end.

Characters in Landolfi who resort to violence are obliged to live with the consequences of their acts. The child murderer in "La muta" ("The Mute") must await the arrival of his executioners. Kafka, imagined in "Il babbo di Kafka" (Kafka's father) as killing his father, who has assumed the form of a spider, can never be certain whether the spider he killed really did contain his father's soul. In like manner, the protagonist of *Cancerqueen* must live forever with the image of Filano grimacing at him from space beyond the window. In seeking to liberate himself, the protagonist has turned himself into a prisoner. Would it not have been better to stay amid the ugly confusion of human society than to seek the rarefied purity of space? The final irony is that the writer has begun to write again, but there is no audience. No one will recover the manuscript. His words are like Filano's corpse, empty husks cast into space.

Passing from the eventual madness of the writer lost in space to that of another, unable to free himself from an obsession, the reader encounters similar concerns in Landolfi's best-known short story, "La moglie di Gogol" ("Gogol's Wife"). This story first appeared in the 1954 collection of short stories and autobiographical pieces entitled *Ombre* (shadows). The title and protagonist are a reminder of Landolfi's lifelong interest in the author of *Dead Souls* (a study of Gogol is included in Landolfi's critical essays, in *Gogol a Roma*), to whom he was drawn for a narrative style that depended less on meticulous observation than on audacious leaps of the imagination. Undoubtedly, Landolfi was also interested in Gogol as an example of an unbalanced mind that descended into religious mania and a fatal melancholy that led to his early death. Like his Gogol, many of Landolfi's heroes fall victim to hallucinations and obsessions, and the author deals convincingly with acute states of psychological isolation, undoubtedly similar to his own.

The tale reads like a surrealistic joke conceived as an entertainment which ultimately reveals much more about its author than was originally intended.

Gogol's wife is an inflatable rubber doll which can be blown up to the size and dimensions chosen by her spouse. She possesses a rudimentary spine and rib cage for rigidity. She is nude at all times, and the narrator, in the guise of an intimate of the great Nikolai, draws attention to the remarkable anatomical exactitude of her exposed genitalia. Yet what appears to be a perfect human replica is only an epidermis, with no inner organs, no mind, no character of her own.

What is the reader to make of this simulacrum of a wife? Since this Gogol is an invention of Landolfi, one is to assume that some of the observable fetishes and the transference of affection from people to objects belong to him. A doll is preferred to a proper wife out of the fear of a real woman's independence and judgment. The doll, naked and placid, with her changes of wigs, able to assume a variety of shapes according to the caprice of the inflator, is quite literally a sex object, ready at all times to satisfy the whims of the husband. The fact that she cannot answer back makes her always passive, subservient and obedient. (The narrator, however, recalls one occasion when she does appear to talk, childishly expressing a desire to go to the lavatory, which throws Gogol into a fit of rage, causing him to deflate her for the evening.) The doll also brings out sadistic impulses in the male; indeed, she seems designed to be humiliated. To inflate her, a pump is inserted in her anus, and she is deflated by forcing one's hand down her throat to release a nozzle.

Subservient as she is, her master is convinced of a stubborn insubordination in her nature, a kind of passive resistance to his whims, perhaps even an unspoken mockery, which he interprets as a challenge to his authority. The wife-doll, Caracas, represents a taunting sexual presence to Gogol which his growing religious mania persuades him to eradicate from his life. She must suffer the same fate as the manuscript of the second part of *Dead Souls*, and in the final conflagration one sees a murderous assault on female sensuality, the world of the flesh and even art (in that Caracas is part muse and the inspirer of the literature of love). In addition, Gogol throws into the flames what appears to be a baby doll of the same material as Caracas, identified as her son. Once more, a father exerts a fearful, fatal authority over his offspring.

Landolfi's symbolism is rich and suggestive, never formulaic or precise. Caracas is a projection of a host of male fears of the female, of the ambiguous relations between the sexes. She offers both physical partnership and challenge to her companion, but the reader can never say with certainty that she equals one value or meaning rather than another. Furthermore, each reading of the tale will yield different levels of interpretation. The story goes well beyond a psychological portrait of Gogol. The fears of the eternal feminine, the impotence of the protagonist, the failure to establish a relationship with another, the sadism of the father—all are familiar themes in Landolfi's fiction. The reader is directed to "La beccaccia" (the woodcock), also in *Ombre*, which focuses on a hunter's cruelty toward an innocent creature following his disappointment in love.

The thematic links between these stories offer a guide to a complete reading of Landolfi's work. In different ways, they deal with aspects of freedom in psychological and aesthetic terms. Tombo introduces into the house of the old maids disturbing motifs of vitality and an alternative form of religious expression. His death is the price he must pay for their lives to remain unruffled. The association of space flight with artistic freedom is quite clear in *Cancerqueen*, but the dream runs into conflict with human limitations, leaving the artist-protagonist suspended in the void. Gogol may immolate his wife to free himself of a degrading dependence, but his creative will is not restored by that brutal expedient. The fate or crisis of the artist is a serious matter for Landolfi.

In *Cancerqueen*, he reveals the ultimate isolation of the writer, who passes with tragic inevitability from dialogue to monologue to silence. Two fellow writers whom he includes in his tales, Franz Kafka and Nikolai Gogol, are presented as being insane, suggesting that this condition accompanies that of the artist. Either one risks mental balance by choosing art as a way of life, or one must be part mad in order to write (or paint or compose). Either way, life in art amounts more to tyranny than to freedom. The caverns and labyrinthine mansions where many of Landolfi's dramas occur suggest that he is interested only in the hidden experience. What lies below the surface of life alone is worth writing about, revealing secret truths of which we are unaware, including destructive impulses that society has a right to control. Landolfi is by no means an aesthete who has chosen literature as a means of refining a style for the pleasure of a handful of insiders. He is a disturbing writer who reveals the cracks in the human façade.

Other major works

NOVELS: *La pietra lunare*, 1937; *Racconto d'autunno*, 1947; *Ottavio di Saint-Vincent*, 1958; *Un amore del nostro tempo*, 1965.

PLAYS: *Landolfo VI di Benevento*, 1958; *Faust '67*, 1969.

POETRY: *Viola di morte*, 1972; *Il tradimento*, 1977.

NONFICTION: *Un paniere di chiocciole*, 1968; *Gogol a Roma*, 1971; *Del meno*, 1978.

MISCELLANEOUS: *La bière du pecheur*, 1953; *Rien va*, 1963; *Des mois*, 1968.

Bibliography

Abruzzi, Giovanna Ghetti. *L'enigma Landolfi*, 1979.
Brew, Claude. "The 'Caterpillar Nature' of Imaginative Experience: A Reading of Tommaso Landolfi's 'Wedding Night,'" in *Modern Language Notes*. LXXXIX, no. 1 (1974), pp. 110-115.

Gathercole, Patricia M. *Studies in Short Fiction*, 1973.
Pandini, Giancarlo. *Tommaso Landolfi*, 1975.
Rosenthal, Raymond. Introduction to *Cancerqueen and Other Stories*, 1971.
Sanguineti, Edoardo. "Tommaso Landolfi," in *Letteratura Landolfi*, 1978.
Secchi, Craziella Bernabo'. *Invito alla lettura di Tommaso Landolfi*, 1978.

Harry Lawton

HENRY LAWSON

Born: Grenfell, Australia; June 17, 1867
Died: Sydney, Australia; September 2, 1922

Principal short fiction

Short Stories in Prose and Verse, 1894; *While the Billy Boils*, 1896; *On the Track*, 1900; *Over the Sliprails*, 1900; *Joe Wilson and His Mates*, 1901; *The Rising of the Court*, 1910; *Mateship: A Discursive Yarn*, 1911; *Triangles of Life and Other Stories*, 1913; *Henry Lawson: The Bush Undertaker and Other Stories*, 1971; *Henry Lawson: Selected Stories*, 1971; *Henry Lawson: Short Stories and Sketches, 1888-1922*, 1972.

Other literary forms

While Henry Lawson is now known primarily for his short stories and prose sketches, he also wrote a substantial amount of verse. Collections of his poetry include *In the Days When the World Was Wide and Other Verses* (1896), *Verses, Popular and Humorous* (1900), and *When I Was King and Other Verses* (1905). *Henry Lawson: Collected Verse* is published in three volumes (edited by Colin Roderick, 1967-1969).

Achievements

Lawson, while at the height of his career in the 1890's, was a truly popular writer: He wrote for and about the common people of Australia, and he was read by those people. Fortune, however, did not follow fame for him, and though his work was published, read, and admired, he lived most of his life in penury and often misery. Even so, he was the first Australian writer ever to receive a state funeral, and his portrait was put on the ten-dollar note in 1965. His reputation, then, has always been high in Australia, though with different people for different reasons at different times; he has yet, however, to receive the recognition he no doubt deserves among readers of fiction in the rest of the world. By any acceptable standard, Lawson, at his best, is a masterful short-story writer.

Biography

Born on the goldfields of New South Wales at Grenfell in 1867, Henry Lawson was the eldest of the five children of Peter Larsen, a former Norwegian sailor, and Louisa Albury, his Australian wife. Henry's name was registered as Lawson and that became the family name. His childhood was not a happy one: From the age of nine he had difficulties with deafness; the family was poor and moved frequently; the parents disliked each other and fought bitterly. Peter and Louisa finally separated by mutual consent in 1883, Louisa taking the younger children to Sydney; Henry remained briefly with his father before joining his mother to help support the family—he was fifteen at the time. Lawson seems to have been fond of his ne'er-do-well father, while he found Louisa overbearing and lacking in human warmth. A number of stories, presumably autobiographical, touch upon this period of his life, especially "A Child in the Dark, and a Foreign Father."

Lawson worked in Sydney as a coach painter and, for a while, went to night school. His mother was ambitious for him and encouraged his intellectual endeavors, for by this time she was herself a considerable figure in feminist and republican circles in Australia. Idealistic in nature, Lawson soon became imbued with lifelong radical and Socialist convictions. As a young writer, Lawson's first break came in 1887, when he published a ballad, "The Song of the Republic," in the prominent magazine *The Bulletin*, which also published his first story, "His Father's Mate," in 1880, a few days before his father died. In 1890, Lawson traveled to Western Australia and worked as a journalist, and in 1891, he moved to Brisbane to write for the radical newspaper *Boomerang*. Before the end of the year, however, he was back in Sydney.

At this point in his career, Lawson began to develop his mastery of the short story; indeed, he was then known more for his poetry than his prose. In 1892, he wrote his first important story sequence, the Arvie Aspinall series, and a number of his most important stories, including "The Drover's Wife" and "The Bush Undertaker." During that same year, he took what became a crucial trip to Bourke, in the Outback, and farther, to "back of beyond." There, on the frontier, the virtues of "mateship" and solidarity, and the terrible realities of Bush life, were impressed upon him and became important thematic features of his subsequent work. Returning to Sydney, Lawson worked at a number of jobs and published his first book, *Short Stories in Prose and Verse*, in 1894. His reputation now growing, he brought out *While the Billy Boils* in 1896, perhaps his best collection of stories, and a volume of verse. That year, he fell in love with, and married, Bertha Bredt. In the midst of the Depression of the 1890's, they went to New Zealand and ran a Maori school until 1896, when again Lawson returned to Sydney. Lawson, by this time, had developed serious alcoholism, which was exacerbated by his frequenting the bohemian Dawn and Dusk Club. Nevertheless, he was able to bring out two more collections of prose in 1900, *On the Track* and *Over the Sliprails*, as well as another book of verse.

Having become dissatisfied with pursuing a writing career in Australia, Lawson took his wife and children to Great Britain, where he hoped to gain recognition. He met with some limited success there, and wrote a number of important stories, particularly the Joe Wilson series. Yet he was not happy; there was still poverty, illness, and drunkenness with which to contend, and increasingly, he and his wife were becoming estranged. In fact, it appears that Lawson had fallen in love with another woman, Hannah Thornburn, before leaving for Great Britain, and his return in 1902 may well have been motivated by his desire to be with Hannah. Upon arrival in Sydney, Lawson learned that Hannah had died several days before. Lawson separated from Bertha and the children, and his life thereafter steadily disintegrated. Not only were there the twin personal tragedies of death and estrangement, there was an artistic crisis as well: His creative faculties were clearly in decline. Added to this was the painful recognition that the Socialist political values he had so long espoused were permanently in eclipse. Whatever relationship each difficulty bore to the other, taken together they were a severe blow, and the remaining twenty years of Lawson's life saw him periodically in prison for indebtedness and drunkenness (out of which comes the famous ballad "One-Hundred-and-Three"), in convalescent or mental hospitals, and simply on the streets. Lawson's friends were generous to him, particularly his landlady, and often helped him; even his political friends assisted with some government support. Lawson continued to write and publish, and his following continued to grow. Yet his best work was now mostly retrospective and autobiographical. In 1921, Lawson had a partially disabling cerebral hemorrhage, though he still wrote, and in 1922, he died at home. He was accorded a state funeral by the government of New South Wales, and a statue was erected in commemoration.

Analysis

Henry Lawson is a popular writer, both with the reading public at large and with professional critics, and for not dissimilar reasons: His limpid and engaging prose style seems a marvel of easy craftsmanship, and his sardonic wit, lively humor, and compassion render his stories attractive. He had a gift for realism that seemed to capture the authentic experience of people, his characters are believable and memorable, and his presentation of the harshness of life in the Bush, with its melancholy overtones of pessimism, has entered into the mythic structures of the Australian consciousness. Lawson mastered the difficult craft of artlessness, allowing the reader to enter into the world of his stories as one might enter a familiar room.

From his earliest collections come many of Lawson's best stories, such as "The Bush Undertaker," "The Drover's Wife," "Rats," and "The Union Buries Its Dead," a frequently anthologized story. In the latter story, Lawson describes the funeral procession in the Outback for a young man who, though a stranger in town, is nevertheless given a funeral because he was a fellow union laborer. This mateship or union solidarity is an ideal that underwrites much of Lawson's thinking, but it is rarely embodied in the world he presents. Most of the gathered crowd are too drunk to follow once the procession begins; the horseman who leaves to join his friend at the bar is an emblem of how good intentions get undermined in the Bush. The tone of the story wavers between an ironic and minimal affirmation of mateship and an almost nihilistic portrayal of the grimness of life on the margins. The comic touches are like gallows humor, and the respects paid to the corpse are the conditioned responses of human indifference. The confusion over the man's identity and name becomes significant: He is a stranger; then he is called James Tyson, according to his union papers; that proves to be a pseudonym; later his real name is learned, but is unfortunately forgotten by everyone. Identity becomes unimportant in the face of the absoluteness of death; it does not matter what his name is. The speaker, both involved participant and distant narrator, refuses the comforts of stock responses and conventions and leaves the reader with a bittersweet regard for the isolation of men striving to survive. The light he casts over the scene is harsh because it is real. As he says, "I have left out the 'sad Australian sunset' because the sun was not going down at the time. The burial took place exactly at mid-day."

In "The Drover's Wife," Lawson delineates the drab and yet dangerous conditions of life for a woman alone in the Bush with her young children while her husband is away for long periods of time. The story is often taken as a tribute to the strength and stoicism of the pioneer woman, but Lawson is less concerned with her character (in certain respects she is a stereotype) than he is with the pattern of life in the Bush. As the drover's wife stands guard against a snake all night, the reader learns about her in a series of flashbacks or reminiscences that reveal the pitiable elements of her lonely life as well as the physical courage and resourcefulness on which she draws. Whether it is fighting a bushfire, trying to stem a flood, or protecting herself from animals and men (the difference is not always clear), the woman does what she must, what she can, because she has slowly adjusted to her existence. There is, however, a cost involved: Though she loves her children, she seems harsh to them. As Lawson puts it, "Her surroundings are not favourable to the development of the 'womanly' or sentimental side of nature." Lawson indicates that her fight with the snake is a symbol of her condition when he writes that the dog, helping her, "shakes the snake as though he felt the original curse in common with mankind." The monotonous Bush, with its "everlasting, maddening sameness of . . . stunted trees," is a false and fallen Eden, and she struggles not with the desire for a forbidden consciousness but with the consequences of male sexuality, with her confinement in isolation and "her worn-out breast."

Lawson never wrote a novel, but his stories often fall into sequences, which, though written in a haphazard order, suggest the outlines of a fragmented novel. Such stories tend to revolve around fictional characters that some critics regard as aspects of Lawson's personality and others see as composite figures from his past. There is Steelman, the clever trickster; his dim-witted sidekick, Smith (whom Lawson spoke of as "my conception of the weaker side of my own nature"); Jack Mitchell, who figures in almost forty pieces, often as an engaging and laconic narrator; Dave Regan, an amusing practical joker who is sometimes his own victim; and Joe Wilson, perhaps Lawson's most complex and developed character. The Joe Wilson series is the closest Lawson came to the expansive connectedness of long fiction; it was written at the height of his career (actually completed during his stay in London), just before his precipitous decline. There are four stories closely interconnected: "Joe Wilson's Courtship," "Brighten's Sister-in-law," " 'Water Them Geraniums,' " and "A Double Buggy at Lahey's Creek." The central story in the sequence, " 'Water Them Geraniums,' " is often regarded as Lawson's finest achievement as a short-story writer.

Like "The Drover's Wife," " 'Water Them Geraniums' " is primarily a story of women in the Bush. Yet it is a deeper, more psychological analysis of what the Bush does to a person than the earlier story. Ostensibly, it is about the narrator, Joe Wilson, and his wife, Mary, and their move to a new home in the Outback. The central portrait, however, is of Mrs. Spicer, a woman in her forties who lives nearby with her children. Like the drover's wife, Mrs. Spicer is often left alone while her husband is away working, but unlike that capable woman, Mrs. Spicer is "haggard," pathetic and even slightly mad, the vitality of her spirit having been eroded by the appalling life she leads. As such, she represents for Mary, Joe's wife, a frightful example of what could become of her; indeed, she and Joe are already experiencing a breakdown in communication with each other, which seems exacerbated by the alienating, dehumanizing force of the Bush itself. More than once, Mary cries out to Joe that this life is killing her: "Oh, Joe! you must take me away from the Bush." The process is one of disintegration, and Mrs. Spicer has succumbed to it. Though she clings to the remnants of respectability, she has been brutalized by the coarseness of her desperate existence. Her death at the end is as pitiful as it is inevitable. Lawson gives his readers a compassionate but dismal rendering of these people, whose lives are not quite redeemed by infrequent touches of tenderness. The fear of madness that constantly surfaces in the story is the fear of losing one's tenuous connection to humanity, of falling into an inward isolation that mirrors the outer circumstances of loneliness. This powerful and affecting story is one of Lawson's most detailed studies of character, and it is impossible not to sense behind it some of his own melancholic desperation with failure.

Lawson's stories are not always grim; his ironic sensibility often carries him into humor, at which he can be extremely successful. Some of his finest stories are his most amusing, in particular "The Loaded Dog," "The Ironbark Chip," and "Bill, the Ventriloquial Rooster." Even when he is comic, however, there is a sense that contact between people is at best precarious and often unsatisfying. For Lawson, the need for camaraderie, for a warmth of relations, is crucial, but it is constantly undercut by the overwhelming difficulties of life. At times, his stories seem to fall into self-pity and sentimentality, but at his best, he maintains a fine balance between an unflinching realism and a compassionate idealism. His easy, colloquial style, with its sardonic self-consciousness, has subsequently become a characteristic and abiding voice in Australian literature and culture.

Other major works

POETRY: *In the Days When the World Was Wide and Other Verses*, 1896; *Verses, Popular and Humorous*, 1900; *When I Was King and Other Verses*, 1905; *The Skyline Riders and Other Verses*, 1910; *For Australia and Other Poems*, 1913; *My Army! O My Army! and Other Songs*, 1915; *Selected Poems of Henry Lawson*, 1918; *Poetical Works of Henry Lawson*, 1925 (three volumes); *Henry Lawson's Collected Verse*, 1967-1969 (three volumes).

NONFICTION: *Henry Lawson: Letters, 1890-1922*, 1970; *Henry Lawson: Autobiographical and Other Writings*, 1972.

MISCELLANEOUS: *Children of the Bush*, 1902.

Bibliography

Clark, Manning. *A History of Australian Literature: Pure and Applied*. Vol. 1, 1984.

Matthews, Brian. *The Receding Wave: Henry Lawson's Prose*, 1972.

Palmer, Vance. "The Writer: Henry Lawson," in *National Portraits*, 1940.

Prout, Denton. *Henry Lawson: The Grey Dreamer*, 1963.

Roderick, Colin, ed. *Henry Lawson Criticism: 1894-1971*, 1972.

Wallace-Crabbe, Chris. "Lawson's *Joe Wilson*: A Skeleton Novel," in *Australian Literary Studies*. June, 1964, pp. 147-164.

Paul Kane

URSULA K. LE GUIN

Born: Berkeley, California; October 21, 1929

Principal short fiction

The Wind's Twelve Quarters, 1975; *Orsinian Tales*, 1976; *The Compass Rose*, 1982.

Other literary forms

Ursula K. Le Guin is best known for her novels, especially the three known as The Earthsea Trilogy (which includes *A Wizard of Earthsea*, 1968; *The Tombs of Atuan*, 1971; and *The Farthest Shore*, 1972), *The Left Hand of Darkness* (1969), and *The Dispossessed: An Ambiguous Utopia* (1974). She has also published poetry, including *Wild Angels* (1975) and *Hard Words and Other Poems* (1981). *The Language of the Night: Essays on Fantasy and Science Fiction* (1979) is an important collection of her critical writing.

Achievements

Le Guin is recognized as a leading American writer of science fiction and fantasy. Her short stories, especially "The Ones Who Walk Away from Omelas," winner of a 1974 Hugo Award, often appear in college literature anthologies, suggesting that her work, like that of Kurt Vonnegut, Jr., stands above much that has been produced in these popular genres. Le Guin has received many awards and honors for her work. *The Left Hand of Darkness* and *The Dispossessed* received both the Nebula and Hugo awards. Volumes of The Earthsea Trilogy earned awards for adolescent literature, including the Boston *Globe* Horn Book Award for *A Wizard of Earthsea*, a Newbery Honor Book Citation for *The Tombs of Atuan*, and the National Book Award for Children's Literature for *The Farthest Shore*. Her other awards include a Hugo for *The Word for World Is Forest* (1976), a Nebula in 1974 for "The Day Before the Revolution," and Jupiters for *The Dispossessed* and "The Diary of the Rose."

Le Guin has been a guest writer at several universities, including the University of Washington, Portland State University, Indiana University, and the University of Reading in England. She has edited several anthologies. In 1980, an adaptation of *The Lathe of Heaven* (1971) was broadcast on public television.

Not all of Le Guin's work has been as well received as her fantasy and science fiction. As literary scholars and critics give more attention to fantasy and science fiction, Le Guin attracts a large share of their interest because she creates possible worlds that cast an informative light on perennial human problems.

Biography

Ursula Kroeber was born on October 21, 1929, in Berkeley, California, the daughter of anthropologist Alfred L. Kroeber and author Theodora Kroeber. She received her B.A. from Radcliffe College in 1951 and her M.A. from Columbia University in 1952. While on a Fulbright Fellowship in Paris in 1953, she married Charles A. Le Guin. She bore three children: daughters Elisabeth and Caroline and a son, Theodore. She taught French at Mercer University and the University of Idaho before settling in Portland, Oregon, in 1959. In 1962, she began publishing fantasy and science fiction. In addition to writing, she has been active in the Democratic Party and in writing workshops.

Analysis

When Ursula K. Le Guin writes about her craft and her works, she often refers to Jungian psychology and Taoist philosophy as major components of her worldview. In her 1975 essay "The Child and the Shadow," Le Guin uses Jungian psychology to support her contention that fantasy is "the language of the night," an important means by which the collective unconscious speaks to the growing individual. In Le Guin's understanding of Jungian thought, consciousness, the part of the self that can be expressed in everyday language, emerges from the unconscious as a child matures. The individual's unconscious is shared in its essentials with all other humans and so is called the collective unconscious.

To become an adult, an individual must find ways of realizing the greatest potential of the unconscious. For Le Guin, these are summed up in the recognition by the individual that on unconscious levels, he or she is identical with all other humans. This recognition releases the irrational forces of social binding, such as compassion, love, creativity, and the sense of belonging to the human community.

A major problem in achieving this recognition is learning to deal with "the shadow." Choosing to be one person involves choosing not to be other persons that one could be. Both the positive and the negative choices must be maintained to sustain an identity; the negative choices become one's shadow. The process of achieving adulthood is blocked by the shadow, an unconscious antiself with which one must deal in order to take possession of the rest of the unconscious.

For Le Guin, a child becomes an adult when he or she is able to cease projecting evil impulses onto others and to recognize that these impulses are part of the self. This process, she believes, is symbolically represented in the many fairy tales and fantasies in which an animal helps the protagonist to discover and attain his true identity. Such stories speak to the unconscious, telling the child by means of myth and symbol how to achieve wholeness of self.

Taoism, a Chinese philosophy expressed about two thousand years ago in the Tao Te Ching, seems closely related to Jungian psychology in Le Guin's mind. This philosophy is expressed in the Circle of Life, or yin-yang symbol. The circle is divided into dark and light halves. Within the light half is a dark spot; within the dark half, a light spot. The dark half represents nonbeing—not nothingness, but rather the potential for all forms of being. That potential for being in nonbeing may be represented by the white spot. Out of this nonbeing comes being, represented by the white half of the circle. Because all that is exists in time and must end, it contains its end within itself, this end represented by the dark spot that refers to nonbeing. The Circle of Life is a diagram of the dynamic relationship between being and nonbeing in the universe.

This metaphysic leads to an ethic of passive activity. All acts in the world of being imply their opposites, the assertion of being activating the potential for nonbeing of the end one seeks. Acts of coercion aimed at controlling human behavior are especially prone to produce equal and opposite reactions. Therefore, the wise person tries not to influence people's actions by direct persuasion or by force, but rather by being a model of the desired activity.

Several of these aspects of Le Guin's worldview appear in "Darkness Box," one of her earliest publications. "Darkness Box" is a fairy tale/allegory that takes place in a world of cycles. In this world, time does not pass. There is no source of light, though it is always mid-morning. Certain events repeat themselves exactly and perpetually. A young prince rides with his army to the seashore to repel an invasion by his rebel brother. The brother always comes from the sea; he is always defeated and killed. At the same time that he leaves, the prince returns to the palace of his father, who exiled the brother. The prince always rides out again with his army to meet the restored and returning invaders. Into this cycle intrudes what appears to be a unique set of events that are sequential rather than cyclical. The son of a witch finds a box on the shore and gives it to the prince. The king recognizes it as a box he cast into the sea and warns the prince not to open it. The prince's longing for music that ends, for wholeness, leads him to knock the box open and restrains him from closing it. Darkness spills out, the darkness of shadows and their opposite, the sun. He begins to experience conflict, death, and the passing of time. Having achieved a shadow, he has entered into time and being.

Read as a Jungian myth of maturation, the tale represents the collective unconscious as a place of unrealized potentials for identity. The prince is a potential ego, his exiled brother a potential shadow, their endless battle a portent of the struggle consciousness must undergo to create a mature personality. Opening the box that lets out darkness becomes a symbolic representation of the birth of the ego, the entrance into time, and self-creation with real consequences for the self, such as the creation of a shadow and the acceptance of mortality.

Read as a Taoist allegory, the tale represents nonbeing, the dark half of the Circle of Life, as a place of unrealized potential for being. Nonbeing is timeless and changeless yet full of possibilities. In this reading, opening the box realizes some of the potentials for being. A real world begins, a world of cause and effect in time, a world bounded by nonbeing as reflected in the introduction of true death. Though not all of Le Guin's stories so directly communicate the Jungian and Taoist aspects of her worldview, many become richer and deeper when viewed in this context.

Le Guin defines fantasy as the manipulation of myths and symbols to communicate with the unconscious. Some of her fantasies she calls psychomyths: "more or less surrealistic tales, which share with fantasy the quality of taking place outside any history, outside of time, in that region of the living mind which . . . seems to be without spatial or temporal limits at all."

"The Ones Who Walk Away from Omelas" is probably her best-known psychomyth. This story combines fiction and essay in an unusual way. The narrator describes the beautiful and happy city of Omelas beginning its summer festival. Gradually, she reveals that this is an imagined city. The narrator cautions the reader against doubting that a utopian city filled with joy might also be a place of dynamic and meaningful life. The reader is encouraged to follow his own fancy in imagining a truly happy city. She suggests attitudes toward technology, sexual pleasure, and drug use that would foster happiness, then returns to a description of the festival.

Guessing that the reader will be skeptical even after helping to imagine this wonderful city, she then reveals two more facts. First, the happiness of Omelas depends upon one small child being locked forever in a dark room, deprived of all comfort and affection. Any effort to provide care and justice for that child would destroy the happiness of Omelas. Second, there are people who cannot bear to accept their happiness under this condition. These are the ones who walk away.

Structured as a mutually imagined myth, this story seems designed to provoke examination of the tendencies of human imagination. Why must people find a dark side of beauty in order to believe in it? Why is happiness unimaginable without suffering? How do people manage to find ways of accepting life under these terms? Why are some people unable to accept that living inevitably entails gaining from the suffering of others? While this story is somewhat different in form from her more typical fantasies, it seems to share with them the central aim of fantasy Le Guin described in "The Child and the Shadow": to reduce the reader's inclination "to give up in despair or to deny what he sees, when he must face the evil that is done in the world, and the injustices and grief and suffering that we must all bear, and the final shadow at the end of all."

Le Guin's science fiction differs from her fantasy and psychomyths in that the distinguishing feature of the story's world is technology rather than magic. Her best science-fiction stories accept the unique technology as a given and center on fully realized characters coming to terms with the problems or implications of that technology. "The Eye Altering" recounts the struggle of colonists trying to adjust to a new planet that does not quite mesh with their metabolism, especially the difficulties they encounter when they discover that they are bearing children who, in fact, are better suited to this new planet than to Earth. In "The Diary of the Rose," the psychoscope, a therapeutic tool, allows a form of mind reading. An apprentice analyst confronts the problem of how to treat a patient who seems perfectly sane but who is accused of political deviation. Several of Le Guin's best science-fiction stories became the seeds of later novels or developed in relation to her novels. "Winter's King" led to *The Left Hand of Darkness*. Written after *The Dispossessed*, "The Day Before the Revolution" is about the death of Odo, the woman who founded Odonianism, the anarchist philosophy of Anarres society in *The Dispossessed*. In "The New Atlantis," Le Guin combines psychomyth and science fiction. While a future America sinks into the sea under the weight of political tyranny and ecological sin, a mythical new world awakens and rises from the sea. In each of these stories, the fates of fully realized characters are more central than the science-fiction settings and technology.

Though Le Guin's stories nearly always contain multiple layers of meaning that repay rereading, they are usually also engaging and entertaining on first reading. She interests the reader in her characters or she sets up her problems in images and symbols that stimulate the imagination and lead to speculation. Many of her stories are also witty. Sometimes the wit is broad, as in "The Author of the Acacia Seeds," which tells of efforts to translate the writings of ants. Sometimes, her wit is more subtle, as in "Sur," an account of the "real" first expedition to the South Pole, made by a group of women who kept their feat a secret to avoid embarrassing Roald Amundsen.

This brief account cannot deal with many of Le Guin's themes. She has shown significant interest in feminism and other political and social themes. Her family background in anthropology has contributed to her interest in imagining cultures and contact between alien cultures. Over the span of her career, she has tended to move from more traditional forms of fantasy and science fiction toward imagining alternative cultures and their interactions. Throughout her career, she has continued to draw themes from Jungian psychology and Taoism.

Other major works

NOVELS: *Rocannon's World*, 1966; *Planet of Exile*, 1966; *City of Illusions*, 1967; *A Wizard of Earthsea*, 1968; *The Left Hand of Darkness*, 1969; *The Tombs of Atuan*, 1971; *The Lathe of Heaven*, 1971; *The Farthest Shore*, 1972; *The Dispossessed: An Ambiguous Utopia*, 1974; *The Word for World Is For-*

est, 1976; *Very Far Away from Anywhere Else*, 1976; *Leese Webster*, 1979; *Malafrena*, 1979; *The Beginning Place*, 1980; *Always Coming Home*, 1985.

POETRY: *Wild Angels*, 1975; *Hard Words and Other Poems*, 1981.

NONFICTION: *The Language of the Night: Essays on Fantasy and Science Fiction*, 1979.

Bibliography

Bittner, James W. *Approaches to the Fiction of Ursula K. Le Guin*, 1984.

Bucknall, Barbara J. *Ursula K. Le Guin*, 1981.

De Bolt, Joe. *Ursula K. Le Guin: Voyager to Inner Lands and to Outer Space*, 1979.

Extrapolation. XXI (Fall, 1980). Special Le Guin issue.

Olander, Joseph D., and Martin H. Greenberg, eds. *Ursula K. Le Guin*, 1979.

Spivak, Charlotte. *Ursula K. Le Guin*, 1984.

Swinfen, Ann. *In Defense of Fantasy*, 1984.

Terry Heller

STANISŁAW LEM

Born: Lvov, Poland; September 11, 1921

Principal short fiction

Sezam i inne opowiadania, 1954; *Dzienniki gwiazdowe*, 1957, 1971 (*The Star Diaries*, 1976, and *Memoirs of a Space Traveler: Further Reminiscences of Ijon Tichy*, 1982); *Inwazja z Aldebarana*, 1959; *Księga robotów*, 1961; *Bajki robotów*, 1964 (partial translation, *Mortal Engines*, 1977); *Cyberiada*, 1965 (*The Cyberiad*, 1974); *Polowanie*, 1965; *Ratujumy kosmos i inne opowiadania*, 1966; *Opowieści o pilocie Pirxie*, 1968 (*Tales of Pirx the Pilot*, 1979); *Doskonala próżnia*, 1971 (*A Perfect Vacuum*, 1979); *Wielkość urojona*, 1973 (*Imaginary Magnitude*, 1984); *Maska*, 1976; *Suplement*, 1976; *Mortal Engines*, 1977; *Golem XIV*, 1981; *More Tales of Pirx the Pilot*, 1982; *Prowokacja*, 1984 (partial translation, *One Human Minute*, 1986).

Other literary forms

Stanisław Lem may well be the best-known Continental European science-fiction writer. He has written teleplays (produced in his native country), but his short stories and particularly his many novels have brought him an even wider circulation. In whatever form, he has concentrated on speculative fictions in which he frequently describes the future of society, combining philosophical argument with imaginative technological fantasies. He has also published book-length studies and collections of essays on technology, general literature, and science fiction. A valuable selection of those essays is available in English translation in *Microworlds: Writings on Science Fiction and Fantasy* (1984), which also includes the autobiographical essay "Reflections on My Life."

Achievements

Lem has been called by a number of critics, Darko Suvin in particular, the best European writer of mature science fiction. A member of the post–World War II Polish "Columbus" generation (a name derived from the novel by Roman Bratney), Lem has been praised for his intellectual abilities, his imaginative writing, and his grasp of modern science. His books, widely popular in Poland, Eastern Europe, and the Soviet Union as well as in the West, have been translated into more than thirty languages. They have sold well, despite the handicap of often being translations of translations: *Niezwycię-zony* (1964; *The Invincible*, 1973), for example, is available for readers of English in a version not from the original Polish but from German; *Solaris* (1961; English translation, 1970), his best-known work in the United States, comes to American readers through the intermediary language of French. Yet these linguistic difficulties have not prevented Lem's talent from being recognized both in his own country and abroad: He won the Polish State Literary Award for 1973, and for a brief and controversial period he was the recipient of an Honorary Membership in the Science Fiction Writers of America.

Biography

Stanisław Lem was born in Poland in 1921, a particularly bad time for countries located between great powers. His study of medicine was interrupted by the German occupation of Poland in World War II, and he did not receive his M.D. until 1946. As the publication dates of his fiction show, he turned to speculative writing early, but his output increased greatly beginning in 1956, when Poland, among other Eastern European countries, offered a brief challenge to Soviet hegemony. During the next twenty years, Lem has commented, he gained a reputation in his own country primarily as a writer of adventure stories for juveniles and was therefore not seriously considered as a writer. Translations of his works, however, were reaching adult audiences both in the Soviet Union and in the West. As sales of the translations mounted and his reputation grew abroad, critical attention followed at home, and today he is recognized as a major European writer within the genre of prose science fiction. His work has appeared in other media as well, even reaching visual media in a number of cases: He has himself written scripts for television adaptations; his first novel, *Astronauci* (1951; the astronauts), was filmed in a joint East German-Polish venture; and his most popular novel, *Solaris*, was made into a motion picture in 1972, at the beginning of the decade that saw his readership increase in Great Britain and the United States.

One result of his increased exposure in the United States was the invitation, in 1973, to become an honorary member of the Science Fiction Writers of America (SFWA), a voluntary association of published writers in the field. Lem accepted, becoming (after J. R. R. Tolkien) only the second writer to be awarded honorary membership in the SFWA. Lem's acid comments on the quality and marketing of American science fiction appeared in print soon after, leading a number of SFWA members to protest his membership and to call for his ouster. The motives for Lem's eventual dismissal depend on who is telling the story, but the full sequence of events, presented from several sides, may be found in the July, 1977, issue of the journal *Science Fiction Studies*. The outcome was that Lem's honorary membership was withdrawn, and he was invited to apply for regular membership, an invitation which he refused.

Lem has strong opinions; he is especially scornful of writers who think of science fiction as mere entertainment. He has great respect for the genre as a valid means of speculating on serious questions, and he resents those who he thinks trivialize it. Many American writers share those opinions, and many protested Lem's treatment in the controversy. In the long run, however, readers will decide for themselves the importance of such biographical incidents to an understanding of the writer's life, and it is most likely that it is Lem's fiction on which his reputation will ultimately depend.

Analysis

Readers fond of the short story will find much both conventional and unconventional in the works of Stanisław Lem. He has published several collections of short stories of the familiar kind; he has also contributed to a form perhaps peculiar to the twentieth century, one that contains all the same elements as a short story or novel—characters, setting, theme, and plot—but which adds an additional fiction that removes the author one step further from his creation. In this form, Lem pretends that the author of the work is someone else; instead of telling the story, Lem summarizes and reviews it.

A Perfect Vacuum and *One Human Minute* consist of just such reviews of nonexistent books, and *Imaginary Magnitude* plays slight variations on the theme, being composed of an introduction to the work, three introductions to nonexistent works, an advertisement for a nonexistent encyclopedia, and a final set of six pieces bearing the general title "Golem XIV." Golem XIV is a reasoning, self-programming supercomputer that has composed several "lectures"; the pieces in this section consist of an introduction and a foreword to those lectures, instructions for consulting the computer, and an afterword. For perfect consistency, Lem should have left the lectures themselves unwritten, but (perhaps unable to resist) he supplies two of them.

Although these forms are unusual, Lem did not create them: He cites the Argentine writer Jorge Luis Borges as his predecessor at the labor of reviewing nonexistent books and suggests that the practice predates even Borges. Lem, however, consistently attempts to add further levels of complication. For example, the introduction to *A Perfect Vacuum* is a brief essay by the same title. "A Perfect Vacuum" (the introduction) functions like the usual preface or foreword, but it is itself also a review and—like the rest of the essays in the book—in part a critique of a work that does not exist. The essay that the reader sees presupposes that the collection *A Perfect Vacuum* begins with an introduction by Stanisław Lem, a fictitious introduction titled "Auto-Momus." What the reader sees, therefore, is at the same time an introduction to the real book in hand and a critique of the nonexistent introduction to that book. Reading "A Perfect Vacuum" is an excellent way to begin one's experience of these unusual forms because it discusses at some length why a writer would choose to write them. A writer, says "S. Lem," may simply be producing parodies or satires, may be producing drafts or outlines, or may be expressing "unsatisfied longings." Yet a final reason is suggested as well:

> Books that the author does not write, that he will certainly never undertake, come what may, and that can be attributed to fictitious authors—are not such books, by virtue of their nonexistence, remarkably like silence? Could one place oneself at any safer distance from heterodox thoughts?

It should be added, however, that in keeping with the convolutions of the form, this opinion is immediately contradicted in the next sentence.

It is tempting to believe that the reviews of fictitious books imply Lem's dissatisfaction with conventional forms; this belief is buttressed by what the author has called "Lem's Law": "No one reads; if someone does read, he doesn't understand; if he understands, he immediately forgets." Lem's Law notwithstanding, it is far safer to resist attributing a motive to so subtle and comic a writer, especially since Lem has also written (and become famous for) the kind of fiction that he here claims no one reads.

In those more conventional short fictions, Stanisław Lem has shown a fondness for stories of two general kinds: those with human space voyagers as the central characters, and those set in a world of robots. There is no hard-and-fast separation; almost all the stories show some kind of man-machine interaction or confrontation. Both types demonstrate that one of Lem's especially noteworthy abilities is his talent for the comic in a field—science fiction—that is not on the whole rich in humor. A second simple preliminary division of Lem's short fiction, in fact, can be made by separating the comic adventures of Ijon Tichy from the serious tales of Pirx the Pilot; both heroes are space travelers of the future, but they inhabit stories quite different in tone and language, although the stories are often similar in the themes they examine.

Lem worked on the stories with Ijon Tichy as a hero for well over a decade, and the publishing history of the work is complicated enough to warrant a word of explanation. There are two Polish versions of the work originally titled *Dzienniki gwiazdowe*: the first was published in 1957, was translated in 1976, and carries the English title *The Star Diaries*. The second Polish edition, that of 1971, contains a number of stories not included in the 1957 collection. These later stories were translated into English and published in 1982 under the title *Memoirs of a Space Traveler*. The two collections in English, *The Star Diaries* and *Memoirs of a Space Traveler*, together with the short novel *Bezsenność* (1971; partial translation in *The Futurological Congress*, 1974), make up the complete adventures of Ijon Tichy available in English.

Tichy, the comic side of Lem's vision, is described by the anonymous narrator not only as the discoverer of 83,003 new stars but also as someone to rank with Baron Münchhausen and Lemuel Gulliver. The literary allusions warn the reader that Tichy's truthfulness is not guaranteed, but since his creator employed him as a character for fifteen years, Tichy must provide a useful vehicle for his author's statements. In fact, many readers may find Tichy the best introduction to Lem: The comedy of the stories is easy to appreciate regardless of the nationality of the reader. The stories are comic not only in their exaggerated space-opera action and in the wildness of their plots but also in their often pointed satire: In these works, Lem parodies an astonishing range of targets. Critics have noted that the author makes fun of his own early attempts at science fiction, and he burlesques many of the more shopworn themes and plots of the genre—for example, time travel. In "Ze wspomnień Ijona Ticheyo IV" ("Further Reminiscences of Ijon Tichy: IV"), in *Memoirs of a Space Traveler*, Tichy is approached by the inventor of a working time machine for capital to continue his research. Greatly impressed, the explorer agrees to approach potential investors, but both to save time and to provide a demonstration of the machine, the inventor offers to go thirty years into the future, find out who the investors were historically, and return with the information on exactly which backers to approach. Unfortunately, the inventor forgets that thirty years in the future he will be thirty years older. He steps into his machine, turns it on, and as he fades from sight before Tichy's eyes in the present, dies of old age. Tichy concludes by observing that everyone travels in time, and if we age when we travel together at the same rate, why not expect that if the speed of travel is accelerated, the speed of aging will also increase? Readers of science fiction will recognize some subtle thrusts at the genre in Tichy's complaint that science fiction, like the inventor, forgets this problem.

Lem satirizes not only science fiction; in fact, critics' most frequent applause is reserved for Lem's linguistic inventiveness as a tool for his satire: His coinage of new words, his skill with names, and especially his fluent parodies of different styles of writing (scientific reports, political speeches) provide commentary on the whole spectrum of the ways in which people communicate (or fail to communicate). In questions of the style of the author, the reader is entirely dependent on the skill of the translator, but even without considering style, the humor of the stories is abundant and genuine.

Two larger targets of the satire of the Tichy stories are human imperfection and human philosophy. The way in which systems of thought have explained or failed to explain human flaws is one of Lem's constant themes. Lem does not hesitate to explore large questions: the purpose of an imperfect creature in a puzzling universe, why evil exists, the possibility of perfection of the human or another species, the utopias for which the human race strives—all these are among the themes that Lem examines in both the comic and the serious stories.

Tichy's serious counterpart is Pirx, a spaceman whose career the reader follows (in *Tales of Pirx the Pilot*) from cadet to commander. Pirx in many ways seems absolutely ordinary as a human being, if not as a literary character. Although in excellent physical condition, he is no superman like Edgar Rice Burroughs' John Carter, but rather a rounded character who changes as he matures. He certainly has reason to change: Through the tales, Pirx is subjected to a series of challenges of increasing difficulty, ones that bring all of his abilities into play. He has courage, skill, and training, but he often confronts as adversaries machines with powers far superior to his. Tichy, by contrast, is frequently only a bystander or an observer of such a machine. In the first tale of Pirx, "Test" ("The Test"), for example, the malevolent machine is the cadet's own ship. Through a series of mechanical failures, it seems to threaten to end his maiden flight by splattering him across the surface of the Moon. Yet Pirx always survives, through intuition when systematic thought is fruitless, through indecision when action fails, or simply through being more adaptable than his adversaries or his competitors.

Pirx is called a dreamer in that first story, but his dreams are sometimes nightmares. In "Patrol" ("The Patrol") two space pilots disappear while routinely surveying an uninhabited region of space. Their disappearance is a mystery until Pirx himself almost falls prey to a mental aberration caused by yet another ship malfunction. The breakdown produces the illusion of a light outside the ship, a will-o'-the-wisp that the two earlier pilots followed to their destruction. Only by using pain to bring himself back to reality is Pirx able to regain control and survive. Here the emphasis is on the fragility of the human endeavor in space: The vulnerable humans inside the ships are totally dependent on the machines that enclose and guard them. They are at the mercy of the machines that make it possible for them to exist. If the machines fail, the humans die. "Albatros" ("The Albatross") drives home this message; in it, the line between safety and disaster is even thinner, because Pirx witnesses a suspenseful but unsuccessful rescue attempt from a luxury passenger liner complete with swimming pools and motion-picture theaters.

Such brief descriptions may make the stories sound pessimistic, but students of Lem have traced in these tales the seemingly contradictory theme that humanity's weakness, its very vulnerability, defines its strength. One might point out that in "The Test," Pirx succeeds when a cadet whom he considers far better qualified fails. The other cadet, Boerst, is handsome and brilliant. Boerst always has the right answers in class and always knows the accepted procedures. Yet the final examination for the cadets aims to test their capacity for innovation and imagination: No procedure covers what to do when a cover falls off a control panel at the same time that a fly has stowed away. No procedure covers what to do when the fly crawls into the open panel and shorts out an electric circuit. In a crisis for which the standard operating procedures are not enough, even perfect knowledge of those procedures is useless. Boerst fails in just such a crisis.

Pirx, by contrast, makes mistakes and—even more important—knows that he makes mistakes. He will not, therefore, stick with a procedure if it does not yield immediate results; rather, since he has failed before, he will assume he is failing again and try something else. With enough tries, he is bound to hit on something that works. The method may seem irrational, but it simply takes into account that humans cannot plan for every eventuality and must therefore leave open an avenue for new solutions. The situation of the electrocuted fly might not occur in a thousand years, but someone in charge of the examination has realized that some unforeseen circumstance is bound to occur, and probably sooner rather than later. One must therefore keep one's mind open. This openness, as Pirx himself comments, results from the fact that we are "the sum of our faults and defects." Pirx's own success in the test can be explained in these terms. Since he lacks superior or outstanding ability in any one dimension, he cannot afford to become one-dimensional; he cannot become a specialist like the humans who fail before him or like the machines that failed them. He must remain open to possibilities from every direction. In short, he must be adaptable. In the final analysis, Pirx is not simply a sympathetic yet bungling hero, as one commentator has called him, nor is his success merely good luck; he is simply human in the best sense—adaptable.

In a third set of stories, Lem asks the question, "What does *simply human* mean?" As Bullpen, one of the instructors at cadet school, likes to remind his pupils, "A computer is only human." Even in the tales of Pirx or of Ijon Tichy, machines sometimes take on human attributes and characteristics. In "Further Reminiscences of Ijon Tichy: V," competing washing-machine manufacturers escalate their competition by building models that seem more and more human: They converse, they instruct, they even make love. By the end of the story, their original purpose has been so submerged that they have room to wash only a handkerchief or two, but they look like Jayne Mansfield. The stories in *The Cyberiad* and *Mortal Engines* carry this development into the far future, when computers and other machines have become only too human. In that distant setting, humans are no longer the central figures in the drama of civilization. Robots occupy the center stage, but the play seems familiar. Although the robots disparage and scorn humans, the robots' fairy tales have the forms and plots of human ones. Endow robots with consciousness and freedom of action, the stories seem to argue, and the meaning of "human" is called into question. The robot societies even show the same weaknesses as earlier human ones. They have their own villains and heroes, who show the same vices and virtues that humans do. There is not much difference between the men and the machines.

Lem reaches the same conclusion as the American science-fiction writer Isaac Asimov, who began his robot stories only a short time earlier: It is behavior, not biology, of which one is proudest in one's best moments and most ashamed in one's worst. Whether the creature is made of flesh or metal is not ultimately the most important factor. Lem may be saying, "Human is as human does," and in his stories, that is ultimately an optimistic definition.

Other major works

NOVELS: *Człowiek z Marsa*, 1946; *Astronauci*, 1951; *Obłok Magellana*, 1955; *Czas nieutracony*, 1957 (three volumes, includes *Szpital przemienienia*,

Wśród umarłych, and *Powrót*); *Eden*, 1959; *Śledztwo*, 1959 (*The Investigation*, 1974); *Pamiętnik znaleziony w wannie*, 1961 (*Memoirs Found in a Bathtub*, 1973); *Powrót z gwiazd*, 1961 (*Return from the Stars*, 1980); *Solaris*, 1961 (English translation, 1970); *Niezwyciężony*, 1964 (*The Invincible*, 1973); *Głos pana*, 1968 (*His Master's Voice*, 1983); *Bezsenność*, 1971 (partial translation in *The Futurological Congress*, 1974); *Katar*, 1976 (*The Chain of Chance*, 1978); *Wizja lokalna*, 1982.

PLAY: *Jacht Paradise*, 1951 (with Roman Hussarski).

POETRY: *Wiersze młodzieńcze*, 1966.

NONFICTION: *Dialogi*, 1957, 1984; *Wejście na orbitę*, 1962; *Summa technologiae*, 1964; *Wysoki Zamek*, 1966; *Filozofia przypadku*, 1968; *Fantastyka i futurologia*, 1970; *Rozprawy i szkice*, 1975.

MISCELLANEOUS: *Noc księżycowa*, 1963; *Niezwyciężony i inne opowiadania*, 1964; *Powtórka*, 1979.

Bibliography

Jarzebski, Jerzy. "Stanisław Lem: Rationalist and Visionary," in *Science-Fiction Studies*. IV (July, 1977), pp. 110-126.

Philmus, Robert M. "The Cybernetic Paradigms of Stanisław Lem," in *Hard Science-Fiction*, 1986. Edited by G. Slusser and E. Rabkin.

Science-Fiction Studies. XIII (November, 1986). Special Lem issue.

Zeigfeld, Richard E. *Stanisław Lem*, 1985.

Walter E. Meyers

NIKOLAI LESKOV

Born: Gorokhovo, Oryol, Russia; February 16, 1831
Died: St. Petersburg, Russia; March 9, 1895

Principal short fiction

Povesti, ocherki i rasskazy, 1867; *Rasskazy*, 1869; *Sbornik melkikh belletristicheskikh proizvedenii*, 1873; *Tri pravednika i odin Sheramur*, 1880; *Russkie bogonostsy: Religiozno-bytovye kartiny*, 1880; *Russkaia rozn'*, 1881; *Sviatochnye rasskazy*, 1886; *Rasskazy kstati*, 1887; *Povesti i rasskazy*, 1887; *The Sentry and Other Stories*, 1922; *The Musk-ox and Other Tales*, 1944; *The Enchanted Pilgrim and Other Stories*, 1946; *The Amazon and Other Stories*, 1949; *Selected Tales*, 1961; *Satirical Stories*, 1968; *The Sealed Angel and Other Stories*, 1984.

Other literary forms

Although Nikolai Leskov's most memorable work was in the shorter forms of fiction, he also attempted to meet the characteristic nineteenth century demand for "major works" with two full-length novels, *Nekuda* (1864; no way out) and *Na nozhakh* (1870-1871; at daggers drawn). Recognizing that novels were not his forte, he also tried to develop a different long form, the "chronicle," the major result of this effort being *Soboriane* (1872; *The Cathedral Folk*, 1924). Leskov also wrote one play, *Rastochitel'* (1867; the spendthrift), and a large body of journalistic nonfiction.

Achievements

Despite the continued output over more than thirty years of much high-quality fiction and despite his popularity among Russian readers, Leskov's immense narrative talent went largely unrecognized by the critics of his time. He was to some extent eclipsed by his great contemporaries: Ivan Turgenev, Fyodor Dostoevski, and Leo Tolstoy. He was also adversely affected by the view that only big novels really "counted." Finally, he was caught in political cross fire and early in his career was virtually read out of literature by certain radical critics for his supposed retrograde views. Nevertheless, the first twelve-volume edition of his collected works (1889-1896) was a symbolic acknowledgment of his status as a classic, and that status has been more and more widely recognized in the decades since his death. New Russian editions of his works are frequent, and there is now a substantial body of scholarship dealing with him. His reputation has also spread abroad, and many volumes of translations and of books about him have been published in English, French, German, Italian, Dutch, Swedish, and other languages. He is regarded as a major narrative artist and a thoughtful critic and moralist, a keen and often caustic observer of Russian society, and an especially penetrating and well-informed commentator on Russian religious life.

Biography

Nikolai Semyonovich Leskov was born on February 16, 1831, in Gorokhovo, a village in Oryol Province. His class background was varied and unusual. His father, a priest's son, had become a government official, receiving
technical membership in the hereditary gentry when he attained the required
rank. His mother was the daughter of an impoverished gentleman married to
a merchant's daughter. Leskov grew up partly in the country, where his father
had bought a tiny estate, and partly in the town of Oryol, where he attended
the *gymnasium*. He did not complete the course, however, dropping out to
take a lowly civil service job, first in Oryol and later in Kiev, where an uncle
was a university professor. Though in later years by wide and incessant reading he educated himself enough for several university degrees, the lack of a
formal one remained a sore point for Leskov. In Kiev, he worked in an army
recruiting bureau, a position that obliged him to witness and take part in
some of the gross injustices and cruelties of Nicholas I's regime. In 1857,
Leskov took leave from the service and entered private business, working as
a factotum for an uncle by marriage, a Russified Scotsman who managed the
estates of some wealthy grandees. This work necessitated much travel within
Russia, and Leskov drew heavily on these experiences in his later writings,
which exhibit a connoisseur's knowledge of colorful nooks and crannies of
Russian provincial life. The success of a few early experiments with writing
convinced Leskov to move to St. Petersburg with the intention of becoming a
professional journalist.

Leskov obtained a position as editorial writer for a leading newspaper, but
in 1862 he fell afoul of the radicals. At issue was an article in which he suggested that a recent series of fires in the capital might actually have been set
by revolutionary arsonists, as had been rumored; he urged the police to make
public its list of suspects so that popular anger would be deflected from the
general body of university students. The threats and attacks on him infuri-
ated Leskov, and he retaliated with an antiradical *roman à clef*, *Nekuda*,
which incensed the radicals against him even more. He struck again with a
second novel, *Na nozhakh*, and there are also antiradical sallies in *The
Cathedral Folk*. In fact, however, despite all the anger and name-calling,
Leskov's views on society and politics were consistently progressive. He
called himself a "gradualist." He hailed the reforms of Alexander II, especially the abolition of serfdom, and he favored equality of all citizens before
the law, freedom of speech and of the press, and an independent judiciary.
Yet he was often discouraged, as were many others, by the enormity of the
country's problems and the inadequacy of the resources, human and material, it could bring to bear on them. The age-old demons of hunger and cold
still haunted the lives of all too many Russians, making other problems seem
trivial luxuries.

As early as 1862, Leskov began to publish short stories, and he soon became convinced that fiction was his true calling. Some of his most famous stories date from this early period; he went through no phase of literary maturation. In the 1870's, after the termination of his long war with the radicals, Leskov produced another series of classic stories. Many were published in the organ of the right-wing ideologue Mikhail Katkov, and for some time Leskov was considered an established member of the Katkov camp. In 1874, Leskov broke with Katkov, ostensibly because of high-handed editing of one of his stories; in fact, their political differences would eventually have led to rupture anyway.

Because of *The Cathedral Folk* and other works with clerical heroes, Leskov had been typed as Russian literature's chief expert on the clergy and its most ardent proponent of Orthodoxy, but actually, by 1875 his own religious development had led him to break with that church. Meditation, rereading of the Gospels, and contacts with Protestants during an extended trip to Western Europe in 1875 brought about this major reorientation. "I no longer burn incense to many of my old gods," Leskov wrote to a friend. His alienation from Orthodoxy only deepened during the remainder of his life. Eventually he went so far as to assert categorically that Orthodoxy was "*not* Christianity." By that time, his ideas had "coincided," as he put it, with those of Tolstoy. Though he acknowledged the brighter light cast by Tolstoy's "enormous torch," Leskov had valid reason to claim that in many respects he became a Tolstoyan even before Tolstoy did. Leskov had suffered from heart disease for several years; he died suddenly on March 9, 1895.

Analysis

Nikolai Leskov, early in his career, developed a characteristic form for his short stories: the "memoir"—half fiction, half fact—with a narrating "I" who regales the reader with tales of the colorful personalities and unusual events that he has experienced in his adventurous life. The border between "fiction" and "fact" is left intentionally blurred—an adroit illusionistic stratagem in an age that claimed the label "realism." In "Ovtsebyk" ("The Muskox"), for example, the narrator is presumably to be equated, at least by unsophisticated readers, with the actual author. Indeed, the story contains, in a lengthy digression, a lyrical account of what are believed to be the actual pilgrimages to monasteries on which the real Leskov as a boy accompanied his grandmother. The main focus of the story, however, is on the mature narrator's encounters with a character who illustrates Leskov's conviction of the futility of the radical intellectuals' efforts to stir the peasantry to revolt.

"Iazvitel'nyi" ("The Stinger") evokes a theme Leskov touched on many times later, the difficulties encountered by the foreigner in Russia. An Englishman working as an estate manager in Russia comes to grief and brings disaster on his peasant charges through his inability to understand their mentality. The story avoids the impression of chauvinism, however, by the narrator's clear recognition that the downfall of the humane Englishman is caused not by any Russian superiority of soul but by the peasants' stubborn barbarism and backwardness.

"Voitel'nitsa" ("The Amazon") remains one of the classic examples of what the Russians call *skaz*, in which a frame narrator, more or less identifiable with the author, hears and records an inner, oral narrative, which is related in picturesque, "marked" language by a folk character. In this case, the inner narrator is one of Leskov's most colorful literary offspring, a Petersburg procuress. Catering to the secret sexual needs of the capital, she has entrée into all levels of society, and her language is a mixture of correspondingly disparate layers, the substratum of local dialect being overlaid with upper-class words, often of Western origin, but not always perfectly understood or accurately reproduced. Her motley language is in perfect harmony with her personality: vulgar, down-to-earth, cynical, yet endlessly vital.

"Ledi Makbet Mtsenskogo uezda" ("Lady Macbeth of the Mtsensk District"), though somewhat atypical in technique, remains one of Leskov's most famous stories; it was the basis for the libretto of Dmitry Shostakovich's opera. Like Turgenev's earlier "Gamlet Shchigrovskogo uezda" ("Hamlet of the Shchigrovsky District"), the title oxymoronically situates a regal Shakespearean archetype in a maximally unromantic, provincial Russian setting; the story itself demonstrates that such human universals know no boundaries of place, time, or class. Presented in a more conventional omniscient-author format than the pseudo-memoirs, "Lady Macbeth of the Mtsensk District" is a lurid tale of adultery and murder in a provincial merchant milieu.

In 1866, Leskov began the most ambitious literary enterprise of his career: to encapsulate in a single artistic work, class by class, the provincial Russia he knew so well. The life of a single town would serve as its microcosm. The huge project was never completed, but the section dealing with the clergy eventually emerged in 1872 as a full-length book, the celebrated novel *The Cathedral Folk*. *The Cathedral Folk* opened up for Russian literature a hitherto unexplored social territory, the provincial clergy, presented in a highly attractive form, with a winning mixture of sentiment and humor. Leskov insisted that *The Cathedral Folk* was not a novel (*roman*), a genre he considered hackneyed in form and limited in content to man-woman "romance," but rather a "chronicle," a genre already made classic in Russian literature by Sergei Aksakov. The chronicle had the advantage for Leskov of legitimizing almost unlimited structural looseness, since its only explicit guiding principle is the sequence of events in time.

Leskov sustained a high level of narrative art through his works of the early 1870's. "Zapechatlennyi angel" ("The Sealed Angel") is one of his most virtuoso performances in the art of *skaz*. Its narrator is a former Old Believer whose speech combines two highly marked linguistic stocks: the religious jargon of the "ancient piety" and the technical language of icon-painting. In this picturesque language, he relates a stirring, skillfully paced tale of his comrades' struggle to recapture a confiscated icon. "Ocharovannyi strannik" ("The Enchanted Pilgrim") is the life story of a monk purportedly encountered by the "author" on a steamer plying Lake Ladoga. This character, Ivan Severyanovich Flyagin, a former serf whose life has been a kaleidoscopic series of extraordinary adventures, is made to epitomize some of the essential qualities of the Russian national character as Leskov perceived it. These generalizations, however, are incarnated in a vivid sequential narrative that grips the reader from beginning to end.

In "Na kraiu sveta" ("At the Edge of the World"), Leskov explored in fictional form an issue concerning which he had strong personal opinions: the missionary activities of the Orthodox Church among primitive tribes in Siberia. It was a risky subject, but Leskov cleverly camouflaged his subversive message by having his tale told by a sympathetic and unimpeachably Orthodox bishop. Intense experiences in Siberia convince the bishop that there is more natural Christianity among the heathen tribesmen than among all the lazy clerics and rapacious, hard-drinking officials then engaged in bringing "civilization" to Siberia. The bishop's tale includes one of the most powerful blizzard stories in Russian literature.

Religious subjects did not occupy Leskov exclusively. "Zheleznaia volia" ("Iron Will") again takes up the theme of the difficulties of the foreigner working in Russia. This time, a German engineer who carries Teutonic discipline and self-control to the point of absurdity is vanquished by the "doughy" formlessness of Russian life. Again, Leskov avoids any impression of chauvinism by showing that it is Russian weaknesses—insouciance, irresponsibility, and hedonism—that bring the German to his doom.

Even when not dealing directly with religious themes, Leskov took very seriously his responsibility to teach morality through literary art. He produced a whole cycle of portraits of *pravedniki* or "righteous ones," people who demonstrate that moral beauty and even sainthood are still possible in the tainted modern world. For all their differences of form and style, these stories are intended to function much like medieval hagiography: While entertaining the reader, they inculcate ideas of virtue. Among the most successful are "Odnodum" ("Singlethought"), "Nesmertel'nyi Golovan" ("Deathless Golovan"), and "Chelovek na chasakh" ("The Sentry"). Leskov took pugnacious pride in his ability to depict virtuous characters. "Show me another writer who has such an abundance of positive Russian types," he demanded. In some of these latter-day moralities, to be sure, artistic performance far overshadows morality. The left-handed hero of the famous "Levsha (Skaz o tul'skom kosom lefshe i o stal'noy blokhe)" ("Lefty: Being the Tale of the Cross-eyed Lefty of Tula and the Steel Flea") is indeed a "righteous one"— not only a craftsman of extraordinary skill but also an (unappreciated) patriot. Yet the principal impact of this classic *skaz* comes from its manner, not its message—its marvelous display of verbal acrobatics. "The Sentry," on the other hand, is cast in a more somber key. There, an omniscient author, moving through a series of terse chapters, builds up extraordinary tension by focusing on the hour-by-hour movement of the clock.

The memoir form employed in many of his stories had many advantages for Leskov. It at least ostensibly transposed a "story" from the realm of fiction to that of history or fact, thus not only enhancing the illusion of reality but also avoiding the charge of deception and even lying that troubled such creators of imaginary realities as Tolstoy. Furthermore, reminiscences of the past provide both philosophical perspective and didactic impetus. The memories Leskov resurrects are drawn mainly from the period of his youth, the reign of Nicholas I. It was not only enlightening to show Russians how far their country had evolved since those dark days, largely through the reforms of Alexander II, but also disturbing to reveal how dangerously reminiscent of the tyrannies of Nicholas' time were the reactionary tendencies prevalent under Alexander III. Finally, the ultimate paradox of the memoir form lies in the nature of art: concrete images, even explicitly dated memories of a vanished past, may be a vehicle for universal, timeless truths about man's nature and fate.

From Leskov's memoir tales of the era of Nicolas I, one could construct a comprehensive sociology of Russia as it was then. Its most egregious evil was serfdom, and in "Tupeinyi khudozhnik" ("The Toupee Artist") Leskov created one of the most searing evocations in Russian literature of the horrors of that institution, especially its corrupting effect on both master and slave. For all his abhorrence of serfdom, however, Leskov never succumbed to the populist tendency to idealize the "people." From the beginning of his career to the end, he demonstrated again and again the "darkness" of the peasant world. Characteristically, the terrible famine of 1891-1892 inspired Leskov to recollect, in "Iudol'" ("Vale of Tears"), the equally terrible famine of 1840. The comparison revealed that society had measurably advanced in that interval: relief measures were now open, energetic, and public. Yet the peasants were as benighted as ever, superstitious and prone to senseless violence. By no means all of Leskov's memoir pieces, however, are so somber. One of the most humorous is "Grabezh" ("A Robbery"), another superb example of *skaz*, which evokes the atmosphere of the prereform provincial merchant class as a setting for comedy.

After his "conversion" to Tolstoyanism, Leskov placed even greater stress on the didactic function of literature. He plumbed a medieval Russian translation of the ancient Greek text *Synaxarion* for materials for an entire cycle of moralistic stories, slyly doctoring their plots to fit Tolstoyan specifications. The most substantial of these stories is "Gora" ("The Mountain"). In another *Synaxarion*-based fable, "Povest' o Fedore-khristianine i o druge ego Abrame zhidovine" (the story of Theodore the Christian and his friend

Abraham the Hebrew), Leskov preached a much-needed sermon of toler-ance and fraternity between Christians and Jews, thus demonstratively reversing the anti-Semitic tendency of some earlier stories.

Perhaps the most memorable and artistically most successful works of Leskov's late years were his satires of contemporary Russian society, which he viewed with deep pessimism, seeing little but corruption and folly among the elite and savagery in the masses. "Polunoshchniki" ("Night Owls") ridi-cules as a fraud (though without naming him) the highly touted Orthodox thaumaturge, Father Ioann of Kronstadt; the contrasting figure is a saintly Tolstoyan girl. In "Zimnii den'" ("A Winter's Day"), Leskov depicts another pure-hearted Tolstoyan girl alone in a degenerate milieu of police informers, extortionists, and sexual delinquents. Perhaps the greatest of these satires, Leskov's swan song, is "Zaiachii remiz" ("The March Hare"). Here, beneath a humorous camouflage—the narrator is a lovable Ukrainian lunatic who re-lates muddled memories of his adventurous youth—Leskov ridicules the "police paranoia" so pervasive in Russia (and elsewhere) at that time and later, the mentality that sees a subversive plotter lurking behind every bush. The camouflage, however, proved insufficient; no magazine editor could be found brave enough even to submit the story to the censors.

In his depiction of nineteenth century Russian life, Leskov's sociological range is broader than that of any other writer before Anton Chekhov. For those who can read him in Russian, his verbal pyrotechnics are simply daz-zling, and his _skaz_ technique has inspired many twentieth century imitators, notably Aleksei Remizov, Yevgeny Zamyatin, and Mikhail Zoshchenko. For non-Russians, such as Walter Benjamin, Leskov remains the storyteller _par excellence_, a practitioner of pure, uncontaminated narrative art. This de-scription would doubtless have surprised and perhaps annoyed Leskov, who set greater store by his efforts as a moralist, but it seems to be the verdict of history.

Other major works

NOVELS: _Nekuda_, 1864; _Oboidennye_, 1865; _Ostrovitiane_, 1866; _Na noz-hakh_, 1870-1871; _Soboriane_, 1872 (_The Cathedral Folk_, 1924).

PLAY: _Rastochitel'_, 1867.

NONFICTION: _Velikosvetskii raskol_, 1876-1877; _Evrei v Rossii: Neskol'ko zamechanii po evreis komu_, 1884.

MISCELLANEOUS: _Sobranie sochinenii_, 1889-1896; _Polnoe sobranie sochine-nii_, 1902-1903 (thirty-six volumes); _Sobranie sochinenii_, 1956-1958 (eleven volumes).

Bibliography
Benjamin, Walter. "The Storyteller," in _Illuminations_, 1968.

Edgerton, William B. "Leskov and Russia's Slavic Brethren," in _American_

Contributions to the Fourth International Congress of Slavicists, 1958.
_____. "Leskov's Trip Abroad in 1875," in *Indiana Slavic Studies*. IV (1967), pp. 88-99.
Eekman, Thomas A. "The Genesis of Leskov's *Soborjane*," in *California Slavic Studies*. II (1963), pp. 121-140.
Howe, Irving. "Justice for Leskov," in *The New York Review of Books*. XXXIV (April 23, 1987), pp. 32-36.
Lantz, K. A. *Nikolay Leskov*, 1979.
Lottridge, Stephen. "Nikolaj Leskov and the Russian *Prolog* as a Literary Source," in *Russian Literature*. III (1972), pp. 16-39.
McLean, Hugh. *Nikolai Leskov: The Man and His Art*, 1977.
Pritchett, V. S. "A Russian Outsider," in *The Living Novel and Later Appreciations*, 1964.

Hugh McLean

CLARICE LISPECTOR

Born: Chechelnik, U.S.S.R.; December 10, 1925
Died: Rio de Janeiro, Brazil; December 9, 1977

Principal short fiction

Alguns contos, 1952; *Laços de família*, 1960 (*Family Ties*, 1972); *A legião estrangeira*, 1964 (*The Foreign Legion*, 1986); *Felicidade clandestina: Contos*, 1971; *A imitação da rosa*, 1973; *Onde estivestes de noite*, 1974; *A via crucis do corpo*, 1974; *A bela e a fera*, 1979.

Other literary forms

Clarice Lispector achieved almost equal success in the short story and the novel. Her novels include *Perto do coração selvagem* (1944; close to the savage heart), *O lustre* (1946; the chandelier), *A cidade sitiada* (1949; the besieged city), *A maçã no escuro* (1961; *The Apple in the Dark*, 1967), *Água viva* (1973; white water), and *A hora da estrela* (1973; *The Hour of the Star*, 1986). Lispector also wrote a limited number of works for children, the most famous of these being *O mistério do coelho pensante* (1967; the mystery of the thinking rabbit) and *A mulher que matou os peixes* (1969; the woman who killed the fish). She has also written nonfiction prose pieces.

Achievements

It is no exaggeration to suggest that Lispector was one of the most original and singular voices to be found in twentieth century Western literature. In a career that spanned more than thirty years, Lispector produced a series of novels and short stories that not only helped lead a generation of Brazilian writers away from the limitations of literary regionalism but also gave Western literature a unique body of narrative work characterized by a highly personal lyrical style, an intense focus on the subconscious, and an almost desperate concern for the individual's need to achieve self-awareness. Though her works earned for her numerous literary awards during her lifetime (including an award she received in 1976 from the Tenth National Literary Competition for her contributions to Brazilian literature), Lispector is only beginning to receive the attention she deserves from critics and readers alike as her spellbinding narratives attract a growing international audience.

Biography

Clarice Lispector was born in the tiny Ukrainian village of Chechelnik on December 10, 1925, while her family was emigrating from the Soviet Union to Brazil. The family settled in the city of Recife in northeastern Brazil before moving to Rio de Janeiro, when Lispector was twelve years old. A precocious child, Lispector began composing stories as early as age six, even attempting to have them published in a local newspaper. A voracious reader in general and a devotee of writers such as Hermann Hesse and Katherine Mansfield in particular, it was a well-read Clarice Lispector who entered the National Faculty of Law in 1940, from which she was graduated in 1944. While in law school, she first took a job on the editorial staff of the Agência Nacional (a news agency) and then as a reporter for the newspaper *A noite*. It was while working for the newspaper that Lispector began writing her first novel, *Perto do coração selvagem*. It was also during this period that she met Lucio Cardoso, an innovative novelist who would serve as her mentor.

Lispector married Mauri Gurgel Valente in 1943 and after being graduated from law school accompanied him to his diplomatic post in Naples, Italy. She followed her husband to Berne, Switzerland, and to Washington, D.C., before separating from him in 1959 and returning with the couple's two children, Pedro and Paulo, to Rio de Janeiro, where she lived and wrote until she died of inoperable cancer only one day before her fifty-second birthday, in 1977.

Analysis

Although Clarice Lispector achieved fame as a novelist as well as a writer of short stories, most critics agree that it is the shorter genre to which the author's storytelling talents, writing style, and thematic concerns are more suited. The bulk of Lispector's stories (particularly those published before 1970, for which the author is most famous) are intense and sharply focused narratives in which a single character (almost always female) is suddenly and dramatically forced to deal with a question concerning an integral part of her existence, and by extension, on a thematic level, human existence itself. Save for a single act that prompts the character to look inward, there is little action in Lispector's stories, as the author seeks not to develop a plot but instead to capture a moment in her character's life. The central event of each story is not nearly so significant as the character's reaction to it, as he or she is shocked out of complacency and forced into a situation that will lead to self-examination and, in most cases, self-discovery.

Because Lispector's stories focus on the rarefied world of her characters' subconscious, many of the short narratives possess a dreamlike quality. Adding to this quality is the lyrical prose in which the stories are written, a prose in which not only every word but the syntax as well seems to have been very carefully selected, frequently making the reading of the pieces more like reading poetry than prose.

In spite of the emphasis on the inner world of her characters and the subjective and highly metaphorical language, Lispector's stories still maintain contact with the world that exists beyond the confines of her characters' minds. While the characters' reaction to a given situation is intensely personal, the theme dealt with in that reaction is always a universal one, such as frustration, isolation, guilt, insecurity, uncertainty, or the coming of age: in other words, fundamental questions of human existence. Also, the events that trigger these questions in the characters' minds are everyday events of modern society. In this way, Lispector manages to examine both private and universal human concerns while still keeping her stories grounded firmly in reality.

Lispector's first collection of short stories, *Alguns contos* (some stories), appeared in 1952 and was immediately praised by critics. In fact, this one collection not only placed the author among the elite of Brazil's writers of short fiction of the time but also showcased her as a leader among the new generation of writers in this genre.

Alguns contos contains six stories: "Mistério em São Cristóvão" ("Mystery in São Cristóvão"), "Os laços de família" ("Family Ties"), "Começos de uma fortuna" ("The Beginnings of a Fortune"), "Amor" ("Love"), "A galinha" ("The Chicken"), and "O jantar" ("The Dinner"). All six narratives are lyri-. cal pieces that focus on the act of epiphany—that is, a single moment of crisis or introspection from which the character emerges transformed. The story most representative not only of this collection but also of all of Lispector's short fiction is "Love." Its central character, Anna, is a basically satisfied, middle-class wife whose world is stable, controlled, predictable. Taking the tram home from shopping one afternoon, however, she spots a blind man chewing gum. For some reason, Anna's world is totally and inexplicably shaken by the sight of him. Disoriented, she gets off the tram well past her stop and finds herself in the relatively primitive and hostile setting of a botanical garden. Feeling out of place and even threatened, she makes her way home and attempts to resume her normal patterns, but while she is happy to be back in the security of her predictable domestic life-style, she has been profoundly affected by her brief and confusing excursion into a world foreign to her own and she wonders if she can ever be as happy in her world as she was before.

This story is a Lispector classic, both because it presents a single character whose normal existence is shaken by a seemingly insignificant event, an event that destroys the stable life-style of the character and takes him or her to a new level of awareness concerning life, and because, in large part a result of its language, the story takes on a dreamlike quality that reflects the disoriented state of the protagonist. This story, however, is not unique; it is simply the best of a collection of six similar tales.

As good as *Alguns contos* is, Lispector's next collection, *Family Ties*, surpasses it. In fact, this collection, the high point of Lispector's work in short fiction, is truly one of the masterpieces of Brazilian literature, regardless of period or genre.

Family Ties is composed of thirteen enigmatic stories, six of which had already appeared in *Alguns contos*, and once again the stories focus on the act of epiphany. For example, in "Preciosidade" ("Preciousness"), a girl going through puberty experiences both fear and confusion after an ambiguous encounter with some boys. This story is particularly interesting in that the event that triggers the protagonist's reaction is never fully described to the reader. The reader sees the character's reaction to the event, however, and it is that reaction, full of anxiety and uncertainty, that constitutes the story, demonstrating that Lispector is not so concerned with the central event of her stories as she is with her characters' reaction to them. By not providing details concerning the event in this particular story, she assumes that her reader's concerns are the same as her own. Another interesting story included in this collection is "O crime do professor de matemática" ("The Crime of the Mathematics Professor"), which recounts the story of a man who buries a stray dog he has found dead in a desperate attempt to relieve himself of the guilt he feels for having once abandoned his own dog. Finally, there is "Feliz anniversário" ("Happy Birthday"), the story of an old woman surrounded by her family on her eighty-ninth birthday. Rather than celebrate, she observes with disdain the offspring she has produced and, much to the shock of those in attendance, spits on the floor to show her lack of respect. All the stories in this collection present individual characters in turmoil and how each deals with this turmoil from the inside out.

Lispector's preoccupation with personal growth through epiphany continues in her third collection of stories, *The Foreign Legion*. Here again, Lispector's protagonists grow as a result of some sort of circumstance in which they find themselves. There is a difference in this collection, however, as the author appears more overtly interested in an existentialist angle concerning her characters' reactions to the situations they confront. For example, in one story, "Viagem a Petrópolis" ("Journey to Petrópolis"), an old woman, told to leave the house in which she has been living, realizes that she is no longer of any use to the world, realizes that she is not only alone but unwanted as well. Her "growth," her manner of dealing with the truth surrounding her existence, is quite fatalistic, existentialist in nature: She dies. In stories in previous collections, the character might well have emerged with some sort of new insight that would have made life more interesting if not better. Here, however, the character merely dies, reflective perhaps of Lispector's growing interest in existentialist thought.

Lispector's fourth collection of stories, *Felicidade clandestina* (clandestine happiness), follows much the same track as her previous collections. The style is still lyrical, the focus is internal, and the thematic concerns are self-awareness and self-discovery. Yet there are some differences between this collection and the earlier ones. In this work, for example, Lispector is more sharply ironic, at times bordering on an almost cruel humor. Also new, or at least intensified, is the author's criticism concerning the condition of both women and old people in modern society, concerns that are present in earlier works but never brought before the reader in such an obvious manner.

After publishing *A imitação da rosa* (the imitation of the rose), a collection of some of her best previously published stories, Lispector published *Onde estivestes de noite* (where were you last night?). While a number of the pieces included in this collection are indeed stories, fictions in the truest sense, several pieces are personal commentaries or reflections by the author, while still others seem to be a mixture of both fiction and commentary. In the pieces that are in fact stories, it is easy to see that Lispector has abandoned neither her thematic concerns nor her interior perspective. This is best seen in the story entitled "A procura de uma dignidade" (the search for dignity), which focuses on a nearly sixty-year-old woman who becomes lost in the maze of halls and tunnels that run beneath the mammoth soccer stadium of Maracanã. While wandering the halls in search of an escape route, she comes to the realization that she is not only physically lost but psychologically lost as well, that it is indeed possible that her life up to this point, a life lived in large part through her husband, may have been a wasted, empty existence. By the end of the story, she is seeking an escape route from both her physical and her psychological confinements.

A via crucis do corpo (the via crucis of the body) is somewhat of a departure from the stories previously published by Lispector—so much so, in fact, that it has confounded critics, most of whom admire it for its quality but nevertheless are left uncertain as to how to interpret it since it does not fit neatly into the Lispector mold. The two main differences between this collection and the others before it is that the stories in this collection contain not only eroticism but also open sexuality, as well as an ample dose of sardonic humor, neither of which is found, at least not to such a degree, in her earlier stories. There is, for example, the story "Miss Ruth Algrave," in which the protagonist is visited by an alien being from Saturn named IXTLAN. He makes love to her and in so doing raises Miss Algrave to a new level of existence. She quits her job and becomes a prostitute while awaiting her extraterrestrial lover's return. Then there is the story "O corpo" (the body), about a bigamist who is murdered by his two wives. Rather than going to the trouble of arresting the two women, the police tell them to leave the country, which they do. This collection is nothing if not entertaining.

Published after her death, *A bela e a fera* (beauty and the beast) is a collection of Lispector stories put together by her friend Olga Borelli. Some of the stories included in this collection were written when the author was a teenager and had never been published. Given the time they were written, these stories and the collection in which they appear are potentially revealing for those interested in the evolution of Lispector the short-story writer. Unlike other collections, however, such as *Alguns contos*, *Family Ties*, and *The Foreign Legion*, *A bela e a fera* is not considered a major collection of the author's stories but rather a literary curiosity piece.

Between 1952 and 1977, Clarice Lispector produced a consistent body of short narratives characterized by a sharpness of focus, a lyrical presentation, and a deep and sincere interest in the psychological growth of the individual human being. These three qualities, which pervade all the author's short stories, are the same ones which form her individual literary voice and which will guarantee that the popularity of her short fiction not only endures but also increases as more readers gain access to it.

Other major works

NOVELS: *Perto do coração selvagem*, 1944; *O lustre*, 1946; *A cidade sitiada*, 1949; *A maçã no escuro*, 1961 (*The Apple in the Dark*, 1967); *A paixão segundo G. H.*, 1964; *Uma aprendizagem: Ou, O libro dos prazeres*, 1969 (*An Apprenticeship: Or, The Book of Delights*, 1986); *Água viva*, 1973; *A hora da estrela*, 1977 (*The Hour of the Star*, 1986); *Um sopro de vida: pulsa ções*, 1978.

NONFICTION: *Para não esquecer*, 1978.

CHILDREN'S LITERATURE: *O mistério do coelho pensante*, 1967; *A mulher que matou os peixes*, 1969.

MISCELLANEOUS: *Selecto de Clarice Lispector*, 1975.

Bibliography

Cook, Bruce. "Women in the Web," in *Review*. LXXIII (Spring, 1973), pp. 65-66.

Fitz, Earl E. *Clarice Lispector*, 1985.

_____ . "Clarice Lispector and the Lyrical Novel: A Reexamination of *A maçã no escuro*," in *Luso-Brazilian Review*. XIV (Winter, 1977), pp. 153-160.

Lindstrom, Naomi. "Clarice Lispector: Articulating Women's Experience," in *Chasqui*. VIII, no. 1 (1978), pp. 43-52.

Patai, Daphne. "Clarice Lispector and the Clamor of the Ineffable," in *Kentucky Romance Quarterly*. XXVII (1980), pp. 133-149.

Keith H. Brower

LU HSÜN
Chou Shu-jên

Born: Shao-hsing, China; September 25, 1881
Died: Shanghai, China; October 19, 1936

Principal short fiction

Na-han, 1923 (*Call to Arms*, 1981); *Ah Q cheng-chuan*, 1923 (in *Na-han*; *The True Story of Ah Q*, 1927); *P'ang-huang*, 1926 (*Wandering*, 1981); *Ku-shih hsin-pien*, 1935 (*Old Tales Retold*, 1961); *Ah Q and Others: Selected Stories of Lusin*, 1941; *Selected Stories of Lu Hsün*, 1960, 1963; *The Complete Stories of Lu Xun*, 1981.

Other literary forms

The bulk of Lu Hsün's writing consists of essays, of which he wrote some six hundred. These essays are mostly "polemical *feuilletons*" which are directed against political, social, or cultural aspects of Chinese society of which Lu Hsün disapproved. Journalistic in design, they are more careless and more varied in style than are Lu Hsün's short stories, which exhibit careful construction, unusual sensitivity, deep emotion, and a high degree of imagination. His essays, written between 1907 and 1936 for publication in magazines or newspapers, were collected from time to time in more than twenty volumes.

Much of Lu Hsün's writing as a whole consists of the translations of foreign authors, a practice he continued during his entire career. His translations were rendered from Japanese or German, the only foreign languages he knew. As early as 1903, he translated the science fiction of Jules Verne. In 1909, he and his brother, Chou Tso-jên, collaborated in publishing *Yü-wai hsiao-shuo chi* (collection of foreign stories). In two volumes, it included works by Anton Chekhov, Leonid Andreyev, Vsevolod Mikhailovich Garshin, Henryk Sienkiewicz, Guy de Maupassant, Oscar Wilde, and Edgar Allan Poe. In the 1930's, Lu Hsün translated works by many other Russian authors. He and his brother also issued an anthology of Japanese authors titled *Hsien-tai Jih-pên hsiao-shuo chi* (1934; a collection of modern Japanese short stories), which included works by Mushakoji Saneatsu, Kunikida Doppo, Mori Ōgai, and Natsume Sōseki.

Lu Hsün produced a volume of autobiographical sketches in *Chao hua hsi shih* (1928; *Dawn Blossoms Plucked at Dawn*, 1976). His volume of prose poems, *Yeh ts'ao* (1927; *Wild Grass*, 1974), also contains reminiscences. Lu Hsün also kept diaries, which have been published as *Lu Hsün jih-chi* (1951; Lu Hsün's diary) in facsimile in twenty-four volumes. His correspondence to his wife and friends has been compiled by his widow, Hsü Kuang-p'ing, and was published in Shanghai in 1946.

Lu Hsün composed verses in *wên-yên* as well as in *pai-hua*. According to Tsi-an Hsia, his classical verses are superior to those in the vernacular and are at least equal to his best *pai-hua* prose. Lu Hsün maintained a lifelong interest in graphic art. In 1929, he published a volume of British wood engravings and another which featured the work of Japanese, Russian, French, and American artists. In 1934, he published selected works of young Chinese artists in *Mu-k'o chi-ch'êng* (the woodcut record). He also published, in collaboration with Chêng Chên-to, two collections of traditional-style stationery by the seventeenth century artist Wu Chêng-yên. He developed a strong interest in the wood engravings of Socialist artists in Western Europe and the Soviet Union, and he published books on the form.

Achievements

Lu Hsün has generally been regarded as one of the most important of modern Chinese writers. His terse, compact, sharp vernacular style was instrumental in shaping the course of modern Chinese prose. His short story "K'uang-jên jih-chi" ("The Diary of a Madman"), modeled on Nikolai Gogol's story of the same title and published in the magazine *Hsin ch'ing-nien* (new youth) in May of 1918, was the first Chinese story written in the style of Western fiction. He was a pioneer in the cause of realism in modern Chinese literature. He later proved himself a master of the satirical tale. His reputation as a writer of short fiction rests primarily on two volumes of stories written between 1918 and 1925: *Call to Arms* and *Wandering*. After these efforts, he wrote practically no fiction, devoting himself mainly to the writing of *tsa-wên*—short, incisive essays on matters of current interest. The story by which he is best known is *The True Story of Ah Q*, a novella (first published in *Call to Arms*) whose antihero, Ah Q, represents the Chinese masses prior to the Revolution of 1911.

Lu Hsün's short fiction has several important merits. As a writer, he worked in the tradition of the Chinese painter, his technique being that of "sketching." With a few deft strokes, he conveys an image of the whole person. He avoids wordiness and elaborate description. Perhaps taking a cue from the spareness of Chinese opera, he makes brief references that suggest the whole scene. He evokes atmosphere without resorting to detail. His satire is biting and bitter, his irony pervasive and often startling.

Yet Lu Hsün's stories often show weaknesses which might have ruined them. He regarded literature as an instrument of moral instruction, social criticism, and revolutionary propaganda. Fortunately, his stories are saved from their didacticism by Lu Hsün's humanity and humanism as well as by the nature of a literary text. Any creative literary text is traversed by a variety of codes that govern its sense and hold meaning for its reader. Lu Hsün's "The Diary of a Madman," for example, written out of class consciousness and class prejudice as an attack on the Chinese semifeudal system and the gentry class, can be interpreted from other viewpoints—as an attack on a tradition-bound society that pronounces the "progressive" individual "insane" or as a commentary on the human condition in general and the individual's conflict with *Das Man*. This sort of ambiguity in Lu Hsün's stories is their saving grace.

The Communists attacked Lu Hsün at first as a bourgeois writer but later accepted him as a proletarian. After they established the Chinese People's Republic in Peking, they considered him to be the Maxim Gorky of China. Mao Tsê-tung referred to him as a "national hero." In 1939, the Communists established the Lu Hsün Academy of Arts in Yenan. Following the fall of Shanghai to the Japanese in 1937, the magazine *Lu Hsün Fêng* (*Lu Hsün's Style*) was started by a group of Communist writers. After Communist troops shattered the Chinese Nationalist defenses of Shanghai in 1949 and occupied the city, the Lu Hsün Museum was established in Peking. Lu Hsün's tomb is located in northeast Shanghai.

Lu Hsün has been translated more than any other modern Chinese writer. Many books and articles have been written about him. For his pioneering efforts in restructuring the Chinese short story and in developing vernacular speech into a new form of written prose, Lu Hsün deserves to be considered the leader of the Chinese Literary Renaissance of 1917-1937. As a writer of short stories, however, he has formidable contenders in such colleagues as Ch'ang T'ien-i, Shên Ts'ung-wên, and Mao Tun.

Biography

Lu Hsün (the pen name of Chou Shu-jên) was born on September 25, 1881, into an upper-middle-class family in the village of Shao-hsing, Chekiang Province, China. He was the eldest of the four sons of Chou Fêng-i (or Chou Po-i), an old-style Chinese scholar, and Lu Jui, the daughter of a minor government official. Of Lu Hsün's three younger brothers, Chou Tso-jên became a writer, Chou Chien-jên became a scientist, and the youngest died of pneumonia at the age of five.

The Chou family was prosperous until 1893, when Lu Hsün's grandfather, Chou Fu-ch'ing, a *chin-shih* (entered scholar), was convicted of attempting to bribe a provincial examination official and sentenced to be beheaded. His execution, however, was postponed until he was fortunate enough to be released from prison under a general amnesty. This scandal and the prolonged illness and death of Lu Hsün's father in 1896 brought the family to the brink of poverty.

Lu Hsün's formal education began at the age of five under the tutelege of his granduncle Chao-lan, who taught him to love books. Grandfather Fu-ch'ing, always unorthodox, required him to read history but encouraged him to read popular novels as well. At the age of eleven, Lu Hsün was enrolled in a private school supported by the Chou clan, where he was obliged to study the Confucian classics known as the Four Books.

Although as late as 1898 Lu Hsün was still practicing the writing of the *pa-ku-wên*, or the eight-legged essay, and the poetry required for the civil service examinations, he decided to pursue an unorthodox path to social advancement. He enrolled in the Kiangnan Naval Academy at Nanking. Dissatisfied with the poor quality of education offered there, however, at the end of the year he returned to Shao-hsing.

Deciding now to attempt the orthodox route, he presented himself at the K'uanchi District examination for the *hsiu-ts'ai* (flowering talent) degree. Although he passed this examination, he never sat for the prefectural examination. Instead, he returned to Nanking and transferred from the Naval Academy to the School of Mines and Railroads attached to the Kiangnan Army Academy. He was graduated in 1901.

Lu Hsün obtained a government scholarship to study medicine in Japan. Arriving in Tokyo in 1902, he entered the Kōbun Institute to study the Japanese language. After being graduated from Kōbun in 1904, he enrolled in the medical school at Sendai, Honshū. In 1906, however, he received a severe shock. In viewing a news-slide of the Russo-Japanese War, he witnessed a bound Chinese man awaiting execution as a spy for the Russians while a crowd of Chinese stared indifferently at him. As a result, Lu Hsün was convinced that the soul and not the body of China needed curing. Withdrawing from medical school, he returned to Shao-hsing. There, he submitted to an arranged marriage to a woman he never afterward regarded as his wife. Then, in company with his brother, Chou Tso-jên, he returned to Japan, this time resolved to devote himself to literature.

The brothers spent their time reading, writing, and translating foreign literature. Although able to read German and Japanese, Lu Hsün used these languages mainly to gain access to the cultures of the "oppressed peoples" of Russia, Eastern Europe, and the Balkans. He also composed essays in classical Chinese on a variety of cultural topics. Near the end of his stay in Japan, the brothers published their *Yü-wai hsiao-shuo chi* (collection of foreign stories), rendered in classical Chinese. Succeeding in obtaining a teaching position at the Chekiang Normal School at Hangchow, he returned to China in 1909.

Lu Hsün quit teaching at Hangchow in 1910 to return to Shao-hsing to serve as the school principal. On October 10, 1911, the Republican Revolution, led by Sun Yat-sen, burst forth, throwing the country into turmoil. With the overthrow of the monarchy in 1911, Lu Hsün composed his first short story—in classical Chinese—which was titled "Huai-chiu" ("Remembrances of the Past") when published in 1913.

When Sun Yat-sen resigned the presidency of China in favor of Yüan Shih-k'ai, Lu Hsün was called to Peking to serve in the ministry of education. Soon disgusted with reform party politics, he buried himself in the study of ancient Chinese texts and inscriptions and developed a strong interest in the history of Chinese literature. This latter interest resulted in his famous volume *Chung-kuo hsiao-shuo shih lüeh* (1923-1930; *A Brief History of Chinese Fiction*, 1959).

Awakened to creative activity by the Literary Revolution of 1917, the following year Lu Hsün wrote his first short story in *pai-hua*, or colloquial Chinese, "The Diary of a Madman," employing Western technique. From this time until 1926, he would write twenty-five such stories that would appear in two collections—fourteen stories in *Call to Arms* and eleven in *Wandering*. His novella *The True Story of Ah Q* brought him national recognition. After 1926, however, Lu Hsün wrote only brief satirical tales, collected in *Old Tales Retold*, devoting himself mostly to writing polemical essays.

Following the massacre of demonstrating students in Peking on March 18, 1926, by the Tuan Ch'i-jui government, Lu Hsün was looked upon as a dangerous radical and was forced into hiding. Leaving Peking, he joined the faculty of Amoy University. In 1927, he moved to Sun Yat-sen University in Canton, where he taught and served as academic dean. Resigning in the spring, Lu Hsün and Hsü Kuang-p'ing, a former student who had become his common-law wife, left Canton for Shanghai.

In 1930, Lu Hsün, having studied Marxism-Leninism, lent his name to the founding of the League of Left Wing Writers. He joined the International Union of Revolutionary Writers. In 1933, he became associated with the Far Eastern Conference against Imperialist War. A close friend of Ch'u Ch'iu-pai, former general secretary of the Communist Party, Lu Hsün provided him with safe haven from arrest and acted as a courier for the Communists. He himself lived in constant fear of arrest and possible execution.

Although by 1930 Lu Hsün had apparently concluded that the Chinese Communist Party rather than the Kuomintang was the only viable force to reform China, he neither accepted Marxist-Leninist dogma fully nor became a member of the Communist Party. Although from 1927 until his death from tuberculosis on October 19, 1936, Lu Hsün produced no original creative work, he has continued to be viewed by many Chinese as China's leading writer of short fiction in the twentieth century.

Analysis

Nearly all of Lu Hsün's short stories were written between 1918 and 1925. The time they deal with is from the eve of the Republican Revolution of 1911 until the May Fourth movement of 1919. The characters they present are mostly men and women whom Lu Hsün considers victims of traditional Chinese society—he calls them "unfortunates"—whether a failed *litteratus*, a *maudit révolté* (cursed rebel), an unlucky ricksha puller, or a young village woman plagued by widowhood. Although Lu Hsün seems more comfortable as a writer when he deals with the downtrodden, he also sometimes concerns himself with certain members of the ruling class, the scholar-gentry either in or out of office, who are opportunists, compromisers, or oppressors of the common people. Although the stories usually focus on a single protagonist and expose either his or her misery or hypocrisy and cruelty, sometimes they also condemn the entire Chinese populace. This view is developed in "The Diary of a Madman," in which the protagonist defies tradition and sees the people as cannibals—the weak devouring the strong. Lu Hsün was a moralist who viewed contemporaneous China as a sick and degenerate society badly in need of treatment. Ironically, the young man's concern for the health of China gains for him the diagnosis of "mad."

Lu Hsün is usually termed a "realist" as a writer of short fiction. Communist critics call him a "critical realist," a "militant realist," and even a Socialist Realist. Although Lu Hsün sought to make his stories conform to reality as he had experienced it and wanted his readers to credit them as based on the truth, he was not realistic in the sense of the fiction of the great European exponents of nineteenth century realism and naturalism, such as Ivan Turgenev, Gustave Flaubert, and Émile Zola, in whom he never showed any interest. His realism was very personal and highly subjective. He was not interested in the material but in the spiritual. In his short stories, he probes into the human spirit as that has been affected by environment and tradition. If one considers the men he took for his intellectual mentors, T. H. Huxley, Max Stirner, Søren Kierkegaard, Henrik Ibsen, Friedrich Nietzsche, Georg Brandes, Lord Byron, Gogol, and Andreyev, one sees a curious thing: The majority are associated with the Romantic spirit of individualism, and only two of them, Huxley and Brandes, with the anti-Romantic spirit of positivism. Lu Hsün had an ironic view of reality that was highly subjective and tempered by strong Romantic elements. It was this view that attracted him to such writers as Gogol and Andreyev, both of whom attempted the fusion of Romanticism and realism and then the fusion of realism and symbolism, and Lu Hsün adopted similar practices. Therefore, as a writer, Lu Hsün might be more usefully termed a subjective realist or an expressionist rather than a social realist. He was surely not a Socialist Realist. One wonders how he would have taken Mao's Yenan Forum Talks of 1942. A satirist must exaggerate, draw sharp contrasts between good and evil. Although he exposed the faults of Chinese society, Lu Hsün never offered any remedy except that it should honor the individual and free the spirit.

Lu Hsün's short stories, for the most part, grew out of his personal experience. He enhanced this subjectivity by the power of his imagination and artistic skill. His artistic skill is of a high order. His stories are characterized by their brevity but above all by their compactness of structure and their pithy, sharp style, in which each word is needed and apposite. His prose is strongly imagistic, especially in its visual appeal. Lu Hsün seldom employs the figures of metaphor or simile; when he does use such a figure, however, it is usually highly effective. He makes use of historical and literary allusion, and one or more such allusions are to be found in the vast majority of his stories. He sometimes resorts to symbolism. Dialogue is usually kept to a minimum. Irony is a pervasive element in nearly all of Lu Hsün's stories, with satire a frequent weapon used in defense of individual freedom. He shows unusual skill in fusing an action with its scene. Although description is suppressed, atmosphere emerges strongly. Perhaps Lu Hsün's major weakness as a writer of fiction is his fondness for nostalgia, his lapses into sentimentality, and his inability always to deal fairly with persons other than the downtrodden.

Of Lu Hsün's stories collected in *Call to Arms*, "The Diary of a Madman," although it made its author prominent, is not one of his best. The first story to be written in the Western manner, it is more clever in conception than effective as a well-constructed tale. As C. T. Hsia, a judicious critic, has pointed out, the story's weakness lies in the author's failure to provide a realistic setting for the madman's fantasies.

The story "K'ung I-chi," about a failed scholar who has become a wine bibber at a village tavern, where he is the butt of jokes, is a much stronger story than "The Diary of a Madman." K'ung I-chi has studied the classics, but he has failed to pass even the lowest official examination. With no means of earning a living, he would have been reduced to beggary except for his skill in calligraphy, which enabled him to support himself by copying. He loved wine too much, however, and he was lazy. When he needed money, he took to stealing books from the libraries of the gentry. For such actions he was frequently strung up and beaten. After being absent from the tavern for a long time, he reappears, dirty and disheveled, his legs broken. Partaking of warm wine, he is the butt of the jokes and taunts of the tavern yokels. He departs from the tavern, but he is never seen again. It is presumed that he has died. As a commentary on the Chinese social order, the story presents a man who is a part of the detritus left by the examination system. At the same time, he must take responsibility for his own weaknesses of character. In addition, the story shows how cruel and unfeeling people can be to those who are less fortunate than they.

"Yao" ("Medicine") is another powerful story. It shows especially careful construction and makes effective use of symbolism. The story concerns two boys who are unknown to each other but whose lives follow equally disastrous courses to become linked after their deaths. Hua Hsiao-chuan is the tubercular son of a tea-shop owner, Hua Lao-chuan, and his wife. The boy is dying. Anxious to save his life, the parents are persuaded to pay a packet of money for a *man-t'ou* (steamed bread-roll) soaked with the blood of an executed man, which is alleged by tradition to be a sure cure for tuberculosis. The beheaded man is young Hsia Yu, the son of the widow Hsia. A revolutionary seeking the overthrow of the Manchu or Ch'ing Dynasty, he was betrayed to the authorities by his conservative Third Uncle, who collected a reward for his treason. Thus, the blood of a martyr and hero, a representative of the new order, is used in the service of a superstitious and useless medical cure. If the parents are ignorant and superstitious, they also truly love their son and try by all the means they know to save him, but he dies, regardless. Nobody has sought to save Hsia Yu from execution; indeed, all the customers at the tea shop highly approve of his arrest and beheading. His widowed mother, who loved him dearly, was powerless to help her son.

Influenced by his admiration for the Russian writer Andreyev, Lu Hsün sought to emphasize the story's purport through the use of symbolism. Since the two boys in the story are linked in the action purely by accident, Lu Hsün reinforces the connection through their surnames, "Hua" and "Hsia," which as "Hua-hsia" literally means "glorious and extensive"; this compound is also an ancient name for China. It is a story of the opposition between the old China—the China of darkness, superstition, and lethargy under foreign rulers—and the new China—the China trying to emerge into the light, the China of the awakened, of the revolutionary. The symbolism is especially dense at the conclusion of the story, when the two mothers meet at the graves of their sons, who are buried opposite each other. Natural flowers are growing on the grave of the Hua boy, but on Hsia Yu's grave has been placed a wreath of red and white flowers. When Hsia Yu's mother perceives the wreath, she cannot understand its presence. She believes that her son has wrought a miracle as a sign of the wrong done to him, that he desires that his death be avenged. Perplexed, she looks around her but sees only a crow perched on a leafless bough. She tells her son that heaven will surely see that a day of reckoning will come. Uncertain of his presence, though, she requests him to make the crow fly on his grave as a sign to her that he is really there. The crow remains still perched on its bough, as if made of iron. Mrs. Hsia and Mrs. Hua have, in their mutual grief, formed a bond of sympathy. Mrs. Hua now suggests that the two of them might as well leave for home. As they depart, they hear a loud caw behind them. Startled, they turn their heads to look behind them. They see the crow stretch its wings and fly off toward the horizon.

The True Story of Ah Q is Lu Hsün's longest and most important story. It originally appeared serially on a weekly basis in the Peking *Ch'en Pao* (weekly post) in its Sunday supplement; these circumstances may have been responsible for its rambling, episodic plot and other literary defects. The story made a powerful impact, however, on its Chinese audience. It saw in the protagonist, Ah Q, what Lu Hsün wanted it to see: the embodiment of all the weaknesses of the Chinese national character, which just prior to the fall of the Ch'ing Dynasty had constituted a national disease. Ah Q is a homeless peasant who lives in the temple of the tutelary god of Wei village. Since no one knows his true surname, the narrator calls him simply "Ah Q"

because the foreign letter "Q" resembles a man's head with a queue, or pig-
tail, hanging down. Thus, "Q" is a pictograph of every Chinese man during
the rule of the Manchus, since the conquerors required Chinese men to shave
their heads and wear queues. Ah Q is a Chinese Everyman.

Ah Q is a dunce whose foolish actions result in repeated humiliating
defeats. He just as repeatedly glosses over these defeats by convincing himself that, if he has been physically overcome, he has nevertheless won a
"spiritual victory." Ah Q is a perfect antihero, but he is an unusual one in
that he is, as William A. Lyell, Jr., has pointed out, "victimizer as well as victim." He is bullied and mistreated by those stronger than he, but he, in turn,
bullies and mistreats those who are weaker. Like the other inhabitants of Wei
village, he follows the Chinese social principle: *P'a ch'iang ch'i jo* (fear the
strong, bully the weak). He is opposed to revolutionaries until he learns that
the village power elite is terrified of them. He tries to join them, but they
arrest him for thievery. He is condemned to death, not by the sword but by
the rifles of a firing squad. He tries to be brave, but, his soul ripped, he is
about to utter, "Help." Yet, as Lu Hsün writes, "Ah Q never said that.
Blackness had already covered his eyes. He heard the shots ring out and felt
his body scatter like a heap of dust."

Ah Q may personify the Chinese social sickness of his time. The people of
the village of Wei, whether ordinary people, the Venerable Chao and his son,
the local *hsui-ts'ai*, or the Venerable Ch'ien and his foreign-educated son, are
no better persons than Ah Q. Lu Hsün shows how the people of Wei village
in general responded to the Republican Revolution of 1911. He suggests as
well why the revolution eventually failed.

On the whole, the stories collected in Lu Hsün's second volume *Wandering*
are superior to those of his first. He himself favored them and pointed out
the reasons for their superiority: his having outgrown his foreign influences;
his more mature technique; his more incisive delineation of reality; and his
having cooled his personal anger and sorrow. Of the eleven stories included
in *Wandering*, four of them are particularly noteworthy: "Chu-fu" ("The
New Year's Sacrifice"), "Tsai chiu-lou shang" ("Upstairs in a Wineshop"),
"Fei-tsao" ("A Bar of Soap"), and "Li-hun" ("Divorce").

"The New Year's Sacrifice" is the story of the tragic lot and cruel treatment
accorded a peasant woman, Hsiang Lin-sao, who, widowed at twenty-six, is
forced to remarry against her will, is then widowed a second time, has her infant son carried off by a wolf, and is hired as a servant by a scholar-gentry
family named Lu. The head of the Lu family, Han-lin, the neo-Confucian
scholar Fourth Uncle Lu, thinks that Hsiang Lin-sao, as a twice-married
widow, is impure and unfit to touch any food or implement connected with
the family ancestral sacrifices. Despite her religious efforts to atone for her
"sin," she is rejected by the Lus and turned into a beggar. She dies in poverty
just as the Lus are about to invoke a New Year's blessing. The news of her

death annoys Fourth Uncle Lu. In anger, he berates her for dying at such an unpropitious time. He remarks to his wife, "You can tell from that alone what a rotten type she is." Thus, this renowned neo-Confucian scholar and rationalist reveals himself to be an inhumane, unfeeling, superstitious, rigid traditionalist whose narrow and inflexible morality is the executioner of a good, simple-hearted peasant woman. A story of remarkable pathos, it evokes a sympathy and a sense of sorrow and compassion that rivals Flaubert's masterpiece "Un Coeur simple" ("A Simple Heart"), the tale of the simple life of Félicité, a country servant whose life is a succession of losses until she is left with only a stuffed parrot, which means so much to her that she dimly confuses it with the Holy Ghost.

"Upstairs in a Wineshop" is the story of the chance reunion one winter evening of two former friends and colleagues upstairs in a village wineshop back home after a ten-year interval. The story is obviously autobiographical and the unnamed narrator a mask for Lu Hsün himself. The narrator arrives at the wineshop alone. He goes upstairs, orders wine and some dishes, and sits drinking and eating while looking out over the snow-covered courtyard outside. The atmosphere here is beautifully evoked by Lu Hsün—inside warm wine and food, outside snow. The snow introduced at the beginning, the symbolism of the crimson camellias blossoming in the snow (suggesting the homeliness of the south as opposed to the strangeness of the north), and the snow and wind at the end that wash away the bittersweet taste of the remembrances of the past give to this story a special pictorial quality in respect to its text—reminiscent of those scholar-painters who did *Wên-jên-hua* (literary men's painting), harmonizing text with picture. When the narrator's old friend and colleague Lü Wei-fu appears by chance, each is surprised at meeting the other, and they greet each other warmly. Both recollect their younger days when they were avid reformers who had rejected the Old Learning in favor of the New. Now they are both middle-aged. To his dismay and disappointment, the narrator learns that his friend is changed, has lost his nerve and rejoined the Confucian establishment. He lives with his mother in a northern province where he tutors the children of a prosperous family in the Confucian classics. He also deceives his mother by making up white lies in order to shield her from a painful reality. Lü Wei-fu has given up "pulling the beards of the gods."

Perhaps the most remarkable feature of "Upstairs in a Wineshop" is Lu Hsün's unwitting undermining of his own anti-Confucian position. As C.T. Hsia has observed, although Lu Hsün undoubtedly intended to present Lü Wei-fu as a weak-kneed, broken man, "the kindness and piety of Lü Wei-fu, however pathetic, also demonstrate the positive strength of the traditional mode of life, toward which the author must have been nostalgically attracted in spite of his contrary intellectual conviction." Hsia concludes that the story, then, with an irony contrary to its author's intention, "is a lyrical confession of his own uncertainty and hesitation."

The strong theatrical character of "A Bar of Soap" has been noted by several critics. Dialogue predominates throughout; indeed, each narrative portion seems like a stage direction for the dialogue that follows, and the whole seems divisible into three or four acts. The story amounts to a sprightly, unmalicious comedy that holds up to ridicule, in a more or less good-natured way, a typical middle-class Chinese family of the early 1920's. It does not reflect Lu Hsün's typical bitterness and sadness but is simply disdainful of the central character, a Chinese Babbitt named Ssŭ-ming, and his family and friends.

Ssŭ-ming, an educated gentleman and a staunch Confucian, has a wife and three young children, a teenage son and two younger daughters. As a youth, he was "progressive." He favored the opening of new schools, half-Chinese and half-Western in curriculum, and the students being taught to speak and write English. He also supported the opening of schools for girls. Now, however, some fifteen or sixteen years later, the "short-haired" schoolgirls disgust him. He thinks the current crop of students fail to apply themselves and remain in a state of ignorance. Moreover, he thinks that they have no morals and that Chinese society has no morals. He and his associates are members of the Moral Rearmament Literary League, which promotes the Confucian classics and the worship of the mother of the philosopher Mencius.

As the title of the story indicates, the centerpiece of the plot is a bar of light-green toilet soap which Ssŭ-ming purchases at a shop and brings home as a gift to his wife. Hitherto she had been washing herself with honey locust pods, which had not proven completely effective. (From Lu Hsün's description, one can infer that the soap in question is a bar of Palmolive toilet soap made by the American firm of Colgate-Palmolive-Peet of Jersey City, New Jersey. This company was an early multinational which by the 1920's had many foreign subsidiaries.)

While in the process of selecting the soap, Ssŭ-ming undergoes two sharp experiences, one which angers him and another which delights him. He is angered when three Chinese students call him what he presumes is a nasty name in English but which he does not actually understand. When he returns home, he finds his son practicing "Hexagram Boxing" (or *T'ai chi ch'üan*, an internal system of kung fu in which each movement corresponds to a particular hexagram of the *I ching*) and interrupts him, since the boy is studying English at school, to ask him the meaning of the "devil's language" that he had heard—namely, "*o-du-fu*," as he thinks it was. The son, Hsüeh-chêng, thinks the expression Chinese and tells his father it means "vicious wife." Ssŭ-ming says that that cannot be right and tells his son to look it up in the dictionary. Finally, Hsüeh-chêng figures that, if English, the expression must have been *o-du-fu-la*, but he says he does not know what this means. (It is the Chinese transliteration of the English "old fool.") The other experience, the one that delights Ssŭ-ming, is the more important of the two. He tells of watching an eighteen- or nineteen-year-old beggar girl assisting her blind grandmother in collecting alms. Admiring the girl for her steadfast filial piety (*hsiao*), the ideal Confucian virtue, he compares his son unfavorably with this model daughter. He predicts that Hsüeh-chêng will grow up like the two "low types" who were leering at the beggar girl, one remarking to the other: "Ah-fa! Don't be put off by the dirt on this piece of goods. If you buy two cakes of soap, and give her a good scrubbing, the result won't be bad at all!" "Think," says Ssŭ-ming to his wife and son, "what a way to talk!" When Ssŭ-ming berates Hsüeh-chêng for trying to deceive him by declaring that he is not sure of the meaning of *o-du-fu-la*, his wife intervenes in defense of the boy, saying, "How can he understand what's in your mind?" and looking angrily at her husband. "If he had any sense, he'd long since have lit a lantern or a torch and gone out to fetch that filial daughter. You've already bought her one cake of soap: All you have to do is buy another. . . ." In other words, she accuses the Confucian moralist of entertaining the same lustful thoughts about the beggar girl as the two "low types" of whom he had disapproved. Her husband replies, "How can you say such a thing? What connection is there? Because I remembered you'd no soap . . . ." She answers, "There's a connection all right. You bought it specially for the filial daughter; so go and give her a good scrubbing. I don't deserve it. I don't want it. I don't want to share her glory." He mumbles, "Really, how can you talk like that? . . . You women . . . ." She counters that men simply all have "dirty minds."

Regardless of this bitter exchange of jealousy and pretended innocence, the next morning Ssŭ-ming finds his wife honoring the bar of soap by using it. Indeed, she continues to use it for nearly six months, during which period her body exudes the pleasant scent of a mixture of palm and olive oil. Then this bar gives way to another, this time one that gives off the fragrance of sandal wood—no doubt a gift of Mrs. Ssŭ-ming to herself.

Thus, Lu Hsün's story "A Bar of Soap" is one of his most amusing and most tolerant satires. It is as if he is saying to himself, "This is the way people are. There may be little hope for them, but there is no use complaining—after all, they're simply being human."

"Divorce" provides a vivid portrait of a tough, uncouth, rebellious country girl as well as a picture of how the power structure of traditional Chinese society works in a rural setting to cow such a female rebel. As the story opens, a family feud has been going on for three years between the Chuangs and the Shihs. The girl, Ai-ku, born a Chuang, married young Mr. Shih. After a time, however, she and her husband did not get along and his parents disliked her. Soon, her husband took up with a young widow and informed his wife that he no longer wanted her. Since that time, she has been living with her father, Chuang Mu-san, and her six brothers. For the past three years, the two feuding families have entered into negotiations several times without any settlement being reached. Preferring to be an unloved wife with honor rather than a dishonored divorcée, Ai-ku has insisted each time that her husband take her back despite an offer of money by the Shihs to effect a separation, and until now her father has supported her position. Father and daughter are now traveling by boat to the village of P'ang, where another meeting between the Shihs and the Chuangs has been arranged by Old Gentleman Wei in a final effort to produce a settlement of the family feud. Meanwhile, to gain face, Chuang Mu-san and his six sons have descended on the Shih household and torn down the family stove. This meeting is seen as crucial because, this time, a prestigious urban relative of the Weis known as Seventh Master, who affects pretensions to scholarship by having delved into the Confucian classics and by being a collector of antiquities in the form of jade and metal anus stoppers formerly placed in corpses to prevent them from decaying too rapidly, is to act as judge and jury at the meeting. Although Seventh Master exchanges cards with the visiting magistrate, he holds no civil service degree, nor does he have any official position.

As the boat carrying Ai-ku and her father moves through the water, the several other rural passengers on board reveal that they are completely familiar with Ai-ku's case. A passenger named Wang informs Chuang Mu-san that he believes the Chuangs are in the right. Encouraged by this remark, Ai-ku begins to reveal her private affairs to Wang when her father utters a curse that silences her. When they arrive at P'ang village, they disembark and walk to Wei's house, where they find the Shihs present. Their attention, however, like everyone else's, is immediately riveted on the dignified, richly dressed gentleman, Seventh Master, who seems to command everyone's respect. Wei announces that Seventh Master, visiting him for the New Year's celebration, has agreed to preside over Ai-ku's case and will attempt to persuade the Chuangs to accept the terms of divorce proposed, with which he, Wei, already agrees. To make the settlement more agreeable, Seventh Master has persuaded the Shihs to add ten dollars to the sum of money already offered to the Chuangs. Although Ai-ku is confident that her father will again reject the divorce proposal, she becomes alarmed when he remains silent. In desperation, she speaks out in her own defense. She insists that in her marriage she was always the proper wife, but her husband was a *ch'u-shêng* (beast) who physically abused her, especially after he fell in love with the widow and wished to get rid of his proper wife. She appeals to Seventh Master for justice, and she threatens to take her case to the highest authorities and ruin everybody if she does not get it.

Seventh Master reminds her, however, that a young person ought to be more compliant in adjusting to reality, for "compliance produces riches." Furthermore, he informs her, since her in-laws have already dismissed her from their presence, she will have to suffer a divorce, regardless of whether there is a money settlement. At this point, Young Shih takes the opportunity to remind Seventh Master that if Ai-ku acts in this manner here, she must have acted much worse in his father's home. He complains that at home she always referred to his father and to himself as "beasts." Indeed, she even called him a *szŭ-shêng-tzŭ* (bastard). Ai-ku breaks in to deny this charge and counters that he called her a *p'in-ch'üan* (bitch).

At Ai-ku's response, Seventh Master cries out a command: "Come in!" Silence immediately follows. Ai-ku is thunderstruck. A servant enters and hurries up to the dignitary, who whispers some order to him which nobody can understand. The man replies: "Yes, venerable sir," and departs. Fearfully, Ai-ku blurts out to Seventh Master that she always meant to accept his decision. Wei is delighted. The families exchange wedding certificates and money. The servant enters and gives something to Seventh Master, who puts his hand to his nose and then sneezes; the whispered order was for snuff. Chuang Mu-san and Ai-ku leave after refusing to take a cup of New Year's wine.

Lu Hsün was a highly sensitive man with a strong sense of justice. He was not content to endure evil with passive indifference. A sedentary literary man (a *wên-jên*), he admired action more than anything else but had no heart for it himself. An acute observer of human nature, but one with a limited range, he had a special knack for sketching what he saw with deft, swift strokes of his pen and with a minimum of words. He was a very gifted writer of short fiction but a mediocre thinker. His thinking fell short of complete clarity. A "wanderer" in the wasteland of hopes and broken dreams, he was at first inspired by Charles Darwin and Friedrich Nietzsche but misunderstood both. His later excursions into Karl Marx and Vladimir Ilich Lenin curtailed his imagination, aroused in him resentment and prejudice, and ran counter to his natural instinct for freedom, independence, and appreciation of individual worth. It was unfortunate that as a creative writer he thought that changing the face of China was more important than painting its portrait. As an individual, he could do little about the former but could have done much about the latter. He never realized this truth until the last year of his life.

If in his short fiction Lu Hsün had depicted humanity as he found it in all its richness, splendor, and nobility together with its poverty, stupidity, and moral degeneracy—in a spirit that extended charity to all and with a sense of the brotherhood of man that included tolerance and a readiness on his part to pardon, leaving moral lessons for others to proclaim and class distinctions for others to condemn—he might have been a great writer rather than simply a gifted one whose full potential as a creative artist was never realized.

Other major works
POETRY: *Yeh ts'ao*, 1927 (*Wild Grass*, 1974).
NONFICTION: *Chung-kuo hsiao-shuo shih lüeh*, 1923-1930 (*A Brief History*

of Chinese Fiction, 1959); *Jê fêng*, 1925; *Hua-kai chi*, 1926; *Fên*, 1927; *Hua-kai chi hsü-pien*, 1927; *Êr-i chi*, 1928; *Chao hua hsi shih*, 1928 (*Dawn Blossoms Plucked at Dawn*, 1976); *San hsien chi*, 1932; *Êrh hsin chi*, 1932; *Wei tzŭ yu shu*, 1933; *Chi-wai chi*, 1934; *Nan ch'iang pei tiao chi*, 1934; *Chun fêng yüeh t'an*, 1934; *Hua pien wên-hsüeh*, 1936; *Ch'ieh-chieh-t'ing tsa wên*, 1937; *Ch'ieh-chieh-t'ing tsa wên êrh chi*, 1937; *Ch'ieh-chieh-t'ing tsa wên mo-pien*, 1937; *Lu Hsün jih-chi*, 1951.

TRANSLATIONS: *Yü-wai hsiao-shuo chi*, 1909 (with Chou Tso-jên; of works by Anton Chekhov, Leonid Andreyev, Vsevolod Mikhailovich Garshin, Henryk Sienkiewicz, Guy de Maupassant, Oscar Wilde, and Edgar Allan Poe); *Hsien-tai Jih-pên hsiao-shuo chi*, 1934 (of short stories by Mushakoji Saneatsu, Kunikida Doppo, Mori Ōgai, and Natsume Sōseki).

ANTHOLOGY: *Mu-k'o chi-ch'êng*, 1934 (two volumes).

MISCELLANEOUS: *Selected Works of Lu Hsün*, 1946-1960 (four volumes); *Silent China: Selected Writings of Lu Xun*, 1973.

Bibliography
Chên, Pearl Hsia. *The Social Thought of Lu Hsün*, 1976.

Hanan, Patrick. "The Technique of Lu Hsün's Fiction," in *Harvard Journal of Asiatic Studies*. XXXIV (1974), pp. 53-96.

Hsia, C.T. "Lu Hsün," in *A History of Modern Chinese Fiction, 1917-1957*, 1966.

Hsü, Raymond S.W. *The Style of Lu Hsün: Vocabulary and Usage*, 1980.

Lyell, William A., Jr. *Lu Hsün's Vision of Reality*, 1976.

Mills, Harriet C. "Lu Xun [Lu Hsün]: Literature and Revolution—from Mara to Marx," in *Modern Chinese Literature in the May Fourth Era*, 1977. Edited by Merle Goldman.

Ting, Yi. "Lu Hsün, Standard Bearer of the Chinese People's New Culture and Communist Thinker," in *A Short History of Modern Chinese Literature*, 1959.

Richard P. Benton

CHRISTOPH MECKEL

Born: Berlin, Germany; June 12, 1935

Principal short fiction

Im Land der Umbramauten, 1961; *Tullipan*, 1965; *Die Noticen des Feuerwerkers Christopher Magalan*, 1966; *Die Gestalt am Ende des Grundstücks*, 1975 (*The Figure on the Boundary Line*, 1983); *Licht*, 1978; *Suchbild: Über meinen Vater*, 1980; *Der wahre Muftoni*, 1982; *Plunder*, 1986.

Other literary forms

Christoph Meckel first gained reknown and critical acclaim for his poetry appearing in such collections as *Nebelhörner* (1959), *Wildnisse* (1962), and *Säure* (1978); he is continually praised as one of the leading poets in contemporary German literature. Furthermore, his graphic art has appeared in more than thirty one-man exhibitions on three continents and has been published in various cycles as woodcuts, engravings, and drawings under several titles, such as *Moël* (1959), *Das Meer* (1965), and *Anabasis* (1983). He has also written several radio plays and essays.

Achievements

Meckel has been most highly regarded for his poetry, having received the prestigious Rainer Maria Rilke Prize for Poetry (1979) and the Georg Trakl Prize of the City of Salzburg (1982), as well as a dozen other prizes or subventions for his writings and honors for his graphic art. In fact, he has been creating prose fiction, as well as poetry and visual art, since the late 1950's. Meckel's early prose works drew curious interest and mixed critical acclaim, earning for Meckel the reputation of a fantast, a comic, even that of a dilettante. Individual short stories were initially placed with various periodicals or appeared in special printings with small publishing houses. The success of his more serious fiction, such as *Licht* and *Suchbild*, has caused him to be recognized as a major writer, and his works now regularly appear with major West German publishers.

Biography

Christoph Meckel was born in Berlin on June 12, 1935, son of the German poet Eberhard Meckel. His early years were spent in the warmth of a loving and well-to-do family, but within ten years he had experienced the collapse of the Third Reich, and with it that of his stable family life. While waiting for his father's return from a French prisoner-of-war camp in North Africa, the family became refugees, frequently moving between Berlin, Erfurt, and Freiburg. Despite poverty and a contentious father, Meckel survived the tumultuous early postwar years.

Though standard biographies report that he studied painting and graphics at the art academies in Freiburg (1954-1955) and in Munich (1956), he admits in *Bericht zur Entstehung einer Weltkomödie* (1985) that he was duly unimpressed with the quality of instruction and thus taught himself the intricacies of his craft through patience and experience. With the exception of the Near East, he has traveled extensively throughout the world: Besides Munich, Paris, and Rome (and his alternating residences in Berlin and southeastern France), he has lived for brief intervals in the United States, Mexico, Africa, Australia, and Southeast Asia. These travels are mirrored in the majority of his works as—in his own term—"vagabondage," the wandering from one landscape or climate to another.

Although Meckel has not written an autobiography as such, several of his works seem to be based on events or experiences from his life. *Suchbild*, for example, relates his childhood, his experiences as a youth at the end of World War II, his relationship with a distraught father, and the eventual literary successes which overshadowed the father's earlier poetry. If the biological father is here rejected, Meckel discovers a more suitable progenitor in *Nachricht für Baratynski* (1981); the forgotten nineteenth century Russian poet is resurrected through biography and fiction as literary kin to Meckel, to clarify the latter's aesthetics and support him in his undertaking. (Incidentally, *Nachricht für Baratynski*, while composed of fictional elements, can best be understood as an essay, rather than as a "story" or literary prose fiction.)

Further biographical information can be gathered in the *Bericht zur Entstehung einer Weltkomödie*. Like other works by Meckel, this so-called report on the origins of a world comedy is not easily categorized in literary terms. While it purports to be a biography of Meckel the graphic artist (and pointedly not that of Meckel the writer), it is scarcely the objective work that a "report" would insinuate, and it is woefully incomplete as a biography: Names and dates are frequently omitted, and the entire narration is superficially divided into three parts, the "report," followed by "notebooks" and an "appendix." Indeed, the reader finds mention of the external events of Meckel's life, his development as a graphic artist, his methods and ultimate goal: to create a World Comedy consisting of nine hundred etchings (*Radierungen*), from the origins of the early collection *Moël* in 1957 to the completion of *Anabasis* in 1982—a period of twenty-five-years.

Still, the literary aspects, the taste of fiction, is familiar to Meckel's readers. He reproduces in words and images the themes which are evident in his visual art: the moods, weather, people and objects, personal recollections, and historical events which underlie his work. This prose piece, like *Suchbild*, can be read as flawed autobiography—though the style and narrative techniques, the evocation of subjectivity through brief anecdotes and mood pictures make a "good story." As autobiography it is disappointingly incomplete; as a report it is fragmented and too subjective. Yet as literature it is evocative, revealing, creating character, mood, and impact which engage the reader. With its irony and humor, *Bericht zur Entstehung einer Weltkomödie* is similar to another of Meckel's fictional biographies, the notes of Christopher Magalan, the fireworks maker.

Analysis

Christoph Meckel's preoccupations with both graphic art and literature have proven to be mutually beneficial. In preparation for an illustration, for example, Meckel collects moods and events in written form as the basis for his visual art. Conversely, his literature benefits from the images that he has seen or "dreamed," as he so often expresses it. To the repeated frustration of literary critics and scholars, Meckel's prose works also elude traditional literary categories. Each is frequently a composite of his complete artistic expression: A prose work may be introduced or illustrated with his own engravings and further enhanced by the inclusion of poems or songs. Especially in his longer fiction, Meckel has insistently avoided the term "novel," preferring instead the broader category of "narration," which allows him more auctorial freedom to combine poetry and graphics with his prose.

Meckel and his works are often characterized as clever, witty, and inventive. Perhaps the most concise description of Meckel's traits comes from his translator and collaborator, Christopher Middleton, who emphasizes Meckel's exuberance. This term is meant to convey not only Meckel's enthusiasm for writing but also his inventiveness and the resultant variety of characters, themes, and forms. A common misconception of Meckel's works centers on precisely this exuberance, this playful aspect of much of his prose. Here several critics have noted that this abundance of imagination often results in no more than interesting tableaux, devoid of a cohesive plot and sustained tension. Others have complained about the aspect of "play," finding no redeeming value in these fanciful creations. In Meckel's defense, this imaginative world is created spontaneously, and, when successful, encourages a similar spontaneity of thought and action on the part of the reader. The world of routine and boredom suddenly is infused with new life; much in the traditional Romantic sense, each reader can create his or her own world through imagination and active participation. It is in this vein that a reader can begin to appreciate Meckel's unique contribution to modern literature.

Meckel's short prose includes both the realistic and the tragic, as well as the fantastic and fanciful. The latter clearly are fictive; with the former, however, the temptation to consider them autobiographical is irresistible: Indeed, they deal with writers or storytellers and are set in locations where Meckel himself has resided. This is the nature of his art: The stories are sensitive, seemingly based on personal experience, thus convincing—yet they must be recognized as fiction.

Meckel's first significant piece of short fiction, *Im Land der Umbramauten*, contains three short stories and twenty-one anecdotal prose pieces centering on the thoughts and deeds of Herr Ucht, a confessed magician. Ucht invents objects and scenarios, purportedly the title story of this volume. Here, in the land of the Umbramauts, the reader learns the geography, topography, characteristics, traditions, and myths—in short, everything one would wish to know in this imaginative travelogue, so reminiscent of Cornelius Tacitus' *Germania* (A.D. 98). Unusual features of this country include wandering mountains and lakes amid the generally barren landscape of a perpetual twilight, fierce winds and giant dogs which threaten the inhabitants. The pivotal chapter, placed exactly in the middle of the narration, concerns Sambai-Sambai, the wandering storyteller. His yarns captivate and entertain the Umbramauts, yet also activate and engage their imaginations, much as Meckel himself attempts to do with this slim volume. Though these stories are the result of a clever and active fantasy, they are not, finally, memorable. They concern the magician's creations—wisps of fancy—not individual characters or events which might capture the reader's sympathy or interest, with which he might identify.

Still, noteworthy in this prose work are the descriptions of the artists, Ucht and Sambai-Sambai, and their function. They are storytellers, creators, magicians, who make life more interesting and thoughtful. Yet their responsibility does not end with the creation of their characters (as is repeated later in the story "Tullipan"). In short, authors must be completely aware of their characters' capabilities before they set them into the world, for otherwise they might inadvertently harm themselves or others.

Following this first major prose publication, Meckel wrote "Die Krähe" ("The Crow"), arguably the most popular and frequently anthologized of Meckel's short pieces. One fine summer day, the narrator happens upon a hunter in the forest, who is seeking to capture a tiger. Agreeing to help, the narrator soon learns that the tiger has metamorphosed himself into a bear, then into an elephant, a wolf, a black fox, and finally a man-sized crow. Eventually, the narrator meets and becomes friends with the crow; together they elude the hunter and make their way through the forests and villages. When they come to a city, however, the crow's unusual size attracts attention, and the two are chased through the streets by an unruly mob. Attempting one last transformation, the crow slowly becomes a huge black cat, blind and thus harmless. The city dwellers, overcome by suspicion and fear, stone the helpless cat to death, while the unharmed narrator quickly leaves the city, never to return. In "The Crow," Meckel's strength as a narrator is evident: Characterized by simplicity of style, an innocent and magical narrative stance leads the reader into a fairy-tale world. This atmosphere of naïveté and innocence, the wondrous mood, are unexpectedly dashed by a grotesque scene of senseless murder, thus earning for the piece the designation as an anti–

fairy tale. Regardless of its literary categorization, the story's implications reflect a timeless moral, as well as a possible reference to contemporary world events.

Tullipan is literally a figment of the narrator's imagination—an invented personality through whom the author can live vicariously—who appears one day at the door. Though harmless and lovable, Tullipan is not a "mature" character; his refreshing innocence estranges him from the townspeople and the narrator. Though Tullipan is able to survive and live happily ever after in a remote castle, the townspeople and the narrator ultimately regret their loss.

Another artist-figure of note is outlined in *Die Noticen des Feuerwerkers Christopher Magalan*, a humorous encomium to the fictitious nineteenth century genius of fireworks. Magalan's brilliant career is cut short during an aerial display, when he suddenly disappears in smoke and flames; the worst is assumed, since he is never seen again. Magalan's biography, written by a certain C. E. McKell, is accompanied by original sketches and an interview with the scholar L. Kuchenfuchs. This playful sketch scarcely conceals its author, Christoph Meckel—in the guises of Christopher Magalan and C. E. McKell—while recalling the Romantic age, Meckel's true artistic and spiritual home.

A more serious investigation of life's meaning is presented in *The Figure on the Boundary Line*. Alone as the houseguest of an absent friend, the protagonist, a writer, observes a lone figure in the woods bordering his property. The writer discovers that this person, seemingly poor and hungry, is perfectly content, that he wants and needs nothing. Gradually, the writer becomes more deeply involved with this man's simple routine, spending more time each day on the border of the property, until one day he completely disappears with the unknown figure, leaving only his diary as a clue to his fate. Metaphorically speaking, both men live at the extreme, at the boundary of property and a complicated, modern life-style. It is precisely this life-style, from which the writer was originally recuperating, that the writer ultimately rejects when he joins the outsider's uncomplicated existence.

The appearance of *Licht* in 1978 marked a new departure for Meckel; this is the first serious narrative of extended length since the novel *Bockshorn* (1973). Its plot is simple: Upon the discovery of a love letter from his companion Dole to an anonymous recipient, the narrator, Gil, sees his world destroyed. Both Gil and Dole, globe-trotting journalists dedicated to their careers, share their spare moments and thus create a separate world of love, hope, and trust. This world is dashed by the presence of the letter. Before Gil can accept and begin to reconstruct their relationship, he receives yet another letter, this one announcing the accidental death of Dole. Reviewers chastised Meckel for the lack of epic narration in the center of the story, while overlooking its necessity: The subjective memories of the narrator throughout the piece purposely clash with the objective reality of the love letter at the beginning and the death notice at the conclusion. Despite the negative reviews, this work established Meckel as a serious writer of prose fiction.

With his next work, *Suchbild*, Meckel enjoyed his greatest success. Perhaps his most ambitious, complex, and compelling work, this "wanted poster" is an attempt to identify his own deceased father, the poet Eberhard Meckel. Initially, the son recounts those many childhood memories which constitute his love for his father. Upon the discovery of his father's war diaries, however, Meckel realizes that the father had compromised his principles and become a conformist to Nazi ideology. The son's faith and trust are shattered, and he must find adequate means of expressing his loss. In addition to introductory quotes, his own engraving as frontispiece, the diary entries and his personal memories, Meckel expands the scope of the work by including an afterword, composed as a fairy tale; in it, the father as magician ultimately destroys the world he loves through thoughtless acts. This narration represents the high point of all those "father books" around 1980, in which children of Nazi sympathizers took their parents to task for betraying their professed ideals under pressure or from conviction.

Der wahre Muftoni provides a humorous respite for Meckel and his readers, following the two previous narratives. The dead brother of the narrator, Susanne, reappears as a diminuitive figure reminiscent of Tom Thumb. As he grows to his former adult size, the two siblings become lovers and lead a scandalous life of glamour and adventure. The brother is a perfect charlatan and lovable thief, a "Muftoni." Finally, however, he begins to shrink, until he is no larger than Susanne's little finger. His final request is that he be placed in a bottle and cast out to sea—until he can return once again in adult size. While Meckel's story can be seen as a delightful parody of sensational adventure novelettes, the "immoral" freedom and spontaneity of the Muftoni inject vitality into an otherwise pedestrian tale.

As defined by Meckel, *Plunder* are those superfluous objects which inhabit one's world. Neither consumer items nor those with practical value, they are the useless, impractical mementos which one invests with value, and which in turn provide one's life with its distinctive meaning. These objects by their subjective appeal—for example, a mildewed spoon, tin soldiers long lost, a stolen bath towel from a favorite hotel—represent a healthy chaos in the ordered ennui of modern society. Interestingly, much of the book consists of anecdotes or stories that the narrator and his companion, Caroline, tell each other. Like the plunder mentioned above, these stories are unique, without utilitarian value, yet in their very telling they represent at once play, trust, mutual esteem, and affection between the man and woman. Aside from content and intent, the act of narration provides a valuable human bond between narrator and listener.

When asked why he writes, Meckel once replied that the best of all possible worlds was not good enough for him, that he wanted to create his own heaven on earth, and to communicate the fact that he was alive. This he has done, even in his less successful works. Though he has written short fiction as brief as a one-page anecdote and as long as a 120-page novelette, his most memorable works are those which engage the reader's sense of play or sympathy, his contemplation and involvement with his fictional world. Only through this shared spontaneity, this exuberance, can we actively create our own worlds and thus escape the stifling regimentation of everyday existence.

Other major works

NOVEL: *Bockshorn*, 1973.

SHORT FICTION: *Ein roter Faden: Gesammelte Erzählungen*, 1983.

POETRY: *Tarnkappe*, 1956; *Nebelhörner*, 1959; *Wildnisse*, 1962; *Säure*, 1978; *Souterrain*, 1984.

NONFICTION: *Nachricht für Baratynski*, 1981; *Bericht zur Entstehung einer Weltkomödie*, 1985.

MISCELLANEOUS: *Werkauswahl: Lyrik, Prosa, Hörspiel*, 1971.

Bibliography

Hanlin, Todd C. "A Biography for the 'New Sensibility': Christoph Meckel's Allegorical *Suchbild*," in *German Life and Letters*. XXXIX (1986), pp. 235-244.

Rockwood, Heidi M. "Writing as a Magician's Game: The Strange Early World of Christoph Meckel," in *Studies in Twentieth Century Literature*. VIII (Spring, 1984), pp. 197-210.

Todd C. Hanlin

ALBERTO MORAVIA

Born: Rome, Italy; November 28, 1907

Principal short fiction

La bella vita, 1935; *L'imbroglio*, 1937; *I sogni del pigro*, 1940; *L'amante infelice*, 1943; *L'epidemia*, 1944; *Due cortigiane*, 1945; *L'amore coniugale e altri racconti*, 1948 (*Conjugal Love*, 1950); *I racconti, 1927-1951*, 1952; *Bitter Honeymoon and Other Stories*, 1954 (selections from *I racconti*); *Racconti romani*, 1954 (*Roman Tales*, 1956); *Nuovi racconti romani*, 1959 (*More Roman Tales*, 1963); *The Wayward Wife and Other Stories*, 1960 (selections from *I racconti*); *L'automa*, 1963 (*The Fetish*, 1964); *Una cosa è una cosa*, 1967 (*Command and I Will Obey You*, 1969); *I racconti di Alberto Moravia*, 1968; *Il paradiso*, 1970 (*Paradise and Other Stories*, 1971; also as *Bought and Sold*, 1973); *Un'altra vita*, 1973 (*Lady Godiva and Other Stories*, 1975; also as *Mother Love*, 1976); *Boh*, 1976 (*The Voice of the Sea and Other Stories*, 1978); *La cosa e altri racconti*, 1983 (*Erotic Tales*, 1985).

Other literary forms

Alberto Moravia has been equally prolific as a novelist and a short-story writer. His novels include *Gli indifferenti* (1929; *The Indifferent Ones*, 1932; also as *The Time of Indifference*, 1953), *Agostino* (1944; English translation, 1947), *La romana* (1947; *The Woman of Rome*, 1949), *Il conformista* (1951; *The Conformist*, 1952), which as adapted as a film in 1970 by Bernardo Bertolucci, *Il disprezzo* (1954; *A Ghost at Noon*, 1955), and *La noia* (1960; *The Empty Canvas*, 1961). Moravia has also written plays, criticism, and many travelogues.

Achievements

In *The Indifferent Ones*, Moravia created the first existentialist novel. With the success of that book, Moravia emerged as one of Italy's leading literary figures; with the translation of *The Woman of Rome* twenty years later, his reputation spread to the English-speaking world. He has received a number of awards for his writing: the Corriere Lombardo Prize for *Agostino* in 1945, the Chevalier de la Légion d'Honneur (1952), the Strega Literary Prize for *A Ghost at Noon*, and the Viareggio Prize for *The Empty Canvas*. Although his fiction rarely strays far from Rome and his themes hardly vary in his many works, he has created an impressive body of work that depicts the plight and struggles of modern man regardless of geographical location.

Biography

Alberto Pincherle Moravia, son of Carlo and Teresa de Marsanich Moravia, was born in Rome, Italy, on November 28, 1907. His Jewish father was an architect, and his Catholic mother was a Dalmatian countess. Hence, he grew up in an affluent and cultured family that kept a box at the opera and retained a chauffeur. Moravia's home life was not happy, though, and his descriptions of bourgeois family conflicts in his fiction mirror his own childhood.

One early escape was storytelling. In 1937, he recalled that as a child,

> I would go off into the fields, or stretch myself out . . . on a couch in a room of the summer villa, and talk to myself. I cannot remember the plots of these solitary narratives; I think they were adventures, dangerous episodes, violent and improbable incidents; I do remember very well, however, that I took up the thread of the story every day at the precise point where I had left it the day before.

At sixteen, tuberculosis of the bone forced him to leave school, and he spent the next several years in bed. A later short story, "Inverno di malato," written in 1930, draws upon his experiences in a sanatorium, and the protagonist, Girolamo, suffers, like his creator, from tuberculosis of the bone. During this long convalescence, Moravia read extensively, and, according to his essay of 1945 "Ricordo degli Indifferenti" ("Recalling *Time of Indifference*"), he was also already demonstrating his writing fluency. In October, 1925, he began *The Indifferent Ones*; by the time he finished the work, he had, in addition, written poems, short stories, and two other novels. "Cortizana stanca," his first publication, appeared in French in the avant-garde magazine *'900* in 1927. It was *The Indifferent Ones*, however, that established his reputation as a leading Italian writer. Moravia later recalled, "Certainly no book in the last fifty years has been greeted with such unanimous enthusiasm and excitement."

When his next novel, *Le ambizioni sbagliate* (1935; *The Wheel of Fortune*, 1937; also as *Mistaken Ambitions*, 1965), angered Italy's Fascist government, Moravia left for the United States, where he taught Italian for a time. A trip to Mexico provided the background for *La mascherata* (1941; *The Fancy Dress Party*, 1947), his only novel set outside Italy. Returning to his native country in 1937, he was soon traveling again, this time to China. Subsequently, he went to the Soviet Union, India, back to China, and to Africa; he has written about each of these places in his various travelogues.

Moravia's difficulties with the government of Benito Mussolini did not end with the 1930's. Il Duce himself ordered the publication of *The Fancy Dress Party*, but he soon recognized the book's anti-Fascist satire and ordered it withdrawn. *Agostino*, Moravia's next novel, was also banned and not published until Italy was liberated in 1944. Following the collapse of the Fascist government on July 25, 1943, Moravia rejoiced in the *Popolo di Roma*, publishing two articles critical of the former regime. Consequently, when the Germans established another Fascist government shortly afterward, Moravia had to flee for his life.

He took refuge in the mountains of Ciociaria, and the nine months he spent there had a deep effect on his writing. As he explained in *The Guardian* (May 31, 1962),

> I had an experience which usually intellectuals don't have. I lived with peasants, ate their food, slept with them, stayed with them all day. So I conceived a great interest in the people, the people who work hard, [and] I tried to write about them.

Heretofore, his characters had been drawn from the middle class, but in the short stories of *Roman Tales* and *More Roman Tales*, and in the novels *The Woman of Rome* and *La ciociara* (1957; *Two Women*, 1958), he drew upon his newfound familiarity with the peasantry.

After World War II, Moravia continued to produce a constant stream of literature: novels, short stories, plays, essays, and travelogues. A resident of Rome, he was elected to the European Parliament in 1984.

Analysis

In his "Frammento d'autobiografia" (Fragment of autobiography), Alberto Moravia writes, "The dominant theme of my work seems to be the relationship between man and reality." Michele, an autobiographical character in *The Indifferent Ones*, elaborates on the difficulty this relationship poses for modern man: "Once upon a time . . . men used to know their paths in life from the first to the last step; but now . . . one's head was in a bag; one was in the dark; one was blind. And yet one still had to go somewhere; but where?" That is the question that Moravia's characters repeatedly attempt to answer. Often the correct response is, "Nowhere."

What Moravia said about his first novel in "Recalling *Time of Indifference*" applies equally well to his early short stories, in which he sought to render the "boredom and impatience" of the Roman middle class, feelings to which he himself was subject. Later stories often deal with the lower classes rather than the bourgeoisie; here, too, though, the characters are trapped by their fears, desires, and lack of direction in a world that has lost all sense of values.

On the cover of *L'imbroglio*, Moravia writes that if the short story "is to rise again from its present state of inferiority, compared with the novel, it must regain its former character, turn back to plot and anecdote, exploit its possibilities for violent dénouements and rapid synthesis, and condense events into natural and concise narrative." In fact, Moravia uses plot and action only as a means of revealing character. Many of his most successful stories revolve around mundane activities—a drive into the country, for example, or a picnic at the seashore—and provide only sufficient detail to demonstrate the characters' moods, usually alienation and existential anxiety.

Moravia uses the family, or male-female relationships, to express this sense of isolation, showing the inability of men and women to communicate with one another. Arguing in 1961 in "Erotismo e letteratura" (eroticism in literature) that sex is "among the few ways of expression and communion available to man," he thus explains what some regard as his obsession with the erotic. *Erotic Tales* might serve as the title to any collection of his fiction, but sex is a means, not an end, for his characters. Their goal is to cure what Adriana in *The Woman of Rome* describes as "absurd, ineffable anguish," and physical coupling is the only way for them to achieve spiritual union. In other cases, sex serves as an escape. Again, *The Indifferent Ones* explains the motivation of many of Moravia's fictional characters when Carla tells why she will accept her mother's lover as her own: "Virtue would merely throw her back into the arms of boredom and the distasteful trivialities of everyday habit... this present adventure... was the only epilogue her old life deserved; afterwards, everything would be new—both life and herself." This desire for escape from the present, whatever the cost, is evident in the story "Inverno di malato" (a sick boy's winter), published in 1935. Girolamo is staying in a sanatorium in the mountains because he is suffering from tuberculosis of the knee bone. A greater affliction, though, is his roommate, Brambilla. This coarse traveling salesman relieves his own boredom by mocking Girolamo as effete. To prove himself, Girolamo decides to seduce Polly, an English girl who has been a sympathetic companion. As so often happens in Moravia's stories, this effort to escape leads only to greater alienation. Girolamo's sexual adventure results in the loss of Polly, and Brambilla still despises him. When Brambilla departs, cured, Girolamo is even more isolated than he was before.

Another early story that exposes the ennui and callousness of the middle class is "Delitto al circolo di tennis," published in 1927 and translated in 1960 as "Crime at the Tennis Club." Members of a tennis club invite an aging countess to a party because they know that she will get drunk and entertain them by making herself ridiculous. This indifference to another's dignity and sensibility turns even more vicious when five of the men lure the countess into a room and try to undress her. Her resistance so angers the self-centered Ripandelli that he hits her on the head with an empty champagne bottle and so kills her. Jancovich easily persuades his colleagues to dispose of the body in the river to make the crime look like an accident, and the young men return to the party to become "indistinguishable... from the other male dancers." They are indistinguishable not only because of their dress but also because none of the other partiers would have behaved better; all seek an escape from the present, whatever the cost may be.

In technique, these stories show Moravia as the contemporary and admirer of Marcel Proust and James Joyce, using realistic details to expose the unreality of man, whose existence is bounded by and composed of bits of time and the objects he perceives. Thus, Moravia details Ripandelli's "starched shirt-front" and the countess' "black shawl embroidered with birds, flowers and arabesques of every possible color." The story "Fine di una relazione" ("End of a Relationship") notes the furniture in Lorenzo's apartment, which includes "the yellow marble top of the sham Louis XV table in the hall." Such description not only grounds these stories in reality but also frequently reveals character. The countess' behavior is as bizarre as her shawl; Lorenzo's sham table and ground-floor apartment in a "small new building at the far end of a still unfinished byroad" indicate the falseness and incompleteness of the character's life.

In the 1940's, Moravia experimented with another form of fiction: Surrealism. Frequently, these pieces are thinly veiled social or political satire. In "L'epidemia" (1944; the epidemic), people's heads begin to give off a putrid odor, but the victims regard the stench as perfume. Moravia here comments on the moral decay that Fascism causes. "Primo rapporto sulla terra dell' Inviato speciale della luna" (1944, first report on Earth of the special envoy from the Moon) purports to be an analysis by a lunar delegate on the two races of man, the rich and the poor. Because this delegate understands nothing about money, he assumes that everyone behaves as he wishes. He therefore concludes that one race prefers "rags to new clothes, . . . cheap furniture to good makes, . . . municipal pools to the sea." Beneath the humor lies the message that the middle class often shares the same attitude as the delegate, both equally ignorant of the true nature of the class struggle.

Although Moravia adopted this surrealistic mode to avoid censorship under the Fascists, it also appealed to his playful nature. Much later he reverted to this form. "Celestina," for example, treats a robot as if it were a girl. The title character "grows up" in a middle-class home, but, despite her own brilliance and her parents' social and economic status, she elopes with an old water heater.

In the postwar period, Moravia's writing changed in two important ways. His earlier writings had concentrated on the middle class, and his protagonists were generally effete intellectuals incapable of acting. Their stories were presented in the third person by an omniscient narrator. Without permanently abandoning any of these literary devices, Moravia in *Roman Tales* and *More Roman Tales* allowed his characters to tell their own stories. The use of the first person allowed Moravia to capture more fully the language of the characters and to demonstrate the limited vision that the individual possesses, thereby indicating that omniscience is too great a fiction even for fiction.

The other change lies in the social class that Moravia turned to consider. As he said in an interview with the *Paris Review* in 1958, "I've tried in these stories . . . to depict the life of the sub-proletariat and the très petite bourgeoisie in a period just after the last war."

The 130 stories collected in these two volumes first appeared in the Milan daily *Corriere della sera* beginning in 1952. This form of publication imposed a brevity and concentration upon these pieces. Yet the sparseness of detail mirrors well the empty lives of the characters and concentrates the reader's attention upon them: A length of some six pages allows for no distractions. While a lesser writer might find this format confining and the large number of stories exhausting, Moravia thrived on the challenge, and these two books contain some of his best stories.

Though the form and characters differ from Moravia's earlier work, the theme does not. Like their prewar bourgeois counterparts, the bartenders, barbers, and dishwashers are trapped in a meaningless world. Typical is the narrator of "Il camionista" ("The Lorry Driver"), who, with his partner, Palombi, regularly drives between Naples and Rome. On one of their runs, they pick up an attractive hitchhiker, Italia. She becomes a frequent passenger, and the narrator quickly falls in love with her. On their drives, he puts one arm around Italia, and they exchange "mere trifles and jokes and lovers' talk." Meanwhile, Palombi "either. . . noticed nothing or. . . pretended not to notice."

One night, the drivers have a minor accident. When they enter a café to get help, they find Italia cleaning up; they also learn that she has a lover, or husband, who is a seafaring hunchback. This discovery is one of two that the narrator makes that night. On the way back to Rome, Palombi tells him, "We were more or less engaged." The narrator correctly observes that "Italia had fooled us both," but the partners have also deceived each other. Though all three sat so close together in the cab of the truck, no one understood the others; their communication indeed consisted of trifles. At the end of the story the two drivers separate, thus confirming the spiritual isolation that had existed all along.

The Fetish, which followed the two collections of Roman stories, returns to third-person accounts of the middle class. The title story reveals one of Moravia's fictional devices, in which a seemingly insignificant event such as a dream at the beginning of a narrative serves as a trenchant commentary on the action that follows. In this case, as Guido waits for the rest of his family to get ready for a picnic, he puts a disc on the phonograph. The machine malfunctions, ruining the record; when Guido tries a second time, the record player works flawlessly.

By now, the family is ready, and as Guido drives he tells about this unusual experience. Jokingly, his wife responds, "Obviously, machines sometimes get fed up with being machines and want to prove that they're not." Nearing the lake that is to be their picnic site, Guido suddenly gets the urge to drive the car off a cliff into the water and so kill himself, his wife, and his two children. He drives off the road but lands in a meadow, an ideal spot for having lunch. Like the record player, Guido had momentarily malfunctioned. He had wanted to assert his individuality, to demonstrate that he is not a machine. In the end, though, he returns to being the predictable husband and father he has always been, unable to escape.

"Il misantropo" ("The Misanthrope") from this collection again stresses a character's entrapment. Another Guido sets off with an acquaintance, Cesare, for a day at the Lagi di Vico. Cesare has provided a date for each of them, but Guido soon tires of his and secretly asks Cesare to trade. His companion agrees, but Guido quickly tires of her, too, and asks to sit beside Cesare. By the time they reach their destination, Guido hates him as well. As they walk to the restaurant overlooking the lake, he sees his reflection in the water and feels such disgust that he throws a stick at it. Once more characters have failed to communicate; Guido is alienated even from himself.

Command and I Will Obey You and *Paradise and Other Stories* serve as companion volumes, the former told by first-person male narrators, the latter by women. The social world of the characters varies: In *Command and I Will Obey You*, Tullio, from the story "Tu mi conosci, Carlo" ("You Know Me, Carlo"), is a beggar, the narrator of "Le cose che crescono" ("The Things That Grow") is a lawyer, and the protagonist of "La cognata" ("The Sister-in-law") is a teacher. Similarly, in *Paradise and Other Stories*, some women are married to rich husbands, others are middle class, and some, like the protagonist in "L'immaginazione" ("Imagination"), are impoverished. Whatever their social class, though, they are alienated and feel reduced to machinery, like Guido in "The Fetish."

A prominent image expressing this condition is the double; like objects, people in the modern world are mass-produced rather than individual. In "Doppioni" ("Doubles"), a student thinks about taking a second apartment in another part of town. He discovers that this place exactly resembles the first, the second landlady has the same name and appearance as the first, and her daughter, who bears the same name as the daughter of his present landlady, behaves exactly like her counterpart. In "Tipo medio" ("A Middling Type"), the narrator regards his apartment, his furnishings, and himself as unique. A flower girl whom he lures to his apartment disabuses him, telling him that everything, even the device he used to attract her in the first place, is identical to the behavior and possessions of the previous occupant.

In his 1941 essay "L'uomo e il personaggio" ("The Man and the Character"), Moravia had remarked, "Modern man seems a mere cipher within mass groupings which are amongst the most formidable humanity has ever known." The narrator of "Doubles" repeats this observation: "We're identical with millions of other people in the world."

The idea of mass-produced humanity informs *Paradise and Other Stories* as well. In "I prodotti" ("Products"), the narrator sees herself as a producer of various kinds of love, such as maternal or conjugal. Even when she sits on her husband's lap, kisses him, or jokes with him, she feels no emotions. Instead, she is like a machine or robot. Hence, when she learns of her husband's infidelity, she remains unmoved, simply deciding to produce one item more—murder. "I am a pretty young woman, wife of a rich young man," the narrator says in "Venduta e comprata" ("Bought and Sold"). Her husband, too, has been unfaithful, indicating that in Moravia's vision of the modern world, fidelity is lacking because the bonds between friends, lovers, and spouses have vanished. Each character is trapped within himself, unable to connect meaningfully and permanently with anyone else. In this story, the woman does not contemplate murder, though; she seeks instead something more fundamental than revenge: herself. Viewing herself as a beautiful object that has been discarded by her husband, she goes into the country each Sunday and pretends to be a prostitute. After a man picks her up, she first takes his money. Then, just as he is about to have sex with her, she feigns illness and returns his payment. In this obsessive way, she tries to buy herself back, selling herself to regain her selfhood.

Moravia's subsequent short fiction has continued to explore questions of sex, interpersonal relations, and man's quest for self-expression "within mass groupings." The title story of *Erotic Tales* again considers the theme of entrapment; here Diana cannot free herself from her cruel lesbian lover. In "La cintura" ("The Belt"), the female narrator had once been struck by her father when she resisted his efforts to save her from drowning. That experience has turned her into a masochist, so the only way she can relate to her husband is to anger him until he beats her. "Il diavolo va e viene" ("The Devil Comes and Goes") expresses a recurring theme in this and other of Moravia's books when the devil says, "Hell isn't suffering more; it's repeating what's already been done."

That is indeed the hell of modern life that Moravia depicts. Characters repeat what they or others have already done. They may think that they are escaping the past, that through violence or love they are breaking out of the circle of repetition, but the reader sees their mistake. Moravia's clinical prose never comments on man's plight; it merely portrays it. In "Recalling *Time of Indifference*," Moravia observed that he had wanted to write tragedy, plays that involved "crime, bloody and insoluble conflict, passion, violence." While he has made his reputation as a writer of understated fiction rather than of melodramatic plays, in one sense he has remained true to that early ambition. His stories and novels do in fact reveal the tragedy of modern man, trapped within himself with no way of finding the exit, if indeed an exit exists.

Other major works

NOVELS: *Gli indifferenti*, 1929 (*The Indifferent Ones*, 1932; also as *The Time of Indifference*, 1953); *Le ambizioni sbagliate*, 1935 (*The Wheel of Fortune*, 1937; also as *Mistaken Ambitions*, 1965); *La mascherata*, 1941 (*The Fancy Dress Party*, 1947); *Agostino*, 1944 (English translation, 1947); *La romana*, 1947 (*The Woman of Rome*, 1949); *La disubbidienza*, 1948 (*Dis-*

obedience, 1950); *L'amore coniugale*, 1949 (*Conjugal Love*, 1951); *Il conformista*, 1951 (*The Conformist*, 1952); *Il disprezzo*, 1954 (*A Ghost at Noon*, 1955); *La ciociara*, 1957 (*Two Women*, 1958); *La noia*, 1960 (*The Empty Canvas*, 1961); *L'attenzione*, 1965 (*The Lie*, 1966); *Io e lui*, 1971 (*Two: A Phallic Novel*, 1972); *La vita interiore*, 1978 (*Time of Desecration*, 1980); *1934*, 1982 (English translation, 1983).

PLAYS: *Gli indifferenti*, 1948; *La mascherata*, 1954; *Beatrice Cenci*, 1955 (English translation, 1965); *Il mondo è quello che è*, 1966; *Il dio Kurt*, 1968; *La vita è gioco*, 1969; *Teatro*, 1958, 1976.

NONFICTION: *Un mese in U.R.S.S.*, 1958; *Saggi italiani del 1959*, 1960; *Un'idea dell'India*, 1962; *L'uomo come fine e altri saggi*, 1964 (*Man as an End: A Defence of Humanism, Literary, Social and Political Essays*, 1965); *La rivoluzione culturale in Cina*, 1967 (*The Red Book and the Great Wall*, 1968); *A quale tribù appartieni?*, 1972 (*Which Tribe Do You Belong To?*, 1974); *Impegno controvoglia: Saggi, articoli, interviste*, 1980.

Bibliography
Cottrell, Jane E. *Alberto Moravia*, 1974.
Dego, Giuliano. *Moravia*, 1966.
Rebay, Luciano. *Alberto Moravia*, 1970.
Ross, Joan, and Donald Freed. *The Existentialism of Alberto Moravia*, 1972.

Joseph Rosenblum

WRIGHT MORRIS

Born: Central City, Nebraska; January 6, 1910

Principal short fiction

Green Grass, Blue Sky, White House, 1970; *Here Is Einbaum*, 1973; *Real Losses, Imaginary Gains*, 1976; *Collected Stories: 1948-1986*, 1986.

Other literary forms

In a career that began in 1942, Wright Morris has published everything but plays and poems. Known primarily as a novelist, he is also a photographer and has created books of photographs such as *The Inhabitants* (1946), with accompanying text, which present his view of the artifacts of American lives. He has even incorporated his photographs into one novel, *The Home Place* (1948). He is an essayist, offering his interpretations of literature and culture in general in such works as *The Territory Ahead* (1958). The first fifty years of Morris' life are examined in three volumes of memoirs.

Achievements

Though often compared with such Midwestern writers as Sherwood Anderson and Willa Cather, Morris is hardly a mere regionalist. He has written about all sections of the United States and many parts of Mexico and Europe. What most distinguishes his fiction are a distinctively original American writing style rooted in the vernacular and a consistently amused response to the efforts of his characters to cope with the daily reality of an increasingly complex world. Frequently categorized as unfairly unheralded, Morris has been given many honors by the literary establishment. *The Field of Vision* (1956) received the National Book Award, and *Plains Song, for Female Voices* (1980) won the American Book Award. He was elected to the National Institute of Arts and Letters and the American Academy of Arts and Sciences in 1970 and was made an honorary fellow of the Modern Language Association in 1975 and a senior fellow of the National Endowment for the Humanities in 1976. He won the Western Literature Association's Distinguished Achievement Award in 1979 and the Robert Kirsch Award of the *Los Angeles Times* in 1981. Morris' most notable achievement is the consistent quality of his writings. He is one of the few American authors to have written as well after he turned fifty as he did before.

Biography

Wright Marion Morris was born in Central City, Nebraska, on January 6, 1910. His mother died six days after his birth, and his father reared him mostly alone in rural Nebraska, Omaha, and Chicago. After briefly attending the City College of Chicago and Pacific Union College, Morris went to Pomona College from 1930 to 1933, leaving to take a year's tour of Europe. He married Mary Ellen Finfrock in 1934 and taught drawing and swimming while he learned to write fiction and take photographs. He lectured at several colleges after becoming a novelist. Divorced in 1961, Morris married Josephine Kantor that year. He was a professor of English at San Francisco State University from 1962 until his retirement in 1975.

Analysis

Wright Morris' novels, to a large extent, are about what it means to be American. They examine the unrelenting grasp of the American Dream and the often bizarre ways in which people attempt to live up to this ideal they only vaguely understand—if it can be understood. His stories are more concerned with the everyday details of life, though these may be bizarre as well. They are stories of character and mood more than plot or theme, written in a style which manages to be distinctive without calling attention to itself.

While the majority of his novels have Nebraska and California as their settings, Morris' short fiction roams all over the United States and Europe, presenting characters with extremely varied social, economic, educational, and ethnic backgrounds. Morris wrote stories sporadically for the first quarter century of his career, taking up the form in earnest only in 1969. Unusual among American writers for having refined his short-story skills after becoming firmly established as a novelist, he has produced his best stories since turning seventy. It is almost as if he created them to meet an artistic challenge he had posed to himself.

These stories look at the quiet side of the emotional turmoil people put themselves through each day. Such themes as the inability to communicate with or understand or feel for one another, loneliness, and the failure of relationships are presented without nostalgia for some simpler past, with little sentimentality or anger. Morris' objective stance toward the world of his characters creates a comic, compassionate, quirkily individualistic body of short fiction.

"The Ram in the Thicket," Morris' first-published and best-known story, is an early version of what became the first two chapters of *Man and Boy* (1951), but it stands on its own as a memorable portrait of one of Morris' frequent subjects in his early fiction: a weak husband in the grasp of a domineering wife. Roger Ormsby and his wife, known as Mother, are depicted preparing to go to the christening of the USS *Ormsby*, named for their only child, Virgil, missing in action during World War II.

The need to conceal emotions characterizes Ormsby and Mother, neither of whom allows the other to guess how they feel about their son's death. Although hearing that Virgil has been killed seems strangely "natural" to his father, Ormsby has "not been prepared to feel what he felt. Mother need never know it unless he slipped up and talked in his sleep." Mother, without saying so, blames Ormsby for the boy's death, since he gave Virgil an air rifle years earlier, thereby conditioning him for war. Since that time, she has considered them united against her, calling them *they* or *you* plural as if they were twin halves of a conspiracy: "Though the boy had been gone two years he still felt him *there*, right beside him, when Mother said *you*."

From the time of the air rifle, both father and son have felt greater emotional distance from Mother, Virgil spending as much time as possible out-of-doors, Ormsby seeking solitude with his pipe in the basement. Once, Ormsby is surprised to find his son in his refuge, and the experience becomes the closest they ever share: "For two, maybe three minutes, there in the dark, they had been what Mother called them, they were *they*—and they were there in the basement because they were so much alike." When Ormsby receives the telegram he knows will tell him of Virgil's death, he takes it to the basement to read.

Mother is nationally prominent for her interest in bird-watching and is constantly involved in that activity, the League of Women Voters, and other organizations and causes. She understands wildlife and politics better than she does those closest to her. She enjoys saying, in jest, that she prefers shoes to men but is actually truthful, since clothing is less complicated than people. Causes are her shelter as much as the basement is her husband's. Yet neither character is being held up to ridicule; the typical Morris character looks for excuses to hide his feelings, for ways of ignoring failures of communication.

The characters in "The Ram in the Thicket" could easily be comical caricatures, but Morris is not concerned with types. His creations come alive through their idiosyncrasies, such as the Oriental rug Mother puts in the bathroom and the leftovers she refuses to throw away, carefully storing them in jars in the icebox, then forgetting about them, leaving Ormsby, when the contents have become moldy, to bury them behind the garage. Such details help create a sense of ordinary lives closely observed.

"The Safe Place" is another Morris story incorporated into his longer fiction, appearing in a different form in *Ceremony in Lone Tree* (1960); it also has characters and situations resembling those in the short novel *War Games* (written in 1951-1952 but not published until 1972). A retired army colonel lives a dull Brooklyn existence with his wife until he is hit by a pie truck and almost killed. The cynical colonel spends his recovery in the hospital contemplating how life is full of senseless violence which ceaselessly swoops down upon the unsuspecting and innocent: "Life, to put it simply, was a battleground." He decides that the only way to avoid the world's dangers and foolishness is to stay in bed—"the only safe place." In many ways, the colonel's view of the absurd world outside the hospital foreshadows that in Joseph Heller's death-obsessed *Catch-22* (1961).

The colonel becomes interested in another patient, Hyman Kopfman, who has had an arm and a leg amputated because of a blood ailment. When Kopfman identifies the problem in his body as America, the colonel senses a kinship between them: "What Hyman Kopfman knew was that the world was killing him." While the colonel is reserved, Kopfman enjoys talking about himself—apparently to himself—"as if he were somebody else." The colonel listens in fascination to Kopfman's account of how his family left Vienna for Chicago when he was a boy, of how Kopfman, as he grew, began wearing his small father's clothes while his brother Paul wore their mother's old skirt and peasant blouse. The boys rarely left their apartment, making it into a self-contained world, a safe place. Below their apartment was another: a walled garden where blind people came to walk.

The colonel decides that Kopfman's life has always been rather hopeless and that this hopelessness makes him lovable. That he is not aware of how hopeless he is touches the colonel even more. The colonel realizes that all Kopfman has ever wanted is to lead "the useless sort of life" that he has himself had. Kopfman's case inspires the colonel to get well despite having nothing to live for while Kopfman, with his hunger for life, gets worse.

"The Safe Place" displays some of the common concerns of Morris' fiction. His characters always seem to be seeking safe places, as with Ormsby's basement, which might not seem to be havens to others. Man survives in this absurd, violent world by tricking himself into believing that he has found a refuge, whether it be a place, a person, a job, a role in society, or a philosophy. "The Safe Place" is also one of several Morris stories contrasting American and European views of life; others include "The Character of the Lover," "Drrdla," "Fiona," "Here Is Einbaum," "In Another Country," "The Customs of the Country," and "Things That Matter." Whether Europeans in America or Americans in Europe, these characters always experience a feeling of dislocation.

Pets are central to Morris' delineation of character. Cats, dogs, and birds appear in the majority of his stories to help underscore certain facets of the humans around them, humans who belong to the pets more than vice versa. Morris' use of animals ranges from the poignant, as in "Victrola," in which an elderly man's dog dies, to the comic, as when a man develops an affection for his neighbors' leghorn pullet in "Fellow Creatures."

Because his characters are independent and eccentric yet crave attention and love, it is appropriate that several Morris stories involve cats. The stray feline in "The Cat in the Picture" causes a marriage to break up. "Drrdla" explores how cats and women are alike as a husband becomes attached to another stray who rejects him for the man's unfaithful wife. "The Cat's Meow" is one of Morris' most effective humorous stories. A writer and his seventeen-pound cat are virtually inseparable, the cat lying on the man's desk during the four hours he writes each day: "The cat faces him, his eyes blinking in the desk light, and the look he gives Morgan, and Morgan returns, is not something to be lightly dealt with, or even when soberly and thoughtfully dealt with, put into words." Morris' animals and humans share this enigmatic quality.

With its whimsical acceptance of the unusual, the unexpected, and the inexplicable, "Glimpse into Another Country" is most representative of Morris' later stories. On the plane from San Francisco to New York, Hazlitt, an elderly academic, is treated rudely by Mrs. Thayer, a fellow passenger, when he tries to make casual conversation with her and her husband. Soon after he arrives in Manhattan, Hazlitt goes to Bloomingdale's, seeing Mrs. Thayer again on the way. In Bloomingdale's, he loses his driver's license and, in a sense, his identity, when the store is closed because of a bomb threat while a clerk is having his check approved.

The next day, he learns from a medical specialist that the health problem about which he has been worried is nonexistent. Considering himself "free of a nameless burden," Hazlitt returns to Bloomingdale's to retrieve his driver's license and impulsively buys an expensive strand of pearls to give to his wife. He cannot afford the gift, but "Writing the numbers, spelling the sum out gave him a tingling sense of exhilaration."

Going to the Metropolitan Museum of Art, Hazlitt sees the ubiquitous Mrs. Thayer in the gift shop. In the museum's basement rest room, a group of boys, seemingly under the influence of drugs, force him to give them the pearls. He returns to the gift shop for an Etruscan pin, the type of gift his wife will consider "sensible." From a bus outside, Mrs. Thayer waves to him, her now-friendly eyes giving him "all the assurances he needed."

Hazlitt, as opposed to the colonel in "The Safe Place," is not perturbed by these events, being slightly bemused by them. Unlike the stereotypical elderly person, Hazlitt also accepts the inevitability of change, as when he discovers that the museum's once-striking Fountain Court lunchroom has been renovated into blandness. More important are the usual Morris concerns, such as the protagonist's inability to communicate with either the relatively nonthreatening Thayers or the drugged youths. In the taxi from the airport, Hazlitt wants "to chat a bit with the driver, but the Plexiglas barrier between them seemed intimidating."

"Glimpse into Another Country" is primarily a comic view of contemporary life. Hazlitt, like many Morris characters, travels through life with an amused tolerance and detachment, refusing to take anything seriously since so many others are willing to assume that burden for him. The unusual and the everyday merge as he moves about as if in a dream. He sees a television picture of a milling crowd in India indifferently passing by dead or sleeping bodies: "The film gave Hazlitt a glimpse into a strange country where the quick and the dormant were accustomed to mingle. Perhaps . . . it was not the walkers but the sleepers who would range the farthest in their travels."

For the Hazlitts of the world, so-called real life is carried on with even less logic than a dream.

With its characters stoically enduring the pains of emotional isolation on the Plains, "The Origin of Sadness" is the Morris story most like his novels, particularly recalling *The Works of Love* (1952). Growing up in Osborn County, Kansas, shy, brooding, self-absorbed Schuler enjoys playing with an Indian companion because they do not have to talk much. He has as a pet a coyote pup, freed from a steel trap, who treats everyone else as an enemy. Schuler is expected to become a country doctor like his late father but is more interested in nature and becomes a paleontologist. Schuler's temperament is suited to an obsession with the remains of the distant past: "He did not find the immediate and shifting flux of time present real at all." As such, he is one of the few Morris characters with some understanding of his sense of displacement.

He marries one of his students, Doreen Oakum, who is part Cherokee, because she shares "both his passion for bones and his talent for silence." Their life becomes "a matter of shared but secret communications." Typically for a Morris couple, there is little romance in their marriage. Doreen seems to feel more strongly about her parrot than her husband. Yet what Schuler loves about her is "her detachment from the world that hummed and buzzed around her, her attachment to the invisible world within her."

Doreen's sudden death drives Schuler back to his birthplace as he experiences despair for the first time. As a snowstorm begins, Schuler, Ice Age expert, makes his way to the arroyo where he had freed the coyote and discovers it to be full of tiny fossils, seemingly undisturbed since his last visit years before. He is concerned that he must bring destruction to the ageless setting by climbing the arroyo. His obsession with the past, his despair at the present, and the innocence of his youth converge as he falls, breaks his hip, and calmly lies awaiting an icy death. His final discovery is that the "deep freeze of all freezes was time itself." By understanding the past and its significance for the present, Schuler has sought to arrest time, and at the end, he recognizes the futility of his efforts.

During a public lecture, Schuler is once asked what he is really seeking; he replies, "What interests me is the origin of sadness." This search is similar to what motivates Wright Morris as he takes ordinary people and situations and peels back the surface layers to uncover the human elements—or their absence—underneath. Morris' stories are unsentimental yet strangely moving, unusually amusing explorations into what it means to be human in the twentieth century.

Other major works

NOVELS: *My Uncle Dudley*, 1942; *The Man Who Was There*, 1945; *The Home Place*, 1948; *The World in the Attic*, 1949; *Man and Boy*, 1951; *The*

Works of Love, 1952; *The Deep Sleep*, 1953; *The Huge Season*, 1954; *The Field of Vision*, 1956; *Love Among the Cannibals*, 1957; *Ceremony in Lone Tree*, 1960; *What a Way to Go*, 1962; *Cause for Wonder*, 1963; *One Day*, 1965; *In Orbit*, 1967; *Fire Sermon*, 1971; *War Games*, 1972; *A Life*, 1973; *The Fork River Space Project*, 1977; *Plains Song, for Female Voices*, 1980.

NONFICTION: *The Inhabitants*, 1946; *The Territory Ahead*, 1958; *A Bill of Rites, a Bill of Wrongs, a Bill of Goods*, 1968; *God's Country and My People*, 1968; *Love Affair: A Venetian Journal*, 1972; *About Fiction: Reverent Reflections on the Nature of Fiction with Irreverent Observations on Writers, Readers, and Other Abuses*, 1975; *Wright Morris: Structures and Artifacts, Photographs, 1933-1954*, 1975; *Earthly Delights, Unearthly Adornments: American Writers as Image-Makers*, 1978; *Will's Boy*, 1981 (autobiography); *Photographs and Words*, 1982; *Picture America*, 1982; *Solo: An American Dreamer in Europe, 1933-1934*, 1983 (autobiography); *A Cloak of Light: Writing My Life*, 1985 (autobiography).

MISCELLANEOUS: *Wright Morris: A Reader*, 1970.

Bibliography

Bird, Roy K. *Wright Morris: Memory and Imagination*, 1985.

Crump, G. B. *The Novels of Wright Morris: A Critical Interpretation*, 1978.

Knoll, Robert E., ed. *Conversations with Wright Morris: Critical Views and Responses*, 1977.

Madden, David. *Wright Morris*, 1964.

Michael Adams

ALICE MUNRO

Born: Wingham, Canada; July 10, 1931

Principal short fiction

Dance of the Happy Shades, 1968; *Something I've Been Meaning to Tell You: Thirteen Stories*, 1974; *The Moons of Jupiter*, 1982; *The Progress of Love*, 1986.

Other literary forms

Alice Munro is principally a writer of short stories, but she has published two novels: *Lives of Girls and Women* (1971) and *The Beggar Maid* (1979), which was originally published in Canada under the title *Who Do You Think You Are?* Whether *The Beggar Maid* is a new kind of novel or an intricately related collection of short stories has been the subject of some debate, but since the ten stories follow the life of one woman over a period of thirty years, from childhood to maturity, it seems reasonable to view it as a novel.

Achievements

Munro has gained recognition as a consummate writer, principally of short psychological fiction. She has received the Governor General's Award (Canada's highest literary award) for *Dance of the Happy Shades* and *The Beggar Maid*. Her novel *Lives of Girls and Women* won the Canadian Booksellers Association International Book Year Award in 1972. She has been nominated for the Booker Prize. She has been compared with Ernest Hemingway for the realism, economy, and lucidity of her style, with John Updike for her insights into the intricacies of social and sexual relationships, with Flannery O'Connor and Eudora Welty for her ability to create characters of eccentric individualism, and with Marcel Proust for the completeness and verisimilitude with which she evokes the past.

Munro is an intuitive writer who is less likely to be concerned with problems of form than with clarity and veracity. Some critics have faulted her for a tendency toward disorganization or diffusion—too many shifts in time and place within a single story, for example. On her strengths as a writer, however, critics generally agree: She has an unfailing particularity and naturalness of style; an ability to write vividly about ordinary life and its boredom without boring her readers; an ability to write about the past without being sentimental or romantic; a profound grasp of human emotion and psychology. Chief among her virtues is her great honesty: her refusal to oversimplify or falsify human beings, emotions, or experience. One of her characters states, "How to keep oneself from lying I see as the main problem everywhere." Her awareness of this problem is everywhere evident in her writing, certainly in the distinctive voices of her narrator-protagonists, who are scrupulously concerned with truth. Finally, her themes—memory, love, transience, death—are significant. To explore such themes within the limitations of the short-story form with subtlety and depth is Munro's achievement.

Biography

Alice Munro was born in the town of Wingham, Ontario, Canada, in 1931. She spent two years at the University of Western Ontario. She was married in 1951 and moved to Vancouver, British Columbia, and she later lived in Victoria, British Columbia. She has three daughters by this marriage. In 1972, she returned to Southwestern Ontario; she lives in Clinton with her second husband.

Analysis

One of Alice Munro's recurring themes is "the pain of human contact . . . the fascinating pain; the humiliating necessity." The phrase occurs in "The Stone in the Field" and refers to the narrator's maiden aunts, who cringe from all human contact, but the emotional pain that human contact inevitably brings is a subject in all of her stories. It is evident in the title story of her first collection, "Dance of the Happy Shades," in which an elderly, impoverished piano teacher, Miss Marsalles, has a "party" (her word for recital) for a dwindling number of her students and their mothers, an entertainment she can ill afford. The elaborate but nearly inedible refreshments, the ludicrous gifts, and the tedium of the recital pieces emphasize the incongruity between Miss Marsalles' serene pleasure in the festivities and the grim sufferings of her unwilling but outwardly polite guests. Their anxieties are intensified by the mid-party arrival of Miss Marsalles' newest pupils, a group of mentally retarded people from a nearby institution. The other pupils and their mothers struggle to maintain well-bred composure, but inwardly they are repelled, particularly when one of the retarded girls gives the only accomplished performance of a sprightly piece called "The Dance of the Happy Shades." The snobbish mothers believe that the idea of a retarded girl learning to play the piano is not in good taste; it is "useless, out-of-place," in fact very much like Miss Marsalles, herself. Clearly, this dismal affair will be Miss Marsalles' last "party," yet the narrator is unable at the end to pity her, to say "Poor Miss Marsalles." "It is the Dance of the Happy Shades that prevents us, it is the one communiqué from the other country where she lives." The unfortunate Miss Marsalles is happy, she has escaped the pain she would feel if she could know how others regard her, or care. She is living in another country, out of touch with reality; she has escaped into "the freedom of a great unemotional happiness."

Few of Munro's characters are so fortunate. In "The Peace of Utrecht," for example, the inescapable emotional pain of human contact is the central problem. Helen, the narrator, makes a trip with her two children to Jubilee, the small town where she grew up, ostensibly to visit her sister Maddy, now living alone in their childhood home. The recent death of their mother is on their minds, but they cannot speak of it. Maddy, who stayed at home to look after their "Gothic Mother," has forbidden all such talk: "No exorcising here," she says. Yet exorcism is what Helen desperately needs as she struggles with the torment that she feels about her sister's "sacrifice," her mother's life, and her own previous self which this return home so vividly and strangely evokes. Mother was a town "character," a misfit or oddity, even before the onset of her debilitating and disfiguring illness (she seems to have died of Parkinson's disease). For Helen, she was a constant source of anxiety and shame, a threat to Helen's own precarious adolescent identity. (Readers who know Munro's novel *Lives of Girls and Women* will find a strong resemblance of Helen's mother to Dell Jordan's bizarre mother. She also appears as recognizably the same character in the stories "The Ottawa Valley," "Connection," "The Stone in the Field," and perhaps in "The Progress of Love.") Recalling the love and pity denied this ill but incorrigible woman, Helen experiences raging guilt, shame, and anger that she and her sister were forced into "parodies of love." Egocentric, petulant, this mother "demanded our love in every way she knew, without shame or sense, as a child will. And how could we have loved her, I say desperately to myself, the resources of love we had were not enough, the demand on us was too great." Finally, Helen and her sister withdrew even the pretense of love, withdrew all emotion: "We took away from her our anger and impatience and disgust, took all emotion away from our dealings with her, as you might take away meat from a prisoner to weaken him, till he died." Still, the stubborn old woman survived and might have lived longer except that Maddy, left alone with her mother and wanting her own life, put her in the hospital. After she tried to run away, restraint became necessary; she did not survive long after that.

Critics have agreed that Munro's strongest works are those which draw on her own small-town origins in Western Ontario, stories of Jubilee, Tuppertown, Hanratty, Dalgleish. Munro has confessed in an interview that "The Peace of Utrecht" is her most autobiographical story and thus was difficult to write. Perhaps its emotional power derives in part from its closeness to her own experience, but it exhibits those qualities for which her writing has been praised: The effortless clarity of style, the psychological penetration of character, the evocation of time and place, the unfailing eye and ear which convey an impression of absolute authenticity—these are the hallmarks of Munro's finest fiction, and they are evident even in her earliest stories. For example, in "The Peace of Utrecht," Helen's visit to two memorable residents of Jubilee, her mother's sisters, Aunt Annie and Auntie Lou, demonstrates a deftness of characterization and a sureness of touch which are remarkable but typical of this writer at her best. Helen finds them spending the afternoon making rugs out of dyed rags. They are very old now. They sit in a hot little porch that is shaded by bamboo blinds; the rags and the half-finished rugs make an encouraging, domestic sort of disorder around them. They do not go out any more, but they get up early in the mornings, wash and powder themselves and put on their shapeless print dresses trimmed with rickrack and white braid.

Later, after tea, Aunt Annie tries to press on Helen a box of her mother's clothing (painstakingly cleaned and mended), seemingly oblivious to Helen's alarm and pain at the sight of these all-too-tangible reminders of her mother. To Aunt Annie, things are to be used up; clothes are to be worn. Yet she is not insensitive, nor is she a fool. Revealing to Helen (who did not know) the shameful facts about her mother's hospitalization against her will, her pitiful, frantic attempt to escape one snowy January night, the board that was subsequently nailed across the bed to immobilize her, and Maddy's indifference to it all, Aunt Annie begins "crying distractedly as old people do, with miserable scanty tears." Despite the tears, however, Aunt Annie is (as Helen is not), emotionally tough, "an old hand at grief and self control." Just how tough she is is conveyed by Aunt Annie's final, quietly understated words: " 'We thought it was hard,' she said finally. 'Lou and I thought it was hard.' "

Helen and Maddy, with less emotional resilience, try to come to terms with their own complex anguish through evasion, rationalization, and, finally, admonishment—"don't be guilty"—but Munro is too honest to imply that they can be successful. In the final lines of the story, Helen urges her sister to forget the past, to take hold of her own life at last. Maddy's affirmation, "Yes I will," soon slips into an agonized question: "But why can't I, Helen? *Why can't I?*" In the "dim world of continuing disaster, of home," there is no Peace of Utrecht, not for Munro's characters, perhaps not for Munro.

The preoccupation in Munro's fiction with family, usually as a "continuing disaster," is striking. Assorted eccentric aunts, uncles, and cousins appear and reappear; a somewhat miscreant brother appears in "Forgiveness in Families" and "Boys and Girls." Sometimes the family portraits are warmly sympathetic, as in the case of the grandmother in "Winter Wind" or especially the gentle father who calmly prepares for his death in "The Moons of Jupiter." Even the neurotic mother and the father in "The Progress of Love" are treated sympathetically. There, the mother's fanatical hatred of her own father leads her to burn the desperately needed money she inherits from him at his death. Clearly, for Munro, family origins matter, sometimes as the source of humor and delightful revelation but more dependably as the source of endless mystery and pain. This is particularly true of "the problem, the only problem," as stated in "The Ottawa Valley": mother. At the story's conclusion, the narrator confesses that

she is the one of course that I am trying to get; it is to reach her that this whole journey has been undertaken. With what purpose? To mark her off, to describe, to illumine, to celebrate, to *get rid*, of her; and it did not work, for she looms too close, just as she always did. . . . She has stuck to me as close as ever and refused to fall away, and I could go on, and on, applying what skills I have, using what tricks I know, and it would always be the same.

Some relationships, some kinds of "fascinating pain," can be recorded or analyzed, but not exorcised. Clearly, these may become the inspiration for significant literature. In Munro's fiction, the view of the emotional entanglements called "family" is unflinchingly honest, unsentimental, but always humane, at times even humorous.

Another important dimension of Munro's short stories is sexual relationship, particularly in the "feelings that women have about men," as she stated in an interview. In "Bardon Bus," the narrator, a woman writer spending time in Australia, meets an anthropologist (known as "X") and begins a deliberately limited affair, asking only that it last out their short time in Australia. After, when both have returned to Canada, she is miserable, tortured by memory and need: "I can't continue to move my body along the streets unless I exist in his mind and in his eyes." Finally, she realizes her obsession is a threat to her sanity and that she has a choice of whether to be crazy or not. She decides she does not have the stamina or the will for "prolonged craziness," and further that "there is a limit to the amount of misery and disarray you will put up with, for love, just as there is a limit to the amount of mess you can stand around a house. You can't know the limit beforehand, but you will know when you've reached it. I believe this." She begins to let go of the relationship and finds "a queer kind of pleasure" in doing this, not a "self-wounding or malicious pleasure," but "pleasure in taking into account, all over again, everything that is contradictory and persistent and unaccommodating about life. . . . I think there's something in us wanting to be reassured about all that, right alongside—and at war with—whatever there is that wants permanent vistas and a lot of fine talk." This seeming resolution, however, this salvation by knowing and understanding all, is subtly undercut by the conclusion of the story. The narrator's much younger friend, Kay, happens to mention her involvement with a fascinating new "friend," who turns out to be "X," the anthropologist. The story ends there but the pain (presumably) does not.

The female protagonist of "Tell Me Yes or No" is also sifting through the emotional rubble of an adulterous affair which has ended, perhaps because of the death of her lover, or perhaps it has merely ended. In this story, it is difficult to distinguish reality from fantasy, and that may be the point. The other lives and other loves of her lover may be real, or they may be a fantasy (as defense mechanism) of the protagonist, but the central insight is the realization of how "women build their castles on foundations hardly strong enough to support a night's shelter; how women deceive themselves and uselessly suffer, being exploitable because of the emptiness of their lives and some deep—but indefinable, and not final!—flaw in themselves." For this woman, none of the remedies of her contemporaries works, not deep breathing, not macramé, and certainly not the esoteric advice of another desperate case: to live "every moment by itself," a concept she finds impossible to comprehend let alone practice. The irony of her difficulty is evident, considering Munro's passionate concern throughout her fiction for "Connection" (the title of one of her stories). Here, it seems that there is some connection, between past choice and present desolation: "Love is not in the least unavoidable, there is a choice made. It is just that it is hard to know when the choice was made, or when, in spite of seeming frivolous, it became irreversible. There is no clear warning about that."

Munro's clear-eyed, self-aware narrators are never easy on themselves. They are constantly requiring themselves to face reality, to be aware of and responsible for the consequences of their own choices. In "Labor Day Dinner," the narrator, forty-three-year-old Roberta, has for the past year been living on a run-down farm with George, a younger man and former art teacher. His ambitious plan is to restore the farm and create a studio in which to do his sculpture. Roberta's daughters Angela, seventeen, and Eva, twelve, are spending the summer with her. The atmosphere is emotionally charged, prickly and tense. George does not approve of the way Roberta indulges her daughters, allowing them to practice ballet instead of doing any work. George does not approve of Roberta, who seems to be indulging herself with tears and moody idleness. On the other hand, Roberta (weeping silently behind her sunglasses) does not approve of George's cooling ardor, his ungallant awareness of her age as evidenced by his request that she not wear a halter top to his cousin's Labor Day dinner because she has flabby armpits. So far, this sounds like the unpromising stuff of the afternoon soaps. (In fact, some of Munro's short stories first were published in popular magazines.) The difference is in what Munro is able to do with her material, the way in which she prevents her characters from deteriorating into stereotypes or her theme into cliché.

Roberta (who has reduced her waist only to discover that her face now looks haggard) reflects mournfully:

> how can you exercise the armpits? What is to be done? Now the payment is due, and what for? For vanity. . . . Just for having those pleasing surfaces once, and letting them speak for you; just for allowing an arrangement of hair and shoulders and breasts to have its effect. You don't stop in time, don't know what to do instead; you lay yourself open to humiliation. So thinks Roberta, with self-pity—what she knows to be self-pity—rising and sloshing around in her like bitter bile. She must get away, live alone, wear sleeves.

The self-awareness, the complex mingling of humor and pathos, the comic inadequacy of the solution, to wear sleeves (rivaling Prufrock's momentous decision to wear his trousers rolled), these lend to the character and to the story a dimension which is generally missing in popular fiction.

Roberta's daughters are close observers of as well as participants in this somewhat lugubrious drama. Angela, watching the change in her mother from self-reliant woman to near wreck and viewing George as a despot who hopes to enslave them all, records in her journal, "If this is love I want no part of it." On the other hand, sensitive Eva, watching her older sister develop the unpleasant traits of a typical adolescent, wants no part of that— "I don't want it to happen to me."

They all nearly get what they want, a way out of the emotional trauma in which they find themselves. On the way home from the Labor Day dinner, the pickup truck in which they are riding (the girls asleep in back) comes within inches of being hit broadside by a car that came out of nowhere traveling between eighty and ninety miles an hour, no lights, its driver drunk. George did not touch the brake, nor did Roberta scream; they continue in stunned silence, pull into their yard and sit, unable to move. "What they feel is not terror or thanksgiving—not yet. What they feel is strangeness. They feel as strange, as flattened out and borne aloft, as unconnected with previous and future events as the ghost car was." The story ends with Eva, waking and calling to them, "Are you guys dead?" "Aren't we home?"

The ending shocks everything in the story into a new perspective, making what went before seem irrelevant, especially Roberta's and George's half-hearted playing at love. For Munro, it seems that the thought of the nearness, the omnipresence, and the inevitability of death is the only thing which can put lives and relationships into true perspective, but this (as Munro states at the conclusion of "The Spanish Lady") is a message which cannot be delivered, however true it may be.

Munro has stated in an interview that her need and desire to write "has something to do with the fight against death, the feeling that we lose everything every day, and writing is a way of convincing yourself perhaps that you're doing something about this." Despite her characteristic concern for honesty and her determination to tell only the truth, it seems in this passage that she may be wrong about one thing: It seems clear that Alice Munro's writing is destined to last for a very long time.

Other major works

NOVELS: *Lives of Girls and Women*, 1971; *Who Do You Think You Are?*, 1979 (U.S. edition, *The Beggar Maid*, 1979).

Bibliography

MacKendrick, Louis K., ed. *Probable Fictions: Alice Munro's Narrative Acts*, 1983.
Miller, Judith, ed. *The Art of Alice Munro: Saying the Unsayable*, 1984.

Karen A. Kildahl

VLADIMIR NABOKOV

Born: St. Petersburg, Russia; April 23, 1899
Died: Montreux, Switzerland; July 2, 1977

Principal short fiction

Vozvrashchenie Chorba, 1930; *Soglyadatay*, 1938; *Nine Stories*, 1947; *Vesna v Fialte i drugie rasskazy*, 1956; *Nabokov's Dozen: A Collection of Thirteen Stories*, 1958; *Nabokov's Quartet*, 1966; *A Russian Beauty and Other Stories*, 1973; *Tyrants Destroyed and Other Stories*, 1975; *Details of a Sunset and Other Stories*, 1976.

Other literary forms

Vladimir Nabokov's fifty-year career as a writer includes—besides his short stories—novels, poetry, drama, memoirs, translations, reviews, letters, critical essays, literary criticism, and the screenplay of his most famous novel, *Lolita* (1955). After his death, three volumes of lectures on literature that he had delivered to students at Wellesley, Stanford, and Cornell were scrupulously edited by Fredson Bowers and published as *Lectures on Literature: British, French, and German* (1980), *Lectures on Russian Literature* (1981), and *Lectures on Don Quixote* (1983).

Achievements

Nabokov occupies a unique niche in the annals of literature by having become a major author in both Russian and English. He wrote nine novels, about forty stories, and considerable poetry in Russian before migrating to the United States in 1940. Thereafter, he not only produced eight more novels and ten short stories in English but also translated into English the fiction that he had composed in his native language, sometimes with the collaboration of his son, Dimitri. Reversing his linguistic field, he translated his *Lolita* into Russian.

Nabokov's work has received considerable critical acclaim; a modern master, he has influenced such diverse literary figures as Anthony Burgess, John Barth, William Gass, Tom Stoppard, Philip Roth, John Updike, and Milan Kundera. Nabokov's fiction is never intentionally didactic or sociological; he detested moralistic, message-ridden writing. Instead, he delighted in playing self-consciously with the reader's credibility, regarding himself as a fantasist, a Prospero of artifice. He manipulates his characters as so many pieces on a chessboard, devising problems for absorbing, intricate games of which he and Jorge Luis Borges are the acknowledged modern masters. His precision of language, lexical command of multilingual allusions, and startling imagery have awed, delighted, but also sometimes irritated critics and readers. Few writers have practiced art for the sake of art with such talent and discipline. Nabokov's advice to students in a college literature course suggests the best approach to his own fiction:

> In reading, one should notice and fondle details. . . . We must see things and hear things, we must visualize the rooms, the clothes, the manners of an author's people . . . above all, a great writer is always a great enchanter, and it is here that we come to the really exciting part when we try to grasp the individual magic of his genius and to study the style, the imagery, the pattern of his novels or poems.

Biography

Vladimir Vladimirovich Nabokov's life divides neatly into four phases, each lasting approximately twenty years. He was born on Shakespeare's birthday in 1899 to an aristocratic and wealthy family residing in what was then called St. Petersburg. His grandfather was State Minister of Justice for two czars; his father, Vladimir Dmitrievich, a prominent liberal politician, married a woman from an extremely wealthy family. Vladimir Vladimirovich, the first of two sons, was reared with much parental love and care, eloquently evoked in his lyrical memoir, *Conclusive Evidence: A Memoir* (1951), later expanded and retitled *Speak, Memory: An Autobiography Revisited* (1966).

In 1919, the October Revolution forced the Nabokovs to flee Russia. Vladimir, who had learned both French and English from governesses during his childhood, enrolled in Cambridge University, took a degree in foreign languages in 1923, and published two volumes of poetry the same year. Meanwhile, his father and the other family members settled in Berlin. There, Vladimir Dmitrievich was assassinated in 1922 by two right-wing extremist Russian expatriates who had intended their bullets for another victim. Vladimir took up residence in Berlin in 1923, and in 1925 married a beautiful Jewish émigré, Véra Slonim, with whom he maintained a harmonious union. Between 1924 and 1929, he published, in Russian-language exile newspapers and periodicals, twenty-two short stories. Many were collected in a 1930 book *Vozvrashchenie Chorba* (the return of Chorb), whose contents were later translated into English and distributed among several collections of Nabokov's short stories.

To avoid confusion with his well-known father, the younger Nabokov assumed the pen name "V. Sirin," after a mythological, multicolored bird featured in ancient Russian literature; he used this name until leaving Europe in 1940. The Nabokovs stayed in Berlin until 1937, even though Vladimir never learned German and usually drew his German fictive personages unfavorably. In his writings during these years, he dramatized the autobiographical themes of political exile from Russia, nostalgia, grief, anguish, and other variations of vagrant rootlessness. His most important novels during the 1920's and 1930's are commonly judged to be *Zashchita Luzhina* (1929; *The Defense*, 1964) and *Dar* (1937-1938; *The Gift*, 1963).

Nabokov's third life-stage began in 1940, when, after a three-year stay in Paris, he was glad to escape the Nazi menace by emigrating to the United States. After a one-term lectureship at Stanford University, he distributed his time for the next seven years between teaching at Wellesley College and working as a Research Fellow in Entomology at Harvard's Museum of Comparative Zoology, pursuing his passion for lepidoptera. During these years, he began to establish himself as an American writer of note and, in 1945, became a naturalized citizen. He published two novels, *The Real Life of Sebastian Knight* (1941) and *Bend Sinister* (1947); a brilliant but eccentric study of the Russian writer who had most deeply influenced him, *Nikolai Gogol* (1944); a number of stories and poems; and sections of his first autobiography. In 1948, Cornell University lured him away from Wellesley by offering him a tenured professorship. He became a celebrated ornament of the Ithaca, New York, campus for ten years, specializing in a course called Masters of European Fiction, alternately charming and provoking his students with witty lectures and difficult examinations.

Nabokov wrote *Lolita* during his summer vacations in the early 1950's, but the book was refused publication by several American firms and was first issued in 1955 by Olympia Press, a Parisian English-language publisher that usually featured pornography. By 1958, the work had become celebrated as well as notorious, and Putnam's issued it in New York. It became the year's sensational best-seller, and Nabokov, taking an abrupt mid-year leave from Cornell, thereupon moved to an elegant hotel on the banks of Switzerland's Lake Geneva for what were to prove nineteen more fecund years.

During this last arc of his career, Nabokov basked in the aura of worldwide recognition as an eminent writer, yet continued to labor diligently: He revised his autobiography; resurrected his Russian long and short fiction in English translations; produced a four-volume translation of and commentary on Alexander Pushkin's novel in verse, *Yevgeny Onegin* (1833; Nabokov's English translation, *Eugene Onegin*, 1964); and wrote several new novels, including two—*Pale Fire* (1962) and *Ada or Ardor: A Family Chronicle* (1969)—worthy of consideration among the twentieth century's leading literary texts. Despite many losses and difficulties in his arduous life, Nabokov never yielded to self-pity, let alone despair. His career demonstrated not only artistic resourcefulness but also the personal virtues of resolution, resilience, and capacity for renewal.

Analysis

Vladimir Nabokov's early stories are set in the post-czarist, post–World War I era, with Germany the usual location, and sensitive, exiled Russian men the usual protagonists. Many are nascent artists: wistful, sorrowful, solitary, sometimes despairingly disheartened. Many evoke a Proustian recollection of their Russian pasts as they try, and often as not fail, to understand an existence filled with irony, absurdity, and fortuity. These tales display Nabokov's abiding fascination with the interplay between reality and fantasy, between an outer world of tangs, scents, rain showers, sunsets, dawns, butterflies, flowers, forests, and urban asphalts, and an inner landscape of recondite, impenetrable, mysterious feelings. He loved to mix the disheveled externals of precisely described furnishings, trappings, and drab minutiae with memories, myths, fantasy, parody, grandeur, hilarity, masks, nostalgia, and, above all, the magic of artistic illusion. He celebrates the unpredictable permutations of the individual imagination over the massive constraints of the twentieth century's sad history. He is the supreme stylist, dedicated to forging his vision in the most dazzling verbal smithy since James Joyce's.

One of his first stories, "Britva" ("The Razor"), is a clever adaptation of motifs used in Gogol's "Nos" ("The Nose") and Pushkin's "Vystrel" ("The Shot"). A White Russian émigré, Colonel Ivanov, now a barber in Berlin, recognizes a customer as the Red officer who had condemned him to death six years before. He toys with his victim, terrorizing him with caustic, cruel remarks, comparing his open razor to the sharp end of a sword, inverting the menace of their previous confrontation in Russia. Yet he shaves his former captor gently and carefully, and finally releases him unharmed. By doing so, Ivanov also releases himself from his burning desire for vengeance. Nabokov uses the multivalent symbol of the razor compactly and densely: The acerbic Ivanov both sharpens and encases his razorlike temperament.

In "Zvonok" ("The Doorbell"), Nabokov delineates a tragic encounter between past and present in a complex tale fusing realism and symbolism. A son, Galatov, has been separated from his mother for seven years, during which time he has fought in the post-1917 Russian Civil War and wandered over Africa, Europe, and the Canary Islands. He learns that his mother's second husband has died and left her some real estate in Berlin. He searches for his mother there, meets her dentist, and through him obtains her address. Structurally, Galatov's visits to the dentist, a Dr. Weiner, anticipates his reunion with his mother: This Weiner is not Galatov's childhood dentist, yet he does happen to be his mother's. When Galatov finally meets his mother, he learns that she, too, is not the mother of his childhood: He meets, in the Berlin apartment, not the faded, dark-haired woman he left seven years earlier but an aged courtesan awaiting the arrival of a lover who is three years younger than her son. Galatov realizes that her fervent greeting of him had been intended for her paramour. When the doorbell announces the latter's arrival, Galatov learns, observing his mother's distraction and nervousness, that her new, déclassé circumstances leave no room for him. He hurriedly departs, vaguely promising to see her again in a year or thereabout. He knows now that not only has the mistress supplanted the mother but also his mother may never have cherished him as dearly as his previous need for her had deluded him into believing. The story's structural symmetry between memory and new reality is impressively achieved.

"Sluchainost" ("A Matter of Chance") is one of Nabokov's most poignant tales. Its protagonist, Aleksey Luzhin—whose surname reappears five years later as that of the hero of *The Defense*—is a Russian exile who, like Galatov, has traveled to many places and worked many jobs. Currently, he is a waiter on a German train; having had no news of his wife, Elena, for five years, he is deeply depressed and has become addicted to cocaine. He plans his suicide for the night of August 1, the ninth anniversary of his wedding and the day of this story. On this particular trip, an old Russian princess, Maria Ukhtomski, is joined in her compartment by a young woman who arrived in Berlin from St. Petersburg the previous day: Elena Luzhina, seeking her lost husband. The story's rising action is full of suspense: Will the unsuspecting spouses find each other on the train? Luzhin sniffs cocaine in the toilet, on the day he has resolved to make his last. The princess has known the Luzhin family and recalls its former aristocratic opulence. Ironically, when the now plebeian Luzhin announces the first seating for dinner, his cocaine-rotted mind can only dimly note the princess; he cannot connect her to his elegant past.

The links between the two plots never interlock. Elena, disturbed by a rudely aggressive fellow passenger, decides to forgo the dinner in the dining car where she would probably have met her husband. She loses her prized golden wedding ring in the vestibule of the train's wagon; it is discovered by another waiter as Luzhin leaves the wagon and jumps to his death before another train: "The locomotive came at him in one hungry bound." Missed chances abound—perhaps too many: Nabokov's uses of coincidence and his insistence on the malignity of haphazard events strain credulity.

Perhaps Nabokov's most accomplished story of the 1920's is "Podlets" ("the scoundrel," retitled by the author "An Affair of Honor" for its English publication). In his foreword to the English translation, Nabokov explains that "'An Affair of Honor' renders, in a drab expatriate setting, the degradation of a romantic theme whose decline had started with Chekhov's magnificent story 'The Duel' (1891)." Nabokov situates the duel within the traditional love triangle. The husband, an affluent banker named Anton Petrovich, returns home early from a business trip to find an arrogant acquaintance, Berg, nonchalantly getting dressed in his bedroom while his wife, Tanya, whom the reader never sees, is taking an interminable bath. Anton Petrovich challenges Berg to a duel. He pulls off his new glove and tries to throw it at Berg. Instead, it "slapped against the wall and dropped into the washstand pitcher." The ludicrous failure of Anton Petrovich's challenge sets the farcical, burlesque tone for the tale.

Anton Petrovich is a loving, tender, hardworking, amiable fellow whose major fault—abject cowardice—becomes his undoing. Chekhov would have treated him gently and compassionately; Nabokov handles him disdainfully and absurdly, emphasizing his fondness for his shiny fountain pen, expensive shoes and socks, and monocle which "would gleam like a foolish eye on his belly." A duel is arranged but does not actually take place. Anton Petrovich, who has never fired a weapon, shakes with increasing fear at the prospect of confronting a former White Army officer who boasts of having killed hundreds. Before entering the woods where the combat is to occur, he and his caricatured seconds stop at a tavern for a round of beers. Anton Petrovich thereupon runs into the bar's backyard, slides and slips ridiculously down a slope, stumbles his way back to a train, and thence rides back to Berlin. He fantasizes that his craven flight will have been overshadowed by Berg's even earlier change of mind about dueling and that his wife will leave Berg and return to him, filled with love, delighted to satisfy him with an enormous ham sandwich.

Abruptly, Anton Petrovich awakens from his fiction. "Such things don't happen in real life," he reflects. He realizes that his reputation, his career, and his marriage are now ruined. He orders a ham sandwich and, animalistically, "grabbed the sandwich with both hands, immediately soiled his fingers and chin with the hanging margin of fat, and grunting greedily, began to munch." Nabokov has here begun to command the art of grotesquerie, precisely observed, relentlessly rendered, contemptuously concluded. Anton Petrovich would serve as a model for Albinus Kretschmar, cuckolded lover and failed artist in the novel *Kamera obskura* (1932; *Camera Obscura*, 1936; revised as *Laughter in the Dark*, 1938). Kretschmar in turn is a prototype for *Lolita*'s Humbert Humbert.

An amusing as well as saddening early exercise in playing mirror games, which were to become more and more convoluted in Nabokov's fiction, is his 1933 story "Admiralteyskaya Igla" ("The Admiralty Spire"). Its narrator addresses a trashy Soviet female writer who uses the pseudonymous male name, Sergey Solntsev. He asserts that her cheap romantic novel, *The Admiralty Spire*, is a vulgar version of his first love affair, sixteen years earlier, with a young woman named Katya, whom the writer has renamed Olga. He accuses her of "pretentious fabrication" and of having "encroached with astonishing insolence on another person's past!" The letter proceeds to lecture the writer on the correct, nostalgic use of the sentimental past, but in the process of recall, the writer admits his distaste for Katya's "mendacity, her presumption, her vacuity" and deplores her "myopic soul" and the "triviality of [her] opinions." He did, however, once love her. The narrator ends with the speculation that the mediocre novelist he is addressing is probably Katya herself, "who, out of silly coquetry, has concocted a worthless book." He hopes against the odds that his presumption is erroneous. The atmosphere of overlapping dimensions of reality established here was to be splendidly employed in such later novels as *Pale Fire* and *Ada or Ardor*.

In "Oblako, ozero, bashnya" ("Cloud, Castle, Lake"), the protagonist, a timid, intellectual bachelor, Vasili Ivanovich, wins a pleasure trip at a charity ball for Russian expatriates in Berlin. He is the kind, meek, saintly soul familiar in Russian literature since Gogol's stories. He does not really want to take the journey but is intimidated by bureaucratic mazes into doing so. Obstacles thwart him persistently: Trying to settle down with a volume of Russian poetry, Vasili is instead bullied by a squadron of husky German fellow travelers, with monstrous knapsacks and hobnailed boots, into forced communal games that prove witless and humiliating. When the group pairs off, no one wants to romance him: He is designed "the loser and was forced to eat a cigarette butt." Unexpectedly, the group comes upon "a pure, blue lake," reflecting a large cloud and adjoining "an ancient, black castle." Overjoyed, Vasili wishes to surrender to the beautiful prospect and remain the rest of his life in the inn from which he can delight in this tableau. Unfortunately for Vasili, the group insists on dragging him back and beats him furiously during the return journey.

The tale is manifestly an allegory mourning the defeat of individuality and privacy in an ugly world determined to enforce total conformity. "Oh, but this is nothing less than an invitation to a beheading," protests Vasili as the group grimly denies him his room with a view. By no accident, Nabokov would soon write his novel, *Priglashenie na kazn'* (1938; *Invitation to a Beheading*, 1959), whose main character, Cincinnatus C., is condemned to death for not fitting into a totalitarian culture. Nabokov may have occasionally presented himself as an arrogant, coldhearted puppeteer lacking any world-mending concerns, but he does clearly condemn all cultures of regimentation and authoritarianism.

"Vesna v Fialte" ("Spring in Fialta") was to become the title work of a collection of Nabokov's short stories; some critics regard it as the masterpiece among his stories, although others prefer "Signs and Symbols." The narrator of "Spring in Fialta," Victor, is a Russian émigré businessman who, over the course of fifteen years, has had sporadic meetings with a charmingly casual, pretty, vital woman named Nina. These encounters are sometimes sexual but never last more than a few hours and occur outside their continuing lives and separate marriages. "Again and again," Victor notes, "she hurriedly appeared in the margin of my life, without influencing in the least its basic text." So, at least, he believes. He has his respectably bourgeois world "in which I sat for my portrait, with my wife, my young daughters, the Doberman pinscher." Yet he finds himself also drawn to Nina's world of carefree sexuality mixed with "lies . . . futility . . . gibberish." This tension that Victor experiences is common in both life and literature, and Nabokov's characters are not immune. Although Nabokov appears to admire uxoriousness, as in the marriages of the Shades in *Pale Fire* or the Krugs in *Bend Sinister*, his protagonists are also mesmerized by *belles dames sans merci*—Margot (renamed Magda) in *Laughter in the Dark*, Lolita, Ada, and many more.

Nina is married to a gifted but repulsive Franco-Hungarian writer, Ferdinand; she also travels with the equally offensive but far less talented writer, Segur. Both men are artist figures, selfish, artificial, buoyant, heartless. Nina, while adaptable and "loyally sharing [Ferdinand's] tastes," is not really his muse: She represents life's vulnerability, and her attempt to imitate Ferdinand's world proves fatal: When the car in which the three ride crashes into a truck, Ferdinand and Segur, "those invulnerable rogues, those salamanders of fate... had escaped with local and temporary injury... while Nina, in spite of her long-standing, faithful imitation of them, had turned out after all to be mortal." Life can only copy art, not replace it.

In "Signs and Symbols," Nabokov wrote his most sorrowful story. An elderly, poor Russian émigré couple intend to pay a birthday visit to their son, institutionalized in a sanatorium, afflicted with "referential mania" in which "the patient imagines that everything happening around him is a veiled reference to his personality and existence." On their way to the sanatorium the machinery of existence seems to malfunction: The subway loses its electric current between stations; the bus is late and crammed with noisy schoolchildren; they are pelted by pouring rain as they walk the last stretch of the way. Finally, instead of being able to see their son, they are informed that he has again attempted suicide and should not be disturbed. The couple return home with the present that they cannot give him, wordless with worry and defeat, the woman close to tears. On their way they see "a tiny, half-dead unfledged bird... helplessly twitching in a puddle."

After a somber supper, the husband goes to bed, and the wife reviews a family photo album filled with the faces of mostly suffering or dead relatives. One cousin is a "famous chess player"—Nabokov's oblique reference to Luzhin of *The Defense*, who commits suicide. In his previous suicide attempt, the son had wanted "to tear a hole in his world and escape." In the story's last section, the time is past midnight, the husband is sleepless and in pain, and the couple decide to bring their boy home from the institution; each parent will need to spend part of each night with him. Then the phone rings: a wrong number. When it rings a second time, the wife carefully explains to the same caller how she must have misdialed. After a while, the phone rings for the third time; the story ends. The signs and symbols in all likelihood suggest that the last call is from the sanatorium, to announce that the son has succeeded in escaping this world.

Artistically, this story is virtually flawless: intricately patterned, densely textured, remarkably intense in tone and feeling. For once, Nabokov the literary jeweler has cut more deeply than his usual surfaces; for once, he has entered the frightening woods of tragic, unassuageable grief; for once, he has forsaken gamesmanship and mirror-play, punning and parody and other gambits of verbal artifice to face the grimmest horrors of a sometimes hopeless world.

Other major works

NOVELS: *Mashenka*, 1926 (*Mary*, 1970); *Korol', dama, valet*, 1928 (*King, Queen, Knave*, 1968); *Zashchita Luzhina*, 1929 (*The Defense*, 1964); *Soglyadatay*, 1930 (novella; *The Eye*, 1965); *Podvig*, 1932 (*Glory*, 1971); *Kamera obskura*, 1932 (*Camera Obscura*, 1936; revised as *Laughter in the Dark*, 1938); *Otchayanie*, 1934 (*Despair*, 1937, revised 1966); *Dar*, 1937-1938, 1952 (*The Gift*, 1963); *Priglashenie na kazn'*, 1938 (*Invitation to a Beheading*, 1959); *The Real Life of Sebastian Knight*, 1941; *Bend Sinister*, 1947; *Lolita*, 1955; *Pale Fire*, 1962; *Ada or Ardor: A Family Chronicle*, 1969; *Transparent Things*, 1972; *Look at the Harlequins!*, 1974.

PLAYS: *Smert'*, 1923; *Dedushka*, 1923; *Polius*, 1924; *Tragediya gospodina Morna*, 1924; *Chelovek iz SSSR*, 1927; *Sobytiye*, 1938; *Izobretenie Val'sa*, 1938 (*The Waltz Invention*, 1966).

SCREENPLAY: *Lolita*, 1962.

POETRY: *Stikhi*, 1916; *Dva Puti*, 1918; *Gorny put*, 1923; *Grozd'*, 1923; *Stikhotvorenia, 1929-1951*, 1952; *Poems*, 1959; *Poems and Problems*, 1970.

NONFICTION: *Nikolai Gogol*, 1944; *Conclusive Evidence: A Memoir*, 1951; *Drugie berega*, 1954; *Speak, Memory: An Autobiography Revisited*, 1966 (revision of *Conclusive Evidence* and *Drugie berega*); *Strong Opinions*, 1973; *The Nabokov-Wilson Letters, 1940-1971*, 1979; *Lectures on Literature: British, French, and German*, 1980; *Lectures on Russian Literature*, 1981; *Lectures on Don Quixote*, 1983.

TRANSLATIONS: *Anya v strane chudes*, 1923 (of Lewis Carroll's novel *Alice in Wonderland*); *Three Russian Poets: Translations of Pushkin, Lermontov, and Tiutchev*, 1944 (with Dmitri Nabokov); *A Hero of Our Time*, 1958 (of Mikhail Lermontov's novel, with Dmitri Nabokov); *The Song of Igor's Campaign*, 1960 (of the twelfth century epic *Slovo o polki Igoreve*); *Eugene Onegin*, 1964 (of Alexander Pushkin's verse novel).

Bibliography

Appel, Alfred, Jr., and Charles Newman. *Nabokov*, 1970.

Field, Andrew. *Nabokov: His Life in Art*, 1967.

Fowler, Douglas. *Reading Nabokov*, 1974.

Lee, L. L. *Vladimir Nabokov*, 1976.

Morton, Donald E. *Vladimir Nabokov*, 1974.

TriQuarterly. No. 17 (Winter, 1970). Special Nabokov issue.

Williams, Carol T. "Nabokov's Dozen Short Stories: His World in Microcosm," in *Studies in Short Fiction*. XII (1976), pp. 213-222.

Gerhard Brand

R. K. NARAYAN

Born: Madras, India; October 10, 1906

Principal short fiction
Malgudi Days, 1941; *Dodu and Other Stories*, 1943; *Cyclone and Other Stories*, 1944; *An Astrologer's Day and Other Stories*, 1947; *Lawley Road and Other Stories*, 1956; *A Horse and Two Goats and Other Stories*, 1970; *Malgudi Days*, 1982 (expanded to include eight new stories as well as stories from previous collections); *Under the Banyan Tree and Other Stories*, 1985.

Other literary forms
Though R. K. Narayan is a short-story writer of distinction and repute, he is known principally as a novelist, chronicler of the mythical South Indian town of Malgudi, which also figures in his short fiction. His novels include *Swami and Friends* (1935), *The Bachelor of Arts* (1937), *The Dark Room* (1938), *The English Teacher* (1945; U.S. edition, *Grateful to Life and Death*, 1953), *Mr. Sampath* (1949; U.S. edition, *The Printer of Malgudi*, 1957), *The Financial Expert* (1952), *Waiting for the Mahatma* (1955), *The Guide* (1958), *The Man-Eater of Malgudi* (1961), *The Sweet-Vendor* (1967; U.S. edition, *The Vendor of Sweets*, 1967), *The Painter of Signs* (1976), *A Tiger for Malgudi* (1983), and *Talkative Man* (1986). *Gods, Demons, and Others* (1964) is a collection of fifteen tales from Indian myth and legend, translated into English and rewritten in Narayan's own terms. Narayan's two autobiographical works are *My Dateless Diary* (1960), a witty journal of his travels across America, and *My Days* (1974), which highlights more than four decades of his writing career and reveals how closely interconnected are his life and his work. Narayan's translations of the two famous Hindu epics—*The Ramayana: A Shortened Modern Prose Version of the Indian Epic* (1972) and *The Mahabharata: A Shortened Prose Version of the Indian Epic* (1978)—successfully capture the spirit of the originals; though the prose translations appear simple, they provide the Western reader with a meaningful introduction to the two of the world's greatest poems.

Achievements
Occupying a prominent place in the literary world for more than half a century, R. K. Narayan, an internationally recognized novelist and the grand patriarch of Indo-Anglian writers (writers of India writing in English), has received a number of literary awards and distinctions. In 1961, he received the National Prize of the Indian Literary Academy (Sahitya Akademi), India's highest literary honor, for his very popular novel *The Guide* (the motion picture of the novel in English and Hindi was also a great success); his other

honors include India's Padma Bhushan Award for distinguished service of a high order, 1964; the United States' National Association of Independent Schools Award, 1965; the English-speaking Union Award, 1975; the Royal Society of Literature Benson Medal, 1980; and several honorary degrees. In 1982, Narayan was made an honorary member of the American Academy and Institute of Arts and Letters.

Narayan invented for his oeuvre the town of Malgudi, considered by critics a literary amalgam of Mysore, where he has lived for several decades, and Madras, the city of his birth. He gently asserts that "Malgudi has been only a concept but has proved good enough for my purposes." In its imaginative scope, Narayan's Malgudi is similar to Faulkner's Yoknapatawpha County, but whereas Faulkner's vision is complex and dark-hued, Narayan's vision is simple, ironic, sad at times, yet ultimately comic.

Biography

Rasipuram Krishnaswami Narayan was born in Madras, South India, on October 10, 1906. Until the family moved to Mysore, he remained in Madras with his grandmother, who supervised his school and college education. In his autobiography, *My Days*, Narayan admits his dislike of education: He "instinctively rejected both education and examinations with their unwarranted seriousness and esoteric suggestions." Nevertheless, in 1930, he was graduated from Maharaja's College (now the University of Mysore).

In 1933, he met a tall, slim girl, Rajam, and immediately fell in love with her. In 1935, after overcoming almost insurmountable difficulties (to begin with, their horoscopes did not match), Narayan and Rajam were married. She was a great help in his creative work, but she lived to see publication of only three novels. She died of typhoid in 1939. Narayan's fourth novel, *Grateful to Life and Death*, dedicated to his dead wife, centers on the trauma of this loss and on a hard-won sense of reconciliation. Rajam is portrayed in some detail as Sushila in that novel and, later, as Srinivas' wife in *The Printer of Malgudi*.

Narayan had not begun his career as a writer without some false starts. Indeed, only after having worked at a number of jobs without satisfaction and success—he worked for a time in the civil service in Mysore, taught for a while, and served as a correspondent for *Madras Justice*—did Narayan finally embark upon writing as a full-time career. In the beginning, many of his writings were rejected—a traumatic experience which he bore with fortitude. He was firm in his resolve to make his living as a writer. Experiencing bitter dejection when several British publishers rejected his first novel, *Swami and Friends*, Narayan instructed a friend not to mail the manuscript back to him in India but to throw it into the Thames. Instead, his friend took the manuscript to Graham Greene, who was successful in finding a publisher for the novel. Thus, from a frustrating experience began the literary career of an eminent Commonwealth writer whose books are known throughout the world, both in English and in translation.

He has published a dozen novels, more than two hundred short stories, nonfiction, a book of stories from Indian myths and legends, and a few critical essays. He lives in Mysore, India, and is involved with Indian Thought Publications, which has published several of his works.

Analysis

R. K. Narayan has said that he found English the most rewarding medium to employ for his writing because it came to him very easily: "English is a very adaptable language. And it's so transparent it can take on the tint of any country." Critics frequently praise the unaffected standard English with which Narayan captures the Indian sensibility, particularly the South Indian ambience. His unpretentious style, his deliberate avoidance of convoluted expressions and complicated grammatical constructions, his gentle and subtle humor—all this gives his writing an elegant, unforced simplicity that is perfectly suited to the portrayal of ordinary life, of all classes and segments of Indian society—household servants, herdsmen, saints, crooks, merchants, beggars, thieves, hapless students.

Narayan is essentially an old-fashioned storyteller. With Addisonian wit, Twainian humor, and Chekhovian irony, he depicts everyday occurrences, moments of insight; while some of his stories are essentially sketches, quite undramatic, others feature the ironic reversals associated with O. Henry. While Narayan's characters are imbued with distinctively Indian values, their dilemmas are universal.

Among the nineteen stories in Narayan's first collection, *Malgudi Days*, there are two stories, "Old Bones" and "Neighbours' Help," that are laced with supernatural elements. This volume includes such memorable stories as "The Gold Belt," "The White Flower," "An End of Trouble," and "Under the Banyan Tree." Some of the stories may be viewed as social criticism; Narayan looks with a satiric eye on various aspects of traditional South Indian society, particularly the dowry system and the powerful role of astrology and other forms of superstition.

One of the finest stories in the collection, "The Mute Companions," centers on the ubiquitous Indian monkey, a source of meager income for poor people and a source of delight for children. Adopting the omniscient point of view yet without moralizing or judging, Narayan portrays the life of Sami the dumb beggar, whose "very existence depended on the behaviour of the monkey." Having taught the monkey several tricks, Sami is able for a time to subsist on the earnings of the clever creature, who is his "only companion." This brief story is an excellent specimen of Narayan's art, revealing his ability to portray a segment of society that typically goes unnoticed. The story emphasizes the passiveness characteristic of the poor Indian, his acceptance of his Karma, or fate. Narayan's gentle social criticism, too, emerges: "Usually he [Sami] avoided those big places where people were haughty, aloof, and inaccessible, and kept formidable dogs and servants." As in many of his stories, Narayan in "The Mute Companions" blends humor and sadness.

Malgudi Days, it should be noted, is also the title of a later collection, published in the United States in 1982. Eight of the thirty-two stories in this collection—"Naga," "Selvi," "Second Opinion," "Cat Within," "The Edge," "God and the Cobbler," "Hungry Child," and "Emden"—were previously uncollected; the remaining stories were selected from Narayan's two earlier volumes, *An Astrologer's Day* and *Lawley Road and Other Stories*.

In his second collection, *Dodu and Other Stories*, Narayan focuses on themes related to motherly love, South Indian marriages, the financial and economic frustrations of the middle class, and childhood. Among the outstanding pieces in this volume of seventeen stories are "Dodu," "Gandhi's Appeal," "Ranga," "A Change," "Forty-five a Month," and "The One-armed Giant." (Originally published in *The Hindu*, a Madras newspaper, as most of his stories have been, "The One-armed Giant" was the first story that Narayan wrote.) The title story, "Dodu," satirically focuses on adult attitudes toward children. "Dodu was eight years old and wanted money badly. Since he was only eight, nobody took his financial worries seriously. . . . Dodu had no illusions about the generosity of his elders. They were notoriously deaf to requests." One of the significant contributions of Narayan is his uncanny ability to portray children—their dreams, their mischief, their psychology. "Ranga," an early tale, is a moving story of a motherless child developing into a disillusioned youth. "Forty-five a Month" is a simple and tender story of the relationship of a father and his family—his wife and their young daughter. The conflict between economic security and the little pleasures of life is evocatively and movingly delineated; indeed, this depiction of a white-collar worker eking out his dreary existence reflects the experience of an entire generation in modern India.

The eighteen stories in Narayan's third collection, *Cyclone and Other Stories*, offer vivid glimpses of Indian life and the Indian character. Perhaps the most notable feature of this volume is the emphasis on surprising twists of plot. One story of this type, "An Astrologer's Day," became the title story of Narayan's next collection, which includes twenty-four stories from earlier volumes and six new stories. Of the latter, "The Watchman," "Crime and Punishment," and "The Tiger's Claw" are particularly noteworthy. "The Tiger's Claw" is narrated by one of Narayan's most engaging recurring characters, whom the people of Malgudi have nicknamed "Talkative Man," or TM for short. Narayan's use of this narrator evokes India's rich oral traditions and lends great charm to the tale.

In *Lawley Road and Other Stories*, Narayan is concerned more with character than with plot. He notes that he discovers "a story when a personality passes through a crisis of spirit or circumstances," but some stories present flashes of significant moments in characters' lives without any dramatic circumstances; others simply show "a pattern of existence brought to view." Many of the pieces in this collection have a reportorial quality—there are sketches and vignettes, character studies and anecdotes. Of the twenty-eight stories gathered here, fourteen are reprinted from previous collections. The title story is delightful. Named after a typical thoroughfare in the fictitious city of Malgudi, the story recounts how Kabir Lane is renamed as Lawley Road. Once again, the narrator is the Talkative Man, who lends distance and historicity to the story. In another strong story, "The Martyr's Corner," the focus is on a humble seller of *bondas*, *dosais* (South Indian snacks), and *chappatis* (wheat-flour pancakes) rather than on the violent action. It is the character of the vendor)—his dreary and drab life and his attitude toward existence—that holds the interest of the reader.

A Horse and Two Goats and Other Stories comprises five stories with illustrations by Narayan's brother R. K. Laxman. Three of the stories, "A Horse and Two Goats," "Seventh House," and "Uncle," originally appeared in *The New Yorker*, in somewhat different form. "A Breath of Lucifer" originally appeared in *Playboy*, while the fifth story, "Annamalai," was first published in *Encounter*. (The latter also appears in the 1985 collection *Under the Banyan Tree and Other Stories*.) The title story deals with Muni, a village peasant, and his meeting with a "red man" from the United States. The language barrier is responsible for confusion about a statue and a pair of goats, with hilarious results. The second story, "Uncle," is a masterpiece; it slowly unfolds the mystery that teases a growing boy about his benevolent but inexplicably sinister "uncle." "Annamalai" and "A Breath of Lucifer" deal with two simple, hardworking, faithful servants. Annamalai is an eccentric gardener who attaches himself to a reluctant master. Sam in "A Breath of Lucifer," with an autobiographical preface, is a Christian male nurse. In the end, both Annamalai and Sam, governed by their own impulses, unceremoniously leave their masters. "Seventh House," perhaps a continuation of "The White Flower" in *Lawley Road and Other Stories*, dealing in astrology and superstitions, touchingly explores a husband's tender devotion to his sick wife. Each of the five stories is a character study; all the stories are embellished with picturesque native customs. The dominant tone throughout the collection is casual, understated.

Under the Banyan Tree and Other Stories is a superb retrospective collection of twenty-eight tales, published specifically for American readers; almost all the stories are drawn from earlier volumes. When the collection appeared on the American scene, several glowing reviews were published in the leading weeklies and periodicals. This collection further confirms Malgudi's place as a great imaginary landscape. The title story, fittingly taken from Narayan's first collection, reaffirms storytelling as a central human activity. The villagers of Somal "lived in a kind of perpetual enchantment. The enchanter was Nambi the story-teller." Yet, having regaled his audience for several years with his tales, Nambi spends the rest of his life in "great consummate silence."

As an old-fashioned storyteller, Narayan has sought to convey the vitality of his native India, a land that is full of humanity, oddity, poverty, tradition, "inherited culture," picturesqueness. Narayan realizes "that the short story is best medium for utilizing the wealth of subjects available. A novel is a different proposition altogether, centralized as it is on a major theme, leaving out, necessarily, a great deal of the available material on the periphery. Short stories, on the other hand, can cover a wider field by presenting concentrated miniatures of human experience in all its opulence." Narayan's concern is the heroic in the ordinary Indian. John Updike affirms that "all people are complex, surprising, and deserving of a break: this seems to me Narayan's moral, and one hard to improve upon. His social range and his successful attempt to convey, in sum, an entire population shame most American authors, who also, it might be charged, 'ignore too much of what could be seen.'" With dignified simplicity, honesty, and sincerity, Narayan infuses his stories with charm and spontaneous humor; he guides the reader through his comic and ironic world with an unobtrusive wit.

Other major works

NOVELS: *Swami and Friends*, 1935; *The Bachelor of Arts*, 1937; *The Dark Room*, 1938; *The English Teacher*, 1945 (U.S. edition, *Grateful to Life and Death*, 1953); *Mr. Sampath*, 1949 (U.S. edition, *The Printer of Malgudi*, 1957); *The Financial Expert*, 1952; *Waiting for the Mahatma*, 1955; *The Guide*, 1958; *The Man-Eater of Malgudi*, 1961; *The Sweet-Vendor*, 1967 (U.S. edition, *The Vendor of Sweets*, 1967); *The Painter of Signs*, 1976; *A Tiger for Malgudi*, 1983; *Talkative Man*, 1986.

NONFICTION: *Mysore*, 1944; *My Dateless Diary*, 1960; *The Reluctant Guru*, 1964; *My Days*, 1974.

TRANSLATIONS: *Gods, Demons, and Others*, 1964 (of tales from Indian myth and legend); *The Ramayana: A Shortened Modern Prose Version of the Indian Epic*, 1972; *The Mahabharata: A Shortened Prose Version of the Indian Epic*, 1978.

MISCELLANEOUS: *Next Sunday: Sketches and Essays*, 1960.

Bibliography

Atma Ram, ed. *Perspectives on R. K. Narayan*, 1982.
Goyal, Bhagwat S. *R. K. Narayan: A Critical Spectrum*, 1983.
Holmstrom, Lakshmi. *The Novels of R. K. Narayan*, 1973.
Raizada, H. C. *R. K. Narayan: A Critical Study of His Works*, 1969.
Sundaram, P. S. *R. K. Narayan*, 1973.

230

Walsh, William. *R. K. Narayan*, 1971.
Westbrook, Perry D. "The Short Stories of R. K. Narayan," in *Journal of Commonwealth Literature*. No. 5 (July, 1968), pp. 41-51.

S. S. Moorty

KENZABURŌ ŌE

Born: Ōse, on the island of Shikoku, Japan; January 31, 1935

Principal short fiction

Kodoku na seinen no kyūka, 1960; "Sebuntīn," 1961; "Seiji shōnen shisu," 1961; *Seiteki ningen*, 1963; *Warera no kyōki o ikinobiru michi o oshieyo*, 1969 (*Teach Us to Outgrow Our Madness*, 1977).

Other literary forms

Although Kenzaburō Ōe first gained attention through his short stories, which are included in many anthologies of postwar Japanese writing, he has also written many novels, such as *Kojinteki na taiken* (1964; *A Personal Matter*, 1968) and *Manengannen no futtoboru* (1967; *The Silent Cry*, 1974). In addition, Ōe has published many essays on literature and politics, the latter reflecting his political activism.

Achievements

Ōe emerged in the late 1950's as one of the leading figures of the postwar generation of writers. His short story "Shiiku" ("The Catch") received the coveted Akutagawa Prize in 1958, while he was still a university student. *A Personal Matter* won the 1964 Shinchōsha Literary Prize and *The Silent Cry* won the Tanizaki Jun'ichirō Prize in 1967. Ōe has also received the Noma Literary Prize and the Osaragi Jirō Prize for other works. He has traveled as an official delegate to China and has visited many other countries as well.

Biography

Kenzaburō Ōe was born on January 31, 1935, in a small village on Shikoku, the smallest of Japan's four main islands. The third son of seven children, he was only six when World War II erupted; he lost his father. Ōe was ten when Hiroshima and Nagasaki were destroyed by atomic attack as the war ended. He entered prestigious Tokyo University in 1954, studying French literature, and burst upon the literary scene while still a student there, publishing a short story, "Shisa no ogori" ("Lavish Are the Dead"), in the magazine *Bungakukai* in 1957. It attracted attention, and his talent was widely recognized when he received the prestigious Akutagawa Prize in 1958 for his "The Catch," which draws upon his experience as a boy in a remote rural village during World War II.

After his graduation, Ōe married Itami Yukari, the daughter of screenwriter Itami Mansaku, in February, 1960. In May of that year he was a member of the Japan-China Literary Delegation, which met with Mao Tse-tung. The next year he traveled in the Soviet Union and Europe, where he met Jean-Paul Sartre.

Drawing upon his childhood, Ōe dealt in his early works with alienation and those on the fringes of society, as well as political issues, contemporary society, and sexual mores. In the summer of 1963, however, his first son was born with serious brain damage, leading him to a new stage in his writing, in which he affirmed hope arising from despair. In five works written between 1964 and 1976, Ōe used the persistent theme of a father dealing with an idiot son: *A Personal Matter* and "Sora no kaibutsu Agui" ("Aghwee the Sky Monster") are notable examples.

In 1965 Ōe traveled to the United States, returning there for another visit in 1968. He also visited Australia, and in 1970 he toured Southeast Asia. He made frequent literary appearances, and in 1975 took part in a two-day fast protesting the treatment of Korean writer and poet Kim Chi Ha. In the late 1970's he wrote two more novels, then turned to short stories in 1980. Throughout his career, Ōe has been a prolific writer; by 1976, his narratives filled two six-volume editions, and sixteen volumes are filled with his collected essays. He currently lives in Tokyo.

Analysis

Prewar Japanese writers such as Jun'ichirō Tanizaki and Yasunari Kawabata, who continued to build their literary reputations after the war, focused on the introspective (notably in the so-called I-novel), but New Left writers such as Kenzaburō Ōe, emerging after the war, are as indebted to Western literary traditions as they are to those of Japan. Like his contemporary Kōbō Abe, Ōe writes about alienation from modern society and the loss of identity in modern Japan. He does so by using as themes his childhood in a small village, the war and subsequent occupation by Americans, and the personal tragedy of his son's birth defect.

In "The Catch," the boy-narrator is combing the village crematory looking for bone fragments with friends when an American plane roars overhead at treetop level. The next morning, the children awaken to an ominous silence. The adults are out searching for downed American airmen. They return late in the day from the mountains, leading an enormous black man. The boy is reminded of a boar hunt as the hunters silently circle around the captive, who has the chain from a boar trap around his legs.

The enemy excites both fear and curiosity among the children. He is put into the cellar of the communal storehouse and a guard is posted. The storehouse is a large building, and the boy and his younger brother live on the second floor with their father, an impoverished hunter. The boy is excited at the thought of sleeping in the same building as the exotic prisoner who has fallen into their midst.

At first the captive is treated as a dangerous animal. The boy goes with his father to town to report the capture. He is uncomfortable in the town, aware of his poverty and dirtiness. The local officials refuse to take the prisoner until they receive orders from the prefecture offices. The boy and his father return to the village at sunset with the unwelcome news.

The boy carries food down into the dark cellar, guarded by his father with shotgun ready. At first the captive only stares at the food, and the boy realizes in shame that the poor dinner might be rejected, but the black man suddenly devours the meal. Gradually the boy loses his fear of the American as they bring him food every day. The children begin to take a proprietary interest in the captive. As time passes, the adults return to their field work, and the children are left with the American. Noticing that the man's leg is wounded from the boar trap, the boy and his friend release him with trepidation, but they find him well-behaved. Even the adults in the village accept the idea that the black man is human, coming to trust him.

Eventually the children let the captive out of the cellar to walk through the village. The adults come to accept this, and he is even allowed to wander around the village alone. The women lose their fear and give him food from their own hands. The children take him to the village spring, where they all strip naked and splash in the water. The boy considers the man a splendid animal, an animal of great intelligence.

Trust and respect evaporate, however, when an official appears on a rainy day. As the adults assemble, the prisoner senses that he is about to be taken away, and he grabs the boy and drags him to the cellar, locking the door behind them. The boy is shocked and hurt as he realizes his sudden danger and sees the airman reverting to the dangerous beast he was when first captured. The grown-ups break into the cellar, and the boy's father plunges a hatchet into the prisoner's skull. They plan to cremate the black man but are ordered to keep the body for identification.

The story ends in irony. Paying another visit, the village official notices the children using the lightweight tail of the American plane as a sled on the grass. In a playful mood, he decides to give it a try, but he hurtles into a rock and is killed. He will be cremated, the villagers using the wood collected to cremate the American captive.

Although the story is set during the war years and the events occur in the context of unusual hardship, its major theme, a youth's coming-of-age, is a universal one: The young boy finds his childhood innocence and trust betrayed by the black captive and the adults who rush to rescue him in a frenzy of hatred. There are echoes of *The Adventures of Huckleberry Finn* (1884) in this story: in the young boys' spirit of adventure, in their unaffected wonder and curiosity, and in their rejection of adult attitudes. (It is not surprising that, during his trip to the United States in 1965, Ōe visited Hannibal, Missouri, the birthplace of Mark Twain.) The coming-of-age theme also underscores another major concern in the story: man's (as opposed to boy's) inhumanity to man: Ōe uses juxtaposition to create a realistic yet somehow absurd view of the world; the young narrator allows him to introduce humorous elements of childish enthusiasm that make the final tragedy all the more appalling.

In the short story "Aghwee the Sky Monster," a young father is haunted by an imaginary baby that flies down from the sky, reminding him of his own baby, whom he killed in the false belief that it had a malignant brain tumor. The story is told through a young college student, who is hired to take care of a banker's son. The student is told that the son, a composer, is having delusions and requires supervision. Needing the money, the student agrees to act as a chaperon, to help keep the son's mind off his delusions. The student accompanies the composer on trips about Tokyo, wary of the possibility that his charge may, at any moment, be joined by the imaginary Aghwee.

He learns that Aghwee is a fat baby, dressed in a white nightgown, who is as big as a kangaroo. From time to time, the composer believes that he sees Aghwee flying down to his side; this naturally alarms the student chaperon, who worries about a possible suicide attempt. In time, the student learns to step aside to leave room for the imaginary baby as they make excursions to bars, motion-picture theaters, and swimming pools, where they invariably turn back without entering the water. When the composer gets his chaperon to take a message to a former lover in Kyoto, the student learns that the lovers were in bed together in a hotel room when a call came from the hospital informing them of the death of the baby, who had uttered only one sound, "Aghwee."

Then disaster strikes. While walking on the Ginza on Christmas Eve with the composer and Aghwee, the student is shocked as they are mysteriously pitched forward into the path of a truck; the student escapes serious harm, but the composer is fatally injured. Visiting the dying composer in the hospital later that day, the student admits that he was about to believe in Aghwee, and the composer smiles. He dies the next day.

Ten years later, the student is suddenly attacked by rock-throwing children who have been mysteriously provoked. One of the rocks hits him in the eye, and he suddenly senses a large white being the size of a kangaroo: Aghwee. He has completed his identification with the dead composer's fantasy.

In his lengthy short story "Mizu kara waga namida o nuguitamau hi" ("The Day He Himself Shall Wipe My Tears Away"), Ōe again writes about a man who is trying to grasp the reality of his youth, this time in an isolated farm village as the war was ending. It is difficult and sometimes frustrating work, and the background of the story is only gradually revealed as the protagonist shifts from the present to a mythical reconstruction of events.

The story opens in a hospital room where the man is dying, or imagines he is dying (this is never resolved), of cancer. What is clear is that the narrator is grappling with a lifetime struggle to free himself from his mother's harsh and stifling influence. He is dictating a history of the events leading to his father's bizarre death in a futile uprising on August 16, 1945, the day after the Japanese surrender in World War II. He attempts to shut his mother and the rest of the contemporary world out by wearing his father's old goggles, which are masked with green cellophane. His identification with his father and his reconstruction of events that he only dimly understood as a six-year-old boy are meant to challenge his mother's sarcastic realism and allow him to relive the most important moment in his life.

The boy's father apparently was involved in right-wing political activities with the military in Manchuria. After Japan's military fortunes took a turn for the worse at Midway and Guadalcanal, the father was involved with an underground group that was against Prime Minister Tōjō. Their plans to change policy failed, for the father suddenly appeared in the valley on January 1, 1943, going straight into seclusion in the storehouse.

The boy's elder stepbrother was sent to war and became the valley's first war casualty. Even though he was not her own son, the narrator's mother took the death as a failure of the father and his politics. Thereafter, his name was never spoken in the family; throughout the story he is referred to as "a certain party," who lived by himself in a shed in back of the main house. His mother also shut herself off from all contact with the neighbors in the valley, ignoring everyone from that day on.

The valley was not a peaceful childhood sanctuary for the young boy, for he was subject to ridicule and hazing by the village children at school. When school bullies taunted him for his impoverished appearance, he stabbed himself in the hand with a hand sickle and threatened to slit his own throat if they attempted to harm him. Confused and appalled, the gang backed off because the boy did not react normally: "He's like a *kamikaze* pilot that didn't get to die!" In the same fashion, the narrator, now thirty-five years old, hopes to upstage his elderly mother by dying of real or imagined cancer.

He was still psychologically wounded by her actions when she caught him attempting suicide when he was almost out of high school. She took his suicide note, stole into the mimeograph room of the school, printed it, and distributed it to all of his teachers and classmates to reveal his weakness. To complete his humiliation, she noted all the incorrect characters he had written in the sentimental will. By making him the fool, she made it impossible for him to consider suicide in the future. Now he believes that cancer can get her attention.

As a boy he both feared and admired his father, wanting to be recognized and accepted, but he was ignored. His father was repugnantly fat, spending his days in semidarkness, sitting in a barber chair, wearing the green goggles. While in Manchuria he had acquired the habit of eating meat, and he had sent the boy to town to buy the only meat Japanese would not eat, oxtails and pig feet. Acquiring his loathsome burden, the boy also had had to visit Korean forest workers to ask for some garlic to flavor the stew his father was going to make. His father had emerged from his dark room to cook the meat outdoors but collapsed on the boy, venting blood and urine. The doctor had been summoned and had diagnosed cancer of the bladder. From that time, the summer of 1944, his father had remained inside the storehouse, his disease slowly progressing.

The critical incident in the story is the appearance in the valley of ten soldiers who had deserted their unit when the surrender of Japan was announced. They came to the house to enlist the support of the former political activist, but also to get the funds that the boy's mother had inherited. That night, the soldiers made plans to go to the city the next day to get money from the bank; they hoped to capture some army planes, disguise them as American planes, and somehow fly to Tokyo and crash them into the Imperial Palace in a final attempt to get the Japanese people to rise up against the invaders. They drank sake and listened over and over to an old German record on the phonograph, a Bach cantata with the line, "His Majesty the Emperor wipes my tears away with his own hand, Death, you come ahead, you brother of Sleep you come ahead, his Majesty will wipe my tears away with his own hand. . . ." It is from this evocation of the prewar imperial ethos that Ōe chose his title.

The next morning, the ten soldiers pulled the father in a hand-built cart to a truck they had stolen and drove to town. The boy's father was bleeding from his terminal cancer and was in considerable pain, but he agreed to lead the quixotic band. The group vowed *junshi*, or death as a sign of allegiance to the emperor. As they emerged from the bank—it was not clear whether they had robbed it or made a withdrawal on the mother's account—they encountered another band of soldiers who opened fire on them, killing all of them except the young boy.

Just as the narrator gets to this crux of the story, the mother suddenly speaks from the corner of the hospital room. She may have been there all along, taking it all in. His mother narrates a different account, describing in cynical terms the soldiers who came after the money and the futility of the make-believe uprising. She shatters the mythical reconstruction the narrator has been trying to build, once again dominating his life and reducing him to a madness that only death will relieve.

One of the most prolific and popular writers in Japan, Ōe, in these and other stories, clearly reflects the concerns of the postwar generation, a generation that saw the fall of old symbols such as the Emperor. The war and defeat of Japan left a void in which his characters try to find themselves, groping for meaning. In "The Catch," the harmony of rural Japan is shattered as a young boy is disillusioned by the adults around him. In "The Day He Himself Shall Wipe My Tears Away," a boy sees his father's death as a sacrifice to the old values. This same hero appears in Ōe's later writing— older, but trying to escape through sex and deviant behavior. Ōe's unique style, heavily influenced by Western traditions and directness, is fresh and controversial, undergirding the issue addressed in most if not all of his fiction: the cultural disharmony that his generation has experienced as a result of World War II and its aftermath. In writing about his own personal crisis, Ōe deals with the larger themes of modernity and meaning in Japan. Like the hero in his favorite novel, *The Adventures of Huckleberry Finn*, Ōe sees life as a quest for adventure, whether in Africa or in the back streets of Tokyo—a quest for truth.

Other major works

NOVELS: *Memushiri kouchi*, 1958; *Warera no jidai*, 1959; *Yoru yo yuruyaka ni ayume*, 1959; *Seinen no omei*, 1960; *Okurete kita seinen*, 1962; *Sakebigoe*, 1963; *Kojinteki na taiken*, 1964 (*A Personal Matter*, 1968); *Manengannen no futtoboru*, 1967 (*The Silent Cry*, 1974); *Kōzui wa waga tamashii ni oyobi*, 1973; *Pinchi rannā chōso*, 1976; *Dōjidai geimu*, 1979.

NONFICTION: *Genshuku na tsunawatari*, 1965; *Hiroshimo nōto*, 1965; *Kowaremono to shite no ningen*, 1970; *Kakujidai no sōzōryoku*, 1970; *Okinawa nōto*, 1970; *Dōjidai to shite no sengo*, 1973; *Jyōkyō e*, 1974.

Bibliography

Wilson, Michiko N. *The Marginal World of Ōe Kenzaburō: A Study in Themes and Techniques*, 1986.

_____. "Ōe's Obsessive Metaphor, Mori the Idiot Son: Toward the Imagination of Satire, Regeneration, and Grotesque Realism," in *Journal of Japanese Studies*. VII (Winter, 1981), pp. 23-25.

Yoshida, Sanroku. "Kenzaburō Ōe: A New World of Imagination," in *Comparative Literature Studies*. XXII (Spring, 1985), pp. 80-96.

Richard Rice

P'U SUNG-LING

Born: P'u-chia-chuang Village, China; June 5, 1640
Died: Tzǔ'ch'uan County, China; February 25, 1715

Principal short fiction

Liao-chai chih-i, 1766 (*Strange Stories from a Chinese Studio*, 1880); *Liao-chai chih-i wei-k'an kao*, 1936; *Chinese Ghost and Love Stories: A Selection from the Liao-chai Stories by P'u Sung-ling*, 1946.

Other literary forms

Although P'u Sung-ling's literary fame rests solely on his collection of short fiction, *Strange Stories from a Chinese Studio* (comprising 431 stories), he was a versatile writer in both classical and colloquial Chinese. He was the author of various works, including a remarkable novel written in the vernacular titled *Hsing-shih yin-yüan chuan* (1870; the story of a marriage to rouse the world). Written under the pseudonym Hsi-Chou-shêng (Scholar of the Western Chou Period), this novel's author remained anonymous for two centuries, until Dr. Hu Shih, in the course of his important studies in the history of Chinese vernacular literature, revealed that the real name of the author was P'u Sung-ling. The earliest known printed edition is dated 1870, but in 1933 a punctuated edition was published to which were added some discussions of the authorship problem by various authors who were in agreement with Hu Shih's finding. The novel is a domestic tragedy, the story of a shrew and the henpecked husband whom she persecutes cruelly and unmercifully. Since this novel contains a million words presented in one hundred chapters, the torturous experiences of this unhappy marriage can be sustained only by the periodic introduction of humorous incidents to relieve the otherwise depressing pathos of the narrative. The author makes no effort to offer any solution for the unhappiness presented. The implication seems to be that according to folk belief such a consequence is simply the result of one's Karma in a previous incarnation. A very unusual feature of this monumental novel is that P'u Sung-ling succeeded in elevating the dialect of his district of Tzǔ'ch'uan—a variety of North China Mandarin—into a literary medium.

P'u Sung-ling's literary efforts were by no means confined to the writing of fiction, whether short or long. A man of parts, he wrote several kinds of poems: *shih* poems in regular meter (*shih-chi*); *tz'ǔ* poems set to preexisting tunes in irregular meter (*tz'ǔ-chi*); folk musical narratives: *ku-tz'ǔ*, or drum songs, and *li-ch'ü*, or folk songs. He wrote plays (*hsi-wên*) and numerous essays (*wên-chi*). He indulged in miscellaneous writings (*t'ung-ch'u*); a lexicon of colloquial expressions in daily use in the Tzǔ'ch'uan district; a treatise on agriculture and sericulture; a treatise on grass and trees; a manual on truancy; a satire on the examination of the self; books on dealing with hungry ghosts; correspondence; and desultory and neglected pieces. Apart from the *Liao-chai chih-i* and the novel mentioned above, all the works now attributed to P'u Sung-ling are included in the two-volume collection, *Liao-chai ch'üan-chi* (1933; complete works from the Chinese studio). *Liao-chai* does not mean "Chinese studio" but more like "casual studio"; Herbert A. Giles's freer translation, however, is not inappropriate.

Achievements

The Ch'ing, or Manchu, Dynasty, between its establishment in 1644 and the Opium War of 1840-1842, gave birth to at least four great literary masterpieces in drama and fiction. Drama produced Hung Shêng's *ch'uan ch'i* style opera, *Chang-shêng tien* (c. 1688; *The Palace of Eternal Youth*, 1955). Long fiction produced two great novels: Ts'ao Hsüeh-ch'in's romance, *Hung-lou mêng* (1792; *Dream of the Red Chamber*, 1929) and Wu Ching-tzǔ's satire, *Ju-lin wai-shih* (1768-1779; *The Scholars*, 1957). P'u Sung-ling's *Strange Stories from a Chinese Studio* is the great masterpiece of short fiction of the Ch'ing era. When he wrote a preface for his collection in 1679, P'u apparently had already assembled most of his tales and sketches, although some may have been written or revised afterward. The collection was never printed during the author's lifetime, but it did circulate in manuscript copies among his friends and acquaintances. A contemporaneous poet, critic, and government official, Wang Shih-chên, was the first to recognize the work as a masterpiece by writing comments on some of its contents. After P'u's death in 1715, the collection was first printed, according to Herbert A. Giles, by his grandson in 1740. The first prominent edition, however, was that collated and edited by his secretary, Yü Chi, in 1766, most authorities regarding this printing in sixteen *chüan* as the first edition. Other editions followed, but the sixteen-*chüan* edition produced in 1842 by Tan Ming-lun, which he collated with that of Yü Chi, became more or less standard and was used by Giles in his English translation.

After the printing of 1766, *Strange Stories from a Chinese Studio* attracted such widespread attention that the author's fame was assured. Educated readers with some literary training recognized that his work represented the perfected culmination of a long tradition of the use of classical Chinese for fictional narrative from the *shên chi* ("records of marvels") of the Wei and Tsin dynasties to the *ch'uan ch'i* ("strange transmissions")—the short prose romances of the T'ang Dynasty, whose range of subject matter is practically identical with that of P'u's stories. His superb handling of the *ku-wên* style, his ability to revivify old plots that had become hackneyed and flimsy through a new "magic realism" that made the improbable and the impossible probable and supernatural creatures, such as flower or fox spirits, seem human, went far beyond what had been accomplished in the past. His stories appealed to an unprecedented number of readers from many walks of life, not simply educated people with some literary training. Consequently, his fictions revived the *ch'uan ch'i* tradition for nearly a century. They inspired many imitations, including the anonymous *Hsing mêng p'i an yan* (late eighteenth century) and Chi Yün's *Yüeh-wei ts'ao-t'ang pi-chi* (1800). Both these works remain untranslated, but their titles in English can be translated, respectively, as "refined words to awaken one from dreams" and "notes of the Yüeh-wei hermitage." Chi Yün criticized P'u for mixing the detailed style of the T'ang *ch'uan ch'i* with the concise and unadorned style of the tales of T'ao Ch'ien (A.D. 365-427) and Liu I-Ch'ing (A.D. 403-444) of the Six Dynasties period. Regardless of such criticism, P'u's tales were admired for their masterly style, which combined terse expression with abundant literary allusions and succeeded in maintaining a contrasting yet harmonious balance between the fantastic and the realistic elements of his fiction.

Biography

P'u Sung-ling was born on June 5, 1640, in the village of P'u-chia chuang, Tzŭ'ch'uan County, Shantung Province, China. Possibly of Mongol ancestry, he was the son of P'u P'an, a merchant, who was also a man of action as well as of some learning. In this old but impoverished family of gentry there were scholars and officials such as P'u's granduncle, P'u Shêng-wên, who held the *chin-shih* ("entered scholar"), the highest, or "doctor's," degree, and was the magistrate of Yu-t'ien, in Chihli. In addition to his family name of P'u and his personal name of Sung-ling, P'u Sung-ling had two *tzŭ*, or "courtesy names," taken at age twenty, by which he was known among his friends— namely, Liu Hsien (Last of the Immortals) and Chien Ch'ên (Knight-errant). He further had two *hao*, or "artistic names," adopted on occasion as names for his library or studio, by which he was popularly known after he became famous: Lo Ch'üan (Willow Spring) and Liao Chai (Casual Studio).

In 1658, at age eighteen, P'u qualified for the lowest, or "bachelor's," degree, becoming a *hsiu-ts'ai* ("flowering talent"), which required him to pass three successive sets of examinations by writing eight or ten *pa-ku wên-chang*, or "eight-legged essays," on themes assigned from the "Four Books and Five Classics," as well as five poems on prescribed patterns. Yet, although he regularly took the provincial examinations for the next highest degree, the *chu-jên* ("promoted man"), or "master's," degree, he consistently failed. Not until 1711, at age seventy-one, did he succeed in being made a senior licentiate. Apparently his diverse interests prevented him from pursuing the traditional program of study rigorously enough.

As a result, P'u Sung-ling spent his life in a variety of activities. In 1670 he was employed as a secretary to Sun Hui, magistrate at Pao-ying, Kiangsu; the following year he accompanied Sun to Kao-yu County, where the latter served for a time as the acting magistrate. By the end of the year, P'u resigned his position and returned to Tzŭ-ch'uan. In 1672 he became secretary to a wealthy friend, Pi Chi-yu, sometime department magistrate of T'ung-chou, Kiangsu, a position which P'u held for nearly twenty years. The rest of his activities consisted of his employment as a licentiate to the district school from 1685 onward, private tutoring in the homes of local gentry, the management of his family affairs (he was happily married to an amiable wife by whom he had four sons, three of whom became licentiates), and the writing of short stories, poems, songs, and miscellaneous essays. His writing of short stories apparently began as early as 1660 and extended to, and possibly beyond, 1679, when he wrote a preface to *Strange Stories from a Chinese Studio*. Although in his day his literary genius was little known beyond the circle of his friends and acquaintances, eventually his fame was to spread over China and even to foreign lands. By 1848, his stories had been translated into Manchu, and by 1880, into English. In this century they have been translated into French, Japanese, German, and Russian.

P'u Sung-ling's preface to *Strange Stories from a Chinese Studio* reveals decided connections between his short stories and his personal life and sentiments. He begins, through references to clothes, by ridiculing the official classes and suggesting that they hold posts for which, from a literary standpoint, they are unfit. Furthermore, in his view, political intrigue in official circles is all too common. The evil machinations of bad and false men often destroy good men and true. As an example, he cites the case of the unfortunate statesman Ch'ü P'ing, who was ruined by the evil machinations of a political rival. As for himself, P'u acknowledges, he is no match for the "hobgoblins" of his time, by which he means the ruling classes. Furthermore, he confesses, he cannot claim the talent of a Kao Pao (fl. 317-323), the author of *Sou shen chi* (c. 320?; *Some Chinese Tales of the Supernatural*, 1941), but rather believes himself mostly inspired by the great poet, essayist, and calligrapher Su Tung-p'o (1036-1102), who liked hearing about the supernatural from others.

Evidently a man much attached to the Buddhist faith, P'u provides a Buddhist interpretation of his existence. He says that just prior to his own birth his father dreamed that a sickly-looking Buddhist priest, whose bare chest was flawed by a black birthmark, entered his chamber. When P'u Sung-ling was born, his chest contained the same kind of black birthmark. When he was a child, he, too, was sickly-looking and unable to hold his own in the struggle for existence. Furthermore, his parents' home was as cold and desolate as the typical Buddhist monastery. When he reached manhood, he attempted to make a living from his pen but remained as poor as a Buddhist priest with an alm's bowl. Although he is familiar with the three states of existence—past, present, and future, according to the Buddhist theory of metempsychosis—no one will listen to his explanations or accept his advice. He often scratches his head in perplexity to think of his low state and wonders whether his lack of success in life is attributable to the influence of a destiny that was determined in a prior existence. He wonders if he might not be a reincarnation of Bôdhidharma (died c. 530), the Indian monk who introduced the Ch'an, or meditation school of Buddhism (called Zen by the Japanese) into China but who failed to convert the Emperor Wu Ti of the Liang (reigned 502-550) to this way of thinking. Mortified at his failure, Bôdhidharma sat meditating for the sake of moral discipline before a blank wall for nine years.

Yet the paths of transmigration are enigmatic, says P'u; he will not complain. He does, however, seem a victim of circumstances, a man "tossed hither and thither in the direction of the ruling wind, like a flower falling in filthy places." This midnight finds him sitting alone in his studio at his dismal table, piecing his tales together below "an expiring lamp, while the wind whistles mournfully without." Vainly he had hoped perhaps to rival Liu I-ch'ing's book about the infernal regions, but conscious of his poor efforts he can only regard himself as an object of pity. "Alas!" he says sadly, "I am but the bird, that dreading the frost, finds no shelter in the tree; the autumn insect that chirps to the moon, and hugs the door for warmth." Like Confucius, as quoted in the *Lun yü* (5th century B.C.; *Confucian Analects*, 1893), his conversations as recorded by his students, P'u inquires, "For where are they who know me?" He himself answers, "They are 'in the bosky grove, and at the frontier pass' wrapped in impenetrable gloom!" That is, like the figure of Li T'ai-po, who is said to have appeared to Tu Fu in a dream, those who know him for what he really is are nonexistent.

In sum, taking the attitudes and sentiments appearing in P'u Sung-ling's preface and the circumstances of his biography and comparing these things with the short stories—their characterizations, themes, satire, and social criticism—leads to the definite conclusion that they embrace, in the words of J. Průšek, "P'u's own dreams and ideals" as well as his "personal view of life and his own philosophy."

In his last years P'u Sung-ling's family fortunes are said to have slightly improved. In 1713, his wife (née Liu) died. He and she had apparently led a happy but uneventful life together. His fondness for her is shown by the sketch of her life he wrote following her death and the several poems he composed dedicated to her memory. In three more years he himself died, on February 25, 1715, at his home in Tzŭ'ch'uan County.

Analysis

In his *Strange Stories from a Chinese Studio*, P'u Sung-ling mostly presents encounters between human beings and supernatural or fantastic creatures. The human beings may be students, scholars, officials, peasants, Taoist or Buddhist priests, fortune-tellers, magicians, maidens, wives, concubines, and so on. Some of these human beings, especially the Taoist or Buddhist priests and the magicians, may possess supernatural powers or illusionary skills of various kinds. The supernatural or fantastic creatures may be animals, birds, flowers, fairies, devils, or ghosts who have assumed human shape, or they may retain their natural forms but have the human powers of speech and understanding. Although when portraying supernatural or fantastic creatures P'u is highly imaginative, in dealing with ordinary mortals he controls his imagination to the degree that they are not exaggerated or unnatural. He appears to seek to make the extraordinary plausible and the ordinary interesting and to press home the point that the ordinary world is endowed always with extraordinary possibilities. His favorite themes seem to be changeableness, in which animals or devils are changed into human form or vice versa; reincarnation; living humans becoming immortals; the dead being brought back to life; male students falling in love with beautiful women; exposure of corrupt or incompetent officials; and criticism of the civil service examination system and of pedantic scholarship. Although P'u imitated the classical short tales of the T'ang Dynasty, he introduced original elements in terms of his personal views and he included criminal and detective stories in his collection. Some of his stories seem to have been written from motives of pure entertainment, but the majority of them state or imply some moral lesson. The early commentator T'ang Mêng-lai alleged that in most of P'u's tales he intended "to glorify virtue and to censure vice." Perhaps more specifically the stories demonstrate P'u's sincere or facetious conviction that in this world evildoers are eventually punished and the kindhearted are in the long run rewarded for their good deeds.

The following are some typical stories from the *Strange Stories from a Chinese Studio*:

"Chao-ch'êng hu" ("The Tiger of Chao-ch'êng") is the story of a tiger who eats the woodcutter son of an elderly widow who has no relations besides her son and depends entirely on him for her support. Thus left to starve to death, the mother indignantly journeys to town, where she enters the magistrate's *yamên* and levels a charge against the tiger. Although the magistrate laughs at her, asking, "Can anyone apply the law to a tiger?" she is not to be put off and insists that he issue a warrant for the tiger's arrest. A lictor named Li-nêng volunteers while drunk to make the arrest but declines after he is sober. Nevertheless, the magistrate insists that he fulfill his duty. One day while Li-nêng is praying at the temple of the local mountain god, the tiger puts in its appearance. When he speaks to the animal, he finds that it understands human speech. He appeals to it to give itself up. It agrees, and Li-nêng leads it, a prisoner, to the court. There the tiger confesses to the crime of having eaten the young woodcutter. The magistrate informs the tiger that it must forfeit its own life unless it can act as the old woman's son and support her in the same manner that he did, in which case the magistrate will allow it to go free. The tiger declares that it can fulfill this obligation. It regularly supplies the old woman with food and money. It becomes tame and is much in her presence. For ten years it takes the best of care of her. When she dies, she leaves enough savings to cover her funeral expenses. The tiger disappears. In conclusion, the narrator warns the reader not to take the story as true; on the other hand, he says, it is not to be considered a joke. Indeed, it is a moral exemplum. Although the tiger is of the brute, it displayed human feelings. Hence it is quite unlike some human beings of the present day, who follow the practice of oppressing orphans and widows and are far from being equal to a member of the brute creation.

In "T'ung-jên yü" ("The Pupils of the Eyes That Talked"), a young scholar, Fang Lien, a married man, has a character weakness: He likes to look at pretty women and girls other than his wife. Out to enjoy himself in this way during the spring festival, his eyes are attracted by the sight of a beautiful young girl who passes by him in a carriage. By the side of the carriage rides a good-looking servant girl on a small pony, and following are ten or more servants. One glance at this beauty causes Fang Lien to lose his heart. As a result, he gallops madly after the carriage to keep her in view. Annoyed at this indignity, the girl in the carriage calls to her maid to pull down the screen so that she is hidden from Fang Lien's ogling. Promptly the maid complies with her mistress' order. Then, turning toward Fang Lien, she condemns his boldness while, at the same time, she stoops to the ground, picks up a handful of dirt, and unexpectedly throws it into his face, blinding him. Although he rubs his eyes, it is clear that he is not going to regain his sight anytime soon.

When Fang Lien returns to his home, he tells his wife what has happened to him. Although a variety of medical remedies are tried over a good period of time, he remains a blindman. Now very worried, he repents of his past sins. He obtains a copy of the Buddhist sutra known as the *Kuang-ming ching* and begins to recite it daily. Although its recitation at first is boring, he eventually experiences a quietude of mind that he has never known before. One day he is startled to hear a small voice speaking in low tones in his right eye, complaining to someone else of the darkness therein. Another small voice then suggests that the two of them exit by his nostrils to see what is transpiring outside. When Fang Lien tells his wife of his extraordinary experience, she greets the news with skepticism. Nevertheless, the next day she secretes herself in the room to observe whatever does transpire. Before long she is astonished to see two tiny men, no larger than beans, come out from Fang Lien's nostrils and leave the house by the door. In a little while she sees them return to the room and reenter her husband's nostrils.

These excursions of the pair continue for several days. Then Fang Lien hears a small voice in his left eye say, "It's not convenient for us to go and come by way of these nostrils. We had each better open a door for ourselves." The small voice in the right eye, however, declares that his wall is too thick to break through. They therefore break through the wall of the left eye.

Immediately the light flows into Fang Lien's darkened orb. To his great delight, he can see again. Although he always remains blind in his right eye, he never ventures to fix his good eye on any woman other than his own wife.

In an annotation to this story, Giles implies that its plot is based partly on a folk belief widely held throughout China—namely, that each of a person's eyes contains a tiny human figure. He thinks this myth originated from one experiencing the reflection of oneself when looking into another person's eyes, or into one's own when viewing oneself in a mirror.

The story "Hua ma" ("The Picture Horse") concerns a Mr. Ts'ui of Liu-ch'ing, who, too poor to keep his garden walls in repair, finds a strange horse—black marked with white and with a scrubby tail—lying in the grass inside his premises. Although he repeatedly drives it away, it persists in returning to the same spot. Since, however, Mr. Ts'ui has a friend who has taken an official appointment in the province of Shensi, a considerable distance to travel, and he has long desired to visit him but has no adequate transportation, he decides to take possession of the horse and ride it to where his friend is located. Having caught it, and saddled and bridled it, he tells his servant that if the owner of the horse should come seeking it he should be informed where he can find it. Then Mr. Ts'ui rides off in the direction of Shensi.

Mr. Ts'ui finds that the horse travels at an astonishingly rapid rate, so that by nightfall they have gone thirty or forty miles. He also finds that the horse does not wish to eat the food he offers. Next day, fearing that the horse may be ill, he attempts to rein it in, but the horse vigorously resists being restrained. When he lets the reins out, the horse proceeds at its previous rapid rate. It is not long before Mr. Ts'ui reaches his destination. When the local prince hears of the speed and endurance of this remarkable horse, he wishes to purchase it. Only after no owner appears to claim the horse over a six-month period does Mr. Ts'ui part with it. Then he buys a mule and returns home on it.

After a time, the prince has business in Liu-ch'ing and rides there on the remarkable horse. Upon his arrival, he leaves it in the custody of one of his officers. The horse breaks away from its custodian and escapes. The officer gives chase. He pursues it to the home of Mr. Ts'ui's neighbor, a Mr. Tsêng, wherein it disappears. The officer accosts Mr. Tsêng and demands the return of the prince's horse, but Mr. Tsêng denies knowing anything about any horse, whereupon the officer bursts into Mr. Tsêng's private quarters. To his dismay, he finds no horse, but upon one wall he observes a picture of a horse exactly like the one he seeks, even with part of its tail burned away by a joss stick. It becomes clear to him and to Mr. Ts'ui that the prince's horse is a supernatural horse. Since the officer is afraid to return to the prince without the horse, he is about to arrest Mr. Tsêng. Mr. Ts'ui, however, intervenes and straightway refunds the purchase price willingly, since it has greatly increased in value. Naturally, Mr. Tsêng greatly appreciates his neighbor's generosity, since he never knew that the horse had been sold in the first place.

According to P'u, the picture of the horse in Mr. Tsêng's apartment was painted by the early T'ang poet and painter Ch'ên Tzŭ-ang, who, although apparently specializing in the painting of horses, was even better known as a writer. In China a close bond existed between painting and scholarship. The object of the painting was to capture the *ch'i*, or the life-spirit and the vitality of a thing, and writing was regarded as "mind painting." The idea of a painted thing having such powerful vitality as to cause it to leave the picture plane and take up an existence in the real world was not original with P'u. Among the historical anecdotes of the early T'ang Dynasty recorded in Liu Tsung-yüan's *Lung ch'êng lu* (c. 796?; untranslated except for short excerpts, as in E.D. Edwards' *Chinese Prose Literature of the T'ang Period, A.D. 618-906*, 1937), one praises Prince Ning as a great painter of horses. Emperor Ming Huang greatly admired a mural depicting horses which the prince had painted, known as *Six Horses in a Dust Storm*, because of the subjects' "fine heads and dappled coats." Every detail of these horses was considered perfect, and their "long, wind-tossed, cloud-like manes" were thought to be unusually realistic. Later, when one of the horses was noticed to be missing from the mural, the absence of the horse led to the belief that its spirit had empowered it to become a living horse. Liu's work was reprinted in the *T'ang tai ts'ung shu* (The T'ang collection of reprints), a collection completed during the reign of the Ch'ing Emperor Ch'ien Lung (reigned 1736-1796). This is the collection from which excerpts are translated by Edwards in his two volumes mentioned above. Some scholars have questioned whether the *Lung ch'êng lu* is by Liu Tsung-yüan (773-819) and have attributed it to Wang Chih of the twelfth century, but the question remains unsettled. Such stories as P'u's "Hua ma" ("The Picture Horse") and that of Liu's account of Prince Ning's painted horses remind one of the American writer Edgar Allan Poe's tapestry horse that comes alive in his story "Metzengerstein" (1832), as well as his "The Oval Portrait" (1842), in which an artist has extracted the life-spirit from his female model and put it into her portrait, thus leaving the former living model dead.

In P'u's story "Hua p'i" ("The Painted Skin"), a Mr. Wang of T'ai-yüan is walking outdoors when he meets a pretty girl. She is walking with difficulty because of her bound feet. He inquires of her who she is and where she is going. She replies that her family loved money and sold her as a concubine. Since the wife of the man to whom she was bound was so jealous of her that she abused her cruelly, she has run away. A runaway, however, has no particular destination. Mr. Wang invites her to his home. She gratefully accepts his offer. He conducts her to a building on his premises that is the library, indicating that she can stay here. She requests him not to tell anyone where she is staying. Although he agrees to keep her secret, he tells his wife of the girl's presence as soon as he sees her. Fearing that the girl may belong to some wealthy and powerful family, Wang's wife advises him that he might better get rid of the runaway, but he refuses to abandon her.

When Wang is out walking again, he encounters a Taoist priest, who asks him if he has met any stranger recently. Wang denies that he has. Walking away from him, the priest calls him a fool and remarks that some people never know when they are in danger of dying. Although Wang thinks that the Taoist is simply trying to land a client, the priest's words make a strong impression on him.

Returning home, Wang goes to the library but finds the door locked. He goes round to the back of the building and peers through the window. Inside he sees a hideous-looking devil with a green face and sawtooth teeth. The devil has spread out a human skin on a table and is painting it with a brush. Having completed the design it is putting on the skin, the devil picks up the skin, shakes it out like a coat, and throws it over its shoulders. To Wang's amazement, he sees that the devil is now the pretty concubine!

Terrified out of his wits, Wang runs off to find the Taoist priest he had encountered. Discovering him in a field, he rushes up to him and falls on his knees before him. He begs the priest to save him from the devil. The Taoist presents Wang with a fly-brush and prescribes that he hang it on the door of the premises occupied by the devil.

Having returned home, Wang carries out the Taoist's directive. After secreting himself in his bedroom, Wang instructs his wife to peep out and observe what happens when the false concubine returns and sees the fly-brush on the door. When the devil appears, Wang's wife sees that it responds to the fly-brush by gnashing its teeth and cursing. It grabs the fly-brush and tears it to pieces. Then, rushing into the room occupied by Wang and his wife, the devil grabs Wang and tears out his heart. Still raging, the devil departs. Wang's wife screams for help. A servant appears with a light. Upon examining Wang, they find him dead.

Wang's wife sends his brother to report the tragedy to the Taoist priest. The priest inquires of him whether any stranger has just come to Wang's house. The brother replying that an old woman has just been hired as a maid, the priest informs him that that person must be the devil in disguise. Taking up his wooden sword, the Taoist accompanies the brother home, where he accosts the presumed maid face-to-face, exposing her as the devil. Calling her a "base-born fiend," he demands the return of the fly-brush. His demand not met, he raises his sword and strikes her. As she falls to the ground, the human skin separates from her body to reveal her devilish hideousness. Then he cuts off the devil's head which turns into a column of dense smoke. The priest uncorks a gourd and throws it into the midst of the smoke. At once a sucking noise is heard and the column of smoke is drawn into the gourd, which the Taoist then corks up. As for the sheet of human skin, complete with eyebrows, eyes, hands, and feet, the priest rolls it up into a scroll. He is about to depart when Wang's wife tearfully pleads with him to restore her dead husband to life. He replies that he does not possess such power, but that if she will apply to the town maniac, he can assist her in such a project. He warns her, however, that no matter how much the maniac insults her or abuses her she must accept such treatment without demur.

Since Wang's brother knows the man to whom the priest alludes, he takes Mrs. Wang in search of him. They find the maniac raving by the roadside. Mrs. Wang approaches the man on her knees. He cries out to her, "Do you love me, my beauty?" She entreats him to restore her husband to life. He laughs at her. Then he gives her a thrashing with his staff. She endures this harsh treatment without a murmur. Then he hands her a distasteful-looking pill and orders her to swallow it. She does so with great difficulty. He cries out, "How you do love me!" and departs.

Returning home, Wang's wife mourns bitterly over her dead husband, greatly regretting the action she has taken. Since none of the servants dare to prepare the corpse, she undertakes to do it herself. As she does so, she feels a great lump rising in her throat which soon pops out of her mouth straight into the open wound of the dead man. She sees that it is a human heart. Excitedly, she closes the wound over it, holding the sides together with her hands. Finding a vapor escaping from the wound, she binds it tightly with a piece of silk. Rubbing the corpse vigorously for a time, she then covers it over with clothes. During the night she inspects the dead man and discovers breath coming from his nostrils. By morning Wang is alive again.

Except for a number of very short sketches, the above stories represent a fair cross section of those in P'u Sung-ling's collection in terms of treatment and plot structure. Apart from the sketches which are mere anecdotes, they range from very simple plots, such as that found in "The Tiger of Chao-ch'êng", to rather complicated ones, such as that of "The Painted Skin." Other tales of special interest might be added to this list: "Tou hsi-shih" ("The Fighting Cricket"), "Lao-shan tao-tzŭ" ("The Taoist Priest of Lao-shan"), "Chih Ch'ing-hsü" ("The Wonderful Stone"), "Niao yu" ("The Talking of the Birds"), "Chan pan" ("Planchette"), "T'ou t'ao" ("Theft of the Peach"), "Chian-no" ("Miss Chian-no"), and "Hua ku-tzŭ" ("The Flower-nymphs"). All these stories are included in Herbert A. Giles's collection of 164 of P'u's stories, *Strange Stories from a Chinese Studio*, which was reprinted in 1969, under the English titles given above. Rose Qong's collection, *Chinese Ghost and Love Stories: A Selection from the Liao-chai Stories by P'u Sung-ling*, contains forty tales. Translations of one or several tales are scattered in various anthologies and periodicals.

P'u Sung-ling weaves together the natural and the supernatural in a more realistic manner than the T'ang authors of *ch'uan ch'i*. In his criticism of

Confucian officialdom, he introduces new moral principles. Yet his treatment of Taoism and Buddhism hardly departs from theirs. He ignores philosophical Taoism to emphasize the superstition, magic, and exorcism of the popular religion of that name, whose founding is attributed to Ling Chang Tao-ling of the second century. This sort of Taoism concerned itself with the alchemical promise of the prolongation of life by discovering the elixir of immortality; with communication with *hsien*, or immortals; with magic pills; and with defeating devils. The Taoist text followed by P'u was not Lao Tzŭ's *Tao tê ching* (fourth century B.C.; *The Way and Its Power*, 1923) but the popular anonymous tract *T'ai-shang kan-ying p'ien* (fifteenth century; *Treatise of the Exalted One on Response and Retribution*, 1906).

In like manner, P'u favors Buddhism over Taoism, giving the Buddhist clergy more integrity, dignity, and respect than he does the Taoist priesthood or Confucian officials. He mainly ignores the intellectual, meditative Buddhist Ch'an sect in favor of the popular Ch'ing T'u, or Pure Land School, which concerns itself with the worship of Buddha Amitabha, who saves into his Pure Land all those who call upon his name in faith. Adhering to the doctrine of Karma and reincarnation, the followers of Ch'ing T'u Buddhism believe in a whole pantheon of Buddhas and Bodhisattvas and in a variety of celestial and terrestrial realms, including heavens and hells. It emphasizes right living and the value of the recitation of favored Buddhist sutras.

In sum, P'u Sung-ling treated the natural and the supernatural in terms of Chinese popular religion, according to which men sought communication with gods and spirits primarily to obtain benefits and avoid calamities.

Other major works
NOVEL: *Hsing-shih yin-yüan chuan*, 1870.
MISCELLANEOUS: *Liao-chai ch'üan-chi*, 1933.

Bibliography
Jên, Fang-chiu. "P'u Sung-ling and *Tales of Liao-chai*," in *Chinese Literature*. No. 1 (January, 1956), pp. 108-114.
Průšek, Jaroslav. "*Liao-chai chi-i* by P'u Sung-ling: An Inquiry into the Circumstances Under Which the Collection Arose," in *Chinese History and Literature: Collection of Studies*, 1970.
_____. "P'u Sung-ling and His Work," in *Chinese History and Literature: Collection of Studies*, 1970.
Tsung, Shu. "An Outstanding Collection of Tales," in *Chinese Literature*. No. 10 (October, 1962), pp. 89-94.

Richard P. Benton

ALEXANDER PUSHKIN

Born: Moscow, Russia; June 6, 1799
Died: St. Petersburg, Russia; February 10, 1837

Principal short fiction
Povesti Belkina, 1831 (*The Tales of Belkin*, 1947); *Pikovaya dama*, 1834 (*The Queen of Spades*, 1896).

Other literary forms
Generally considered the greatest poet in the Russian language, Alexander Pushkin is known not only for his lyrical and narrative poems but also for his brilliant verse novel *Evgeny Onegin* (1825-1833; *Eugene Onegin*, 1881), as well as his play *Boris Godunov* (1831; English translation, 1918), which was the inspiration for the opera by Modest Mussorgsky.

Achievements
Often termed the father of Russian literature, Pushkin occupies a unique position in Russian literary history. During his age, the language of the Russian aristocracy was French, not Russian, and Pushkin's literary sensibility was largely formed by French writers, particularly writers of the eighteenth century. He combined their classical approach with the Romantic elements of the English poet George Gordon, Lord Byron, and native Russian materials such as folktales in a transformation that produced a number of masterpieces, primarily in poetry. Yet Pushkin's general influence on nineteenth century Russian prose writers is immeasurable because his primary contribution was neither to character type nor to technique but to the very language of fiction itself. Precision and brevity, he believed, are the most important qualities of prose—elements which the eighteenth century French essayists also held in high regard—and his tales are characterized by a concise, plain language which set the standard for Russian prose writers who followed. Although character analysis was not Pushkin's primary achievement, his insight into the protagonist in *The Queen of Spades* is considered a precursor to the development of the psychological analysis of character which was the hallmark of the great Russian novelists of the nineteenth century. Ivan Turgenev, Leo Tolstoy, and Fyodor Dostoevski all acknowledged the influence of various aspects of his work. Russian critics have long expected Pushkin's reputation to become more firmly established in other countries, but since Pushkin's primary achievement is in poetry, and his particular, precise language is so difficult to translate, his reputation outside Russia has remained limited.

Biography
Alexander Sergeyevich Pushkin was born into the Russian aristocracy and lived the relatively privileged life of a member of the nobility. One element

which set him apart from other aristocrats who gathered around the czar was his heritage on his mother's side: His great grandfather was the black slave Hannibal, whom Peter the Great bought in Turkey and brought back to Russia. At an early age, Pushkin's poetic talents were recognized, but the subject of some of his poetry was the desire for liberty, and for political reasons the czar banished him from Moscow to his mother's estate when he was twenty years old. Although Pushkin eventually was called back to Moscow by the czar, for the remainder of his life he was subject to the czar's direct censorship. At the height of his literary powers, Pushkin died a tragic death. He married a woman who was in favor with many members of the czar's court because of her beauty; she was not an intellectual, however, and did not appreciate Pushkin's writing. When Pushkin discovered that she was secretly meeting a member of the court in a liaison, he challenged the man to a duel in which Pushkin was wounded in the stomach. He died two days later.

Analysis

Alexander Pushkin's short fiction exhibits the classic characteristics of the Romantic tale. The focus is on event, on plot, with character portrayal subordinated to dramatic action. These cleverly plotted, entertaining stories have much in common with such early masters of the modern short story as Sir Walter Scott, Washington Irving, Edgar Allan Poe, and Honoré de Balzac. As Romantic tales, Pushkin's stories have been termed perfect. Yet his reputation as one of the developers of the modern short story rests on a remarkably small body of work: the five tales which make up the collection *The Tales of Belkin* and the masterpiece *The Queen of Spades*. In addition to these completed stories, a number of fragments were published after his death which illustrate Pushkin's struggle in writing fiction. In contrast to his early achievements in poetry, his technical mastery of fiction required a long, difficult period of apprenticeship.

One of Pushkin's most challenging technical problems was the appropriate management of point of view, and in *The Tales of Belkin* he finally solved that problem. He framed the tales with an opening device, as Scott had done in a series of novels titled "Tales of My Landlord" (1816-1819) and as Irving had done in his *Tales of a Traveller* (1824)—works popular in Russia at the time that Pushkin began writing fiction. Pushkin's tales are presented as stories told by various people to one Ivan Petrovich Belkin, who wrote them down; upon his death, they were passed on to a publisher. The opening section of the collection is not a story but an address to the reader by this fictitious publisher, who comments on the background of the tales in a short paragraph and then presents a letter by a friend of Belkin which describes Belkin's life. This elaborate device does function to place the tales together in a coherent arrangement wherein Pushkin's voice carries consistently from one tale to the next.

The opening tale of the collection is "Vystrel" ("The Shot"), one of the most widely anthologized tales in short fiction. Within that single story, Pushkin exhibits a master's manipulation of point of view, with a central narrator who, in turn, relates narration by two other characters. The central narrator is a young army officer, Lieutenant I. L. P., who describes the conditions of his regiment in a small, isolated town. The young officers spend their evenings gambling at the house of a thirty-five-year-old civilian named Silvio, who is a Byronic figure—a Romantic hero, detached and proud, somewhat ironic and cynical, with an obsessive personality. When Silvio is insulted by a newcomer, everyone expects Silvio to kill the brash young newcomer in a duel, for Silvio is a renowned shot who practices daily. Silvio passes up the opportunity, however, and the incident is forgotten by everyone but the lieutenant/narrator, who secretly cannot forgive Silvio for what he considers his cowardice.

Later, however, when Silvio learns that he must leave town, he calls the lieutenant aside and explains his reason for passing up the duel by relating a series of previous events, thus becoming a second narrator in the story. Six years previously, as a hussar himself, Silvio had a duel with another young officer, a brilliant count of great social position and wealth. From the details which Silvio relates, it is obvious that subconsciously he was jealous of the man. The conditions of the duel were such that the two men drew lots for the first shot; Silvio's opponent won, but his shot missed, passing through Silvio's cap. As Silvio prepared for his shot, the young count possessed such aplomb that he ate cherries, calmly spitting out the seeds, as he waited. Angered by this show of superiority, Silvio made the strange request that he be allowed to take his shot at some future date, at any time he should choose to do so; the young count, with his great poise, agreed without any sign of apprehension. Now, Silvio has learned that the count is to be married, and Silvio is leaving to take his revenge. Because of this previous commitment to his honor, Silvio was forced to allow the recent insult to go unchallenged; consequently, the lieutenant learns that Silvio is not a coward after all. After Silvio relates these events, however, the lieutenant has strange, contradictory feelings about him: What kind of a man would do such a thing? An antihero in the Byronic tradition, Silvio is an elevated figure who believes that he is beyond the common sensibilities of society; the response of the narrator illustrates his ambivalence toward that Byronic role, an ambivalence which reflects Pushkin's own attitude.

The first section of the story ends with Silvio's departure, and the second begins four or five years later, when the lieutenant has left the army to return to his country estate. His neighbor, a Countess B., has been absent from her estate, but when she returns with her husband, the narrator visits them to relieve his boredom. In a short while, the narrator discovers that the husband is the same man whom Silvio left to kill, the brilliant young count, and he becomes the third narrator as he relates the events that followed Silvio's departure at the end of the first section of the story. Silvio indeed did appear at the estate, finding the count enjoying his honeymoon, but when Silvio claimed his shot, the count agreed. Silvio, however, in the spirit of the duelist, determined that they should draw lots once more. Once more, the count wins the first shot, but once more he misses, his stray shot striking a painting on the wall. Yet as Silvio readies himself to fire the deciding shot, the countess rushes in and, seeing her husband in danger, throws her arms around his neck. This action is too much for the count, and he angrily demands that Silvio shoot. Silvio, now satisfied that he has broken the count's poise, fires his shot off to one side, into the same painting that the count struck. The story ends with the comment by the central narrator that Silvio was killed some years later in a military battle. The portrayal of Silvio that emerges from the separate narrators of this highly crafted tale is that of a principled, intriguing figure. There is a new twist to this tale, however, which deviates from the literary type of the day: The Byronic antihero has been bested by a straightforward, decent man. Although Pushkin actually began this story as a parody on the Byronic figure, his technical proficiency enabled him to explore the larger meanings of that figure, and "The Shot" became a masterpiece.

The two stories which follow "The Shot" in the collection, "Metel" ("The Blizzard") and "Grobovshchik" ("The Undertaker"), are not as complex. "The Blizzard" revolves around a case of mistaken identity, which was a popular subject for Romantic tales at the time. A young heroine, Maria Gavrilovna, who has been brought up reading French novels, falls in love and sneaks off to marry her lover at night. Without her knowledge, a blizzard causes her lover to lose his way while going to the church, and she marries a man who, unknown to her, is not her lover. She returns to her parents' home and four years later learns that her lover—whom she believes is her husband—was killed in the War of 1812. Afterward, she meets a Colonel Burmin, a veteran of the same war, and falls in love with him. He responds to her love but declares that one night on a whim he married an unknown woman who mistakenly thought he was someone else, and thus he cannot marry. The situation recalls that of Irving's "The Spectre Bridegroom," not only in its mistaken identities in marriage but also in its tone; as in Irving's story, all ends happily as the events eventually reveal the true identities: The heroine is, indeed, the unknown woman whom Colonel Burmin married that night. The events in Pushkin's story move much more quickly than those in Irving's, for they are presented without Irving's relaxed digressions; the influence of the occasional essayist was much stronger in Irving's work, and his tales, in general, do not have the quickly paced dramatic action of Pushkin, in whose stories one seldom finds superfluous material or inessential detail.

"The Undertaker" is a humorous tale about an undertaker who is visited one night by the corpses he has buried, in response to an invitation he impulsively made at a party the previous night. The descriptions of the corpses are the highlight of this supernatural story, which ends with the undertaker waking from what proves to have been a dream. The tone and events of this story, particularly the corpses who come back to haunt the living, were to influence Nikolai Gogol—Pushkin's younger contemporary, another major prose writer of the period—in his famous "Chinel" ("The Overcoat"). Gogol had read Pushkin's collection and thought highly of it. One specific aspect of Pushkin's "Stantsionnyi smotritel" ("The Station Master") influenced Gogol: the character of the "little man." The story, narrated by government official "Titular Counsellor A. G. N.," is about a poor post-office stationmaster of low rank, Samson Vyrin, a "little man," who has a beautiful daughter, Dunya. When the narrator was traveling one day, he happened to stop at Samson's station for horses; there he noticed a series of pictures on the wall depicting the story of the Prodigal Son. He also first saw the girl Dunya, who was fourteen at the time. Her beauty deeply impressed him, and one day some years later, when he happens to be in the same district, he remembers her and stops at the same station. He asks about her, and the stationmaster, now a broken man, relates her story, thus becoming a second narrator.

Three years previously, the stationmaster tells the traveler, a hussar named Captain Minsky stopped at the station and, seeing the beautiful Dunya, pretended to be too ill to continue his journey. The hussar remained at the station several days, with Dunya nursing him, and then, one day when the stationmaster was away, fled with her. The stationmaster followed, until it became obvious that Dunya had willingly run off with Minsky. Later, the stationmaster takes a two-month leave and, on foot, traces the pair to St. Petersburg. There he discovers the pair living in a fancy hotel, and he confronts Minsky alone, demanding the return of his daughter before she is ruined. Yet Minsky declares that he is in love with Dunya and that neither she nor the stationmaster could ever be happy with each other because of what has happened. The stationmaster leaves, but he returns to find his daughter, and he discovers her enjoying her elegant surroundings as she tenderly winds her fingers in Minsky's hair. When she sees her father, she faints, and Minsky drives the father away.

The stationmaster's narration at this point in the story is ended, and the original narrator, the government official, tells how the stationmaster has now taken to drink. In the closing scene of the story, some years later, the official returns once more to the station house and discovers that the stationmaster has, indeed, died from drink. In asking directions to the grave, he learns that a wealthy lady recently visited the area with her children in a coach-and-six and also asked for the stationmaster. On learning of his death, she began weeping and then visited the grave herself; the woman was the daughter Dunya.

The twist of the young daughter returning not lost and ruined but happy and in good spirits creates the dramatic irony in these events. On one level, the story is thus an attack on the sentimental tales of the day about the young daughter gone to ruin. Once again, Pushkin elevated a story begun in parody to a masterpiece—many critics consider it the finest in the collection. The foolishness of the stationmaster in drinking himself to death for his lost daughter becomes the object lesson of the events as it completely reverses the story of the Prodigal Son.

The last story in the collection, "Barishnya krestyanka" ("The Squire's Daughter"), is a lighthearted and delightful tale, related to Belkin by "Miss K. I. T.," the same source as for "The Blizzard." As in "The Blizzard," events revolve around a case of mistaken identity. Two landowners are at odds; one has a seventeen-year-old daughter, Liza, and the other a young son, Alexey, home from the university, where he has picked up the Byronic posturing so common to the age. Here, Pushkin gently satirizes that behavior, in contrast to his probing of it in "The Shot." Liza seeks to meet the young man, and learning that he likes peasant girls, she dresses up one morning as such a girl and goes to a forest through which she knows he will be passing. He sees her, is attracted by her, and they begin to meet regularly at the same place in the forest, she continuing with her disguise. Meanwhile, the two landowners reconcile their differences, and Alexey's father demands that he marry the other landowner's daughter. Alexey refuses because of his love for the "peasant" girl, but at the crucial moment, Liza's true identity as the landowner's daughter is revealed, and all ends happily in light comedy.

The Queen of Spades, written after *The Tales of Belkin* was published, remains one of the most widely known stories in the history of short fiction. In this complex story, Pushkin uses an omniscient point of view, moving from one character to another as the situation demands; the narrative is divided into six sections and a conclusion. The story opens after an all-night game of cards with a young officer named Hermann, a Russified German, learning that the grandmother of a fellow officer, an old countess, supposedly has special knowledge of the three cards what will appear in faro—a gambling game in which only someone with supernatural powers can predict the cards and their sequence before they appear. Hermann himself cannot play cards; he can only watch, for his financial circumstances would not allow him to lose. At heart, however, he is a gambler who feverishly longs to play, and the countess' supernatural ability fires his imagination. He begins to hang around the street where the countess lives, his imagination dwelling on her secret. Then, one night after a compelling dream about winning at cards, he wakes and wanders the streets until he finds himself mysteriously before the house of the old countess. He sees in the window the face of a fresh, young woman, Lizaveta, and that moment seals his fate. She is the ward of the countess, and she is receptive to Hermann's advances. He uses her to gain entrance one night to the countess' bedchamber, where he surprises the countess as she is going to bed. He pleads with the countess to tell him the secret, but she insists that the story is only a joke, that there is no secret. Hermann becomes agitated, convinced that she is lying, and when she refuses to talk to him, he draws a pistol to scare her into answering. This threat is too much for her, and she suddenly collapses in death.

Hermann confesses the situation to Lizaveta, and they conceal the real events of the countess' death. At the funeral, Hermann hallucinates that the old countess is winking at him from the coffin. That night, her corpse, or "ghost," visits him, and in exchange for the promise that he will marry Lizaveta tells him the winning sequence: three, seven, ace. The device of the returning corpse, or ghost, has been popular in literature from William Shakespeare's *Hamlet* (c. 1600-1601) to Charles Dickens' *A Christmas Carol* (1843), and, as in both of those works, the returning ghost indicates an unnatural situation and a disturbed personality. In this Pushkin story, the reader is to assume that the ghost is not "real" but rather an indication of Hermann's disturbed mind. It is this aspect of the tale that was to influence the psychological analysis of character that became the hallmark of the great Russian novels, especially Dostoevski's *Prestupleniye i nakazaniye* (1866; *Crime and Punishment*, 1866). The three cards are perpetually in Hermann's mind and on his lips, and one night he takes all the money he has in the world to a famous gambling house, where he bets on the three; he wins and returns the following night to stake everything on the seven; again he wins, and the third night he returns to bet on the ace. A large crowd gathers, having heard of his previous success. This night, however, instead of the ace appearing, the queen of spades is the chosen card, and Hermann sees the face of the old countess in the figure on the card, smiling up at him. The short paragraph of the conclusion relates that Hermann is now at a mental hospital, where he simply repeats, over and over, "Three, seven, queen! Three, seven, queen!" Lizaveta, however, has married a very pleasant young man and is happy. In the opera by Pyotr Tchaikovsky, based on this story, the events differ somewhat. In the opera, Hermann and Lizaveta become lovers, and when he leaves her to gamble, she throws herself into the river; after the appearance of the queen, Hermann stabs himself. During the remainder of his life, Pushkin was never to equal the dramatic intensity of this story. It remains a classic, one of those tales that helped shape the direction of modern short fiction.

Other major works

NOVELS: *Evgeny Onegin*, 1825-1833 (*Eugene Onegin*, 1881); *Arap Petra velikogo*, 1828-1841 (*Peter the Great's Negro*, 1896); *Kirdjali*, 1834 (English translation, 1896); *Kapitanskaya dochka*, 1836 (*The Captain's Daughter*, 1846); *Dubrovsky*, 1841 (English translation, 1896); *Egipetskiy noche*, 1841

(*Egyptian Nights*, 1896); *Istoria sela Goryukhina*, 1857 (*History of the Village of Goryukhino*, 1966).

PLAYS: *Boris Godunov*, wr. 1824-1825, pb. 1831 (English translation, 1918); *Skupoy rytsar*, wr. 1830, pb. 1852 (*The Covetous Knight*, 1925); *Kamyenny gost*, wr. 1830, pb. 1839 (*The Stone Guest*, 1936); *Motsart i Salyeri*, pb. 1832 (*Mozart and Salieri*, 1920); *Pir vo vryemya chumy*, pb. 1833 (*The Feast in Time of the Plague*, 1925); *Stseny iz rytsarskikh vryemen*, wr. 1835, pb. 1937; *Rusalka*, pb. 1837 (*The Water Nymph*, 1924); *Little Tragedies*, pb. 1946 (includes *The Covetous Knight*, *The Stone Guest*, *Mozart and Salieri*, and *The Feast in Time of the Plague*).

POETRY: *Ruslan i Lyudmila*, 1820 (*Rusland and Liudmila*, 1974); *Gavriiliada*, 1822 (*Gabriel: A Poem*, 1926); *Kavkazskiy plennik*, 1822 (*The Prisoner of the Caucasus*, 1895); *Bratya razboyniki*, 1824; *Bakhchisaraiskiy fontan*, 1827 (*The Fountain of Bakhchisarai*, 1849); *Graf Nulin*, 1827 (*Count Nulin*, 1972); *Tsygany*, 1827 (*The Gypsies*, 1957); *Poltava*, 1829 (English translation, 1936); *Domik v Kolomne*, 1833 (*The Little House at Kolomna*, 1977); *Skazka o mertvoy tsarevne*, 1833 (*The Tale of the Dead Princess*, 1924); *Skazka o rybake ir rybke*, 1833 (*The Tale of the Fisherman and the Fish*, 1926); *Skazka o tsare Saltane*, 1833 (*The Tale of Tsar Saltan*, 1950); *Skazka o zolotom petushke*, 1834 (*The Tale of the Golden Cockerel*, 1918); *Medniy vsadnik*, 1841 (*The Bronze Horseman*, 1936); *Collected Narrative and Lyrical Poetry*, 1984.

NONFICTION: *Istoria Pugacheva*, 1834 (*The Pugachev Rebellion*, 1966); *Puteshestviye v Arzrum*, 1836 (*A Journey to Arzrum*, 1974); *The Letters of Alexander Pushkin*, 1963.

MISCELLANEOUS: *The Captain's Daughter and Other Tales*, 1933; *The Works of Alexander Pushkin*, 1936; *Polmoe sobranie sochinery*, 1937-1959 (seventeen volumes); *The Poems, Prose, and Plays of Pushkin*, 1943; *The Complete Prose Tales of Alexander Pushkin*, 1966; *Pushkin Threefold*, 1972; *Alexander Pushkin: Complete Prose Fiction*, 1983.

Bibliography

Bayley, John. *Pushkin: A Comparative Commentary*, 1971.
Beckwith, Martha Warren, et al. *Pushkin: The Man and the Artist*, 1937.
Cross, Samuel H., and Ernest J. Simmons, eds. *Centennial Essays for Pushkin*, 1937.
Debreczeny, Paul. *The Other Pushkin: A Study of Alexander Pushkin's Prose Fiction*, 1983.
Magarshack, David. *Pushkin: A Biography*, 1967.
Troyat, Henri. *Pushkin*, 1970.
Vickery, Walter N. *Alexander Pushkin*, 1970.

Ronald L. Johnson

JEAN RHYS
Ella Gwendolen Rees Williams

Born: Roseau, Dominica; August 24, 1894
Died: Exeter, England; May 14, 1979

Principal short fiction

The Left Bank and Other Stories, 1927; *Tigers Are Better-Looking*, 1968; *Sleep It Off, Lady*, 1976.

Other literary forms

Jean Rhys wrote five novels, *Postures* (1928), which was published in the United States in 1929 under the title *Quartet*; *After Leaving Mr. Mackenzie* (1931); *Voyage in the Dark* (1934); *Good Morning, Midnight* (1939), which was dramatized for radio by the British Broadcasting Corporation (BBC) in 1958; and *Wide Sargasso Sea* (1966), which many consider to be her masterpiece. She also wrote *Smile Please: An Unfinished Autobiography* (1979). Her letters were published in 1984.

Achievements

During the first decade of her writing career, Rhys achieved only limited success. Although her books were well received by critics, they attracted only a small readership. After years of neglect, however, interest in her work increased dramatically following the publication of *Wide Sargasso Sea*. She was elected a Fellow of the Royal Society of Literature; her novel won the W. H. Smith literary award and the Award for Writers from the Arts Council of Great Britain. Throughout the 1970's, her reputation grew, and she now holds a secure place in the first rank of female twentieth century novelists. Her work is notable for its unsparing exploration of a particular character type: the dispossessed, dependent, exploited single woman, struggling to survive in a society in which she has no roots, no money, no power, and often, no hope.

Biography

Jean Rhys was born Ella Gwendolen Rees Williams on August 24, 1894, in Roseau, Dominica, in the West Indies. Her father was a Welsh doctor, and her mother a Creole (the name given to longstanding white settlers in the West Indies). In 1910, she was sent to England to live with an aunt in Cambridge, and she later studied acting at the Royal Academy of Dramatic Art. When her father died, she was forced to make her living as a chorus girl in touring musical companies. In 1919, she married a French-Dutch poet and journalist and went to live on the Continent, where the couple led a bohemian life. The marriage ended in divorce in 1927. In 1938, she married again and settled in Cornwall, England. Following her second husband's death in 1945, she married for the third time in 1946. Her literary career flourished moderately in the late 1920's and 1930's, but she disappeared entirely from the literary scene during World War II and did not reappear until 1958, when the BBC adapted *Good Morning, Midnight* for radio. Encouraged by the new interest in her work, she began writing again, and her reputation was still growing at her death in 1979, at the age of eighty-four.

Analysis

The range of Jean Rhys's stories, as in her novels, is narrow. She focuses on the world of the lonely, the outcast, the vulnerable. Her central characters are all women, who live in a world they cannot control, which regards them with indifference and cruelty. Communication is often found to be impossible, and the protagonists' fragmented, tormented world is perpetually on the verge of falling apart. The dominant note is of isolation, dependency, and loss, with more than a smattering of self-pity.

Rhys's first collection, *The Left Bank and Other Stories*, consists of twenty-two stories, most of them short sketches, of life on the Parisian Left Bank. A few stories, "In the Rue de l'Arrivée," "A Night," and "Learning to Be a Mother," end on an optimistic note, as does "Mannequin," in which a young girl, at the end of her first day as a mannequin, feels a surge of happiness as she steps into the street and merges into the vibrant life of the city. She is one of the few heroines in Rhys's fiction who discovers a sense of belonging. The dominant mood of the collection, however, is one of helplessness and troubled uncertainty, and as such it sets the tone for Rhys's later work. The stories focus on characters who inhabit the fringes of society: artists, exiles, misfits, deprived women. "Hunger," for example, is a despairing, first-person monologue of an English woman who is down and out in Paris. She takes the reader, day by day, through her experience of five days without food.

"La Gross Fifi" is a more ambitious story, one of a group at the end of the collection which are set outside Paris—in this case, on the French Riviera. Fifi is a huge, vulgar woman who keeps a gigolo half her age in a sleazy hotel. The other main character is a young woman named Roseau. The name, she explains, means reed, and her motto in life is "a reed shaken by the wind" (a motto which might adequately describe virtually all of Rhys's helpless and vulnerable heroines). Roseau can survive, she says, only as long as she does not think. Unhappy and lonely, without home, friends, or money, she is comforted one night by Fifi, who reveals herself to be infinitely kind and understanding. She knows the foolishness of her own situation, yet she genuinely loves her man, however irregular and unhappy the relationship appears. When her lover abruptly leaves her, she faces the hostile world with dignity, still attracting men and still cheerfully defying the darker elements in her life. Roseau feels protected by her presence, which is so full of life that she cannot help but feel gladdened by it. The story reaches a climax when Roseau learns that Fifi has been stabbed to death in a quarrel with her lover.

Fifi's almost tragic grandeur serves as a measure of Roseau's inadequacy. She knows that she can never love with such full abandon or live so whole-heartedly. She decides to leave the hotel, and the story ends with her packing (a typical activity for the rootless Rhys heroine) while the yellow sunshine—yellow always carries negative connotations for Rhys—streams through the window.

Rhys wrote no more short stories until the early 1960's, and eight of them were published in *Tigers Are Better-Looking*. These stories are longer, more complex, the characters more fully realized, but Rhys's vision has become even more bleak and despairing than it had been in *The Left Bank and Other Stories*. "The Lotus," told with a taut economy and a ruthless fidelity to what Rhys saw as reality, is one of the bleakest. Lotus Heath is an eccentric middle-aged poet and novelist. Ronnie Miles invites her for drinks one evening, since they live in the same apartment building. His wife Christine dislikes Lotus, however, and her frequent cruel insults sabotage Ronnie's attempts to be polite and sociable. When Ronnie helps Lotus down to her own small, ill-smelling apartment, her cheerful guise suddenly drops and she reveals her own despair and frustration. Later, Ronnie sees Lotus running naked and drunk (she is one of many Rhys heroines who drink too much) down the street, soon to be escorted away by two policemen. When one of the policemen inquires at the Miles's about Lotus, Ronnie denies that he knows much about her, and no one else in the building will admit to knowing her either. An ambulance takes her to the hospital. Christine, who found her own insults highly amusing, ignores the whole affair, lying in bed smiling, as if Lotus' eclipse has somehow made her own star rise. The story ends when Ronnie, his kindness revealed as shallow and ineffectual, begins to make love to Christine—cruelty has its reward, and compassion is snuffed out without a trace. Nor can there be any escape or consolation through art, which is represented inadequately by Lotus, and is mocked by Christine. In this story, the only arts which flourish are popular songs preserved on secondhand gramophone records.

The best-known story in the collection is probably "Till September Petronella." It opens with the heroine and narrator, Petronella Grey, performing a typical action—packing. She dislikes London, with its gray days, and heartless people, a recurring theme in Rhys's fiction. Typically also, Petronella has no money and has cut herself off from her family. She admits to herself that she has never lived in a place that she liked, and the story chronicles the directionless drift of her life. She visits her boyfriend Marston in the country, and his guests Frankie and her lover Julian. During a lunch loosened by drink, they fall to pointless quarreling. Petronella decides to return to London, and Marston says that he will see her in September. The date of their parting is significant: July 28, 1914.

In London, she is befriended by an eager young man, Melville, and during their evening together she recalls that her career as a chorus girl failed because she could not remember the only line she had to speak. The incident keeps coming back to her; it is a parable of her life. She has lost her connections, the threads which bind her to the rest of life and society. She cannot fit smoothly into the flow of life. When Melville tells her that he, too, is going away until September, their lighthearted farewell does not disguise for the reader the dangerous period of loneliness which Petronella is about to enter. Not only does the story emphasize her dependence on men, who provide her with distractions but not fulfillment, but also it makes it clear that Petronella enters her private wasteland just as Europe begins to tear itself apart in World War I. Her aimlessness is somehow linked to a wider spread of chaos. There will be no September reunions.

Much of the story's power comes through Rhys's gift for subtle suggestion rather than overt statement. The reader is forced to penetrate beyond the apparently trivial nature of the dialogue, which makes up nine-tenths of the story, to the darkness which lies behind it and threatens to engulf it. When the story ends with Petronella sitting quietly, waiting for the city clock to strike, the moment has acquired an ominous quality, as if the striking clock will inaugurate some dreadful Day of Judgment which she, waiting passively, can do nothing to avert.

Sleep It Off, Lady consists of sixteen stories. They are predominantly tales of regret and loss and fall into a rough chronological sequence which resembles the chronology of Rhys's own life. The first five take place in the West Indies at the turn of the century. Two of these ("Pioneers, Oh, Pioneers," and "Fishy Waters") deal with the difficulties of white settlers in the West Indies, isolated in the land they were responsible for colonizing. A strongly autobiographical middle group centers on a young female protagonist who goes to school in Cambridge, England, trains as an actress, and becomes a member of the chorus in a touring company. Three stories toward the end of the collection ("Rapunzel, Rapunzel," "Who Knows What's Up in the Attic?" and "Sleep It Off, Lady") feature elderly female protagonists.

There is probably no more quietly horrifying story in English literature than "Sleep It Off, Lady." Told with an unsentimental, almost clinical precision, it centers on an elderly heroine, Miss Verney, a spinster who lives in one of the poorer parts of the village, where she does not really belong. The central action consists of her attempts to rid herself of a dilapidated old shed which stands next to her cottage, but she cannot persuade any of the local tradesmen to pull it down. She feels increasingly helpless, and the shed begins to acquire a sinister power over her. She dreams of it as a coffin.

One day, she sees a rat in the shed, and the powerful rat poison which Tom, her neighbor, puts down seems to have no effect. The rat walks unhurriedly across the shed, as if he is in charge of everything (while she feels herself to be in charge of nothing). Tom suggests that the rat must be a pink one, the product of her excessive drinking. She feels trapped and misunderstood and retreats into a closed world of her own. She stops going for walks outside. Letters remain unanswered, and she rejects the good-neighborliness of Tom.

What makes the story so poignantly effective is that just before her inevitable demise she undergoes a form of rebirth. On her birthday, she awakes feeling refreshed, happy, and young again. It is a windless day, with a blue sky overhead. Poised between one year and the next, she feels ageless, and she makes plans to reach out to other people once more when her new telephone is installed. Yet her optimism is misplaced. Later in the day, as she struggles to move a garbage container back to the shed, she falls and loses consciousness. When she awakes it is nearly dark, and she is surrounded by the contents of the trash can, including broken egg shells (symbolizing the failure of her rebirth). When she calls to some passing women for help, the wind drowns out her cries. Even nature has turned against her. A local child named Deena finds her but refuses to help and makes it clear that Miss Verney is despised in her own neighborhood. The next morning, Miss Verney is discovered by the postman, who is carrying a parcel of books for her. The parcel—like the telephone, a symbol of communication with the outside world—comes too late. She dies that evening. Her individual will to live proves useless in the face of the hostility and indifference of her neighbors. Regarded as trash, she dies surrounded by trash. Her feeling of renewal was only the last and the cruellest trick that life was to play upon her.

The last story in the collection, only one-and-a-half pages, serves as an appropriate epitaph for all of Rhys's stories. "I Used to Live Here Once" features an unnamed protagonist who in later life returns to her childhood home in the West Indies. She crosses a stream, using the stepping stones she still remembers well, and approaches her old house. In the garden, she sees a young boy and a girl under a mango tree and calls to them twice, but they do not answer. When she says hello for the third time, she reaches out, longing to touch them. The boy turns to her, looks her directly in the eye, and remarks how cold it has suddenly become, and he and the girl run back across the grass into the house. The story ends with the pregnant sentence "That was the first time she knew."

She knows that she cannot return to the freshness and vitality of her youth. She also knows that the coldness emanates from her, and therefore she must have frozen into a kind of living death. Yet beyond this, it is as if she knows everything that Rhys's stories have depicted, time after time: the pain of final separation, the loneliness of exile, the failure of people to connect with one another, the horrible realization of what life can become. Jean Rhys's stories do not elevate the spirit but rather reveal the gradual strangulation of the life force. They do not make easy or comfortable reading. Rhys's merit lies in her quiet but devastating presentation of the hopeless and the forgotten. She looks on despair and futility with an unblinking eye; she does not flinch or sentimentalize, and she does not deceive.

Other major works

NOVELS: *Postures*, 1928 (U.S. edition, *Quartet*, 1929); *After Leaving Mr. Mackenzie*, 1931; *Voyage in the Dark*, 1934; *Good Morning, Midnight*, 1939; *Wide Sargasso Sea*, 1966.

NONFICTION: *Smile Please: An Unfinished Autobiography*, 1979; *Jean Rhys Letters, 1931-1966*, 1984.

Bibliography

Angier, Carole. *Jean Rhys*, 1986.
Davidson, Arnold E. *Jean Rhys*, 1985.
James, Louis. *Jean Rhys*, 1978.
Staley, Thomas. *Jean Rhys: A Critical Study*, 1979.
Wolfe, Peter. *Jean Rhys*, 1980.

Bryan Aubrey

IHARA SAIKAKU

Born: Osaka, Japan; 1642
Died: Osaka, Japan; September 10, 1693

Principal short fiction

Saikaku shokoku-banashi, 1685; *Kōshoku gonin onna*, 1686 (*Five Women Who Loved Love*, 1956); *Honchō nijū fukō*, 1686; *Futokoro suzuri*, 1687; *Nanshoku ōkagami*, 1687; *Budō denraiki*, 1687; *Buke giri monogatari*, 1688 (*Tales of Samurai Honor*, 1981); *Nippon eitaigura: Daifuku shin chōja-kyō*, 1688 (*The Japanese Family Storehouse: Or, The Millionaire's Gospel Modernised*, 1959); *Honchō ōin hiji*, 1689 (*Tales of Japanese Justice*, 1980); *Seken munezan' yō*, 1692 (*Worldly Mental Calculations*, 1965; also as *This Scheming World*); *Saikaku okimiyage*, 1693; *Saikaku oridome*, 1694 (*Some Final Words of Advice*, 1980); *Saikaku zoku tsurezure*, 1695; *Yorozu no fumihōgu*, 1696.

Other literary forms

Ihara Saikaku's best-known work is the picaresque novel *Kōshoku ichidai otoko* (1682; *The Life of an Amorous Man*, 1964). He first won fame as a poet, however, with *Ikudama manku* (1673; ten thousand verses at Ikudama), a compilation that includes *haikai* (comic linked verse) of Saikaku and more than two hundred of his associates. His solo *haikai* performances are recorded in *Dokugin ichinichi senku* (1675; solo verses, one thousand in one day), *Saikaku haikai ōkuzaku* (1677; Saikaku's haikai, a great many verses), and *Saikaku ōyakazu* (1681; Saikaku's a great many arrows). Saikaku also wrote two puppet plays, *Koyomi* (calendar) and *Gaijin Yashima* (triumphant return from Yashima), both of which were staged in 1685.

Achievements

With the publication of *The Life of an Amorous Man* in 1682, Saikaku established himself as the most popular storyteller of his time, and indeed to this day among Japanese writers of fiction he ranks second only to Murasaki Shikibu, the author of *Genji monogatari* (c. 1004; *The Tale of Genji*, 1925-1933, 1935). In the last decade of his life, he published more than two dozen major works that dealt with a wide spectrum of the life of the city dwellers in seventeenth century Japan. These works are distinguished by acute observations of the foibles of man, which are portrayed with humor and empathy. Saikaku was a daring individual, who relished being called Saikaku the Hollander. He was an innovator, a highly original writer who graced his stories with a unique, terse style derived from his training as a *haikai* poet. Indeed, with the appearance of his first prose work, he created a new genre, which came to be called *Ukiyo-zōshi* (booklets of the floating world), certainly a measure of the high respect due him.

Biography

Little is known of Ihara Saikaku's personal life. He was most certainly born in Osaka in 1642, there being sufficient indication that he considered this city to be his hometown. His real name was, according to one source, Hirayama Tōgo; Ihara was, most likely, his mother's maiden name, which he later adopted for his professional name. "Saikaku" is the last of a series of noms de plume that he used. According to the same source, he was a merchant in an unspecified trade who could afford to leave the management of the business to trusted clerks and devote his life to literary pursuits and to travel.

He took an early interest in *haikai* and is believed to have qualified in his twenty-first year to become a *haikai* teacher (*tenja*). In the early 1670's, he became a disciple of Nishiyama Sōin (1605-1682), the head of the Danrin school of *haikai* and a major challenger to the traditional Teimon school. By 1673, when *Ikudama manku* was performed, Saikaku had established himself as a leading force under Sōin.

Traditionally, *haikai* poetry is composed in linked sequences by several poets as a ritualized social and literary activity. Saikaku was by no means the first to break from this tradition—there had been others before him, most notably Arakida Moritake (1473-1549), who is credited with *Dokugin senku* (compiled 1536-1540; a thousand verses composed by one man). Nevertheless, he was the first to compose one thousand verses in a single day in 1675. The occasion was an emotional one: a memorial tribute to his young wife, who had died after a brief illness. Saikaku titled the compilation *Dokugin ichinichi senku*. This effort was followed in 1677 by *Saikaku haikai ōkuzaku*, another solo performance in which sixteen hundred verses were composed in a single day and night. When rivals bested him, first with eighteen hundred verses, then with twenty-eight hundred, Saikaku returned in 1680 with a public performance of four thousand verses in a single day and night. The record of this feat was published the following year as *Saikaku ōyakazu*. When rivals reported besting him again, Saikaku was determined to put an end to all such rivalry. In 1684, he assembled an audience, and in the presence of referees and scribes he composed 23,500 verses in a twenty-four-hour period. Unfortunately, he delivered the verses so fast that the scribes could only draw hash marks for each verse.

Saikaku proved his point, and as a result the Danrin school embarked on a path of self-destruction. It was not, however, the end of Saikaku. As long as linked verse remained a group activity, fettered by the constraints of traditional versification, it allowed little room for the genius of any single individual to bloom. It is not surprising that Matsuo Bashō (1644-1694) and Saikaku, the two leading men of the Danrin school, discovered a way to free themselves from these limitations and so unleash their talents. Bashō's concentration on the opening verse (*hokku*) of the *haikai* sequence allowed him to reach unsurpassed heights in his endeavor. As for Saikaku the raconteur, performing rapid-fire solo *haikai* gave him experience in weaving together *haikai* sequences with something approaching narrative content and led the way to the development of an idiosyncratic narrative that displayed *haikai* techniques.

With the death of his teacher Sōin in 1682, Saikaku was emboldened to proceed with the publication of his first attempt at fiction, *The Life of an Amorous Man*. The work was so well received that publishers encouraged him to continue; he was thus embarked on a brief but prolific career as a writer of fiction, producing more than two dozen novels and collections of short stories in the last decade of his life. When he died in 1693, one of his disciples moved into his residence as a caretaker; he edited and possibly made additions to the unfinished manuscripts he found before he had them published. Saikaku's enormous popularity can be seen in that a succession of works purporting to be sequels or written in a style and vein emulating Saikaku's began to appear almost immediately and continued to be published for decades after his death.

Saikaku's last words summarize his attitude toward life. Noting that he had exceeded man's allotted span of fifty years, he gave thanks in this deathbed poem:

> The moon of this Floating World
> I have enjoyed a surplus
> These last two years

Analysis

Ihara Saikaku was a poet who turned to writing prose fiction late in his life. As a *haikai* poet he had distinguished himself as a daredevil maverick with his rapid-fire performances. Yet his focus in *haikai* was the real world of the commoner's life. Unlike the poems of his contemporary Bashō, which tended to be sublimated, Saikaku's poems deal squarely with the diurnal activities of the men and women of the cities. When he turned to fiction, he continued to draw his materials directly from the commercial, urban society of his day.

Saikaku was a consummate storyteller who told his stories with relish. He was also a supreme stylist who wrote in a terse, innovative style that was emulated by his contemporaries and followers. To a large extent, Saikaku's style derived from his training as a *haikai* poet whose medium required communication by splashes of imagery rather than articulated narrative. (Unfortunately, such matters of style are usually lost in translation and can be seen only in the original text.) Saikaku's genius lay in the brilliant insight with which he wrote about sex and money in the life of the townsmen. His earliest work was imbued with optimism and an exuberant air, while his later works turned increasingly pessimistic. Yet throughout his writing career,

Saikaku displayed a rare talent of intermingling the comic with the tragic.

Five Women Who Loved Love is generally considered to be Saikaku's masterpiece. It is a rather carefully crafted collection of five scandalous love stories. In contrast to Saikaku's other works on "love," which were in reality about mere sexual encounters, these are stories that dwell more extensively with the portrayals of men and women in love and the often tragic consequences which follow. All but the last of these love stories end tragically; the protagonists pay for their indiscretions with their lives. Punishments for crimes considered subversive to the hierarchical order were harsh in the Tokugawa period. A hired hand who had illicit intercourse with his master's daughter, for example, could have been sentenced to death. Adultery by a married woman was also punishable by death, and a husband who caught his wife in the act could kill her and her lover on the spot. Death was also often the penalty for kidnaping, or even for the embezzlement of ten *ryō* or more. These stories acquired additional poignancy as each of them was based on actual scandals, some still very fresh in the minds of Saikaku's readers. Saikaku freely altered and embellished the incidents and, in typical Saikaku style, added comical touches.

The first story is that of Onatsu, the younger sister of a shopkeeper in the regional town of Himeji, who falls in love with Seijūrō, a clerk in her brother's employ. At an outing carefully staged by Seijūrō, they fulfill their desire. The liaison cannot go unnoticed, however, and fully aware of the penalty for Seijūrō, they flee by boat to reach Osaka but are tracked down and brought back to face the consequences. When Seijūrō is executed, Onatsu loses her mind; at one point she tries to kill herself but is restrained. She then becomes a nun in order to care for Seijūrō's grave, and she prays for his soul day and night. Saikaku comments, "This then is my creation, a new river and a boat for the lovers to float their love downstream, like bubbles in this sad fleeting world." He makes no comment on the harshness of the punishment or the injustice of the law. Yet this final line makes it clear where his sympathy lay: They had violated no moral law; they were simply two hapless lovers caught in an unreasonable legal system.

The second story is about adultery between a barrelmaker's wife, Osen, and her neighbor Chōzaemon. Osen is falsely accused of adultery by Chōzaemon's wife. Incensed, she vows to give the accuser real cause to worry. Her desire for revenge, however, soon turns to lust. One evening after a party, when Chōzaemon follows her home, she invites him in. They are no sooner in bed when the barrelmaker appears and discovers them in the act. Chōzaemon flees the scene, only to be caught and later executed. Osen chooses a more heroic path to death, plunging a carpenter's chisel-like plane into her heart. Osen had acted out of vengeance, rather than love. Chōzaemon's conduct, too, was deficient. Saikaku comments, "The scoundrel's and her corpse too were put on public display at Togano to expose their shame. Their names, through countless ballads, spread to faraway provinces; there's no escaping from one's own misdeeds. Frightful, this world of ours!" Although Osen is spared the indignity of public execution, Saikaku leaves no doubt as to his disapproval of the conduct of Osen and Chōzaemon: unmitigated adultery stemming from revenge or lust.

The third and perhaps most effective of the five stories is about Osan, the beautiful wife of an almanac-maker, and Moemon, a clerk in her husband's Kyoto shop. The almanac-maker has hired Moemon specifically to look after the shop and Osan while he takes an extended business trip to Edo. During her husband's absence, Osan and her maid Rin, who is attracted to Moemon, play a trick on him. The prank backfires, however, and Osan ends up in bed with Moemon. Moemon has come to Rin's bed in response to a note from her; meanwhile Osan has taken Rin's place in her bed to surprise him. Osan, however, falls asleep and is taken unawares. In the morning, when Osan realizes what has happened, she is mortified about the "shame" as well as the nature of her transgression. The only honorable way to salvage the situation, she believes, is to "sacrifice her life in order to save her honor," and she asks Moemon to "join her in her journey to death." They elope, stage a mock suicide to fool pursuers and flee to a mountain hamlet where they find momentary bliss. One day, unable to suppress an urge to reconnoiter the situation back in the capital, Moemon slips back into the city and is spotted; the misadventure leads to their demise: They are paraded through the streets and executed.

In spite of the essentially tragic nature of the incident, the story is told with humorous turns of phrases and is sprinkled with comic interludes. In less skilled hands, it could easily have become a farce; in Saikaku's, it has been crafted into a thoroughly enjoyable tragicomedy. The adultery is unintended, but Osan has made an irrevocable mistake. To validate her good-faith effort to maintain her honor, Saikaku portrays her as an admirable woman, truly in love with Moemon. She is further portrayed as a spirited woman, full of life, who makes the most of the last days of her life and does not regret her action. Saikaku's final comment: "At dawn of the twenty-second of the Ninth Month they met their end as in a fleeting dream, an end far from dishonorable. Their story is widely known and even today the name of Osan is remembered as vividly as her lovely figure in the pale-blue robe she wore to her death."

The fourth story unfolds with a greengrocer's family taking temporary refuge in a temple when their shop is destroyed by fire. As they await the rebuilding of the shop, an adolescent love affair develops between Oshichi, the fifteen-year-old daughter, and Kichisaburō, a temple page from a samurai family. When the shop is rebuilt and the family returns to their new quarters, Oshichi yearns to see Kichisaburō again. Blinded by love, she sets fire to the new building, believing that the family will then return to the temple again.

The fire is arrested at an early stage, but Oshichi is paraded about the city and eventually burned at the stake. Saikaku comments, "No one should ever commit such an evil act. Heaven does not tolerate it." He continues,

> Since it was something Oshichi had done with conviction, knowing full well its consequences, she did not allow herself to waste away. Instead, each remaining day, she had her black hair done up and looked as beautiful as ever. Early in the Fourth Month, alas at sixteen she was in the spring of her youth, as the cherry blossoms were falling to the ground and even the cuckoos cried out in unison their songs of lament, she was finally told that her time had come. She remained as calm and collected as ever, ready to accept life as an illusory dream of an existence and earnestly awaited rebirth in the Land of the Buddha. How very sad!

Saikaku is emphatic in his condemnation of the grave crime of arson and does not question the harshness of the punishment. Yet he allows an outpouring of sympathy for Oshichi. Although she has been illogical and foolish, she has acted out of pure love, Saikaku seems to suggest, when the more common cause of criminal transgressions are greed, jealousy, and spite. Her motive is honorable. Furthermore, faced with death, Oshichi conducts herself with dignity. Saikaku portrays her as showing no remorse, but as being sincere in her acceptance of death as the consequence of her act.

Saikaku continues the story beyond the death of the heroine, relating an aspect of the young man's life that had only been hinted at earlier: his homosexual relationship with another youth. Kichisaburō had been so weakened with lovesickness that he had not been told of Oshichi's fate. When he learns of it, he quickly reaches for his sword, but the monks restrain him from killing himself, reminding him of the pledge of homosexual love that he has made to his "sworn brother." He is torn between his obligation to his lover and what he believes is his duty to the girl he once loved. He is relieved, however, when his sworn brother releases him from the obligation, counseling him to join the priesthood to look after Oshichi.

Saikaku's aim was to cover the spectrum of love "in all its varied forms" and particularly to show how duty, honor, and dignity play key roles in the relationships among men. The homosexual segment here anticipates the fifth story, in which a handsome young man who has suffered the loss of two male lovers is relentlessly pursued by a young woman. Madly in love with him, she visits him dressed as a young boy to attract his attention. In the end, they marry, inherit a fortune, and, presumably, live happily ever after.

The success of *Five Women Who Loved Love* and Saikaku's stories in general derives from the wry humor and detachment with which he tells his stories. He maintains a distance from his characters yet manages to portray them sympathetically. The women in these stories are portrayed as independent and strong-willed, undaunted by the harsh laws of society and able to risk their lives for love.

Saikaku traveled extensively around the country and wrote hundreds of short stories which were published over the years as collections, usually with specific themes. Legends and tales with strong local flavor, for example, were brought together in *Saikaku shokoku-banashi* (Saikaku's tales of the provinces), a collection of thirty-five stories told with typical Saikakuesque humor. This short-story form, rooted in the oral tradition and no more than several pages long, was to become with appropriate refinement Saikaku's favorite and most effective form in the years to come. With Saikaku's background and genius in *haikai* versification and with his talent as a raconteur, it was inevitable that he would abandon the novel in favor of the short story. In time, he began to produce collections of short stories with more distinct themes.

As the Bakufu mounted a renewed campaign to encourage filial piety in the early 1680's, Saikaku responded characteristically with the publication in 1686 of his *Honchō nijū fukō* (twenty cases of unfilial conduct in Japan), a gleeful collection of stories about the most reprehensible sort of children, sons and daughters who plot against one another and who would even murder their parents for money. Though doomed by the very odious nature of the stories, the work opened the way for Saikaku to explore the use of themes as a unifying device for other collections of stories. Saikaku returned to the theme of male homosexuality in earnest with the publication of *Nanshoku ōkagami* (the great mirror of manly love) in 1687. In this collection of forty stories, he focused on two groups: samurai and their "sworn brothers" and Kabuki actors and their townsmen patrons. In these stories, particularly in the former group, conflicts arise from triangular relationships, with honor and dignity playing key roles in their resolution. Samurai morality, especially as it pertained to the codified vendetta of the Tokugawa period, is the theme for the thirty-two stories in *Budō denraiki* (the transmission of martial arts), while it is the gnarled notion of samurai honor that serves as the thematic unifier for the twenty-six stories in *Tales of Samurai Honor*. These works of the samurai world are usually criticized as being inaccurate depictions of the samurai mind-set. Yet viewed as humorous portrayals of the strange world of the samurai, they are as entertaining as the bulk of Saikaku's writing.

While Saikaku had begun his career as a novelist with an unmistakable optimism, he entered a new phase in 1688 with the publication of *The Japanese Family Storehouse*. Perhaps he had become disillusioned with life under the Tokugawa regime; certainly, the seemingly unlimited economic opportunities that were in evidence earlier were rapidly disappearing. His focus took a pragmatic turn, and he began to write stories that revolved almost exclusively around the economic life of the townsmen. The theme to which he turned for *The Japanese Family Storehouse* was the economic life of the wealthy merchants. Of its thirty stories, seventeen are lively, humorous stories on how to become a millionaire, while the remaining thirteen serve as warnings to the merchants on how easy it is to lose their fortunes. Interestingly, many of the stories were based on true stories. Here, Saikaku unabashedly exhorts his fellow merchants not to neglect their family trade, to pay close attention to their business on a daily basis, advising them on how to manage their household finances. The didactic tone, however, is held in check by Saikaku's skill as an effective storyteller.

While there are positive aspects to *The Japanese Family Storehouse*, the success stories are by and large based on events that had taken place decades earlier. In the late 1680's, the economic outlook was bleak; it was no longer easy to amass a fortune. Saikaku's next important work, the last to be published during his lifetime, was *Worldly Mental Calculations*, whose theme concerns the merchants' year-end struggle to settle their accounts. Here, Saikaku turns his attention to the poor merchants, portraying their struggles to escape the harangues of the bill collectors. With irony, detachment, and humor, Saikaku tells tales of the poor, who will manage, by hook or by crook, to see the New Year in even when they have no resources except their wits. To Saikaku's credit, even the bleakest story somehow ends on a light note.

In both his earliest works, which dealt with the themes of pleasure and sensuality, and his latest, which dealt with economic realism, Saikaku had turned from the optimistic to the pessimistic. In his last memorable work, *Saikaku okimiyage* (Saikaku's parting present), published in 1693, a few months after his death, Saikaku returned to the men who squander their fortunes on the denizens of the pleasure quarters. They are portrayed as living in poverty, typically with the courtesans on whom they spent a fortune to ransom them from their indentured service. They show no remorse and, significantly, although they are penniless in the slums, they have not lost their self-respect: They are managing their lives with dignity.

Saikaku was, above all, a raconteur who wrote to entertain. He was a highly original writer, and he wrote in a distinct individual style, a combination of the oral tradition and the ornate literary style. His use of subject matter drawn from contemporary society as well as his use of seventeenth century colloquialism for dialogue contributes to a sense of realism. Saikaku's stories, especially the novels, are weak in plot development; it must be remembered, however, that the concept of plot construction is largely alien to traditional Japanese literature. Saikaku's stories, and much of traditional Japanese literature, must be appreciated more as segments in sequence than in consequence.

Other major works

NOVELS: *Kōshoku ichidai otoko*, 1682 (*The Life of an Amorous Man*, 1964); *Shoen ōkagami*, 1684; *Wankyū isse no monogatari*, 1685; *Koshoku ichidai onna*, 1696 (*The Life of an Amorous Woman*, 1963).

PLAYS: *Koyomi*, 1685; *Gaijin Yashima*, 1685.

POETRY: *Ikudama manku*, 1673; *Dokugin ichinichi senku*, 1675; *Saikaku haikai ōkukazu*, 1677; *Saikaku ōyakazu*, 1681.
NONFICTION: *Yakusha hyōbanki*, 1683?

Bibliography
Befu, Ben. "Some Observations on the Structure of Ihara Saikaku's *Seken Munezan'yō*," in *Monumenta Serica*. XXVII (1968), pp. 385-397.
Callahan, Caryl. "Tales of Samurai Honor: Saikaku's *Buke Giri Monogatari*," in *Monumenta Nipponica*. XXXIV, no. 1 (Spring, 1979), pp. 1-20.
Hibbett, Howard. *The Floating World in Japanese Fiction*, 1959.
_____. "The Japanese Comic Linked Verse Tradition," in *The Harvard Journal of Asiatic Studies*. XXIII (1960/1961), pp. 76-92.
_____. "Saikaku and Burlesque Fiction," in *The Harvard Journal of Asiatic Studies*. XX, nos. 1/2 (June, 1957), pp. 53-73.
Keene, Donald. *World Within Walls: Japanese Literature of the Pre-Modern Era, 1600-1867*, 1976.
Lane, Richard. "Postwar Japanese Studies of the Novelist Saikaku," in *The Harvard Journal of Asiatic Studies*. XVIII (June, 1955), pp. 181-199.
_____. "Saikaku and Boccaccio: The *Novella* in Japan and Italy," in *Monumenta Nipponica*. XV, nos. 1/2 (1959-1960), pp. 87-118.
_____. "Saikaku's Contemporaries and Followers: The Ukiyo-zōshi 1680-1780," in *Monumenta Nipponica*. XIV, nos. 3/4 (1958-1959), pp. 125-137.
_____. "Saikaku's Prose Works: A Bibliographical Study," in *Monumenta Nipponica*. XIV, nos. 1/2 (1958), pp. 1-26.
Leutner, Robert. "Saikaku's Parting Gift: Translations from *Saikaku Okimiyage*," in *Monumenta Nipponica*. XXX, no. 4 (Winter, 1975), pp. 357-391.
Marcus, Virginia. "A Miscellany of Old Letters: Saikaku's *Yorozu no fumi hōgu*," in *Monumenta Nipponica*. XL, no. 3 (Autumn, 1985), pp. 257-282.

Ben Befu

BRUNO SCHULZ

Born: Drohobycz, Poland; July 12, 1892
Died: Drohobycz, Poland; November 19, 1942

Principal short fiction

Sklepy cynamonowe, 1934 (British edition, *Cinnamon Shops and Other Stories*, 1963; U.S. edition, *The Street of Crocodiles*, 1963); *Sanatorium pod klepsydrą*, 1937 (*Sanatorium Under the Sign of the Hourglass*, 1978).

Other literary forms

Two collections of stories were the only literary works Bruno Schulz published during his lifetime. Since 1964, all of his extant works have been published in Poland; these have included prose sketches, essays and critical reviews of other literary works, and letters. The main collections in Polish are *Proza* (1964; Prose), *Księga listów* (1975; collected letters, edited by Jerzy Ficowski), and *Okolice sklepów cynamonowych* (1986; outskirts of the Cinnamon shops, edited by Ficowski). All of his papers, and sketches for a work titled "Mesjasz" (the messiah), were destroyed during World War II.

Schulz was also an artist of great talent. Many of his drawings were conceived as illustrations for his stories and consequently have literary as well as graphic interest.

Achievements

Schulz created an original prose style and a mode of narration like those of no other writer of the twentieth century. He was unquestionably one of the finest Polish prose writers of the period between the two world wars. *Cinnamon Shops*, his first book (translated in the United States as *The Street of Crocodiles*), was immediately recognized by Polish literary critics and honored by the Polish Academy of Literature. Since World War II, Schulz's works have been translated into more than a dozen languages. His influence on contemporary writers has been very strong, and he has been compared to the greatest of twentieth century authors. Isaac Bashevis Singer, winner of the Nobel Prize for Literature in 1978, has written:

> Schulz cannot be easily classified. He can be called a surrealist, a symbolist, an expressionist, a modernist. . . . He wrote sometimes like Kafka, sometimes like Proust, and at times succeeded in reaching depths that neither of them reached.

Schulz's impact on writers of longer fiction and novelists has been as great as his influence on short-story writers. One example, among many, is Cynthia Ozick's novel *The Messiah of Stockholm* (1987), partly based on Schulz's life and writings. It is difficult to define the exact genre of his prose. In *Cinnamon Shops* each of the fifteen parts has a title, and Schulz occasionally refers to them as "tales" (in Polish, *opowiadania*). Yet the term is loose. Three of the parts are an extended "Traktat o manekinach" ("Treatise on Tailors' Dummies"), and the whole has unity of character, place, time, and tone. In the book, Schulz broke decisively with the traditional forms of both the short story and the novel.

In a letter written to the Polish playwright and novelist Stanisław Ignacy Witkiewicz, in 1935, Schulz wrote:

> To what genre does *Cinnamon Shops* belong? How should it be classified? I consider it an autobiographical novel, not merely because it is written in the first person and one can recognize in it certain events and experiences from the author's own childhood. It is an autobiography—or rather, a genealogy—of the spirit. . . . since it reveals the spirit's pedigree back to those depths where it merges with mythology.

Schulz created a new genre of prose that belongs to him alone.

Biography

When Bruno Schulz was born, in 1892, Drohobycz was a small Polish town in Galicia, then a province of the Austro-Hungarian Empire. Poland had lost its independence and was partitioned; it became independent in 1918, when Schulz was twenty-six years old. Drohobycz had a population of about thirty thousand, largely Jewish and Polish.

Schulz's family was Jewish and spoke Polish. His father, Jakub, was the owner and bookkeeper of the textile fabrics shop described in his son's stories. Bruno was the youngest of three children; he was educated at home and in a school named for Emperor Franz Joseph. The merchant profession to which his parents belonged separated them from the Hasidim, and Schulz never learned Yiddish; although he knew German he wrote in Polish, the language of his immediate family. After completing high school, he studied architecture in Lwów for three years, until the outbreak of World War I. He taught himself to draw and produced graphics, hoping to make art his career. Instead, he obtained the post of teacher of drawing and handicrafts at the state high school, or *gimnazjum*, named for King Władysław Jagiełło, in Drohobycz. He was to teach in the school for seventeen years, until his death in 1942.

In the 1920's it was only drawing and painting that Schulz practiced openly, in full view of his friends; he kept his literary works to himself, sharing them with few people in Drohobycz. It was through correspondence with friends in distant cities that Schulz began his literary career. *Cinnamon Shops* began in the letters he sent to Deborah Vogel, a poet and doctor of philosophy who lived in Lwów. Fragment by fragment, episode by episode, the book progressed, embedded in Schulz's letters; she urged him to continue, until the book took the form it now has. Schulz gained the support of the eminent novelist Zofia Nałkowska, who helped him in the publication of the book.

Stanisław Witkiewicz in Kraków became an early enthusiast of Schulz's work, and a correspondent; other admirers and correspondents came to include the novelist Witold Gombrowicz, the poet Julian Tuwim, and the German writer Thomas Mann.

After his literary success, Schulz continued to live in Drohobycz. Because of his prize from the Polish Academy of Letters, a "golden laurel," his school gave him the title of "professor" but no raise in salary. His brother died in an accident in 1936, and Schulz's financial responsibilities grew; he became the sole supporter of his widowed sister, her son, and an aged cousin. Schulz became engaged, but his fiancée was Catholic, there were religious complications, and their relationship eventually ended. With the help of friends in Poland and France, Schulz managed to travel to Paris in the summer of 1938, and he stayed there for three weeks—it was his first trip abroad.

War broke out in Poland in September, 1939. According to the Molotov-Ribbentrop secret pact, Germany attacked western Poland on September 1, and their ally, the Soviet Union, had agreed to attack eastern Poland simultaneously. Drohobycz was in eastern Poland, and the Red Army with the NKVD invaded it on September 17. For the next twenty months, they occupied the town. Schulz continued to teach drawing in his high school; he had stopped writing. In the summer of 1941, the Germans attacked their Soviet allies, occupying Drohobycz in turn. Together with other Jews, Schulz was confined to the ghetto. One day in November, 1942, he ventured with a special pass to the "Aryan" quarter; he was bringing home a loaf of bread when he was recognized by a Gestapo officer, who shot him dead on the street. That night, a friend recovered his body and buried it in the nearby Jewish cemetery.

That cemetery no longer exists. In addition, the manuscripts of Schulz's unpublished works, given to a friend for safekeeping, are lost—they disappeared along with their custodian. Schulz's major work was to have been the novel titled "Mesjasz." No trace of this work remains either.

Analysis

Very high claims have been made for Bruno Schulz's work ever since Stanisław Witkiewicz's enthusiasm about *Cinnamon Shops*; Schulz's reputation as a twentieth century Polish writer has been consistently high. Czesław Miłosz, in his *History of Polish Literature*, stressed Schulz's humor, intuition, and the metaphorical richness of his language, confirming that "today, Schulz is regarded as one of the most important prose writers between the two wars." Isaac Bashevis Singer has called him "one of the most remarkable writers who ever lived," and Cynthia Ozick has written that Schulz had "one of the most original imaginations in modern Europe." The Yugoslav writer Danilo Kiš has said, "Schulz is my god." These are very high estimates. On what are they based?

The twentieth century has witnessed a number of literary movements that have claimed to have a special relation to reality, or a hold upon it: surrealism and hyper-realism, ultraism, expressionism. In theory or in practice, the movements attempted to combine the individual and the world around him in a new synthesis, to combine in a single outlook both subject and object in all their breadth. In practice, and with a minimum of theory or dubious abstraction, Schulz seemed to achieve that synthesis. It is true that Schulz developed a theory of the mythical transformation of the everyday world that he described in his correspondence and in his essay "Mityzacja rzeczy-wistości" (mythization of reality), but of infinitely greater importance was the artistic synthesis itself, displayed above all in his book *Cinnamon Shops*.

The basic cast of characters is simple. The narrator is a boy—and the man he came to be—describing events using the first-person pronoun. His father Jacob is perhaps the most important character, owner of the dry-goods shop which is the major source of torment as well as the basis for the livelihood of the family. The mother is of far lesser importance; Adela, a practical, sensuous servant, dominates the family. In addition there are shop assistants, diverse relatives, the huge, amorphous presence of the house with its many rooms, and the town. Although the father is an unusual character, the basic situation is ordinary, familiar, everyday. Even boredom is taken into account, taking up the time that becomes a major ingredient of the book.

One of Schulz's major innovations is his use of a child narrator and adult narrator merged into a single viewpoint. Ever since the nineteenth century, a traditional device of European and American fiction was an observing narrator through whose consciousness and senses the events of the novel were filtered. This consciousness was different from that of the author; the narrative consciousness was aware of some things the author might know but unaware of others. Usually the narration did not completely coincide with this consciousness, because if it did it would be too chaotic and disorderly, private, and undirected. Instead, this consciousness—what might be called a fictional construct—was located just outside the point of view of the narrative consciousness, in the middle distance. In *Cinnamon Shops*, the young boy provides this narrative consciousness, but only partly. It is difficult to pinpoint the boy's age, which might be anywhere between five and twelve. This ambiguity builds on the important presence of the house and rooms, which have accumulated the associations stored up over many years. More important, the childhood consciousness is overlaid by that of an adult and artist. The book was written by an author already approaching forty. The narration is a highly synthetic—and successful—mix of different developmental stages. The density of the sense of reality is thicker, more solid and opaque, than that available to most observers confined to a single moment in space and time. Because of the book's subtle artistry, this often goes unrecognized by the reader. Yet the resurrection of the shop, and the reconstruction of childhood with all its emotional riches, took place only after the father and the business had long disappeared.

For Schulz, this is not linear. Whether time is "really" linear is for the individual reader to judge. It might be that time's linearity is a tradition which our culture has found convenient, that it is a fictional construct that is difficult to judge objectively. Certainly Schulz's synthetic time provides the reader with a shock of recognition; it is strikingly real, or realistic. In "Pan," Schulz evokes intense, midsummer heat before presenting the young narrator's encounter with a vagabond:

> It was there that I saw him first and for the only time in my life, at a noon-hour crazy with heat. It was at a moment when time, demented and wild, breaks away from the treadmill of events and like an escaping vagabond, runs shouting across the fields. Then the summer grows out of control, spreads at all points all over space with a wild impetus, doubling and trebling itself into an unknown, lunatic dimension.

In the title story, the reader is told, "Amidst sleepy talk, time passed unnoticed. It ran by unevenly, as if making knots in the passage of hours, swallowing somewhere whole empty periods. Without transition, our whole gang found ourselves on the way home long after midnight. . . ." Schulz constantly calls calendar time into question. The story "Noc wielkiego sezonu" ("The Night of the Great Season") begins, "in a run of normal uneventful years that great eccentric, Time, begets sometimes other years, different, prodigal years which—like a sixth, smallest toe—grow a thirteenth freak month."

These are not merely verbal effects. They underlie a uniquely solid and sensuous concept of reality and psychology. Schulz's descriptions of interiors, of rooms, closets, and walls, are among the finest and most evocative that exist in literature. Like the Dutch painter Jan Vermeer, he renders simple concrete details with superb suggestiveness: "his eyes, like minuscule mirrors, reflected all the shining objects: the white light of the sun in the cracks of the window, the golden rectangle of the curtains, and enclosed, like a drop of water, all the room with the stillness of its carpets and its empty chairs" (from, "Pan Karol," "Mr. Charles"). Schulz is particularly good at describing the blurred transitions between different psychological states; here his aptitude is similar to that of Marcel Proust. His descriptions of boredom and the revolt against boredom ring with truth—and of waking, going to sleep, or the sheer softness of a bed and bedclothes, a sleeper who "still hung on to the verge of night, gasping for breath, while the bedding grew around him, swelled and fermented—and again engulfed him in a mountain of heavy, whitish dough." His use of metaphor is always evocative, rendering the associations memory imparts to physical objects. In describing the bolts of cloth in his father's shop, Schulz writes of "the powerful formations of that cosmogony of cloth, under its mountain ranges that rose in imposing massifs.

Wide valleys opened up between the slopes . . . the interior of the shop formed itself into the panorama of an autumn landscape, full of lakes and distance." The blend of subject and object becomes almost seamless. The density of psychological association—or investment—and palpable concrete objects come together in some of the most sensuous descriptions in literature.

Probably the key to these passages is memory. For Schulz, memory is like an onion, providing layer after layer of physical growth. Objects and memory of objects become interchangeable. It is the father who explains that in old apartments there are rooms which are sometimes forgotten, and, unvisited for months on end, "they wilt neglected between the old walls and it happens that they close in on themselves, become overgrown with bricks, and, lost once and for all to our memory, forfeit their only claim to existence . . . they merge with the wall, grow into it, and all trace of them is obliterated in a complicated design of lines and cracks" (in the "Treatise on Tailors' Dummies: Conclusion"). For Schulz, "Reality is as thin as paper and betrays with all its cracks its imitative character." Reality is always fluid, it is dense, shifting, frequently "half-baked and undecided," constantly threatened by possibilities that approach fulfillment and then retreat again, on the verge of realization. Reality is in a constant fermentation, participating in the psychology of multiple observers with their preoccupations, memory, and fantasy. The narrator's father speaks of the "make-believe of matter which had created a semblance of life," and physical objects have as much solid palpability—as much feeling—as people have. He asks, "How much ancient suffering is there in the varnished grain, in the veins and knots of our old familiar wardrobes? Who would recognize in them the old features, smiles, and glances, almost planed and polished out of all recognition?" As the father asks this question his own wrinkled face appears to be an old plank, full of knots and veins, from which all memories had been planed away.

Was Schulz influenced by Sigmund Freud and by psychoanalysis? Probably only to a limited extent. After World War I, the movement enjoyed a great vogue; Bruno Bettelheim has described how, for many, it became an all-encompassing way of life that occupied all the free time of its enthusiasts. Schulz was interested in psychoanalysis, but his verdict was largely negative; the description of the psychoanalysis of his Uncle Edward is a savage parody that concludes the *Cinnamon Shops*, ending with the uncle's complete loss of personality, reduction to the state of an automaton responding only to the ringing of a bell, and, ultimately, death. Schulz was responding to some of the same historical currents that produced psychoanalysis and the later movement of Surrealism, but his attitudes toward the subconscious, as revealed in *Cinnamon Shops*, were entirely his own. What he stressed above all was the synthetic, cumulative function of memory and growth. Linear cause and effect and the somewhat rigid, theoretical mechanisms of Freud have little place in Schulz's world. On the other hand, he subjected the inner world of the psyche to one of the most sustained, probing explorations of his time.

Schulz's second collection of stories, *Sanatorium Under the Sign of the Hourglass*, did not provoke the same excitement that met the first collection. It is a virtuoso performance, especially the title story, but differs in important ways from the *Cinnamon Shops*. First, its mode of composition was different. *Cinnamon Shops* was elaborated in correspondence with Deborah Vogel, and Schulz was oblivious to the presence of any other reader or larger audience. The intensity of the attention riveted upon his experience is unhindered, uninterrupted. The author of the stories in *Sanatorium Under the Sign of the Hourglass* was famous, and he became intimidated by what he felt was a spotlight shining on him, intruding on his act of writing. Now he was writing for a public, and it made him uncomfortable. Also, as with other mature writers, he was subjected to powerful literary influences from the past. He read widely—Rainer Maria Rilke, Thomas Mann, and Franz Kafka, among others—and borrowed what he found useful for his own stories. The story "Sanatorium Under the Sign of the Hourglass" incorporates successfully ideas from Mann's *Der Zauberberg* (1924; *The Magic Mountain*, 1927); in some ways Schulz even goes beyond Mann in his evocation of atmosphere and in his concept of human transformation. In "Ostatnia ucleczka ojca" ("Father's Last Escape"), the metamorphosis of the father into a kind of crustacean or crab shows an obvious debt to Kafka's *Die Verwandlung* (1915; *The Metamorphosis*, 1936). Schulz's own translation of Kafka's *Der Prozess* (1925; *The Trial*, 1937) appeared in 1936. Schulz's stories in his second collection are on a consistently high plane, yet they do not represent an advance. Schulz was now a writer of fiction. He was branching out; his focus was less exclusively on his own childhood. His Ovidian transformations occur with a certain ease, as when the irritated father turns into a buzzing fly, or when Simon, the old age pensioner, is subject to an assumption and rises into the sky. Many of the effects are allegorical; they are partly willed by the intellect, yet the transformations do not engage the author's sense of an all-encompassing reality. The allegory is more abstract and brittle than it was in *Cinnamon Shops*. Some stories are frankly experimental, as when Schulz uses an obtuse first-person narrator and an arch, *faux naïf* speaking voice in "Emeryt" ("The Old Age Pensioner") and "Samotność" ("Loneliness"). The stories "Dodo" and "Edzio" ("Eddie"), on the other hand, are extremely realistic, almost naturalistic. No doubt it is good that he was experimenting in new directions; his new undertakings were certain to lead to new forms of synthesis in the future.

In the late 1930's, however, his creative work began to slacken. More and more frequently he fell into barren and agonizing states of depression. His isolation and solitude in Drohobycz had advantages but also great disadvantages. Still, he continued to work on his project for "Mesjasz." Two parts originally destined for it—"Księga" (the book) and "Genialna epoka" (the age of genius)—found their way into the collection *Sanatorium Under the Sign of the Hourglass*. During the war, he read aloud to his friends sections of "Mesjasz"; in this work, the myth of the coming of the Messiah was to symbolize a return to the happy perfection that existed at the beginning—the return to childhood.

One cannot know what artistic form this return would have taken. Friends of Schulz returned to Drohobycz in 1944 and 1945 to search for his papers. They had no success. All of Schulz's manuscripts, records, letters, and papers were lost, with a single exception: One drawing was found.

Other literary forms

NONFICTION: *Proza*, 1964; *Księga listów*, 1975 (edited by Jerzy Ficowski); *Okolice sklepów cynamonowych*, 1986 (edited by Ficowski).

Bibliography

Bayley, John. "Pioneers and Phantoms," in *The New York Review of Books*. XXV (July 20, 1978).

Bereza, Henryk. "Bruno Schulz," in *Polish Perspectives*. IX (June, 1966).

Ficowski, Jerzy. Introduction to *The Street of Crocodiles*, 1977.

Lukashevich, Olga. "Bruno Schulz's *The Street of Crocodiles*: A Story in Creativity and Neurosis," in *The Polish Review*. XIII (Spring, 1968).

Miłosz, Czesław. *The History of Polish Literature*, 1969, 1983.

Taylor, Colleen M. "Childhood Revisited: The Writings of Bruno Schulz," in *Slavic and East European Journal*. XIII (December, 1968).

John Carpenter

SIR WALTER SCOTT

Born: Edinburgh, Scotland; August 15, 1771
Died: Abbotsford, Scotland; September 21, 1832

Principal short fiction

"Wandering Willie's Tale," 1824; *Chronicles of the Canongate*, 1827; "Death of the Laird's Jock," 1828; "My Aunt Margaret's Mirror," 1828; "The Tapestried Chamber," 1828.

Other literary forms

A giant of European Romanticism, Sir Walter Scott made important contributions to many literary forms. He wrote the Waverley novels (1814-1831), a series that virtually created the historical novel. Particularly admired are the Scottish novels, including *Waverley: Or, 'Tis Sixty Years Since* (1814), *Old Mortality* (1816), *Rob Roy* (1817), *The Heart of Midlothian* (1817), *The Bride of Lammermoor* (1819), and *Redgauntlet* (1824). Scott also wrote extremely popular poetry, including *The Lay of the Last Minstrel* (1805), *Marmion: A Tale of Flodden Field* (1808), and *The Lady of the Lake* (1810). He also collected ballads in the two-volume *Minstrelsy of the Scottish Border* (1802), published critical editions of the works of John Dryden (1808) and Jonathan Swift (1814), and wrote histories, essays, reviews, criticism, and plays.

Achievements

Scott's life was a series of remarkable achievements. In literature, he was a pioneer whose works still stand on their own merits. He collected ballads for the *Minstrelsy of the Scottish Border*, a milestone in the study of Scottish antiquities. From 1805 to 1810, Scott wrote the most popular poetry in Great Britain, setting unprecedented sales records. In 1813, he was offered the poet laureateship, which he refused. His greatest achievement came in the field of fiction. The Waverley novels virtually created a new genre, the historical novel, and made Scott one of the two most popular novelists of the century. He was knighted in 1819. Scott was also an accomplished writer of short fiction, and three of his six stories are generally acknowledged to be among the best in the genre. Finally, Scott wrote a series of literary prefaces, criticisms, and reviews that made him an important literary theorist.

Biography

Walter Scott was born in Edinburgh, Scotland, on August 15, 1771, and attended Edinburgh Royal High School and Edinburgh College. In 1786, he signed indentures to become a Writer to the Signet and, in 1792, he became a Scottish Advocate. In 1797, he married Charlotte Carpenter, with whom he had four children. He became Sheriff-Deputy of Selkirkshire in 1799 and

Clerk to the Scottish Court of Session in 1806. From 1805 to 1810, h. published best-selling poetry. In 1812, he bought Abbotsford, his home for life. Two years later, Scott published *Waverley*, the first in the series of remarkably successful and influential Waverley novels. He became a baronet in 1819, and later, in 1822, he arranged and managed the visit to Scotland of King George IV. Four years following this peak in his social career, Scott's wife died and he suffered bankruptcy, which he struggled to overcome during the remainder of his life. In 1827, he acknowledged publicly his authorship of the Waverley novels, and, in 1829, he began publication of the "Magnum Opus," a forty-eight-volume edition of the Waverley novels. He died at Abbotsford on September 21, 1832.

Analysis

Sir Walter Scott is known primarily as a novelist and secondarily as a poet. He wrote only six short stories. Nevertheless, he remains an important figure in that genre, too. In *The Short Story in English* (1981), the distinguished critic Walter Allen begins his survey of the genre with Scott's story "The Two Drovers," which he calls "the first modern short story in English." In addition, three of his stories (as mentioned above) are generally acknowledged to be among the masterpieces of the form.

Scott uses the same methods and explores the same subjects in his stories as in his novels. He places his characters in concrete historical situations; they are social beings rooted in a particular time and place. Conflicts between individuals symbolize larger issues—the conflict between past and present, the conflict between national traditions and temperaments, the tragedy of cultural incomprehension. Scott presents these themes more starkly, however, in his stories. The demanding form of the short story forced him into a directness and concision often lacking in his novels. Thus, to many readers, Scott's short stories may be the most satisfactory works he ever wrote.

Scott's first short story, "Wandering Willie's Tale," appeared in the novel *Redgauntlet*. Although it attains its full significance only in the context of that larger work, this universally admired tale stands on its own merits. It presents a comic version of serious Scott themes. Steenie Steenson, the grandfather of the narrator, goes on a strange odyssey. When he brings his rent to his landlord, Sir Robert Redgauntlet, the old persecutor dies in burning agony just before giving Steenie a receipt. The silver disappears. Sir John Redgauntlet, the son and successor, threatens to evict Steenie from his hereditary home unless he can produce either rent or receipt. Poor Steenie, tossing off a mutchkin of brandy, makes two toasts: the first to "the memory of Sir Robert Redgauntlet, and might he never lie quiet in his grave till he had righted his poor bond-tenant"; the second, "a health to Man's Enemy, if he would but get him back the pock of siller." Immediately afterward, riding through the dark wood of Pitmurkie, Steenie is accosted by a strange gentleman who takes him to Redgauntlet Castle, where dead Sir Robert is revelling with a set of ghastly persecutors. Avoiding various temptations, Steenie demands and obtains his receipt. When Sir Robert insists that he return every year to pay homage, Steenie cries, "I refer myself to God's pleasure, and not to yours." Losing consciousness, he awakens in this world. He brings the receipt to Sir John and, acting upon a hint from Sir Robert, unlocks the mystery of the missing silver.

This comic tale of diablerie has a serious side. The portrayal of Sir Robert and his cohorts from "the killing times" is a grim reminder of Scotland's bloody past. Like other Scott heroes, Steenie cannot evade the past but must come to terms with it. When the past demands his unconditional loyalty, however, he struggles to retain his freedom. Nor is the present time idealized. Sir John, the advocate, can be just as tyrannical as his father. As wartime Scotland evolves into civil peace, physical coercion gives way to legal. Scott balances the evils of the past against those of the present. In like manner, he balances the natural against the supernatural. He suggests the possibility of a rational explanation for the extraordinary events; perhaps Steenie was having a drunken dream. Where did the receipt come from, though, and how did Steenie know where to recover the silver? As usual, Scott suggests something at work beyond the rational.

"Wandering Willie's Tale" is a gem of formal art. The onward rush of events is played off against the balanced structure. For example, Steenie's first meeting with Sir Robert is contrasted with his first meeting with Sir John. Scott highlights the contrast by focusing on the account book in each scene. The second meeting with Sir Robert also necessitates a second meeting with Sir John. The short-story form allows Scott to achieve a superb structure that is lacking in his novels. Finally, it is generally acknowledged that Scott writes his freest, raciest, most humorous prose when he is writing in Scots dialect. His only story related wholly in the vernacular, "Wandering Willie's Tale" is his one sustained masterpiece of prose.

"The Highland Widow" first appeared in *Chronicles of the Canongate* (which also includes "The Two Drovers"). It is the tragedy of Elspat MacTavish, who must live with the guilt of having caused the death of her only son. She is compared to Orestes and Oedipus, and the inevitability and starkness of her drama are indeed Sophoclean. Yet the method is unmistakably Scott's. The tragedy arises out of particular historical circumstances.

Scott's narrator declares that his object is "to throw some light on the manners of Scotland as they were, and to contrast them, occasionally, with those of the present day." Elspat MacTavish grew to womanhood in the years before the rebellion of 1745, when the Highlands were a law unto themselves. She became the wife and faithful companion of the famous MacTavish Mhor, who did not hesitate to take anything, lawfully or not, that he desired to have. The morality of husband and wife is that of the old Highland, one of "faithful friends and fierce enemies." In Scott, however, the old order changes, yielding place to new. MacTavish Mhor is killed by soldiers, the rebellion of 1745 is foiled, the Highlands are pacified, and military violence is replaced by civil order. Only Elspat MacTavish, dwelling in the wildest recesses of the Highlands, remains unconscious of the great change. Even her son, Hamish Bean, mingling more with people in this world, understands that his father's trade of cateran is now dangerous and dishonorable. To provide for his mother and himself, he enlists in a new Scottish regiment. Living in the past, Elspat finds Hamish's actions incomprehensible—to be a soldier, to fight under a Campbell, their hereditary enemies, and to support the government of Hanover. Conditioned by her historical environment, acting by her own best lights, she determines to save Hamish from dishonor.

The tragic climax comes inexorably. Elspat drugs Hamish's parting drink, preventing him from returning to his regiment in time. She knows that her son retains enough of the old Highland traditions to consider the promised scourging for lateness as appropriate only for dogs. Caught between his duty to his new masters and his old Highland dread of dishonor, and urged on by his mother, Hamish kills the sergeant sent to secure him. He himself is speedily apprehended, found guilty, and executed. Hamish's fate is sad, but that of Elspat is tragic. She continues to live with the knowledge that she killed her only child. The parallels with Orestes and Oedipus suggest not only the mental torment that results from such epic crimes but also the deep love between mother and son.

Once again, the strict demands of the short-story form compelled Scott into a concentration of effort and intensity of effect that are absent from his novels. Everything is directed toward the tragic end. The opening description of old Elspat and her crime eliminates all suspense about what happened but stimulates wonder as to how it happened. It also gives the following story of long ago a sense of inevitability. In like manner, although there are occasional references to Fate, the action develops inevitably out of the characters of the two major figures, who are themselves products of their historical environments. Finally, Scott raises the language of Elspat to the heroic level, partly to suggest her Gaelic speech but mostly to give her the tragic tone.

"The Two Drovers" also appeared in *Chronicles of the Canongate*. Whereas "The Highland Widow" is based on a conflict between different times, "The Two Drovers" is based on a conflict between different places. Robin Oig M'Combich is a Highlander, Harry Wakefield a Yorkshireman. The two are best of friends but, because neither understands the national traditions or temperament of the other, tragedy results.

The story begins with an ominous instance of second sight. Robin's aunt warns him not to undertake the cattle drive because she sees Saxon blood on his dirk. Robin's reply, "All men have their blood from Adam," indicates that he is unaware of the great national differences between men. He gives his weapon to Hugh Morrison, but the sense of doom hangs over him.

The story modulates into the realistic mode. Scott quickly establishes the genuine friendship between the two drovers. When Robin unintentionally gains possession of the very field that Harry had been seeking for his own cattle, however, the simple Yorkshireman suspects the canny Scot of duplicity. Even when Robin offers to share the field, Harry's hurt pride makes him refuse. His anger is increased by his drinking, the wretchedness of the pasturage he finally obtains, and the taunts of his English cronies "from the ancient grudge against the Scots." Consequently, when Robin arrives at the inn, Harry challenges him in characteristic English fashion, "a tussle for love on the sod . . . and we shall be better friends than ever." To a Highlander, however, to be beaten with fists stains a man with irremovable dishonor. When Robin tries to leave, Harry knocks him down.

The story hastens to its inevitable climax. Despite the sense of doom, the tragedy can be understood entirely in terms of the actors and their backgrounds. Robin walks ten miles to obtain his dirk from Hugh Morrison, tells Harry, "I show you now how the Highland dunnièwassel fights," and plunges his dagger into Harry's heart. Throwing the fatal weapon into the turf-fire, he exclaims, "take me who likes—and let fire cleanse blood if it can." His aunt's vision was accurate: The imagery of blood, prominent from the start, ends here. Before leaving, though, Robin looks "with a mournful but steady eye on the lifeless visage" of his friend and remarks, "He was a pretty man!" Scott's capacity for expressing the most intense dramatic emotions in the simplest language, his realistic eloquence, justifies his title to be called the most Shakespearean of prose writers.

The story ends with the trial judge's lengthy summation, which reflects Scott's own view of historical tragedy. No villains are involved. The crime arose from an "error of the understanding . . . men acting in ignorance of each other's national prejudices." The judge also points out that, if Robin had had his dirk and killed Harry immediately, he would have been guilty of manslaughter. Ironically, his aunt's second sight caused him to commit murder. Robin acknowledges the justice of the death sentence, and the story closes on his simple but resonant monosyllables: "I give a life for the life I took, and what can I do more?"

Scott's last three short stories were published in *The Keepsake* (a Christmas gift-book published annually) of 1828. "My Aunt Margaret's Mirror" and "The Tapestried Chamber" are ghost stories; "Death of the Laird's Jock" is a sketch of "a subject for the pencil" of an artist. None is significant literature.

In contrast, Scott's first three stories set the highest standards for the newly emerging genre. "Wandering Willie's Tale," a marvelous comic tale, was regarded by Dante Gabriel Rossetti and Andrew Lang as the finest short story in English. "The Highland Widow" and "The Two Drovers" triumph on a nobler plane, reaching the heights of tragedy. All three stories exemplify Scott's major contribution to British fiction: the portrayal of man as a social and historical being.

Other major works

NOVELS: *Waverley: Or, 'Tis Sixty Years Since*, 1814; *Guy Mannering*, 1815; *The Antiquary*, 1816; *The Black Dwarf*, 1816; *Old Mortality*, 1816; *Rob Roy*, 1817; *The Heart of Midlothian*, 1817; *The Bride of Lammermoor*, 1819; *A Legend of Montrose*, 1819; *Ivanhoe*, 1819; *The Monastery*, 1820; *The Abbot*, 1820; *Kenilworth*, 1820; *The Pirate*, 1822; *The Fortunes of Nigel*, 1822; *Peveril of the Peak*, 1823; *Quentin Durward*, 1823; *St. Ronan's Well*, 1824; *Redgauntlet*, 1824; *The Betrothed*, 1825; *The Talisman*, 1825; *Woodstock*, 1826; *The Fair Maid of Perth*, 1828; *Anne of Geierstein*, 1829; *Count Robert of Paris*, 1831; *Castle Dangerous*, 1831.

PLAYS: *Goetz von Berlichingen*, 1799 (translation); *Halidon Hill*, 1822; *Macduff's Cross*, 1823; *The Doom of Devorgoil*, 1830; *Auchindrane: Or, The Ayrshire Tragedy*, 1830.

POETRY: *The Chase, and William and Helen: Two Ballads from the German of Gottfried Augustus Bürger*, 1796 (translation); *The Eve of Saint John: A Border Ballad*, 1800; *The Lay of the Last Minstrel*, 1805; *Ballads and Lyrical Pieces*, 1806; *Marmion: A Tale of Flodden Field*, 1808; *The Lady of the Lake*, 1810; *The Vision of Don Roderick*, 1811; *Rokeby*, 1813; *The Bridal of Triermain: Or, The Vale of St. John, in Three Cantos*, 1813; *The Lord of the Isles*, 1815; *The Field of Waterloo*, 1815; *The Ettrick Garland: Being Two Excellent New Songs*, 1815 (with James Hogg); *Harold the Dauntless*, 1817.

NONFICTION: *Minstrelsy of the Scottish Border*, 1802 (two volumes); *The Life and Works of John Dryden*, 1808; *A Collection of Scarce and Valuable Tracts*, 1809-1815 (thirteen volumes); *The Life and Works of Jonathan Swift*, 1814; *Lives of the Novelists*, 1821-1824; *Chronological Notes of Scottish Affairs from the Diary of Lord Fountainhall*, 1822; *Lays of the Lindsays*, 1824; *The Life of Napoleon Buonaparte: Emperor of the French, with a Preliminary View of the French Revolution*, 1827; *Tales of a Grandfather: Being Stories Taken from Scottish History*, 1828-1830 (four volumes).

Bibliography

Hayden, John O. *Scott: The Critical Heritage*, 1970.
Johnson, Edgar. *Sir Walter Scott: The Great Unknown*, 1970.
Lockhart, John Gibson. *Memoirs of the Life of Sir Walter Scott*, 1837-1838.
Lukács, Georg. *The Historical Novel*, 1937, 1962. Translated by Hannah Mitchell and Stanley Mitchell.
Wilt, Judith. *Secret Leaves: The Novels of Walter Scott*, 1985.

Mark A. Weinstein

VARLAM SHALAMOV

Born: Vologda, Russia; 1907
Died: Moscow, U.S.S.R.; January 17, 1982

Principal short fiction

Kolymskie rasskazy, 1978 (*Kolyma Tales*, 1980, and *Graphite*, 1981).

Other literary forms

Varlam Shalamov was primarily a writer of short stories, although the particular nature of the genre he developed is unique. His stories are a blend of fiction and nonfiction. Shalamov was also a poet, and his only works to be published in the Soviet Union have been poems. A collection of poems titled *Shelest List'ev* (rustling of leaves) was published in 1964 and *Tochka kipeniia: Stikhi* (boiling point: poems) appeared in Moscow in 1977. Shalamov has also written essays, in particular *Ocherki prestupnogo mira* (n.d.; essays on the criminal world).

Achievements

Shalamov's achievements cannot be measured by ordinary standards or norms. Certainly, his greatest achievement was to stay alive during his seventeen years in what he calls the "death camps"—as opposed to ordinary camps—in Kolyma in northeastern Siberia. He survived: Although he was indelibly marked by the experience, it did not break him.

The quality of his short stories, which are a subtle blend of fiction and nonfiction, is on an extraordinarily high level. John Glad, who translated most of the *Kolymskie rasskazy* into English in two volumes, *Kolyma Tales* and *Graphite*, claimed in 1981 that Shalamov was "Russia's greatest living writer." Although this might seem excessively enthusiastic, particularly in view of the achievements of Aleksandr Solzhenitsyn, the claim is not to be lightly dismissed. The stories are strikingly original in their use of the short-story form. Solzhenitsyn himself had the highest regard for Shalamov's talent. When he first read Shalamov in 1956, he later recalled, he felt as if he had "met a long-lost brother" and believed that in some ways Shalamov's experience surpassed his own. "I respectfully confess," Solzhenitsyn wrote, "that to him and not to me was it given to touch those depths of bestiality and despair towards which life in the camps dragged us all." Solzhenitsyn writes relatively little about the mining camps of Kolyma in *Arkhipelag gulag* (1973-1975; *The Gulag Archipelago*, 1974-1978) or about the infamous "numbered" death camps that had no names but only numbers to designate them.

The critic Grigori Svirski has well described the shock experienced by Russian readers when Shalamov's first stories were circulated in samizdat form in the 1960's:

It was truth and not perfect style that was required of Shalamov, and in each new story he uncovered new pages of truth about convict life with such power, that even former political prisoners who had not witnessed such things were struck dumb. The truth revealed by Shalamov shocks because it is described by an artist, described with such skill, as they used to say in the nineteenth century, that the skill is invisible.

Biography

Varlam Tikhonovich Shalamov was born and reared in Vologda, a town in north-central European Russia. Shalamov's adult life was largely spent in prisons and camps, but ironically even his childhood was spent in a region affected by the Russian penal system. He has written of Vologda that "over the centuries as a result of the banishment to the area of so many protesters, rebels, and different critics of the tsars, a sort of sediment built up and a particular moral climate was formed which was at a higher level than any city in Russia." In 1919, Kedrov, the Soviet commander of the northern front, had two hundred hostages shot in Vologda. Little is known of Shalamov's life, but he says in a story that one of the hostages killed was the local chemistry teacher—as a result, Shalamov never learned chemistry or even the formula for water.

Shalamov was married, and in 1937, he was arrested for declaring that Ivan Bunin, the winner of the 1933 Nobel Prize for Literature, was "a Russian classic." Shalamov spent the next seventeen years in labor camps, mostly in Kolyma, in northeastern Siberia, where the prisoners worked in gold mines. The Soviet Union is the second largest producer of gold in the world, largely because of these mines, which utilized prison and slave labor; it is estimated that more than three million people have died there from cold, hunger, and overwork. In *The Gulag Archipelago*, Solzhenitsyn calls Kolyma "the pole of cold and cruelty"; the British author Robert Conquest argues in *Kolyma: The Arctic Death Camps* (1978) that these killings were the conscious result of a policy of extermination.

Shalamov was released in 1954 and returned to Moscow. His stories were first circulated in manuscript form in the Soviet Union and were later published in Russian in the émigré journals *Grani* and *Novyi Zhurnal*. Some samizdat authors in the Soviet Union at the time were establishing regular contact with Western journalists and even obtaining Western lawyers to protect their rights, but Shalamov, old and ill, could do nothing to ensure more adequate publication of his works. A French version of his stories was published in 1969. It was not until 1978, however, that a complete Russian edition of the stories was brought out by Overseas Publications Interchange in London. The Soviet authorities forced Shalamov to denounce publicly the publication of his stories.

Shalamov was ill during the last decades of his life. A contemporary observer described Shalamov in Moscow: "On the speaker's rostrum stood a man with a completely fixed expression on his face. He appeared dried up and curiously dark and frozen like a blackened tree." Shalamov died of heart failure on January 17, 1982.

Analysis

It is natural to compare Varlam Shalamov's work to that of Solzhenitsyn; there are similarities in their subject matter, and they had great respect for each other. Solzhenitsyn was among the first to recognize Shalamov's talent in the early 1960's, when Shalamov's brief sketches of life in the Kolyma labor camps began to trickle into the embryonic samizdat network just beginning to form in Moscow, Leningrad, and a few other cities. Recognizing their importance, Solzhenitsyn invited Shalamov to share the authorship of *The Gulag Archipelago*, the multivolume "experiment in literary investigation" on which he was working. Shalamov was too ill, however, to accept Solzhenitsyn's invitation.

Unlike Solzhenitsyn, Shalamov does not aim at a panoramic view of the camp world. Also, his language is quite different from that of Solzhenitsyn. On the surface, at least, he does not appear to maintain a high pitch of passionate indignation and invective; he adheres to a deliberately cool and neutral tone. In contrast to the passionately self-righteous, not-to-be-intimidated Solzhenitsyn, with his steely courage and seemingly infinite capacity for resistance, Shalamov appears chilly, remote, preferring a miniature canvas that is fragmentary and almost incomplete. Rhetoric is left behind, the writer taking refuge in a kind of passive quietism. This first impression, however, is almost entirely false.

If Shalamov lowers his voice, it is to be even more direct, precise, and more telling. His experience was quite different from that of Solzhenitsyn. Arrested in 1937, Shalamov was in Kolyma throughout World War II and observed the war only by means of the new arrivals of prisoners. Solzhenitsyn was arrested at the war's end, in 1945. Shalamov's camp experience was twice as long, and harsher; he knew no *sharashka*, or special projects camp, like that described in Solzhenitsyn's *V kruge pervom* (1968; *The First Circle*, 1968). Instead, Shalamov was designated for extermination and according to all expectations should have died.

It is difficult for the Western reader, with current notions of history and modernity, to understand Kolyma. In the United States, slavery ended with the Civil War; in Russia, the serfs were emancipated at about the same time. Though readers may think of themselves as skeptical and as not believing in unabated progress, still, old habits die hard; many realities of the contemporary world and of foreign countries appear to be impossible. In the mid-1930's, the Soviet government began to exploit its underground gold seams by means of slave labor of an unprecedented kind. Slaves, as is well-known, are relatively unproductive; the NKVD, however, resolved to overcome the reluctance of their prisoners to work through the goad of hunger, by deliberately undernourishing them unless they achieved high production norms. The result was that most of the prisoners died. Then again, the NKVD paid nothing for its captives and could always replace dead ones by enslaving new people. Kolyma was the ultimate pole of this murderous system, cut off from continental Russia yet attached to it by its need for laborers.

Shalamov was arrested for calling Ivan Bunin a "Russian classic"; others were arrested for still more trifling reasons—for example, writing to a fiancée. Once in Kolyma, the captives' immediate overseers would be thieves and common criminals, officially described by the Soviet government as "friends of the people" or "socially friendly elements." In the story "Esperanto," Shalamov describes one of his jobs: "On the very first day I took the place of a horse in a wooden yoke, heaving with my chest against a wooden log." Shalamov observes wryly that man has more endurance than any other animal. In the story "Zhitie inzhenera Kipreeva" ("The Life of Engineer Kipreev"), a prisoner, Kipreev, declares that "Kolyma is Auschwitz Without the Ovens"; the inscription over the prison gates—strikingly similar to the German "Arbeit macht frei" at Auschwitz—is "Labor is honor, glory, nobility, and heroism." Few survived the first three years in Kolyma; the narrator observes in the story "Kusok mysa" ("A Piece of Meat"), "two weeks was a long time, a thousand years." The area contained innumerable mass graves. In the frozen taiga, dead bodies did not decompose; in the chilling story "Po Lend-licu" ("Lend Lease"), a recently arrived bulldozer—a gift from the United States government—has as its first task to cut a trench to hold a mass grave of bodies that is slowly sliding down the frozen side of a mountain.

In conditions such as these it would be unrealistic to expect a sustained attitude of vituperation like that of Solzhenitsyn. The prison conditions described by Fyodor Dostoevski in *Zapiski iz myortvogo doma* (1861-1862; *Buried Alive: Or, Ten Years of Penal Servitude in Siberia*, 1881; better known as *House of the Dead*, 1915) were considered to be almost luxurious in comparison with those of the camps in Kolyma, and the same applied to Anton Chekhov's 1894 description of the penal colony on Sakhalin Island. In one of Shalamov's stories, a general, sent to Kolyma at the close of World War II, notes that the experience of the front cannot prepare a man for the mass death in the camps. One character, informed that the Soviet Union has signed the United Nations resolution on genocide in 1937, asks with caustic irony, "Genocide? Is that something they serve for dinner?" ("The Life of Engineer Kipreev"). The conditions were closer to those described by Bruno Bettelheim in *The Informed Heart: Autonomy in a Mass Age* (1960) and Eugen Kogon in his *Der SS-Staat* (1947; *The Theory and Practise of Hell*, 1950), although as Shalamov observes, "there were no gas furnaces in Kolyma. The corpses wait in stone, in the permafrost." It should be remembered that Shalamov was not there for one year, like Bettelheim, or seven years, like Kogon, but seventeen years.

The key to the unique tone in these stories can be found in the story titled "Sententsiya" ("Sententious"), which describes a prisoner on the verge of death who gradually revives. The evolution of feelings that pass through his semiconscious mind (he is the story's narrator) is of extraordinary interest. At the beginning he is a walking dead man, one of those who were called *Musselmänner* in Nazi concentration camps, "wicks" in the Soviet camps. The narrator observes, "I had little warmth. Little flesh was left on my bones, just enough for bitterness—the last human emotion; it was closer to the bone." His greatest need is for forgetfulness and sleep. Later he improves, and he notes, "Then something else appeared—something different from resentment and bitterness. There appeared indifference and fearlessness. I realized I didn't care if I was beaten or not." As he steadily improves there is a third stage: fear. Then a fourth stage follows: "Envy was the name of the next feeling that returned to me. I envied my dead friends who had died in '38. I envied those of my neighbors who had something to chew or smoke." The narrator says bitingly that after this point, the feeling of love did not return:

> Love comes only when all other human emotions have already returned. Love comes last, returns last. Or does it return? Indifference, envy, and fear, however, were not the only witnesses of my return to life. Pity for animals returned earlier than pity for people.

The passage suggests that the evolution of feelings did not stop there, but continued. It gives a valuable insight into Shalamov's own attitudes. The narrator of the story has to learn language and individual words all over again. Each thought, each word "returned alone, unaccompanied by the watchful guards of familiar words. Each appeared first on the tongue and only later in the mind."

Henceforth, this particular bitterness would stay with Shalamov as a substrate; in the foreground or almost hidden in the background, it provides his unique tone. John Glad has noted that Shalamov's tone sometimes seems neutral, distant, or passive. Yet it is never truly neutral. Usually it is closer to the bitterness described above: a dark, profoundly reverberating irony that no other author has expressed as well as Shalamov, and is "closer to the bone."

Shalamov's range often goes beyond this. He can surprise with his sense of humor. His description of the visit of an American businessman, Mr. Popp, to the Soviet Union, the hasty preparation of the authorities to receive him, and his meeting with the "Commandant" of a hotel, Tsyplyakov, are as funny as Mikhail Zoshchenko at his best. The variety of people in Shalamov's stories is great. He describes naïve people such as the young peasant Fedya in "Sukhim paikam" ("Dry Rations"), the omnipresent criminals, religious fanatics, Esperantists, heroic officers from World War II such as "Pugachov" who were swept into the camps in 1945 and died attempting to escape, bureaucrats, guards, doctors, women, and the most ordinary people. Like Solzhenitsyn, he is particularly good at describing the special kind of meanness, or sadism, of one person toward another, cultivated by the totalitarian system and by the widespread presence of informers and spies. Even prisoners trying to recruit other prisoners for escape attempts were likely to be hired informers. Some of the stories are especially effective because of the variety and solidity of the characters. There is not only a single protagonist and a few other one-dimensional characters used as foils, but also the unexpected breadth of real life. In the story "Nadgrobnoe slovo" ("An Epitaph"), a group of prisoners fantasize about what they will do when they leave prison and return to normal life. No two dreams are the same. One peasant wants to go to the Party headquarters, simply because there were more cigarette butts on the floor there than he had seen anywhere else: He wants to pick them up and then roll his own cigarette. The last words are given to a person hitherto silent who slowly, deliberately, expresses unrelieved hatred: " 'As for me,' he said in a calm, unhurried voice, 'I'd like to have my arms and legs cut off and become a human stump—no arms or legs. Then I'd be strong enough to spit in their faces for everything they're doing to us.' "

There is real artistry in these stories, and it is of an unexpected, nontraditional kind. Shalamov has been compared to Chekhov ("the Chekhov of the camps"), and although the comparison is apt there are real differences between the two writers. Both show economy, sparingly sketch in a background, and lead toward a single dramatic point or realization at the end. Shalamov's stories, however, are less obviously fictional than Chekhov's. Although Shalamov uses a variety of narrators in the stories, a majority have a speaker who resembles Shalamov himself. There is an air of casualness about the stories, both old-fashioned and at the same time extremely modern. Far more frequently than with Chekhov, the reader is unsure of the direction in which a narration is leading, although usually the story has a hidden but inexorable direction. At the end of the story "Perviy zub" ("My First Tooth"), a storyteller tries out several alternate versions of a story on a listener; the technique is similar to that used by Akira Kurosawa in his film *Rashomon* (1950). The story ends:

> "I don't like that variation either," I said.
> "Then I'll leave it as I originally had it."
> Even if you can't get something published, it's easier to bear a thing if you write it down. Once you've done that, you can forget. . . .

As an ending this is disarming, seemingly casual, although the sharp edge of irony should not be missed. Shalamov sometimes says that he wants nothing more than to forget; often when he describes an experience he will admit that he simply did not care what would happen. Yet these attitudes are incorporated into the subject matter of the stories. Shalamov the writer, the artist, remembers and cares intensely. Western readers often miss the deeply under-stated irony in these passages: It is unique, subtle, and extremely powerful.

Shalamov's stories have interested many readers because of their unusual subject matter. On the verge of nonfiction, they are invaluable as documents. Their greatest value, however, is probably in their original use of form and their artistry. Stories such as the allegorical "Domino" ("Dominoes") and "Zagavor yuristov" ("The Lawyers' Plot") achieve a concentrated depth of meaning that is truly remarkable. Like Elie Wiesel, Shalamov is a survivor and a witness who also happens to be an excellent artist. By his own admission, he subordinates art to the truth of experience. Yet his art only gains from this.

Other major works

POETRY: *Shelest List'ev*, 1964; *Tochka kipeniia: Stikhi*, 1977.
NONFICTION: *Ocherki prestupnogo mira*, n.d.

Bibliography

Conquest, Robert. *Kolyma: The Arctic Death Camps*, 1978.
Glad, John. "Art out of Hell: Shalamov of Kolyma," in *Survey*. CVII (1979), pp. 45-50.
_____. Foreword to *Graphite*, 1981.
_____. Foreword to *Kolyma Tales*, 1980.
Hosking, Geoffrey. "The Chekhov of the Camps," in *The Times Literary Supplement*. October 17, 1980, p. 1163.
_____. "The Ultimate Circle of the Stalinist Inferno," in *New Universities Quarterly*. XXXIV (Spring, 1980).
Svirski, Grigori. *A History of Post-war Soviet Writing: The Literature of Moral Opposition*, 1981.

John Carpenter

LESLIE MARMON SILKO

Born: Albuquerque, New Mexico; March 5, 1948

Principal short fiction
Storyteller, 1981.

Other literary forms
Leslie Marmon Silko is known most widely for her novel *Ceremony* (1977). An early collection of poetry, *Laguna Woman* (1974), established her as an important young Native American writer, and most of the lyric and narrative poems in that book are integrated with the autobiographical writings and short stories that make up *Storyteller*. Silko has also adapted, with Frank Chin, one of her short stories into a one-act play of the same title, *Lullaby*, which was first performed in 1976. Silko has also written film scripts; in one, she adapted a Laguna Pueblo myth, "Estoyehmuut and the Kunideeyah (Arrowboy and the Destroyers)," for television production in 1978. Earlier, she wrote a film script for Jack Beck and Marlon Brando that depicted, from a Native American viewpoint, the Francisco Vásquez de Coronado expedition of 1540 (the script was sent to Hollywood in 1977 but was not used).

Several of Silko's critical essays and interviews provide useful insights into her short fiction, as does her correspondence with the poet James Wright, which is collected in *The Delicacy and Strength of Lace* (1986). Two particularly useful essays are "An Old-Time Indian Attack Conducted in Two Parts," published in *The Remembered Earth: An Anthology of Contemporary Native American Literature* (1981), and "Language and Literature from a Pueblo Indian Perspective," published in *English Literature: Opening Up the Canon* (1979). Silko's interviews often supply autobiographical and cultural contexts that enhance the understanding of her work; among the most insightful are "Leslie Silko: Storyteller," in *Persona* (1980), "Two Interviews with Leslie Marmon Silko," in *American Studies in Scandinavia* (1981), and the videotape *Running on the Edge of the Rainbow: Laguna Stories and Poems* (1979), which offers Silko reading from her work and is interspersed with her commentary on Laguna culture. A collection of Silko's work and related material is housed at the University of Arizona library in Tucson.

Achievements
Silko, along with Louise Erdrich, N. Scott Momaday, Simon Ortiz, and James Welch, is regarded by critics as among the best of the more than fifty Native American writers with significant publications to have emerged between the mid-1960's and the mid-1980's. While she is well-read in the canonical tradition of Anglo-American writing, having delighted particularly,

at an early age, in Edgar Allan Poe, John Steinbeck, William Faulkner, Flannery O'Connor, and, later in college, William Shakespeare and John Milton, she brings to her own work the sensibility and many of the structures inherent in the Laguna oral tradition, creating, for example, a subtext of re-visioned Laguna mythology to the more conventional aspects of her novel *Ceremony*. Although, in a manner similar to that of other American writers drawing upon an ethnic heritage, Silko chooses to place her work in the context of Laguna culture, her work appeals to diverse readers for its insights not only into the marginal status of many nonwhite Americans but also into the universal celebration of the reciprocity between land and culture.

Formal recognition of Silko's fiction came quite early in her career. Her story "Lullaby" was included in *The Best American Short Stories, 1975*, and "Yellow Woman" was included in *Two Hundred Years of Great American Short Stories* (1975), published to commemorate the American bicentennial. In 1974, she won the *Chicago Review* Poetry Award, and in 1977 she won the Pushcart Prize for Poetry. She has also been awarded major grants from the National Endowment for the Humanities and the National Endowment for the Arts for her work in film and in fiction. In 1981, Silko received a five-year fellowship from the MacArthur Foundation, permitting her the freedom to pursue whatever interests she wished to develop. In addition, Silko has held writing residencies in fiction at several universities and has been invited for lectures and readings at schools from New York to California.

Biography

Leslie Marmon Silko was born in Albuquerque, New Mexico, on March 5, 1948, the descendant of Laguna, Mexican, and Anglo peoples. Silko's mixed ancestry is documented in *Storyteller*, in which she recounts the stories of the white Protestant brothers Walter Gunn Marmon and Robert G. Marmon, her great-grandfather, who, with his older brother, settled in New Mexico at Laguna as a trader, having migrated west from Ohio in 1872. Her great-grandmother Marie, or A'mooh, married Robert Marmon, and her grand-mother Lillie was a Model A automobile mechanic. Both were well educated and well informed about both Anglo and Laguna life-styles. Growing up in one of the Marmon family houses at Old Laguna, in western New Mexico, Silko inherited from these women and from her grandfather Hank Marmon's sister-in-law Susie Marmon a treasury of Laguna stories, both mythological and historical. Indeed, "Aunt Susie" is created in *Storyteller* as Silko's source for many of the traditional stories that shaped her childhood.

Silko's early years were spent in activities that neither completely included her in nor fully excluded her from the Laguna community. She participated in clan activities, but not to the same extent as the full-bloods; she helped prepare for ceremonial dances, but she did not dance herself. Attending the local day school of the Bureau of Indian Affairs, she was prohibited from using the Keresan language which her great-grandmother had begun teaching her. She had her own horse at eight, and she helped herd cattle on the family ranch; at thirteen, she had her own rifle and joined in the annual deer hunts. From the fifth grade on, Silko commuted to schools in Albuquerque. After high school, she entered the University of New Mexico, also in Albuquerque, and, in 1969, she was graduated summa cum laude from the English department's honors program. After three semesters in the American Indian Law Program at the same university, Silko decided to pursue a career in writing and teaching. For the next two years, she taught English at Navajo Community College in Tsaile, Arizona. She spent the following two years in Ketchikan, Alaska, where she wrote *Ceremony*. She returned to teach in the University of New Mexico's English department for another two years before she moved, in 1980, to Tucson, where she became a professor of English at the University of Arizona and where she lives, teaches, and writes.

Analysis

Leslie Marmon Silko's short fiction is "told" in the context of her personal experience as a Laguna Pueblo and serves as a written extension, continuation, and revitalization of Laguna oral tradition. Blurring the genre of the short story with historical anecdotes, family history, letters, cultural legacies, photographs, and lyric and narrative poems, *Storyteller* includes most of Silko's published short stories and poems. While the stories certainly stand on their own, and, indeed, many of them are included in various anthologies, Silko's matrix of thick description, conveying the mood of events as well as describing them, testifies to the essential role of storytelling in Pueblo identity, giving the people access to the mythic and historic past and relating a continuing wisdom—about the land, its animals, its plants, and the human condition—as an integral part of the natural process. About her collection, Silko has said, "I see *Storyteller* as a statement about storytelling and the relationship of the people, my family and my background to the storytelling—a personal statement done in the style of the storytelling tradition, i.e., using stories themselves to explain the dimensions of the process."

In unifying the past and the present to illuminate the kinship of land and people, Silko's story "Lullaby" evokes both beauty and loss. Set north of the Laguna Reservation, the story traces the life of an old Navajo couple, Chato and Ayah, from whose point of view the story is told by an omniscient narrator. While Ayah sits in the snow, presiding over her husband's death, she recalls various episodes in her own life just as if she were sharing in Chato's last memories. She is wrapped in an old army blanket that was sent to her by her son Jimmie, who was killed while serving in the army. She recalls, however, her own mother's beautifully woven rugs, themselves symbolic of stories, on the hand loom outside her childhood hogan. Again contrasting the past with the present, Ayah gazes at her black rubber overshoes and remembers the high buckskin leggings of her childhood as they hung, drying, from the ceiling beams of the family hogan.

What Ayah remembers seems better than what she has at present—and it was, but she does not escape into nostalgia for the old ways. Ayah remembers events and things as they were, for they have brought her to the present moment of her husband's death. She remembers Jimmie's birth and the day the army officials came to tell Chato of his death. She remembers how doctors from the Bureau of Indian Affairs came to take her children Danny and Ella to Colorado for the treatment of tuberculosis, which had killed her other children. Despite their good intentions, the white doctors frightened Ayah and her children into the hills after she had unknowingly signed over her custody of the children to them. When the doctors returned with reservation policemen, Chato let them take the children, powerless in her protest that she wanted first to try the medicine men. Chato had taught her to sign her name, but he had not taught her English. She remembers the months of refuge in her hatred of Chato for teaching her to sign her name (and thus to sign away her children) and how she fled to the same hill where she had earlier fled with her children. She remembers, too, Chato's pride during his years as a cattlehand and how, after he broke his leg in a fall from a horse, the white rancher fired him and evicted them from the gray boxcar shack that he had provided for the couple.

As Ayah recalls these losses, she also recalls the peacefulness of her own mother, as if she were rejoining her mother in contrast to the alienation of her own children from her after they had been away from home and learned to speak English, forgetting their native Navajo and regarding their mother as strangely backward in her ways. Now, with Chato reduced to alcoholism, senility, and incontinence, the old couple lives in the hogan of Ayah's childhood, and her routine is interrupted only by her treks to Azzie's bar to retrieve her husband. Ayah now sleeps with Chato, as she had not since the loss of Danny and Ella, because only her body will keep him warm. Fused with the heat of her body is the heat of her memory, as Ayah recalls how the elders warned against learning English: It would endanger them.

Ayah's recollection is presumably in Navajo (though Silko writes in English): The language is the story of her life and her relationship with the land on which she lived it. Place dominates her values; an arroyo and a cowpath evoke precise memories, yet the evocation of her life culminates in her decision to allow Chato to freeze to death rather than see him suffer through the last days of his degradation. She wraps him in Jimmie's blanket and sings a lullaby to him which her grandmother and her mother had sung before her: "The earth is your mother,/ she holds you./ The sky is your father,/ he protects you./ Sleep. . . ./ We are together always/ There never was a time/ when this/ was not so." Ayah's closing song in the story joins birth with death, land with life, and past with present. Through her story, Ayah creates an event that supersedes the oppression of the white rancher, the stares at the Mexican bar, the rejection of her acculturated children, and the apparent diminution of traditional ways: The story continues the timeless necessity of the people to join their land with the sacredness of their language.

In a later story set in Alaska, Silko focuses even more emphatically on the power of the story to create and to sustain the life of a people. By shifting from Laguna characters to Navajo characters and, finally, by using an Eskimo context, Silko stresses the universality of storytelling among peoples who codify the world through an oral tradition. Further, her contrast of orality with literacy is also a contrast in consciousness and values: In orality, meaning resides in the context of the linguistic event, be it in Keresan or Yupik, and that context implies an identification yet a diversity of nature and culture; in literacy, meaning resides in the coding of the script or print itself, be it the sign in English or in Chinese, and that coding implies a compartmentalization that permits abstract categories in both nature and culture. In short, orality encourages a holistic perspective while literacy seeks to preserve duality. The title story of the collection seeks to explore the ramifications of just such divergent ways of seeing the world (or hearing it), and, at the same time, the story models the process of the oral tradition: It is not a Yupik story so much as it is one that is written as if it were a Yupik story.

"Storyteller," like "Lullaby," begins *in medias res*, as do many stories in any oral tradition. It, too, is told from the point of view of a woman, but the Eskimo protagonist is a young girl, anonymous though universal as the storyteller. She is in jail for killing a "Gussuck" (a derogatory term for a white person) storekeeper. According to Anglo law and logic, however, the girl is innocent. Through juxtaposed flashbacks, Silko's omniscient narrator reconstructs the events that have led to her imprisonment. Moving away from the familiarity of a Pueblo context, Silko sets the story in Inuit country on the Kuskokwim River near Bethel, where she spent two months while she was in Alaska; she brings, then, her own attentiveness to the land to her fashioning of the story about attentiveness to storytelling. The imprisoned girl grew up with an old couple who lived in a shack outside the village, and she was nurtured by the stories of her grandmother. Although the girl had attended a "Gussuck school," she was sent home for refusing to assimilate, having been whipped for her resistance to speaking English. Sexually abused by the old man, the girl takes the place of her grandmother in the old man's bed after her death. Before the grandmother's death, however, the girl had learned about the death of her parents, who had been poisoned with bad liquor by a trader who was never taken to court for the crime. Her grandmother had not told her the complete story, leaving much of it ambiguous and unfinished. While the girl witnesses the destruction of village life by oil-drillers and listens to her "grandfather" ramble on and on with a story of a polar bear stalking a hunter, she recalls her grandmother's last words: "It will take a long time, but the story must be told. There must not be any lies." The girl believes that the "story" refers to the old man's bear story, but, in fact, it is the story which the girl herself will act out after the grandmother's death.

Bored by sex with the old man, the girl begins sleeping with oil-drillers, discovering that they are as bestial as the old man, who sleeps in a urine-soaked bed with dried fish while he adds to his story throughout the winter. When she is about to have sex with a red-haired oil-driller, he tapes a pornographic picture of a woman mounted by a dog to the wall above the bed, and then in turn mounts the girl. When she tells the old man about it, he expresses no surprise, claiming that the Gussucks have "behaved like desperate people" in their efforts to develop the frozen tundra. Using her sexuality to comprehend the strange ways of the Gussucks, the girl stalks her parents' killer as the old man's bear stalks the hunter. The Gussucks, seemingly incapable of grasping the old man's story, fail in their attention to the frozen landscape; they do not see or hear the place, the people, or the cold, blue bear of the story.

That failure to grasp the analogy of the bear story to the impending freeze of winter is what finally permits the girl to avenge the death of her parents. She lures the "storeman" from his store, which doubles as a bar, to the partially frozen river. Knowing how to breathe through her mitten in order to protect her lungs and wrapped in her grandmother's wolf-hide parka, the girl testifies mutely to the wisdom of her grandmother's stories. She knows where it is safe to tread on the ice and where it is not—she hears the river beneath her and can interpret the creaking of the ice. The storekeeper, taunted by her body, which is symbolic itself of her repository of knowledge for survival, chases her out onto the ice, trying to catch her by taking a single line to where she stands on the ice in the middle of the river. Without mittens and parka and oblivious to the warning sounds from below the ice, the storeman ignores the girl's tracks that mark a path of safety and crashes through the thin ice, drowning in the freezing river. He has had many possessions, but he lacked a story that would have saved him.

When the state police question her, the girl confesses: "He lied to them. He told them it was safe to drink. But I will not lie. . . . I killed him, . . . but I don't lie." When her court-appointed attorney urges her to recant, saying, "It was an accident. He was running after you and he fell through the ice. That's all you have to say in court," the girl, disregarding the testimony of children who witnessed the man's death, insists: "I will not change the story, not even to escape this place and go home. I intended that he die. The story must be told as it is." Later, at home under a woman trooper's guard, the girl watches as the old man dies, still telling his story even as it evokes the death of the hunter; his spirit passes into the girl, herself now continuing the story of the bear's conquest of the man.

Now the storyteller herself, the girl has become her story: The story has taken revenge on both the storeman and the old man, her first seducer, through her actions, namely the telling of the stories. The story, then, does not end, but returns to itself, the bear turning to face the hunter on the ice just as the myth of natural revenge turns the story against the storeman and the seductive power of the story turns against the storyteller, the old man. Even, however, with a new storyteller, the girl, the story has no beginning and no end: It continues as long as the people and the land continue. Indeed, the story's survival is the survival of the people; ironically, the girl's story will provide the lawyer with a plea of insanity, ensuring the survival of the story and the storyteller despite the degradation involved in charging her with madness.

While Silko's stories are about the characterization of individuals, of a culture, of the land's significance to a people and their values, and of discrimination against a people, they are most fundamentally about the oral tradition that constitutes the people's means of achieving identity. Storytelling for Silko is not merely an entertaining activity reminiscent of past glories but an essential activity that informs and sustains the vitality of present cultures, shaping them toward survival and bestowing meaning for the future. The people, simply put, are their stories: If the stories are lost, the people are lost.

Other major works

NOVEL: *Ceremony*, 1977.

PLAY: *Lullaby*, 1976 (with Frank Chin).

POETRY: *Laguna Woman*, 1974.

NONFICTION: *The Delicacy and Strength of Lace: Letters Between Leslie Marmon Silko and James A. Wright*, 1986 (edited by Anne Wright).

Bibliography

Blicksilver, Edith. "Traditionalism vs. Modernity: Leslie Silko on American Indian Women," in *Southwest Review*. LXIV (Spring, 1979), pp. 149-160.

Lincoln, Kenneth. *Native American Renaissance*, 1983.

Lucero, Ambrose. "For the People: Leslie Silko's *Storyteller*," in *Minority Voices*. V (Spring-Fall, 1981), pp. 1-10.

Ruoff, A. LaVonne. "Ritual and Renewal: Keres Traditions in the Short Fiction of Leslie Silko," in *MELUS*. V (Winter, 1978), pp. 2-17.

Seyersted, Per. *Leslie Marmon Silko*, 1980.

Vangen, Kate S. "The Devil's Domain: Leslie Silko's 'Storyteller,'" in *Coyote Was Here: Essays on Contemporary Native American Literary and Political Mobilization*, 1984.

Veile, Alan R. *Four American Indian Literary Masters*, 1982.

Michael Loudon

GERTRUDE STEIN

Born: Allegheny, Pennsylvania; February 3, 1874
Died: Neuilly-sur-Seine, France; July 27, 1946

Principal short fiction

Three Lives, 1909; *Tender Buttons*, 1914; *Portraits and Prayers*, 1934; *Mrs. Reynolds and Five Earlier Novelettes, 1931-1942*, 1952; *As Fine as Melanctha, 1914-1930*, 1954; *Painted Lace and Other Pieces, 1914-1934*, 1955; *Alphabets and Birthdays*, 1957.

Other literary forms

It is difficult to classify Gertrude Stein's writings, because she radically upset the conventions of literary genres and because she worked in many different forms. Traditional generic labels simply do not describe individual works. Even when Stein names the genre in a work's title (*Ida, a Novel*, 1941, for example), the conventional form only marks how far Stein has digressed from the norm. Works such as *Ida* and *Mrs. Reynolds* are Stein's version of the novel, while *The Autobiography of Alice B. Toklas* (1933) and *Operas and Plays* (1932), among other works, encourage comparison with other genres. Stein became famous in America with *The Autobiography of Alice B. Toklas*, and her success encouraged her to experiment further with the genre (*Everybody's Autobiography*, 1937). Even when writing "autobiography," however, Stein did not adhere to conventional restrictions, using multiple viewpoints in the composite work. Similarly, although Stein wrote many plays, some of which have been performed, they do not follow dramatic conventions, for frequently they lack plot and character. Stein also wrote meditations and other quasi-philosophical and theoretical musings, and in numerous essays she attempted to explain her theories of composition and her notions of art. In addition, she experimented in verse and developed a special genre which she called portraits. Regardless of the form, however, the style is unmistakably Stein's and serves as a signature to all of her works.

Achievements

Stein's greatest achievement was her wily and strong independence, which revealed itself as much in her life-style as in her work. She was a creative person with a strong personality, a gift for conversation, and a good ear, and her home became a center for the avant-garde circle of artists in Paris during the early 1900's. Perhaps this salon would not be so famous were it not for the fact that those associated with it were later accepted as the outstanding figures of the modern art world. In time, artists as different as Ernest Hemingway, Sherwood Anderson, Virgil Thomson, Henri Matisse, and Pablo Picasso became associated with Stein. Those working in the visual medium as well as literary figures were drawn to the discussions and activities that took place in the Stein home. Among contemporaries she was recognized as a fascinating individual, a woman of strong opinions and definite views, a lively intelligence and vibrant mind; among the cultural historians who came later, she was acknowledged to be a person of enormous creative influence and empowering force.

Stein's achievements were not limited to her role as a cultural catalyst, however, for she was a pioneering writer in her own right. Working from a sense that the present moment of consciousness is supreme, Stein increasingly radicalized her writing to focus on the here and now, on the mystery of consciousness, and ultimately on the enigma of language and words. This drive led Stein increasingly away from the conventions of language as commonly understood and practiced through the structures and preoccupations of genre, through the patterns and assumptions of syntax, and finally even through the basic referential quality of words. Repetition—of sounds and words themselves—became the hallmark of Stein's writing. Some contemporaries thought her experimental language to be foolish and childlike, but others hailed her efforts as truly pioneering literary breakthroughs. Most of the key terms in the criticism of modern literature have been applied to Stein at one time or another—abstractionist, cubist, minimalist, and so on. Indeed, most historians of the period agree that her work and her personality must be acknowledged before any serious discussion of any of these movements can proceed. However her work is defined, regardless of whether one likes or dislikes it, it has made a significant impact on the development of modern literature.

In addition to its variety and inventiveness, the sheer bulk of Stein's canon should not be overlooked as an accomplishment. Richard Bridgman's *Gertrude Stein in Pieces* (1970) lists nearly six hundred titles in the Stein bibliography, some very short pieces but others significantly longer. She was prolific, flexible, and varied—at her best in the unclassifiable writings that mingle verse, prose, and drama into a unique species of art that bears the imprint of Gertrude Stein alone.

Stein had the misfortune of living through two world wars. During the first she obtained a Ford van, which she drove for the American Fund for French Wounded. In 1922, she was awarded the Médaille de la Reconnaissance Française for wartime activities.

Biography

When Daniel Stein and Amelia Keyser were married in 1864, the seeds of Gertrude Stein's future independence were sown, for the couple had some unusual ideas about child rearing and family life. Perhaps most psychologically damaging to the children was the parents' firm decision to have five children—no more and no fewer. Consequently, Gertrude's beloved older brother Leo and she were conceived only after the deaths of two other Stein children. In *Everybody's Autobiography* Stein says that the situation made her and her brother feel "funny." Knowing that one's very existence depends on the deaths of others surely would have some psychological effect, and some biographers attribute Stein's lifelong interest in identity to her knowledge of her parents' decision about family size.

Daniel Stein was apparently as quarrelsome and independent as his daughter was to become. Operating a successful cloth and clothing business in Baltimore with his brothers, Daniel and another brother broke up the partnership by moving out to Pittsburgh to open a new business. When Daniel had earned enough money, he moved the family across the Ohio to Allegheny, and it was there that Gertrude Stein was born in 1874. She was the last child the Steins were to have, completing the unit of five children. Michael Stein was the oldest child (born in 1865); Simon was next (1867); then came Bertha (1870) and Leo (1872). When Allegheny was hit with fire and flood, Daniel once again moved the family, this time to Austria, having decided that the older children needed the benefits of a European education.

The family went first to Gemünden and then to Vienna. Although not wealthy, they lived well and were able to afford a nurse, a tutor, a governess, and a full domestic staff. The children were exposed to music and dancing lessons, and they enjoyed all the sights and activities of the upper-middle class in Europe at the time. In his concern for the education of his children, Daniel resembles Henry James, whose educational theories also featured the advantages of the European experience to a developing mind. During this period, letters from Amelia and her sister Rachel Keyser, who accompanied the Steins, reveal that the baby was speaking German and experiencing an apparently contented, pampered, and protected infancy.

The roaming continued. In 1878, the family moved to Paris, and Stein got her first view of the city she would later make her home. When the Steins returned to the United States in 1879, they lived at first with the Keyser family in Baltimore, but Daniel was set on living in California. By 1880, the family had relocated to Oakland, where they stayed for some time (until 1891), long enough for the artist to develop an attachment to the place. It was Oakland that Stein always thought of as home.

The unsettled life of the Steins continued with the death of Amelia when the artist was fourteen. Three years later (in 1891), Daniel died, leaving Michael head of the family. He moved the family to San Francisco that year, but by the following year the family was dispersed—Michael and Simon remaining in San Francisco, Gertrude and her sister Bertha going back to Baltimore to live with their mother's sister, and Leo transferring from the University of California at Berkeley to Harvard. In the fall of 1893, Gertrude Stein herself entered Harvard Annex (later renamed Radcliffe College), thus rejoining the brother to whom she had grown so attached. Their strong bond was to survive into adulthood, being broken only by Gertrude's lifelong commitment to Alice B. Toklas and her ascendancy in Parisian art circles.

Stein was at Harvard during a wonderful period in that institution's history. She had the good fortune to study under William James, whose theories of psychology intrigued the young woman and initiated a lifelong interest in questions of personality, identity, and consciousness. Stein's later attempts to present in her writing awareness of a continuing flux in the present, the immediacy of present existence, and the inclusiveness and randomness of consciousness can be traced in part to James's influence. Stein's first publication came out during this Harvard period. "Normal Motor Automatism," co-authored with Leon M. Solomons, was published in *Psychological Review* in September, 1896. Although this essay was primarily Solomons', Stein published her own work on the subject in the *Psychological Review* of May, 1898—"Cultivated Motor Automatism: A Study of Character in Its Relation to Attention." Stein's early interest in automatic writing has led some readers to believe that the method directed her own subsequent writing, but that claim has been generally discredited. Harvard did more to focus her attention on the consciousness behind the work than on the techniques and strategies of the writing process.

The Harvard experience was not, however, completely successful. In the spring of 1897, Stein failed the Radcliffe Latin entrance examination and consequently was not awarded her bachelor's degree. Undaunted, in the fall of 1897 she entered The Johns Hopkins School of Medicine, and she received the Harvard degree in 1898, having been privately tutored in Latin so that she could pass the examination. It was William James who encouraged her to take the Harvard degree and to continue her education; Johns Hopkins seemed a likely choice both because it was funded to accept women into the program on a basis equal to men and because her brother Leo was studying there. The first two years of medical study went well, but after that, Stein complained of boredom and began to dislike her classes. In the end, she did not pass her final examinations and never took the degree. She had learned what she wanted to learn and had no interest in practicing medicine.

For some time, Stein had been spending her summers in Europe with Leo, so it seemed natural that they would settle in London in September, 1902. In February of the following year, Stein sailed back to the United States, this time staying in New York until rejoining Leo once again for summer travel. In the fall of 1903, they occupied the house at 27 rue de Fleurus, the address which was to become famous as an artistic mecca. *Quod Erat Demonstrandum*, or *Q.E.D.* (1950, as *Things as They Are*), was written there, although Stein then overlooked the work for some thirty years.

In 1904, Gertrude and Leo began purchasing paintings by men destined to become the leading figures of modern art. Having studied the great masters throughout the museums of Europe, the Steins were not automatically impressed with the world of modern art, yet something about Paul Cézanne's work struck Leo, and to a gallery of his works he took his sister. After the purchase of their first Cézanne, they were soon given freer rein to look among the canvases of the Paris art dealers. They purchased works by Honoré Daumier, Édouard Manet, Pierre-Auguste Renoir, Henri Toulouse-Lautrec, Paul Gauguin, and others. Thus Leo and Gertrude Stein laid out a new direction in their own cultural life and established a new model for American art collectors. People began to go to the rue de Fleurus address to see the paintings and then to talk about art and to socialize. The cultural center of modern art was born.

During this time, Stein was also writing. *The Making of Americans* (1925) and *Three Lives* date to this period, *Three Lives* being published in 1909 as Stein's first book. Another important event of the period was Stein's meeting Alice Toklas in September, 1907; Toklas moved into the Stein household on rue de Fleurus early in 1909. Her presence hastened the deterioration of the relationship between Stein and her brother (he finally left in 1913) and facilitated Stein's writing, because Toklas learned to type and transcribed Stein's work. She was Stein's companion for the remainder of the artist's life.

In June, 1914, *Tender Buttons* was published. The work marks a significant movement on Stein's part toward abstractionism, as she focuses more on things than on people and blurs the distinction between poetry and prose. When war broke out, Stein and Toklas were houseguests of the Alfred North Whiteheads in Lockridge, and they did not return to Paris until October of that year. In 1915, they left Paris for Spain, returning in 1916. In 1917, Stein obtained a Ford van from the United States, which she drove for the American Fund for French Wounded as a supply truck, and Stein's preoccupation with automobiles, especially Fords, began. She contributed to the war effort in France in various ways and in various areas of France, not returning to Paris "permanently" until May of 1919.

After the war, writing and socializing could once again begin in earnest. In 1922, she met Hemingway and became godmother to his son born the following year. Stein continued to write and began also to lecture during this period; she continued also to cultivate her interest in cars (she was now on her third) and in pet dogs. In 1931, *Lucy Church Amiably* was published, and in 1932, *The Autobiography of Alice B. Toklas* was written at Bilignin. It became a literary sensation in 1933, and it continues to be the most widely read and appreciated of all Stein's writings. Early in 1934, the first public performance of *Four Saints in Three Acts* (1932) took place in Hartford, Connecticut. Performances in other cities soon followed, and Stein began a lecture tour in the United States that established her reputation.

When Paris was occupied in 1940, Stein was advised to leave, which she did, not returning until December of 1944. In the following year, she toured United States Army bases in occupied Germany and lectured in Belgium and elsewhere. In July of 1946, en route to a friend's summer house, Stein fell ill and was admitted to the American hospital at Neuilly-sur-Seine. On July 27, she died following an operation for cancer. Her brother Leo died a year later, almost to the day, and Toklas, Gertrude Stein's dearest companion, survived another twenty-two years. A chapter in the history of modern art had come to an end.

Analysis

Gertrude Stein's work has never been easily accessible to the reader. During her lifetime, her work was both ridiculed and celebrated, and indeed these two attitudes continue to prevail among Stein's readers. Now that historical distance has provided a supportive context for Stein's work, however, and now that readers can see Stein in a milieu of highly creative artists devoted to wrenching art from the restrictions of realism and verisimilitude, her work is more easily appreciated for the inroads it makes against conventions, although perhaps not more easily understood. Stein was a powerful initiator, a ruthless experimenter, and a bold and forthright manipulator of words.

Having already written *Things as They Are*, *Three Lives*, and *The Making of Americans*, Stein was in full command when she made the surprising innovations of *Tender Buttons*. The author herself always rated the work highly, considering it to be one of her most significant writings despite the ridicule and scorn it received from those who did not agree that it added a new dimension to literature. Prior to *Tender Buttons*, Stein had grown increasingly abstract in her writing. *Tender Buttons* marks something of a culmination in this progressing abstractionism, for here she produces a set of "still lifes," each of which sustains abstraction. The subject matter, too, has changed from earlier writing. In *Tender Buttons*, Stein moves from people to things. The book is divided into three sections: "Objects," "Food," and "Rooms." While the divisions classify, the effect is still that of eclecticism, for no perceptible principles of order determine either the arrangement within each section or the sequencing of the sections themselves.

The title of *Tender Buttons* indicates some of the ironies of the collection. A button is something hard, concrete, and functional, while the word "tender" as an adjective suggests the opposite—something soft. "Tender" can also be a verb, and in this sense, the collection is Stein's offering of discrete bits of prose. "Tender" may suggest an emotional state, but, if so, the emotion must emanate from the reader, for the hard little buttons of prose in *Tender Buttons* do not themselves develop an emotional state. In the title, as in the name of each passage within the work, Stein seems to be offering the reader something tangible, something realistic, but she does so only to challenge the reader's notions of reality and to tease the mind.

The verbal fragments in *Tender Buttons* reveal a variety of strategies, and it is the flexibility of language and idea that keeps one reading. Each entry is titled; "A Red Stamp," "A Plate," "Roastbeef," "Sugar," and "Oranges" are typical examples. Entries range in length from a single short line to the approximately twelve pages of the undivided section "Rooms." In some of the entries, the title shapes the suggestions and hints, while in others, the title seems to bear little or no relationship to what follows. Stein's prose does not describe the objects realistically, but rather, opens the mind to the flow of thoughts that the title evokes. In these verbal fragments there is no logic, no sequence; sometimes an entry shows accretion, but no line of thought is developed. Indeed, even the logic of syntax is refused in favor of phrases and, ultimately, in favor of single words.

The work is abstract not only because it collects seemingly discrete verbal fragments but also because it seems to follow one of Stein's axioms about abstract painting: that a painting has its own existence, its own life. Aesthetic value does not derive from a work's referential quality but rather from itself. In modern painting, the focus is on the colors of the paint, the shapes, the textures, the forms. In *Tender Buttons*, the focus is on the words themselves, their sounds, juxtapositions, and the life that emanates from their unconventional arrangement. Stein recognized that words bring with them a whole series of associations that are different for each reader and uncontrollable by the artist, so she deliberately aimed to remove words from their usual contexts to reduce their associational qualities and to cause new associations to arise from novel juxtapositions. A reader of Stein's work must surrender selfhood to the text and accept the linguistic experience offered.

In naming volume 4 of the Yale edition of Stein's writings *As Fine as Melanctha*, the editors draw attention to one of Stein's short pieces of prose that takes the appearance of a short story but turns out to defy the conventions of that genre, just as Stein defies other literary conventions. "As Fine as Melanctha" was Stein's answer when requested to write something "as fine as 'Melanctha,'" one of the three pieces that constitute *Three Lives*. Yet "As Fine as Melanctha" is radically different from the earlier work. The 1922 piece has no characters, no setting, no plot, and no chronology. The opening line announces that it is "a history of a moment," but a moment has no history. "As Fine as Melanctha" is a moment out of time, or rather many moments out of time, moments so common as to be timeless and timely simultaneously.

"As Fine as Melanctha" is a good example of Stein's perfected verbal strategies throughout the decade of the 1920's as she attempted to make immediate and alive the verbal moment. She ignores, for example, the rules of syntax, mingling phrases and clauses and sentences indiscriminately. The only punctuation mark in the piece is the period, and it closes sentence fragments and sentences alike. Even questions end in a period rather than the expected question mark. The effect is that syntax no longer aids communication; consequently, the reader must release his fierce hold on sentence structure as a way to capture meaning. Where, however, can he turn in his desperate drive to understand? The logical next step is the word itself. Yet the reader is so accustomed to thinking of words as they relate to one another that when Stein violates expected word order as well as the rules of syntax, the reader confronts the stunning reality that words themselves are empty. Since everything one knows is understood through context, the removal of context both in the larger areas of character development and plot and in the smaller areas of language renders the reading of "As Fine as Melanctha" something of an existential experience.

Reading Stein's work puts the reader in tension with the text; that is when the sparks fly for those willing to accept the challenge. Repeatedly, and in a variety of ways, Stein makes language meaningless. One of the hallmarks of Stein's work is repetition. Yet repetition does not contribute to communication by stressing meaning; instead, it reduces meaning. The following sentence from "As Fine as Melanctha" uses internal repetition: "I mean that it has been noticed again and again that abundance that in abundance that the need of abundance that there is therein a need of abundance and in this need it is a necessity that there is stock taking." A reader is grateful to emerge from the tangled web in the inner core of the sentence—repetition of "abundance," "need," and "need of abundance." The sentence seems to accumulate words that lose meaning in the process of being accumulated. Even the apparent meaning at the end (the necessity of stocktaking) vanishes in the light of "abundance." The repetition so confuses the reader that the end of the sentence seems to have meaning because it apparently follows normal English syntax, yet even that meaning reduces itself to the redundancy of "stock taking" and "abundance." The reader is left with a single, uncontextualized word, systematically emptied of meaning and association.

There are other kinds of repetition in "As Fine as Melanctha." Repetitions of sounds as well as words prevail in a passage such as the following: "How dearly clearly merely is she me, how dearly clearly merely am I she. How dearly is she me how dearly is she me how dearly how very dearly am I she." The words "dearly," "clearly," "merely," "she," and "me" are repeated in varied arrangements that challenge syntax. The sounds of the words tend to flatten them, to make them anonymous. Repetition of the sound "erely" eventually is reduced to repetition of the "e" sound, as in "me." The sentence shows Stein's progressive reductionism: The meanings of different words are reduced to sounds; the repetition of multiple sounds is reduced to a single sound. Not only do the words become meaningless when repeated in such close proximity, but characters, as well (the difference between "she" and "me"), become such close approximations of one another that identity is destroyed. Language here is subversive and destructive.

In another example, repetition is used to change syntax: "The difference between humming to-day yesterday and to-morrow is this, it always means more. The difference between humming to-day yesterday and to-morrow is this. It always means more." The reader yearns to believe that this variation of syntax is meaningful, because that is the way readers have been taught to read. Yet once again, the repetition is used to destroy meaning. When Stein's reader puts mind against text, the mind returns as a wet noodle, aware only of its own limpness. Such awareness, however, is knowledge of one's fleeting consciousness, and Stein's objective is achieved.

"Brim Beauvais" represents Stein's work during the decade of the 1930's, when she became increasingly minimalist. In this work, her paragraphs are shorter, most being only a single line, and formal sections come from division into chapters, although such divisions are useless. Many chapters have the same identifying label: For example, three sections are identified as "Chapter X"; two are "Chapter Ten." Furthermore, the numbers are not always sequential. More confusion in the structure occurs through embedding. Several pages into "Brim Beauvais" appears the heading "Beauvais and His Wife: A Novel." There are labeled episodes within sections, although neither the chapter headings nor other labels contribute to communication. The work has a "Part II," but no Part I. All these devices are merely added to the verbal disruptions seen in earlier work. Even the opening of "Brim Beauvais" suggests how much further Stein has gone in her developing abstractionism. The work begins with the single word "once." It functions elliptically to suggest the "once upon a time" opening of fairy tales. Yet the second line truncates that suggestion. "Always excited to say twice" forces the reader to understand "once" in a numerical framework and thus to count something he does not know; similarly, the adjective "excited" describes a person not yet introduced. Stein is a master at invoking emptiness. Like the cubists, she presented a part without feeling it necessary to fill in or even suggest the surrounding whole. She believed that the mind partakes of the world through fragments, not through complete systems, and that her writing was an open window on this process.

By the winter of 1940, another war had begun in Europe, and Stein was finding it difficult to carry on any sustained writing project. "To Do: A Book of Alphabets and Birthdays" (published in 1957 as *Alphabets and Birthdays*) provided a structure while allowing for the intermittent composition that met Stein's needs during this period. The structure was provided by the alphabet, which Stein marched progressively through, assigning four names to each letter and creating episodes, events, and nonsense rhymes around each. The work has the fantastic actions and situations that children love, and Stein had children in mind when she wrote it. On the other hand, some publishers have insisted that the work is really more appropriate for adults than for children. If so, it must be adults who are young at heart, for the work has a delightful lightness, a happy flippancy, and a joy of language that emerges from repetition of sounds and words. The alphabet book shows Stein's skill at duplicating the rhythms and sounds of conversation and thoughts as people silently talk to themselves. Stein's ear for speech has often been noted, and here the speech of conversation conveys a swiftness and easy familiarity that make the work especially pleasant to read. At the same time, it remains true to the developing minimalism throughout Stein's career, for the letter is a reduction of the word.

Stein adhered to her principles throughout her life, always finding new ways to bring the meaning of her craft to the reader's awareness—even if this meant shocking the reader out of the lethargy of language. When she began to attract more people than her brother, Leo's support deteriorated and he claimed to find her work silly. His evaluation is shared by many. Stein is not a woman for all readers. Indeed, she tends to attract only coterie groups. Because her work is amenable to literary critics practicing deconstruction, however, and because the feminist movement has brought lesbian relationships into the open and searches out the quiet subversions such a lifestyle encouraged, both the work of Gertrude Stein and the artist herself have been looked at anew. The new reader and the returning reader alike will find Stein's work ever fresh, ever varying, ever innovative, and ever shocking, and for that reason alone it will always have enthusiastic readers somewhere, someplace.

Other major works

NOVELS: *Three Lives*, 1909; *The Making of Americans*, 1925; *Lucy Church Amiably*, 1930; *A Long Gay Book*, 1932; *The World Is Round*, 1939; *Ida, a Novel*, 1941; *Brewsie and Willie*, 1946; *Blood on the Dining Room Floor*, 1948; *Quod Erat Demonstrandum*, or *Q.E.D.*, 1950 (as *Things as They Are*); *A Novel of Thank You*, 1958.

PLAYS: *What Happened: A Five Act Play*, wr. 1913, pb. 1922; *White Wines*, wr. 1913, pb. 1922; *Do Let Us Go Away*, wr. 1916, pb. 1922; *For the Country Entirely: A Play in Letters*, wr. 1916, pb. 1922; *Counting Her Dresses*, wr. 1917, pb. 1922; *Geography and Plays*, pb. 1922; *Capital Capitals*, wr. 1922, pr. 1929, pb. 1932 (libretto; music by Virgil Thomson); *Four Saints in Three Acts*, wr. 1927, pb. 1932, pr. 1934 (libretto; music by Thomson); *Operas and Plays*, pb. 1932; *Doctor Faustus Lights the Lights*, wr. 1938, pb. 1949, pr. 1951; *Yes Is for a Very Young Man*, pr., pb. 1946; *The Mother of Us All*, pr. 1947, pb. 1949 (libretto; music by Thomson); *Last Operas and Plays*, pb. 1949.

POETRY: *Bee Time Vine and Other Pieces: 1913-1927*, 1953; *Stanzas in Meditation and Other Poems: 1929-1933*, 1956.

NONFICTION: *The Autobiography of Alice B. Toklas*, 1933; *Lectures in America*, 1935; *The Geographical History of America*, 1936; *Everybody's Autobiography*, 1937; *Picasso*, 1938; *Paris, France*, 1940; *Wars I Have Seen*, 1945; *Four in America*, 1947.

MISCELLANEOUS: *The Gertrude Stein First Reader and Three Plays*, pb. 1946; *The Yale Edition of the Unpublished Writings of Gertrude Stein*, 1951-1958 (eight volumes, edited by Carl Van Vechten).

Bibliography

Bridgman, Richard. *Gertrude Stein in Pieces*, 1970.

Brinnin, John Malcolm. *The Third Rose: Gertrude Stein and Her World*, 1959.

Copeland, Carolyn Faunce. *Language and Time and Gertrude Stein*, 1975.

DeKoven, Marianne. *A Different Language: Gertrude Stein's Experimental Writing*, 1983.

Dubnick, Randa. *The Structure of Obscurity: Gertrude Stein, Language, and Cubism*, 1984.

Hoffman, Michael J. *The Development of Abstractionism in the Writings of Gertrude Stein*, 1965.

_____. *Gertrude Stein*, 1976.

Mellow, James R. *Charmed Circle: Gertrude Stein and Company*, 1974.

Stewart, Allegra. *Gertrude Stein and the Present*, 1967.

Sutherland, Donald. *Gertrude Stein: A Biography of Her Work*, 1951.

Walker, Jayne. *The Making of a Modernist: Gertrude Stein from "Three Lives" to "Tender Buttons,"* 1984.

Paula Kopacz

JUN'ICHIRŌ TANIZAKI

Born: Tokyo, Japan; July 24, 1886
Died: Yugawara, Japan; July 30, 1965

Principal short fiction

"Kirin," 1910; "Shisei," 1910 ("The Tattooer," 1963); "Shōnen," 1910; Hō-kan," 1911; "Akuma," 1912; "Kyōfu," 1913 ("Terror," 1963); "Otsuya goroshi," 1913; "Watakushi," 1921 ("The Thief," 1963); "Aoi Hano," 1922 ("Aguri," 1963); *Tade Kuu mushi*, 1928-1929 (*Some Prefer Nettles*, 1955); "Mōmoku monogatari," 1931 ("A Blind Man's Tale," 1963); "Ashikari," 1932 (English translation, 1936); "Shunkinshō," 1933 ("A Portrait of Shunkin," 1936); *Hyofu*, 1950 (collection); *Kagi*, 1956 (*The Key*, 1961); "Yume no ukihashi," 1959 ("The Bridge of Dreams," 1963); *Yume no ukihashi*, 1960 (collection); *Fūten rojin nikki*, 1961-1962 (*Diary of a Mad Old Man*, 1965); *Kokumin no bungaku*, 1964 (collection); *Tanizaki Jun'ichirō shu*, 1970 (collection); *Seven Japanese Tales*, 1981.

Other literary forms

For Western readers, Jun'ichirō Tanizaki is best known for his short stories and short novels. Throughout his career, however, he was a prolific writer of plays, essays, and translations as well. Many English readers favor his long novel *Sasameyuki* (1949; *The Makioka Sisters*, 1957) as his best work. It is the story of a family's efforts to arrange a marriage for Yukiko, the third of four daughters in a respectable Osaka family. Tanizaki has written a number of plays, and also noteworthy are his two translations into modern Japanese of Murasaki Shikibu's *Genji monogatari* (c. 1004; first English translation, *The Tale of Genji*, 1925-1933). The earlier translation was restricted by the severe censorship during the time of the war with China; the later one was in more liberal and colloquial language.

Achievements

The modern Japanese writers most commonly suggested as comparable to Tanizaki for the quality of their fiction are the 1968 Nobel Prize winner Yasunari Kawabata, and Yukio Mishima. It is widely believed that Tanizaki was Kawabata's chief rival for the Nobel Prize that year. Mishima's easier fiction gains more readers but cannot match Tanizaki's more innovative complexity. From his earliest years, however, Tanizaki has had his detractors, as many found his youthful "demoniac" works offensive. Throughout his career, for that matter, his frank portrayal of unconventional, even bizarre sexual and marital relationships among his characters caused consternation. In spite of such reservations, Tanizaki was elected to the Japanese Academy of Arts in 1937. He was awarded the Mainichi Prize for Publication and Culture for *The*

Makioka Sisters and the Asaki Culture Prize and the Imperial Cultural Medal, both in 1949. These are the most important awards the Japanese can give a writer.

Biography

Jun'ichirō Tanizaki, whose father owned a printing establishment, was born in Tokyo on July 24, 1886. He attended the Tokyo Imperial University, studying classical Japanese literature, but had little interest in attending lectures and did not earn a degree. Even at the university, however, he wrote stories and plays for small magazines, some of them serialized; indeed, he continued to be productive throughout his life. In his early years, he was noted for dissolute habits, and some readers blamed him for what they believed was worship of women. His three marriages were unconventional, the experiences of which some will say are hinted at in his short fiction. The suggestion is made occasionally that Tanizaki's moving from Tokyo to the Kansai after the earthquake of 1923 contributed to changes in his writing, but changes in phrasing, characterization, or dialogue in these different years are not easy to see in English translations. As one reviews the publications of his life, one finds no time when he was unproductive. In fact, he continued writing to the time of his death, on July 30, 1965, in Yugawara.

Analysis

The dominant theme in Jun'ichirō Tanizaki's best work is love, but few writers so successfully explore this universally preferred topic with such unconventional revelations. Commentators often identified his earliest writings as "demoniac"; his later work they might have characterized as "sardonic." As labels prove to be insufficient for most good writers, however, one must struggle to understand Tanizaki's probing style as he uncovers complicated motives for lovers, spouses, family members, and friends, who continually surprise one another. In addition, as one finishes reading Tanizaki's works of fiction, most characteristically, one finds oneself more than a little uncertain as to how things really work out. The disputes, the rivalries, or the resentments always seem resolved or brought to a close; most commonly, though, the reader finds himself needing to fill in indeterminate gaps using his own imagination. This challenge, in fact, contributes to much of the pleasure in reading Tanizaki's fiction.

In his early sensational tale, "The Tattooer," the exceptional tattooer, Seikichi, behaves much like a sadist in his attitudes toward some of his customers, as he revels in the excruciating pain they endure for the honor of having such an artist adorn their bodies. He outdoes himself in embellishing the back of a beautiful young woman with a huge black widow spider. Readers are told that "at every thrust of his needle Seikichi . . . felt as if he had stabbed his own heart." After he assures the woman that he has poured his soul into this tattoo and that now all men will be her victims, she accepts this prophecy, turns her resplendently tattooed back to him, and promptly claims the tattooer himself as her first conquest.

With similar emphasis upon intimate revelation of pain, and with similarly ambivalent implications for the suffering endured, in "Terror," a young man describes his peculiar phobia for riding in a train or any other vehicle. For the occasion in the story, he must travel by train to take a physical examination for military duty. His nervous trembling almost drives him mad and certainly drives him to excessive alcoholic consumption. With the combination of neurotic fearfulness and drunkenness, he seems unlikely to pass his physical; the reader, however, hears a doctor reassuring the young man: "Oh, you'll pass all right. A fine husky fellow like you." Such open-endedness in Tanizaki's short fiction seems practically his trademark.

The probing into the psychology of nonconforming personalities reveals itself also in "The Thief." In this story, a young man shares the discomfort and embarrassment with his university dormitory roommates as one by one they admit their shame at having suspected the narrator as the perpetrator of recent thefts. Readers can hardly avoid sympathizing with the young man as he reveals his private thoughts about the unfortunate, painful admissions by others who suspect and distrust him. Then one suddenly discovers that this sensitive young man, in fact, truly is the thief. In fact, the thief boasts that, with an outward show of innocence, he can deceive not only roommates and readers but even himself.

In the story "Aguri," Tanizaki goes further, with his presentation of a self-conscious narrator brooding over his fears and inadequacies. The middle-aged Okada, accompanied by his slim, shapely mistress on a shopping trip, describes in extravagant detail how he is wasting away physically while the young woman, Aguri, craves the most expensive luxuries. As in "The Thief," the narrator of this story carries the reader along with him in his imagination, momentarily at least, with a painful scene of ruinously expensive purchases for Aguri, followed by Okada's fainting embarrassingly in public from weakness. Almost before one realizes the change, however, the reader learns that these disasters were merely an imagined vision. The man and woman end up making modest purchases and with no physical collapse.

In what is probably Tanizaki's most widely read work, *Some Prefer Nettles*, readers are shown a husband and wife, Kaname and Misako, who seem to torture each other with continuing irritations, discomfort, and worry for lack of ability to speak candidly to each other about their heartfelt desires; neither is capable of a forthright decision. Both incline partially toward Western culture and convention-free social values. Kaname prides himself on tolerant generosity when he learns of his wife's interest in another man and encourages her to experiment with this affair until such a time when the two of them can rationally decide whether to dissolve their own marriage or to renew it again with no hard feelings. Readers are limited, however, to the thoughts of Kaname for speculation about what causes the current division. Both these young people look on at contrasts in social relationships as Misako's father, accompanied by a complacent, obedient mistress, indulges himself as a connoisseur of puppet shows. As the story continues, one receives hints that Misako's extramarital romance offers no future hopes for her; Tanizaki intrigues readers more obviously, however, in showing that Kaname desires to follow the older man's conservative style of life. He, too, wants to be waited on with the flattering attentions of an old-fashioned, obedient woman. At the conclusion, readers are told that Kaname is joined at night by a woman whom the narrator does not name, bearing old-style Japanese books; most commentators assume that the old man has sent his mistress to Kaname as a generous gift, but the woman could just as plausibly be Misako adapting to the old-fashioned role to recover their marriage.

In "A Blind Man's Tale," Tanizaki offers what might be his boldest experiment in narrative point of view. A blind masseur, while massaging a nobleman, recalls the insight he gained thirty years before into a complicated series of events in sixteenth century Japanese history. What he knows he learned largely through the experience of serving as masseur for a beautiful noblewoman. The blind man depends upon his own intuition, overheard conversations, and confidential hints. His story not only opens up multiple perspectives on historical events, interesting for their own sake, but also leaves readers pondering choices in judging these acts as honorable, cowardly, or opportunistic.

In "Ashikari" the author appeals to easy emotionalism by beginning with a sentimental narrator taking a walk, visiting the Shrine of Minase and then, in the evening, enjoying the moonlight on the river. His detailed observations of ancient scenes and nostalgic thoughts about the past are accompanied by recitation of favorite verses, Chinese and Japanese. He also composes verses of his own, reciting them aloud while admiring the moonlight. Soon, however, this simple sentimentalism gives way.

The brash visitor, Serizawa, who appears suddenly, dominates the scene from this point. Serizawa tells the story of his father's love for the elegant widow Oyu, a woman surrounded by symbols of refinement. This leads to the self-sacrificing of both the father and Oyu's younger sister Oshizu, who marry but remain chaste in respect for the love between Oyu and the father. The three of them remain close companions in this setting for two or three years. In retrospect, though, one is left intrigued with the mystery of what kind of satisfaction either the father or the son gained from their limited sharing in the Lady Oyu's aristocratic way of life.

"A Portrait of Shunkin" invites attention for another narrative technique favored by Tanizaki, the use of abundant circumstantial detail to lend an initial air of credence to the unusual love story that follows. At the beginning, the narrator gives precise descriptions of a pair of tombstones in a temple graveyard and then of a privately printed biography, and the only known photograph of the beautiful, blind woman Shunkin, famous for her samisen lessons. With this narrator, however, one discovers Tanizaki's characteristic ambivalence as the storyteller regularly admits uncertainty about how to interpret the evidence he has found. One suspects that Shunkin gained pleasure from tormenting Sasuka, her disciple, who may have been, in effect, her slave, but quite possibly he also was her lover. The most startling event, Sasuka's blinding of himself following the cruel, disfiguring scalding of Shunkin by an assailant, invites a great range of speculation about Sasuka's motives: to preserve the memory of her beauty, to gain a measure of acceptance from her, or to distract her from demanding so much of him because of her own handicaps.

Tanizaki varies the formula for an epistolary novel in fine comic style in *The Key*, by representing two supposed diarists, husband and wife, emphatically directing their intimate confessions to each other while insisting that they never will read each other's secret thoughts. Yet the diaries for each are readily accessible, as is the conspicuously misplaced "key" to which the title refers.

The love relationships, as each character defines them, are challenges to imaginative reader response. The husband's poor health and troublesome combination of great sexual desire with limited ability contrasts with the wife Ikuko's apparent lack of interest in sex compensated by her considerable talent and durability. With each sexual act, which she presumably tries to avoid, she exposes her husband's gullibility and endangers his life because it causes his blood pressure to rise. The young gentleman, Kimura, kept on the scene as a marriage prospect for the daughter Toshiko, actually interests the mother and functions both as a substitute for the deficient husband and to provoke his high blood pressure further with jealousy. At the conclusion, Ikuko confesses her motives more explicitly than is usual in Tanizaki, but the continuing family relationship—with the plan that Kimura will marry Toshiko so that the three can live together—invites the usual, wide range of speculation.

Certainly one of Tanizaki's most difficult tales is "The Bridge of Dreams," the story of a boy's affectionate memories of his mother and stepmother with resulting family complications. The most striking images in Tadasu's few recollections of his mother are of her sitting by the pool soaking her pretty feet in the water and of her permitting him to suckle her breasts at night when they were in bed together. This was when he was nearly five years old. The new mother, who had been a geisha, was chosen for her striking resemblance to Tadasu's real mother. She even took the same name and adopted similar habits as a full replacement. In time, as the boy grew old enough to marry, he had difficulty distinguishing the two mothers in his memory. When the second mother has a son, too, the new baby is sent off for adoption. The narrator even relates that Tadasu sucked the milk from his stepmother's swollen breasts after she had given up the child. Following the deaths of his father and second mother, Tadasu adopted his stepbrother with a vow to protect him from loneliness. In this story, with the powerful emphasis on family protectiveness, readers can hardly avoid pondering the relative gains and losses from the characters' exceptional watchfulness over their loved ones.

Another excellent comic representation of obsessive love reveals itself in Tanizaki's novella *Diary of a Mad Old Man*. In this story, Utsuki, a sickly old man, age seventy-seven, fits into the traditional family pattern as the unchallengeable head of the family, whose word is law. The narrative comes across mostly through the old man's notes in his diary. Tanizaki leaves indeterminate the private thoughts of Utsuki's wife and grown children, but they know of his squandering wealth and affection on his daughter-in-law, the scheming Satsuko. The family had been suspicious of her as a bride for the son, Jokichi, right from the start, because of her background as a lowly cabaret dancer. In fact, as the story begins, Jokichi has already lost interest in her anyway, and Satsuko is visited frequently by another young man, Utsuki's nephew, Haruhisa. Nevertheless, the old man's dotage reveals itself in expensive gifts for her, including a cat's-eye ring costing three million yen, the plan to enshrine her footprints on his gravestone, and niggardliness toward his own children. One's disgust for the old man grows with the combination of abundant references to Utsuki's medicines, drugs, and treatments and Satsuko's obvious contempt for him. After Utsuki boldly kisses her on the neck one time, she tells him that she felt as if she had "been licked by a garden slug." Near the end, the narrative trails off with a long series of notes attesting the failing health of an apparently dying man. Then, in the final entry, one reads that Utsuki recovered enough to supervise excavation of the garden to construct a swimming pool for his darling Satsuko. Even in his last years, Tanizaki never lost his ability to catch his readers off guard.

Other major works

NOVELS: *Chijin no ai*, 1924 (*Naomi*, 1985); *Kōjin*, 1926; *Manji*, 1928-1930; *Yoshinokuzu*, 1931 (*Arrowroot*, 1982); *Bushuko hiwa*, 1935 (*The Secret History of the Lord of Musashi*, 1982); *Sasameyuki*, 1949 (*The Makioka Sisters*, 1957); *Shōshō Shigemoto no haha*, 1950 (*The Mother of Captain Shigemoto*, 1956).

PLAYS: *Aisureba koso*, 1921; *Okumi to Gohei*, 1922; *Shirogitsune no yu*, 1923 (*The White Fox*, 1930); *Mumyō to Aizen*, 1924; *Shinzei*, 1949.

NONFICTION: *Bunsho no dukohon*, 1934; "In'ei raisan," 1934 ("In Praise of Shadows," 1955); *Kyō no yume, Ōsaka no yume*, 1950.

TRANSLATION: *Genji monogatari*, 1936-1941, 1951-1954 (of Murasaki Shikibu's medieval *Genji monogatari*).

MISCELLANEOUS: *Tanizaki Jun'ichirō zenshu*, 1930 (twelve volumes); *Tanizaki Jun'ichirō zenshu*, 1966-1970 (twenty-eight volumes).

Bibliography

Keene, Donald. *Dawn to the West: Japanese Literature of the Modern Era: Fiction*, 1984.

Petersen, Gwenn Boardman. *The Moon in the Water: Understanding Tanizaki, Kawabata, and Mishima*, 1979.

David V. Harrington

WILLIAM TREVOR
William Trevor Cox

Born: Mitchelstown, County Cork, Ireland; May 24, 1928

Principal short fiction

The Day We Got Drunk on Cake and Other Stories, 1967; *The Ballroom of Romance and Other Stories*, 1972; *The Last Lunch of the Season*, 1973; *Angels at the Ritz and Other Stories*, 1975; *Lovers of Their Time and Other Stories*, 1978; *Beyond the Pale and Other Stories*, 1981; *The Stories of William Trevor*, 1983; *The News from Ireland and Other Stories*, 1986.

Other literary forms

Though probably best known as a writer of short stories, William Trevor has also written television and radio scripts, plays, and numerous novels. Among Trevor's novels, *The Old Boys* (1964), *Miss Gomez and the Brethren* (1971), *Elizabeth Alone* (1973), and *The Children of Dynmouth* (1976) have been particularly praised.

Achievements

Trevor is widely regarded as one of the finest storytellers and craftsmen writing in English. In Great Britain, his work has long been widely and favorably reviewed and has frequently been adapted for radio and television broadcast by the British Broadcasting Corporation (BBC). In 1964, Trevor's second novel, *The Old Boys*, was awarded the Hawthorden Prize; his fourth collection, *Angels at the Ritz and Other Stories*, was hailed by Graham Greene as "one of the finest collections, if not the best, since Joyce's *Dubliners.*" In addition, Trevor has won the Royal Society of Literature Award, the Allied Irish Banks' Prize for Literature, and the Whitbread Prize for Fiction; he is also a member of the Irish Academy of Letters. In 1979, "in recognition for his valuable services to literature," Trevor was named an honorary Commander, Order of the British Empire. In the United States, knowledge of Trevor's work increased markedly when *The Stories of William Trevor*, an omnibus collection, was published in 1983 and received wide and highly enthusiastic reviews.

Biography

Born William Trevor Cox in Ireland's County Cork, William Trevor, the son of a bank manager, spent much of his childhood living in small Irish towns and attending a series of boarding and day schools that included St. Columba's in Dublin. After earning a B.A. in history from Dublin's Trinity College, Trevor, a Protestant, began work as a sculptor and schoolmaster, taking his first job as an instructor of history in Armagh, Northern Ireland. In 1952, Trevor married Jane Ryan and moved to England, where he spent the next eight years teaching art at two prestigious public schools—first at Rugby and then at Taunton. Between 1960 and 1965, Trevor worked as a copywriter at an advertising agency in London; he simultaneously began devoting an increasing portion of his free time to the writing of fiction. By the early 1970's, following the appearance of several novels and a steady stream of stories in such publications as *Encounter*, *The New Yorker*, and *London Magazine*, Trevor's reputation was secure. The father of two sons, Trevor resides in Devon and writes full-time.

Analysis

Like his novels, William Trevor's short stories generally take place in either England or the Republic of Ireland. For the most part, Trevor focuses on middle-class or lower-middle-class figures whose lives have been character- ized by loneliness, disappointment, and pain. Many of Trevor's characters are trapped in jobs or familial circumstances that are dull or oppressive or both; many retreat frequently to fond memories or romantic fantasies. Trevor rarely mocks the men and women who inhabit his fiction, nor does he treat them as mere ciphers or automatons. In fact, like James Joyce, to whom he is often compared, Trevor assumes a detached authorial stance, but occasion- ally and subtly he makes it clear that he is highly sympathetic to the plight of underdogs, self-deluders, and the victims of abuse and deceit. Invariably, his principal characters are carefully and completely drawn—and so are the worlds they inhabit. Few contemporary writers of short fiction can render at- mosphere and the subtleties of personality as precisely and as tellingly as William Trevor. Few can capture so accurately and wittily the rhythms and nuances of everyday speech. Though its themes can be somber and settings quite bleak, Trevor's brilliantly paced and carefully sculpted fiction consis- tently moves, amuses, and invigorates.

One of Trevor's earliest stories, "The General's Day," illustrates with par- ticular clarity the darkest side of his artistic vision. Contained in *The Day We Got Drunk on Cake and Other Stories*, "The General's Day" centers on a decorated and now retired military man who, at seventy-eight, has never quite come to grips with his retirement and so spends his days wandering around the local village looking for something to do. On the day of the story, a sunny Saturday in June, General Suffolk greets the day with energy and resolution but ends by simply killing time in the local tea shop, where he musters what is left of his once-celebrated charm and manages to convince a woman—"a thin, middle-aged person with a face like a faded photo- graph"—to join him for drinks at the local hotel. There, fueled by gin, Gen- eral Suffolk flirts so blatantly and clumsily with the woman that she flees, "her face like a beetroot." Fueled by more gin, the lonely man becomes increasingly obnoxious. After suffering a few more rejections and humiliations, he finally stumbles back home, where he is mocked further by his "unreliable servant," Mrs. Hinch, a crude woman who habitually cuts corners and treats herself to secretive swigs of the general's expensive South African sherry. In the story's final scene, General Suffolk, "the hero of Roeux and Monchy-le-Preux," is shown leaning and weeping on his cleaning woman's fat arm as she laughingly helps him back to his cottage. "My God Almighty," General Suffolk, deflated, mutters; "I could live for twenty years."

Trevor often portrays older men and women who make stoic adjustments to the present while living principally in the past. He also sometimes focuses on children and adolescents who use vividly constructed daydreams as a means of escaping dreary surroundings or obtuse parents who are themselves sunk in the deadness of their cramped and predictable lives. In "An Evening with John Joe Dempsey," from *The Ballroom of Romance and Other Stories*, Trevor's central figure is a boy of fifteen who lives in a small house in a small Irish town where, daily, he sits in a dull classroom in preparation for a dead-end job at the nearby sawmills. John Joe lives with his widowed mother, a wiry, chronically worried woman whose principal interest in life is to hover protectively about her only son. John Joe escapes his mother's smothering solicitations by wandering about the town with one Quigley, a rather elderly dwarf reputed to be, as one local puts it, "away in the head." Quigley likes to fire John Joe's already active imagination by regaling the boy with detailed descriptions of the sexual vignettes he claims to have witnessed while peeping through area windows. In his own daydreams, John Joe dallies with many of the same sizable matrons that Quigley likes to portray in compromising positions. One of them, Mrs. Taggart, "the wife of a postman," is a tall, "well-built" woman who in John Joe's fantasies requires repeated rescuing from a locked bathroom in which she stands unblushingly nude. Like many of Trevor's characters, John Joe is thus a convincing mix of the comic and the pathetic. If his incongruous sexual fantasies are humorous, the rest of his life looks decidedly grim. In the story's particularly effective closing scene, Trevor portrays John Joe in his bed, in the dark, thinking again of impossible erotic romps with wholly unobtainable women, feeling "more alive than ever he was at the Christian Brothers' School . . . or his mother's kitchen, more alive than ever he would be at the sawmills. In his bed he entered a paradise: it was grand being alone."

In "Nice Day at School," from the same collection, Trevor's principal character is a girl of fourteen, Eleanor, who lives on a housing estate with her cranky, chain-smoking mother and her father, a former professional wrestler who now works as a nightclub bouncer and likes to claim that his work has made him the trusted friend of many celebrities, including Rex Harrison, Mia Farrow, Princess Margaret, and Anthony Armstrong-Jones. Though Eleanor is embarrassed by her father's obviously exaggerated accounts of his encounters with the rich and famous, she is much given to vivid imaginings of her own. Bombarded daily by saccharine pop songs and the more blatantly sexual chatter of her friends, Eleanor thinks obsessively of her ideal lover:

> a man whose fingers were long and thin and gentle, who'd hold her hand in the aeroplane, Air France to Biarritz. And afterwards she'd come back to a flat where the curtains were the colour of lavender, the same as the walls, where gas fires glowed and there were rugs on natural-wood floors, and the telephone was pale blue.

Subtly, however, Trevor indicates that Eleanor is not likely to find a lover so wealthy and suave. Like her friends and most girls of the same social class, this daughter of a bloated bouncer and a bored, gin-sipping housewife will instead wind up with someone like Denny Price, the young butcher's apprentice with "blubbery" lips, who once moved his rough hand up and down her body "like an animal, a rat gnawing at her, prodding her and poking."

Trevor often focuses on women who find themselves pursued by or entangled with insensitive or calculating males. In "Office Romances," from *Angels at the Ritz and Other Stories*, Trevor's central character is Angela Hosford, a typist who works quite anonymously in a large London office appointed with "steel-framed reproductions" and "ersatz leather" sofas and chairs. At twenty-six, Angela is pleasant but plain and myopic: She wears contact lenses that give her eyes a slightly "bulgy look." Her pursuer, Gordon Spelle, is, at thirty-eight, tall and "sleek," but his left eyelid droops a bit, and the eye it covers is badly glazed. While watching old films on television when she was fourteen, Angela had developed a crush on the American actor Don Ameche and had imagined "a life with him in a cliff-top home she'd invented, in California." Now, she finds herself drawn to the deliberately "old fashioned" Spelle, and at one point imagines herself "stroking his face and comforting him because of his bad eye." One day, after his flatteries succeed in rendering Angela both "generous and euphoric," Spelle manages to lure her into a dark and empty office, where—muttering "I love you" repeatedly—he makes love to her, inelegantly, on the floor. Angela finds this experience "not even momentarily pleasurable, not once," but afterward, she basks in the memory of Spelle's heated professions of love. Angela eventually takes a job elsewhere, convinced that Spelle's passion for her "put him under a strain, he being married to a wife who was ill." Like many of Trevor's characters, she understandably decides not to look past her comforting delusions; she refuses to accept the well-known fact that Spelle was "notorious" and "chose girls who were unattractive because he believed such girls, deprived of sex for long periods of time, were an easier bet."

The vast gulf that often separates romantic fantasy from unsavory fact is similarly revealed in the title story of *Lovers of Their Time and Other Stories*. In this piece, set during the 1960's, Trevor's lovers are Norman Britt, a mild-mannered travel agent with "a David Niven moustache," and a young woman, Marie, who tends the counter at Green's the Chemist's. Norman and Marie meet regularly in one of Trevor's favorite fictional locations—a dark pub filled with a wide array of drinkers, talkers, and dreamers. In that same place, in "The Drummer Boy," the two listen to Beatles songs and talk of running away with each other to some romantic foreign country—an event they realize is not likely to materialize. Marie is single, but Norman is married to the loud and bawdy Hilda, who spends the better part of her life sipping cheap wine and watching police dramas on the television and who has previously hinted that she is quite content in the odd marital arrangement that Norman loathes. Thus, at Norman's instigation, the two lovers begin to rendezvous more intimately at the nearby hotel, the Great Western Royal. More specifically, they begin to sneak into a large, infrequently used bathroom, "done up in marble," on the hotel's second floor. Here, luxuriating in an enormous tub, they talk hopefully of happier days that, unfortunately, never arrive. Hilda dismisses her husband's request for a divorce by telling him, "You've gone barmy, Norman"; Marie, tired of waiting, weds "a man in a brewery." Thus, as the years pass, Norman is left with a nostalgic longing not only for Marie but also for that brief period in the 1960's when playful risk-taking was much in the air. Often, while riding "the tube" to work, Norman

> would close his eyes and with the greatest pleasure that remained to him he would recall the delicately veined marble and the great brass taps, and the bath that was big enough for two. And now and again he heard what happened to be the sound of distant music, and the voices of the Beatles celebrating a bathroom love, as they had celebrated Eleanor Rigby and other people of that time.

This allusion to a popular and bittersweet Beatles song is especially appropriate in yet another Trevor story about two thoroughly average and lonely people whose lives have not often been marked by episodes of great passion.

In "Flights of Fancy," also from *Lovers of Their Time and Other Stories*, Trevor's principal character, Sarah Machaen, is yet another Eleanor Rigby–like character destined, one assumes, to spend the rest of her life uneasily alone. Sarah, a clergyman's daughter, is an executive secretary in a large London firm that manufactures lamps; she visits museums, sings in a Bach choir, and is "a popular choice as a godmother." Well into middle age, Sarah is quite content with the externals of her life and gradually has become "reconciled to the fact that her plainness wasn't going to go away." Sometimes, however, she gets lonely enough to daydream of marriage—perhaps to an elderly widower or a blind man. Ironically, the one person who does express a romantic interest in Sarah is another woman, a young and pretty but unschooled factory worker called Sandra Pond. Sarah is shocked at the very idea of lesbianism, yet she cannot stop her mind from "throwing up flights of fancy" in which she pictures herself sharing her flat with Sandra and introducing her to London's many cultural delights. Though her shyness and acute sense of propriety prompt her to reject Sandra's clumsy but clearly genuine professions of love, Sarah is haunted by the sense that she has perhaps passed up her last chance for passion and romance.

"Broken Homes," also from *Lovers of Their Time and Other Stories*, is one of Trevor's most powerful stories. Its principal character, Mrs. Malby, lives with her two budgerigars in a little flat that is scrupulously neat and prettily painted. Mrs. Malby, a widow, lost both of her sons thirty years earlier during World War II; now, at eighty-seven, she has come to terms with her own impending death and wants nothing more than to spend her remaining days in familiar surroundings, her faculties intact. Unfortunately, Mrs. Malby's flat is destroyed and her serenity threatened by a squad of loud and insensitive teenagers from a nearby comprehensive school—"an ugly sprawl of glass and concrete buildings," Mrs. Malby recalls, full of "children swinging along the pavements, shouting obscenities." As part of a community relations scheme, these teenagers have been equipped with mops and sponges and brushes and sent out into the neighborhood in search of good deeds to perform. Mrs. Malby politely asks these obnoxious adolescents to do nothing more than wash her walls, but they treat her with condescension and contempt, and while she is out, they proceed to make a complete mess of her apartment, splattering its walls and floors with bright yellow paint. The students' "teacher," an obtuse and "untidily dressed" bureaucrat, patronizingly assures Mrs. Malby that the damage is slight. He reminds her that, in any event, one must make allowances for the children of "broken homes."

Perhaps more than any of his other stories, "Broken Homes" reveals Trevor's sympathy for the plight of the elderly and his acute awareness of the infirmities and insecurities that accompany old age. The story certainly reveals a strong suspicion that, by the mid-1970's, the British welfare state had become both inefficient and rudely intrusive. Indeed, "Broken Homes" is informed by the subtly expressed sense—not uncommon in Trevor's later fiction—that contemporary Great Britain and Ireland have grown increasingly crass and tacky and that the old social fabric is rapidly and perhaps deleteriously unraveling.

Arguably, "The Paradise Lounge," from *Beyond the Pale and Other Stories*, is Trevor's most representative story. Set principally in the small bar of Keegan's Railway hotel, in "a hilly provincial town" in the Republic of Ireland, "The Paradise Lounge" shifts its focus between two recognizably Trevoresque figures. One of them, Beatrice, is thirty-two; the other, Miss Doheny, is in her eighties. Beatrice—who wanted to be an actress, once— drives often to Keegan's and its adjoining Paradise Lounge to rendezvous with her lover, a middle-aged businessman already married. Miss Doheny, one of the locals, goes regularly to the lounge for a bit of company and several good, stiff drinks. The two have never formally met. Yet Beatrice—

observing Miss Doheny from across the room—is convinced that the old woman is an intriguing figure with a fascinating and no doubt satisfyingly romantic past; she does not realize that Miss Doheny is not only lonely but also full of anger and regret. Miss Doheny, in turn, envies Beatrice's freedom—her ability, in a more liberated and enlightened age, to enter into a friendly sexual affair without running the risk of paralyzing guilt and ostracism. She does not realize that the younger woman's affair has grown stale and mechanical and that by her own estimation Beatrice is about to engage in nothing more than a "dirty weekend"—the final fling in a relationship that, "stripped of love," was nothing more than a "mess of deception and lies."

Like all of Trevor's stories, "The Paradise Lounge" features tight organization and lean but detailed prose. Its very "average" characters are made interesting by Trevor's careful attention to the traits and quirks that make them individuals, to the memories and regrets they have of the past. Trevor, often wry and always detached, refuses to sentimentalize Miss Doheny and Beatrice; he does not, however, subject them to ridicule. "The Paradise Lounge" reveals once again that Trevor understands that for most people expectation and reality infrequently coincide and that among men and women a periodic yearning for adventure and escape is surely universal.

Other major works

NOVELS: *A Standard of Behaviour*, 1958; *The Old Boys*, 1964; *The Love Department*, 1966; *Miss Gomez and the Brethren*, 1971; *Elizabeth Alone*, 1973; *The Children of Dynmouth*, 1976; *Other People's Worlds*, 1980; *Fools of Fortune*, 1983.

PLAYS: *The Elephant's Foot*, 1965; *The Girl*, 1967; *A Night Mrs. da Tanka*, 1968; *Going Home*, 1970; *The Old Boys*, 1971; *A Perfect Relationship*, 1973; *The 57th Saturday*, 1973; *Marriages*, 1973; *Scenes from an Album*, 1975; *Beyond the Pale*, 1980.

Bibliography
Gitzen, Julian. "The Truth-Tellers of William Trevor," in *Critique*. XXI (1979), pp. 59-72.
"William Trevor," in *The Writer's Place: Interviews on the Literary Situation in Contemporary Britain*, 1974. Edited by Peter Firchow.

Brian Murray

VOLTAIRE
François-Marie Arouet

Born: Paris, France; November 21, 1694
Died: Paris, France; May 30, 1778

Principal short fiction

Le Monde comme il va, 1748, revised as *Babouc: Ou, Le Monde comme il va*, 1749 (*Babouc: Or, The World as It Goes*, 1754; also as *The World as It Is: Or, Babouc's Vision*, 1929); *Memnon: Ou, La Sagesse humaine*, 1749 (*Memnon: Or, Human Wisdom*, 1961); *La Lettre d'un Turc*, 1750; *Le Blanc et le noir*, 1764 (*The Two Genies*, 1895); *Jeannot et Colin*, 1764 (*Jeannot and Colin*, 1929); *L'Histoire de Jenni*, 1775; *Les Oreilles du Comte de Chesterfield*, 1775 (*The Ears of Lord Chesterfield and Parson Goodman*, 1826).

Other literary forms

Voltaire's writings are vast, spanning more than one hundred volumes of letters, literature, and scholarship. He wrote in both French and English, publishing his works in several countries, depending on the prevailing political climate.

Voltaire has been remembered most for his incisive short stories, which convey complex philosophical ideas. During his own age, however, he was noted as a political satirist, playwright, and poet. He was a master of the epic poem, and his *La Henriade* (1728; a revision of *La Ligue*; *Henriade*, 1732) revived the popularity of this genre. His plays were renowned throughout France, and *Œdipe* (1718; *Oedipus*, 1761), produced when Voltaire was only twenty-four, received critical acclaim. His major philosophical work, *Dictionnaire philosophique portatif* (1764; *A Philosophical Dictionary for the Pocket*, 1765; also as *Philosophical Dictionary*, 1945), was an ambitious compendium of philosophical ideas and terms. In addition, his historical writings, such as *Le Siècle de Louis XIV* (1751; *The Age of Louis XIV*, 1752), have earned for him a reputation as one of the first modern historians.

Achievements

During his lifetime, Voltaire was both revered and rejected. He was alternately honored by kings for his brilliance and exiled or imprisoned for his radical political views. He was welcomed into the courts of George I and Princess Caroline of England, Frederick II of Prussia, and Louis XV of France. Louis XV appointed him as Royal Historiographer and as Ordinary Gentleman of the King's Bedchamber in the 1740's. In 1746, Voltaire realized one of his greatest ambitions when he was elected to the prestigious Académie Française. In the 1750's, Frederick II gave him a medal of merit, made him a chamberlain, and considered Voltaire to be his personal tutor and court philosopher until a bitter disagreement caused Voltaire to leave Prussia.

Voltaire's scathing attacks on intolerance, injustice, and superstition scandalized many of the powerful in the government and the French Roman Catholic Church, but his humor, imagination, and daring in expressing his opinions won for him numerous followers as well. When he was living in Switzerland in his later years, people made pilgrimages to his home and stood outside it hoping to catch a glimpse of him. At the end of his life, Voltaire returned to Paris to the acclaim of crowds of admirers. Yet, even in death, he stirred controversy: His body had to be smuggled out of Paris to allow him the decent burial in consecrated ground that the French Catholic hierarchy denied him.

Voltaire was one of the foremost philosophes of the French Enlightenment, and his influence went far beyond his long and successful lifetime. His ideas on the freedom and dignity of the individual are credited with having had a strong influence on the French Revolution of 1789. His satirical and irreverent wit gradually eroded some of the religious and political intolerance of eighteenth century France. Many who have fought for toleration, justice, and equality have looked back to the spirit of Voltaire's writings. He summarized his own sense of satisfaction about the successes of his and other philosophes' writings in a letter to Jean Le Rond d'Alembert dated July 18, 1766, in which he rejoiced that

> the Church of Wisdom is beginning to develop in our neighborhood where, twelve years ago the most somber fanaticism ruled. The provinces are becoming enlightened, the young magistrates are thinking boldly. . . . One is astonished by the progress that human reason has made in so few years.

Biography

Voltaire was born François-Marie Arouet on November 21, 1694, the son of a *grand bourgeois* lawyer. From 1704 to 1711, he attended a Jesuit boarding school, after which he pursued the study of law until his political writings earned for him his first exile from Paris in 1716 and his first imprisonment in the Bastille in 1717. From that time on, he devoted himself to his writing, beginning with plays and poetry and expanding to literature, philosophy, and history. He was socially and intellectually precocious, associating with many aristocratic and libertine men in the Société du Temple (Society of the Temple) by the time he was twelve. Voltaire was brilliant, witty, a talented writer, and, in later years, a social activist. Yet he could also be impulsive and hotheaded, which resulted in his arrest on several further occasions. Voltaire lived in various parts of France, England, Holland, Prussia, and Switzerland, moving in and out of these countries as his political sentiments and personal temperament made it unwise or impossible for him to stay where he was. He spent the last years of his life living near the Swiss border, between his French homeland and the freer intellectual environment of Geneva, allowing himself an escape route to either country.

Voltaire was as untraditional in his personal life as in his political and philosophical ideas. His freedom from the norms of society, however, seemed to sustain his creative energies. In 1734, Voltaire met Madame Émilie du Châtelet, who would be his mistress and intellectual partner for the next fifteen years. He moved in with her and her husband at their estate at Cirey, where he wrote and studied with the "divine Émilie." Even after Voltaire's widowed niece, Madame Denis, had become his new mistress, he maintained an intellectual relationship with Madame du Châtelet which would inspire him until her death in 1749. Her death saddened and depressed Voltaire for many years, contributing to the growing skepticism about the goodness of the world that is evident in his later fictional works, such as *Candide: Ou, L'Optimisme* (1759; *Candide: Or, All for the Best*, 1759). Throughout his life, Voltaire had suffered from bouts with ill health and severe hypochondria. He lived to be eighty-three, however, and was one of the most energetic and prolific authors in history.

Analysis

Voltaire's wit and insight into the human condition found a memorable forum in his short stories. These stories were not merely entertaining fantasies but were works of philosophical and social reflection as well. By allowing his readers to see the world through his characters' eyes, Voltaire taught new ways of thinking about the attitudes and situation of humanity.

Voltaire's fiction ranges from extremely short pieces to the longer works *Zadig: Ou, La Destinée, Histoire orientale* (1748; originally as *Memnon: Histoire orientale*, 1747; *Zadig: Or, The Book of Fate*, 1749), *Le Micromégas*, (1752; *Micromegas*, 1753), *Candide*; and *L'Ingénu*, (1767; *The Pupil of Nature*, 1771; also as *Ingenuous*, 1961). While those longer works are the primary stories for which he is remembered, his shorter tales contain many of the same themes in a tightly crafted and inventive form.

Voltaire was fascinated throughout his life with the issues of good and evil, freedom and determinism, and the nature of Providence. A Deist to the end of his life, convinced that God had created the world and left it to run according to an original plan, Voltaire yet struggled with the concepts of fate and Providence from the human perspective. The view of Gottfried Wilhelm von Leibnitz and others that this is the best of all possible worlds fit with Voltaire's Deism but not with his experience of the world. Voltaire's stories show a continually deepening sense of the evil and folly in life, in which it is difficult to find the good. His protagonists often undertake long and bizarre journeys, on which they learn tolerance from the experience of the universality of human suffering. Human goodness does not seem to be rewarded in the long run, and no obviously overarching plan shows itself to his heroes. It appears that existence is a pointless interplay of events in which evil people seem to be quite happy and successful, and the good often suffer miserably. Yet Voltaire always allows for the possibility that some good may be present in the worst of situations, even if that good is well hidden.

Within Voltaire's longer stories, this theme is quite obvious. In *Zadig*, the protagonist encounters a continually changing cycle of fortunes and misfortunes until he finally decides in despair that goodness will never be rewarded. An angel in disguise teaches him that the ways of Providence are inscrutable and all that happens in life creates the best possible world as a whole. Once Zadig realizes that the evil in the world is part of the divine plan, and that the world would be less perfect without it, he is freed from his ignorance and becomes the happy man that he had always believed he would be. He ends up a king, ruling more justly and compassionately because of the wisdom gained from his misfortunes. In the later work, *Candide*, Voltaire's growing pessimism is evident. Candide is an innocent and optimistic young man who undergoes an incredible series of cruel and painful disasters. Considering the enormity of the ills which meet him from all sides—he is exiled, drafted, beaten, robbed, and continually loses the woman he loves—he is amazingly slow to question his optimistic view of the world. By the end of his life, however, Candide settles down on a small farm with the woman he sought all his life (now grown quite ugly and disagreeable), and he brushes aside his original belief that things are all ordered for the best. He recognizes that the attempt to try to ignore the inevitability of suffering and evil in life leads to a tragic failure: the failure to try to improve the world in whatever ways are possible. He is now more content with the attitude that "we must cultivate our garden," thus abandoning the question of the good of the whole universe for the task of alleviating the misery of existence in his small corner of the world.

In Voltaire's shorter tales *Babouc* and *Memnon*, the issue of the apparent dominance of evil over good receives an answer similar to that given by *Zadig* in 1747. As in the novel *Zadig*, the protagonists learn that this world is imperfect but that it plays its appointed role in a universe that is ordered by Providence.

In *Babouc*, the jinni Ithuriel descends to earth to send Babouc on a fact-finding journey to Persia. Babouc is to travel throughout Persepolis to see if the Persians are worthy of punishment or destruction because of their evil actions. Babouc sets off and soon finds himself in the midst of a war between Persia and India. This war, begun over a petty dispute, has been ravaging the country for twenty years. Babouc witnesses bloody battles, treachery, and cruelty on both sides. He also witnesses many amazing acts of kindness and humanity. His journey continues in this vein. For every set of abuses in religion, politics, sexual conduct, and education, he finds also some good and noble elements. His cry of surprise echoes throughout the piece: "Unintelligible mortals! . . . How is it that you can combine so much meanness with so much greatness, such virtues with such crimes?" By the end, he agrees with a wise man whom he meets that evil is prevalent and good people are rare, yet the best is hidden from a visitor and needs to be sought more diligently. As he examines the society, he finds that those who have obtained positions of power through corrupt means are capable of devotion to their work and often pursue their careers with devotion and justice. He gains compassion for the people and their leaders and devises a way in which to communicate what he has learned to the jinni. He has a metalsmith fashion a statue out of every kind of stone, earth, and metal and takes this figure back to Ithuriel, asking, "Will you break this pretty little image, because it is not all gold and diamonds?" Ithuriel immediately comprehends and pardons the Persians, deciding not to interfere with "the way the world goes." Even though the world is not fully good, it contains enough good to merit its continued existence.

In *Memnon: Or, Human Wisdom* (not to be confused with *Memnon: Histoire orientale*, the original title of *Zadig*), Voltaire takes a different path to a similar moral. In this humorous tale, a young man named Memnon plans to become perfectly wise by ridding himself of all of his passions. He decides to renounce love, drinking, wasting money, and arguing. He is assured that this will lead him to financial and emotional security, remove all hindrances to the exercise of his reason, and thus make him happy. After he forms this plan, he looks out his window and sees a young woman in tears. He rushes to counsel her, sheerly out of compassion, and ends in her embrace. Her uncle enters, and only a large sum of money convinces him not to kill Memnon. Memnon then has dinner with his friends and consoles himself by getting drunk and gambling, which leads to an argument in which he loses an eye. "The wise Memnon is carried back home drunk, with no money, and minus an eye." He recovers a bit, only to find that his investors have bankrupted him. He ends up sleeping on a pile of straw outside of his house and dreams that a six-winged heavenly creature, his good jinni, comes to him. Memnon wonders where his good jinni was the night before and is told that he was with Memnon's brother, who was blinded and imprisoned. Memnon comments that it is worthwhile "to have a good genie in a family, so that one of two brothers may be one-eyed, the other blind, one lying on straw, the other in prison." The jinni helpfully points out that the situation will get better if Memnon abandons his ridiculous attempt to be perfectly wise. This world is only one of many others, all of which are ordered by degrees of perfection, and the earth is far down near the craziest end of the scale. All is well, the jinni assures him, when one considers the arrangement of the universe as a whole. Memnon says that he will believe that all is well when he can see that it is with both eyes.

Although Voltaire's fiction depicts a crazy world where fortunes are uncertain, evils abound, and goodness does not ensure happiness, there are two things which are valued in most of his stories—the search for knowledge and the companionship of trusted friends. In *Jeannot and Colin*, Voltaire examines the worth of friendship and learning over the illusory happiness to be gained from wealth and power. Jeannot and Colin are friends and roommates at school until Jeannot's father sends for him to come home and enjoy the new family wealth. Jeannot does so, scorning his old friend and turning with relish to his new life of leisure. His mother and father discuss his future with a tutor, but each area of study, whether philosophy, mathematics, or history, is judged of no use to a young man of society who now has servants to do as he wishes. They decide to teach him to dance and be attractive, so that he can shine in social graces. He becomes a vaudeville singer and charms all the ladies of breeding. This, however, does not last: His father is bankrupted, his mother forced to become a servant, and Jeannot himself is homeless. In a state of distress, he runs into his old friend, Colin, whom he had snubbed. Colin is overjoyed to see him and offers to take Jeannot into his home and his business and to help Jeannot's mother and father out of their difficulties. Colin's kindness and forgiveness change Jeannot's heart and allow Jeannot's natural goodness to grow, free from the ravages of society. Jeannot lives happily, assisting his parents and marrying Colin's equally sweet-tempered sister.

Philosophical reflections and social satire weigh down the plots of some later stories, such as *The Ears of Lord Chesterfield and Parson Goodman*, making them tedious. These stories show the drier side of Voltaire's satire. At his best, however, Voltaire offered his readers richly woven tales which critiqued society, satirized pretensions, expressed new philosophical ideas, and simply entertained. The stories include much humor and piercing insight into the common follies of humanity. These philosophical tales succeeded, as no straightforward philosophy could, in offering many people new perspectives on reason, experience, and humanity.

Other major works

NOVELS: *Zadig: Ou, La Destinée, Histoire orientale*, 1748 (originally as *Memnon: Histoire orientale*, 1747; *Zadig: Or, The Book of Fate*, 1749); *Le Micromégas*, 1752 (*Micromegas*, 1753); *Histoire des voyages de Scarmentado*, 1756 (*The History of the Voyages of Scarmentado*, 1757; also as *History of Scarmentado's Travels*, 1961); *Candide: Ou, L' Optimisme*, 1759 (*Candide: Or, All for the Best*, 1759); *L'Ingénu*, 1767 (*The Pupil of Nature*, 1771; also as *Ingenuous*, 1961); *L'Homme aux quarante écus*, 1768 (*The Man of Forty Crowns*, 1768); *La Princesse de Babylone*, 1768 (*The Princess of Babylon*, 1769).

PLAYS: *Œdipe*, 1718 (*Oedipus*, 1761); *Artémire*, 1720; *Mariamne*, 1724 (English translation, 1761); *L'Indiscret*, 1725 (verse); *Brutus*, 1730 (English translation, 1761); *Ériphyle*, 1732; *Zaïre*, 1732 (English translation, 1736); *La Mort de César*, 1733; *Adélaïade du Guesclin*, 1734; *L'Échange*, 1734; *Alzire*, 1736 (English translation, 1763); *L'Enfant prodigue*, 1736 (verse; *The Prodigal*, 1750? prose translation); *Zulime*, 1740; *Mahomet*, 1742 (*Mahomet the Prophet*, 1744); *Mérope*, 1743 (English translation, 1744, 1749); *La Princesse de Navarre*, 1745 (verse; music by Jean-Philippe Rameau); *La Prude: Ou, La Grandeuse de Cassette*, 1747 (verse; based on William Wychereley's play *The Plain-Dealer*); *Sémiramis*, 1748 (*Semiramis*, 1760); *Nanine*, 1749 (English translation, 1927); *Oreste*, 1750; *Rome sauvée*, 1752; *L'Orphelin de la Chine*, 1755 (*The Orphan of China*, 1756); *Socrate*, 1759 (*Socrates*, 1760); *L'Écossaise*, 1760 (*The Highland Girl*, 1760); *Tancrède*, 1760; *Olympie*, 1763; *Le Triumvirat*, 1764; *Les Scythes*, 1767; *Les Guèbres: Ou, La Tolérance*, 1769; *Sophonisbe*, 1770 (revision of Jean Mairet's play); *Les Pélopides: Ou, Atrée et Thyeste*, 1772; *Les Lois de Minos*, 1773; *Don Pèdre*, 1775; *Irène*, 1778; *Agathocle*, 1779.

POETRY: *Poème sur la religion naturelle*, 1722; *La Ligue*, 1723; *La Henriade*, 1728 (revision of *La Ligue*; *Henriade*, 1732); *Le Temple du goût*, 1733 (*The Temple of Taste*, 1734); *Le Mondain*, 1736 (*The Man of the World*, 1764); *Discours en vers sur l'homme*, 1738-1752 (*Discourses in Verse on Man*, 1764); *Poème de Fontenoy*, 1745; *Poème sur les événements de l'année 1744*, 1745; *Poème de la loi naturelle*, 1752 (*On Natural Law*, 1764); *La Pucelle d'Orléans*, 1755, 1762 (*The Maid of Orleans*, 1758; also as *La Pucelle*, 1785-1786); *Poème sur le désastre de Lisbonne*, 1756 (*Poem on the Lisbon Earthquake*, 1764); *Poème sur la loi naturelle*, 1756; *Le Pauvre Diable*, 1758; *Épître à Horace*, 1772.

NONFICTION: *Histoire de Charles XII*, 1731 (*The History of Charles XII*, 1732); *Lettres philosophiques*, 1734 (originally published in English as *Letters Concerning the English Nation*, 1733; also as *Philosophical Letters*, 1961); *Discours de métaphysique*, 1736; *Éléments de la philosophie de Newton*, 1738 (*The Elements of Sir Isaac Newton's Philosophy*, 1738); *Vie de Molière*, 1739; *Le Siècle de Louis XIV*, 1751 (*The Age of Louis XIV*, 1752); *Essai sur les mœurs*, 1756, 1763 (*The General History and State of Europe*, 1754, 1759); *Traité sur la tolérance*, 1763 (*A Treatise on Religious Toleration*, 1764); *Dictionnaire philosophique portatif*, 1764 (*A Philosophical Dictionary for the Pocket*, 1765; also as *Philosophical Dictionary*, 1945); *Commentaires sur Corneille* 1764; *Avis au public sur les parracides imputés aux calas et aux Sirven*, 1775; *Correspondence*, 1953-1965 (102 volumes).

MISCELLANEOUS: *The Works of M. de Voltaire*, 1761-1765 (thirty-five volumes), 1761-1781 (thirty-eight volumes); *Candide and Other Writings*, 1945; *The Portable Voltaire*, 1949; *Candide, Zadig, and Selected Stories*, 1961; *The Complete Works of Voltaire*, 1968-1977 (135 volumes; in French).

Bibliography

Aldridge, Alfred Owen. *Voltaire and the Century of Light*, 1975.
Bottiglia, William F., comp. and ed. *Voltaire: A Collection of Critical Essays*, 1968.
Mason, Haydn Trevor. *Voltaire: A Biography*, 1981.
Richter, Peyton E., and Ilona Ricardo. *Voltaire*, 1980.

Mary J. Sturm

ALICE WALKER

Born: Eatonton, Georgia; February 9, 1944

Principal short fiction

In Love and Trouble: Stories of Black Women, 1973; *You Can't Keep a Good Woman Down*, 1981.

Other literary forms

Alice Walker is known for her achievements in both prose and poetry; in addition to her two short-story collections, she has published several novels, several volumes of poetry, and a collection of essays. *The Third Life of Grange Copeland* (1970), *Meridian* (1976), and *The Color Purple* (1982) examine the struggles of blacks against destruction by a racist society. Her poetry is collected in *Once* (1968), *Five Poems* (1972), *Revolutionary Petunias and Other Poems* (1973), *Goodnight, Willie Lee, I'll See You in the Morning* (1979), and *Horses Make a Landscape More Beautiful* (1984). *In Search of Our Mothers' Gardens: Womanist Prose* (1983) is a collection of essays which are important to an understanding of what is important to Walker, of her purposes and methods. Walker also wrote for children *Langston Hughes: American Poet* (1974) and edited an anthology of writing by Zora Neale Hurston, *I Love Myself When I'm Laughing . . . and Then Again When I'm Looking Mean and Impressive: A Zora Neale Hurston Reader* (1979).

Achievements

From the beginning of her career, Walker has been an award-winning writer. Her first published essay, "The Civil Rights Movement: What Good Was It?" won first prize in *The American Scholar's* annual essay contest in 1967. Her first novel was written on a fellowship at the MacDowell Colony in New Hampshire. *Revolutionary Petunias and Other Poems* was nominated for a National Book Award and won the Lillian Smith Award of the Southern Regional Council in 1973. *In Love and Trouble* won the Richard and Hinda Rosenthal Award from the American Institute of Arts and Letters in 1974. *The Color Purple*, which remained on *The New York Times* list of best-sellers for more than twenty-five weeks, was nominated for the National Book Critics Circle Award and won both an American Book Award and the Pulitzer Prize for Fiction. Walker's many honors include a National Endowment for the Arts grant in 1969, a Radcliffe Institute Fellowship in 1971-1973, and a Guggenheim Fellowship in 1978. She has been praised for her ability to get inside the minds of passive, inarticulate characters, to combine cruelty and compassion, the weight of oppression and the buoyancy of affirmation so that they are deeply felt and keenly understood at once. Unfavorable reviews of Walker's work usually complain that she always makes the men villains and the women heroes. Walker herself confirms her "womanist" bias. Despite some demurs about a feminist slant, the response to *The Color Purple* was overwhelmingly positive, and there is increasing critical attention being paid to her work. Walker is an inspired writer who continually dares to confront the worst and celebrate the best in the Afro-American experience.

Biography

Alice Malsenior Walker was born in Eatonton, Georgia, to sharecropper parents on February 9, 1944. She attended Spelman College in Atlanta on scholarship, transferring to Sarah Lawrence in New York, where she was graduated in 1965. While working in the Civil Rights movement in Mississippi in the summer of 1966, she met Melvyn Rosenman Levanthal, an attorney, whom she married in 1967. After residing for seven years in Jackson, Mississippi, the couple returned to the East in 1974, where Walker served as a contributing editor for *Ms.* magazine. The two were divorced in 1976, sharing joint custody of a daughter, Rebecca. Walker moved to California in 1978, where she continues to write and remains politically active.

Analysis

The heroism of black women in the face of turmoil of all kinds rings from both volumes of Alice Walker's short stories like the refrain of a protest song. *In Love and Trouble* reveals the extremes of cruelty and violence to which poor black women are often subjected in their personal relationships, while the struggles in *You Can't Keep a Good Woman Down* reflect the social upheavals of the 1970's.

Such subjects and themes lend themselves to a kind of narrative that is filled with tension. The words "love" and "trouble," for example, in the title of the first collection, identify a connection that is both unexpected and inevitable. Each of the thirteen stories in this collection is a vivid confirmation that every kind of love known to woman brings its own kind of suffering. Walker is adept at pairing such elements so as to create pronounced, and revealing, contrasts or intense conflicts. One such pair that appears in many of these short stories is a stylistic one and easy to see: the poetry and prose that alternate on the page. Another unusual combination at work throughout the short fiction may be called the lyrical and the sociological. Like the protest song, Walker's stories make a plea for justice more memorable by giving it a poetic form. She breathes rhythmic, eloquent language into the most brutish and banal abuses.

These two elements—similarity of subject matter and the balance of highly charged contraries—produce a certain unity within each volume. Yet beyond this common ground, the stories have been arranged so as to convey

a progression of interconnected pieces whose circumstances and themes repeat, alternate, and overlap rather like a musical composition. The first three
stories of *In Love and Trouble*, for example, are all about married love; the
next two are about love between parent and child; then come three stories in
which black-white conflict is central; the fourth group concerns religious
expression; and the last three stories focus on initiation. Other themes
emerge and run through this five-set sequence, linking individual motifs and
strengthening the whole. Jealousy is one of those motifs, as is the drive for
self-respect, black folkways, and flowers, in particular, the rose and the
blackeyed Susan.

The four stories to be discussed suggest the breadth of Walker's imagination and narrative skills. "Roselily" is a good place to begin, being the first
story of *In Love and Trouble* and striking an anticipatory note of foreboding.
"The Child Who Favored Daughter" is an equally representative selection,
this time of the horrific destruction of the black woman. The third selection,
"The Revenge of Hannah Kemhuff," is as cool and clear as "The Child Who
Favored Daughter" is dark and fevered. The narrator recounts a tale of voodoo justice, specifically crediting Zora Neale Hurston, author of *Mules and
Men* (1935). The last story of this collection, "To Hell with Dying," is an affirmative treatment of so many of the themes Walker has previously developed
more darkly.

"Roselily" takes place on a front porch surrounded by a crowd of black
folk, in sight of Highway 61 in Mississippi during the time it takes to perform
a wedding ceremony. As the preacher intones the formal words, the bride's
mind wanders among the people closest to her there—the bridegroom, the
preacher, her parents, sisters, and children. His religion is different from
hers, and she knows that he disapproves of this gathering. She speculates
uneasily about their future life together in Chicago, where she will wear a veil
and sit on the woman's side of his church and have more babies. She is the
mother of four children already but has never been married. He is giving her
security, but he intends, she realizes, to remake her into the image he wants.
Even the love he gives her causes her great sadness, as it makes her aware of
how unloved she was before. At last, the ceremony over, they stand in the
yard, greeting well-wishers, he completely alien, she overcome with anxiety.
She squeezes his hand for reassurance but receives no answering signal from
him.

The ambivalence felt by the bride in this magnetic mood piece is intensified by poetic and fairy tale elements. First, there are the ceremonial
resonances of the words between the paragraphs of narrative, stately and
solemn like a slow drumbeat. As these phrases alternate with Roselily's
thoughts, a tension develops. At the words "*Dearly Beloved*," a daydream of
images begins to flow, herself a small girl in her mother's fancy dress, struggling through "a bowl of quicksand soup"; the words "*we are gathered here*"

suggest to her cotton waiting, ready to be weighed, a Mississippi rural countriness she knows the bridegroom finds repugnant; *"in the sight of God"* creates in her mind the image of God as a little black boy tugging at the preacher's coattail. Gradually, a sense of foreboding builds. At the words *"to join this man and this woman,"* she imagines "ropes, chains, handcuffs, his religion." The bridegroom is her rescuer, like Prince Charming, and is ready to become her Pygmalion. Like Sleeping Beauty, Roselily is only dimly aware of exchanging one form of confinement, of enchantment, for another. At the end of the ceremony, she awakes to his passionate kiss and a terrible sense of being *wrong*.

While "Roselily" is a subtle story of a quiet inner life, "The Child Who Favored Daughter" records the circumstances of a shocking assault. It begins, also, on a front porch. A father waits with a shotgun on a hot afternoon for his daughter to walk from the school bus through the front yard. He is holding in his hand a letter written by her to her white lover. Realizing what her father knows, the girl comes slowly down the dusty lane, pausing to study the blackeyed Susans. As his daughter approaches, the father is reminded of his sister, "Daughter," who also had a white lover. His intense love for his sister had turned to bitterness because she gave herself to a man by whom he felt enslaved; his bitterness poisoned all of his relationships with women thereafter. He confronts the girl on the porch with the words "White man's slut!" then beats her with a stable harness and leaves her in the shed behind the house. The next morning, failing to make her deny the letter and struggling to suppress his "unnamable desire," he slashes off her breasts. As the story ends, he sits in a stupor on the front porch.

This story of perverted parental love and warring passions is about the destructive power of jealousy and denial. Its evil spell emanates from the father's unrepented and unacknowledged desire to possess his sister. He is haunted by her when he looks at his own daughter. Once again, a strongly lyrical style heightens the dominant tone, in this case, horror. Short lines of verse, like snatches of song, are interspersed with the narrative, contrasting sharply in their suggestion of pure feeling with the tightly restrained prose. The daughter's motif associates her with the attraction of natural beauty: *"Fire of earth/ Lure of flower smells/ The sun."* The father's theme sounds his particular resignation and doom: *Memories of years/ Unknowable women— /sisters/spouses/illusions of soul/.* The resulting trancelike confrontation seems inevitable, the two moving through a pattern they do not control, do not understand.

In "The Revenge of Hannah Kemhuff," a woman who has lost husband, children, and self-respect, all because a charity worker denied her food stamps, comes to the seer, Tante Rosie, for peace of mind. Tante Rosie assures the troubled woman that the combined powers of the Man-God and the Great Mother of Us All will destroy her enemy. Tante Rosie's apprentice, who narrates the story, teaches Mrs. Kemhuff the curse-prayer printed in Zora Neale Hurston's *Mules and Men*. Then she sets about to collect the necessary ingredients for the conjure: Sarah Sadler Holley's feces, water, nail parings. Her task seems to become almost impossible when her mentor tells her that these items must be gained directly from the victim herself. Nevertheless, with a plan in mind, the young woman approaches Mrs. Holley, tells her that she is learning the profession from Tante Rosie, and then asks her to prove that she, as she claims, does not believe in "rootworking." It is only a short while until Mrs. Kemhuff dies, followed a few months later by Mrs. Holley, who had, after the visit of the apprentice, taken to her bedroom, eating her nails, saving her fallen hair, and collecting her excrement in plastic bags and barrels.

This is the first story in the collection in which the black community comes into conflict with the white. It is a conflict of religious traditions and a strong statement in recognition of something profound in African folkways. Mrs. Holley failed Mrs. Kemhuff years before in the greatest of Christian virtues, that of charity. Mrs. Kemhuff, though now reconciled with her church, cannot find peace and seeks the even greater power of ancient conjure to restore her pride. Like other Afro-American writers who have handled this subject, Walker first acknowledges that voodoo is widely discounted as sheer superstition, but then her story argues away all rational objections. Mrs. Holley does not die as the result of hocus-pocus but because of her own radical belief, a belief in spite of herself. There is something else about this story that is different from those at the beginning of the collection. Instead of a dreamy or hypnotic action, there are alert characters speaking and thinking purposefully, clearly. This is one strand of many evolving patterns that emerge as the stories are read in sequence.

"To Hell with Dying" is the last story in the collection and a strong one. A more mellow love-and-trouble story than most preceding it, it features a male character who is not the villain of the piece. Mr. Sweet Little is a melancholy man whom the narrator has loved from childhood, when her father would bring the children to Mr. Sweet's bedside to rouse him from his depression with a shout: "To hell with dying! These children want Mr. Sweet!" Because the children were so successful in "revivaling" Mr. Sweet with their kisses and tickling and cajoling ways, they were not to learn for some time what death really meant. Years pass. Summoned from her doctoral studies in Massachusetts, the twenty-four-year-old narrator rushes to Mr. Sweet's bedside, where she cannot quite believe that she will not succeed. She does induce him to open his eyes, smile, and trace her hairline with his finger as he once did. Still, however, he dies. His legacy to her is the steel guitar on which he played away his blues all those years: that and her realization that he was her first love.

It is useful to recognize this story as an initiation story, like the two that precede it, "The Flowers" and "We Drink the Wine in France." Initiation stories usually involve, among other things, an unpleasant brush with reality, a new reality. A child, adolescent, or young adult faces an unfamiliar challenge and, if successful, emerges at a new level of maturity or increased status. Always, however, something is lost, something must be given up. As a very small girl, the narrator remembers, she did not understand quite what was going on during their visits to the neighbor's shack. When she was somewhat older, she felt the weight of responsibility for the dying man's survival. At last, after she has lost her old friend, she is happy, realizing how important they were to each other. She has successfully negotiated her initiation into the mysteries of love and death, as, in truth, she had already done, to the best of her ability, at those earlier stages.

This often-reprinted story is a culmination of the struggle between Death and Love for the lives of the girls and women, really for all the blacks of *In Love and Trouble*, one which well represents Walker's talent and demonstrates her vision of blacks supporting and affirming one another in community.

If *In Love and Trouble* is Walker's tribute to the down-and-out black woman, then *You Can't Keep a Good Woman Down* is her salute to black women who are pushing ahead, those who have crossed some barriers and are in some sense champions. There are black women who are songwriters, artists, writers, students in exclusive Eastern schools; they are having abortions, teaching their men the meaning of pornography, coming to terms with the death of a father, on one hand, or with the meaning of black men raping white women, on the other. Always, they are caught up short by the notions of whites. In other words, all the political, sexual, racial, countercultural issues of the 1970's are in these stories, developed from what Walker calls the "womanist" point of view.

This set of stories, then, is somewhat more explicitly sociological than the first and somewhat less lyrical, and it is also more apparently autobiographical, but in a special sense. Walker herself is a champion, so her life is a natural, even an inescapable, source of material. Walker-the-artist plays with Walker-the-college-student and Walker-the-idealistic-teacher, as well as with some of the other roles she sees herself as having occupied during that decade of social upheaval. Once a writer's experience has become transformed within a fictive world, it becomes next to impossible to think of the story's events as either simply autobiography or simply invention. The distinction has been deliberately blurred. It is because Walker wants to unite her public and private worlds, her politics and her art, life as lived and life as imagined, that, instead of poetry, these stories are interspersed with autobiographical parallels, journal entries, letters, and other expressions of her personality.

There are three stories that deserve special attention, "Nineteen Fifty-five," "Fame," and "Source." To begin with, they serve as checkpoints for the collection's development, from the essentially simple and familiar to the increasingly complex and strange, from 1955 to 1980. Furthermore, these stories are independently memorable.

The opening story, "Nineteen Fifty-five," is presented from the perspective of a middle-aged blues singer, Gracie Mae Still, whose signature song, recorded by a young white man named Traynor, brings him fame and fortune. Gracie Mae records her impressions of Traynor in a journal, beginning with their first meeting in 1955 and continuing until his death in 1977. Over the years, the rock-and-roll star (obviously meant to suggest Elvis Presley) stays in touch with the matronly musician, buying her lavish gifts—a white Cadillac, a mink coat, a house—and quizzing her on the real meaning of her song. From the army, he writes to tell her that her song is very much in demand, and that everyone asks him what he thinks it means, really. As time goes by and his life disappoints him, he turns to the song, as if it were a touchstone that could give his life meaning. He even arranges an appearance for himself and Gracie Mae on the Johnny Carson Show, with some half-developed notion of showing his fans what the real thing is and how he aspires to it. If he is searching for a shared experience of something true and moving with his audience, however, he is to be disappointed again. His fans applaud only briefly, out of politeness, for the originator of the song, the one who really gives it life, then squeal wildly for his imitation, without any recognition of what he wanted them to understand. That is the last time the two musicians see each other.

In part, this story is about the contribution that black music made to the spirit of the times and how strangely whites transformed it. The white rock-and-roll singer, who seems as much in a daze as some of the women of *In Love and Trouble*, senses something superior in the original blues version, but he misplaces its value, looking for some meaning to life that can be rolled up in the nutshell of a lyric. In contrast to the bemused Traynor, Gracie Mae is a down-to-earth champion, and her dialect looks forward to Walker's masterful handling of dialect in *The Color Purple*. She repeatedly gives Traynor simple and sensible advice when he turns to her for help, and she has her own answer to the mystery of his emptiness: "Really, I think, some peoples advance *so* slowly."

The champion of "Fame" is Andrea Clement White, and the events take place on one day, when she is being honored, when she is being confronted by her own fame. She is speaking to a television interviewer as the story begins. The old woman tells the young interviewer that in order to look at the world freshly and creatively, an artist simply cannot be famous. When reminded by the young woman that she herself is famous, Andrea Clement White is somewhat at a loss. As the interview continues its predictable way, the novelist explaining once again that she writes about people, not their color, she uneasily asks herself why she does not "*feel* famous," why she feels as though she has not accomplished what she set out to do.

The highlight of the day is to be a luncheon in her honor, at which her former colleagues, the president, and specially invited dignitaries, as well as the genially detested former dean, will all applaud her life accomplishments (while raising money). All the while, the lady of the hour keeps a bitingly humorous commentary running in her mind. Her former students in attendance are "numbskulls," the professors, "mediocre." Out loud, she comments that the president is a bore. No matter how outrageous her behavior, she is forgiven because of her stature; when she eats her Rock Cornish hen with her hands, the entire assembly of five hundred follows suit. At last, however, the spleen and anxious bravado give way to something out of reach of the taint of fame: a child singing an anonymous slave song. Recalled to her dignity, the honored guest is able to face her moment in the limelight stoically.

In this comic story of the aggravations and annoyances that beset the publicly recognized artist, Walker imagines herself as an aging novelist who does not suffer fools gladly. She puts the artist's inner world on paper so that something of her gift for storytelling and her habits of mind become visible. The stress of the occasion and being brought into forced contact with her former president and dean trigger her aggressive imagination, and her innate narrative gift takes over. She visualizes using her heavy award as a weapon against the repulsive kissing dean, hearing him squeal, and briefly feels gleeful. The story, however, is something more than simply a comic portrait of the artist's foibles. When Andrea Clement White questions herself about her own sense of fame, admits her own doubts, she is searching for something certain, as Traynor is searching in "Nineteen Fifty-five," though not so blindly. Like him, she is called out of the mundane by a meaningful song.

The last story of *You Can't Keep a Good Woman Down* is "Source," and in it Walker brings the social conscience of an antipoverty worker in Mississippi into relationship with the expanding consciousness of the alternative life-style as practiced on the West Coast. This is the story of two friends, Irene and Anastasia, who had attended college together in New York. When funding for Irene's adult-education project was cut, she traveled to San Francisco for a change of scene, to be met by Anastasia, who was living on welfare with some friends named Calm, Peace, and their baby, Bliss, all under the guidance of a swami named Source. The two young women were unable to find any common ground, Irene believing in collective action and Anastasia believing that people choose to suffer and that nothing can be changed. After walking out on a meeting with Source, Irene was asked to leave. Years later, the two meet again in Alaska, where Irene is lecturing to educators. Anastasia is now living with an Indian and passing for white. This time, the two women talk more directly, of color, of Anastasia's panic when she is alone, of her never being accepted as a black because of her pale skin. Irene is brought to face her own part in this intolerance and to confess that her reliance on government funding was every bit as insecure as had been Anastasia's reliance on Source. Their friendship restored and deepened, the two women embrace.

The title of this story suggests a theme that runs throughout the entire collection, the search for a center, a source of strength, meaning, or truth. This source is very important to the pioneer, but it can be a false lure. When Irene recognizes that she and Anastasia were both reaching out for something on which to depend, she states what might be taken as the guiding principle for the champion: "*any* direction that is away from ourselves is the wrong direction." This final portrait of a good woman who cannot be kept down is a distinctively personal one. It is women not distracted by external influences, true to themselves, and able to open themselves to one another, who will triumph.

Walker's short fiction adds a new image to the pantheon of American folk heroes: the twentieth century black woman, in whatever walk of life, however crushed or blocked, still persevering. Even those who seem the most unaware, the most poorly equipped for the struggle, are persevering, because, in their integrity, they cannot do otherwise. The better equipped know themselves to be advocates. They shoulder their dedication seriously and cheerfully. They are the fortunate ones; they understand that what they do has meaning.

Other major works

NOVELS: *The Third Life of Grange Copeland*, 1970; *Meridian*, 1976; *The Color Purple*, 1982.

POETRY: *Once*, 1968; *Five Poems*, 1972; *Revolutionary Petunias and Other Poems*, 1973; *Goodnight, Willie Lee, I'll See You in the Morning*, 1979; *Horses Make a Landscape More Beautiful*, 1984.

NONFICTION: *I Love Myself When I'm Laughing . . . and Then Again When I'm Looking Mean and Impressive: A Zora Neale Hurston Reader*, 1979 (editor); *In Search of Our Mothers' Gardens: Womanist Prose*, 1983.

CHILDREN'S LITERATURE: *Langston Hughes: American Poet*, 1974.

Bibliography

Cooke, Michael G. "Intimacy: The Interpenetration of the One and the All in Robert Hayden and Alice Walker," in *Afro-American Literature in the Twentieth Century: The Achievement of Intimacy*, 1984.

Davis, Thadious M. "Alice Walker's Celebration of Self in Southern Generations," in *Women Writers of the Contemporary South*, 1984. Edited by Peggy Whitman Prenshaw.

Harris, Trudier. "Folklore in the Fiction of Alice Walker: A Perpetuation of Historical and Literary Traditions," in *Black American Literature Forum*. XI (1977), pp. 3-8.

O'Brien, John, ed. *Interviews with Black Writers*, 1973.
Pryse, Marjorie. Introduction to *Conjuring: Black Women, Fiction, and Literary Tradition*, 1985. Edited by Marjorie Pryse and Hortense J. Spillers.

Rebecca R. Butler

ROBERT WALSER

Born: Biel, Switzerland; April 15, 1878
Died: Herisau, Switzerland; December 25, 1956

Principal short fiction

Fritz Kochers Aufsätze, 1904; *Aufsätze*, 1913; *Geschichten*, 1914; *Kleine Dichtungen*, 1914; *Der Spaziergang*, 1917 (*The Walk and Other Stories*, 1957); *Prosastücke*, 1916; *Kleine Prosa*, 1917; *Poetenleben*, 1917; *Seeland*, 1920; *Die Rose*, 1925; *Selected Stories*, 1982 (foreword by Susan Sontag); *Aus dem Bleistiftgebiet: Mikragramme aus den jahren 1924-1925*, 1985.

Other literary forms

Robert Walser's reputation as a prose miniaturist long obscured his achievement as a novelist. He published three novels, *Geschwister Tanner* (1970; the Tanner siblings), *Der Gehülfe* (1908; the assistant), and *Jakob von Gunten* (1909; English translation, 1969). The latter is generally acknowledged to be the most impressive work. *Der "Räuber"-Roman* (1972; the "robber" novel), a boldly personal, experimental work, was published posthumously. His most important dramatic works were published in the volume *Komödie: Theatralisches* (1919; comedy: theatrical writings). He also wrote poetry, the merit of which has been the subject of some controversy.

Achievements

In the early decades of this century, critics praised the psychological complexity and stylistic finesse of Walser's stories and essays. The novelist Robert Musil even asserted that Franz Kafka's first book, *Betrachtung* (1913; *Meditation*, 1940) was a "special case of the Walser type." Walser's fiction appeared both in avant-garde reviews and in newspaper *feuilletons*. By the 1920's, however, his increasingly experimental prose had begun to alienate the editors and newspapers on whom he depended for a living. After he ceased writing in 1933, his work fell into oblivion.

Critics in Germany and Switzerland rediscovered Walser in the 1960's. The edition of collected works by Jochen Greven, which began appearing in 1966, gathered together for the first time all the short fiction that had appeared in scattered newspapers and reviews. Readers could appreciate for the first time the range and versatility of his prose. Walser is now widely regarded as one of the most significant writers in twentieth century German literature. Although English translations by Christopher Middleton appeared as early as 1957, what brought Walser's work to the attention of English-speaking readers was the publication in 1982 of the *Selected Stories*, with a foreword by Susan Sontag.

One of Walser's greatest gifts as a writer was his ability, as Christian

Morgenstern put it, to "see the world as a continuous wonder." He made no attempt to separate perceptions that are "significant" from those that are "trivial." While some readers find this rejection of conventional discriminations frustrating, others find its heterodoxy refreshing. In a brief but now classic essay of 1929, Walter Benjamin evoked the enigma of Walser's seemingly artless art: "While we are used to seeing the mysteries of style emerge out of more or less fully developed and purposeful works of art, here we are faced with language running wild in a manner that is totally unintentional, or at least seems so, and yet that we find attractive and compelling. A letting go, moreover, that ranges through all forms from the graceful to the bitter."

Biography

Robert Otto Walser was born in Biel, Switzerland, on April 15, 1878. His father, Adolf Walser, a bookbinder by trade, was, by all accounts, a convivial individual, if a rather lackluster businessman. His mother, whose maiden name was Elisa Marti, was socially ambitious but psychically labile. She died in 1894, when Robert was sixteen.

Walser spent his active years as a writer in four cities: Zurich (1896-1905), Berlin (1905-1913), then his native Biel (1913-1921), and, finally, Bern (1921-1929). His work falls into four phases, which coincide with the periods he spent in those cities. Frequently switching both jobs and addresses, he lived on what he himself described as "the periphery of bourgeois existences." He sold much of his short fiction to newspapers and reviews, some of which he later published in book form. He supplemented this meager income mostly through menial clerical jobs. While in Berlin, he attended a school for servants. For a brief period he was employed as a butler at Dambrau Castle in Upper Silesia.

The years in Berlin were crucial for his artistic development. Through his brother Karl, a painter and illustrator, he came into contact with leading intellectual figures. Yet, although cosmopolitan Berlin left its mark on his increasingly sophisticated prose, he never lost the outsider's contempt for the established order. His relations with the writers Hugo von Hofmannsthal and Frank Wedekind and the industrialist and politician Walter Rathenau were stormy.

Walser's three Berlin novels attracted some favorable critical attention but relatively few readers. He could not interest publishers in further novels, and some manuscripts were lost. After his return to Biel in 1913, he turned his back on the novel and continued writing *feuilleton* essays and short stories. During his lifetime he wrote more than thirteen hundred individual pieces of short prose. In 1921 he moved to Bern, claiming that he wished to make his prose more cosmopolitan in outlook. His style became increasingly experimental, and editors began to reject his submissions. In the mid-1920's his anxiety about writing literally paralyzed his hand, leading him to invent what he called his "pencil method" of composition. In a tiny script, he wrote texts now known as microgrammes. A selection of hitherto unpublished microgrammes, which had been deciphered painstakingly by scholars in Zurich, was published in 1985 under the title *Aus dem Bleistiftgebiet.*

By the late 1920's, Walser was leading the life of a recluse and hearing persecuting voices from which he could find no escape. On January 25, 1929, he was admitted to the Waldau asylum, near Bern. At first, he appears to have reached almost thankfully for the new role of inmate, which he was to play diligently, mending sacks and refusing special concessions, for the remaining twenty-seven years of his life. Yet, at times, he longed to be set free. In 1933, in apparent protest against his transfer from Waldau to the asylum at Herisau, in the canton of Appenzell-Ausserrhoden, he gave up writing altogether. He died at the age of seventy-eight, on Christmas Day, 1956.

Analysis

Robert Walser's early reputation as a miniaturist was misleading. His essays and stories actually form the nucleus of a larger work, which he once described as a "sliced-up or torn-apart novel of myself." The main protagonist in this autobiographical "novel" is not so much Walser as his poetic self. This self adopts a wide variety of roles, such as that of the servant, the artist, and the child. Yet Walser never identifies for long with these fictional alter egos. His stance toward them is ironic, haughty, or nonchalant. Having adopted them with the flick of a pen, he can discard them just as swiftly. More crucial than their individual identities is their unmistakable voice, which remained remarkably constant throughout his career. By turns effusive and reticent, self-effacing and self-inflating, long-winded and laconic, solitary and convivial, this voice determines the cadences of his prose.

Throughout his career, Walser struggled to reconcile his modernist practice with his conservative ideals. His literary values were firmly rooted in Swiss literary tradition. Among Walser's idols was the civic-minded nineteenth century novelist Gottfried Keller, who is renowned for his lyrical realism. Walser's own prose, however, is closer to the self-conscious experimentation of modernists such as Virginia Woolf.

While not a major achievement, his first book, *Fritz Kochers Aufsätze* (Fritz Kocher's essays), is a characteristic product of the Zurich phase. Walser adopted the persona of a schoolboy writing compositions on hackneyed themes such as friendship and nature. These neo-Romantic effusions are tongue-in-cheek, but tiresome nevertheless. Walser's stylistic dexterity only becomes apparent when he lets the schoolboy mask slip. Alternating with the purple prose of Fritz Kocher are stretches of sophisticated, and self-conscious writing, which poke fun not only at the convention of schoolboy essays but also at language itself.

The tone becomes more urgent in the final piece in the collection, "Der

Wald" (the forest). Kocher intimates that he is driven into the forest by unspecified woes, but this oblique confession ends abruptly. Kocher claims that he must be careful not to divulge too much about himself. Here he is clearly speaking on behalf of Walser himself, the Walser who does not want readers to recognize the self lurking behind his numerous personas. This attitude is stated unequivocally in "Das Kind" ("The Child"): "Nobody has the right to treat me as if he knew me."

It has been said of Kafka's stories that they are alienated fairy tales. This is true also of Walser's. His two Zurich fairy tales in free verse are indispensable for an understanding of his short prose. In *Aschenbrödel* (1901; *Cinderella*, 1985) and *Schneewittchen* (1901; *Snowwhite*, 1985), which Benjamin called "one of the most profound compositions in recent literature," Walser's heroines rebel against the script of the Grimm Brothers by refusing to allow themselves to be rescued. They owe their creativity to the sisters and stepmother who torment them. Without that hostility, they would be lost. Happiness and recipocrated love would destroy what they most prize in themselves. Thus, they chase away the Prince Charmings.

There are examples in the short prose both of this bleak vision and of a radiant counterpoint. In "Seltsame Stadt" ("A Strange City"), for example, Walser conjures up a Utopian society. The inhabitants of this singular city are dolls, relatives, perhaps, of the graceful puppets that Heinrich von Kleist describes in his essay "Über das Marionettentheater" (About the Marionette Theater"). They revere life and treasure the senses and can thus dispense with preachers and artists. Surfacing here is the conviction that in a truly civilized society the professional artist would be superfluous. The narrator dwells in a rather fetishistic manner on the shoes and trousers of the women. These obsessions recur in the short prose, most flagrantly, perhaps, in "Hose" ("Trousers"), which is less about women's emancipation than about Walser's trousers fetish.

The story "Oskar" is uncharacteristically forthright. Written in Biel but reflecting back on the Zurich years, it describes the origins of Walser's stylization of himself as a self-denying hermit. Oskar discovers within himself a need for solitude. He is not content to satisfy this need, and he feels compelled to make life harsher by denying himself such creature comforts as a warm room in winter. His shaping of this idiosyncratic persona is partly involuntary, partly willed. The rationale for his seemingly masochistic behavior is aesthetic. He expects the solitude to sharpen his appetite for life. As Oskar's isolation intensifies, however, the narrator intimates the human cost of his wayward odyssey.

In Berlin, Walser retained the pose of the naïve provincial, but his prose became increasingly sophisticated. The theater stimulated his imagination, and he wrote frequently for the influential review *Die Schaubühne*. Although he was ostensibly commenting on the plays of Wedekind, Gerhart Hauptmann, and others, his real subject was the self-impersonation that he himself practiced in the medium of prose. Ideally, he wanted his fiction to enact an appealing version not only of himself but of life itself. He was, however, fully aware that this quest for life in art raises tortuous epistemological questions. Even as early as 1902, in the dramatic sketch *Die Knaben* (1902; the boys), an actor is chided for confusing life with appearances and "the body with its reflexes."

In "Beantwortung einer Anfrage" ("Response to a Request"), Walser illustrates graphically the exploitation of the self on which his art is based. The narrator offers advice to an actor who has asked him for a sketch that he can perform. Instead of giving the actor a script, the narrator advises him to use his body as his material. Carefully choreographed gestures will enable him to manipulate the audience's response. If physical pain is to horrify the spectator, then it must be elegantly enacted. The uncharacteristically violent self-immolation at the end of the story anticipates the lurid effects of the later Expressionists. More important, however, the execution of this sketch mirrors the workings of Walser's prose. It, too, manipulates images of the self, relying for its effects on emotional dissonance and stylistic incongruity.

In Biel, Walser regressed stylistically. He did not always distance himself successfully from the neo-Romantic clichés that once again invaded his prose. In "Die Einfahrt" (the journey in), for example, the description of his return to the fatherland aboard a train full of noble workers is downright mawkish. Nature affords him a screen onto which he can all too easily project the fulfillment of secret desires. In "Wald" (the wood), the forest becomes the setting for an illusionary erotic encounter. This sketch could be contrasted with the less self-indulgent treatment of the same motif in *Fritz Kochers Aufsätze*.

The Walk and Other Stories is an exceptional chronicle of the Biel years. Walser is more candid than elsewhere about the darker emotions underlying his surface exuberance. The title "The Walk" evokes both a physical activity and a philosophy of life, as "the Way" evokes Christianity and Taoism. This hero is as self-evasive as his fictional cousins of this period, but he, at least, reflects about the gaunt figure of Tomzack, a personification of the dark forces within him. Walser subjects his neo-Romantic motifs to probing scrutiny. It is fear that drives the stroller into the center of a fairy-tale forest. The prose reflects upon this evasion even as it narrates it.

Walser was at his most innovative formally during the years in Bern. In moving to that city in 1921, he openly rejected the pastoral idylls that mar the Biel prose. His aim was to reflect the internal workings of human consciousness. While the artist figure remains prominent, the landscape through which he now strolls is that of his own mind. Some readers find this "aimless ambling" (Walser) as infuriating as others find it intriguing. One early example of the former type of response was provided by a critic who attacked Walser for misrepresenting the nineteenth century playwright Georg Büchner in "Ein Dramatiker" (a dramatist). Walser responded by describing the offending text as "an imaginary, small, short, thin, slim, nervous, healthy, cheeky, timid story," composed in the manner of "carpet weaving, of a game with words, of something mosaic-like" in the hope that readers would detect "the novella-likeness of his apparent essay."

Eine Ohrfeige und Sonstiges (1925; *A Slap in the Face et cetera*, 1985) is one of the most provocative texts of the Bern years. It is hard to assign it to any one genre. Walser showers the reader with an assortment of diary-like entries, anecdotes, aphorisms, fragmentary stories and miniature fairy tales. The opening paragraph forces the reader to plunge immediately into a narrative that juxtaposes events as if they were elements in a collage. Elsewhere in his final collection, *Die Rose* (the rose), Walser suggests that this free-wheeling method of composition allows him to play on "the instrument of his fancies."

The opening lines of *A Slap in the Face et cetera* represent clipped renderings of actual impressions prompted by a brief visit to Biel. Instead of developing the initial allusions to a schoolteacher and a sergeant, however, the narrator flits into the tiny auditorium of a theater, which immediately suggests its opposite, a giant railway station he has recently observed. He teases the reader by withholding key information, such as the name of the playwright, who turns out to be Oscar Wilde. Walser perceives an affinity between his fate and that of the Irishman. Later, in the middle of a meditation on the vagaries of the literary marketplace, he invokes the eighteenth century poet Friedrich Hölderlin, who suffered a mental breakdown and spent the last thirty-six years of his life in seclusion.

Walser strews fragmentary fictions amid diary-like entries of this kind. One of these miniature stories is a grotesque fairy tale about a mother, Lady Hypocrite, and her son, "little trouserlegs." Walser is playing here on the register of unacknowledged childhood traumas. Lurking beneath such fairy-tale figures as the passionately wicked mother is an autobiographical substratum that he banishes from the surface of his prose. Instead, he finds refuge in his own playfulness, indulging in whimsical allusions to high culture and reveling in his own power to mold the fairy tale any way he chooses. He clings to this high-wire exuberance, which cannot, however, entirely distract the attention of the reader from the abyss below.

These fragmentary fictions often reveal as much as they conceal. In a final fiction, introduced by a banner headline, Walser develops the motif of the romantic triangle toward an ingenious anticlimax. His heroes often have a weakness for Platonic relationships in which they can indulge their fantasies without fear of losing them to a paltry reality. In this fragment, the narrator's totally imaginary infatuation with a married woman, whom he has never met, suggests the fragility of the threads linking an isolated dreamer—the narrator and behind him, of course, Walser himself—to the world of others.

Skepticism about the epistemological status of fiction had been a feature of Walser's prose ever since the Zurich years, but the debate within him about his poetic principles intensified in the mid-1920's. The incomprehension that greeted the verbal playfulness of the Bern prose affected him deeply. He edged slowly toward silence. In *A Slap in the Face et cetera*, he could still transmute his skepticism about fiction into verbal high jinks, but by the late 1920's his tone had changed. In "Brief an einen Besteller von Novellen" ("Letter to a Commissioner of Novellas"), he explains somewhat defensively why he cannot deliver works that conform to the traditional genre. In mock-bureaucratic language, he argues that traditional novellas can no longer do justice to contemporary life, which has turned into "something tentative, cautiously groping." In "Für die Katz" ("For Zilch") he wryly conceded the pointlessness of his literary productivity. In 1933, he renounced literature for good.

Other major works

NOVELS: *Geschwister Tanner*, 1907; *Der Gehülfe*, 1908; *Jakob von Gunten*, 1909 (English translation, 1969); *Der "Räuber"-Roman*, 1972.

PLAYS: *Aschenbrödel*, 1901 (fairy-tale play; *Cinderella*, 1985); *Schneewittchen*, 1901 (fairy-tale play; *Snowwhite*, 1985); *Die Knaben*, 1902 (sketch); *Komödie: Theatralisches*, 1919.

POETRY: *Gedichte*, 1909; *Unbekannte Gedichte*, 1958.

MISCELLANEOUS: *Eine Ohrfeige und Sonstiges*, 1925 (*A Slap in the Face et cetera*, 1985); *Das Gesamtwerk*, 1966-1975 (thirteen volumes).

Bibliography
Avery, George. *Inquiry and Testament: A Study of the Novels and Short Prose of Robert Walser*, 1968.
Benjamin, Walter. "Robert Walser," in *Robert Walser Rediscovered*, 1985. Edited by Mark Harman.
Hamburger, Michael. "Robert Musil, Robert Walser, Franz Kafka," in *From Prophecy to Exorcism: The Premisses of Modern German Literature*, 1965 (reprinted in *A Proliferation of Prophets*, 1984).
Harman, Mark. "Introduction: A Reluctant Modern," in *Robert Walser Rediscovered*, 1985. Edited by Mark Harman.
Walser, Martin. "Unrelenting Style," in *Robert Walser Rediscovered*, 1985. Edited by Mark Harman.

Mark Harman

SYLVIA TOWNSEND WARNER

Born: Harrow, Great Britain; December 6, 1893
Died: Maiden Newton, Great Britain; May 1, 1978

Principal short fiction

Some World Far from Ours, and Stay Corydon, Thou Swain, 1929; *Elinor Barley*, 1930; *Moral Ending and Other Stories*, 1931; *The Salutation*, 1932; *More Joy in Heaven, and Other Stories*, 1935; *The Cat's Cradle Book*, 1940; *A Garland of Straw and Other Stories*, 1943; *The Museum of Cheats*, 1947; *Winter in the Air, and Other Stories*, 1955; *A Spirit Rises*, 1962; *A Stranger with a Bag, and Other Stories*, 1966 (U.S. edition, *Swans on an Autumn River: Stories*, 1966); *The Innocent and the Guilty: Stories*, 1971; *Kingdoms of Elfin*, 1977; *Scenes of Childhood*, 1981; *One Thing Leading to Another: And Other Stories*, 1984.

Other literary forms

In addition to the short stories for which Sylvia Townsend Warner is best known, she wrote seven novels: *Lolly Willowes: Or, The Loving Huntsman* (1926), *Mr. Fortune's Maggot* (1927), *The True Heart* (1929), *Summer Will Show* (1936), *After the Death of Don Juan* (1938), *The Corner That Held Them* (1948), and *The Flint Anchor* (1954). She also wrote five collections of poetry, which were published as *Collected Poems* (1982), a biography, a travel guidebook, and a volume of literary criticism, and she translated two books from French into English.

Achievements

Warner's first novel was the first selection of the Book-of-the-Month Club; her second was an early selection of the Literary Guild. Her later novels did not attain the same popularity, but her short stories, 144 of which were published in *The New Yorker* over a period of four decades, gained for her a wide readership.

In 1967, she became a Fellow of the Royal Society of Literature (she wryly commented that it was the first public acknowledgment she had received since she was expelled from kindergarten) and in 1972, an honorary member of the American Academy of Arts and Letters. Her short story "The Love Match" was awarded the Prix Menton for 1968.

No full-length critical assessment of Warner's achievement as novelist, short-story writer, and poet has been produced. John Updike noted in a favorable review that her "half century of brilliantly varied and superbly self-possessed literary production never won for her the flaming place in the heavens of reputation that she deserved." As far as her achievement in the short story is concerned, however, she certainly ranks alongside H. E. Bates and V. S. Pritchett, her two British contemporaries, whose work most resembles her own.

Biography

Sylvia Townsend Warner was born in Harrow, Middlesex, on December 6, 1893. She was educated mostly at home (her father was a schoolmaster), having been considered a disruptive influence in kindergarten. Her early talent was for music, and in 1914 she was set to travel to Vienna to study under Arnold Schönberg, but the outbreak of World War I prevented it. In 1916, after the death of her father, she moved to in London and was a member of the editorial committee which compiled the ten-volume *Tudor Church Music* (1922-1929). Her first publication was a collection of poetry, *The Espalier*, in 1925, a time when she thought of herself primarily as a poet. In the 1920's, she met the novelist T. F. Powys, who proved to be influential on her early poetry and fiction. In 1930, Warner moved to the country and lived with her friend Valentine Ackland in a Dorset village. During the 1930's, she and Ackland became involved in left-wing politics, joining the Communist Party and serving with the Red Cross in Barcelona during the Spanish Civil War. In subsequent years, Warner lived the quiet life of an English gentlewoman in rural Dorset, managing to sustain her literary output up to her final years. She died in 1978.

Analysis

One of the notable features of Sylvia Townsend Warner's short stories is her elegant, precise, epigrammatic, and witty prose. These qualities are particularly noticeable when she focuses on what she knows best: the niceties of English middle- and upper-class life as they reveal themselves in day-to-day domestic and social routines, and the sudden disruption of those routines. As in the novels of her British contemporary, Barbara Pym, her detached and humorous observance of the oddities of humanity is one of the chief pleasures to be gained from her stories. She has a sharp but sympathetic eye for eccentricity of all kinds, and her stories cover a wide range of situations and points of view.

Perhaps because of the variety of her fiction, it would be misleading to pinpoint specific themes or leading ideas. Warner's stories do not reveal a consistent or dominant mood or atmosphere. She does not espouse a philosophy or champion a cause. Her subject matter is the infinite variety of human nature, its follies, regrets, hopes, deceits, compromises, its small defeats and victories, the tidy chaos of the average human life. The stories frequently develop out of an apparently insignificant event or chance encounter or an incident or memory from the protagonist's past, which resurfaces to affect the present. A sudden rift is produced in the otherwise smooth fabric of daily life, and often an ironic twist at the end will reveal a new dimension to a relationship or to the inner life of the protagonist.

Warner is a traditionalist. She does not experiment with modern techniques (her chief technical device is the flashback); her stories succeed through strong characterization and plotting. There is an old-fashioned quality about her and her fictional world. Almost all of her stories are set in England, with a carefully evoked spirit of place (perhaps this accounts in part for her success in *The New Yorker*, since she usually portrays a timeless, civilized England that popular American culture has tended to idealize).

Warner has a Hardy-like awareness of the ironies of fate (Thomas Hardy was a major influence on her early poetry) and of the tricks that time plays. Many of her stories (for example "The Sea Is Always the Same," "Johnnie Brewer," and "A Second Visit") center on the protagonist's return, after a gap of many years, to a former home or place of memories. In *"Hee-Haw!"* from *Winter in the Air, and Other Stories*, Mrs. Vincent returns to the village in Cornwall, where for three years, thirty years previously, she had lived turbulently with her first husband, Ludovick, a young artist who was later to gain eminence. The first sound she hears on her return is the unchanging, regular sound of the foghorn from the lightship (*Hee Haw! Hee Haw!*), which seems to span the thirty years of her absence, giving a sense of permanence and familiarity to the external environment. What of her internal environment? She is introduced to an old man in the hotel bar, who needs little prompting to recall the famous artist. His recollections, however, shock her. He tells her that Ludovick and his wife (or girlfriend, he did not know which) were the happiest couple he had ever seen, and he relates several incidents in which they were playing and laughing together. Mrs. Vincent, however, knowing how stormy her relationship with Ludovick was, assumes without question that the old man must be referring to another woman. In a wave of jealousy, she realizes that she has discovered, thirty years after the event, her husband's infidelity. She is left to her anger and her melancholy; an old wound has been reopened in a way that she would not have imagined possible

The strength of *"Hee-Haw!"* is in the contrast between the ease with which the reader guesses the truth (although the truth is never overtly established) and the inability of Mrs. Vincent to recognize that her relationship with Ludovick might have looked quite different from the outside. It is at once a poignant tale of reminiscence and a reminder of the subjectivity of the experience of life. Appearances are not what they seem, and memory is only shifting sand.

"Winter in the Air" also focuses on a return. A middle-aged woman, Barbara, returns to live in London after a twelve-year absence, following the breakup of her marriage. The story consists of a series of flashbacks to the final stages of her marriage two months previously, interspersed with Barbara's thoughts as she arranges the furniture in her new apartment. The reader is given the minimum of clues regarding the reasons for the divorce, and the chief interest of this otherwise slight, although typical story, lies in the fact that nine-tenths of its emotional force lies below the surface. Deep emotions surface only momentarily.

What Barbara really feels, though, is contained in the half-remembered snatches of a quotation from William Shakespeare's *The Winter's Tale* (1623) which flash into her mind: the dignified, despairing speech of Hermione, the wronged wife, whose chief comfort in life, the favor of her husband, has gone, though she does not know how or why it went. As Barbara sits down to write to Willie, she knows that in real life one does not say such things, and all she is prepared to commit to paper is a platitude about her new char-woman; this, however, is as unsatisfactory to her as confessing her true feel-ings, and she tears up the letter and throws it away. Neither truth nor plati-tude can be uttered, and the deeper emotional terrain of her life must remain as silent as the silence which she notices enveloping her new apartment. Si-lence will hide secrets and heal pain, and life will go on. The story finishes with Barbara projecting herself into the mundane thoughts of the char-woman about the weather: Winter is in the air. This final thought has a slightly ominous connotation; whether it hints at Barbara's future loneliness, old age, or simply the demise of emotional honesty and communication, Warner rightly leaves to the reader to decide.

Swans on an Autumn River contains what is often regarded as Warner's finest story, "A Love Match." It centers on a quiet conservative couple, Jus-tin Tizard and his elder sister Celia. Justin returns on leave after the Battle of the Somme in 1916, in which Celia's fiancé has been killed. He stays at her apartment in London, but during his sleep he relives the terrible scenes of battle, raving incoherently. Celia, sleepless, listens in horror in the adjoining room. The following day, as they stroll casually around London, an old woman mistakes them for man and wife. The incident is one of several foreshadowings of what is to come. Two nights later, Celia is again awakened by Justin's ravings. She goes to his side to comfort him, and the combination of her compassion and his distress drives them into the physical expression of love.

Afterward, they feel no regret, and as the years go by they find happiness together. They possess an intuitive insight into each other's feelings, feel no need to impress each other, and are not particularly concerned with each oth-er's likes and dislikes. Their common childhood memories act as a bond be-tween them. They also become practiced at shielding their true relationship from their neighbors in Hallowby, the English village to which they move in 1923, and soon become one of the most respectable of couples.

Their lives are upset in the 1930's when Celia, who has become bored with local society and developed a reputation for supporting unusual causes, receives a series of anonymous letters which claim that her secret is common knowledge in the village. The letters turn out to be only idle gossip from one of Justin's disappointed female admirers, and he soon puts a stop to them. Nothing has changed, and the secret remains intact.

The final outcome is carefully developed to produce the maximum effect. During World War II, Hallowby is bombed. Rescue workers entering a bombed house find a bedroom floor deep in rubble. Slates from the roof have fallen on the bed, crushing the two bodies that lay there. One of the villagers at the scene offers the opinion that Justin went into Celia's bedroom to comfort her. Others agree, and the coroner accepts this hypothesis as truth.

Warner's comment that the story's success was a victory for "incest and sanity" was only partly tongue-in-check. Rarely has incest been so sympathetically portrayed. Warner places subtle emphasis on the ease with which the lovers communicate and the depth of their love. The very criminality of their liaison adds to its preciousness for them. The ambiguity of the conclusion is also important. It is not made explicit whether the villagers genuinely believe their own explanation, whether they simply cannot comprehend the implications of what they see, or whether they guess the truth but, out of common human decency, desire to shield the lovers from shame. The open-endedness of this conclusion reflects the necessary mixture of emotions which the story has raised and left unresolved. The image of the two lovers in death, locked together in the tenderness of their illegal union and surrounded by the debris of their ruined house, remains vividly in the reader's mind.

"Swans on an Autumn River" also culminates in a strong visual image, which juxtaposes opposites to suggest the unattainable nature of an ideal. Norman Repton, an engineer in his late sixties, visits Ireland for the first time on a business trip. It is a country for which he always felt a romantic longing, fueled by the poetry of William Butler Yeats. The country does not meet his expectations, however, and he soon discovers that he is an alien in an unfamiliar land.

Repton is attracted to the river, which is one of two central symbols in the story. It is as if the river has power to compensate him for his old age, his weak physical condition, and the dissatisfaction with life that he feels. At night, he leaves the curtain of his room undrawn, so he can see the river, which also casts its lightly dancing reflection on the ceiling. In spite of this, he is aware of neither, being alternately sunk heavily in sleep or at the mercy of his bladder and digestion. His low vitality is a strong contrast to everything that the flowing river and its reflection suggests. In its ease, serenity, and sparkling movement, it represents another realm of being, but it is a realm which is forever closed to him, however much he longs for it.

This theme is restated and developed by another powerful symbol in the climax of the story. When he wakes in the morning, he sees a gathering of swans on the river. He looks at them enraptured, as if they were his own treasure. He grabs some bread and rushes out of the hotel, by which time eighteen swans have collected. The swans come flocking toward him as he excitedly tosses them the bread. He notes how skillfully they swim "without check or collision" (unlike his own troubled and unsatisfactory life). When the feeding is interrupted by a swarm of gulls competing for the bread, Repton strikes at one of them and becomes so angry that he loses all thought of where he is. He only succeeds in making a fool of himself, falling down and hitting his head on the pavement. To two passersby, he is nothing more than a corpulent old Englishman behaving eccentrically, and the story ends with a policeman arranging for an ambulance to take him away.

The poetry of Yeats may well have been in Warner's mind when she wrote this story. The swans resemble those in "The Wild Swans at Coole" which "drift on the still water,/ Mysterious, beautiful." In their effortlessness, they seem to belong to a realm of eternity, and they are contrasted in the story with the frequent emphasis on the limitations and restrictions of ordinary bodily life. Repton himself calls to mind the lines from Yeats's "Sailing to Byzantium": "An aged man is but a paltry thing,/ A tattered coat upon a stick, unless/ Soul clap its hands and sing. . . ." Repton cannot clap his hands and sing, however, and he cannot be gathered into the "artifice of eternity" which the swans on the river symbolize. "Swans on an Autumn River" thus becomes a tragic story of the disparity between the infinity of human desire and the finite realities within which it must operate.

The Innocent and the Guilty is the only one of Warner's collections to be organized under a specific theme. She had confessed to an "obsessive" concern with this theme, but the title is wholly ironic ("Perhaps one day, I shall . . . write a story where the innocent are charming and the guilty nauseating"). The ironic purpose is clear from "Truth in the Cup," in which a group of self-righteous villagers, celebrating in the local hotel on a stormy night, lament the moral decay of the young. Like sinful man in Genesis, however, they become victims of a catastrophic flood. It is also clear in "The Quality of Mercy," in which a drunken young woman and the local toughs who help her home are more virtuous than the "respectable" sister who greets them with abuse and recrimination.

The distinctions between innocence and guilt become blurred in "But at the Stroke of Midnight," one of Warner's most ambitious stories. It is a mysterious tale, with a hint of the supernatural, and it centers on the motif of rebirth. The protagonist is Lucy Ridpath, an undistinguished middle-aged woman who escapes from her dull marriage to seek a new life. Adopting the name Aurelia, she goes through a number of adventures in London and becomes like "a nova—a new appearance in the firmament, the explosion of an aging star." She has a powerful effect on everyone she meets. A clergyman sees her as a tranquil, spiritual woman; others find themselves curiously attracted to her and do her unexpected favors.

Leaving London to stay at a guesthouse, she adopts a stray cat and calls it Lucy. (Cats appear with somewhat alarming frequency in Warner's fiction.) She moves to a country cottage and successfully tries her hand at being a landscape artist. It seems that her rebirth is accomplished. The title, however, with its Cinderella connotations, suggests that it will not last. So it turns out. One cold wet night, Lucy returns late, mortally injured, and the moment it dies, Aurelia realizes that she is no longer Aurelia but Lucy Ridpath once more. When morning breaks, she goes outside to bury the cat, but she finds herself immersed in floodwater. Walking toward the road, she has a half-conscious desire to drown, and as she wades deeper in the water, she falls and is swept away by the current.

This curious but stimulating story, a mixture of realism and fantasy, is one of Warner's very few attempts to deal with an archetypal theme. It does not entirely succeed. The ending is abrupt and the reason for Lucy's death is unexplained. The cat, it seems, mysteriously embodies her former self, to which she must return when the cat dies. It is quite possible that Warner intended such a supernatural implication. In one of her early stories, "Early One Morning," from the collection *The Salutation*, an old woman dies and her soul immediately passes into one of the local greyhounds. Perhaps the tragedy of "But at the Stroke of Midnight" is that having once known rebirth, Lucy cannot lapse back into a former state. Caught between two selves, the old and the new, she can be neither.

In "Oxenhope," Warner returns to a favorite theme, the effects of the passing of time, as experienced by a protagonist who returns to former haunts. As the story develops, it becomes a subtle meditation on the presence of mortality and the longing for immortality.

William, a man in his sixties, returns to the village where he had stayed for a month when he was seventeen. As he drives through, he recognizes everything in the landscape. He thinks about the old shepherd he had known, with his prodigious memory that seemingly would never die, and he wants to know all the changes that the unchanging valley has seen. As he reminisces, the narrative passes freely between present event and past remembrance; past and present seem to merge. He finds the gravestone of the woman who had befriended him and cleans it so that the name stands out, just as he had done with the other family gravestones so many years previously. He notices, however, that the most recent name is the least visible, as if the woman had not expected to be remembered.

Fully aware of the imprint of mortality, he decides that the past is irrecoverable and that there is no purpose in staying. Then comes the ironic twist in the tale, so characteristic of Warner. He meets a local boy, who talks to him about local legends. One story is of a man who "set fire" to the loch and sent flames leaping up around his boat. William immediately realizes that the man was him—out in a rowing boat he had taken a match to bubbles of marsh gas as they rose to the surface of the water, and the fire had been the result. He leaves the village satisfied, with no need even of a backward glance, realizing that he is lodged in the collective memory of the locality, which lends him a kind of immortality. The subtlety of the observed paradox and its implications reveal Warner's fiction at its best. Human life remains embedded in the past even when the past has seemed to vanish or to be vanishing, and yet the knowledge of this fact paradoxically frees the present from the past's stifling grip.

Two more collections are worthy of comment. *Kingdoms of Elfin* is a collection of fantasies about fairy kingdoms. The product of Warner's final creative years, these stories display considerable ingenuity (and Warner clearly relishes the telling of them), but few rank with her best work. The fantasy setting does not supply the moral bearings necessary in order to feel and respond fully to the odd adventures of the fairy protagonists. Warner invents her own fairy lore with considerable aplomb, but the kingdoms she describes are not mystical or otherworldly. On the contrary, they tend to parallel human institutions, particularly the hierarchical structure of medieval or Renaissance society. In consequence, much of the pleasure to be gained from them is in the occasional acid comment about the superstitions of religion, or in the gentle mocking of the social pretenses and snobbery and the political plotting and maneuvering that bedevil both human and fairy world.

Scenes of Childhood is a posthumous collection of Warner's reminiscences about her upbringing in Edwardian England, a time "when there was a Tzar in Russia, and scarcely an automobile or a divorced person in Mayfair." Impressionistic sketches rather than fully developed stories, they display her epigrammatic style to best advantage. Extracting much harmless fun from the eccentricities of upper-middle-class English life, she parades an assortment of odd characters ranging from her parents to great aunts, nannies, retired majors, French teachers, and a butler whose smile was so ghastly that he had to be got rid of (he revenged himself by joining the fire brigade and ruining the Warner's kitchen while putting out a minor fire).

At their best, Sylvia Townsend Warner's short stories constitute a quiet exploration of the oddities and ironies of the human condition, as it unfolds itself in time, fate, and circumstances. She is an acute observer, but she is careful not to judge. Her humor, always tart, is never malicious. She is a realist, and few of her stories end in unqualified optimism. She is aware of the pain of loss and the mockery that time makes of human ideals. She notes the human capacity for self-deceit but also the ability to make peace with limitations. Rarely faltering in the smoothness of her controlled, elegant, economical prose, she is a craftswomen whose finely wrought stories entertain and delight.

Other major works

NOVELS: *Lolly Willowes: Or, The Loving Huntsman*, 1926; *Mr. Fortune's Maggot*, 1927; *The True Heart*, 1929; *Summer Will Show*, 1936; *After the Death of Don Juan*, 1938; *The Corner That Held Them*, 1948; *The Flint Anchor*, 1954.

POETRY: *The Espalier*, 1925; *Time Importuned*, 1928; *Opus 7*, 1931; *Whether a Dove or a Seagull: Poems*, 1933; *Boxwood*, 1957; *Twelve Poems*, 1980; *Collected Poems*, 1982.

NONFICTION: *Jane Austen*, 1951; *T. H. White: A Biography*, 1967; *Letters*, 1982.

Bibliography

Harmon, Claire, ed. "Sylvia Townsend Warner, 1893-1978: A Celebration," in *PN Review*. VIII, no. 23 (1981), pp. 30-61.

Strachan, W. T. "Sylvia Townsend Warner: A Memoir," in *London Magazine*. (November, 1979), pp. 41-50.

Updike, John. "The Mastery of Miss Warner," in *The New Republic*. CLIV (March 5, 1966), pp. 23-25.

Vannatta, Dennis, ed. *The English Short Story, 1945-1980*, 1985.

Bryan Aubrey

JESSAMYN WEST

Born: North Vernon, Indiana; July 18, 1902
Died: Napa, California; February 23, 1984

Principal short fiction

The Friendly Persuasion, 1945; *Cress Delahanty*, 1953; *Love, Death, and the Ladies' Drill Team*, 1955; *Except for Me and Thee: A Companion to the Friendly Persuasion*, 1969; *Crimson Ramblers of the World, Farewell*, 1970; *The Story of a Story and Three Stories*, 1982; *Collected Stories of Jessamyn West*, 1986.

Other literary forms

Best known for her first collection of short stories, *The Friendly Persuasion*, during her long literary career Jessamyn West also published eight novels, including *Leafy Rivers* (1967), set on the frontier in nineteenth century Ohio, and *South of the Angels* (1960), set, like many of her short stories, in Southern California. West also published an opera libretto based on the life of John James Audubon, *A Mirror for the Sky* (1948), and a collection of poems, *The Secret Look: Poems* (1974). Among her screenplays was that for the film *Friendly Persuasion*, written in collaboration. Her autobiographical writings include an account of the production of that film, *To See the Dream* (1957); *Hide and Seek: A Continuing Journey* (1973), the story of her early life; *The Woman Said Yes: Encounters with Life and Death—Memoirs* (1976), dealing with her illness with tuberculosis and her sister's sickness and suicide; and *Double Discovery: A Journey* (1980), a travel diary. She edited *The Quaker Reader* in 1962.

Achievements

Ever since the publication of her first book, West has had a large and loyal following. Critics praise her craftsmanship: her clear prose, her vivid realization of the natural setting, her historical accuracy, her effective creation of characters who are complex human beings beneath their seemingly simple surface. Her accomplishments have been recognized by the Indiana Authors' Day Award in 1957, the Thormod Monsen Award in 1958, and the Janet Kafka Prize in 1976, as well as by the awarding of honorary doctorates both in her native Midwest and in her longtime home, California. West's works are divided between the Midwestern frontier of her family's past and the new frontier of twentieth century Southern California. The fact that her fiction is authentically regional does not limit her appeal, however, for her themes transcend local color, dealing as they do with survival as a moral and loving being in a difficult and dangerous world.

Biography

Jessamyn West was born in North Vernon, Indiana, on July 18, 1902. After moving with her parents to California, she completed her education at Fullerton High School, at Whittier College, where she received a B.A. in English in 1923, and at the University of California, Berkeley. Although she had published short stories based on her family's Quaker past, she did not collect them in a book until 1945, thus publishing her first book at the age of forty-three. Later, she taught at numerous universities and at Breadloaf. Her last book, *The State of Stony Lonesome* (1984), was completed shortly before her death, on February 23, 1984, at her longtime home in Napa, California.

Analysis

Jessamyn West's short stories fall into two categories: those which treat various episodes in the lives of a single family and are gathered in a single volume, and those which more conventionally are quite separate in plot and character, gathered in the customary collections. The books *The Friendly Persuasion*, *Except for Me and Thee: A Companion to the Friendly Persuasion*, and *Cress Delahanty* fall into the first category. Although some critics have called them novels, the sketches of which each volume is composed are obviously separate. The fact that an acknowledgment preceding *The Friendly Persuasion* refers to "stories in this book" which had been published in various magazines makes West's own assumptions clear. In the introduction to *Collected Stories of Jessamyn West*, Julian Muller calls those earlier volumes "novels," while admitting that the chapters could stand alone, and thus he omits those sketches from his collection. A complete analysis of West's short fiction, however, must include the consideration of those works on an individual basis, even though a study of her long fiction might also include them.

The *Collected Stories of Jessamyn West* included all the stories from two previous volumes, *Love, Death, and the Ladies' Drill Team* and *Crimson Ramblers of the World, Farewell*, along with eight additional stories which Jessamyn West wished to have included. According to the editor, those stories which were omitted, West believed, needed revision.

The focus in all of West's work is a basic tension in human life. On the one hand, man yearns to be free of restraints; on the other hand, he desires to love and to please the beloved, thus voluntarily to accept limitations on his individuality. The beloved is not only his human partner; the term also suggests divinity, speaking to his spirit directly, in the Quaker tradition. Although social or religious groups may presume to judge the conduct of West's characters, the final judgment must be their own, guided by their separate and sacred consciences. According to the editor of the *Collected Stories of Jessamyn West*, West's first published story was "99.6." Set in a tuberculosis sanatorium, the story reflects West's own experience. The protagonist, Marianne Kent, desperately watches her temperature, hoping for the change which would signal some improvement in her health. Aware of her own feverish condition, the consumption which is truly consuming her, she wishes that the nurse would help her with an illusion, with the suggestion that perhaps the heat she feels comes from warmer weather outside, not from her own fever. Although the obvious antagonists are Marianne Kent and her disease, at the conclusion of the brief story the protagonist turns to God, pleading with Him for some sign of hope, for some reduction from 99.6. Thus, the real struggle is a spiritual one. Mrs. Kent must accept what divinity permits.

In *The Friendly Persuasion*, stories set in the nineteenth century among the Indiana Quakers of the Ohio River Valley, conscience is always a consideration. The Irish Quaker Jess Birdwell, a devout man but one who has a mind of his own, is married to Eliza Cope Birdwell, a stricter Quaker—in fact, a Quaker minister, who must consider the community's judgment of her as well as God's. "Music on the Muscatatuck" illustrates the stresses on the relationship between Jess and Eliza, which result from their differences in temperament and convictions. After describing the natural beauty of the Birdwell farm, the comfort and plenty of their pretty home, the goodness of Eliza as a wife, and Jess's own prosperity, West sets the problem: Jess likes music; as a Quaker, he is supposed to have nothing to do with it.

Jess's temptation comes when, like Eve in the Garden, he is separated from his mate. On a business trip to Philadelphia, he meets an organ salesman; already seduced by his own love of music, he stops by the store. The result is inevitable: He orders an organ.

When Jess returns home, he cannot find the words to tell Eliza, who follows the Quaker teachings about music, what he has done. Unfortunately, when the organ arrives, Eliza makes a miscalculation about Jess's male pride: She commands him to choose between the organ and her. Jess moves the organ in the house, and Eliza is left in the snow, pondering her next course of action. Fortunately, Eliza knows the difference between her domain and that of the Lord. She compromises, and the organ goes in the attic. All goes well until a church committee comes to call just when the Birdwell's daughter Mattie has slipped up to the attic to play on the organ. Surely God inspires Jess Birdwell in this crucial situation, for he prays and continues praying until the music stops. The committee concludes that angels have provided the accompaniment; Jess suspects that the Lord, who has kept him praying for so long, has made His statement. Just as Eliza is about to announce her triumph, however, the music once again comes from the attic, and Jess again responds.

The story is typical of West. The human beings involved live close to their natural setting; they are ordinary people, neither rich nor poor. Although they may disagree with one another and although they often have much to learn, they are usually basically good, and at the end of the story, some resolution of their conflict with one another and with their spiritual scruples is suggested. The tone is also typical. Perhaps one reason for West's popularity is that, in an age when many writers do not seem to like their own characters, and for good reason, she is honestly fond of hers. As a result, she can laugh at their foibles and follies, their deficiencies in wisdom, and their mistakes in judgment without negating the fact of their basic goodness.

One of the endearing qualities of the Birdwell family is that, despite their strict religious convictions, they accept differences within the family; each member is expected, above all, to follow his own conscience. In the Civil War story "The Battle of Finney's Ford," what was supposed to be a fight against Morgan's raiders proves to be no fight at all, because Morgan's raiders change their route. In the meantime, however, the Birdwell boys must decide whether to fight. One of them, Joshua, says that he is willing to kill, if necessary; the other, Labe, will not join the town's defenders. Ironically, at the end of the story, Josh says that the reason he must fight is that he so dislikes fighting, while Labe admits that he must not fight because he truly enjoys fighting. Thus the real "Battle of Finney's Ford" has been a battle of conscience for the boys, and for the parents, a struggle to let them make their own decisions. The slightness of the external plot, typical of many of West's stories, does not reduce the magnitude of the internal action. For Jess, Eliza, Josh, and Labe, there is a major spiritual battle; as usual, the element of love is present in the resolution of the conflict.

Although *Cress Delahanty* is set in twentieth century California rather than nineteenth century Indiana, and although it lacks the specific Quaker religious background, the importance of the natural setting, the basic goodness of the characters, and the emphasis on spiritual problems are similar to the stories in *The Friendly Persuasion*. For example, "Fifteen: Spring" deals with Cress's selfish encounter with death, just as in the previous volume "The Meeting House" had followed Jess Birdwell through a similar crisis. In "Fifteen: Spring," Cress has developed a schoolgirl crush on a dying man, the father of sons her age. In her egotism, she wishes to be important to him, even to die in his place, if necessary, but after a visit to his home, after realizing that God is in charge, not Cress, she learns that she is not of major importance to her beloved, nor is her love of any help to him. Ironically, the final consolation comes from his wife, who recalls her own lost youth and, from her own tragic situation, finds pity for foolish Cress.

Many of West's stories deal with young people who are being initiated into life. In *Love, Death, and the Ladies' Drill Team*, "A Time of Learning" describes the encounter of nineteen-year-old Emmett Maguire, a talented sign- and housepainter, with his first love, Ivy Lish. Emmett loves the seemingly perfect girl with all of his heart. When he paints her picture, it is an act of total commitment. Unfortunately, Emmett must learn that the beloved is not always worthy of the emotion she inspires. As other men know, Ivy is consistently unfaithful. When Emmett learns that she has given his painting to another lover, his immediate impulse is toward revenge: He will paint her on the barn, as ugly as she has proved herself to be, for all to see. Then comes his spiritual crisis. Somehow, he finds, he cannot paint ugliness, or perhaps he cannot hate. When he paints a larger-than-life picture of her on the barn, he finally forgets about her in the joy of realizing that he is indeed a good painter. Thus, finally, his love of art is more important than her betrayal of him, and his wish to love defeats his temptation to hate.

West clearly believes, however, that it is not only the young who must learn about life. One of the optimistic elements in her stories is the suggestion that life is learning itself. Because most of her major characters are willing to expand their consciousnesses, anxious to revise their judgments, they are appealing. Thus, in *Except for Me and Thee: A Companion to the Friendly Persuasion*, the Quaker preacher Eliza Birdwell, a stubborn woman with a strict conscience, must deal with the issue of fugitive slaves. In the long story "Neighbors," Eliza must not only decide whether to obey the law, as her religion dictates, by turning over the fugitive slaves who seek refuge with her, or to hide them and defy the law of her country; she must also come to terms with Jess's involvement in running slaves to freedom, at the risk of his life and his liberty. The decision is not easy, but in changing her mind about the law and in acquiescing to the demands of Jess's conscience, Eliza herself grows spiritually.

Not all of West's stories have so hopeful a conclusion. In "The Condemned Librarian," from *Crimson Ramblers of the World, Farewell*, an embittered teacher, who believes that she has not been able to realize her dreams, consults a woman doctor who, against all odds, has risen from being a high school librarian to her present profession. Perversely, the teacher refuses to reveal her symptoms to the doctor, and, despite all of her efforts, the doctor fails to diagnose tuberculosis. As a result, the teacher nearly dies, but to her delight, the doctor must abandon her practice and go back to being a high school librarian. The title "The Condemned Librarian" makes it clear that hatred has, in this situation, had a great triumph, but ironically, the person most trapped is the bitter teacher, who must live with the knowledge that she herself is condemned. Although she feels happy thinking of the doctor's misery, she admits that the old magic is gone from her teaching. Clearly, by her spite she has corroded her own soul.

Other stories of that collection, however, end with understanding and reconciliation. For example, "Live Life Deeply" begins with the disappearance of fourteen-year-old Elspeth Courtney, who has turned up at the maternity ward of the local hospital. Her distraught father, pursuing her, discovers that she had been on Reservoir Hill early that morning, contemplating suicide because, as she confided to the troubled man she met there, a teacher she admired had made fun of her for a composition titled "Live Life Deeply." The stranger had been worrying about his wife's cesarean section, while Ellie had been worrying about her humiliation. When the baby is born, the stranger's problem is solved. Then, the new father solves Ellie's problem by pointing out that she wants to live life fully and that her pain is as much a part of a full life as the excitement and joy of the birth. Convinced, Ellie begins to plan her next composition, which will deal with her experiences in the maternity ward. Now that she understands that pain and joy are both a part of life and that both are necessary to make life interesting, she can move ahead, accepting even her setbacks.

In all of Jessamyn West's stories, whether the setting is the past or the present, Indiana or California, an individual, young or old, has the opportunity to grow spiritually. If, like the teacher in "The Condemned Librarian," one chooses to hate instead of to love or if one refuses to permit freedom of conscience to others, one's life will be miserable. Many ordinary people, however, live lives as meaningful and as exciting as those of Jess Birdwell, Cress Delahanty, and Elspeth Courtney. In her carefully crafted accounts of everyday life, Jessamyn West has revealed the drama of spiritual conflict in these later centuries as compellingly as did the productions of *Everyman* in medieval times.

Other major works

NOVELS: *The Witch Diggers*, 1951; *Little Men*, in *Star Short Novels*, 1954; *South of the Angels*, 1960; *A Matter of Time*, 1966; *Leafy Rivers*, 1967; *The Massacre at Fall Creek*, 1975; *The Life I Really Lived*, 1979; *The State of Stony Lonesome*, 1984.

PLAY: *A Mirror for the Sky*, 1948 (libretto).

SCREENPLAY: *Friendly Persuasion*, 1956.

POETRY: *The Secret Look: Poems*, 1974.

NONFICTION: *To See the Drama*, 1957; *Hide and Seek: A Continuing Journey*, 1973 (autobiography); *The Woman Said Yes: Encounters with Life and Death—Memoirs*, 1976; *Double Discovery: A Journey*, 1980.

ANTHOLOGY: *The Quaker Reader*, 1962.

Bibliography
Library Journal. Review of *Collected Stories of Jessamyn West*. CXI (December, 1986), p. 140.

The New York Times Book Review. Review of *Collected Stories of Jessamyn West*. October 26, 1986, p. 54.

Publishers Weekly. Review of *Collected Stories of Jessamyn West*. CCXXX (September 26, 1986), p. 66.

Shivers, Alfred S. *Jessamyn West*, 1972.

Rosemary M. Canfield-Reisman

YEVGENY ZAMYATIN

Born: Lebedyan, Russia; February 1, 1884
Died: Paris, France; March 10, 1937

Principal short fiction
Povesti i rasskazy, 1963; *The Dragon: Fifteen Stories*, 1966.

Other literary forms
Yevgeny Zamyatin's most important piece of fiction was his novel *My* (wr. 1920-1921, pb. 1952; *We*, 1924). A satirical examination of a future utopian state, the novel affirms the timeless value of individual liberty and free will in a world which places a premium on conformity and reason. This work exerted a significant influence on George Orwell's *Nineteen Eighty-Four* (1949). Zamyatin also wrote plays, adaptations, and film scenarios. His early dramatic works are historical plays—*Ogni svyatogo Dominika* (1922; *The Fires of Saint Dominic*, 1971) and *Attila* (wr. 1925-1927, pb. 1950; English translation, 1971)—while a later work, *Afrikanskiy gost* (wr. 1929-1930, pb. 1963; *The African Guest*, 1971), provides a comic look at philistine attempts to cope with Soviet reality. The author's most successful adaptation for the screen was a version of Maxim Gorky's *Na dne* (1902; *The Lower Depths*, 1912), which Zamyatin transformed into a screenplay for Jean Renoir's film *Les Bas-fonds* (1936; *The Lower Depths*, 1937).

Achievements
Although Zamyatin is best known in the West for his novel *We*, it has been his short fiction that has been most influential in the Soviet Union, since *We* has never been published there. In his short fiction, Zamyatin developed an original prose style that is distinguished by its bold imagery and charged narrative pacing. This style, along with Zamyatin's writings and teachings about literature in the immediate postrevolutionary period, had a decisive impact on the first generation of Soviet writers, which include such figures as Lev Luntz, Nikolay Nikitin, Venyamin Kaverin, and Mikhail Zoshchenko. In addition, Zamyatin's unswerving defense of the principle of artistic and individual freedom remains a vivid element of his literary legacy.

Biography
Yevgeny Ivanovich Zamyatin was born on February 1, 1884, in Lebedyan, a small town in the Russian heartland. The writer would later point out with pride that the town was famous for its cardsharpers, Gypsies, and distinctive Russian speech, and he would utilize this spicy material in his mature fiction. His childhood, however, was a lonely one, and as the son of a village teacher,

he spent more time with books than with other children.

After completing four years at the local school in 1896, Zamyatin went on to the *gymnasium* in Voronezh, where he remained six years. Immediately after he was graduated, Zamyatin moved to St. Petersburg to study naval engineering at the Petersburg Polytechnic Institute. Over the next few years, Zamyatin became interested in politics and joined the Bolshevik Party. This political involvement led to his arrest late in 1905, when the student was picked up by the authorities who were trying to cope with the turbulent political agitation that swept the capital that year. Zamyatin spent several months in solitary confinement, and he used the time to write poetry and study English. Released in the spring of 1906, Zamyatin was exiled to Lebedyan. He soon returned to St. Petersburg, however, and lived there illegally until he was discovered and exiled again in 1911.

By this time he had been graduated from the Institute and had been appointed a lecturer there. He also had made his debut as a writer: In 1908, he published the story "Odin" ("Alone"), which chronicles the fate of an imprisoned revolutionary student who kills himself over frustrated love, and in 1910, he published "Devushka," another tale of tragic love. Although neither work is entirely successful, they both demonstrate Zamyatin's early interest in innovative narrative technique. A more polished work of his was *Uezdnoe* (1913; *A Provincial Tale*, 1966), which Zamyatin wrote during the months of renewed exile in 1911 and 1912. Zamyatin's penetrating treatment of ignorance and brutality in the Russian countryside was greeted with warm approval by the critics. On the other hand, his next major work, *Na kulichkakh* (1914; at the end of the world), provided such a sharp portrait of cruelty in the military that the publication in which the story appeared was confiscated by the authorities.

In 1916, Zamyatin departed Russia for Great Britain, where he was to work on seagoing icebreakers. His experience abroad provided the impetus for two satires on the British middle class—*Ostrovityane* (1918; *The Islanders*, 1972) and "Lovets chelovekov" ("The Fisher of Men"). Zamyatin returned to Russia after the abdication of Czar Nicholas in 1917, and embarked upon a busy course of literary endeavors. The period from 1917 to 1921 was a time of remarkable fecundity for the writer: He wrote fourteen stories, the novel *We*, a dozen fables, and a play. This body of work evinces an impressive diversity of artistic inspiration. Zamyatin subjects range from the intense passions found in rural Russia ("Sever," "The North") to the dire conditions afflicting the urban centers during the postrevolutionary period ("Peshchera," "The Cave"; "Mamay"; and "Drakon," "Dragon") to ribald parodies of saints' lives ("O tom, kak istselen byl inok Erazm," "How the Monk Erasmus Was Healed").

In addition to his own literary creation, Zamyatin dedicated himself to encouraging the literary careers of others. He regularly lectured on the craft of writing to young writers in the House of Arts in Petrograd, and he took part in numerous editorial and publishing activities. Among those whose works he helped to edit were Anton Chekhov and H. G. Wells. For many of these editions, he also wrote critical or biographical introductions, and such writers as Wells, Jack London, O. Henry, and George Bernard Shaw received Zamyatin's critical attention. As a result of this editorial work and his involvement in such literary organizations as the All-Russian Union of Writers, which he helped to found, Zamyatin's own productivity began to decline after 1921, particularly his prose.

At the same time, Zamyatin found himself in the awkward position of having to defend himself against those who perceived something dangerous or threatening in the ideas his work espoused. In his prose fiction and in numerous essays, Zamyatin consistently articulated a belief in the value of continual change, innovation, and renewal. Seizing upon the thermodynamic theory of entropy—the concept that all energy in the universe tends toward stasis or passivity—Zamyatin warned against the dangers of stagnation in intellectual and artistic spheres. Exhorting writers to be rebels and heretics, he argued that one should never be content with the status quo, for satisfaction with any victory can easily degenerate into stifling philistinism. By the same token, Zamyatin denounced conformist tendencies in literary creation and decried efforts to subordinate individual inspiration to predetermined ideological programs.

Given the fact that one of the ideological underpinnings of the new Soviet state was a belief in the primacy of the collective over the interests of the individual, Zamyatin's fervent defense of individual freedom could not help but draw the attention of the emerging establishment. The writer was arrested in 1922 along with 160 other intellectuals and became subject to an order for deportation. Yet without his knowledge, and perhaps against his will, a group of friends interceded for him and managed to have the order withdrawn. After Zamyatin's release in 1923, he applied for permission to emigrate, but his request was rebuffed.

During the latter half of the 1920's, the political climate in the Soviet Union became more restrictive, and Zamyatin was among a number of talented writers who were singled out for public denunciation and criticism. He found that the doors to publishing houses were now closed to him and that permission to stage his plays was impossible to obtain. Zamyatin did not buckle before the increasingly vituperative attacks directed toward him. Indeed, he had once written that "a stubborn, unyielding enemy is far more deserving of respect than a sudden convert to communism." Consequently, he did not succumb to pressure and make a public confession of his "errors," as some of his fellow writers were forced to do. On the contrary, he stood up to this campaign of abuse until 1931, when he sent Joseph Stalin an audacious request for permission to leave the Soviet Union with the right to return "as soon as it becomes possible in our country to serve great ideas in literature without cringing before little men."

With Gorky's help, Zamyatin's petition was granted, and he left the Soviet Union with his wife in November, 1931. Settling in Paris, he continued to work on a variety of literary projects, including translations, screenplays, and a novel entitled *Bich bozhy* (1939; the scourge of God). Because of his interest in film, he envisioned a trip to Hollywood, but these plans never materialized. He died on March 10, 1937.

Analysis

Perhaps the most distinctive feature of Yevgeny Zamyatin's short fiction is its charged, expressive narrative style. The writer characterized the style of his generation of writers in a lecture entitled "Contemporary Russian Literature" (delivered in 1918). Calling the artistic method of his generation Neorealism, he outlined the differences between Neorealist fiction and that of the preceding Realist movement. He states:

> By the time the Neorealists appeared, life had become more complex, faster, more feverish.... In response to this way of life, the Neorealists have learned to write more compactly, briefly, tersely than the Realists. They have learned to say in ten lines what used to be said in a whole page.

During the first part of his career, Zamyatin consciously developed and honed his own unique form of Neorealist writing. Although his initial experimentation in this direction is evident in his early prose works (and especially in the long story *A Provincial Tale*), this tendency did not reach its expressive potential until the late 1910's, when it blossomed both in his satires on British life and in the stories devoted to Russian themes. The stories *The Islanders* and "The Fisher of Men" provide a mordant examination of the stifling philistinism permeating the British middle class. The former work in particular displays the tenor and thrust of Zamyatin's satiric style. The first character introduced into the tale is a minister named Vicar Dooley, who has written a *Testament of Contemporary Salvation*, in which he declares that "life must become a harmonious machine and with mechanical inevitability lead us to the desired goal." Such a vision raises the specter of death and stasis, not energy and life, and Zamyatin marshals his innovative narrative skills to expose the dangers that this vision poses for society.

One salient feature of Zamyatin's style is the identification of a character with a specific physical trait, animal, or object that seems to capture the essence of the character being depicted. Through this technique, the writer can both evoke the presence of the character by mentioning the associated image and underscore that character's fundamental personality type. What is more, once Zamyatin has established such an identification, he can suggest significant shifts in his characters' moods or situations by working changes on the associated images themselves. In *The Islanders*, this technique plays a vital role in the narrative exposition, and at times the associated images actually replace a given character in action. Thus, one character's lips are compared at the outset of the story to thin worms, and the women who attend Dooley's church are described as being pink and blue. Later, a tense interaction between the two is conveyed in striking terms: "Mrs. Campbell's worms twisted and sizzled on a slow fire. The blues and pinks feasted their eyes." Similarly, the central protagonist is compared to a tractor, and when his stolid reserve is shattered by feelings of love, Zamyatin writes that the tractor's "steering wheel was broken." Through this felicitous image Zamyatin not only evokes his hero's ponderous bulk but also suggests the unpredictable consequences which follow the release of suppressed emotion.

As striking as his satires on British conservatism are, however, it is in the stories that he wrote on Russian subjects that Zamyatin attained the apex of his vibrant expressionistic style. In his lecture on contemporary Russian literature, he spoke of his desire to find fresh subjects for literary treatment. Contrasting urban and rural settings, he declared: "The life of big cities is like the life of factories. It robs people of individuality, makes them the same, machinelike." In the countryside, Zamyatin concludes, "the Neorealists find not only genre, not only a way of life, but a way of life concentrated, condensed by centuries to a strong essence, ninety-proof."

As if to illustrate this premise, in 1918 he wrote the long tale entitled "The North." This story celebrates the primal forces of nature: In a swift succession of scenes, Zamyatin depicts a passionate yet short-lived affair between a true child of the forest—a young woman named Pelka—and a simple fisherman named Marey. Pelka is perhaps the closest embodiment of the ideally "natural" character in all of Zamyatin's works. She talks with the forest creatures, keeps a deer for a pet, and loves with a profound passion that cannot understand or tolerate the constraints imposed by civilized man. Sadly, her brief interlude of love with Marey is threatened by his foolish obsession with constructing a huge lantern "like those in Petersburg." Marey's desire to ape the fashions of the city destroys his romantic idyll with Pelka. After she vainly tries to stir Marey's emotions by having a short fling with a smug, callous shopkeeper named Kortoma, Pelka engineers a fatal encounter between herself, Marey, and a wild bear: The two lovers die at the hands of the natural world.

To illuminate this spectacle of extraordinary desire and suffering, Zamyatin utilizes all the tools of his Neorealist narrative manner. Striving to show rather than describe, Zamyatin avoids the use of such connectors as "it seemed" or "as if" in making comparisons; instead, the metaphorical image becomes the illustrated object or action itself. Especially noteworthy in "The North" is Zamyatin's use of charged color imagery. By associating particular characters with symbolic visual leitmotifs, the writer enhances his character portrayals. Thus, he underscores Pelka's naturalism by linking her to a combination of the colors red (as of flesh and blood) and green (as of the vegetation in the forest). Zamyatin compared his method to Impressionism: The juxtaposition of a few basic colors is intended to project the essence of a scene. At times, Zamyatin allows the symbolic associations of certain colors to replace narrative description entirely. Depicting the rising frenzy of a Midsummer Night's celebration, Zamyatin alludes to the surging flow of raw passion itself when he writes: "all that you could see was that . . . something red was happening."

Zamyatin's attention to visual detail in "The North" is matched by his concern with auditory effects. He thought that literary prose and poetry were one and the same; accordingly, the reader finds many examples of alliteration, assonance, and instrumentation in his work. He also gave careful consideration to the rhythmic pattern of his prose, revealing a debt to the Russian Symbolist writers who emphasized the crucial role of sound in prose. Seeking to communicate his perceptions as expressively and concisely as possible, he tried to emulate the fluidity and dynamism of oral speech. One notes many elliptical and unfinished sentences in Zamyatin's prose at this time, and his narratives resemble a series of sharp but fragmentary images or vignettes, which his readers must connect and fill in themselves. Zamyatin explained: "Today's reader and viewer will know how to complete the picture, fill in the words—and what he fills in will be etched far more vividly within him, will much more firmly become an organic part of him."

Zamyatin's other works on the deep recesses of the Russian countryside reflect his calculated attempt to evoke deep emotions and passionate lives in elliptical, allusive ways. The story "Rus'" ("In Old Russia"), for example, is narrated in a warm colloquial tone in which the neutral language of an impersonal narrator is replaced by language that relies heavily on the intonations and lexicon of spoken Russian. This technique, called *skaz* in Russian, was popularized by writers such as Nikolay Leskov and Alexey Remizov, and Zamyatin uses it to good effect in this tale. His narrator's account of the amorous activities of a young married woman named Darya is accented with notes of sly understanding and tolerance. As the narrator describes her, Darya cannot help but give in to the impulses of her flesh. At the very outset, she is compared to an apple filling up with sap; when spring arrives, she unconsciously feels the sap rising in her just as it is in the apple and lilac trees around her. Her "fall," then, is completely natural, and so, too, is the ensuing death of her husband only a few days later. Again, Zamyatin's narrator conveys the news of the husband's death and the gossip that attended it in tones of warm indulgence. In the deep backwaters of Russia, he indicates, life flows on; such events have no more lasting impact than a stone which is dropped into a pond and causes a few passing ripples.

While Zamyatin was drawn to rural Russian subjects, he did not ignore urban themes: Two of his most striking works of 1920—"The Cave" and "Mamay"—exhibit his predilection for expressive imagery and his nuanced appreciation of human psychology. In "The Cave," Zamyatin depicts the Petrograd landscape in the winters following the Russian Revolution as a primordial, prehistoric wasteland. This image dominates the story, illustrating the writer's own admission that if he firmly believes in an image, "it will spread its roots through paragraphs and pages." Yet while the overarching image of Petrograd's citizens as cave dwellers creates a palpable atmosphere of grimness and despair in "The Cave," the images with which Zamyatin enlivens "Mamay" are more humorous. This story continues a long tradition in Russian literature of depicting the life of petty clerks in the city of St. Petersburg. The protagonist here is a meek individual who bears the incongruous name of Mamay, one of the Tatar conquerers of Russia. Mamay's wife is a stolid woman so domineering that every spoonful of soup eaten by Mamay is likened to an offering to an imperious Buddha. The sole pleasure in little Mamay's life is book collecting, and it is this mild passion that finally stirs the character into uncharacteristic action. He had been gathering and hiding a large sum of money with which to buy books, and at the end of the story he discovers with dismay that his stockpile has been destroyed by an enemy. Enraged, he is driven to murder. This contemporary Mamay, however, is only a pale shadow of his famous namesake: The intruder proves to be a mouse, and Mamay kills it with a letter opener.

Zamyatin's pursuit of a charged, expressive narrative manner reached a peak in the early 1920's, and in at least one work, "Rasskaz o samom glavnom" ("A Story About the Most Important Thing"), the writer's ambition resulted in a work in which stylistic and structural manipulation overwhelm semantic content. Zamyatin creates a complex narrative structure in which he shifts back and forth among three plot lines involving the life of an insect, revolutionaries in Russia, and beings on a star about to collide with the Earth. The tale forcefully conveys the writer's sense of the power of the urge to live and procreate in the face of imminent death, but in certain passages, his penchant for hyperbole and intensity of feeling detracts from the effectiveness of the work as a whole.

Later in the decade, however, Zamyatin began to simplify his narrative techniques; the result can be seen in the moving story "Navodnenie" ("The Flood"), perhaps the finest short story of this late period. Written in 1928, "The Flood" reveals how Zamyatin managed to tone down some of his more exaggerated descriptive devices, while retaining the power and intensity of his central artistic vision. One finds few of his characteristic recurring metaphors in the story, but the few that are present carry considerable import. The work's central image is that of flooding, both as a literal phenomenon (the repeated flooding of the Neva River) and as a metaphorical element (the ebb and flow of emotions in the protagonist's soul). The plot of the story concerns a childless woman's resentment toward an orphaned girl named Ganka, who lives in her house and has an affair with her husband. Sofya's rising malice toward Ganka culminates on a day when the river floods. As the river rises and a cannon booms its flood warning, Sofya feels her anger surging too: It "whipped across her heart, flooded all of her." Striking Ganka with an ax, she then feels a corresponding outflow, a release of tension. Similar images of flooding and flowing accompany Sofya's childbirth, the feeding of her child, and the rising sensation of guilt in her heart. In the final scene of the story, the river again begins to flood, and now Sofya feels an irrepressible urge to give birth to her confession. As she begins to reveal her murderous secret, "Huge waves swept out of her and washed over. . . everyone." After she concludes her tale, "everything was good, blissful . . . all of her had poured out."

The recurring water images link all the major events in "The Flood," and Zamyatin achieves further cohesiveness through additional associations such as birth and death, conception and destruction. The tight austerity of his later fiction endows that body of work with understated force. The writer himself commented on the conscious effort he made to achieve this kind of effective simplicity: "All the complexities I had passed through had been only a road to simplicity. . . . Simplicity of form is legitimate for our epoch, but the right to simplicity must be earned."

The oeuvre that Zamyatin left behind provides an eloquent testament both to the man's skill as a literary craftsman and to the integrity and power of his respect for human potential. His innovations in narrative exposition exerted a palpable influence on his contemporaries, and his defense of individual liberty in the face of relentless repression holds timeless appeal for his readers.

Other major works

NOVELS: *Uezdnoe*, 1913 (novella; *A Provincial Tale*, 1966); *Na kulichkakh*, 1914 (novella); *Ostrovityane*, 1918 (novella; *The Islanders*, 1972); *My*, wr. 1920-1921, pb. 1952 (*We*, 1924); *Bich bozhy*, 1939.

PLAYS: *Ogni svyatogo Dominika*, 1922 (*The Fires of Saint Dominic*, 1971); *Attila*, wr. 1925-1927, pb. 1950 (English translation, 1971); *Afrikanksiy gost*, wr. 1929-1930, pb. 1963 (*The African Guest*, 1971); *Five Plays*, 1971.

SCREENPLAY: *Les Bas-fonds*, 1936 (*The Lower Depths*, 1937; adaptation of Maxim Gorky's novel *Na dne*).

NONFICTION: *Litsa*, 1955 (*A Soviet Heretic*, 1970).

MISCELLANEOUS: *Sobranie sochinenii*, 1929; *Sochineniia*, 1970-1972.

Bibliography

Brown, Edward J. *"Brave New World," "1984," and "We": An Essay on Anti-Utopia*, 1976.

Collins, Christopher. *Evgenij Zamjatin: An Interpretive Study*, 1973.
Richards, D. J. *Zamyatin: A Soviet Heretic*, 1962.
Shane, Alex M. *The Life and Works of Evgenij Zamjatin*, 1968.

Julian W. Connolly

MIKHAIL ZOSHCHENKO

Born: Poltava, Russia; August 10, 1895
Died: Leningrad, U.S.S.R.; July 22, 1958

Principal short fiction

Rasskazy Nazara Ilicha, gospodina Sinebryukhova, 1922; *Uvazhaemye grazhdane*, 1926; *Nervnye lyudi*, 1927; *O chem pel solovei: Sentimentalnye povesti*, 1927; *Siren' tsvetet*, 1929; *Lichnaya zhizn'*, 1933; *Golubaya kniga*, 1935; *Russia Laughs*, 1935; *The Woman Who Could Not Read and Other Tales*, 1940, 1973; *The Wonderful Dog and Other Tales*, 1942, 1973; *Scenes from the Bathhouse and Other Stories of Communist Russia*, 1961; *Nervous People and Other Satires*, 1963.

Other literary forms

Although the fame of Mikhail Zoshchenko rests almost entirely on his short stories, he produced a few works in other genres that are often discussed as important facets of his opus, most notably longer stories (*povesti*), which are almost invariably treated as short novels outside Russia. Two of these, *Vozvrashchennaya molodost'* (1933; *Youth Restored*, 1935) and *Pered voskhodom solntsa* (1943, 1972; *Before Sunrise*, 1974), show a different Zoshchenko from that seen in his short stories—an author who is attempting to rise above the everyday reality of his stories. The first of these novels is a variation on an age-old theme—a desire to regain lost youth, with a humorous twist in that the old professor renounces his restored youth after failing to keep up with his young wife. In *Before Sunrise*, Zoshchenko probed deeper into his own psyche, trying to discover his origins, going back even to the prenatal time. In order to achieve this, he employed the psychoanalytical methods of Sigmund Freud and Ivan Pavlov, which were and still are a novelty in Russian literature. His other longer stories (a few occasional pieces written at the behest of Soviet authorities in order to conform with the political trends of the time) and playwriting attempts do not enhance his stature; on the contrary, they detract from his reputation so much that they are generally ignored by critics and readers alike.

Achievements

Zoshchenko was fortunate to enter literature in the 1920's, when Russian writers were relatively free to choose their subject matter and to express themselves. His kind of writing—humorous stories and satire—seems to have been possible only in that decade. One of Zoshchenko's most significant achievements is making his brand of humor and satire unmistakably his, not an easy task in a nation known for its exquisite sense of humor. With an ear to the ground, he demonstrated an infallible understanding of human habits and foibles. He was able to see humor in almost every situation, although his humor is often suffused with sadness deriving from the realization that life is not as funny as it often seems. He frequently spoke for the Soviet people when they were not permitted to speak freely, yet he did it in such a way that it was very difficult to pin on him a political bias or hidden intentions until very late in his career. Just as important was his ability to reproduce the language of his characters, a curious concoction of the language of the lower classes and the bureaucratese of political parvenus trying to sound politically sophisticated or conformist. As a consequence, his several hundred short stories serve as a gold mine for the multifaceted study of the Soviet people in the first decades after the revolution. In this respect, Zoshchenko's writings resemble those of Damon Runyon, Edward Lear, and perhaps Art Buchwald. That he was able to achieve all this without sinking to the level of a social or political commentator of the period reveals his artistic acumen, which has not been equaled before or after him.

Biography

Mikhail Mikhailovich Zoshchenko was born on August 10, 1895, in Poltava, Russia, to a lower-gentry, landowning family. His father was a painter of Ukrainian origin, and his mother was a Russian actress. Zoshchenko was graduated in 1913 from a high school in St. Petersburg, where he spent most of his life; one of the worst grades he received was in Russian composition. Later, he studied law at the University of Petersburg. World War I interrupted his studies, and he volunteered for service in the czarist army, became an officer, and was injured and gassed in 1916. In 1917, he volunteered again, this time for the Red Army, although his military duties were limited because of his former injuries. After the revolution, Zoshchenko settled in St. Petersburg (later Leningrad), trying several professions and not settling on any of them until he decided to be a free-lance writer. For short periods of time he was a railroad ticket agent, a border-guard telephone operator, an instructor in rabbit- and poultry-raising, a militiaman, a census taker, a detective, a carpenter, a shoemaker, a clerk-typist, and a professional gambler, among other professions. This plethora of jobs served Zoshchenko later as a source of material for his stories; it also explains the authenticity of his fiction as well as his deep understanding of human nature. In 1921, he joined the famous literary group of writers calling themselves the Serapion Brothers, who gathered periodically to discuss their own works. His affiliation with this group would have far-reaching effects on him, lasting long after the group had ceased to exist. Being apolitical and having as its main goal the purely artistic improvement of its members, the society contributed significantly to the development of Russian literature at that time; it also left a stigma on its members, however, that would especially haunt Zoshchenko two decades later.

Zoshchenko wrote his first story in 1907 but did not publish anything until 1921. His first book, a collection of short stories, was published in 1922. He immediately became one of the most popular Soviet writers, publishing several additional collections and hundreds of stories. He continued as a freelance writer in the 1930's, his output unabated and his reputation high. Yet the new political and cultural climate, manifested especially in the demand on the writers to follow the dictates of Socialist Realism, forced him to alter his style. His fiction from that time consequently suffered in quality. He tried his pen in new genres, such as psychological and documentary fiction, with varying success. During World War II, he was active during the siege of Leningrad and was decorated for his performance. Later, he was evacuated to Alma-Ata, where he spent the rest of the war, mainly writing *Before Sunrise*. In 1946, the enmity between Zoshchenko and the regime, which had been simmering below the surface throughout his writing career, burst into the open when the party cultural czar, Andrei Zhdanov, viciously attacked him, together with the poet Anna Akhmatova, for their "antisocial" and "dangerous" writings. The attack meant removal from the literary scene—a punishment from which Zoshchenko never fully recovered. He disappeared until Joseph Stalin's death in 1953, and even then he was able to publish only a few anemic stories, from which the old spark and power were gone. He died in Leningrad on July 22, 1958. Since then, his reputation has been restored, and his stories are republished regularly. His works, though somewhat dated, are still held in high esteem, especially among literary critics.

Analysis

A typical Zoshchenko story is a four-to-six page sketch about a seemingly unimportant event in the lives of ordinary Soviet citizens. Most of his stories take place in Leningrad, and most of his characters come from the lower-middle class—managers, clerks, workers, artists—and the intelligentsia of both sexes, although peasants often appear as well. The episodes usually involve an exaggerated conflict in which the characters reveal their thoughts and attitudes about everyday reality. This dramatic conflict is presented in humorous tones that endear the characters to the reader; its resolution makes the reader chuckle, sometimes laugh aloud, but it seldom leaves him bitter, angry, or demanding decisive action.

This outward innocence, however, quickly dissipates after a closer look at the characters and their vexing problems. The reader realizes that the author does not always mean what he says and does not say what he means, and that much more lurks beneath the surface. In the story "Spi skorei" ("Get on with the Sleeping"), for example, a traveler has difficulties finding a suitable room in which to sleep, and when he does, his problems begin to unfold: A window is broken and a cat jumps in because it mistakes the room for a rubbish dump, a pool of water lies in the middle of the floor, there is no light ("you're not thinking of painting pictures in it?" he is asked both innocently and sarcastically by the innkeeper), the traveler has to use a tablecloth for a blanket and slides down the bed as if it were an iceberg, and, finally, the room is infested with bedbugs and fleas. At the end of the story, a woman's passport is returned to him by mistake. This comedy of errors, neglect, and incompetence is mitigated by the traveler's last words that the passport's owner "proved to be a nice woman, and we got to know each other rather well. So that my stay at the hotel had some pleasant consequences after all."

The inconveniences portrayed in Zoshchenko's tale are not tragic but rather amusing, and the author's habit of soothing conclusions—whatever their motives—tends to smooth over the rough edges. In "Melkii sluchai iz lichnoi zhizni" ("A Personal Episode"), the protagonist, after realizing that women no longer notice him, tries everything to become attractive again, only to discover that he has grown old. It is all lies and Western nonsense, anyway, he consoles himself. "Semeinyi kuporos" ("The Marriage Bond") shows a young wife who leaves her husband following a fight; after failing to find a suitable place to live, she returns to him. The author again moralizes, "There is no doubt, though, that this question of living accommodation strengthens and stabilizes our family life. . . . The marriage bond is rather strong nowadays. In fact very strong." The husband in the story "Rasskaz o tom, kak zhena ne razreshila muzhu umeret'" ("Hen-Pecked") falls ill and is about to die, but his wife will not let him die, as they have no money for a funeral. He goes out and begs for money and, after several outings, regains his health. "Perhaps, as he went outside the first time, he got so heated from excitement and exertion, that all his disease came out through perspiration." In another story, "Bogataia zhizn'" ("The Lucky Draw"), a married couple win a huge sum in a lottery but become very unhappy because they have nothing to do afterward. In "Administrativnyi vostorg" ("Power-Drunk"), an assistant chief of the local police is so overzealous in his off-duty efforts to punish a poor woman who allowed her pig to roam the streets that he arrests his own wife because she interceded for the woman. In story after story Zoshchenko makes seemingly insignificant events so important to his characters that they find in them the moving force of their lives. The reader, however—usually a person who has been exposed to such chicanery at one time or another—cannot help but understand that there is something basically wrong with one's life when such trivial events, against which one feels so helpless, are often repeated in various forms, that such occurrences are not really trifles, and that the primary aim of Zoshchenko's satire is not only to amuse or to exercise social criticism but also to point, rather subtly, at the philosophical meaning of existence.

Zoshchenko's reputation primarily as a social satirist is still perpetuated by both the connoisseurs of his stories and the Soviet authorities who condemn him, the former saying that Zoshchenko's criticism of the Soviet reality is justified and the latter that it is too harsh and ideologically motivated, even if sugarcoated with humor. There is no doubt that such an interpretation of his approach to reality is possible. Bureaucrats in particular are singled out for scorn. In "Koshka i liudi" ("The Stove"), a committee in charge of maintenance for an apartment building refuses to repair a fuming stove, pretending that nothing is wrong, even though one of them falls unconscious from the fumes. In "Bania" ("The Bathhouse"), checks for clothing are issued after the clothes are taken away, wrong clothes are returned, and there are not enough buckets. In the story "Butylka" ("Bottle"), a bottle lies broken on the street and nobody picks it up. When a janitor sweeps it aside, he is told by the militiaman to remove it altogether. "And, you know," the author chimes in, "the most remarkable thing is the fact that the militiaman ordered the glass to be swept up."

In perhaps Zoshchenko's harshest criticism of bureaucracy, "Kamennoe serdtse" ("A Heart of Stone"), a director demands of his business manager a truck for his personal needs. When the manager tells him that no truck is available, the director threatens to fire him, but the manager retorts, "Now, if you were a product of the old order, an attitude like that toward your subordinate would be understandable, but you are a man of the proletarian batch, and where you got a general's tone like that I simply can't understand." Nevertheless, the director succeeds in getting rid of the stubborn manager. The not-so-subtle implication here is that the revolution has changed little and that vulgarity (*poshlost'*) is as strong as ever. In all such stories, the bureaucrats, who seem to run the country, are satirized for their unjustified domination and mistreatment of their fellowmen.

Seen through such a prism, Zoshchenko's attitude toward social problems in his country two decades after the revolution can be seen as direct criticism. In fact, Zhdanov used exactly such an interpretation to attack Zoshchenko in 1946 for his alleged anti-Soviet writings. Singling out one of the stories written for children, "Prikliucheniia obeziany" ("The Adventures of a Monkey"), Zhdanov excoriated the author for writing that a monkey, after escaping from a zoo in Leningrad during the war and experiencing many troubles with human beings, decides to return to the zoo because it is easier for him to live there. The question of whether Zoshchenko wrote this story simply to amuse children or as an allegory of the inhumane (or perhaps too human) conditions in the Soviet society remains unanswered. It is quite possible that the author meant to say the latter. Yet he refused to admit political ulterior motives or an ideological slant in his writings:

> Tell me, how can I have 'a precise ideology' when not a single party among them all appeals to me? . . . I don't hate anybody—there is *my* precise ideology. . . . In their general swing the Bolsheviks are closer to me than anybody else. And so I'm willing to bolshevik around with them. . . . But I am not a Communist (or rather not a Marxist), and I think I never shall be.

If one is to believe his words, one must assume that the political or ideological criticism was not foremost on his mind. As for social criticism, he saw no crime in it; on the contrary, he believed that it was his duty to try to remedy ills and shortcomings by poking fun at them, as all satirists have done throughout history.

It is more likely that Zoshchenko was primarily interested in criticizing the morals of his compatriots, and in this respect he is no better or worse than any other moralist. He himself said that for the most part he wrote about the petty bourgeoisie, despite the official claims that it no longer exists as a separate class: "For the most part I create a synthetic type. In all of us there are certain traits of the petty bourgeois, the property owner, the money grubber. I write about the petty bourgeoisie, and I suppose I have enough material to last me the rest of my life." When some of the stories containing such criticism are examined, it is hard to disagree with Zoshchenko and even harder to see them as simply political criticism of the new regime. It is the moral behavior of his characters rather than what the government tells them to do that fascinated Zoshchenko. As a natural satirist, he was attracted mostly to the negative traits in human nature. Foremost among these traits is marital morality or, rather, the lack thereof. Infidelity seems to be rampant among Zoshchenko's marriage partners and, what is even more interesting, they have few qualms about it. In one example of a marital merry-go-around, "Zabavnoe prikliuchenie" ("An Amusing Adventure"), three couples are intertwined through their infidelity, somewhat incredibly, to be sure, but in a way symptomatic of the loosening of moral fiber within Soviet society. Dishonesty and cheating also seem to be rampant. In "Ne nado spekulirovat" ("The Greedy Milkwoman"), a young milkmaid, eager to pocket a large reward, recommends her husband to a widow seeking a new husband, mistakenly believing that after the marriage ceremony things will return to normal. The husband, however, likes the new arrangement and refuses to return to his lawful wife. Hypocrisy is revealed by workers who praise a deceased fellow worker even though they had not said a kind word about him when he was alive in "Posledniaia nepriiatnost'" ("A Final Unpleasantness"). Bribery is still abundant despite the official disclaimers, and thievery seems to be as common as winter snow. In two stories, "Telefon" ("The Telephone") and "Dobrorozhelatel'," the occupants of an apartment building are called away on urgent business only to find upon their return that their apartments have been robbed and ransacked. In "Akter" ("The Actor"), a reluctant actor is robbed right on the stage by fellow performers who pretend that their crime is part of the play.

Zoshchenko hints at an explanation for such behavior in the persistent discrepancy between the ideal and the real, between the official façade and reality, and between appearance and substance. Another explanation can be found in the perpetual clash between an individual and the collective.

In a charming one-page sketch, "Karusel'" ("The Merry-Go-Round"), the author destroys the myth that everything can be free in a society by having a young fellow ride a wooden horse, simply because it is free, until he almost dies. Another likely explanation can be found when untenable living conditions require several people to share not an apartment but a single room: Those who live in the room are packed like sardines; all the tenants rush to the scene whenever even the smallest incident happens, and the room's occupants have completely lost any sense of privacy. How, it is implied, can a person preserve his own dignity and respect for others when he is given a bathroom for an apartment, in which his wife, a small child, and a mother-in-law struggle to live while thirty-two other tenants use the same bathroom ("Krizis"; "The Crisis")? Or when the tenants collectively pay the electricity bill until they almost come to blows because some use more and some use less electricity ("Letniaia peredyshka"; "Electricity in Common")? Similarly humiliating struggles are presented in "Istoriia bolezni" ("History of an Illness"), in which a person prefers to be ill at home rather than in a hospital because there he is thrust in the same bathtub with an old, deranged woman and contracts whooping cough while eating from the same plate that the sick children next door have used. Regardless of whether the Soviet citizens will ever learn to adjust to this omnipresent communal life, they are paying a terrible price in overwrought nerves and general misanthropy.

Perhaps the best explanation for the immorality portrayed in Zoshchenko's stories, however, is simply the imperfection of human nature. Many of Zoshchenko's characters display the same weaknesses found in all ages and societies, which a political system can only exacerbate. His characters are egotistical and selfish to the core, as in the story "Liubov'" ("Love"), in which a young man declares his undying love for a girl on a night stroll, but when they are attacked by a robber he protests when the girl is not robbed at all. Zoshchenko's characters are also often insensitive toward one another: A man on a train mistreats his woman companion; when people protest, he is surprised, saying that it is only his mother. Other characters are greedy, taking advantage of others: An innocent man is arrested by the secret police, and his relatives sell all of his possessions, even his apartment allotment; he returns, however, in a few hours. In another story, "Vodianaia feeriia" ("A Water Ballet"), when a man comes to a city, all of his acquaintances pay him a visit mainly to take a bath in his hotel. The characters are jealous (an illiterate woman finally agrees to learn how to read only after she stumbled upon a fragrant letter her husband had received from a teacher urging him to arrange for his wife's reading classes), and they are vain (a woman defends her moonshining husband before the judge but balks when the husband reveals that she is older than he). All these traits demonstrate that Zoshchenko's characters are normal human beings sharing the same weaknesses and problems with people everywhere. One can read into these traits the corroding impact of a repressive governmental system, but more likely, these characters would behave the same way regardless of the system under which they lived. Nor does Zoshchenko believe them to be beyond salvation. In one of his best stories, "Ogni bol'shogo goroda" ("Big-City Lights"), a peasant father visits his son in Leningrad with the intention of staying there permanently. When everyone makes fun of his peasant ways, however, the old man becomes irritated and starts to cause problems for everyone, until one day he is treated with deep respect by a militiaman. This causes the old man to change his ways, and he returns happily to his village. In the words of an intellectual in the story, "I've always been of the opinion that respect for individuals, praise and esteem, produce exceptional results. Many personalities unfold because of this, just like roses at daybreak." Whether Zoshchenko is revealing his naïveté here or is adding a didactic touch to mollify the ever-present censors is immaterial; in these few words he diagnoses one of the gravest ills of any totalitarian society.

There is another strain in Zoshchenko's storytelling that, again, sets him apart from other humorists and satirists: his penchant for the absurd and grotesque. Many of his characters and situations lead to a conclusion that in essence life is absurd more often than one thinks. As a result, some of his stories are paragons of an absurd set of circumstances that no one can fathom or untangle. In "Ruka blishnego" ("My Brother's Hand"), for example, a nice person, wishing to shake hands with all people, finds out belatedly that one person who was extremely reluctant to shake hands is a leper. The best story depicting this absurdity shows a shipwrecked man during the war unknowingly holding on to a floating mine, happy about his salvation and making plans about his future ("Rogul'ka"; "The Buoy"). The pessimism and pervasive sadness of Zoshchenko's fiction break through in stories such as these despite the humor, proving the old adage that often there is only one step between laughter and tears.

There are other facets of Zoshchenko's short-story repertoire that are less significant, stories that are simply humorous without any pretense or deeper meaning, parodies of other famous literary pieces, stories showing the Russians' veneration of everything foreign, and others. They contribute to a multicolored mosaic of a life rich in human idiosyncrasies, in emotions and weaknesses, in lessons for those who need or seek them which offers plain enjoyment to connoisseurs of good literature. In this respect, Zoshchenko made a significant contribution to the wealth of both Russian and world literature, ranking among those first-rate humorists and satirists—Nikolai Gogol, Nikolay Leskov, and Anton Chekhov—who influenced him.

Other major works
NOVELS: *Vozvrashchennaya molodost'*, 1933 (*Youth Restored*, 1935); *Pered voskhodom solntsa*, 1943, 1972 (*Before Sunrise*, 1974).

Bibliography

Alexandrova, Vera. "Mikhail Zoshchenko," in *A History of Soviet Literature*, 1963.

Domar, Rebecca A. "The Tragedy of a Soviet Satirist: Or, The Case of Zoshchenko," in *Through the Glass of Soviet Literature*, 1953. Edited by E. J. Simmons.

McClean, Hugh. Introduction to *Nervous People and Other Satires*, 1963.

Masing-Delic, Irene. "Biology, Reason, and Literature in Zoshchenko's *Pered vosxodom solntca*," in *Russian Literature*. No. 8 (1980), pp. 77-101.

Mihailovich, Vasa D. "Zoshchenko's 'Adventures of a Monkey' as an Allegory," in *Satire Newsletter*. IV, no. 2 (1967), pp. 84-89.

Monas, Sidney. Introduction to *Scenes from the Bathhouse and Other Stories of Communist Russia*, 1961.

Slonim, Marc. "Mikhail Zoshchenko: The Condemned Humorist," in *Soviet Russian Literature: Writers and Problems*, 1964.

Von Wiren-Garzynski, Vera. "Zoshchenko's Psychological Interests," in *Slavic and East European Journal*. No. 11 (1967), pp. 3-22.

Vasa D. Mihailovich

UPDATES

UPDATES

Asimov, Isaac
BORN: Petrovici, Russia; January 2, 1920
SHORT FICTION
Casebook of the Black Widowers, 1980
The Union Club Mysteries, 1983
The Winds of Change and Other Stories, 1983
Banquets of the Black Widowers, 1984
The Disappearing Man and Other Mysteries, 1985
The Edge of Tomorrow, 1985 (short stories and essays)
Alternative Asimovs, 1986
The Best Mysteries of Isaac Asimov, 1986
The Best Science Fiction of Isaac Asimov, 1986

Asturias, Miguel Ángel
BORN: Guatemala City, Guatemala; October 19, 1899
DIED: Madrid, Spain; June 9, 1974

Ballard, J. G.
BORN: Shanghai, China; November 15, 1930
SHORT FICTION
Low-flying Aircraft: And Other Stories, 1976
The Venus Hunters, 1980
Myths of the Near Future, 1982
News from the Sun, 1982

Beckett, Samuel
BORN: Foxrock, near Dublin, Ireland; April 13, 1906
SHORT FICTION
Pour finir encore et autres foirades, 1976 (*Fizzles*, 1976)

Bellow, Saul
BORN: LaChine, Quebec, Canada; June 10, 1915
SHORT FICTION
Him with His Foot in His Mouth and Other Stories, 1984

Borges, Jorge Luis
BORN: Buenos Aires, Argentina; August 24, 1899
DIED: Geneva, Switzerland; June 14, 1986
SHORT FICTION
Six problémes pour don Isidoro Parodi, 1967 (*Six Problems for Don Isidoro Parodi*, 1981)
El libro de arena, 1975 (*The Book of Sand*, 1977)

Bowles, Paul
BORN: Long Island, New York; December 30, 1910
SHORT FICTION
Midnight Mass, 1981

Caldwell, Erskine
BORN: White Oak, Georgia; December 17, 1903
DIED: Paradise Valley, Arizona; April 11, 1987
SHORT FICTION
Stories of Life: North and South, 1983
The Black and White Stories of Erskine Caldwell, 1984

Calisher, Hortense
BORN: New York, New York; December 20, 1911
SHORT FICTION
Saratoga, Hot, 1985

Calvino, Italo
BORN: Santiago de las Vegas, Cuba; October 15, 1923
DIED: Siena, Italy; September 19, 1985
SHORT FICTION
Fiabe italiane, 1956 (*Italian Folktales*, 1980)
Marcovaldo: Ovvero, Le stagioni in città, 1963 (*Marcovaldo: Or, The Seasons in the City*, 1983)

Gli amori difficili, 1970 (*Difficult Loves*, 1984)

Capote, Truman
BORN: New Orleans, Louisiana; September 30, 1924
DIED: Los Angeles, California; August 25, 1984
SHORT FICTION
One Christmas, 1983

Cassill, R. V.
BORN: Cedar Falls, Iowa; May 17, 1919
SHORT FICTION
Three Stories, 1982

Clarke, Arthur C.
BORN: Minehead, Somerset, England; December 16, 1917
SHORT FICTION
Best of Arthur C. Clarke, 1973

Connell, Evan S., Jr.
BORN: Kansas City, Missouri; August 17, 1924
SHORT FICTION
Saint Augustine's Pigeon, 1980

Cortázar, Julio
BORN: Brussels, Belgium; August 26, 1914
DIED: Paris, France; February 12, 1984
SHORT FICTION
Queremos tanto a Glenda y otros relatos, 1980 (*A Change of Light*, 1980, and *We Love Glenda So Much*, 1983)

Dahl, Roald
BORN: Llandaff, South Wales; September 13, 1916
SHORT FICTION
The Best of Roald Dahl, 1978
More Tales of the Unexpected, 1980
A Roald Dahl Selection: Nine Short Stories, 1980

Davenport, Guy
BORN: Anderson, South Carolina; November 23, 1927
SHORT FICTION
Eclogues: Eight Stories, 1981
Apples and Pears and Other Stories, 1984

Dick, Philip K.
BORN: Chicago, Illinois; December 19, 1928
DIED: Santa Ana, California; March 2, 1982
SHORT FICTION
I Hope I Shall Arrive Soon, 1985
The Collected Stories of Philip K. Dick, 1987 (5 vols.)

Disch, Thomas M.
BORN: Des Moines, Iowa; February 2, 1940
SHORT FICTION
The Man Who Had No Idea, 1982

Elkin, Stanley
BORN: New York, New York; May 11, 1930
SHORT FICTION
Early Elkin, 1985

Gallant, Mavis
BORN: Montreal, Canada; August 11, 1922
SHORT FICTION
Home Truths, 1981

García Márquez, Gabriel
BORN: Aracataca, Colombia; March 6, 1928
SHORT FICTION
Collected Stories, 1985
ACHIEVEMENTS
Nobel Prize for Literature, 1982

Gardner, John
BORN: Batavia, New York; July 21, 1933
DIED: Susquehana, Pennsylvania; September 14, 1982

SHORT FICTION
The Art of Living and Other Stories, 1981

Garrett, George
BORN: Orlando, Florida; June 11, 1929
SHORT FICTION
An Evening Performance, 1985

Gold, Herbert
BORN: Cleveland, Ohio; 1924
SHORT FICTION
Stories of Misbegotten Love, 1985
Lovers and Cohorts: Twenty-seven Stories, 1986

Golding, William
BORN: Cornwall, England;
   September 19, 1911
ACHIEVEMENTS
Nobel Prize for Literature, 1983

Goyen, William
BORN: Trinity, Texas; April 24, 1915
DIED: Los Angeles, California;
   August 30, 1983
SHORT FICTION
Had I a Hundred Mouths: New and Selected Stories, 1947-1983, 1985

Grau, Shirley Ann
BORN: New Orleans, Louisiana; July 8, 1929
SHORT FICTION
Nine Women, 1986

Hawkes, John
BORN: Stamford, Connecticut;
   August 17, 1925
SHORT FICTION
The Universal Fears, 1978
Humors of Blood and Skin: A John Hawkes Reader, 1984
Innocence in Extremis, 1985

Heinlein, Robert A.
BORN: Butler, Missouri; July 7, 1907
SHORT FICTION
Expanded Universe, 1980

Himes, Chester
BORN: Jefferson City, Missouri; July 29, 1909
DIED: Moraira, Spain; November 12, 1984

Laurence, Margaret
BORN: Manitoba, Canada; July 18, 1926
DIED: Lakefield, Ontario, Canada;
   January 6, 1987

Lavin, Mary
BORN: East Walpole, Massachusetts;
   June 11, 1912
SHORT FICTION
Selected Stories, 1981

McCarthy, Mary
BORN: Seattle, Washington; June 21, 1912
SHORT FICTION
The Hounds of Summer and Other Stories, 1981

Malamud, Bernard
BORN: Brooklyn, New York; April 26, 1914
DIED: New York, New York; March 18, 1986
SHORT FICTION
The Stories of Bernard Malamud, 1983

Maltz, Albert
BORN: Brooklyn, New York; October 28, 1908
DIED: Los Angeles, California; April 26, 1985

Oates, Joyce Carol
BORN: Lockport, New York; June 16, 1938
SHORT FICTION
A Sentimental Education, 1981
Last Days, 1984
Wild Saturday and Other Stories, 1984
Raven's Wing, 1986

O'Brien, Edna
BORN: Tuamgraney, County Clare,
Ireland; December 15, 1930
SHORT FICTION
Returning: Tales, 1982
A Fanatic Heart: Selected Stories, 1984

O'Faoláin, Seán
BORN: Cork, Ireland; February 22, 1900
SHORT FICTION
The Collected Stories of Seán O'Faoláin,
1980

O'Flaherty, Liam
BORN: Aran Islands, Ireland; August 28,
1896
DIED: Dublin, Ireland; September 7,
1984
SHORT FICTION
The Pedlar's Revenge and Other Stories,
1976
The Wave and Other Stories, 1980

Ozick, Cynthia
BORN: New York, New York; April 17,
1928
SHORT FICTION
Levitation, 1982

Paley, Grace
BORN: New York, New York;
December 11, 1922
SHORT FICTION
Later the Same Day, 1985

Pritchett, V. S.
BORN: Ipswich, Suffolk, England;
December 16, 1900
SHORT FICTION
Collected Stories, 1982
More Collected Stories, 1983

Pynchon, Thomas
BORN: Glen Cove, New York; May 8,
1937
SHORT FICTION
Slow Learner, 1984

Shaw, Irwin
BORN: New York, New York;
February 27, 1913
DIED: Davos, Switzerland; May 16, 1984
SHORT FICTION
Five Decades, 1978

Sillitoe, Alan
BORN: Nottingham, England; March 4,
1928
SHORT FICTION
Down to the Bone, 1976
The Second Chance and Other Stories,
1981

Singer, Isaac Bashevis
BORN: Leoncin, Poland; July 14, 1904
SHORT FICTION
*The Collected Stories of Isaac Bashevis
Singer*, 1982
Image and Other Stories, 1985

Spark, Muriel
BORN: Edinburgh, Scotland; February 1,
1918
SHORT FICTION
*Bang-bang You're Dead and Other
Stories*, 1982
The Stories of Muriel Spark, 1985

Stuart, Jesse
BORN: W-Hollow, Riverton, Kentucky;
August 8, 1907
DIED: W-Hollow, Riverton, Kentucky;
February 17, 1984

Sturgeon, Theodore
BORN: Staten Island, New York;
February 26, 1918
DIED: Eugene, Oregon; May 8, 1985

Taylor, Peter
BORN: Trenton, Tennessee; January 18,
1917
SHORT FICTION
Old Forest and Other Stories, 1985

Tuohy, Frank
BORN: Uckfield, Sussex, England;
  May 2, 1925
SHORT FICTION
The Collected Stories of Frank Tuohy,
  1984

Updike, John
BORN: Shillington, Pennsylvania;
  March 18, 1932
SHORT FICTION
*Your Lover Just Called: Stories of Joan
  and Richard Maple*, 1980
Bech Is Back, 1982
The Beloved, 1982
ACHIEVEMENTS
Pulitzer Prize in Letters, 1982, for *Rabbit
  Is Rich*

Welty, Eudora
BORN: Jackson, Mississippi; April 13,
  1909
SHORT FICTION
Thirteen Stories, 1965
The Collected Stories of Eudora Welty,
  1980
Moon Lake and Other Stories, 1980
Retreat, 1981

Williams, Tennessee
BORN: Columbus, Mississippi; March 26,
  1911
DIED: New York, New York;
  February 25, 1983
SHORT FICTION
Collected Stories of Tennessee Williams,
  1985

INDEX

I